THE SILENT DEBATE:
Asian Immigration and Racism in Canada

179-180
193

Chinese workers on board a Canadian Pacific ship. Their labor was used to service Pacific-based C.P. steamships at their facility in Kowloon. The kichen staff and lower-rank seamen were also Chinese.
— Vancouver Public Library

THE SILENT DEBATE:
Asian Immigration and Racism in Canada

179

EDITED BY
Eleanor Laquian
Aprodicio Laquian
Terry McGee

Institute of Asian Research
The University of British Columbia, Vancouver, B.C.

Canadian Cataloguing in Publication Data

Main entry under title:

The silent debate

Papers presented at the conference, Asian immigration & racism in Canada, held in Vancouver, B.C., June 24–27, 1997.
Includes bibliographical references and index.
ISBN 0-88865-167-8

1. Canada--Emigration and immigration--Government policy--Congresses.
2. Asia--Emigration and immigration--Congresses. 3. Racism--Canada--
Congresses. I. Laquian, Eleanor R., 1939- II. Laquian, Aprodicio A., 1935-
III. McGee, T. G. (Terence Gary) IV. University of British Columbia. Insti-
tute of Asian Research. V. Title: Asian immigration & racism in Canada.
JV7285.A8S58 1998   325'.25'0971   C97-910875-6

 This book is printed on recycled paper.

To all Asian Immigrants who have embarked on this journey . . .

Krishna Chariot Festival at Stanley Park, Vancouver, B.C., August 1996.

*Group portrait of East Indian workers at the North Pacific Lumber Co. Ltd., Barnet (near Coquitlam),
B.C. about 1900.* — Vancouver Public Library

Contents

Illustrations

Figures

Tables

Tables

Tables

Foreword

I recognize that the theme of this book, Asian Immigration and Racism in Canada, is important to UBC, to British Columbia and to Canada. The current period of globalization and increased economic growth, particularly in Asia, has precipitated an unprecedented outflow of people from the region. Some of them are making permanent moves while others are just visiting. While the economic impact of tourism is significant, the socio-economic impact of permanent migration is even more so.

As a fourth generation Canadian, I know that immigration is not a new phenomenon. However, since the 1980s, a great number of immigrants have enriched Canada with both financial and human capital. Indeed, many including myself, argue that their contribution to B.C.'s economy in the eighties and nineties has been the main economic salvation of the province at a time of dramatic fluctuation in prices of natural resources. Today, in the municipalities of Vancouver, Burnaby, and Richmond, it is conservatively estimated that Asian migrants make up from 20 to 30 per cent of the population. Last year a survey showed that some 47 per cent of first year entrants to UBC came from homes where Asian languages were spoken. This shift from European to Asian migration, and the resulting mix, present many challenges to Canadian society.

Increased Asian immigration and, with it, the perceived rise in racism are important policy considerations in Canada today. While Canadian immigration policies go some way to address these issues, it is important that public discussions focus on racism from both the perspective of Canada as a receiving country, and from the perspective of the Asian countries of origin. There are those who argue that the best offensive to racism is information on how Asian immigrants meet the objectives of Canada's immigration policy. Education has a key role to play in overcoming prejudices. "Objective" information about other cultures leads to better understanding and breaks down ignorance and racism.

Beyond the formal education system which is controversial in B.C. because of the cost of teaching English as a second language, immigration must become an issue for public discussion and debate so our citizens know the main benefits and costs of immigration to this country. However, there is reticence on the part of average Canadians to discuss ethnicity and race.

They are afraid to risk misunderstanding and be branded racists. During the last elections, our political leaders studiously avoided discussing immigration even though public opinion polls indicate that it is ever-present in people's consciousness. I think it is about time that we stop avoiding the issue and engage in a discussion which is central to the future health and well-being of our nation.

As you read this volume, keep in mind that Canada's policies on immigration are a balance of the uneasy tension between idealism and pragmatism: our idealism about multiculturalism and its search for a kinder gentler and freedom-loving society on the one hand *versus* our pragmatic view of immigration as an instrument for economic growth and an answer to our demographic problems.

Canada is committed to multiculturalism, to providing a better life for refugees and to keeping families together through the family reunification program. Immigration serves to bring us the knowledge and skills of people who can contribute to the country's development. After all, with Canada's fertility rate way below replacement levels and the country's population aging rapidly, immigration assures us that the country has a productive work force. The current debate on immigration is a result of this tension between idealism and pragmatism. By exploring the dynamic tension between these two polarities, this book can serve to enhance our understanding and point to future policy solutions.

As the world population approaches the six billion mark and globalization increases interaction among people, immigration will continue to be one of the critical policy issues. Canada, as one of the few countries in the world that still accepts immigrants, will be under increased pressures to rethink its immigration policies. There are some Canadians who believe that Canada is nearly full — that, somehow, the optimal population size for this country is about 33 or 34 million and that we are fast approaching that limit. There are others, who believe that Canada, as the "best country in the world to live in" according to United Nations' assessment, should share its bounties with the rest of the world and accept more immigrants. While it will not be possible to resolve these issues in the immediate future, we can expect to move closer to some kind of policy solution and develop strategic opportunities for making a difference.

I believe that this book will contribute to a greater understanding of immigration issues leading to a more tolerant and mutually respectful society in B.C. and Canada. I am pleased that UBC has brought together scholars, business and public policy leaders to begin the process of this debate and facilitate the development of public policy.

Shirley Chan
Chair, UBC *Board of Governors*

Message

As Secretary of State for Multiculturalism and the Status of Women, I welcome this book's interest in the effects of immigration, the phenomenon of racism and the concept of multiculturalism. These issues are of global concern and deserve the attention that this book brings to them. The results of discussions on the themes covered in this publication will be of enormous assistance in furthering our common goals for humankind.

If we have a multiculturalism policy in Canada, it is because we are willing to acknowledge openly that every member of every Canadian community has helped to build this country. Men and women from all backgrounds came here to invest themselves and their labor in building Canadian society and, in doing so, became Canadian. They continue to labor and build in every area of Canadian life. Their presence is felt in politics, education, literature, visual arts, business. These Canadians, from their varied backgrounds, can easily envision the multitude of possibilities that will be open to their children and grandchildren in Canadian society.

They call themselves Canadian and are Canadian, but in being so, do not have to forget their origins.

This is the balance that we think brings Canadian society closer than ever to the democratic ideal that we are striving for. It is a balance that the Government of Canada, through its Multiculturalism Program, is working to encourage throughout the whole of our society.

In 1971 when the Multiculturalism Policy was first announced, we were breaking new ground in acknowledging, through an appreciation of cultural differences the diverse groups who had helped to develop our country. As time passed, it became clearer that, for Canada to thrive, we needed the full participation of all Canadians working collectively to change our institutions and attitudes. We had to ensure not only that opportunities were available to Canadians but that Canadians had access to those opportunities whether it was a case of doing better business, receiving higher education or further training, or just being able to communicate effectively — with a boss, an employee, a doctor, a banker or a neighbor.

At the same time, we realized that Canada benefited from an unprecedented range of skills, talents and knowledge that put us far ahead of the competition. We realized both what a great untapped resource we had been ignoring and what a tremendous disservice we were perpetrating by not devoting greater efforts to providing Canadians with the means to become full participants in the society where they spend their lives.

Today, 25 years later, we can look back and congratulate ourselves on the development of an innovative multiculturalism policy. But, we can also take pride in the fact that it has not remained static. Today we have multiculturalism policy objectives that will help ensure our ability to meet the demands of the 21st century. In fact, we don't have to wait that long. With 1997 being Canada's Year of Asia Pacific, we have the perfect opportunity to appreciate, right now, that we depend, more than ever, on the ability of all Canadians to contribute to our growth and development.

But, we do not want to rely on unwilling participants. We want to create a climate that favors willing cooperation.

Our first objective, therefore, is to foster a society that respects its cultural diversity, so that all Canadians feel a sense of belonging and attachment to the country they call home. Demographic projections tell us that, by 2006, 43 per cent of Canadians will have at least one origin other than British, French or Aboriginal, significantly expanding the scope and nature of diversity in Canada.

Second, we want to develop an active citizenry, which has both the capacity and opportunity to participate in shaping the future of our communities and our country.

And, third, we want to ensure fair and equitable treatment that accommodates people of all origins with respect and dignity.

These are the fundamentals. These are goals that apply to all Canadians. These are the equalizers. For that is what we believe is central to life in Canada: that we all have a share in what happens in this country and that we are all being asked to take an active role in deciding what happens. Despite our outward differences, it is clear that we are all driven by the same needs; to know who we are, to provide security for ourselves and our families, and to join others in ensuring the future of our country.

There are practical means at hand, through the Multiculturalism Program of the Department of Canadian Heritage, to help Canadians respond to these needs. We can, for example, make sure that diversity issues are recognized across the federal government, other levels of government and public institutions, so that national policies in all areas reflect the needs of a diverse population.

The Multiculturalism Program can also help to improve public understanding and acceptance of diversity. A prime component of the Program is the March 21 anti-racism campaign which is essentially an educational program aimed at encouraging Canadians to accept and value the cultural diversity that enriches our country.

As well, in this regard, we work closely with community groups and institutions to develop appropriate responses to specific needs, particularly in the areas of education, health services, policing and the justice system. Over the years the Program has contributed to a number of projects that have had the very positive and practical effect of opening Canadian society to the advantages of a diverse population.

In 1994, the Asia Pacific Foundation of Canada published the report *Asian Canadians: A Hidden Advantage*, and the Race Relations Advisory Council on Advertising produced the effective document *The Color of Your Money*. In 1995, the Canadian Ethnocultural Council, working with the Conference Board of Canada and the Department of Canadian Heritage, published a discussion paper entitled *Ethnocultural Diversity: A Source of Competitive Advantage*. There is the Metropolis Project, which was inaugurated last year. It is a partnership between researchers and governments from a number of countries, to carry out policy research and to exchange information on best practices in the areas of immigration, integration and program development.

Many of the Multiculturalism Program's activities are directed at children whose only experience is the culturally diverse society. They are predisposed to the idea that cultural differences are inconsequential when viewed against the inherent worth of the individual, who can add to the pool of skills, knowledge and talent that will further our development as a society. One such annual project is the Matthew da Costa Award, which encourages elementary and secondary school children to find out about the varied people who have contributed to Canada's development from earliest times to the present.

I am pleased to report, as well, that the Canadian Race Relations Foundation, after a number of delays, was inaugurated last year. The Foundation is ready and able to work with other organizations in Canada, to strengthen the efforts being made to vanquish racism — organizations such as UBC's Institute of Asian Research, Centre for Human Settlements, Canada Asia Pacific Research Initiatives (CAPRI) and the China Program for Integrative Research and Development (CPIRD).

A recent initiative, headed by my department, with the cooperation of the Department of Justice and Solicitor General, was the National Planning Meeting on Hate Crime and Bias Activity. Reaction to date indicates that our efforts are showing progress. I am confident that, with the cooperation of stakeholders, enforcement and justice officials, we will be successful in dealing effectively with hate crime and bias activity.

Individuals, institutions and organizations across the country are working to facilitate the integration of Canadians into the economic, political, social and cultural spheres of Canadian life. Many of the activities that have been undertaken have kept in step with the times by taking into consideration the specific needs of women, seniors and youth.

And, in the Canadian context, of utmost importance is the collaboration among Canadians of different origins, whose experiences are nonetheless similar. The bonds holding Canadians together can be defined in terms of our common needs. Our strength lies in our willingness to work together to fulfill those needs. It is easy to envision how this concept of collaboration and partnership applies equally to the global context.

If the Multiculturalism Policy has evolved to become a more effective instrument for social change, it is because Canadians have spoken out and demanded justice — demanded that all Canadians stand on an equal footing. We cannot say that Canadians value human rights, civic rights and responsibilities, and the right of citizens to participate in their society and call ourselves a role model for the world — if we do not ensure that our deeds match our words.

The Honorable Hedy Fry, P.C., M.P.
Secretary of State for
Multiculturalism and the Status of Women

Preface

The Institute of Asian Research (IAR) at the University of British Columbia focuses its research and other academic activities under its Public Policy Program on contemporary policy issues encompassing the processes of cultural, economic, political, social and technological change in Asia. One such issue is the "Asian diaspora" and this book, *The Silent Debate*, is one of the key activities pursuing this theme.

The contents of this book grew out of an international conference on Asian immigration and racism sponsored by the IAR on 24–27 June 1997. In that conference, discussions focused on the perspective of countries receiving migrants (Canada, Australia, New Zealand, United States) as well as sending countries (China, Hong Kong, Malaysia, Philippines, Sri Lanka and other South Asian countries).

This book is divided into four parts. *Part One* starts with a chapter on policy options by **Aprodicio and Eleanor Laquian** that focuses not only on Canada but the Asian situation as well. It is followed by an analysis of Asian immigration and racialized social conflict in Canada, particularly in Toronto, by **Alan Simmons. Elliot Tepper** evaluates Canada's multiculturalism policy and **Meyer Burstein** then ventures into a rethinking of Canada's immigration policies, with special focus on the Metropolis project which he heads for Citizenship and Immigration Canada.

Part Two of the book indicates the view from Asian countries of origin. **Zeng Yi** from Peking University looks at factors in China that are influencing migration to Canada and other countries. Policies and programs related to export of human resources are analyzed by **Sisira Pinnawala** for Sri Lanka and Ambassador **Jose Brillantes** for the Philippines. The prospects for South Asian migration to Canada are studied by **Azfar Khan** and intra-regional migration in Southeast Asia are viewed from the Malaysian experience by **Azizah Kassim**.

Shifting to other countries receiving migrants, *Part Three* highlights the findings of **Graeme Hugo** on migration and mobilization in Asia. **Manolo Abella** correlates structural change in Asia with emigration pressures. And immigration policies and programs in receiving countries like Australia and New Zealand are reviewed by **Gavin Jones** and **Andrew Trlin** respectively. **Angelica Tang** then provides a detailed look at immigration policies and programs to serve immigrants in New York City.

Part Four evaluates the effects of immigration on Canada. **Thomas Hutton** relates Asian immigration to structural changes in Vancouver. **Edward Woo** reviews the business program involving investors and entrepreneurs from Hong Kong. The rhetoric of racism as reflected in housing choices in Vancouver is studied by **David Ley**. **Kogila Moodley** discusses the role of education in combating racism in Canada and relates her findings to educational policies. Finally, **Terry McGee** relates Asian immigration to globalization and looks at the implications of research findings to policy.

In holding the conference and editing this book, we acknowledge with thanks the funding support from UBC's Canada Asia Pacific Research Initiatives (CAPRI), China Program for Integrative Research and Development (CPIRD), the Centre for Human Settlements, and the Metropolis Project of Citizenship and Immigration Canada in Ottawa. Special thanks are due to the Department of Canadian Heritage for a grant to print this book.

We are indebted to the paper writers who came to Vancouver from Asia, North America and Europe to share their thoughts and research findings. We are also grateful to the session chairs: **Mike Harcourt, Paul T.K. Lin, Olav Slaymaker, Walter Uegama,** and other speakers like **Dennis Pavlich, Shirley Chan** and the Honorable **Hedy Fry,** Canada's minister of state for multiculturalism and the status of women.

The conference logo and book cover were designed by **Lisa Kwan** who also formatted all the tables and figures. **Sue Ahn** did the final book formatting and photos while **Dulce Amba** organized the chapter references and bibliography. **Jason Colantonio** had the painstaking job of indexing this big red book. **Kate Chang** and **Natalie McArthur** helped with proofreading. **June Kawaguchi** and Dulce set up the *Quick Asia* web sites project on immigration and racism that enabled us to access valuable information from the Net. Efficient logistical support was rendered by **Karen Jew, Marietta Lao** and **Pierre Fallavier,** of the Institute of Asian Research. **Ian Slater** and **Jackie Garnett** promoted the book in *Pacific Affairs*. Finally, the photos were contributed by Asian immigrants, affiliated with the Institute, who are proud to share their families' immigration experience. We are grateful for the pleasure of working with all of them.

It is our hope that in publishing this book, the silent debate on Asian immigration and racism in Canada will become more open, honest,and constructive. Perhaps, in this way, positive policy measures can be evolved. We acknowledge with thanks the help of all the people who made the publication of this book possible but the authors and editors assume full responsibility for errors of fact and interpretation.

Eleanor Laquian
Aprodicio Laquian
Terry McGee

Part One

The Receiving Country Perspective

1 Asian Immigration and Racism in Canada — A Search for Policy Options

Aprodicio A. Laquian and Eleanor R. Laquian

In the past 145 years (from 1852, when Statistics Canada started publishing records, to1997) Canada added about 14.9 million immigrants to its population. Of this number, 1.2 million were admitted in the last five years alone, almost two-thirds coming from Asia. Most Asian immigrants have settled in Toronto, Vancouver and Montréal. Between 1981 and 1991, about 4.3 million out of 26.6 million Canadians (16.3 per cent) were foreign born. (Citizenship and Immigration Canada,1997: 3).

The increasing number of non-white immigrants in Canada's population has heightened awareness about the changing ethnic mix of Canadian society. However, there is an apparent reticence on the part of many Canadians to discuss immigration as a political or social issue. During the June 1997 elections, for example, it was observed that "polls show Canadian concerns over immigration levels but the political debate on the issue is missing" (Gardner, 1997: 1).

It has been suggested that this reticence is due to the changed nature of the migrants themselves — a shift from the traditional white, Anglo-Saxon, and European peoples to Asian and other visible minorities. In 1993, 44.3 per cent of the 255,819 immigrants to Canada came from seven Asian countries: Hong Kong, Philippines, India, China, Taiwan, Sri Lanka, and Vietnam (See Table 1). Aside from these countries, others sending emigrants to Canada are: Afghanistan, Bangladesh, Bhutan, Brunei, Cambodia, Indonesia, Japan, South Korea, Laos, Macau, Malaysia, Mongolia, Myanmar, Nepal, Pakistan, Singapore, Thailand, and Tibet. In 1994, a total of 142,997 Asians were admitted to Canada, making up 63.8 per cent of the total number of immigrants. Citizenship and Immigration Canada includes under the Asian category, immigrants from Iran, Lebanon, Iraq, Saudi Arabia, Israel, United Arab Emirates, Kuwait, Bahrain, Cyprus, Jordan, Oman, Palestine, Qatar, Syria and Yemen.

3

Canadian Reactions to Immigration

In her book on Canadian immigration, Hawkins (1972: 34) said that "in Canada, immigration is neither a national myth nor . . . an essential element in national development." She noted that, "as an area of public policy, immigration has evoked conventional support but little real enthusiasm." Hawkins attributed this lack of enthusiasm to the fact that, unlike Americans, who view their country as a "nation of immigrants," Canadians see themselves as having descended from "two founding nations." To Hawkins, the relationship between these two solitudes is "the central fact of Canadian history."

More than 25 years after the publication of Hawkins' book, it is apparent that immigration has become a key issue in Canada. Not only are immigrants arriving in greater numbers, they are also not coming from the two founding nations anymore. In British Columbia, the traditional landing place for most Asian immigrants, almost 80 per cent of new arrivals in 1996 came from Asia. Immigrants from Great Britain to British Columbia made up only 3.9 per cent of 1994 arrivals. (Citizenship and Immigration Canada, 1997: 58–60).

Public opinion polls indicate that many Canadians are against current levels of immigrant intake. There are also signs of opposition to immigration in general. An Angus Reid poll in January 1996 found that 49 per cent of respondents thought immigration levels were "too high." However, subse-

Table 1: Top Ten Countries of Last Permanent Residence among Canadian Immigrants

Country	1993	Per cent	1994	Per cent	Rank
Hong Kong	36,574	14.3	44,169	19.7	1
Philippines	19,772	7.7	19,097	8.5	2
India	20,472	8.0	17,225	7.7	3
China	9,466	3.7	12,486	5.6	4
Taiwan	9,867	3.9	7,411	3.3	5
Sri Lanka	9,103	3.6	6,671	3.0	6
U.S.A.	8,014	3.1	6,234	2.8	7
Vietnam	8,301	3.2	6,230	2.8	8
Great Britian	7,159	2.8	5,971	2.7	9
Bosnia-Hercegovina	-	-	4,905	2.2	10
Poland	6,877	2.7	-	-	10
Total Top Ten	135,605	53.0	130,399	58.2	
Others	120,214	47.0	93,476	41.8	
Grand Total	**255,819**	**100.0**	**223,875**	**100.0**	

Source: Citizenship and Immigration Canada, Citizenship and Immigration Statistics, 1994: x.

quent probing found that quite a few who said immigration levels were fine were actually concerned but were hesitant to say so. As a result, Angus Reid concluded that the opposition level is actually around 60 per cent. These findings are considerably higher than the 31 per cent in February 1989 who thought that there were "too many" immigrants accepted to Canada. Don DeVoretz, co-director of the Centre of Excellence for Immigration Studies in Vancouver has noted that in 1985, only 25 per cent of people polled thought immigration levels were too high compared to 40 to 50 per cent holding the same view in recent polls (*Vancouver Sun*, 9 October 1997).

While a majority of Canadians express the view that a pluralist and free society should not discriminate against the immigration of people because of their color or racial characteristics, more than a fifth see problems arising from too many Asians coming in. Public consultations conducted by the Department of Citizenship and Immigration in 1994 revealed a strong desire among Canadians to see immigrants assimilated into Canadian society rather than integrated under the official policy of multiculturalism. They believed that "Canada should replace its 'mosaic' with a 'melting pot'" (Citizenship and Immigration Canada, 1994: 41).

Henry and Tator (1994) explain the negative response to immigration as the inherent conflict between "democratic liberalism" with its pluralist and equity ideals and a "racist ideology" rooted in Canadian history and tradition. This conflict creates a "fundamental dissonance" in Canadian society. They suggest that, as a result, an ideology of "democratic racism" has evolved to permit some Canadians "to justify and maintain two apparently conflicting sets of values." From time to time, however, there are increased or decreased manifestations of racism in response to changing economic and political circumstances.

A key question posed in this book is: has the past decade, which is marked with an unprecedented increase in Asian immigration, witnessed a rise in racism in Canada especially in the two major destination cities of Toronto and Vancouver?

Douglas Palmer, in a 1997 report to Immigration Canada reviewed the results of national polls conducted between November 1996 and February 1997. Of particular interest in his study was the reaction to the statement: "Non-whites should not be allowed to immigrate to Canada." The answers to this attempt to measure racial tolerance indicated that respondents from Toronto were the most intolerant of immigrants while Vancouverites were the least racist. At the same time, British Columbians as a whole were slightly more racist than the national average. (*Vancouver Sun*, 7 October 1997). Palmer, in interpreting this, said that the two feelings were not mutually exclusive: "Just because virtually all bigots are opposed to immigration does not mean all people opposed to immigration are bigots." He added that people may have a number of reasons for opposing immigration that are not based on racism. (*Vancouver Sun*, 9 October 1997).

Another interpretation of the survey findings was offered by Lloyd Stanford. Noting that respondents from Toronto had the highest scores on intolerance, Stanford said that this may be due to the complexion of the immigrants: "Intolerance tends to be greater the darker the skin color." He noted that there are more blacks in Toronto and that "People who are inclined to judge things in terms of color would obviously feel strongest against people who are black, as against people who are brown or a mixture." (*Vancouver Sun*, 6 October 1997).

Racism in Canada

To clarify the issue of racism in Canada, it is important to start with a definition of some concepts. In this regard, it is useful to begin with what Canadians consider the basic shared values in their society. In discussions sponsored by Citizenship and Immigration Canada, participants have observed that Canada is committed to being an equitable society that "celebrates the individual" and recognizes that each person is a unique human being with a distinct character.

In an equitable society, every person has a choice but choices are governed by attitudes, traditions, and culture. When such factors limit opportunities because of people's race or national origin, *discrimination* arises. Limiting of opportunities is often rooted in stereotypes, prejudice and racism. Simply put, *stereotypes* are generalized conceptions of a group of people resulting in a conscious or unconscious categorization of each member of that group as having specific characteristics. *Prejudice* is similar to stereotypes in that the prejudiced person has already made a judgment of another person's characteristics based on incorrect information. Often, prejudiced attitudes are used to rationalize unequal treatment of people which reinforces stereotypes and racism.

According to Li (1994), *racism* fundamentally involves "a form of exclusion, in which the dominant group prevents subordinate groups from equal access to economic, political, social and cultural life." To Simmons (See Chapter 2) racism is based on the process of "othering" where one group of people (racists) draw attention to some distinctive physical attributes of another group (skin color) and associated ethnic characteristics (accent, clothing) and treat them as different, outsiders, and less deserving of the normal benefits of membership in society.

Li (1994) makes a distinction between the attitudinal and the structural aspects of racism. In the former, racism is seen as arising mainly from the development of hostility and faulty generalizations about racialized groups. To Li, however, this psychological approach to racism was an insufficient basis for understanding the phenomenon. He stressed that "political and economic benefits derived from racial prejudice and discrimination" arising from "unequal relationships between dominant and subordinate groups" were a better explanation for the presence and persistence of

6

racism. Li pointed to the importance of "institutional racism," which refers to the discriminatory effects of institutional operations, as a key explanatory variable.

Many students of racism agree that the phenomenon tends to be concrete and specific — it has, in the words of Brandt (1986: 67–68), "a geographic, social and historical specificity." Goldberg (1992) observed that ". . . subject, objects and modes (of racism) alter . . . Developments and changes in racist discourse are demonstrated to be functions of dominant interests, aims, and purposes." Hall (1978) stressed that ". . . racism is always historically specific . . . whatever common features it may appear to share with other similar social phenomena . . . it always assumes specific forms which arise out of the present — not the past — conditions and organization of society."

Moodley, like Simmons and Li, traces the origins of racism to attribution of inferior characteristics to people who are physically different from the racist group (Chapter 19). Thus, European colonialism and slavery during the 19th century were justified because of the supposedly inherent superior nature of the colonizers over the genetically inferior backward peoples they ruled and enslaved. Moodley noted that racism and racist characteristics have been held not only by Europeans — other groups (the Japanese, Indians, Chinese) also had racist attitudes and behavior.

The history of Canada, rooted as it is in the "two founding nations" theory, has been characterized by explicit, systemic and institutional racism. As noted by Li (1988), Jones (1978), and Sunahara (1981), "In the history of Canada, institutionalized discriminatory practices against minority groups were common, for example, in the enslavement of blacks in Nova Scotia in the pre-Confederation days, the disenfrachisement of Japanese Canadians in British Columbia until 1949, and the exclusion of Chinese between 1923 and 1947." Racism and discrimination were applied to aborigines, temporary laborers and immigrants, in accordance with the prevailing beliefs and values of the times.

Students of Canadian immigration like to cite the fact that the first Asian migrants to Canada probably crossed the Bering Strait during the last Ice Age and became Canada's First Nations. Subsequent waves of migrants included Chinese laborers, Japanese fisherfolk, Sikh farmers, other South Asians who came as agricultural settlers, and Southeast Asian refugees. The subjugation of the First Nations by the Founding Nations and the exploitation of early Asian workers by the new European settlers show that unequal treatment of Asians in Canada is of long standing.

From the start of European colonization,the dominant position of the English and French in Canada has resulted in prejudicial and racist treatment of minority groups. As observed by Henry and Tator (1994), "The racist heritage of Canada has bequeathed to both earlier and present generations of Canadians a powerful set of perceptions and behavioral patterns regarding people of color. A deeply entrenched hegemonic system of White group dominance exists and perpetuates inequity and oppression by those who use power, privilege and resources against those who are powerless and socially and economically disadvantaged." Other cases of racist incidents are shown in the following examples:

- From 1927 to 1951, it was illegal for more than three First Nations people to gather in one place to discuss land claims. To raise money for land claims was punishable by imprisonment. Until 1951, it was a criminal offense to hold a potlatch in First Nations communities. First Nations people were not allowed to vote until 1960.
- In 1912, the Saskatchewan legislature passed the "white women's labor law" that prohibited the employment of white women by Asian-Canadian males. In 1924, the Regina City Council voted to deny a certain Yee Clun a license that would have allowed him to hire white female waitresses in his restaurant. When Yee went to court, the Supreme Court of Canada upheld the legality of the statute. The law was not repealed until 1940 in Manitoba, 1947 in Ontario and 1968 in British Columbia (Backhouse, 1994).
- In 1907, the Asiatic Exclusion League led riots against Chinese and Japanese communities in Vancouver; they destroyed property and beat up people until repelled by residents of Japan Town.
- In 1911, Vancouver Island parents succeeded in excluding Japanese and Chinese children from one school because their "lack of English" was holding back the progress of their children.
- Under the War Measures Act (1942), Japanese males aged 19 to 45 were interned in camps and their properties were confiscated. Later, the Act interned all Japanese immigrants and Canadians of Japanese descent. When the camps were closed in 1946, almost 4,000 people of Japanese descent were deported to Japan. Canadians of Japanese descent were allowed to vote only in 1948 (Sunahara, 1981).
- As late as 1954, home buyers in the exclusive British Properties enclave in Vancouver had to sign a covenant that they would not resell "to a Jew or an Oriental."

It may be noted that these incidents were products of the specific historical periods within which they occurred. The racism against Asians in the past could be explained by such factors as the lower economic status of the immigrants, their relatively small numbers, and the influence of racist movements in the United States and elsewhere. However, economic and social conditions in Canada have changed dramatically since those times. A different type of Asian immigrants has come to Canada in the last decade. Many of them are well-educated, highly skilled, upwardly mobile, aware of their rights and responsibilities, and active participants in the democratic processes of the land. Are they faring better than their ancestors?

The New Asian Immigrants

Canada's immigration laws were changed in 1962 to admit more people from Asia and other non-white, non-European countries. As a result, millions of Asians, especially from Hong Kong, Taiwan, China, South Asia and the Philippines, immigrated to Canada.

The latest waves of Asian immigrants are a varied lot: arrivals in Vancouver in 1993 showed that 41.3 per cent of the immigrants spoke Cantonese or Mandarin Chinese, 16.9 per cent Hindi or Punjabi, 13.1 per cent Tagalog, and 6.2 per cent Vietnamese. Since that year, the proportion of immigrants with Chinese ancestry has increased rapidly. At current rates of immigration, "visible minorities" are projected to make up 39 per cent of all B.C. residents by 2005 and most of those will be Chinese.

A survey of Chinese business immigrants in Vancouver (Chow, 1995), revealed their characteristics as follows:

a) 72 per cent live in single-detached homes and 80 per cent own their homes outright;
b) 12 per cent drive luxury cars and 77 per cent paid cash for their vehicles;
c) 33 per cent have university level education; and
d) 23 per cent have U.S. dollar bank accounts.

It is obvious that recent Chinese immigrants to Canada are very different from their ancestors who came to Canada to work on the rail road, operate laundry shops or run restaurants.

Quite a number of Chinese immigrants have come in under the economic class (investors and entrepreneurs). It has been estimated that business immigrants to British Columbia brought in $3 billion in investments in 1991 and $4 billion in 1992. Each investor is estimated to have brought in an average of $2 million and each entrepreneur $1 million, despite the fact that the minimum requirement was only $350,000. These economic inputs have had varied effects. In 1988, about 25 per cent of all houses sold in Vancouver were bought by Hong Kong immigrants.

Asian immigration has contributed to the prosperity and cultural diversity of Vancouver making it the ideal multicultural society that other cities wrestling with urban unrest would envy. As an article in the *Vancouver Sun* stated:

> One of Vancouver's selling points — aside from being a city that's considered safe, clean, friendly and lively — is that it conveys a sense of many cultures living together harmoniously . . . that apparently strife-free multiculturalism is visible through Chinatown and the proliferation of ethnic restaurants.

With the new characteristics of Asian immigrants, the obvious wealth, education and skills they brought and the adoption of Canada's multicultural policy, have there been changes in Canadian attitudes and behavior toward Asians? Evidence from recent media reports do not show this. In fact, there are indications of a resentment against Asians, as seen in the following cases:

- Immigrants are blamed for skyrocketing prices for housing in cities like Toronto and Vancouver. In Vancouver, Asians are accused of buying small treed lots, knocking down the wooden frame houses traditionally built on those lots, cutting down trees, and building "monster houses." A number of communities have passed zoning codes and building regulations to stop the building of such houses in efforts to legislate taste and aesthetics. While these events can be interpreted in terms of housing economics and community politics, racism has also colored the debate.
- Asian immigrants are accused of taking advantage of welfare regulations, allegedly by "sponsoring" their relatives and then reneging on their responsibilities.
- Asian immigrants are said to impose their own values on Canadian society and show lack of respect for Canadian traditions and symbolic values as in the insistence of Sikhs to wear their turbans instead of the RCMP Stetson hat. Asian immigrants are also criticized for bringing their traditional and political conflicts back home to Canada.
- Canadian mass media regularly highlight news about Asian youth gangs, criminal activities of triads, the involvement of some Asians in the drug trade, and the propensity of Asians to resort to violence (as in the recent troubles at a Vancouver Sikh temple). Other sensationalized accounts have been made of dowry burnings, wife beating, drive-by shooting and other "unacceptable" cultural practices attributed to Asians.
- It has been estimated that about 56 per cent of students entering Vancouver public schools for the first time do not speak English at home (88 languages are spoken by students within the Vancouver school system). There are charges that the low language capability of Asian immigrants is somehow "holding back" the learning progress of non-Asian Canadians.
- Some immigrant parents are branded as "astronauts" and their children "parachutists" because the former commute to Hong Kong or Taiwan to look after their businesses while leaving the children and their spouses behind. These commuters are accused of taking advantage of Canadian basic services without paying taxes. The reluctance of some Asian immigrants to declare their overseas assets is seen as proof of their lack of commitment to Canada.
- The proliferation of Asian megamalls has been criticized by quite a number of people. Objections to them range from concern about heavy traffic to noise pollution. Again, some proposals on zoning codes and planning regulations have been made in local councils to deal with these issues.

In reacting to cases of immigrant backlash, many Asian immigrants, especially those with access to the ethnic press, have voiced their strong objections to what they perceive as racist accusations. They say, for example, that the rapid increase in house prices is due not so much to the buying propensities of Asian immigrants but to the greed of property sellers and local developers. The large houses are justified in terms of the larger size of Asian families. They ask why very large houses built by white Canadians are acclaimed as beautiful "Tudor classics" while their large houses are called "monster homes."

The accusation that Asian immigrants are "welfare cheats" is deeply resented by most immigrants. They point to studies that reveal that Asian immigrants find jobs soon after arrival, even if such jobs are below their educational and skill levels. Because they are employed, Asian immigrants are not likely to go on welfare. (A 1996 study found that only 13.8 per cent of people drawing unemployment insurance were immigrants, compared to 17.5 per cent of native-born Canadians). Asian immigrants generally fulfill their obligations as sponsors of relatives. They consider as symptomatic of racism the wide publicity given by the media to rare cases where Asians have been found to "abuse" the welfare system.

The "sensational" treatment by the mainstream media (owned and dominated by Anglo-Canadians) of news related to Asian immigrants is also resented. For example, the Asian origin of people involved in crimes of murder, rape, riots, spousal abuse, drug dealing and violence is often mentioned in news items even when it has little relevance to the story. On the other hand, when the news is positive (an athletic triumph, a scientific breakthrough), individuals are immediately designated Canadians without mentioning their country of origin.

A very active ethnic press in Canada has taken great efforts to ease the tensions between immigrants and mainstream Canadians. Articles have been printed admonishing immigrants to adjust and not insist on living the way they did back home. Quite a number of nongovernmental organizations have been set up by Asian immigrants to help ease problems of transition, offer courses in English, assist immigrants in finding jobs and housing, and generally attempt to smooth out the adjustment to Canadian life. David Lam, former B.C. lieutenant governor, in a recent book (Roy, 1996), likened immigrating to Canada to crossing a bridge — "once crossed, the bridge should be burned."

Despite these positive efforts, however, many Asian immigrants write letters to editors complaining that they have been subjected to discrimination and unfair treatment. The activities of racist organizations such as the Heritage Front, skinheads, neo-Nazis, and other white supremacists are increasing. Anti-Asian graffiti has become quite visible in parks and other public places. There are also signs of "benign racism" reflected in sometimes not-so-polite private discussions of Asian immigrants among like-minded people.

To an increasing number of Asian immigrants in Canada, careful distinctions on whether the reactions to them are due to stereotypes, prejudice, backlash effect, psychological racism, symbolic racism, systematic racism, or institutional racism is so much academic hair splitting. What matters to them is how they are regarded in Canadian society. When they feel unwelcome in their own neighborhood, insecure in their places of work, humiliated on the streets (spat upon or verbally abused), cowardly attacked by grafitti and threatened by anonymous hate mail sent to their homes — the message is as clear as a graffiti commonly seen on Wreck Beach near UBC: Chinks Go Home.

As noted by Henry and Tator (1994):

> In real life, experiences of racism are presented to victims as integrated parts of an oppressive system. Victims of racism experience . . . it in many spheres of life: neighborhoods, schools, work sites, and . . . other public settings. Prejudicial attitudes and discriminatory actions are often intertwined. As such, racism as experienced by victims is integrated into actions and meanings, and from their standpoint, racism would appear as emerging from the same objective reality which systematically treats "race" as undesirable.

Links Between Asian Immigration and Racism

The issue of racism and its possible links to Asian immigration is extremely difficult for Canadians to discuss openly because it goes against the moral philosophies and official policies that are considered basic to Canadian liberal ideas. Many Canadians find it hard to talk about immigration because they are afraid to be called racists or bigots (Bergman, 1993).

> Nice, polite, open-minded — Canadians wear these stereotypes of civility like a badge of honor. And according to the results of a national poll on attitudes towards racial and ethnic minorities . . . The Canadian predilection for good manners may extend into the murky realm of racism. Of 1,200 people polled by Decima Research, two-thirds declared that one of the best things about Canada is its acceptance of people from all races and ethnic backgrounds. At the same time, however, more than half of the respondents admitted that they harbor negative views of some minorities — even though they insisted that they would never act on or express those views.

A close look at the history of Canadian immigration reveals outright racist policies. In the words of Taylor (1991): "Canada's immigration law from 1885 until 1962 was explicitly racist in wording and intent: non-white, non-European immigration was openly discouraged and/or prohibited." As proof of this claim, Taylor cited the following:

- Between 1875 and 1923, the government of British Columbia passed a number of laws restricting the civil rights of Chinese immigrants. The original 1885 Chinese Immigration Act imposed a "head tax" on Chinese immigrants. Originally set at $50, it rose to $100 in 1900, and to $500 in 1904. The 1923 revision of the 1885 act effectively terminated immigration from China. This exclusionary law was not lifted until 1947. As indicated by a resolution of the New Democratic Party of B.C. ". . . these 38 years of oppressive restrictions and 24 years of exclusion were clearly racist in motivation and effect . . ." (NDP, 1995).

- The 1906 Act on Immigration empowered the government to prohibit the landing in Canada of any unspecified class of immigrants.
- The 1931 general regulations of the Immigration Act prohibited independent immigrants from Asia and specified that admissible immigrants were to be "British subjects from the 'white' Commonwealth countries, U.S. citizens, wives and children of male residents of Canada, and agriculturists with sufficient means to farm in Canada."

Recent attitude surveys have shown that some people in Canada still hold some degree of prejudicial attitudes (Environics, 1988; Angus Reid Group, 1989; Economic Council of Canada, 1991; Canadian Council of Christian and Jews, 1993; Angus Reid Group, 1994). However, as Henry, Tator, Mattis and Rees, (1995) indicated, most Canadians holding these attitudes recognize that these are unacceptable in a democratic society. Henry and Tator (1994) cited a Maclean's/Decima poll in July 1993 that showed a third of Canadians felt that new immigrants should be encouraged to maintain their distinct culture while the majority felt that they should blend in with the larger society and "be more like them."

Other national surveys confirm the presence of racist attitudes among Canadians. The 1989 Angus Reid poll found that about 80 per cent of Canadians believed that multiculturalism is one of the best things in the country. At the same time, however, about 41 per cent of those polled also believed that Canada was changing too quickly because of all the minorities that have come in. The poll concluded that about 13 per cent of Canadians could be considered "ethnocentrists" based on their negative attitudes towards immigrants and refugees. Their negative attitudes appeared largely cultural — they were concerned with "the threat to Canadian culture" associated with "multiculturalism" and high immigration levels (Angus Reid Group, 1989: 7–8).

Another Angus Reid poll in 1993 found that 57 per cent of Canadians felt that new immigrants should assimilate into Canadian life instead of bringing their problems back home to the new country. About 15 to 20 per cent of Canadians surveyed could be described as "hard core" racists who wanted to preserve a "white Canada" (Angus Reid Group, 1994).

Do these survey findings indicate, then, that racism is on the increase in Canada and that it is reflected in people's reactions to immigration? The available evidence suggests that racism in Canada has actually been declining. Compared to the open racism in the past, current attitudes and behavior are evidently less racist. As Moodley stated, the 15 to 20 per cent anti-immigrant groups in Canada are just about the same proportion as the right wing supporters of LePen in France, the National Front in Britain or the neo-Fascist parties in Germany. What is important, in her view, is not the absolute proportion of these anti-immigrant and openly racist groups but the pressures they exert on establishment parties and public institutions.

Current laws on immigration in Canada are officially committed to achieving a liberal and egalitarian society. The policy of multiculturalism envisions the integration of immigrants into Canadian society instead of their full assimilation. Unlike the United States, Canada has never set immigration quotas based on ethnic classifications. Rather, Canada has selected immigrants on the basis of their educational, language proficiency, health and skills backgrounds, basing the acceptance of immigrants on the human resource needs of the country.

Since 1962, Canadian immigration law has emphasized humanitarian goals. These were to be accomplished by accepting more refugees and the implementation of the family reunification program. In 1967, however, the Revised Immigration Act introduced the point system which allocated specific points for individual characteristics of immigrants. For example, 12 points were given an immigrant's educational level, 15 points for vocational training, 10 points for age, etc. The types of immigrants accepted (Table 2) and their numbers each year were determined by an estimate of the types and numbers of workers needed by the Canadian economy rather than a commitment to humanitarianism.

In addition to Canada's idealistic goals on immigration, therefore, the new immigration laws officially view immigration as a means for promoting economic growth in Canada. As one official said, "250,000 new immigrants every year can only benefit Canada," especially since the education and training of most of those immigrants have been paid for in their countries of origin. It was not an accident that, until recently, Canada's immigration was administered by the Department of Manpower and Immigration.

Immigration in Canada has also been viewed as a demographic factor. The latest version of the Canadian Immigration Act, approved by Parliament in 1976 and proclaimed in force in 1978, set as one of its objectives: "to support the attainment of such demographic goals as may be established by the Government of Canada from time to time in respect of size, rate of growth, structure and geographic distribution of the Canadian population" (Employment and Immigration Canada, 1988).

Between 1976 and 1986, Canada's average rate of natural increase (the difference between births and deaths) was 0.81 per cent per year. More than a fifth of Canada's annual population growth is due to net inmigration. As a Minister of Citizenship and Immigration once said, "without immigration, the last Canadian would die in about 175 years." Canada's total fertility rate — the probable number of children that a female child born in Canada would have within her lifetime was 1.6 in 1985, way below the replacement level of 2.1.

An important demographic fact is the aging of Canada's population (Foot, 1986). From 1971 to 1981, the median age of Canadians increased from 26.2 years to 31.1 years. Statistics Canada projects that the median age will rise to 37 years by the year 2000. This phenomenon has prompted some authors to suggest that "Every effort should be made to consider using immigration policy to smooth out the current age imbalance in the Canadian population."

The tensions among humanitarian ideals, economic pragmatism and demographic realities provide the primary context for discussing policy options related to immigration in Canada. In good times Canada's humanitarian ideals practically soar. During periods of international trouble, such as the collapse of the Soviet Union, the war in the Balkans, the civil war in Sri Lanka, and the Vietnam War, Canada has been one of the first countries to open its doors to refugees and displaced persons.

During times of economic stress, however, immigration becomes a contentious issue in Canada as people express their concern about the country's ability to absorb and integrate new immigrants into the economic system. During these times, complaints are heard that newcomers take jobs away from native Canadians, refugees take advantage of Canada's generous welfare system, immigrants force their cultural ways on the country, the price of integrating immigrants into the society through language training and other services is too high, and that Canada's fragile environment cannot support all the newcomers. As one participant in the Canadian immigration consultation said, "It must be realized that Canada is not an empty country waiting to be filled up. We have a fragile ecology." Some even suggest that the country is already full.

The 1990s in Canada seem to be a time of such economic and social stress. As a result, the immigration debate, quiet as it is, is preoccupying people's minds. In November 1994, Canada's Immigration Minister announced new immigration policies that created a great deal of controversy. These changes included the following:

- Reducing the number of immigrants for 1995 to 190,000–215,000 compared to a target set in 1994 for 230,000.
- Greater emphasis to attracting "economic immigrants" to Canada who could bring in entrepreneurial skills and wealth.
- Expecting immigrants to pay more of the expenses involved in their coming and settlement in the country.
- Cracking down on abusers of the immigration system, especially people with criminal records.
- The possibility of requiring a bond as a financial guarantee by the sponsoring families.
- Making knowledge of English or French a "critical element" in the immigration selection process.
- Imposing a moratorium on immigrant investor funds and redesigning the program.

Table 2: Immigrant Class by Year of Landing

Class	1993	Per cent	1994	Per cent
Family Class	112,266	43.9	93,882	41.9
Refugees	30,382	11.9	20,384	9.1
Assisted Relatives	22,918	8.9	27,459	12.3
Entrepreneurs	16,666	6.5	14,166	6.3
Self-employed	3,384	1.3	2,736	1.2
Investors	12,576	4.9	10,463	4.7
Retired	7,733	3.0	7,426	3.3
Live-in Caregivers	3,001	1.3	4,951	2.2
Others	46,893	18.3	42,408	19.0
Total	**255,819**	**100.0**	**223,875**	**100.0**

Source: Citizenship and Immigration Canada, *Citizenship and Immigration Statistics*, 1994, p. 61.

- Setting up a separate management system for refugees and stressing the settlement of women and children in Canada.
- Setting the target for refugees at around 24,000 to 32,000 in 1995.

The immediate reaction to the Immigration Minister's proposals were quite negative. It was claimed that the proposed changes "conveyed a negative image of immigrants and reinforced people's exclusionary thinking and prejudicial attitudes" (Li, 1994). It was argued that the changes tended to perpetuate the image that immigrants were the ones causing social problems when, in fact, Asian immigrants were often the victims of abuses.

A particularly thorny issue highlighted in the reactions to the Minister's announcement focused on the proposed policy on family reunification. In accordance with Canada's humanitarian goals, family reunification has been given a lot of emphasis in past years. There were fears that the proposal to limit the number of immigrants in 1995 would be achieved by de-emphasizing family reunification. The suggestion of a bond to be posted by sponsoring families was interpreted as a lack of trust that such families would meet their obligations. The proposal to shift the burden and costs involved in settling in the country to immigrants was also seen in the same vein.

The proposed emphasis on attracting "economic migrants" was criticized by some as self-serving. It raised the issue not only of possible "brain drain" from developing countries but "capital drain" as well. To those who favored the program on family reunification, the importance given to economic migrants was seen as implying that family members reunited with their relatives in Canada did not make any economic contributions to the country.

The proposal that attracted the most criticism was the making of English and French as "critical" factors in the selection process. To many critics, falling back on the language of the two founding nations policy was discriminatory against people from Asia. Some Chinese-speaking immigrants, especially, felt they were being singled out by the emphasis on English and French as most of them did not have facility in these languages.

Finally, changing the targets on the number of refugees to be accepted was seen by many as a backing down from the humanitarian ideals of the country. It was interpreted as discriminatory against a group which, in most instances, represented people in most need of help. Some individuals pointed out that alleged abuses in Canada's policies on refugees were caused by political patronage in the Refugee Board and bureaucratic incompetence and should not be blamed on refugees and immigrants. They argued that appointments to the refugee board should not be used to court ethnic votes.

It is apparent that despite the ambivalence and silence that characterize discussions on immigration and racism, many Canadians and immigrants have strong feelings about these issues. As pointed out by Burstein (Chapter 4), the majority of Canadians still think of immigration as a positive force for nation-building. However, there seems to be a perception held by a significant number of Canadians that the immigration program has been managed from too narrow a perspective and that it has primarily served the interests of minority ethnic groups and not the broader public interest. Burstein considers this view dangerous because it serves to undermine public support for immigration-related programs that serve "to integrate new immigrants and combat the tensions produced by rapid social change — particularly racism and discriminatory treatment."

It is obvious from the uneasiness expressed by Asian immigrants that there is a need to openly discuss the relationship between immigration and racism. In this, they do not reflect the official stands of Canadian political parties who seem to have retreated from the debate. As indicated by Tepper (Chapter 3), although Canada's multiculturalism policy began with nearly universal bipartisan support, the term multiculturalism is now rarely mentioned in the platforms of the major parties. The two opposition parties — Reform and the Bloc Québécois both reject multiculturalism. To the Bloc, multiculturalism undermines Canada's commitment to the "two founding peoples" concept and is a "betrayal of . . . bilingualism and biculturalism." To the Reform Party, sensitive to charges that it is racist, the problem of multiculturalism is precisely rooted in the "two founding peoples" concept which "takes away from the equality" of all individuals in Canada. Both the Liberal and Conservative Parties have decided to minimize discussions on multiculturalism in their platforms. To one observer, this meant that "the politics of the local pub, the coffee shop and shopping mall are not reflected by party platforms and electioneering" (Gardner, 1997).

Policy Options: Other Countries and Places of Origin

In searching for policy options related to immigration and racism, it is important to remember that the issue cannot be dealt with by Canadian policies and programs alone. There are complex developments in Asia and other countries that directly and indirectly affect the movement of people to Canada. The experience of other receiving countries such as Australia, New Zealand and the United States may provide certain insights. There are also trends and patterns in sending countries that need to be understood if Canadian policy options are to be effective.

As Jones (Chapter 14) and Trlin, Henderson and Pernice (Chapter 13) show in their chapters, there are many parallels between immigration in Canada and those in Australia and New Zealand. To begin with, there is a strong parallelism among the levels of so-called "hard core" anti-immigrant groups in all three countries — roughly constituting from 13 to 25 per cent of total populations. There are also very similar levels of people's objection to immigration levels (roughly 40 to 60 per cent against), despite the fact that public debate in Australia and New Zealand on immigration is a lot more open while it is largely silent in Canada.

One aspect of Canadian international development policy recommends that official development assistance of Canada should be targeted to specific countries in Asia in order to improve conditions in those countries enough so as to encourage people to stay there. It is suggested that if life in the developing countries is improved, people will not be motivated to emigrate. It has even been argued that improved conditions in a country might encourage immigrants in Canada to return to those countries and contribute to national development in their places of origin.

The view that in-country development would inhibit immigration to Canada, however, is an unrealistic one. Studies of potential and actual migrants have shown that a certain element of psychological predisposition exists among immigrants and that immigration, as a voluntary act, is often self-selective. Also, development programs tend to make information about Canada and other destination countries more readily accessible to people in developing countries. In this era of rapid globalization, this additional information often triggers off outmigration.

In the Asia Pacific region, a number of policy regimes have tended to influence immigration to Canada and other countries. Among the more important of these trends and policies have been the following:

1) *Migrant Streams and Migration Bridges.* A number of Asian countries have traditionally been sources of immigration (e.g., China, India, Japan). Older streams of migrants tend to act as bridges for the new migrants. Barring a drastic change of immigration policy in a receiving country, the traditional source of migrants would continue to contribute to higher immigration levels. In Canada's policy of family reunification, countries that

have contributed many immigrants to Canada will continue to send disproportionately more migrants to the country.

While important migration streams and migration bridges make immigration to Canada easier and more efficient, there may be a tendency to rely heavily on such well known streams to the point where immigrants from a specific country would become dominant and thereby attract racist reactions. This may be seen, for example, in the case of immigrants from Hong Kong, Taiwan, China and India, which, in recent times, seem to have been receiving the brunt of anti-immigrant feelings. The drawing of a specific type of immigrant from a country (like the recruitment of live-in caregivers mainly from the Philippines and Sri Lanka) also tends to develop certain racial stereotypes. Perhaps, balanced and proportional spreading out of certain types of immigrants might help to ease racist tendencies in the future.

2) *Overseas Employment Programs.* A number of countries such as the Philippines, Bangladesh and Sri Lanka have official policies and programs that encourage temporary emigration. Considerations in establishment of such policies include: a) high unemployment and underemployment rates in the country because of the inability of the local economy to absorb more people into the labor force; b) the considerable foreign exchange remittances sent in by the immigrants; and c) the perceived training and other benefits arising from people's experiences abroad. In pursuance of these policies and programs, formal mechanisms have been organized by the Government, often supported by NGOs and other cause-oriented sectors, to lend support to such ventures.

Policies on temporary migration might have an indirect effect on more permanent immigration because the migration experience, even of a temporary nature, often leads to a tendency to move more permanently. For example, it has been shown that quite a number of Filipino live-in caregivers going to Canada are coming from Singapore, Hong Kong, and some Middle Eastern countries. Other live-in caregivers applying from the Philippines have lived abroad as temporary workers before. The experience of having lived abroad has given them some of the financial resources, language abilities and the confidence to apply for more permanent immigration. Such migrants have also proved to be quite successful in their adjustment to conditions in Canada.

From the perspective of the sending country, labor outmigration can be quite costly in that the country's investments in the education and skills development of the emigrant are enjoyed by the receiving country. As noted by Brillantes (See Chapter 9), quite a number of Filipino migrants to Canada have much higher educational and other qualifications than those required by the live-in caregiver program. Because of the nature of jobs found in Canada by these migrants, a process of de-skilling occurs. Still, Philippine

Government policies cannot really stop the emigrants from leaving because there are very few job opportunities in the country. Besides, the remittances of Filipinos working abroad, estimated at more than $4 billion a year, are important to the country's development.

In formulating its immigration policies, Canada needs to be sensitive to policies in sending countries in order to ensure that the interests of both countries as well as those of the migrants are upheld. In the case of countries with overseas employment programs, it must be realized that temporary migration based on contractual arrangements eventually triggers permanent migration. The wishes and welfare of the migrants should also be given due consideration, above and beyond the need of the sending country for foreign exchange and the receiving country's need for labor.

3) **E*thnic Conflicts and Civil Strife*.** Ethnic conflicts and civil strife, not to mention nature-made calamities and upheavals that tend to negatively affect the welfare of people, serve as triggers to outmigration. The Vietnam War, political unrest in China after the Tiananmen incident, the civil war in Sri Lanka, and other conflicts have tended to push people away from countries of origin and those people who had the opportunity emigrated from the country. Conflicts also create refugees, quite a number of whom are accepted into Canada.

Canada's humanitarian policies have supported the acceptance of refugees fleeing from ethnic conflicts and civil strife. It has been found, however, that many refugees, unlike independent immigrants, do not have the education and skills required for easy integration into Canadian society. Although Canada continues to accept refugees, therefore, the numbers have been declining, perhaps, as a result of the many difficulties associated with the adjustment of refugees in the country. Such difficulties may indicate advantages in separating immigration policies from that of refugees.

4) **Po*licies in Other Receiving Countries*.** Since Canada is not the only country that traditionally receives immigrants, the movement of people to this country might be influenced by the policies of other receiving countries. For example, the perceived hardening attitude toward Asian immigration in Australia and, to a lesser extent, New Zealand, might affect the volume and pace of immigration to Canada.

A review of changing conditions in Australia reveals a striking similarity with the situation in Canada. After abandoning the "White Australia" policy in 1972, Australia started admitting immigrants from Hong Kong, Vietnam and the Philippines. The Pauline Hanson incident, however, where a member of Australia's Parliament formally made pronouncements that can be interpreted as anti-immigrant if not racist, has brought to the surface the latent racist feelings of many Australians. The complaints against Asian immigrants sound remarkably the same as those heard in Canada: immigrants are stealing jobs away from locals, they flaunt their wealth by building huge houses and driving around in expensive cars, they are raising the cost of education because their children have to be taught English, they have brought Asian crime and gambling into the country, they have no commitment to Australia and refuse to pay taxes locally, they leave their children unattended while they fly as "astronauts" between Asia and Australia, and they stick to themselves and refuse to integrate into the mainstream culture. In Australia, as in Canada, a number of studies have shown the tremendous contribution of immigrants to the country's economy and society but such information does not seem to be considered at all by people who have developed negative attitudes towards the immigrants.

In the literature on racism in Australia, there is a hint that quite a number of white Australians considered the aborigines as inferiors — even sub-human. In Canada, the First Nations are recognized as the original settlers and their culture is highly appreciated. In British Columbia, there is even an effort to base the cultural symbols and images of the province on the art and aesthetics of the First Nations. To some extent, therefore, the regard for aborigines in Canada is very similar to the situation in New Zealand where the images and symbols of the Maori have been adopted by the mainstream culture.

Immigration to Canada has been traditionally linked to that in the United States. In the past, there has been an observed tendency for Asian immigrants to use Canada as a stepping stone to the United States. More recent studies have been showing, however, that for many immigrants, Canada is their final destination (Laquian, 1973). In fact, there has been a perceived tendency for Asian immigrants in the United States to move to Canada permanently for various reasons.

Key Issues and Policy Options

In considering Canadian immigration policy and its links to racism, it is important to identify a number of key issues that need to be analyzed in order to come up with options that may be considered by policy makers and the general public. Some of the key issues in a search for policy options include the following:

1) *The Silent Debate.* The reticence of Canadians on issues related to Asian immigration and racism is not helping the process of formulating proper policies and programs. The avoidance of the issue for political expediency by major political parties is inimical to the process of policy making. The budgetary emasculation of the federal multiculturalism program is resulting in less support for open discussion. Raising the issue once a year on

21 March (global day against racism and discrimination) is an ineffective way of encouraging debate.

If Canada is to face up to the challenges of immigration, multiculturalism and racism, the Canadian people need to lose their reticence in discussing what is obviously a policy area of high saliency. This is precisely why support for the federal multiculturalism program is needed. The program brings to people at the community, school, work place and local government levels the opportunity to openly discuss Asian immigration and its effects and consequences. In the words of Tepper (1997), the multiculturalism program "helps civil society to help itself." It assists vulnerable groups, among them many immigrants, to get involved in the process of policy making. Most important of all, by bringing concerned stakeholders together, it embodies the Canadian commitment to pluralism and the coming about of a polyethnic society.

2) **Ultimate Goals of Immigration.** The seeming tension between the idealistic and the pragmatic goals of immigration to Canada needs to be resolved. At present, the pragmatic approach that links immigration types, levels and pace to the economic and social demands in Canada (especially human resources needs) seems to have greater acceptance. Some people have questioned, for example, if the Government should continue setting targets for immigration in advance or whether a more pro-active approach should be used that determines the numbers and types of immigrants to be accepted based on a continuing analysis of human resource needs.

As seen in the public response to immigration changes proposed by the government in 1994, recent emphasis on more pragmatic aspects of immigration (such as the stress on accepting more economic migrants) has generated considerable criticism. The changes seem to suggest a retreat from the traditional humanitarian and liberal policies pursued by Canada. There are even hints that the changes might be influenced by a growing opposition to the admission of more visible minorities in Canada — a position that may be seen by some as having roots in racism. On this issue, a clear pronouncement from the government of the main goals of immigration in Canada is called for.

If, indeed, Canadian authorities feel that a more "pragmatic" approach to immigration is needed, then, this should be openly acknowledged and the humanitarian goals of the immigration policy may be formally de-emphasized. Continuing to uphold the idealistic humanitarian banner on the one hand and pushing for economic programs on the other suggests double-talk and dishonesty. Canada, after all, is one of only a handful of countries still open to immigration. With more than half of its citizens silently critical of its immigration policies, it will not lose international stature and prestige if it responds to what its people wish and openly adopts a more pragmatic and utilitarian immigration policy that serves its own national interests. The issues related to the real objectives of immigration and multiculturalism need to be given the highest priority in the upcoming review of the Immigration Act by the legislative task force commissioned by the Minister of Citizenship and Immigration.

3) *Immigrants and Refugees.* In the search for a more pragmatic immigration policy, there is a need to differentiate between how Canadian policy should deal with immigrants and refugees. If Canada wants to continue to uphold humanitarian objectives, it can continue to pursue current policies on refugees. However, refugee acceptance and flows should be separated entirely from immigrants because refugees require different program approaches.

Precisely because refugees are admitted into Canada because of real or potential dangers to themselves, they require more resources and assistance. As such, specific programs need to be formulated for them. It should be specified that such programs are different from those applied to immigrants. In this way, the public will not be confused with the effects and impact of the two programs and attitudes and behavior applied to each group will not be generalized.

4) *Family Reunification.* The question has been raised whether family reunification is a basic human right of immigrants (some of whom claim that extended families are inherent parts of their family traditions) or whether this is a part of the "pragmatic" determination of immigration needs.

Canadian policy needs to uphold the fact that sponsorship of a family member is a "legal obligation" and that sponsors should show concrete evidence of their ability to support the incoming family members. Resolving this issue will go a long way toward eliminating the charge that immigrants are abusing Canadian programs on health and social assistance by not living up to their sponsorship obligations.

Consistent research findings that, in general, the educational levels, professional backgrounds, and technical skills of immigrants have been declining call for a reconsideration of the family reunification policy. For example, a 1984 study revealed that immigrants who came in 1980–85 had incomes that were 25 per cent below the national average while those who came before 1961 maintained income levels above the national average. Similarly, a study by Statistics Canada found that between 1981 and 1991, the proportion of immigrants falling in the category of professional and management classes fell from 32 to 25.9 per cent. Among immigrants from Asia, Africa and the Middle East, the proportion fell from 34 to 16.3 per cent (Campbell, 1996).

It is quite obvious that family reunification, while a good humanitarian policy, has had the effect of lowering the "quality" of immigrants. This is not surprising because sponsored immigrants, usually made up of the very young and the very old, do not have the same qualifications as independent immigrants who are selected in accordance with the point system. If Canada's immigration policy is to support the country's economic program, therefore, there is a critical need to take a second look at the family reunification program.

5) *Language Education.* An important aspect of multiculturalism in Canada is language education. However, there is considerable controversy surrounding language education, especially the English as a second language (ESL) program. Immigrants have the responsibility to learn the language of their adopted country and should not expect the process to be subsidized by the government. Many Asian immigrants have the financial means to learn English or French on their own. In this regard, the policy statement of the Minister of Immigration that the capacity to use English and French should be used as a "critical" element in selecting immigrants seems reasonable. The government should review the current ESL program which is becoming a major cause of racial tension. Perhaps Canada can learn from New Zealand (Trlin, Chapter 13) where language instructions are not free.

The multiculturalism program provides an image of Canada's diversity. It provides a symbolic acceptance of pluralism as an important element in statehood. The Canadian formulation that it is a state with two official languages but not one official culture, as reflected in the multicultural policy, stipulates that people coming to live in Canada should achieve facility in either English or French even as they maintain their own culture and traditions.

6) *Economic Contributions of Immigrants.* It is generally accepted that one of the benefits from immigration is the economic contribution of immigrants. The business immigration program involving entrepreneurs, self-employed and investors categories has attracted more than 30,000 people to Canada between 1992 and 1996. About 80 per cent of these immigrants came from Asia: in 1996, 37 per cent came from Hong Kong, 20 per cent from Taiwan, and about 7 per cent each from South Korea and China. The investors program alone has brought in more than $3.7 billion into Canada and created 33,000 jobs since 1986. The entrepreneur program, in turn, has brought in $435 million and employed 12,850 workers (Woo, Chapter 17).

Despite these contributions, economic migrants have caused policy controversies. Those who favor the programs point to the wealth brought in by immigrants and the jobs they have created. Those who are against, however, see the lack of commitment of the immigrants to Canada since about 25 per cent of them regularly commute between Canada and Asia and that quite a number are planning to return to Asia after they get the "insurance" of a Canadian passport. Again, Canada may learn something from New Zealand which has solved the shortcomings of their business program by amending its points system (Trlin, Chapter 13).

There have been serious problems about management of investors' funds — one estimate indicated that more than a fourth of the funds had suffered serious losses. Business immigrants have also complained about the fact that income taxes in Canada average around 54 per cent, compared to 15–20 per cent in Hong Kong. Labor costs in Canada are also high. Finally, a proposal to require Canadian residents to declare overseas assets worth over $100,000 has been considered by many immigrants as a problem.

There is a serious concern over studies showing that the economic performance of immigrants in general has been declining compared to native-born Canadians. It is not clear what is causing this decline — reasons advanced include the declining level of education of recent immigrants mainly due to the increased admission of young and old people through the family reunification program, the changing nature of the Canadian job market that is shifting more to the services sector, the inability of immigrants to read, speak and understand English or French, and the difficulties met by migrants to achieve accreditation and certification in Canada of their educational and professional qualifications. Whatever the reasons, the declining economic performance of immigrants will be particularly serious if, as in the United States, low income immigrants are not able to help their children to become upwardly mobile (Tang, Chapter 15). This will create a low income underclass, especially in very large cities.

7) **Institutional Coordination.** At present, a number of federal, provincial and municipal agencies are directly or indirectly involved in immigrant and racism issues. At the federal level, coordination is needed among Citizenship and Immigration Canada, Human Resources Development Canada, Statistics Canada, Canadian International Development Agency, Foreign Affairs and International Trade and Canadian Heritage as to what each agency is supposed to do and how the combined activities of all agencies can be arranged in such a way that synergy can be achieved.

The allocation of responsibilities, resources and authority over immigration between the federal and local governments needs to be resolved. The Canada-Québec Accord on immigration is quite unique — it is not clear whether it should be seen as an exception or it can be used as a model for what provinces can and should do in the immigration field. Many provinces are complaining that they are increasingly being asked to provide services to immigrants while they are not in a position to influence immigration policies, which are entirely carried out at the federal level. Many municipalities are also responsible for providing immigrant services despite the fact that they have no influence over the policies and forces that send immigrants their way.

Officials in Canadian diplomatic missions abroad bear a great deal of the load for processing immigration applications but there are indications that quite a number of those officials are not fully aware of the effects and consequences of their day to day decisions. While the federal government in Ottawa assigns "targets" of the number of immigrants, each diplomatic mission in 37 countries has the capacity to process, the actual determination of who gets accepted or rejected lies mostly with the diplomatic mission officer. Despite guidelines for the use of the points system, there is a great deal of leeway for each officer in choosing from among 2,000 or more job classifications that have to be weighed before an applicant gets accepted or turned down.

8) **Information for and about Immigrants.** Current immigration assistance and service programs have been shown to be generally unknown and/or inaccessible to new immigrants. This may be because immigrant services are needed at the local or municipal level while information tends to be generated and disseminated at the central or regional government level.

General information about immigrants, based on even a cursory evaluation of mass media messages, tends to be biased. Thus, a content analysis of news and feature articles about immigration and immigrants reveals that most information is sensationalized, colored and one-sided. More information about negative aspects of immigration is published compared to more positive treatment. Media coverage also tends to highlight stereotypes about ethnic groups with incomplete information, and in some cases, even wrong information.

There are some critics of immigration programs who believe that better education, better communication or intercultural understanding are motherhood words that will not help combat racism and discrimination. However, programmatic experience shows that providing accurate and timely information to the general public about immigrants helps to ease tension as what happened in New York City (See Tang, Chapter 15). If mainstream Canadians can read more about the history, culture and backgrounds of immigrants by including such materials in the curricula of schools, as part of Canadian history and culture, it might foster better understanding and appreciation of other cultures. Encouraging the growth of the ethnic press also enhances multiculturalism and better cultural understanding.

9) **NGOs and CBOs Concerned with Immigrants.** Studies have shown that immigrant groups tend to be well organized and that many voluntary services are made available to new immigrants by such established groups. While there are federal and local government programs linked to these nongovernmental and community based organizations (NGOs and CBOs), there is a general tendency to ignore them. In view of the known benefits arising from the activities of such groups, many of

whom have immigrant roots themselves, some public resources should be allocated to encourage them.

Public assistance, however, should be designed in such a way that it fosters self-reliance rather than dependence. Thus, initial support may be given to NGOs and CBOs but these organizations should prove their capability to be sustainable in the long run. Government assistance should be based on this criterion. One of the laudable traits of Asians is their capacity for self-reliance. This is a trait that needs to be encouraged among Asians who are starting to pick up the un-Asian attitudes of "entitlement" and dependence on government subsidies.

10) **Immigration and Racism.** Immigration can be, and should be, treated separately from racism from a policy perspective. A serious policy problem arises from the fact that there is a tendency to link the two elements together. A careful analysis of the cultural, political and ideological forces that are using the semantics and symbols of racism to win points in the immigration debate is therefore needed.

Canada's official commitment to multiculturalism is the main policy handle in the immigration question. From an operational point of view there seems to be a need for information to be disseminated both on the underlying objectives of the policy and the processes by which it is being implemented. For example, there seems to be a dearth of information on how educational, informational and organizational aspects of the program are being carried out. Regarding immigration, especially Asian immigration, accurate data on who the immigrants are, what they bring into the country, what they contribute to development and how they facilitate the processes leading to multiculturalism are not readily and widely available. There is conflicting information on whether the contribution of immigrants to the Canadian economy are significant or not. There is also variable information on what is happening to the economic contribution of immigrants through time. It is important that such information be made available because prejudice, stereotypes and racist views are often formed in the absence of facts.

Asian immigration to Canada, Canada's immigration policy, and how to deal with a perceived increase in racism in this country are legitimate spheres of policy debate. Discussions on Asian immigration and immigration policy, however, are colored by ethnic and racial considerations that place policy options within the emotional context of racism. In this debate, racially-tinted incidents in Canada's history are brought out. In the efforts of actors and protagonists to push their individual points of view, discussions of policy options are muddied by bringing in charges and counter-charges of racist tendencies and motives.

Despite the current concern about immigration and racism, one can conclude that compared to the past, racism in Canada has declined. The estimate that about 15–20 per cent of Canadians are "hard core ethnocentrist" is probably accurate. Although the group is small, its influence is more widely perceived because of the higher levels of Asian immigration, the greater visibility of immigrants, the government's policies on equity and human rights, and a general concern with political correctness.

In the final analysis, the success or failure of Canada's immigration policies depend on a resolution of the ultimate vision of Canadian society. Canadian history is going through a transition from the two founding nations concept to the multicultural society ideal. The question remains, however, whether the multicultural approach means integration of new immigrants into the English or French social fabric or whether a new multicultural configuration is possible. In many ways, the increasingly multicultural makeup of Canadian society due to increased immigration from Asia is serving to blur the polarizing effect of the two founding nations concept and the bilingual and bicultural policies of the past. Asian immigration and the coming in of visible minorities have contributed, and continue to contribute, to the achievement of multiculturalism in Canada. It is, perhaps, in the eventual evolution of a new Canadian identity that Canada's immigration and racial dilemma will be resolved.

2 Globalization and Backlash Racism in the 1990s: The Case of Asian Immigration to Canada

Alan B. Simmons

This chapter concerns the implications of recent Asian immigration for racism and racialized social conflict in Canadian society. It argues that Asian immigration to Canada is centrally involved in the shifting struggle between racist and anti-racist movements. There are two sides to this involvement. Firstly, the inflow of large numbers of Asian immigrants, including many well-educated and affluent individuals, increases the strength and influence of the main Asian-origin communities in Canada. Skilled immigration, natural increase and upward social mobility combine to make these communities better able to collectively challenge old racist stereotypes and help to break them down.

Secondly, when racists in Canadian society are faced with social and economic changes associated with unfamiliar immigration and globalization, they respond with "reactive" (backlash) forms of racist imagination and practice. Growing Asian communities and Asian immigrants have been major targets of reactive racism. They are accused of fostering "offensive" dress (turbans and daggers), "inappropriate" housing ("monster homes"), and negative social impacts (unaffordable real-estate, etc.). Such allegations arise from a complex mix of factors, including real changes in cultural practices fostered by Asian-origin citizens, cultural resistance by European-origin and other citizens, anxieties associated with globalization, and racist distortions that build on these other factors. This mix must be examined critically and the racist distortions countered in anti-racist initiatives. The challenge arising from recent developments can be better understood within a broader historical perspective on racism and nation building policies in Canada.

The preceding arguments are developed in four sections. Part one outlines a theoretical approach linking racism, nation building and economic globalization. Part two examines the impact of immigration from Asia on the growing size and influence of Asian-origin communities in Canada. Part three analyzes how Asian-origin peoples in Canada have fared in overcoming the continuing legacy of economic discrimination and related ethnic stratification.

A fourth and concluding part discusses the nature of racist backlash against ethnic-Asian communities in Canada and the need for counter strategies.

THEORY: THE CHANGING CHARACTER OF RACISM

Racism is based on "othering," a process in which one group of people (racists) draw attention to some distinctive physical attributes (such as skin color) and associated ethnic characteristics (accent, values, clothing, etc.) of other people and treat them as different, less deserving and outsiders with respect to the normal benefits of membership in society. Rejection can be social ("shunning"), economic (exclusion from productive activity or subordination in low-paid, dirty, dangerous jobs), cultural or physical ("deportation" and "genocide"). Usually it is some combination of these.

The origins of racism in any society where it is found are complex and involve cognitive processes, socialization and the struggle between different groups in society for power, resources and cultural dominance. When such struggle becomes racialized (that is, based on racist imagery and teaching) it may take different forms. The most extreme form involves genocide: a definitive elimination of an "other" who is viewed as so worthless or dangerous that he/she must be eradicated. More common historically is partial incorporation of "an inferior but useful other" in a subordinated position (slave, menial worker, etc.). Sometimes the incorporation can be much greater, as when the other is viewed as extremely useful and even admirable in certain respects (say, business skills) and accorded significant prestige, while at the same time excluded socially, rewarded less, and always faced with exclusion when their valuable work is no longer required. These various outcomes may be understood as points on a continuum between full and complete incorporation of "others" and their complete and definitive exclusion.

Racism that serves to incorporate "an inferior but useful other" is generally linked to institutional practices and stereotypes that sustain a political-economic system. The system may be formally established in state policies supporting racist segregation, or it may be informally organized in a context where state policies are non-racist while permitting (or not sufficiently opposing) racist labor recruiting and employment patterns in civil society. It has been argued by some observers that the employment of undocumented migrant farm workers and immigrants working in the urban-informal sector in the United States is informally structured to reinforce racism and the subordination/exploitation of these workers (Sassen 1983). With respect to Canada, the charge has been made that the recruitment of migrant "domestic workers" (nannies, housemaids, etc.) is driven by a combination of racist and sexist values in Canadian society, and that the state is complicit in the matter because it acquiesces to pressures in society and continues to support policies that permit domestic workers (all female, virtually all non-white) to be brought in on contract from less developed countries (Jakubowski 1994, Simmons 1997).

Racism that falls short of complete exclusion, always involves a tension involving the extent of incorporation. Sometimes the incorporation is hidden. What appears as total exclusions (say, in the form of policies that ban all immigration) can mask indirect inclusion (say, of foreign labor in foreign countries through colonial and neo-colonial practices). What appears as complete subordinated inclusion is often maintained with the threat and occasional application of total exclusion (deportation or genocide).

In particular historical instances, racism generally involves a mixture of incorporative and exclusionary practices working together. The balance between these practices may vary from one case to another and shift over time. Consider these illustrations:

1) *Threat of exclusion and genocide can be used by the powerful to insure that racialized minorities continue to work for low wages.* In the history of Canadian nation-building, native peoples have been primarily excluded (on "Indian Reserves") and selectively incorporated (through Residential Schools, extensive adoption of children to non-natives, etc.) in ways that have genocidal overtones. Such practices also meant that native women, for example, were economically dependent and available for low-wage cannery jobs.

2) *Selective exclusion of female immigrants can prevent a racialized-minority from reproducing, hence reinforce its weak power-base and economic subordination.* Several tens of thousands of Chinese men were admitted to Canada in the first decade of the 20th century in order to fill hard, dangerous, low-wage jobs in railroad building and mining (See figure 2, ahead). But their wives and children were not admitted, in a move to prevent reproduction and growth or survival of a Chinese community in Canada. Exclusion of the wives and children and insuring that the Chinese community was shrinking tended to reinforce the subordination of early Chinese male settlers in Canadian society.

3) *Complete exclusion of ethnically distinct immigrants can serve to maintain racist ideologies within nations and to promote a racist division of labor internationally.* Exclusion would seem logically to preclude racists from gaining an economic advantage, since it would tend to limit or eliminate the presence of minority-group workers. But this logic does not stand up in a world of trade. Japan has pursued a deeply racist nation-building policy in the post War period by prohibiting virtually all immigration. Meanwhile, jobs were exported to other Asian nations in the form of off-shore industry — that is, Japanese investments were used to build manufacturing plants for export production in neighboring low-wage nations. The approach was integral to a high level of national economic growth and the retention of cultural homogeneity and pervasive ethnocentrism within Japan.

European nations individually and now collectively have been characterized by exclusionary-racist immigration policies (particularly since the mid-1960s) that show some similarity to the Japanese model. Some extremely xenophobic groups in Canadian society would like to move in the same direction.

From the above, we may conclude that historically and in the contemporary world common forms of racism involve varying degrees of incorporation of an alleged "inferior other." Racism may be understood therefore to be a series of practices promoted by self-interested groups in pursuit of a mix of material and cultural goals. The material and cultural goals are frequently imbedded in nation-building projects, and structured around state policies. In some historical instances the material and cultural goals of a racist imagination can be pursued without any strain between them. In other cases, strain arises between these goals. The Canadian case provides illustrations of different patterns over time.

1) For much of its history Canada was deeply exclusionary with respect to non-European peoples. Such exclusion took place within an international system that brought indirect benefits to Canada through British (later U.S.) political-economic domination of non-European nations. In Canada, native peoples were mostly marginalized and excluded (on Reserves), although the early period and some later instances when natives were subordinated and incorporated in the fur trade and the fish canning industry should not be forgotten. Non-Europeans were, with minor and partial exceptions, prohibited from settling. After Confederation in 1867, Canada as a minor player in the North-Atlantic system of nations, pursued self-directed colonization (its own immigration laws and practices). But the goals remained the same: the construction in the Americas of a new European nation, settled by Europeans, linked to Europe in trade and commerce, benefiting indirectly from the British/American domination of colonies and dependent nations in Africa, Asia, the Caribbean and Latin America, and founded on dominant European values, institutions and traditions (Christianity, capitalism, democracy, etc.). This system with its highly ethnocentric and racist elements remained in place in Canada until 1962, although some signs of transition began to appear as early as 1947.[1]

2) Canadian nation-building in the period since the early 1960s has sought to incorporate non-Europeans through immigration and permanent settlement. The reasons, timing and abruptness of the change in direction are best understood in terms of broad changes taking place in the international system and Canada's place in it. Some of the main elements were: a) The dismantling of the European colonial system, the rise of

new independent nations in Africa, Asia and the Americas, and the desire by political leaders to end racism in order to expand international cooperation and build a Western alliance against the threat of Soviet communism; b) a declining European interest in emigration, associated with rising incomes and falling population growth in that region; c) continuing labor demand in the main immigrant receiving countries; and d) low incomes, economic uncertainty and associated political unrest in many non-European nations.

The main Western immigrant receiving nations — Australia, Canada and the United States — were all subject to the changes in international circumstances. All shifted away from Euro-centric immigration policies in the early 1960s. At the same time, all three nations adopted policies that were far more open to immigration from other parts of the world. However the origins of the new flows varied according to specific circumstances (Figure 1). Immigration from Asia increased dramatically to each of these nations. Latin Americans and Caribbean emigrants went principally to the United States, but many also came to Canada.

3) Canadian self-colonization through selective immigration and related policies and practices that developed after 1962 were to begin with somewhat biased in favor of non-European immigrants who would take jobs in "lower-middle" and "middle" level positions. This bias — and associated ethnic stratification in Canada — inserted many immigrants in Canadian society at levels above Canadian-born manual workers; it also insured that few of

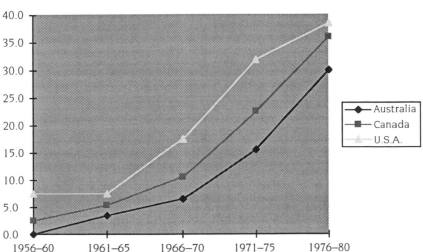

Figure 1: Asian Immigrants as a Per cent of all Immigrants Admitted to Australia, Canada and the United States, 1956–1980

the new immigrants would compete with Canadian-born elites. This outcome reflects the joint influences of state policy, ethnic stratification in Canadian society, and labor force demand.

Following the adoption of the "points system" in 1967, Canada has officially sought settlers who would "adapt" readily to Canadian society. In practice this has meant encouraging (through selection and other practices) individuals with skills and resources that will allow them to quickly find work and become self-sufficient and productive. When the "points system" for selecting immigrants was first put in place, the demand was high for workers in various less-skilled and middle-skilled categories: construction, industrial workers (machine operators, mechanics, etc.) nursing, teaching, and diverse clerical and administrative categories of government employment (in a period of expansion of state services). Immigrants admitted in the 1960s and 1970s tended to have skills for these position; often their skills were higher than those required, so they ended up in positions lower than those for which they had been trained.

4) Beginning in the 1980s, the impact of economic globalization began to be felt more deeply in Canada. This resulted in a further shift in "Canadian 'nation-building' and 'colonization' policies."[2] Immigration policies began to place increasing emphasis on the need to attract individuals with high level skills, business experience and investment resources. Such developments took place in a context of slowing Canadian economic growth, a struggle to attract international investment capital (as it began to flow to more profitable international locations), and problems in the national balance of payments as Canadian exports faltered.

In the early 1980s, business immigrants (investors and entrepreneurs) began to be specifically recruited. Few individuals with the combination required (wealth, and an interest in emigrating to Canada) can be found in most parts of the world. However, large numbers can be found in Hong Kong and Taiwan, with the result that the vast majority of business immigrants to Canada come from these countries. Over the early and mid 1990s various changes were made to immigration regulations with the objective of increasing the proportion of worker immigrants, reducing sponsored-family immigrants, and increasing the share of application and landing costs paid by the immigrants themselves. The latter have been referred to as "entrepreneurial" immigration policies, since they seek ready-made, self-financed, just-in-time human resources for a privatizing, export-led economy. Such policies tend to increase the proportion of highly skilled professional and business immigrants who have the resources to challenge racist practices and ethnocentric biases in Canadian society.

In sum, racism has taken different forms in Canadian society. Until 1962 it was embedded in state policies on immigration and nation building. When the state moved to a so-called "non-racist" immigration policy in 1962,[3] racism remained widespread in civil society as a series of informal practices that restricted the mobility of recent immigrants and non-Europeans. While the legacy of this widespread informal racism has not disappeared, the dominant form of racism in contemporary Canadian society appears to be the reactive, backlash kind. It reflects resentment of the success and economic power of non-European immigrants and cultural communities in Canada. The main characteristics of these transitions are in Figure 2.

Economic globalization plays a dual role in the recent transformation of struggle between anti-racist values and racist backlash. It reinforces certain aspects of anti-racist struggle. At the same time, it creates conditions in which the new reactive racism can arise. These paradoxical outcomes emerge through diverse specific mechanisms, as summarized in Figure 3. For example, the very emergence of former colonized nations as NICs (newly industrializing countries) with increasing influence in international commerce and financial institutions is reinforced by global investment and trade patterns. The fact that these nations are non-European has a direct impact countering old racist imagery. The fact that such countries also may vigorously oppose racism (at least as it affects their expatriate communities abroad) is also important in countering official racist practices. When, in the context of globalization, Canadian policies and international circumstances combined to favor

Figure 2: Historical Forms of Racism in Canada

Period and main form of racism	Associated incorporation of Non-European labor	Associated Exclusion of Non-Europeans from membership
Until 1962 *Offical "Colonial" Racism*	Indirectly, through division of labor in European Colonial system	Major thrust of laws and practices affecting natives and immigrants
1962–1970s *Widespread informal Racism in civil society*	Directly, through admission of many lower and middle level non-European immigrants, and through multicultural policy.	Partial exclusion, in economic and cultural arenas. Non-European immigrants took jobs below their skill levels and moved up to better jobs more slowly.
1980s–1990s *Backlash racism from threatened groups in society*	Directly, as above, with increasing priority given to highly skilled professional and business immigrants.	Still partial. Some non-European immigrants and their descendants are moving to elite positions, while facing new "backlash" racism.

immigration to Canada of professionals and wealthy individuals from these former colonial nations, old racist views and teachings are further challenged.

At the same time, globalization leads to other outcomes that reinforce racist backlash. Many who wish to move in an international system that is changing due to rapid shifts in investment, production and employment from one region to another are less skilled and poor. When they ignore official immigration policies and move anyway, they become very vulnerable to exploitative hiring and racialized treatment abroad. They are often viewed in host societies as "job stealers" and become the target of racist action. Since skilled workers in receiving societies are also often made insecure by changing employment prospects as globalization unfolds, they too may resent the skilled and wealthy immigrants, if the immigrants are viewed as competitors for jobs and other scarce resources (housing, attractive neighborhoods, etc.).

The following sections provide some empirical evidence on the patterns of shifting immigration and racial discrimination corresponding to the arguments and hypotheses discussed to this point.

GLOBALIZATION AND THE GROWTH OF ASIAN-ORIGIN COMMUNITIES

Immigrants come to Canada from virtually every nation in Asia, but the great majority are from South Asia (mostly from India) or of Chinese ethnicity (from Hong Kong, Taiwan and China). Immigration figures for 1994 are indicative of the dominance of these flows over others (Table 1). In that year more than 44,000 immigrants from Hong Kong entered Canada; this represented nearly a third of the total inflow from all of Asia. Considered

Figure 3: Globalization, Anti-Racism and Racism

GLOBALIZATION	
ANTI-RACISM	NEW RACISM AND RACIST BACKLASH
At *Global level*: • Rise of NICs • Expanding trade contacts • New geo-political alliances • Rising commercial travel • Elite South-North migration	Racism: • Treatment of undocumented migrants • Treatment of low-skilled visa workers • Export of low-skilled jobs
At *national level*: • Human rights movements • Multiculturalism • Growing "voice" of minorities • Rising non-white elites	*Racist backlash* • Displacement of previously privileged • Ethno-class competition • Job and status insecurity

**Table 1: Asian Immigration to Canada, 1994,
by Country of Last Permanent Residence**

Country	Number	Per cent
Hong Kong	44,169	31.2
Philippines	19,097	13.5
India	17,225	12.1
China (People's Rep.)	12,486	8.8
Taiwan	7,411	5.2
Sri Lanka	6,671	4.7
Vietnam	6,230	4.4
Pakistan	3,746	2.6
Korea (South)	2,946	2.1
Iran	2,694	1.9
Lebanon	2,674	1.9
Iraq	1,931	1.4
Saudi Arabia	1,780	1.3
Israel	1,615	1.1
United Arab Emirates	1,357	1.0
Bangladesh	1,224	0.9
Kuwait	1,029	0.7
Other*	7,302	5.2
Total	**141,587**	**100**
Total Immigrants to Canada	**223,875**	
Asian immigrants as % of Total	**63.2**	

* "Other" Asian countries from which immigrants came are: Afghanistan, Bahrain, Bhutan, Brunei, Cambodia, Cyprus, Indonesia, Japan, Jordan, Laos, Macau, Malaysia, Mongolia, Myanmar, Nepal, Oman, Palestine, Qatar, Singapore, Syria, Thailand, Tibet, and Yemen

together, Chinese from Hong Kong, China, and Taiwan provided more than 45 per cent of all Asian immigration and more than one quarter of all immigration to Canada. The flow from South Asia (India, Sri Lanka, Pakistan and Bangladesh) was smaller (just over 20 per cent of the total movement from Asia), but still appreciable. Immigration from the Philippines (13.5 per cent of the Asian total) was also large.

Immigration of Chinese and South Asians to Canada has a long history, dating back to the late 19th century (Table 2). The volume of flows changed over time in direct response to shifts in Canadian immigration policy. In the period 1906 to 1908 some 5,000 "East Indians" (South Asians) were admitted for low-wage labor. Between 1906 and 1924, approximately 45,000 Chinese were similarly admitted; virtually all of these immigrants were men. In all other years between 1900 and 1947, only a handful of additional East Indians and Chinese were admitted — the doors were essentially closed tight by racist policy.

Table 2: Immigration of Chinese and South Asians to Canada

Year	Chinese	South Asians
1906–24	43,470	5,381
1924–46	7	598
1947–62	21,877	4,836
1963–67	18,716	9,707
1968	8,382	3,932
1969	8,272	6,579
1970	5,377	6,847
1971	5,056	6,499
1972	6,322	6,479
1973	14,722	11,893
1974	13,083	15,710
1975	12,035	12,678
1976	11,548	9,141
1977	7,169	7,298
1978	5,384	6,415
1979	8,024	5,751
1980	11,245	9,508
1981	13,002	9,210
1982	10,747	10,153
1983	9,559	8,750
1984	10,782	7,686
1985	10,287	5,832
1986	8,496	9,938
1987	18,795	14,909
1988	26,258	15,925
1989	24,695	15,505
1990	37,327	18,140
1991	34,046	24,051
1992	49,339	29,132
1993	46,042	**33,768**
1994	**56,655**	27,642
1968–1994	**472,649**	**339,371**

Sources: Prior to 1968, figures compiled by Bolaria and Li (1978: tables 5.1 and 7) from various official documents. Figures from 1968–1994 from Immigration Statistics (annual reports).
Notes: Annual figures are arrivals by country of last permanent residence. Chinese include those from China and Hong Kong. South Asians include those from India, Pakistan, Sri Lanka and Bangladesh.

Figure 4: Chinese in Canada by Selected Year

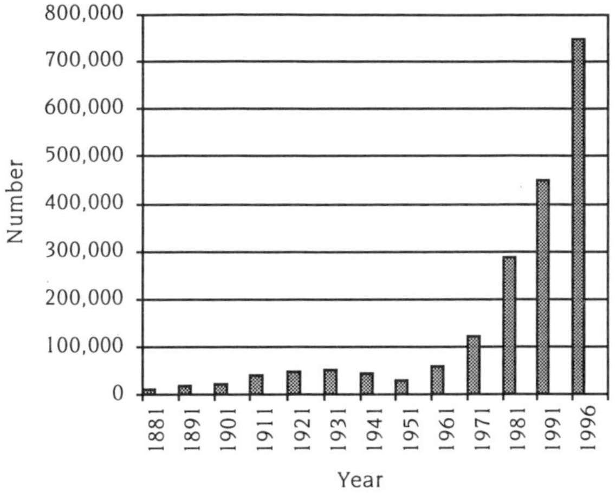

Table 3: Per cent Distribution of Chinese and South Asian Immigrants by City of Destination, 1994

	Chinese	South Asian	Other	Total
Destination				
Vancouver	32	27	11	19
Toronto	34	36	26	29
Montréal	4	8	13	10
All other places	30	29	50	42
Total	**100**	**100**	**100**	**100**
(N)	56,655	31,307	135,913	223,875

Source: Citizenship and Immigration Statistics, 1994. Ottawa: Minister of Public Works and Government Supplies, 1997. Table IM21.

Notes: Figures show intended destination of immigrants arriving in 1994, classified by country of last permanent residence. Chinese are those from China, Hong Kong and Taiwan. South Asians are those from India and Sri Lanka.

Table 4: Wages of Chinese and White Labor, circa 1900

	Wage period	Wages paid to Chinese	Wages paid to Whites	Chinese wages as % of White
Agricultural labor	month	$20–25	$30–40	64.3
Cannery workers	month	$40–50	$80–90	52.9
Lumber workers	day	$1.25	$2.25–3.75	35.7
Coalminers	day	$1.25	$3.00–4.00	35.7
Railway workers	day	$1.00	$1.25–1.50	72.7

Source: Report of the Royal Commission on Chinese and Japanese Immigration, 1902.

A very modest resumption of immigration from Asia between 1947 and 1962 reflected a change in Canadian policy: restrictions on sponsorship of family members by previous Asian immigrants were lifted, leading to modest inflows of wives and children. However, the really important rise in Asian immigration did not take place until two associated policy shifts in the 1960s: the elimination of the country preference system for selecting immigrants in 1962, and the introduction of the points system in 1967.

Asian-origin ethnic communities in Canada are growing through immigration and natural increase. The size of the communities can only be roughly estimated from self-declared ethnic origin in past censuses and population projections taking into account immigration levels. From this, it would appear that the Chinese ethnic population in Canada in 1996 is in the range of 750,000 people (Figure 4). Together Chinese- and South Asian-origin peoples represent somewhat more than 3 per cent of the Canadian population. Since the Asian-origin immigrants settle overwhelmingly in Montréal, Toronto and Vancouver (Table 3), the proportion of the population of Asian origin in these cities is many times higher than the nation as a whole. The Chinese and South Asian ethnic communities are the largest non-European origin groups in Canada.

Immigrants from Asia prior to the 1960s were brought into the country for low-wage and dangerous work in fields such as coal mining and railway construction. They also found niches in low-income commerce: laundry services, restaurants, and convenience stores. Wage comparisons from the early 20th century are informative in this regard (Table 4). Over time, many of the early Chinese immigrants gradually shifted from manual work in logging, railways and mines to commercial activities, as proprietors of small stores and restaurants (Li, 1988).

The surge in Asian immigration in the period following the establishment of the points system in 1967 included individuals who varied widely in terms of education and occupation. Some were managers and professionals, others clerks and assembly workers. However, the proportion at the higher end of this occupational spectrum (namely managers, professionals, skilled workers) was from the beginning relatively high. In consequence of the skills of immigrants and the high schooling aspirations of their children, since the 1960s about one-sixth (17 per cent) of Chinese-origin workers in Canada have been professionals, compared with 10 to 11 per cent in the population at large (Kalbach and Kalbach 1995).

Changes in Canadian immigration policy in the 1980s led to efforts to encourage the immigration of highly skilled workers and business class immigrants, including managers, investors and entrepreneurs. In 1994, for example, more than 11,000 immigrants came to Canada as entrepreneurs, investors and managers (Table 5). More than one-fifth of all Chinese immigrants destined for the labor force who entered Canada in 1994 were entrepreneurs, investors or managers. This is approximately three times higher

**Table 5: Intended Occupation of Chinese and
South Asian Immigrants, 1994**

	Entrepreneur	Investor	Manager	**Sub-total**	Other	**Total**	<u>N</u>
Chinese	6.6	7.4	6.9	**21.0**	79.0	**100.0**	28,918
South Asians	1.2	0.2	2.1	**3.5**	96.5	**100.0**	11,556
All other	2.3	0.6	4.4	**7.3**	92.7	**100.0**	68,330
Total	**3.3**	**2.4**	**4.8**	**10.5**	**89.5**	**100.0**	**108,804**

Source: Citizenship and Immigration Statistics, 1994. Table IM19.
Note: Sub-total is sum of per cent intending to work as entrepreneurs, investors and managers.

**Table 6: Destinations of Entrepreneurial, Investor and
Managerial Immigrants, 1994**

	B.C.	Ontario	Québec	All other	Canada	<u>N</u>
Entrepreneurs	31.2	29.9	14.5	24.3	100.0	3,643
Investors	61.1	22.9	7.5	8.5	100.0	2,576
Managers	24.6	54.3	10.4	10.7	100.0	5,234
Sub-total	**34.9**	**39.5**	**11.0**	**14.5**	**100.0**	**11,453**
All others	19.4	55.3	12.4	12.9	100.0	97,351
All immigrants	**21.1**	**53.6**	**12.2**	**13.1**	**100.0**	**108,804**

Source: Citizenship and Immigration Statistics, 1994. Table IM23.
Note: Totals are limited to those destined for the labor force.

than the proportion in these three occupations among all immigrants. It is more than six times higher than the proportion in these elite occupations among South Asians.

Immigrants entering in the business class tend to settle primarily in British Columbia and Ontario (Table 6). Most go to Vancouver and Toronto, the main cities in these provinces. As the majority are ethnically Chinese, this concentrates the impact of well-to-do Chinese-origin immigrants on Canadian society in two large cities, principally.

Not all Asian immigrants who enter the business class are necessarily leaders in the business world. Some investors, for example, have rather modest business skills, despite having accumulated sufficient capital to meet Canadian entry requirements. This became evident in news reports following the tragic murder of a former Hong Kong cab driver who was able to come to Canada as an investor after selling his car and apartment in Hong Kong (Wong 1997). He was murdered outside his attractive and expensive home in Vancouver. Initially neighbors and reporters could not believe that he actually made his living in Canada delivering newspapers. While this may be a major exception, it is instructive regarding misunderstandings that can arise about who constitutes an investor. Other Asians immigrating to Canada in the business class are clearly multi-millionaires and important international investors, as is evident from reports on the amount of capital they bring and invest in Canada. The government of Ontario reports that business immigrants from Hong Kong alone established 500 business and invested $68 million in that province between 1986 and 1991 (estimates from Business Immigration Section, Ministry of Industry, Trade and Technology, Government of Ontario).

In summary, the principal Asian-origin ethnic communities in Canada are large and growing rapidly through new immigration arising from the intersection of Canadian policies and international circumstances in a globalizing international system. The communities include individuals in a very wide range of occupations and income groups, some of whom have advanced professional training and/or significant capital and business experience. It is understood that their children are achievement oriented and upwardly mobile. If so, the rising economic power and potential for political influence of Asian-origin individuals and their communities should be evident in their levels of schooling, jobs and incomes. The chapter turns to evidence on this question in the next section.

THE ACHIEVEMENTS OF ASIAN-ORIGIN CITIZENS

Evidence on the extent to which Asian-origin people in Canada have been able to overcome racist institutional barriers to achievement in schooling, jobs and income is indirect. Conclusions in this area involve inference from scattered studies of ethnic stratification and mobility. In these studies, racism is not measured. Nor is achievement motivation, ambition, support-networks and other factors that bring about success. Rather, the studies measure outcomes — how Asian origin citizens, for example, make out in jobs and incomes compared to those of European or other origin. Despite their many limitations, such data do allow a general assessment of the relative educational and occupational achievements of Asian-origin individuals and communities in Canada, even though they do not permit anything more than inferences and speculation on the factors that led to these outcomes. The objective of examining recent data on outcomes or performance of Asian-origin immigrants and the Canadian-born of Asian ethnic background is to assess their transforming status in Canadian society and their potential for further challenging old racist stereotypes.

Schooling

Asian immigrants, like others arriving in Canada in recent years, have high levels of schooling reflecting in considerable part the selection procedure for independent (worker) immigrants and the likelihood that their families also have high levels of schooling. In addition, children in Asian-origin

Table 7: Highest Level of Schooling, Individuals Aged 20–25 of South Asian Ethnicity by Place of Birth and the Total Population, Toronto, 1991.

	Ethnic South Asian by Place of Birth				Total (all foreign and Can. born)
	Caribbean	Asia	Canada	Total	
Females by level of schooling					
Primary	3.3	3.8	2.1	3.6	1.7
Secondary	44.5	35.3	12.5	34.9	32.8
Technical	38.3	18.3	12.5	21.3	26.1
University	13.9	42.6	72.2	40.3	39.3
Total	**100.0**	**100.0**	**100.0**	**100.0**	**100.0**
N=	1,370	5,505	720	7,590	120,130
Males by level of schooling					
Primary	4.1	1.6	0.0	1.8	1.6
Secondary	46.8	34.0	19.7	34.5	39.4
Technical	26.1	18.0	12.7	18.9	23.5
University	23.4	46.5	66.9	44.9	35.5
Total	**100.0**	**100.0**	**100.0**	**100.0**	**100.0**
N=	1,090	4,830	710	6,630	115,665

Source: Special tabulation of the 1991 census for the Toronto CMA.
Notes: Ethnicity is self-defined. South Asian place of birth includes India, Pakistan, Bangladesh and Sri Lanka. Caribbean place of birth includes Greater and Lesser Antilles plus Guyana. Individuals classified by level of schooling have completed the level shown except for Primary (which includes individuals who have no schooling or primary incomplete) and University (which includes individuals who have some university training as well as those who have a degree).

families, including particularly those born in Canada, are known to be keenly interested in school achievement. Table 7 provides some select data in this regard for ethnic South-Asians aged 20–24 living in Toronto. Overall, levels of schooling for males and females in this group are similar to the population at large in Toronto: about one-third have only high school or less, indicating that not all Asian-origin youth in Canada have gone on to college or university. Further examination of the data indicate large differences within the ethnic South Asian community. Those of South Asian ethnic background who were born in the Caribbean are part of a mass-migration from their home countries (mostly Guyana and Trinidad) to North America. Levels of schooling in this group are far lower than among those born in Asia, who are part of a more select stream of immigration. Levels of university study among the ethnic-Asian youth born in Canada are extremely high. For example, 70 per cent of the women in this group have completed at least some university studies as opposed to only 39 per cent in the population at large.

Table 8: Employment Income for Asians Born in Canada, by Period of Arrival and Date of Census

Date	Index of Average Employment Income (Can. born = 100)						
	All periods	1985–89	1980–84	1975–79	1970–74	1965–69	1960–64
Males							
1981 Census	79.0	n.a.	n.a.	65.9	75.1	85.6	91.5
1986 Census	76.5	n.a.	57.3	71.1	79.6	88.5	94.4
Females							
1981 Census	85.7			72.4	85.1	95.6	95.2
1986 Census	83.8		64.2	79.5	88.7	98.6	97.1

Source: Ravi Verma and Chan Kwok Bun. "The Economic Adaptation of Asian Immigration to Canada." Paper presented at the Symposium on Immigration and Integration, October 25–27,1996, Department of Sociology, University of Manitoba.
Notes: Figures for 1981 and 1986 include people living in Census Metropolitan Areas only. Figures for 1991 include all people in Canada. Average employment income is for all work in the year prior to the census, with the exception that the 1991 data are based on individuals who worked full time for the entire preceding year. n.a. is not applicable.

Income From Employment

Several studies have examined job, promotion and income discrimination affecting visible minorities in Canada from the perspective of their wages, controlling other variables likely to affect income, such as sex, age, education, metropolitan residence and period of residence in Canada. Findings from analysis of the 1981 census show that Asians who arrived prior to 1960 and who hence had lived in Canada for 20 years or more had incomes almost as high as Canadian men and women with similar education, ages, and residence (Beaujot et al. 1988). However, Asian immigrants who had arrived more recently had lower levels of wages, but the reason why is not known. It may be that incomes rise over time as immigrants adapt culturally and learn to overcome racism; or it may be that more recent immigrants face greater challenges.

The income findings described above have recently been replicated for 1981 and extended to 1986, where a similar pattern is found (Table 8). Comparing the incomes of same arrival cohorts in 1981 and 1986 lends credence to the argument that experience in the Canadian labor market pays-off in higher relative incomes. Incomes rose for all cohorts between these two years. The data also support the view that Asian immigrants who arrived just before the recession in the early 1980s had particularly low incomes relative to Canadian born (compare the relative income for the recently arrived in 1981 with those for the recently arrived in 1986).

Data on the income from employment among South Asians in Toronto confirms that the pattern of rising income with longer residence in Canada

Table 9: Employment Income of South-Asian Born, Living in Toronto, by Sex and Period of Arrival, 1990

	1981–90	1971–80	< 1971
Males	0.62	0.85	1.08
Females	0.71	0.88	1.08

Source: Special tabulation of the 1991 census of Canada
Notes: Average annual income is for full time workers, employed for the entire year. South Asians are those born in India, Pakistan, Bangladesh and Sri Lanka. Toronto is the Toronto CMA (Greater Toronto). The index is the average income for South Asian workers divided by the average income for all workers.

continued to hold for 1990 (Table 9). These data show that incomes of those who had been in Canada the longest were actually somewhat higher than those of average workers in Toronto. The comparison does not control for level of education nor age. The higher than average incomes of the South Asian workers who have been in Canada since 1970 or earlier reflect in part the fact that they are older and more experienced than the average worker.

Economic Success

One of the limitations of most previous efforts to analyze the economic success of the Asian-born in Canada is that it collapses Asian-born immigrants in a single category, regardless of country of origin. Data recently reported by Verma and Kwok Bun (1996) overcome this by pointing to major differences between the employment income of different national-origin groups (Table 10). Immigrants from Hong Kong and India have average employment incomes above those of Canadian born. In contrast, those born in Vietnam and China have incomes far below this average. Female immigrants from the Philippines have incomes that are 96 per cent of those of Canadian born women; while males from the Philippines have average incomes only 81 per cent of Canadian born males.[4] These data do not control for other relevant variables, such as age, schooling and metropolitan residence, so they should also be read with care.

While the preceding evidence is partial and incomplete it points generally to the relative success that Asian immigrants and their children born in Canada have had in schooling and earnings. Their success does not mean that they did not face discrimination, nor that they feel themselves to be fully integrated into Canadian society. In fact, as the evidence in the next section argues, discrimination and social integration are more complex and unresolved issues.

Table 10: Average Employment Income by Place of Birth, 1990

Place of Birth	Income		Index (Can.=1.00)	
	Males	Females	Males	Females
Canada	38,321	26,092	1.00	1.00
U.K.	48,353	29,212	1.26	1.12
U.S.A.	47,399	30,699	1.24	1.18
Germany	43,801	23,845	1.14	0.91
Netherlands	41,700	25,651	1.09	0.98
Italy	39,326	24,188	1.03	0.93
Portugal	33,007	24,105	0.86	0.92
India	39,738	24,752	1.04	0.95
Hong Kong	38,750	28,170	1.01	1.08
China	31,957	21,784	0.83	0.83
Philippines	31,151	25,088	0.81	0.96
Vietnam	26,742	20,048	0.70	0.77

Source: Ravi Verma and Chan Kwok Bun, "The economic adaptation of Asian immigration to Canada." Paper presented at the Symposium on Immigration and Integration, October 25–27,1996. Department of Sociology, University of Manitoba. (Mimeo, Statistics Canada). The data are from a special run of the 1991 Census of Canada.
Note: Employment income in calendar 1990 for individuals who worked full time over the full year.

OVERCOMING RACIST SOCIAL BARRIERS

In the colonial and neo-colonial eras of Canadian history (up until the 1960s), racist imagery was based largely on an "othering" of non-European peoples to insure that any living in Canada (and these were to be few) were limited to low-wage and/or dangerous jobs. The assumption was that non-Europeans were not morally or mentally suitable for more skilled and remunerative roles in the Canadian economy. In the post-colonial and global periods of Canadian history (from the 1960s to the present) these old stereotypes are being replaced by a new imagery. Racism against Asians is increasingly based on allegations of unacceptable cultural differences. These include: wearing turbans in places where "hats" are traditionally forbidden, carrying ceremonial daggers in violation of rules against "weapons," building "monster" houses, and engaging in exclusionary business practices. Asian-origin immigrants are also blamed for destroying the "life style" of European-origin Canadians, by changing the ethnic composition of schools and by contributing to rising real-estate prices that make housing unaffordable to children in the neighborhoods where they grew up.

Contemporary racism is based on the stigmatization of people who cannot be faulted in terms of their work-ethic or productive contributions. It is "reactive," based increasingly on resentment or "backlash" against more affluent and successful immigrants. Issues of concern by leaders of the backlash are diverse. They rest on cultural biases, fears, distortions and misunderstandings that must be examined. They emerge in a particular political-economic phase of nation-building that may both offer and constrain anti-racist strategies, so the context of future-oriented efforts must also be taken into account. Among the questions to be considered are the following:

Will the current racist reaction to Asian immigration gain strength and lead to policies designed to reduce Asian and other non-European inflows? The rise in anti-immigration sentiment and racism in many economically advanced countries in recent years points to this possibility. Given the interdependence of nations in the international system, nations that seek to cut off immigration at least in part to address ethnocentric and racist sentiment in their societies will do so in a way that hides the racist motivation. They will typically claim that the reasons are entirely economic, to do with concerns about the impact of immigrants on job availability for the native born, for example. Rather than cut immigration of some particular group, such as Asians and other non-Europeans, they will reduce or eliminate all immigration. Europe redefines itself so that movement within the EEC is no longer international migration; it then greatly restricts all immigration to Europe (from outside) thereby responding perfectly to racist pressures while claiming that it is acting on other grounds. Since a high proportion of all immigration to Canada comes from non-European sources, any overall reduction in immigration levels would primarily serve to reduce these flows. This logic has not been lost on racists in Canada, and seems to be reflected in the policies to reduce all immigration that some citizens would like to see implemented and has likely had some effect in the setting of immigration targets in Canada and Québec (Simmons, in press).

If Canada is able to resist and counter racist-based pressures to reduce immigration, on what grounds will it do so? Canadian exceptionalism in immigration policy currently rests on a set of incompletely tested assumptions related more broadly to Canadian nation-building and the national economy. These include:

- immigrants create jobs for the native-born rather than take them away;
- skilled and business immigrants create highly paid jobs, which is what Canada primarily needs;
- the new export-led economy in Canada will provide a context in which such skilled immigrants will make the greatest contribution, thereby assuring that they will find Canada attractive and that the native born will want them to stay; and

- adjustment to the new global system through success in entrepreneurship and exports will create opportunity for all Canadians and hence contribute to national solidarity and to a reduction in ethnic, regional, linguistic and class conflict.

These assumptions are potentially plausible, but in some cases they do not correspond to recent experience. It seems that the current quest for higher national economic growth (measured in trade and gross national product) may be based on policies that, by themselves and without counter measures, tend to increase income inequality, regional economic disparities and ethnic tensions. The so-called "economic recovery" following the recession of the early 1990s has been characterized by all these strains and seems to have reinforced the efforts by some to racialize social tensions. Racialized immigrants are viewed as job-stealers, even when the evidence shows they generally contribute over time somewhat to net national employment (Economic Council of Canada 1991) and that an immediate effect on unemployment is likely to be small (Marr and Siklos 1994). Ethnicized immigrants are blamed for blocked political aspirations, and so on.

Can the "backlash" attacks on skilled immigrants be countered directly through evidence and public education? This seems to be one of the most promising areas for anti-racist strategy, but the specifics need to be thought out and developed more fully. Consider the following arguments used by opponents of immigration and carried forward by those who hold racist views:

- *Inflated real-estate values.* Well-to-do immigrants are frequently blamed for rising real estate values and the inability of young Canadian-born to afford houses in the communities where they grew up. However, the evidence on this matter suggests that immigrants are at most contributors to a problem that is created in the first instance and to the greatest degree by internal migration in Canada.
- *"Monster houses."* The term "monster house" denotes the shock and opposition that people feel to significant changes in architectural style in their neighborhood. It may be non-racist in origin for many users of the term, but is then picked by others and racialized: only (unwelcome) foreigners build monster homes. Yet the entire issue needs to be thought through more fully. Western urban architecture also includes many very old styles — such as the Brown-Stone houses of New York or the Gray-Stone houses of Montréal — suited to high density, high land-price areas. The houses stretch forward to the sidewalk, have small or no side alleys, and have smaller enclosed gardens, if any. Such housing is almost inevitable in desirable, land-scarce urban areas. Immigrants have not been and are not likely to be the only promoters of such housing. Historically as well, the very wealthy in Canada have lived in large houses on large lots in prestigious communities within the major cities (e.g., Westmont in Montréal, Forest Hill in Toronto, etc.). The fact that very

wealthy recent non-European immigrants may also do this is nothing new. More needs to be researched and said on these matters. Much of what is blamed on non-European (particularly Asian) immigrants with respect to "monster homes" seems to be the outcome of more general trends that are not caused by the immigrants primarily. These trends include: rising pressure on "old stock" housing (leading to the demolition of smaller houses on valuable property and their replacement with larger homes) and shift in housing preferences among the affluent in Canada in general (the movement to very large homes with impressive entrance foyers in prestigious new suburbs of large cities).

- *So-called "offensive dress"*: *daggers and turbans.* It seems that many Canadians, perhaps the majority, now clearly distinguish turbans from "hats" and ceremonial daggers from "knives." They also know that a sharp pencil can be used as a dangerous weapon, but given its understood use no one would think of banning pencils from public places. Yet racists continue to resist such logical distinctions. Racism that is based on distortions and misperceptions of this resistant kind may be very hard to counter through education alone, since it seems to be based on some deeper fear of difference or perhaps the economic threats of immigrants.

- *"Job stealers."* Evidence that immigrants have at least a modest net positive impact on employment comes primarily from general models of the Canadian economy. Unfortunately, such models are rather abstract and remote, hence may have little impact on public perceptions. Public education needs to incorporate more concrete cases and illustrations covering the mix of impacts including the positive ones.

In sum, Canadians of Asian origin, like other non-European origin peoples in Canada, find themselves in a paradox. As they make progress in breaking down the old stereotypes, they find themselves facing a "backlash" in the form of new "reactive" racist hostilities and resentments. The contemporary situation is one in which the old battle to eliminate racism with respect to access to schools, jobs and business opportunities is not yet complete. At the same time, a new battle is emerging to counter racism in the area of "rights" — the right to build a house or place of worship that looks different, or to wear ethnic head-dress in places where "hats" are forbidden, and in other respects to become accepted socially and culturally. The context in which the struggle is being waged — namely, export-led nation-building in the new globalization and expanded competition between nations — is one that gives rise to hope and concern at the same time. Increasing success of Asians and others in their home countries and as immigrants to Canada gives them greater prestige and resources to counter racism, just as it provides a pretext for new racist attacks by individuals and groups made insecure and threatened by global developments. Countering the new attacks will require specific new strategies at various levels.

Endnotes

[1] Canada's explicitly ethnocentric and implicitly racist "country preference" system for selecting immigrants was terminated in 1962. Increasing numbers of non-Europeans began to immigrate to Canada immediately thereafter. The "points system" for selecting immigrants was adopted in 1967 and led to a further expansion of non-European flows. These major policy shifts were preceded by several minor ones. In 1947, the law excluding the admission of wives and children of Asians was repealed, leading to the inflow of several thousand Chinese and South Asians (Figure 2). In 1956, Canada initiated a visa system for recruiting domestic workers (nannies and housekeepers); this sparked annual inflows of hundreds of Caribbean and other women, many of whom later became immigrants when the "national preference system" for immigrant selection was terminated.

[2] The reader should be aware that my use of the terms "nation-building" and "colonization" to describe current economic and immigration policy trends is not usual, but hopefully justified in order to place these policy trends in a broader historical perspective. Current neo-Liberal restructuring in Canada (policies to cut social expenditures, attract investment through declining industrial taxes, promote economic growth through exports, etc.), has much in common with previous Canadian nation-building policies in that the restructuring is oriented toward Canada's place in the international economic system and tends to polarize regions and social classes insofar as they represent relative winners and losers in the emerging nation. Similarly, the term colonization is normally used to denote an externally imposed settlement by foreign elites over an existing "native" underclass. While Canadian colonization has certainly included European-led colonization in relation to Amerindians and other indigenous peoples, the process has also long included what might be called self-colonization, a process by which Canadian elites (and others) seek to encourage whatever kind of settlement they feel will benefit their interests. What changes over time is not the dynamics promoting foreign settlement or "colonization" but the shifting international economy, Canada's place in it, and related views on the ideal immigrant.

[3] The official position of Canadian immigration policy and practice since 1962 has been "non-racist," yet more careful reviews of policy in practice years after the policy shift took place (and by which time any lingering racism based on earlier policies should have disappeared) have concluded that many specific features of Canadian immigration policy — such as the setting of immigration targets, the special program for foreign domestic workers, etc. — reflect in part racist influences in Canadian society making themselves evident through policy practices (see, for example, Jakubowksi 1994 and Simmons, in press).

[4] Similar gender differences in income achievement (relative to the Canadian born) have been noted for the Caribbean immigrants in Canada (Beaujot et al, 1988: table 24; Simmons and Plaza, 1995) but the reasons for such differences are unknown and may involve links between gender and racism. For example, do non-white immigrant women do relatively well compared with other women because women in general are disadvantaged with respect to higher income jobs, such that color has diminished importance in discrimination affecting salaries and promotions?

3 Multiculturalism and Racism: An Evaluation

Elliot L. Tepper

The "Asian fact" is now an obvious and important part of Canada's mosaic. However, just as the impact of Asia is being felt increasingly in the county, as a domestic reality, the policy designed to deal with diversity is under attack. Multiculturalism is 25 years old as a government activity. However, just when a policy for diversity is most needed, the support for government involvement in managing change is being weakened. This chapter looks at Multiculturalism in several aspects. The term multiculturalism has at least three possible meanings: a description of empirical reality, a government activity, and symbolic representation of the polity.[1] This chapter discusses all three, with specific reference to themes of this book: Asian immigration, racism, and public policy. After presenting some demographic data relating to the "Asian fact," as an empirical reality, an evaluation of Multiculturalism will be given, from several perspectives. The chapter concludes with some aspects of Multiculturalism as it applies to race relations; and to the role of government as regulator of the moral and symbolic order.

This chapter suggests that multiculturalism as an empirical reality, including the Asian presence in Canada, is going to increase, with implications for the country's self definition; it suggests that as government policy, multiculturalism has always been most important at the symbolic level rather than just as an activity of government; and that both at the symbolic and practical level, a public policy such as Multiculturalism is required. Multiculturalism as a policy bears considerable weight for preparing Canada for the next millennium. If there is a single message in this chapter it is this: If you are concerned about racism in Canada, then support Multiculturalism.

ORIGIN, EVOLUTION AND DEFINITION OF THE POLICY

Conceptually, Multiculturalism is rooted in blending together two separate visions of the state. One is the vision of society as a mosaic. This is based in part on the desire to distinguish Canada from its melting pot neighbor to the South. Canada's self image as a mosaic goes back at least to the 1930s. (See Gibbon, 1938). Academic and policy currency was given to this image in 1965 by John Porter who implanted it in modern discourse with his monumental study, demonstrating that Canada is indeed a mosaic, but a mosaic of structured inequality. (See Porter, *Vertical Mosaic*, 1965). From the mosaic image originates legitimacy of an integrative rather than an assimilative strategy of state formation.

The other vision, of course, is acceptance of the dualistic nature of Canada's origins, and the need to accommodate subsequent evolution of the polity. Prime Minister Trudeau's formula in 1971 was to define the evolving state as having two official languages, but no official cultures. The origins of the policy and the program lie in his formulation in Parliament that Canada is "a multicultural country within a bilingual framework." This legitimates collective as well as individual rights, and the role of government in promoting both multiculturalism and bilingualism. Conceptually, Multiculturalism as policy is the product of blending dualism with pluralism.

Chronologically, the roots of government involvement in diversity issues goes back at least to the war years. (Joshee, 1995; Hillmer, 1988). The wartime effort required a rallying of the population, which by then was already undeniably diverse, though diversity was not yet conceptually incorporated into the national self-definition of the state. Crystallization of the policy did not come until many years later, as a response to the recurring need to accommodate Canada's dualism, while confronted with the post war sensibility of fair play amidst a steadily more diverse population.

The policy is driven by political and demographic necessity. Coping with a large state founded by "the Conquest" and nurtured by immigration, has proven to be a formidable political task. It has been successful so far in part by largely ignoring the original conquest, that of Canada's indigenous inhabitants, and also by drawing on the inherent wealth of the land. Hard work by a constantly refreshed population is clearly a factor. Effective political management should be acknowledged as well. The task of effective governance is made increasingly difficult by the demographic situation of declining birth-rates at home and wide-ranging sources of immigration from abroad. Multiculturalism is thus a political activity of the state made in response to empirical reality and the need for effective governance in a plural society.

Changing Social Reality: The Asian Fact

Canada is now in a position to assess social reality more closely. We know that Canada has been a diverse society from the outset, far more so than is generally realized, or incorporated into the national consciousness. Groups thought of as new to the country have in fact been present almost from the beginning (see Tepper, in *Canada 2000: Race Relations as Public Policy*, 1989). However the dimensions of diversity have deepened considerably since the change in immigration practice in the 1960s. That is why there is a need for a publication such as this, to assess the policy implications of the rapid ethno-demographic transformation of Canada's largest urban centres. With the Metropolis Project, there will soon be a flood of new research on the impact of the changes in the past thirty years or so. In the meantime, as more data become available from the 1991 census, a clearer snapshot is available of the ethno-demographic bases of Canadian society. New data that has become available at press time shows that indeed, immigration patterns have shifted so markedly to Asia and other areas, such as the Middle East, that newcomers from there now comprise over half the foreign-born in Canada. This is a watershed in Canadian history. As recently as the 1981 census, European immigrants comprised 67 per cent of all immigrants in Canada; now, they are less than half the total, at 47 per cent. Moreover the foreign-born overall are now at a fifty-year high level, as a proportion of the Canadian population. As of the 1996 Census, the total foreign-born have risen to 17.4 per cent of the population, with Asian immigrants a conspicuous and rapidly increasing part of the total. Some issues relating to multiculturalism as policy and reality are also more clearly answerable.

Empirically Canada is becoming more diverse. Moreover while multiculturalism is accused of being a policy which encourages divisiveness, of encouraging lack of identification with Canada, the data show that the opposite is occurring. Thus perception, need and reality may be growing farther apart. For a country historically considered pragmatic, not ideological, this is a dangerous trend.

There are at least several dimensions of diversity relevant to our discussion. They include the sheer magnitude and direction of ethno-demographic change. Figure 1 shows the present Canadian "pie" and the proportions of the population by region of origin. Figure 2 shows recent immigration by source area, with policy implications for this volume. It shows that immigration from Asia and the Pacific is at 42 per cent, double the rate from Europe. In addition, if the country is to grow, it must rely on immigration, as birth rates at home are well below replacement rates. Between 1995 and 1996, Canada grew by only 1.34 per cent, and that was entirely due to the arrival of newcomers. The bulk of the newcomers were from Asia: China (20,935), Hong Kong (24,868), India (18,227) and the Philippines (15,804).[2] So far in 1997, immigration patterns further reinforce the impact of Asia on Canada. Midway through the year, the top five source countries for immigration are: 1) Hong Kong: 18,200; 2) People's Republic of China: 14,000; 3) India: 13,000; 4) Taiwan: 10,375; and 5) Pakistan: 8,200.

No matter how you slice it, the Canadian pie shows "the other" as the biggest single slice, with the Asian component an important element. Of course there is no homogeneity within these large census aggregates. However it is clear that given immigration trends, the Asian component will only increase as a proportion of the Canadian population.

Figure 3 shows where the country may be going in the near term. While trends often confound the academic fortune tellers, these figures are based on solidly established drifts in the demographic currents, and project only a few years into the future. As you can see, the projections for Asia are quite startling. Figure 4 tells the story in a more compelling fashion. In a country with a declining birth rate, the country's children are a critical indicator of the ethno-demographic makeup of the future. The large population of original settlers will ensure they remain numerically predominant for the foreseeable future. But they are heading for an absolute decrease in proportion of school age children, while other groups are anticipated to have significant increases; Asians top this list with Chinese at 98 per cent and South Asians at 73 per cent.

Collectively, these charts hint at the degree to which "the Asian fact" is increasingly the Canadian fact. Canada is a plural society with ever deepening dimensions of ethno-demographic diversity. Much of that diversity is "visible" and an increasing amount of that visibility comes from Asia.

MULTICULTURALISM: AN EVALUATION

How is Multiculturalism doing in its mandate to help Canada adjust to social reality, which includes demographic transformation? The Program was reviewed internally in a year-long exercise (see the Brighton Report), and, since its inception, has been reviewed externally by the media, academics and political parties. From the range of possible vantage points, we can provide a few indicators of the activity of Multiculturalism as an activity of the state.

Empirical Indicators

Let us start with at least some empirical evidence. What can the census snapshot tell us about how well immigrants are adapting to Canada? Large aggregates may be crude indicators, but they are sometimes useful. Multiculturalism is often faulted for creating divisiveness, for keeping people in groups, and groups separate from each other. There is an urge to make new-

Figure 1: Ethnic Origins, Canada, 1991

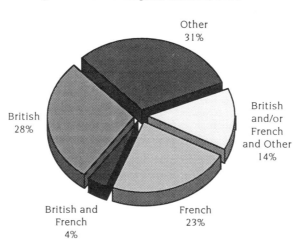

Figure 2: Immigration by Source Area, 1991

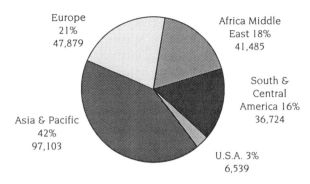

Europe 21% 47,879

Africa Middle East 18% 41,485

South & Central America 16% 36,724

U.S.A. 3% 6,539

Asia & Pacific 42% 97,103

Figure 3: Selected Ethnic Origins, Children < 15 Canada, 1991–2006

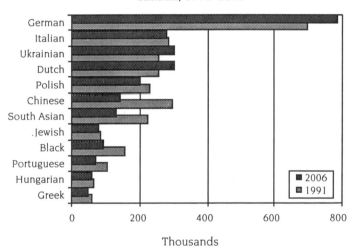

German
Italian
Ukrainian
Dutch
Polish
Chinese
South Asian
.Jewish
Black
Portuguese
Hungarian
Greek

0   200   400   600   800

■ 2006
▩ 1991

Thousands

Figure 4: Percentage of School-aged Children by Ethnic Origin

Percentage changes among school-aged children with selected ethnic origins other than British/French/Canadian expected to range from -16% to +98%.

Newer groups show higher rates of increase:
Chinese (98%), South Asian (73%), Black (51%) and Portuguese (47%).

Decreases in Ukrainian (-16%), Dutch (-14%) and German (-11%) groups.

Source: Statistics Canada, Catalogue 93-315 and 94-327; Teega, Population Projections of Ethnic Groups in Canada to the Year 2016, Statistical Supplement.

comers conform to Canada and to blame Multiculturalism for allowing minorities to not identify with Canada. The census suggests exactly the opposite. What common sense should tell us, and the census confirms, is that by and large, people come to Canada in order to become Canadians. A high proportion of those eligible for citizenship have become citizens, after the mandatory three year residence requirement. Moreover, that proportion has *increased* noticeably in the past decade, exactly during the time period that Multiculturalism has come under increasingly strident attacks for keeping Canada divided, by encouraging people to not identify with the country. Asians are among the early adopters of citizenship. Moreover, most of the late adopters are from the U.K. and the U.S. — precisely those who do not have difficulty in appearing to adapt to Canada. During the time period of government involvement in assisting immigrant adaptation, and the period of significant increase in nontraditional sources of immigration, those opting to associate with the county have increased steadily. Once again, Asians tend to lead the list (Tables 1 and 2).

There are other empirical indicators and they all point in the same direction: "whether we look at naturalization, political participation, official language competence, or intermarriage rates, we see the same story. There is no evidence to support the claim that multiculturalism has decreased the rate of integration of immigrants, or increased the separatism or hostility of ethnic groups" (Kymlicka, 1997: 4).

Stakeholders

The official review of Multiculturalism produced other ways to evaluate the policy. In an internal examination, a number of suggestions and criticisms were presented. (See Strategic Evaluation Of Multicultural Programs, Final Report, Corporate Review Branch, March, 1996. This is commonly referred to as the Brighton Report, after its principal investigator). Its central thrust, after extensive interviewing and research, was to reform the policy to emphasize themes central both to the actual operation of the policy over its existence, and to core values of Canadians: Identity, Civic Participation, and Social Justice. These were accepted by the government and now form the broad policy guidelines for Multiculturalism.

As part of the Review process, a number of submissions were sent in by groups familiar with the Program. Opinions varied considerably. The Ukrainian Canadian Congress recommended ending the Department and Program funding altogether, and placing Multiculturalism more into mainstream Departments of government, while emphasizing language training (presumably heritage languages), in a decentralized program. (The Ukrainian Canadian Community and Multiculturalism, November, 1995). The German Canadian Council was supportive of Multiculturalism but concerned that the new policy goals focus exclusively on one pillar of Multiculturalism, social issues, and "abandons the Multiculturalism Act

Table 1: Rate of Eligible Immigrants Becoming Citizens, Canada
1981–1991

Year	Per cent
1981	75
1986	79
1991	81
1996	83

Source: Census of Canada, *The Daily*, 8 Dec. 1992, and 4 Nov. 1997

Table 2: Naturalizations by Country of Former Allegiance:
Top 20 Countries

Country of Former Allegiance	Persons Granted Citizenship	Average Number of Years since Immigration
All Countries	217,333	5.6
Top 20 countries		
Hong Kong	17,112	4.2
Stateless	16,512	4.5
Poland	16,384	4.4
Lebanon	15,876	3.8
China	14,232	3.8
United Kingdom	12,620	10.6
Philippines	11,508	4.3
India	8,953	7.0
Sri Lanka	5,768	3.8
El Salvador	5,314	4.1
U.S.A.	5,247	13.4
Vietnam	5,223	4.5
Iran	5,124	3.8
Portugal	4,795	10.7
Jamaica	4,159	7.8
Trinidad & Tobago	3,369	8.9
Guyana	3,177	5.9
Pakistan	2,597	4.2
Somalia	2,420	3.1

Source: Census of Canada, *The Daily*, 8 Dec. 1992, and 4 Nov. 1997

and . . . Policy to an alarming degree." It wants a balanced approach, also emphasizing cultural Identity and Interculturalism. (Full Multiculturalism: A Model for Canada, The German Canadian Congress, December 1996). It appears that the concern of the organization representing the largest "other" population in Canada is for continued support for cultural retention (development of ethnic groups in isolation) and activities which allow sharing of cultures to "promote the values of tolerance . . . and mutual appreciation." Folkfests and the Canadian Ethnocultural Council are offered as examples (ibid., page 3).

Organizations representing groups much newer in Canada, in terms of large numbers, took a different tack. The Canadian Arab Federation joined the Ukrainians and the Canadian Jewish Congress in noting the long history of their members' presence in Canada. Then, based on a survey of its members, it concluded "multicultural policies should be about removing barriers for people to become citizens of equal rights and status, to contribute . . . to the Canadian Society. In this context, Multiculturalism is not obsolete because barriers that inhibit full participation . . . are still intact and in some instances growing, a fact that justifies even more support for Multiculturalism programs." The brief also then supports the full range of ongoing Programs, including "support for and funding of ethno-specific community organizations because they are in a better position than governmental agencies to understand the needs of their communities and to effectively serve them." (The Canadian Arab Federation's Submission on Multiculturalism Policies, November, 1995).

The Chinese Canadian National Council was also strongly supportive of Multiculturalism, opening its submission on the subject with the statement that it "supports the continuation and enhancement of multicultural programs and policies. In our view, Multiculturalism not only strengthens our country but is absolutely essential to creating and maintaining a fair, just, harmonious and flourishing nation. "It buttresses the support with arguments that Multiculturalism is an integral part of efforts to eradicate racism, as well as being essential to the well being, empowerment and participation of all sectors of society. It adds comments on the economic aspects of the policy, noting that "Canada's future economic prosperity is very much dependant upon our success in developing a healthy Multicultural society . . . to interact with and understand our global partners." Its evaluation of the policy is summed up in the conclusion of its paper:

> It must be recognised that the public funds supplied in support of Multiculturalism are truly minuscule and nominal given the stated aims of the Multicultural Act. The truth is that Multiculturalism has been and will continue to be realized by the incredible efforts of dedicated volunteers from many different groups in our society who have a common belief in the greatness and potential of this country which we call home. For this reason Canada reaps an enormous dividend for every dollar it spends on

Multiculturalism and thus this program and policy should continue and be enhanced. The Chinese Canadian National Council is of the firm belief that Multiculturalism is an indispensable element in our struggle to achieve a truly egalitarian society. (CCNC Position Paper-Multiculturalism, June 1996).

Political Parties

The verdict on Multiculturalism is much more mixed from the view of Canada's political parties. The policy began with nearly universal partisan support. Introduced as a policy under the Liberals, the Multiculturalism Act was passed under the Conservatives, and a Department with a full fledged Minister was implemented. Canadian Race Relations was added to the Department's mandate under one regime and maintained through alternating governments right up till the separate Programs were amalgamated as part of the downsizing and review process. The Race Relations Foundation was pledged and legislation was passed under the Conservatives, but proclaimed under the next Liberal administration. The NDP has been a consistent supporter. However, that consensus was not to last. Evaluation of Multiculturalism can be seen in the positions of Canada's major parties, over time.

Backlash against Multiculturalism, and indeed against diversity issues in general, has become increasingly apparent. Political parties have reflected and in some cases led the reaction. The term Multiculturalism presently is rarely used in public discourse by any of the parties, and related terms such as race relations are no longer in the forefront. The reasons for this have been speculated upon by others: "a policy area that has had relatively meagre financial and support structures has been vilified as the root cause of such varied problems as Canadian unity and racism. The speed with which a consensus on the orthodoxy of multiculturalism within the political mainstream has been transformed into a rough-and-tumble free-for-all is breathtaking."[3]

The Liberal Party said little about Multiculturalism in its 1993 election platform and even less in the recently concluded election. Here are the Red Book (campaign platform) promises regarding diversity issues:

- One of the core values of Canadian society is a strong belief in the equality of our citizens. Canadians are proud of our linguistic duality and our multicultural diversity.
- At a time when racial intolerance and ethnic hatred are in resurgence around the world, a Liberal government will take measures to combat hate propaganda and will enhance the programs of the Department of Multiculturalism and Citizenship that promote tolerance and mutual understanding.
- In February 1991, Parliament passed the Canadian Race Relations Foundation Act. Although the legislation received unanimous approval in Parliament, the Conservative regime has not to date proclaimed it. A Liberal government will proclaim this law and create the Canadian Race Relations Foundation, to work at the forefront of efforts to combat racism and all forms of racial discrimination in Canada.

During the recent election campaign in 1997, the topic of multiculturalism was rarely mentioned. While the issue of immigration and the treatment of immigrants as a security matter received some commentary, very little was raised about the disappearance of the just created Department of Multiculturalism and Citizenship.

As noted, the Red Book in 1993 promised to enhance the Programs of the Department of Multiculturalism which deal with hate propaganda and that promote tolerance and mutual understanding; to proclaim the Race Relations Foundation; to apply the Employment Equity Act to include the federal public service, and to give the Canadian Human Rights Commission the authority to initiate investigations of Employment Equity issues. In its first mandate it did fulfill all of these commitments.[4] In the 1996 successor, the so called "Red Book 2," no specific pledges were made on this or most other issues. However the government has maintained the presence of Multiculturalism within government, albeit with a reduced budget (along with all other Departments and agencies) despite the strong objections to Multiculturalism of the Official Opposition Party and the sensitivity of the governing party to such opposition, on other matters.

Multiculturalism is now under direct threat from both the present and former Official Opposition Parties in Parliament. Interestingly, the sharply divergent views of the Bloc Québécois and the Reform Party coalesce on this one issue, and the convergence is more than superficial. The Bloc's perspective can be given succinctly: "the position of the Bloc Québécois is very clear on the federal government's multiculturalism policy. We believe this policy . . . should be abolished." (Cristine Gagnon, Bloc Québécois: Integration rather than Multiculturalism. In Cardozo and Musto, eds, 1997: 42). She cites with approval the Deputy Premier of Québec, "Although the Québec government acknowledges the fact that Québec is multi-ethnic, it favors a policy of cultural convergence in one common culture, fortified by foreign sources."

The policy of the Reform party is strikingly similar, and rests on an oddly symmetrical logic. Though its language differs it also wants to see funding for Multiculturalism to end, and policies of cultural convergence (unhyphenated Canadians, promotion of a "national culture") to replace it. (Party Blue Book, 1990). While the party is often accused of being "racist" and is sensitive to that charge, at a conceptual level its position is a mirror to that of its nemesis, the party it has now replaced as the Royal Opposition in Parliament. Underlying the party position of the Bloc is a fundamental insistence that Canada return to the concept of "two founding peoples." The Bloc spokesperson just cited quotes with approval a long time opponent of the Bloc within Québec, the provincial Liberal leader Robert Bourassa. In his objection to the announcement of Multiculturalism in 1971, in an open letter to the Prime Minister, the Québec Premier says: "This proposal was a betrayal of the work done by the (Royal) Commission, whose focus had been on bilingualism and biculturalism, and thus the equal status of the two founding peoples. Québec never changed its position, although leaders and political options changed regularly over the years."

The Reform Party's rejection of Multiculturalism comes from just the opposite direction. The party's Director of Policy, a political theory professor, noted: "first it must be emphasized that multiculturalism is not the major concern of the Reform Party. Our policies are addressed to the constitutional, fiscal and political crises that now grip Canada. The root of much of this trouble is the pernicious "two founding nations" concept of Canada, of which multiculturalism is a confused and confusing echo." Though supposedly not a major concern for the Party, in this year's election platform, Resolution Number One was a rejection of any consideration of group rights and the elimination of anything which takes away from the equality of the individual. This may be fairly viewed as an attack on the notion of Employment Equity and Multiculturalism.

The Conservative Party of Canada, which provided the first (and only) full fledged Minister of Multiculturalism in an independent Department, has turned away from its earlier support as well. It has adopted a policy very similar to the Reform Party, perhaps because it is Reform which is seen as likely to replace it as the alternative national political party.[5] At its Policy Advisory Conference in July 1996, it also rejected any funding for "institutionalized Multiculturalism," and rejected an amendment that would have affirmed the Party as "accepting the need to foster understanding, equality of opportunity and common Canadian values within the spirit of the Multiculturalism Act" (Amendment No 325, A Multicultural Society).[6]

Public Opinion

Is the attack on Multiculturalism by political parties based on widespread public disillusionment? I do not have access to the inner thoughts of Canada's political elite, and more importantly to the private polling undertaken by politicians of all the major parties. There are a number of public sources to examine, to see if the general public has given up on the vision of the country as a multicultural mosaic.

However, comparing polling data from disparate sources is a bit of a mugs game. Given enough sources and enough questions, almost any position may be supported. For present purposes, we will focus on the largest public opinion polls, which do allow comparability. Angus Reid conducted large scale polls in both 1974 and 1991. They were based on extensive prior discussion with leading academics, and used many comparable questions in both instruments. Thus the two polls give us a rare opportunity to obtain a longitudinal view of attitudes toward multiculturalism in Canada. Concerns over divisiveness are apparent. But so too are solid indicators of increasing support over time for multiculturalism and its goal of an integrative strategy in managing diversity.

A considered conclusion may be reached, based on extensive review of data obtained over time. John Berry, the co-designer of the largest surveys, says "We may conclude that Canadian attitudes are clearly not assimilationist; rather they support some degree of cultural maintenance along with some degree of sharing and accommodation on the part of ethnic groups, a pattern we refer to as the integrationist option."[7]

PROGRAM CONSIDERATIONS

There are other ways to evaluate the Canadian approach to diversity. It should be kept in mind that Multiculturalism is not the only way that governments have attempted to deal with diversity. There is an elaborate set of Human Rights Commissions, federally and provincially, hate laws, Employment Equity legislation, etc. None have achieved such public opprobrium, from such sources as those indicated above. Sustaining Multiculturalism in the future will be a difficult task.

My own evaluation is that Multiculturalism as a state policy is essential. It does not create diversity; it does provide a means to deal with it. Recent response to polyethnic reality has been to attack the policy meant to deal with it. Several aspects of the present situation are worth noting.

1) **Administrative size**

Multiculturalism must appear to be a giant among its peers as an activity of the state. The amount of attention it has generated, especially negative attention in recent times, suggests a major venture in social engineering by the state. The backlash presently in view must be based on a major push by government to legislate social change. Of course the reality is exactly the opposite. Measured by any reasonable yardstick, multiculturalism as an actual activity of the centre is picayune. Even people who are close to the program, might be surprised by the meagre resources devoted to the policy. The entire budget devoted to multiculturalism programming at the time when it was so fiercely attacked from so many quarters was 27 million dollars, with another 10 million for personnel. The total number of officers in headquarters was only 60 persons, with another 40 or so scattered across the country in Regional Offices. The budget has now been cut even further, with the prospect of even further reductions in the future. Staff reductions are of similar magnitude.

One conclusion seems inescapable. Extravagant expense is not the source of discontent with Multiculturalism in Canada.

2) **Administrative opportunity**

Change is not always negative. The reabsorption of Multiculturalism within a much larger Department of Canadian Heritage, and the combining of its three programs into one, opens new options, perhaps, which a separate but small department lacks. It may assist "Mainstreaming

Multiculturalism" which is part of its mandate. It is arguably better to be a small part of a large Ministry than to be a small Ministry on its own. And it does maintain its visibility by having a Minister of State for Multiculturalism and Status of Women, at a time when it could have been abolished altogether.

3) **Administrative disarray**

Perhaps it is not known how thorough the reorganization is in regard to Multiculturalism. In the short span of a few years, it has moved from a Sector within the Department of the Secretary of State, to a Department with a Junior Minister within the Department of the Secretary of State, to a full fledged and legislatively based Department of Multiculturalism and Citizenship, to an all but invisible element within the short-lived Campbell government to a minor but visible element within Canadian Heritage, with part of a reconstituted junior minister. Within the last few years it has lost its Department status, its Minister in Cabinet, a Deputy Minister, an ADM, and one of its two DG's positions. The three Multiculturalism Program areas have been combined into a single Program, within a milieu of uncertainty. Making a single functioning Department out of four or five merging corporate cultures, with a fiscal and constitutional crisis in the offing, bodes ill for Multiculturalism as a policy or activity of the central government.

Analysing Multiculturalism is a difficult task. As a program, it is deeply involved with the processes of society, evolving in an almost unconscious fashion which keep pace with the evolution of Canadian society itself. Of course there are clear program guidelines, forms, budgets and periodic reviews. Of special interest is the program in race relations, one of the three program areas of the agency (along with community participation and heritage languages and literature. All these names change over time). Race relations was added as an activity in 1981 when the very term was controversial, and quite early in the life of the department. Its first activity was to study the race relations climate in 11 Canadian urban centres. The Brixton riots in England provided the backdrop, and the motivation to ensure if possible that Canada did not follow suit. Over time it evolved numerous strategies and engagement with institutions and localities across the country. Its best known, most apparent activity is the annual March 21st campaign as part of the global day against racism and discrimination. That activity consumes about half its budget and involves anti-racism activities through partnerships with hundreds of schools and other local units. The race relations program works year round with numerous government and nongoverment channels. It has developed "firefighting" capacity, mobilizing teams to work with local community organizations as race relations problems arise.

Even this thumbnail sketch fails to capture the scope of the program. Much of the activity to combat racism is nearly invisible; or too numerous to catch in an overview as they occur in localities across the country; or were carried out by other branches of the program and not even labelled "race relations" but literary or research or community participation. For example substantial support is given to multicultural education. Some themes cross cut the program areas, such as "institutional change" which permits work across government and with such strategic organizations as the Federation of Canadian Municipalities. Capturing the full range of race relations activities of the program would require a separate study.

CONCLUSION

In conclusion it is better to stand back from the details of the various programs and present a conceptual or functional perspective of Multiculturalism in Canada. It seems to me that the myriad small projects and large activities perform three functions.

1) **Help civil society to help itself**

   Cross cutting the various program thrusts is an underlying goal. As an activity of government, Multiculturalism is engaged in strengthening the infrastructure of Canada's adaptive capacity. The country has so far adjusted to very significant ethno-demographic changes with remarkably limited turmoil and muted backlash. This is primarily due to the operations of a robust civic society, lightly guided and assisted by government. The process of adaptation in Canada is a two way street. Multiculturalism has worked with civil society to help newcomers adapt to society, and to help society adjust to the presence of new and very diverse elements.

2) **Assist the vulnerable**

   Underlying the policy is a philosophy that individuals should be permitted to play an active, and an equal, role in society. The Programs to foster that end involve assistance to those who might otherwise miss out, or remain marginalized. Thus assistance is given in some instances to allow individuals to form groups, and the groups to become viable as members of the community. Other times help is given to organizations that assist vulnerable individuals, such as battered immigrant women. New voices are encouraged in privileged fora in the arts. Again, at almost an instinctual level, various components of the program assist the inclusiveness of those who might otherwise be excluded. Canadian history has shown that being a minority, especially a visible minority, can lead to exclusion. Thus the programs of Multiculturalism have an emphasis on the potentially marginalized.

3) **Manage the symbolic order**

   Standing back from the program elements and looking at the functions this public policy performs, it becomes evident that its most important role is to reconceptualize the political community. As Raymond Breton has reminded us (see Breton, 1984 and 1985), government has the task of managing the symbolic order. Most important of the functions of Multiculturalism is to provide an image, a definition, of the state which validates diversity. However short the goal is from attainment, and we know in Canada that we are far from the goal, Multiculturalism provides a symbolic acceptance of pluralism as a constituent element of statehood. The formulation that this is a state with two official languages but no official cultures, is a way to bring policy in line with reality. It also prepares the country for its much more polyethnic future.

We should have anticipated an attack on pluralism, in a country under economic and political stress. As concern for national unity goes up and the economy goes down, tolerance of being different thins out. And make no mistake: diversity is indivisible. Those who dislike or fear "the other," who insist on conformity and assimilation, are as unlikely to accept new roles for women, tolerate linguistic duality, regional distinctiveness or religious differentiation. Retrenchment in one area, such as lowered acceptance of newcomers or the visibly different, will lead to backsliding in all areas of acceptance of diversity. It will not be only Asians in Canada who will suffer if the reaction to diversity is to weaken the Programs which provide assurance of acceptance. But all those who are different, especially visibly different, will become more vulnerable. The urge to return to, or to sustain what is left of, the vertical mosaic, remains strong in the land. Rapid change is unsettling, and concern for its impact is legitimate. What must not happen is to disarm ourselves in the face of change.

Eliminating multiculturalism or race relations from the vocabulary and programs of the state would not eliminate multiculturalism or race as a social reality. It just makes the future of Canada more problematic. Multiculturalism may need transforming, a process now well underway. But the country's leaders need to revalidate diversity in order to lead the polity successfully into the next millennium. The reality of multiculturalism needs to be reintroduced as a legitimate part of the public discourse in Canada.

Endnotes

[1] When referring to government programs, the word Multiculturalism will be capitalized; at other times it will be spelled in the lowercase.

[2] *Ottawa Citizen.* 1997. "Canadian population up, thanks only to immigrants." (Reporting on a study released by Statistics Canada). (March 26).

[3] Yasmeen, Abu-Laban, and Daiva Stasiulis. 1992. "Ethnic pluralism under siege: Popular and partisan opposition to Multiculturalism." In *Canadian Public Policy* 18 (4) (December): 381. See also Wilson, 1993, The Brighton Report, 1996.

[4] Creating opportunity: The liberal plan for Canada, equality in diversity, 1993. In the same section it also pledged to target immigration levels of "approximately" one per cent of the Canadian population per year. This it did not achieve.

[5] See Cardozo, Andrew L., n.d., "Chain reactionaries: How Reform Party policies on immigration and multiculturalism have influenced the Tory and other parties," Discussion paper released by the Council of Canadians and the Asian Canadian Caucus, Draft 2.

[6] Report of the policy advisory committee (July 1996): 82. See also "Tories want to discourage diversity, but not in Québec," *The Toronto Star* (31 July 1996): A5

[7] Kalin, Rudolf, and John W. Berry. 1991. "Ethnic and multicultural attitudes in Canada, outside Québec," Draft prepared for *State of the art review of research on Canada's multicultural society* (September): 7. See also: Berry, J. W., and Rudolf Kalin,1993, "Multicultural and ethnic attitudes in Canada: An overview of the 1991 National Survey," presented at Canadian Psychological Association Annual Meetings, Montréal (May).

4 Rethinking Canada's Immigration Policies

Meyer Burstein

Rethinking immigration policy sounds rather episodic and seems to imply that major change is just around the corner. However, there seems to be no major changes about to be announced or hiding in the development pipeline. Which is not to say that important questions are not being raised about immigration both inside and outside government. Indeed, questions are being asked and many of these raise basic issues regarding the immigration program and its strategic directions.

The act of questioning is not in itself unusual. People who have worked in the policy field know that there is never a time when policy is not being rethought or reengineered. However, it is also known that policy change rarely occurs smoothly and without inflection. Policy — like evolution — often goes through long periods of stasis before undergoing rapid transformation. The issue is whether immigration is entering such a period. And if it is, what are some of the issues we will need to deal with?

The majority of Canadians still think of immigration as a positive force for nation-building. There is, however, an emerging view that for the program to continue to be successful it will need to be managed more carefully.

There is a perception held by a significant number of Canadians — that first the immigration program has been managed from too narrow a perspective — that the focus has been on managing numbers rather than consequences — and second that immigration has primarily served the interests of minority ethnic groups and that it needs to be rebalanced so it can operate more firmly in the broader public interest. Now this perception — whether it is true or not — is dangerous because what it does is to undermine public support for the complex of immigration-related programs. Programs that are essential if Canada is to successfully integrate new immigrants and combat the tensions produced by rapid social change — particularly racism and discriminatory treatment.

Challenges to Immigration Policy

Changing the perception and fostering broad public support for immigration is probably one of the most important challenges that faces immigration policy makers over the medium to long-term. And to meet this challenge successfully it will require vision. It will require creativity. And It will require courage, including political courage. Canada is not alone in this task. Much the same set of challenges exists in Australia, in the United States, in Israel and in Western Europe where, in several instances, the debate has already begun. And what is interesting here is that the discussions are so similar whether the countries are the traditional immigrant receiving countries — that is, Canada, the U.S. and Australia which have an instrumental view of immigration — or whether the countries are those that define themselves in terms of their ethnic affiliation (like most of Europe). When this debate in Canada will be fully joined is open to speculation, however it is a debate that we must have and one for which we will need to prepare ourselves.

Perhaps the first opportunity for a more fulsome discussion of the issues will arise when the legislative review task force that was commissioned by Mme. Robillard, the Minister of Citizenship and Immigration, to review the Immigration Act, to simplify it and to modernize its provisions, reports at the end of the year. And while the report will focus primarily on the Immigration Act, the ensuing debate, public consultations and discussions will likely raise broad issues of public policy and of fundamental direction. Here are some of the factors — the issues — that will need to be considered:

1) **Increasing international migration.** International migration has, for some time, been steadily increasing and that, in light of the factors that drive it, it will continue to increase for decades. The reasons are well known:
   - Medical and agricultural improvements have generated rapid population growth particularly among the youth;
   - Changes in agriculture have freed up rural workers;
   - Trade liberalization has boosted manufacturing and has stimulated large scale rural to urban migration;
   - Most importantly, population growth that has outstripped, and will continue to outstrip, job creation in developing economies.

   At the same time new communication technologies and mass media have alerted people to economic opportunities in the West which vastly improved air links have made accessible.

   Put bluntly, what this means for North America and for Europe is that the question of whether or not to have an immigration program is moot. Because, while countries can, in a technical sense, insulate themselves from migration, they cannot accomplish this without sacrificing their most basic tenets of liberalism, social justice and an efficient civil society.

Now at one level, this is all somewhat besides the point. There is virtually nobody — at least not in Canada — who would close the doors to international migration. Nevertheless, casting immigration as something inevitable rather than as something to be chosen, does change the way in which we think about migration and the role of government. Because if immigration is inevitable, it becomes more apparent that the role of government is to manage social change. It is also to find innovative ways to expand absorbtive capacity so we can accommodate immigration and, ensure broad public support for the program itself and for the related complex of programs that are needed to integrate immigrants fully into Canadian society.

For immigration to work, it cannot be seen as divisive — as something that prevents Canada from acting in a cohesive way to address national and international problems and from undertaking large scale public investments in our social infrastructure.

2) *Economic role of immigrants.* A second thing that needs to be taken into account is the fact that the relative economic performance of immigrants to Canada has been declining. The same is true for the United States and also for Australia. This is troublesome, especially since there is as yet no consensus explanation as to why it is happening, how serious the problem is and whether it will persist. Some explanations invoke changes in the relative education levels of immigrants and the native born; others invoke ambition, changing sources of immigration and racism.

One prominent explanation focuses on globalization and some of the resulting changes that are taking place in urban labor markets. Changes that make it more difficult for immigrants to find employment. Specifically, some analysts feel that North American labor markets are assuming an hourglass shape with manufacturing jobs — jobs that have traditionally employed immigrants and provided them with a stepping stone — being squeezed out, thus relegating immigrants to marginal personal service jobs at the bottom of the labor market. There is also, in this scenario, a real risk that immigrants and non-integrated minorities will find themselves in competition with other labor market entrants and with persons who have been affected by restructuring and are now competing with them for a diminishing pool of low end jobs.

Whatever the reason, if this declining relative performance persists over the economic recovery and, more importantly, if it turns out to be transgenerational — that is, if it prevents immigrants from equipping their children to participate on a full and equal basis in the labor market — then we have a very real problem on our hands and the possibility that Canada is forming a social underclass. If the evidence firms up, public policy will have to make every effort to interrupt the cycle and to prevent this from happening. The challenge would be to mobilize resources for significant public investment at a time of fiscal restraint and competition for scarce funds.

3) *Racism and xenophobia.* A third challenge that we urgently need to come to grips with, one of principal conference themes, is racism. It is no secret that immigration to Canada is not only diverse, it is visible.

Racism and xenophobia are major preoccupations in Europe. They need to become major preoccupations in Canada as well, notwithstanding the more benign domestic environment. Canada is by no means free of racist sentiment. Given that immigrants are highly concentrated in major urban centres, it would be disastrous if, for involuntary reasons, we were to form large concentrations of visible migrant populations who are excluded from good job opportunities, from decent housing, from education and from equal access to public services through racism and prejudice. The outcome: unemployment, poverty, crime and social dysfunction would only reinforce negative stereotyping and set up a destructive cycle that would ultimately produce intractable urban ghettos.

Some people may think of this as an alarmist portrayal but it is not one that is alien to a good number of living rooms across Canada. We don't have a great deal of information to go on here, but some of the findings from public attitude research are disturbing. Toronto, where the greatest proportion of visible minority immigrants settle, displays greater levels of racism than any other part of the country. Which is not to say that racism elsewhere is not a problem. Even though only a small minority of persons express blatantly prejudiced attitudes — say places like Vancouver where tolerance scores are particularly high — substantial numbers of people are still affected by racist views and are subject to discrimination.

It is interesting to note in this regard that, while crime and immigration tend to be associated in the public mind with crime by immigrants, the real problem lies with discrimination and with hate and bias crime that is directed against immigrants and visible minorities. How to combat this, how to counter racist sentiment and to promote social cohesion is a task that governments will need to focus on.

Combating racism will need to go well beyond the responses that we are already familiar with, namely: public education, culturally sensitive services, sensitivity training and so on. We will likely need to focus active citizenship measures on participation and membership and on building organizations at the neighborhood level. In particular, we will need to focus attention on producing unified activities that require the energy of diverse people to reach a shared goal: housing and recreation are good examples. Existing organizations should be enlisted in this effort and should consciously seek ways to cross group boundaries and identify common projects. Special events and public festivals can also create a more tolerant tone, especially when diverse groups are involved in planning these.

4) *Citizenship.* A fourth policy issue concerns citizenship. There are competing views regarding the way in which Canadian citizenship should be interpreted in a globalized world. Some feel that a looser interpretation of citizenship is inevitable, indeed, desirable while others feel that it would devalue citizenship, provide unwarranted and unsustainable access to social services and that it would be used as insurance against political and other forms of insecurity. The debate reflects growing concern with social cohesion and a view that immigration has contributed significantly to the breakdown of this social cohesion. There are many competing views of what this means and what a cohesive society would look like — how it would be organized and function — but in all of them what is at stake is the definition of the nation state expressed in terms of the rights and responsibilities of its members.

Here too globalization plays a complicating role. One issue receiving increasing attention is the rise of transnational communities or networks. Some of these networks straddle several nations and they challenge policy makers in a variety of ways by virtue of their economic wealth, the political power they wield and the human capital they embody. An important example here is the overseas Chinese network with a combined economic output in the neighborhood of $600 billion. In trying to come to grips with these networks, nation states must first understand the ways in which policy decisions in the area of taxation, foreign investment, immigration, citizenship, education and access to public services impact these populations. Issues become triangulated involving the ethnic group, the homeland state and the country where the group resides.

Further complicating the issue of citizenship is the fact that new technologies — satellite television, video recorders and the internet — permit transnational groups and transnational religious communities to maintain a unique cultural identity that challenges the capacity of the nation state to effect uniform patterns of national identity and social control.

5) *Immigration policy and demographics.* A fifth issue concerns immigration policy and demographics. Canada's population growth is slowing and the Canadian population is aging. As net population gain from domestic sources slows, immigration becomes an ever more important component of national and provincial population growth and of growth in

the labor force. This will become increasingly evident in the largest cities where the bulk of immigrants are concentrated. At the 1% rate identified in the redbook, net immigration would increase population by roughly one million persons every four years with 2/3 of this flow destined to Montreal, Toronto and Vancouver. What is the rationale for a movement of this size? To what extent could it be controlled? Should Canada articulate a population policy? And if so, what should it be? Should environmental concerns be factored in as these are linked to population pressures?

6) **Immigration and economic objectives.** How should immigration be linked to Canada's economic objectives? What role should selection play? Should the emphasis be placed on broad human capital endowments — on adaptability, on numeracy and on literacy? Or should selected Immigration be targetted on occupational niches and skill gaps.

What role should be assigned to job readiness? To language skills? To education? Do we need more highly skilled human capital?

The macro-economic evidence is mixed but there are virtually no large scale studies that argue for massive benefits. Most studies conclude that immigration produces small, albeit positive, economic benefits. Is this the only way to think about the economic advantages conferred by immigration? What of the entrepreneur and investment programs? What advantages do they confer on Canada? There are some who argue that the gains are minimal. That international capital markets are sufficiently flexible to provide Canada with all the capital it needs. And that Immigrant investment is not risk investment. Others argue that by encouraging entrepreneurship and immigrant investors, Canada is acquiring a stake in the emerging global economy — particularly in and around the Pacific Rim. If this is true, what are the policies that are needed to sustain this investment? How can Canada nourish immigrant entrepreneurship and benefit from the potential trade and export links that it affords us? What are the implications for governance? With the exception of Quebec, the federal government controls immigration flows but many of the implications associated with immigration impact on provincial governments and on municipalities. Issues involved are health, education, training, transportation, land use policies and recreational facilities.

How should policy be organized and coordinated to maximum effect. Given the complexity of immigration and the fact that it touches every sphere of public and private life, for policy to be successful and to address the challenges before us, it is essential that all the stakeholders operate from a shared strategic platform. What is needed is leadership and, as I indicated before, vision, creativity and courage. What is also critically needed is knowledge.

The Metropolis Project

To shed light on some of the issues raised above, there is a recent international initiative called Metropolis that some of you already know about. Metropolis has as its goal: to stimulate research on immigration and integration; to focus that research on public policy issues; and to encourage its use in decision making.

The project's unit of analysis is the city — on how international migration impacts cities and how, in turn, immigrant integration is affected by urban processes. The project is international in scope and the partnership now includes: Canada, U.S., New Zealand, Argentina, Israel, Sweden, Norway, Denmark, France, the U.K., the Netherlands, Italy and — soon — Germany, Portugal and Greece. It also includes several international organizations — the OECD, the EC and UNESCO. Financial and organizational support has been drawn from amongst the membership and from the international organizations.

Strategic directions for the project internationally have been set at a conference in Milan attended by ministers, decision-makers and academics from the participating states. And these directions are used to focus research to be reported at the second conference in Copenhagen in the fall. They are spatial concentration and social economic mobility; and economic impacts and labor market participation. And they will be examined through a comparison of 10 cities.

Other events are planned for Jerusalem and Vancouver. And we anticipate deepening the involvement of the partnership through workshops and seminars bringing together academics and decision-makers.

At the core of this alliance is the idea that countries face similar issues notwithstanding different ideologies, different policies and different legal regimes. Within Canada, core funding for the project has been provided by a group of federal departments in concert with SSHRC. Based on this support, four academic centres have been created, centred in Vancouver, in Edmonton, in Toronto and in Montreal. Each centre is a consortium of major universities and each is plugged in — in a variety of ways — into the policy and broader stakeholder community.

Research under the Metropolis banner started only recently so it is still too early to assess impacts. However, it is fair to say that governments have noticed the project. Not only the line departments with specific policy responsibilities but also the central agencies of government that are looking at the project with a view to seeing if it offers lessons for how to mobilize expertise outside of government circles to help in addressing the major social challenges that face us. And herein lies the real answer to rethinking immigration policy. Because the answer does not lie in any particular formulation of issues or academic papers. The answer lies in the process, the process of mobilizing knowledge to help define issues, to provide options and arguments for decision-makers to use and in public education.

Part Two

The View from Asian Countries of Origin

The Laquians

The Del Rios

The Ahns

The Jadavjis

The Folleros

The Wings

The Yuens

The Wing Yuens

5 Conditions in China Influencing Outmigration

Zeng Yi and Zhang Qinwu

China has opened its door to the outside world since the end of the 1970s. With increasing exchanges with other countries, outmigration, temporary as well as permanent, has been increasing tremendously. This chapter will try to shed some light on the factors in China that influenced outmigration. It will have four parts: a brief introduction, a historical background, a review of characteristics and trends of current migration, and an analysis of future perspectives.

The Historical Background

The scale of Chinese outmigration flow was not large as compared with its population size before the end of the 18th century (Skeldon, 1996). During the period 1801–1925, however, a large number of Chinese workers went abroad, with a migration peak around 1851–1875. Chen (1963) estimated that the number of outmigrant workers during the period 1801–1930 was about 3 million. However, Zhu (1989) estimated that the figure would have been about 10 million. Such a large difference in estimates by different scholars demonstrated that the historical statistics about Chinese outmigration were very scanty and unreliable.

The world-wide economic crisis during the 1930s resulted in a large number of immigrants returning to China. For example, the number of returning Chinese migrants in the 1930s was about 550,000, while the outmigrants during the same period were about 280,000 (Zhu, 1989: 76). The Second World War disrupted the normal migration streams and the data became even more unreliable after that.

After 1949, China's door to the outside world was essentially closed except for some exchanges with the former Soviet Union and other socialist countries. In the 1950s and 1960s, there was an official regulation on immigration for overseas Chinese who wished to return, but no detailed law or regulations governed outmigration since it was so rare at that time. Outmigration was very limited in the 1950s and 1960s involving mainly Chinese citizens who went abroad to take over property of their old parents or relatives, students who were sent to study in the former Soviet Union and

Eastern European countries, and some official delegations visiting other countries. During the Great Cultural Revolution between 1966 and 1976, Chinese international migration was further reduced, mainly due to political and administrative problems. During this period of disaster, the political obstacles for going abroad and returning from abroad were much larger. The most important precondition for official approval to go abroad at that time was to pass the political evaluation. Those who had a non-revolutionary family background were not allowed to go abroad. The governmental administrative agencies could not normally perform their functions which also caused a lot of difficulties for people to get official papers for international migration.

Development of Policies about Outmigration

In the middle of the1970s when the cultural revolution was close to the end, the State Council issued a note relaxing the policy for going abroad. It stated that as long as the official permit for immigration from another country was ensured, a Chinese citizen who was not a criminal should be allowed to leave. This was implemented at a larger scale after Deng Xiaoping launched the economic reforms by the end of the1970s.

In November 1985, the Chinese People's Congress passed a law on outmigration and immigration, effective from Feb. 1986. The detailed regulations for implementing this new law were issued in Dec. 1986. It was stated in the law and the detailed regulations that Chinese citizens' application for going abroad for private purpose should be approved if the necessary official documents (e.g., invitation, financial support etc.) were presented, except for criminals and those who may potentially hurt the national security or benefits speculated by a relevant governmental agency at ministry level. It also stated that the official approval or disapproval should be issued to the applicants within 30 days, or within 60 days in the remote areas. This waiting time was further reduced to 15–20 days for large and middle size cities, and 40 days for remote areas in Dec. 1996 (People's Public Security Newspaper, Dec. 5, 1992). Starting from Dec. 1990, the State Council announced that authorized travel agencies could organize tourist trips for Chinese people. The destinations of such trips were mostly Southeast Asian countries in early 1990s, but these are now spreading to Europe, North America and other countries.

Until July 1992, Chinese citizens who went abroad not only needed a passport and a valid visa issued by the foreign country, but also a Chinese official note approving the trip. Since July 1992, such official note was no longer needed. Those with a multiple-entry visa issued by another country, and those Chinese citizens who have residence permits in another country can go in and out of China anytime. Starting from August 1993, all Chinese students, sent by the government or having other financial support to study abroad, were allowed to hold an ordinary/private passport issued by the agencies of public security rather than a passport for public affairs issued by the

Ministry of Foreign Affairs. Quite recently, university faculty, students and other Chinese citizens who go abroad for short-term visits such as for collaborative research are allowed to hold ordinary/private passport. An ordinary/private passport is valid for five years and easy to extend when it expires, but a passport for public affairs is usually valid for one or two years only and much more difficult to extend. Furthermore, persons who hold a passport for public affairs are not allowed to submit their visa applications to the foreign consulate general in China. Their applications must go through the work unit, related ministry or provincial government and the Ministry of Foreign Affairs, which takes at least 2.5 months. The relaxation of the policy on who holds what kind of passport indicates the trend that the government is simplifying the bureaucratic procedures and reducing limitations for Chinese citizens' applications for going abroad.

With the economic reform and implementation of the new policy on outmigration as part of the general policy of opening to the outside world, the number of applications approved by the Chinese public security agencies for outmigrations due to private reasons such as inheriting property, marriage, visiting relatives, private business, self-supported study, tourism. etc., has increased tremendously (see Figure 1): 80,000 in 1986 to 970,000 in 1995, and 710,000 in the first half of 1996 (People's Public Security Newspaper, 5 Dec. 1996). In the period 1979–1990, the total number of applications for going abroad due to private reasons, as handled by the public security agencies, was 1.55 million, and among these, 1.35 million were approved, (an approval rate of 87.1 per cent). In 1990, however, the number of application for going abroad due to private reasons was 290,235, and among these, 278,988 were approved, an approval rate of 96.1 per cent (*People's Daily*, overseas edition, 21 May 1991).

Although previous limitations on citizens' going abroad have been removed, China is still one of the countries which has effective official control over outmigration. Only those Chinese who have foreign invitation and financial support documents are allowed to apply for a private passport, which serves to limit outmigration.

The data shown in Figure 1 and discussed above do not include the large number of Chinese citizens visiting abroad for public affairs approved by various ministries and foreign offices of provincial governments. They include delegations for business or academic activities, scholarly visits or collaborative research supported by either Chinese institutions or foreign institutions. It is difficult to compile statistics on this since many agencies at ministry or provincial level can approve such visits.

Starting in 1990, illegal outmigration became observable in China. In March 1994, the Chinese People's Congress passed a law seriously punishing persons who organize illegal outmigration. The law was implemented effectively and illegal outmigration has become less serious in recent years. Liang and Ye conducted a study on illegal outmigration from Fujian province in China to New York city in the United States. They concluded that the size of undocumented Fujianese immigration to the U.S. was relatively small and the mass media accounts of the "Golden Venture" episode was much exaggerated (Liang and Ye, 1997: 26).

Outmigration For Private Purposes

Very little data on reasons given by people when applying for outmigration for private purposes are available. Data from two local surveys shed some light on this issue. Table 1 and Table 2 list the reasons for outmigration based on a survey conducted in 1935 and another survey conducted in 1989. It should be noted that the data listed in Table 1 and Table 2 are not very compatible since the 1935 survey covered both rural and urban areas while the 1989 survey only referred to one urban district in Shanghai. Another problem is that the investigators of the Shanghai survey in 1989 discovered that the real purpose of a large number of applicants going abroad to "study" (especially those going to Japan and Australia who stated their reason as learning the language), were actually going "to work for making money" rather than "study."

Nevertheless, we have listed their reasons in Tables 1 and 2. One very interesting point is that one of the most important factors in Chinese outmigration is the relationship with overseas relatives, which accounts for about 20 per cent of all permanent and temporary outmigrations in both the 1930s and 1980s. Chinese culture emphasizes helping each other especially among family members and relatives. Once a man or a woman settles down in another country where the income is higher and other conditions are better, he or she feels responsible to help other family members and relatives to avail themselves of the new opportunities. Having other family

Figure 1: Number of Applications for Going Abroad for Private Reasons Handled by the Agencies of Public Securities

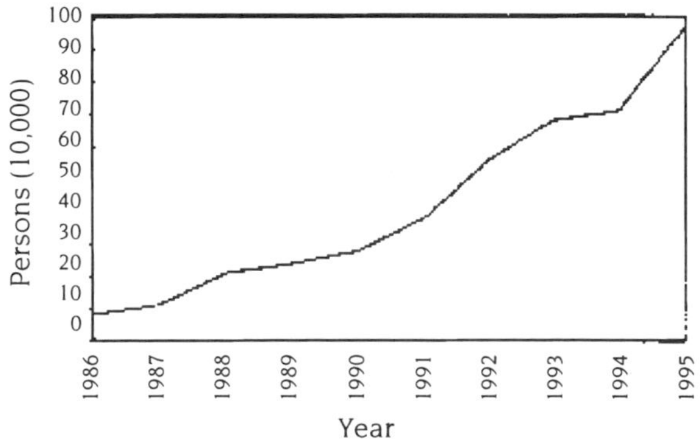

Source: *People's Public Security Newspaper*, 21 Nov. 1995 and 5 Dec. 1996.

78

members and relatives join them helps to empower their social and economic status and may be another motivation to assist relatives' migration. This is important for receiving countries like Canada. It may be important to conduct indepth study targeting the landed immigrants to analyze their characteristics such as place of origin, family and kinship structure and other socio-economic attributes, which will be useful for forecasting the flows of incoming migration.

Table 1. Reasons for Outmigration for Private Purposes

Reasons	# of cases	%
Study abroad	901	58.0
Visit relatives	311	20.0
Permanent outmigration to another country	209	13.5
Visiting Worker	43	2.8
Tourism	30	1.9
Visiting scholar	23	1.5
Accompany spouse or another relative	8	0.5
Marriage	4	0.3
Not clear	24	1.5
Total	**1553**	**100.0**

Source: a survey conducted by Population Research Institute of Social Science Academy in Shanghai. See Sha Jichai (1995) "International migration and mobility", In: Sha Jichai and Chao Jin Chun (eds.). *Studies on Population Problems during the Process of Economic Reform and Opening the Door to the Outside World*. Beijing: Peking University Press. Page 250.

**Table 2. Reasons for Outmigration Based on a Survey
by China Pacific Association, 1935**

Reasons	Per cent
Economic pressures	69.95
Attractions/help/relationship of overseas relatives	19.45
To escape famine	3.43
Development of enterprises	2.87
To escape trouble due to behavior that is unacceptable to the local community	1.88
Insecurity in the local area	0.77
Fighting within family	0.77
Others	0.88

Source: Chen Da (1939), p. 285.

Economic pressure and other life difficulties were the main reasons why Chinese migrated to other countries in the 1930s. This is not the case in China anymore. Although differences of income among individuals are increasing, almost everyone in China today has no major difficulties obtaining basic living necessities such as food and clothing. Liang and Ye (1997) discovered that absolute poverty is not the cause for the undocumented outmigration from Fujian province to New York City. The motivation for outmigration now is to seek better opportunities, to study or work and to improve living standards. For this reason, most of the contemporary Chinese outmigrants have higher education and skills.

Studying Abroad and the Brain Drain Problem

Figure 2 presents the data on students and scholars who went abroad to study with financial support from the Chinese government. This is only part of the picture, because the figures do not include those who went abroad to study on their own or with overseas support. Before the economic reform and the policy of opening to the outside world started in the late 1970s, the number of government-sponsored Chinese students abroad was very small and limited to the former Soviet Union and some other Eastern European countries. After 1978, however, the number has been increasing very steadily. The rising trend was reversed in the period of 1989–1991 mainly because of the Tiananmen Square Incident. Since 1992, the number has been rising again.

The number of students and scholars who went abroad to study with financial support from the Chinese government reached a peak of 19,000 in 1994, which was almost double the number in 1993. The figures shown in Figure 2 do not include those students and scholars supported by foreign institutions through exchange programs or by their own private resources. According to the statistics, the total number of students and scholars who went abroad to study supported either by Chinese government or by foreign institutions through exchange programs approved by the Ministry of Foreign Affairs was about 170,000 in the period 1978–1991. Among them, almost half went to the United States (47 per cent of the total), 15.9 per cent went to Japan, 7.1 per cent went to Canada, 5.9 per cent to Germany, 4.7 per cent to U.K., and 4.1 per cent to France. In the period 1978–1990, the Chinese students who went abroad to study with their own resources approved by the public security agencies were about 140,000, and again the main host countries were United States, Japan, Canada, Australia and some European countries.

The flow of students going abroad with their own resources has been steadily increasing in recent years. The figures cited above clearly show China's increasing interests in sending students and scholars abroad to learn advanced scientific knowledge and new technology. However, a large majority of the Chinese students who have gone abroad to study have not come back to serve the country. This is the so-called brain drain problem due to the extremely large income differences for technical professionals

Figure 2: Number of Students and Scholars Who Went Abroad to Study with Financial Support from the Chinese Government

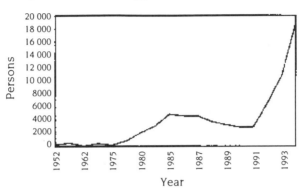

Source: China Statistical Yearbook (1995) *and A Statistical Survey of China* (1996)

between China and developed countries. China needs to worry about this problem and implement policies to provide good living and working conditions to attract overseas Chinese students to return. This is what the government has been doing since the middle of the 1980s. This campaign has had some effects but not at a large enough scale to be fully successful due to financial and political limitations.

Many people have realized that the current Chinese brain drain problem may not be that bad in the long run. For example, many Taiwanese students stayed to work in North America or Europe after they received their advanced degrees in the1950s and 1960s when Taiwan's economic development level was low. In the1970s when Taiwan's economy took off and the income, living standards and working conditions improved, many Taiwanese scholars, managers and engineers with up-to-date knowledge/technology and working experience came back either permanently or temporarily to make major contributions to the economic take off of Taiwan. Therefore, the current brain drain problem in China may have its positive effects in the future (Ma, 1993).

With the rapid economic growth especially in the Southeast coastal areas, the opportunities for making money and business or professional career development are improving. According to our impression (no survey data are available), more and more people feel that it is not necessary to permanently immigrate to get rich and have a good business or professional career, since this goal can be realized in China with no langauge and cultural difficulties. This kind of change in the push-pull mechanism of Chinese international migration will continue and it is possible to attract more and more overseas Chinese scholars, managers and technicians to return to China in the future if the economic development and the political reform continue in the right directions.

81

Labor Services Export To Other Countries

Before 1979, China sent technical laborers to developing countries as international aid for political reasons. Starting from 1979, Chinese commercial labor services export to other countries has developed very quickly. According to official statistics, the cumulative number of persons/times for labor service in other countries in the period 1979–1994 was about 0.98 million. The destination countries increased from eight in 1979 to 178 in 1995. Number of contracts increased from 36 in 1979 to 19,321 in 1995 (see Figure 3), and the estimated value (U.S. dollars) of this export increased from 0.17 billion in 1980 to 6.6 billion in 1995 (see Figure 4). The Chinese labor services export has been mainly concentrated on Singapore, South Korea, and former Soviet Union countries. The main fields of the exported labor service work have been construction, agriculture, forestry, and light industry. Construction is a major area. Most Chinese labor services exports have followed the principle of "do what contract states; high quality of work, and relatively low benefits to attract more contracts," so that the Chinese labor service exports generally enjoy a good reputation especially in developing countries.

However, the educational level and technology training of the Chinese export laborers are generally low. The management and market analysis as well as the international language skills are also poor. This is why it has been difficult for the Chinese labor industry to enter the market of developed countries. Even at its traditional markets of labor export (Middle East and Southeast Asia) it is facing serious challenges.

It is estimated that China has about 250 million surplus labor in rural areas, and about 20 million workers who were laid off from the state-owned enterprises due to economic deficits. The labor resources in China are very rich today and in the near future. If China puts more emphasis on improving its education and professional training programs, the potential for the Chinese labor service export industry is bright, which may benefit people from both China and other countries.

Outmigration For Permanent Residence

Some of the temporary migrants may become permanent residents or even citizens of another country later. But outmigration for permanent residence refers to those who specify their intention for permanent migration at the beginning of the process of their application. Permanent outmigration for family reasons (such as inheriting property, joining close relatives etc.) has been going on for hundreds of years. According to the statistics of the public security agencies, permanent outmigrants for such reasons were roughly 20,000 per year between 1985 and 1990. The pre-condition for permission of permanent outmigration is the official approval from the destination country. The law states that those who make false documentations for illegal outmigration will be punished.

Conclusion

It is estimated that about 30 million overseas Chinese are either permanent residents or citizens of other countries. The overseas Chinese especially those who live in developed countries may play a pulling role for their relatives in China to migrate. Higher income and better opportunities in the developed countries are also attracting factors.

Considering cultural and language preferences, the conditions in China will strongly influence the future trend of Chinese outmigration. With the relaxation of the policy and simplification of the procedures for applying for governmental approval, it will be easier for Chinese people to travel abroad

Figure 3: Number of Contracts of the Labor Services Export to Other Countries

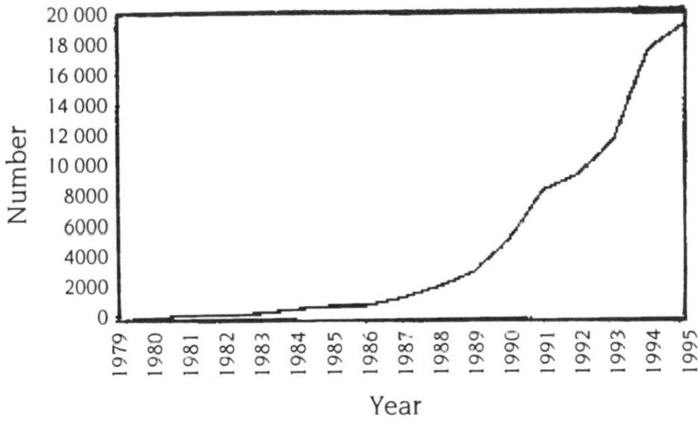

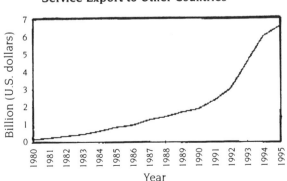

Source: China Statistical Yearbook (1995) and A *Statistical Survey of China* (1996)

Figure 4: Fulfilled Values of the Chinese Labor Service Export to Other Countries

Source: China Statistical Yearbook (1995) and A *Statistical Survey of China* (1996)

(Liang and Mandel, 1997). With expected further socio-economic develop-ment in China, living standards and working opportunities of Chinese peo-ple are expected to continuously improve. If this trend is not reversed, the pushing factor in China for outmigration will gradually become weaker, and the pulling factor of attracting overseas Chinese students, business men and professionals to return to China may gradually increase. Some coastal cities (Shanghai, Guangzhou and Shen Zhen) have already started to attract over-seas Chinese. However, if China had a large scale famine, internal war or serious political instability, and the Chinese people's living standards sharply decline, a lot of Chinese would go to other countries as refugees or other kinds of outmigrants.

The population of China today is about 1.25 billion and it will be about 1.5 billion around the middle of the next century. The scale of refugees and other outmigration flow based on such a huge population will be extremely large if national famine, internal war or other serious political instability occur in China, which will certainly affect other countries' stability and sustainable development. To avoid such disasters by continuing the trend of socio-economic development in China is, therefore, not only good for China itself but also useful for the stability and development of the world as a whole. This is the historical responsibility of all Chinese people in the 21st century.

6 From Brain Drain to Guest Workers and Refugees: The Policies and Politics of Outmigration from Sri Lanka

Sisira Pinnawala

An examination of the patterns of outmigration from Sri Lanka reveals several important trends since the sixties when exodus of the educated and the professionally-qualified was a controversial political and social issue. In the seventies not only did the pattern of migration change but some important shifts and reassessments of the official policies on migration also occurred. Since then the restrictive policies that were introduced in the sixties to control the outflow of the professionally qualified personnel have given way to liberal policies promoting migration of labor, especially those who belong to semiskilled and unskilled categories. The changes in the official policies on the one hand reflect the changes in attitudes toward migration among politicians and policy makers. On the other, they are also a result of changes in the economic strategies and socio-economic conditions. The socio-economic changes in the country coupled with the changing pattern of demand for labor in the international labor market[1] have resulted in changing composition of the labor outflow from one that was predominantly professional and educated to one of unskilled labor with a very high composition of women. Further, in recent years refugees from the Tamil community who are fleeing the civil war in the Northeast of the country have become important components of the outmigration.

In the early days western countries, including Australia and North America, were the major recipients of migrants from Sri Lanka. The economic upsurge in the Middle East in the 1970s as a result of the petro-dollars changed this. Today the bulk of Sri Lankan labor leaving for overseas employment head for the Gulf region. The refugees go mainly to India or to European countries but North America, especially Canada, and Australia are also favored destinations of the refugees.

This chapter examines the changes in the patterns of outmigration from Sri Lanka since the 1960s in relation to a) changes in the official policies towards migration and b) political and ideological determinants of the migration process. It argues that in deciding official policies, ideologies and political interest of the state and state actors, namely the policy makers and the bureaucracy are given priority over the interests of the migrants. It also argues that in deciding refugee policies transnational and interstate relations, namely, ethnic connections, domestic political pressure and security interests are more important than moral and humanitarian concerns that are outlined in international conventions. The chapter concentrates mainly on Sri Lankan guest workers in the Middle East and Sri Lankan Tamil refugees in India.

An Overview of Outmigration from Sri Lanka

Outmigration from Sri Lanka started during the colonial period. In 1867 the Colonial government of Malaya invited Ceylonese who responded to this call favorably. Except for a few traders from the Sinhalese community almost all those who responded to this invitation were Tamils from Jaffna. The Tamils were mainly white collar workers (De Fontgalland 1986). The exact number of those who migrated during this period is not available. The 1931 Malayan census shows that there were 18,490 Ceylonese-born people living in the country (De Fontgalland 1986).

After independence, the members of the mixed European community who are popularly known as Burghers started leaving the country. The majority of them went to Australia which by then had relaxed its strict white Australia policy. Anglophile locals, both Tamil and Sinhalese, also joined the exodus later. These migrants were well-educated; many of them were professionally-qualified people. The main reasons for the migration of these two groups were the sweeping changes in the country's social organization, mainly the changes in the educational and language policy. However, the state during this period was not concerned about the outflow of labor as the loss of skills was not perceived as a serious problem for the country (Karunathilake 1987: 190).

In the late sixties highly qualified professionals and technical personnel became the major component of the migrant outflow. The popular destination of these professionals was England. The colonial link was the main reason for preferring England to other counties. In the 1970s other countries, mainly the U.S.A. and Australia, also became recipients of professional migrants from Sri Lanka. The migration of professionals led to government-imposed restriction on migration.

The sixties saw another important development in the outflow of labor from the country. In 1964 the government finalized an agreement with India called the Sirima-Shastri Pact to repatriate some half a million Tamils who were living in the plantations. These people whose citizenship was taken away in 1949[2] were technically stateless persons and had been a controversial issue in the diplomatic and political relations with India. In 1964 the two governments signed the Sirima Shastri Pact under which India undertook to give citizenship to 525,000 of over 700,000 so called stateless people. Repatriation started under the terms of this pact in 1968 and by 1986 459,410 people numbering 115,458 families had left the country (De Fontgalland 1986: 40).

Except for the repatriation of the so-called stateless Tamils which involved a large number of people, outmigration from Sri Lanka was in a small scale up to the '70s. This situation changed in the mid-1970s with the start of labor migration to the oil rich economies in the Middle East. According to estimates of the Sri Lanka Bureau of Foreign Employment (SLBFE), in 1994 there were over 500,000 contract workers overseas and of them over 95 per cent were in the Middle East. The largest number of Sri Lankan migrant workers is in Saudi Arabia which has an estimated Sri Lankan work force of 200,000 at present. This is followed by Kuwait and UAE with 80,000 and 75,000 respectively (Ruhunage 1996: 7).

Guest workers from Sri Lanka belong mainly to semiskilled and unskilled categories. The majority are women and are employed as housemaids in the Middle East (Ruhunage 1996, Ariyawansa 1989: 10, Korale 1984). Recently there has also been a movement of workers to newly emerging economies in Southeast Asia. The majority of the workers who are in the Middle East today are in the category of unskilled labor, namely housemaids. This special nature of the Sri Lankans employed abroad has been discussed by several authors who have seen it as a reason for Sri Lanka not being greatly affected by the reduction of job opportunities in the mid-1980s (Eelens and Speckmann 1990: 299, Lakshman 1993: 149).

Refugees leaving the country became a significant component of the outflow of migrants in the mid 1980s with the escalation of the civil war. The refugees from Sri Lanka are almost exclusively Tamils fleeing the war in the Northeast. The flow of refugees which started after the escalation of violence in 1983 was first to India. In the latter part of the year and in early 1984 the refugee movement was directed to the West as well. By 1986 according to some estimates there were about 130,000 Tamil refugees in India. Though estimates vary there were also about 50–70,000 refugees in the West (De Fontgalland 1986: 328, Greenberg 1986). Germany and France were the countries with the largest Sri Lankan refugee populations in 1986 (De Fontgalland 1986). In the 1990s with the start of the so-called Eelam War II,[3] there was a second wave of refugees from Sri Lanka. Some estimates say that during this period some 122,064 refugees arrived in India from the island (*Tamil Times*[4] Oct. 15, 1991: 6). According to Indian Home Ministry Annual Report for 1990–91 there were 210,944 Tamils living in India (*Tamil Times* Oct.15, 1991: 6) by the end of 1991. Europe received more Tamil refugees during the second phase. According to some estimates there were 130,000 asylum seekers in Europe in 1990 (*Tamil Times*, November 15, 1990: 6). Europe, according to reports published in *Tamil Times*, received 20,000 Sri Lankan asylum seekers on average annually during the period between 1990–1992.

From Control to Promotion of Outmigration — Policies and Politics

The official policy of the Sri Lankan state on the outmigration of labor has changed from a policy of control and restrictions in the early 1960s to one of promotion in the late 1970s. During the period immediately after independence when outmigration from Sri Lanka consisted mainly of Burghers and the Anglophile Sinhalese and Tamils, there was no official reaction to it though there was considerable outflow of well-educated and skilled personnel. The outflow was not considered as having any impact on the economy and hence it was not considered a major problem (Karunathilake 1987: 190). In the late sixties when professionally and technically qualified people started leaving in considerable numbers thus affecting sectors such as the health service, engineering service and universities, the government began to take notice of the problem. The state for the first time saw outmigration of labor as a loss of a valuable resource that is needed for the country's development. This led to controls of migration of certain categories of people, especially the professionals. The situation changed in the mid-seventies when the government started following a policy of promoting outmigration of labor. These policy changes need to be understood in relation not only to the socio-economic conditions but also to dominant political ideologies and interests of the state and the state actors of the period concerned.

Political Ideology vs. Policy of Migration Control

The first policy measure on outmigration, introduced by the Sri Lankan state, can be more appropriately called a policy reaction. In the late sixties,as stated earlier, professionals started moving out of the country in significant numbers. It is important to note that the reason for their migration was not unemployment but a host of other factors (Sessional Paper 10, 1974). For many who left the country during this period dissatisfaction with the working conditions including inadequate rewards were the main reasons for the decision to migrate (Karunathilake 1987). The socio-economic changes that were taking place, especially the changes in the educational policies and the movement of the country towards socialism were also reasons for the professionals to leave. Between May 1971 and June 1974, 1,705 professionals left the country (Karunathilake 1987: 211). The number of professionals leaving the country between 1979 and 1981 showed an increase of 20 per cent (Ministry of Planning 1985). In some fields, such as medicine and engineering, the annual outflow was more than the annual production according to data compiled by government sources.

The state in this context had two policy options: to control outmigration by negative interventionist policies or to provide solutions to the causes of migration. The policy adopted was control and restrictions which lasted up to the mid-1970s. The control measures were in the form of passport control and foreign exchange limitation. During this period professionals leaving the country were issued a passport valid for one journey only. Medical and engineering graduates were required to sign a bond with the government to serve the country for a period of five years before leaving the country. The migration controls, though strictly enforced, did not bring the expected result of stopping the outflow of professionals. According to observers, controls only worsened the situation as these gave professionals one more reason to leave the country. At best the controls and restrictions only delayed the departure of the individuals who wanted to leave and were therefore not a solution to the brain drain.

The other policy option available to the state was to address the causes that made the professionals leave the country. According to a Cabinet Sub-Committee Report (Sessional Paper 10) in 1974, the main reason for the exodus of professionals was not unemployment. Brain drain was caused by a host of social factors including the stepmotherly treatment the professionals received at work and the failure of the country to provide them with facilities and material incentives. The unsatisfactory occupational status and the lack of incentives for professionals in the country during the period was well documented in the 1971 ILO inter-agency report on Sri Lanka which highlighted the salary differentials in the government sector which highly favored the civil service and clerical occupations against the professionals (ILO Report 1971: 118–119).

The question that arises then is why the state failed to look into the above option as a solution to the brain drain and resorted to unproductive and unpleasant controls that did not work. Here one can speculate on the two main reasons. The first is the vested interests in the powerful top bureaucracy of the country which benefited from the situation. The other was the political ideology of the state which was socialist during most of the period and nationalist all throughout. The state and the state actors, i.e., the civil service interests in the bureaucracy, were protecting their interests and were not mindful of addressing the real issues.

Sri Lanka inherited a powerful bureaucracy from the British colonial rulers. Bureaucrats enjoyed a privileged position in the public sector and were better off both financially and status-wise than the professionals (ILO Report 1971). The bureaucracy dominated by the civil service personnel did not want their position equaled and powers challenged by giving the professionals better facilities and pay. Any changes in the service facilities and rewards would have affected their position and privileges. Therefore it was understandable that they were not interested in recommending policies that could have affected their position and privileges negatively. The interests of the powerful top bureaucracy therefore have played an important role in the failure of the government to adopt policies that were favorable to the professionals.

The political ideology of the day which was predominantly nationalist and socialist was also responsible for the government adopting controls. The strong nationalist ideology which was brought into the political forefront in 1956 dominated the two largest national political parties that have alternatively ruled the country since independence. The party that was in power for over 15 years out of the 20-year period between 1956 and 1977 was not only nationalist but also socialist. This mixture of socialist and nationalist ideologies which is the hallmark of the Third World brand of socialism was on the one hand inward looking in its policies. On the other hand, true to the socialist ideology there was very strong support for controls. It was the political ideology and the interest of the state that were responsible for the state preferring controls and regulations to solve the brain drain problem.

State Interests and Workers Welfare in the Promotion of Migration

The restrictive policies of the state on Sri Lankans leaving the country for employment abroad changed in the mid-1970s. This change was caused by several factors. First, the opportunities made available to overseas workers in the newly emerging petro-dollar economies in the Middle Eastern countries were attracting Asian workers including Sri Lankans. The majority of job opportunities were mainly in the fields that were outside of those restricted by the state. Therefore the government could not see any rationale in restricting the movement of these workers for employment abroad . Second, the economic and social benefits of the labor migration were also in the minds of the policy makers. Foreign employment was seen as a solution to poverty and as a measure to alleviate some negative effects of rising unemployment and helping the foreign currency reserves of the country (Lakshman 1993, Dias 1986). At the same time the government that came into power in 1977 adopted open economic policies as the basis of its development strategy and under the economic liberalization that followed, restrictions and control of all forms had to go. All these led not only to lifting of restrictions on foreign employment but also to a policy of active promotion of labor migration. Promoting foreign employment became part of the activities of the country's diplomatic missions after 1977 (Labor Migration 1977: 15–16).

With the increasing outflow of guest workers and the value of remittances to the country, the government introduced several measures to facilitate migration for work. These included welfare programs for workers and their families and training programs for workers. Further, several parliamentary acts were passed simplifying migration procedures and easing foreign exchange regulations to facilitate remittance of money. The government brought in the Foreign Employment Agencies Act No. 32 of 1980 strengthening government control on the agencies. This act required the employment agencies to take financial responsibility for their contract workers by requiring the agencies to make a deposit with the government towards that end. The regulations were further tightened by the Sri Lanka Bureau of Foreign Employment Act No. 21 of 1985 which established the Sri Lanka Bureau of Foreign Employment (SLBFE) to oversee migration of labor overseas. Under this act in addition to further strengthening the state control over the employment agencies and increasing their responsibilities, a welfare fund was also established which is partly financed by a tax levied on employment agencies.

Both the welfare program and the training program serve mainly the workers in unskilled categories. The training program especially caters to women who are employed as housemaids.[5] This is important as the majority of these women come from either rural areas or from under-privileged urban communities. They naturally are not familiar with the working conditions or not suitably equipped in the language of the host country. The training covers areas such as handling of kitchen equipment, social and cultural adjustment, basic knowledge of English and Arabic and banking functions and how to access welfare facilities. There were 13 such training centres under the SLBFE in 1996.

The above measures however were not always successful in helping the migrants. There are several reasons for this. For example intervention of the state in regulating employment agencies by requiring them to register with the SLBFE did not produce expected results as people still use informal channel, i.e., through contacts made by friends etc. to go abroad for work. Though estimates vary there is a sizable number who do not go through registered agencies. Between January to May 1997, 23.85 per cent of those who went abroad for work did not use registered employment agencies or the SLBFE according to SLBFE data sources. This situation often results in problems in providing redress to employees in trouble. This was clearly evident during the Gulf crisis.

The above is evidence of the state's interest in the promotion of foreign employment for its citizens and its concern about the welfare of the migrant labor force. But the question is whose interests are better served by these measures or in other words who is the real beneficiary. Though it may sound speculative it is quite logical to ask whether the government would have done all this had it not been for the value of the migrants to it. Migrants provide a substantial portion of the country's foreign exchange. Therefore what the state is doing by adopting these measures is promoting its own interests, i.e., helping to keep the labor market to continue the flow of foreign exchange. The protection of workers is only an outcome of that effort. One could argue that the government is protecting the goose that lays the golden eggs.

The state's concern for its own interests more than those of the migrants is further evident by the fact that it has been slow in adopting measures to protect and find ways to give redress to those who face problems abroad. The state started paying attention to these issues only recently. Most Middle East countries, being authoritarian regimes, provide the migrants with only very limited protection (Labor Migration 1996: 14). Further, the migrants from Sri Lanka are most vulnerable as they are mainly women and unskilled workers. It is very common to hear abuse of laborers especially those who are working in the domestic sector. In 1995 according to some estimates nearly 5,000 complaints were received from the Middle East out of which the Saudi Arabia and Kuwait had the largest share (Labor Migration 1996: 15). The diplomatic missions in the region have since started taking interest in attending to these problems but critics are not satisfied with the work they do. At present there are labor welfare officers in four embassies, namely, in Saudi Arabia, Kuwait, Abu Dhabi and Oman. Steps are taken to post them in embassies in countries where there are more than 25,000 Sri Lankan workers. However the emphasis of the state is on promoting migration. The critics say the diplomatic missions are more interested in looking for job vacancies than protecting the workers already there (Labor Migration 1996: 15).

The state is interested in the overseas migrant labor for two reasons. First, it is seen as a safety valve on the employment front (Lakshinan 1993: 148) though analysts do not agree that this has made any direct impact on unemployment (Dias 1986). The reason that is given for the failure of the guest workers to make an impact on unemployment is the fact that the majority of these migrants are from a category of people who are not directly involved in the labor market i.e., housewives and young women. The second reason for the interest of the state is that guest workers are major contributors to the country's foreign earnings. Data on foreign exchange brought into the country by migrant workers clearly demonstrate their importance in the economic front. According to studies the contribution of the guest worker remittance to the GNP has increased steadily and significantly in recent years. For example the ratio of foreign remittance by guest workers rose from 0.7 per cent in 1977 to 4.9 per cent in 1991 (Wickremasekera 1993: p). Similarly the share of employee remittance of the export earnings of the country has risen from 2.2 per cent in 1976 to 22.3 per cent in 1991 (Ruhunage 1996). Today worker's remittance is second only to the foreign exchange earned by the garment industry (Ruhunage 1996). The guest workers therefore were a blessing in disguise for the government which was looking for foreign exchange to help the balance of payment situation. All these show that promotion of migrant labor is in the interest of the state.

Repatriation and Politics of Ethnicity

During the 1960s Sri Lanka started a program of repatriation of Tamil workers in the estates. The 1964 Sirima-Shastri Pact agreed that India will accept the majority of the so-called stateless people from Sri Lanka. This pact which was implemented in 1968 went against the restrictive policies of labor migration of the period. Though these workers could not be called skilled in the strict sense of the term, the work they performed needed a special skill, for example plucking of tea. The very nature of the jobs they performed in the plantations made them an essential component of the Sri Lankan economy. Further, they performed a task that the majority of the locals, especially the majority of the Sinhalese in the surrounding villages were not willing to undertake. Then the question arises as to why the government that was adopting a restrictive policy on professionals with the argument that the loss of their skills would be negative to economic development did not take the same argument into consideration in the case of the estate workers.

One may argue that there was no labor shortage and actually the estates were experiencing a labor surplus. It is true that when the Sirima-Shastri Pact was signed there was a labor surplus in the estates. But the true situation went beyond that. If the Pact worked the way it was intended and had the government succeeded in repatriating the numbers it intended to repatriate, there would have been a shortage of labor (ILO Report 1971: 123) and that would have affected tea production. Why this eventuality was not considered can be explained only if one looks at the ethnic politics involved in the repatriation of Tamil workers.

One may not be able to argue that the loss of estate workers and its impact is negative on the economy due to the nonavailability of data. But it is true that the production of tea went down during the late sixties, a trend that has continued until recently. There are a host of factors ranging from drought to price declines in the market that have been put forward as responsible for this situation (Central Bank 1970). However it is reasonable to assume that repatriation was also contributory to this. The policy of repatriation of Tamil estate workers was therefore influenced by other concerns than the logical evaluation of the economic impact. In other words, ethnic factor was one reason for the state not paying attention to the possible economic impact of the repatriation.

Refugee Policies and State Interests

Refugees are a category of migrants who are covered by several international conventions and a UN protocol defining their status and rights. According to the 1951 UN Convention Relating to the Status of Refugees, refugees are persons who, owing to a well-founded fear of being prosecuted for reasons of race, religion, nationality, membership of a particular social group or political opinion, are outside of the country of their nationality and are unable to or, owing to such fear, unwilling to avail themselves of the protection of that country; or who having a nationality and being outside the country of their former habitual residence as a result of such events, are unable or, owing to such fear, are unwilling to return to it (UN 1951). Since then other conventions have adopted definitions expanding the principles of the UN convention (Newland 1993: 82).

International conventions however do not always determine the policies of states on refugees. Scholars have identified several forces that are important in deciding refugee policies in different context. Security issues, both national and international, transnational relations, namely, irredentas and diasporas are some of them. In addition, what is now known as the international refugee regime has greatly influenced refugee policies of states

(Jacobsen 1996). It consists of the nongovernmental organizations looking after the interests of refugees and the media that have taken over the responsibility of promoting the moral and humanitarian aspects of refugee phenomenon, an aspect often neglected by the state.

The Sri Lankan government sees the ethnic problem as creating displacement but the refugees are also a problem created by the Tamil militants to get India involved in the conflict and to get the international community to exert pressure on the Sri Lankan government. The government therefore does not accept the genuineness of the majority of the Tamil refugee claims, especially those who leave the country. Sri Lanka's official policy towards those who are displaced by the war is somewhat complex and ambiguous. The Sri Lankan government does not accept that Tamils are victimized and have reasonable grounds for leaving the country. The argument of the government is that Tamils are safely living in southern parts of the country and also in refugee camps in the North and East. Therefore it has always used diplomatic pressure on host governments to discourage accepting Tamil refugees. The government policy on refugees is therefore closely associated with its political interests.

Tamil refugees who started arriving in India, particularly in Tamilnadu are one of the major policy and political concerns faced by both the Sri Lankan and the Indian governments. When the displaced Tamils from Sri Lanka first arrived in Tamilnadu the Indian government readily accepted them as refugees. The reasons range from Indian security and political concern for the region to the pressure exerted by domestic political groups, particularly those in Tamilnadu. Tamils from Sri Lanka have long-standing cultural links with the Tamils in South India. The presence of refugees therefore can create difficult situations for the Indian government. Further, due to the close transnational links, Tamilnadu politics and Sri Lankan Tamil conflict have closely interacted since 1980, a relationship which has been mutually beneficial for both parties until recently.

Despite all this, Sri Lankan Tamil refugees are a burden to India both politically and economically. It is however the political burden that is the main reason for the recent changes in Indian policies towards the refugees from Sri Lanka. When the displaced Tamils from Sri Lanka arrived in India in 1984, the Indian reaction was to accept them and offer them refugee status. India not only welcomed them but also was active in international circles in promoting the flight of the refugees during these early days. The transnational links the Sri Lankan Tamils have with Tamilnadu which is an important actor in Indian politics and India's alleged role in the Tamil militancy in Sri Lanka during the early phase (Sivarajah n.d.,) were the reasons for this Indian reaction. It is therefore not correct to say that humanitarian obligations were the only reason for India's ready acceptance of Sri Lankan Tamils as refugees. This political consideration as the basis of policy is further illustrated by the fact that the Indian government did not show the same favorable reaction to the arrival of Tamil refugees in India after the Indo-Lanka accord, especially after the assassination of Rajiv Gandhi, allegedly by the LTTE. With the assassination of Rajiv Gandhi, which took place in Tamilnadu, even Tamilnadu politicians were unwilling to promote Tamil militancy in the Indian context as they did in the past. Since then India's reaction was a mixture of indifference to outright rejection of Tamil refugees.

Treatment of refugees and India's policy on Tamil refugees, therefore, changed with the changing political climate in Tamilnadu and the nature of Indian involvement in Sri Lanka. Indian intervention and the subsequent Indo-Lanka Agreement started a process of repatriation. After the Indo-Lanka accord of 1987 and the Indian Peace Keeping Force fiasco and especially after the killing of Rajiv Gandhi, Indian policy towards Sri Lankan Tamil problem changed. With that the Indian policy towards Tamil Refugees also changed. Now India actively supports Sri Lanka's attempt to stem the flow of refugees to India. The co-operation the Indian navy has extended to the Sri Lankan navy to block refugees crossing to India in the recent past is a good example of this. The change of policy towards the refugees from that of support before 1987, when India was promoting the Tamil militants, to active discouragement today, illustrates the fact that Indian domestic and regional interests are the deciding factors in its policy with regard to refugees from Sri Lanka.

What is clear from the above is the importance of political interest in deciding refugee policies. Though refugees are accepted as an international obligation in both political and moral terms, pragmatic concerns have always influenced countries to adopt policies according to the needs of given situations. In here the security needs of the host country and its domestic political concerns often come into operation. Therefore refugee policies are not merely legal and administrative actions upholding moral principles outlined in international conventions but political actions determined by national and local interests.

Conclusions

It is not a new argument that policy decisions are influenced by ideological factors and other interests. Ideologies and interests are part and parcel of policies and therefore policies and politics are inseparable. The important issue this chapter was attempting to highlight is what takes priority in a given situation and whose interests are taken into consideration in deciding policies. As was illustrated in the above discussion, in relation to labor migration from Sri Lanka and to the exodus of refugees, the interests of the state have always taken priority. In relation to outmigration of labor, the Sri Lankan state by supporting migrants is actually promoting its own interests. Promotion of the interests of the migrants in this regard is the result not the end objective of state policy. Political ideologies also play a part in deciding policies as illustrated in relation to the repatriation of Tamil estate workers.

In relation to refugees both the host country and the home country have played politics and were more interested in the political advantages than the humanitarian aspects of the refugee phenomenon. The humanitarian aspects were given attention only as part of politics. Again the interests of the refugees were the result not the end objective of the policies.

What the above shows is important in throwing some light onto the much broader issue of the state and its function. The classical argument that the purpose of the state is to promote the well being of the citizens or the common good (Diggs 1974) is indirectly questioned in this paper. Morality and ethics as part of the existence of the state are also brought up here though not directly. The Sri Lankan state using, or more appropriately put, exploiting, the migrants particularly the most vulnerable of the disadvantaged groups among them — women — for its own good, questions the morality of the state actions. Though these are not immediately related to policy making they are nevertheless important to understand the legitimacy of the policy making process.

Endnotes

[1]   In the mid-1973s OPEC countries raised the price of oil resulting in an economic boom in the region. This had a tremendous impact on the international labor market generating large demands for skilled and unskilled labor.

[2]   When the British left the country in 1948 giving Sri Lanka independence, the Tamil workers who were brought into the country to work in the tea plantations and other people of Indian and Pakistani origin received automatic citizenship and voting rights. One of the first acts of the post-independence government was to introduce a bill called the Indo-Pakistani citizenship act in Parliament to remove the citizenship rights of these people.

[3]   The renewal of violence after the breakdown of peace talks between the Sri Lankan government and the Liberation Tigers of Tamil Eelam (LTTE) in 1990 is called the Eelam War II.

[4]   *Tamil Times* is a publication by the Tamil Times Ltd. in Surrey, England. Though it caters to the Sri Lankan Tamil diaspora in the west it presents a moderate view of the ethnic problem in Sri Lanka.

[5]   According to SLBFE data for 1996 of the 162,572 who left for work overseas 110,593 (68.03 per cent) were housemaids. About 13.37 per cent were unskilled workers. There were only 0.37 per cent professionals among them.

7 In the Maelstrom of Hope and Despair; The Prospects for South Asian Migration to Canada[1]

Azfar Khan

There are two truisms about voluntary migration in a market system. The first is that people move because they see some improvements in doing so, be it in income and economic position, social position and/or relative situations of security. The other is that their movement is essentially influenced by structural imbalances between their place of origin and the place(s) of destination(s). These two factors have governed the movement of people from South Asia, or for that matter from any other part of the world over the last two centuries.

The movement within and beyond national frontiers is attended upon by causal and enabling conditions. However, though there may be little, or no, institutional restrictions on movements within national boundaries, the transnational movements of people are governed by certain juridical concerns. Migration of South Asians to Canada is two-sided. It is primarily a movement of those who are "selected" by an immigration policy(ies) of the host country and it is determined to a large extent by the economic, social and political processes that bring about situations of relative deprivation and give vent to the motivation to migrate.

A particular environment of migration is then enabled by a certain harmonization of the established dictates of demand and supply. Thus, though the immigration legislation in the host country may describe, to varying degrees, the receptivity of the movers, it is not so that all those who have a need to move would migrate. Once the causal influences suggest a movement, the choice of a destination is facilitated by four considerations: the relevant information the movers have; their financial resources; the institutional and personal support they can count on; and their socio-economic profile. This is a framework within which the past and future movements of South Asians to Canada need to be considered.

97

Canadian Immigration Policy and South Asian Migration

Canadian immigration policy has been more circumspect than policies generally adopted by most other countries of the North. In Canada, the immigration of foreigners has been managed to fundamentally reflect the demographic and economic needs of the country, but these have also not been without their racial and ethnic overtones. A retrospective look at the migratory flows suggests that while the Europeans were preferred in the earlier "settler" phase of the movements, the latter major movements from the developing countries were motivated essentially by economic considerations. Although it must be admitted that in the settler phase of immigration, economic concerns also played a major role leading to the recruitment of Chinese and Japanese labor to work on the railroads, in the lumber industry and in other public sector projects.

The migration of South Asians to Canada dates back to the turn of the century. The early migrants, mainly Sikhs, were soldiers of the British Empire (see Tatla 1995) and recruits in the many steamship companies (Tinker 1977) who settled in the lands by official consent. They migrated as single men, mainly to the western provinces, and later were able to arrange for the migration of their families. Over the years a small community, largely ethnically monolithic, took shape. Their numbers were not very significant and as such their presence constituted a minor aberration in the general migration picture. Immigration in Canada, apart from the presence of the Chinese labor in the western provinces, was largely characterized by the movements of people from Europe.

This seems to have changed in the early sixties, when migration of non-Europeans was also invited by the Canadian government which considerably relaxed the racial and ethnic barriers and removed nearly all privileges for immigrants from Europe. It could be surmised that the new immigration legislation was enacted to cement Canada's avowed "neutral" status, with a general appeal to the principles of human rights, in a changing world structure. But this was by no means an open door policy as such, for the migrants were vetted by an objective selection criteria based on a points system which established the suitability of the movers to the needs of the economy (Samuels and Jansson 1988). However, what this did was expand the base of migration from South Asia, where previously immigration to Canada was largely confined to North India, and particularly Punjab, the latter flows incorporated the other regions and ethnic communities of South Asia. As such, the general South Asian community which is now to be found in Canada is no longer monolithic but is ethnically and culturally very diversified. Furthermore, the destinations of the migrants also diversified in the post-'60s phase of migration. Whereas, well up to the '60s, the western provinces — particularly British Columbia — were the places where most people of South Asian origin were to be found, in the latter phase, the eastern provinces, particularly Ontario and to a lesser extent Quebec, were the major chosen destinations. So much so, that the present censal picture, with regards to South Asian population, indicates that a vast majority is to be found in the two eastern provinces mentioned above.

The 1960s and the early '70s were perhaps, the heyday of migration from South Asian countries — particularly India and to a lesser extent Pakistan — and given the relative leniency in admitting foreigners, a broad amalgam of occupational categories of independent migrants is noted whose numbers were also fairly high. The independents were basically migrants who had no family connections in the host country and migrated to take up paid employment in Canada. They were selected by allocating points for the make-up of their socio-economic profiles, i.e., education, age, knowledge of the working languages and, quite astutely, skills. The last is an extremely important concern, for it is here where a certain manipulation could take place depending upon Canada's requirement for particular skills at different points in time.[2] Besides the fact that the base of migration expanded, there was also a qualitative shift in the socio-economic profile of people hailing from the region. Whereas, in the earlier period, the South Asian Sikh "settlers" essentially followed the labor from the orient in blue collar occupations, i.e., on the railroads and with the lumber companies, the latter stream was basically composed of relatively high skilled white collar workers who also included many professionals in their ranks.[3] It could be posited that this particular migration stream from South Asia, contributed significantly to the "brain drain" from the source countries. It hardly included any unskilled among its numbers for, given the legislation, it was inconceivable for an unskilled worker to be considered — let alone admitted — for immigration into the country in the category of "independents."

Migration in the "independents" category was significantly curtailed in the post-1976 period, when the economy was getting into the throes of an economic recession. At this point, the points system was made more stringent, presumably with the explicit intention of protecting the job market for those already residing in Canada, and these controls remained in force till the late 1980's. Data from the last decade show that independent migrants again gained in importance as the decade progressed consequent upon a relaxation in the controls on immigration. For example, whereas in 1983 immigration of independents accounted for 30 per cent of total immigration in Canada, in 1988 the proportionate share of the category rose significantly to 51 per cent (Immigration Canada 1990). But even then, the numbers were much less than those noted for the 1960s.

To throw a quantitative gloss on the picture, in the 1980s, migrants from Asia accounted for an average of 45 per cent of total immigrants, however, the majority of these came from the Southeast Asian region and not South Asia.[4] Taking an average over the decade, it seems that migration of South Asians to Canada has, at best, been no more than 9 per cent of the total yearly flows, and about 17 per cent of the Asian immigration. As regions of provenance go, India is by far the most important country and has, over the period of two decades, consistently been among the top five source areas.

Though the immigration of independents may have gone up, the major type of movements from South Asia over the last decade have been for family reunification, which have accounted for almost 80 per cent of all immigration. Immigration for "family reunification" includes the movement of immediate family members (i.e., children, parents, spouses, fiances and to lesser extent, siblings) and this migration is accorded the highest priority. However, it should be clear that the "family reunification" immigration is predicated upon the significant flows of "independent" South Asians in the ten-year period following the inception of the points system in Canadian immigration legislation, and certainly also of the earlier settlers. Family reunification movements also have a basis in the naturalization of those who were admitted temporarily, particularly on student visas. This distinctive pattern of South Asian immigration is as much culturally, as it is historically, determined and is reflective of the social structures which have mediated migration from the region.[5]

The Development Context of Migration in South Asia

Emigration pressures are fundamentally derived in the wider developments taking place in the countries of the region. All the economies are undergoing a massive structural transformation and in one — Sri Lanka — the economic outcomes are exacerbated by civil strife which has pitted the country's two largest ethnic communities in a bloody war for well over a decade. The movements of refugees arising from this are time bound and require attention in their own right. However, our concern is more with the patterned flows incumbent upon the processual social and economic transformations in the countries of the region.

The "structural transformations" in the four major countries of the region (India, Pakistan, Bangladesh and Sri Lanka) are noted to have, more or less, a similar context. The transformations arise from a debt crisis which confronted the economies in the latter part of the '80s. The origins of the crisis are essentially located in the heavy borrowing undertaken by the developing countries on the world markets to finance investments and the deficits in their trade and balance of payments, consequent upon a deteriorating terms of trade structure in the '70s and the '80s. By the end of the '80s, these deficits had grown to alarming levels. The external debt, given the structural base of the countries, also could not be serviced efficiently. Something needed to be done.

As a crisis of financial solvency hit the debtor countries, they looked for viable solutions. One was that they could extricate themselves from the situation by borrowing in the international markets. However, once the debt crisis surfaced most of the private and bilateral sources dried up overnight. The second was that they could tighten their belts by putting up restrictions on imports and cutting capital expenditures to balance their accounts. But this was an option with pronounced economic, political and social costs and not many were willing to take the risks, lest they alienate the population and invite a response which they would not be able to control. The third which seemed logical was to adjust their economies to the changed circumstances of the world economy. Though this was the path chosen, it must be noted that the transformation included some aspects of the first two options as well.

The "bail out" programs which were then introduced, with the assistance of the two Bretton Woods institutions, i.e., the International Monetary Fund (IMF) and the World Bank, are what are typically described as "structural adjustment packages" or SAPs. In return for the countries' willingness to accept the packages, the IMF and the World Bank would help the countries to tide over their immediate financial constraints and also find mechanisms for rescheduling the repayment of debt and provide some debt relief. However, the programs came with certain conditions; the adjustments were to be undertaken in a framework of "globalization," the dynamics of which were decreed by the adoption of a freer structure of international trade and a focus on economic growth basically to earn foreign exchange to pay off their outstanding external debt. Consequently, the countries' production structures would need to orient themselves towards a growth imperative, which required liberalization and market deregulation and the removal of state controls on production which were deemed inefficient.

Employment Impact of Adjustment Reforms and Migration

The general assessment after almost a decade of experience under the adjustment regimes is that, in the short term, the adjustment reforms have had a uniformly adverse impact in nearly all countries of the region. The impacts of pursuing such a policy are, of course, differentiated because of the different make-up of the production base and commensurately, the different potential of income generation. In this regard the costs to those economies, such as Pakistan, Bangladesh and Sri Lanka, which do not have a very diversified manufacturing and trade base and have to rely on few commodities for export earnings are higher, than for a country like India, which has a relatively more diversified production base, even though it may be more heavily indebted in absolute terms.

Whatever the macro requirements of the adjustment reforms, our basic endeavour is to establish how the processes are affecting the livelihoods of the people and fostering outmigration tendencies from the region. One aspect of this, and perhaps the most important, is to assess their impact on employment in the various sectors of the economy. Employment, or the lack of it, plays a critical role in generating migration impulses, primarily because it is the most significant determinant of income generation and therefore, as a corollary, of the welfare of the people. It is also important from a point of view of a common, and persuasive, argument in migration analysis which holds that creating jobs at origin and improving the income earning potential would dampen the pressures on migratory flows.

1) **Employment and the demographic concern.** The basic link of employment in South Asia is with demographic concerns. All the countries of the region are characterized by very high population growth rates, and although some successes have been achieved in lowering fertility levels, the momentum inherent in the population pyramids of the South Asian countries, suggests that the population of the region would be well in excess of 1.5 billion by the end of the century. Furthermore, the population structure suggests a very large number in the working phase of their lives. It is estimated that 50 per cent, if not more, of the population of the region is below 15 years of age, which emphasizes the pressures on the economies to create jobs in the future to absorb the potential entrants in the labor force. Given that the present rate of growth of the labor force is, and would continue to be for some time, greater than the rate of growth of employment suggests continual addition to the backlog of unemployment.

2) **The situation of formal sector employment.** The situation as regards the development of absorptive capacity(ies) makes for a dismal reading. In the Indian case, for example, even prior to the inception of the adjustment reforms, the rate of growth of employment fell while the rate of growth of output rose. This led one researcher to remark that ". . . the most striking fact is that the '80s have been the best decade in terms of economic growth but the worst decade in terms of employment generation" (Ghosh 1992: 95). At the point of introduction of the adjustment and liberalization packages, Mundle (1992) estimated the employment impact of adjustment policies by developing low growth and high growth scenarios for the Indian economy and his projections showed that in either case unemployment levels were likely to go up. The numbers of unemployed were in the 1991–92 period projected to vary between 12 to 18 million persons. However, it should be kept in mind that Mundle's reference is only to formal "organized" sector employment which only makes up around 8 per cent of total employment, plus the fact that it is only to overt unemployment. If some estimates of underemployment are added to this, the figures obtained can only be described as colossal.[6] The general trend is also reflective of the situation in Pakistan, Bangladesh, Sri Lanka and Nepal.

    But what can be made of this situation at the sectoral level? Of course, it may be stated that the impact across sectors is likely to vary as well, depending upon the priorities accorded by a country's development policies to different sectors in keeping with the dictates of the reforms which require a switching of expenditures to activities which have a higher growth and profitability potential. But even then a general decline in rate of growth of employment across sectors is noted. From the data available it seems that in India, the decline was particularly severe in agriculture and manufacturing. In other countries of the region, which have a relatively less diversified economic structure, the situation could be worse. So far as agriculture is concerned, the argument could be made that the sector has reached the limits of its absorption potential. However, the decline in the manufacturing sector employment growth rate is indeed, a cause for concern especially so since, within the context of modern sector development, it is the sector with the key carrying capacity. This does not bode well for the future, as labor absorption in agriculture being at a point where it essentially represents a stasis, suggests an accelerating migration towards the cities. What this is likely to do is buttress the surplus labor force in the urban areas and add significantly to the growth of people living on the margins in the cities; the growth of urban slums all across the region attest to the trend.

There are some sectors which have benefited in the period of adjustment. The opening up of the economies, which globalization has entailed, has also seen inflows of capital in the form of foreign direct investment. However, there are two points to consider here. Firstly, much of this investment is in the form of companies setting up commercial operations in capital intensive industries and tieing up with local entrepreneurs in the growing sectors — such as telecommunications and microprocessors industry in India — to take advantage of the low cost high quality labor. Thus, though they may provide opportunities for the absorption of those who are fairly high skilled, their potential in the overall scheme of employment generation is minor. Secondly, even in the consideration of high skilled work, the absorptive capacity created is nowhere near being adequate enough to employ the majority of the available labor stock.

3) *The privatization option.* The dwindling of formal sector employments is noted in all the four large countries of the region, i.e., India, Pakistan, Bangladesh and Sri Lanka. There are reasons for this, of course. Firstly, a good deal of the decline may be attributed to retrenchments through public expenditure cuts. Secondly, the move towards liberalization and privatization though it may have been beneficial for growth, has also suggested a weak potential for employment. In the Indian case, Mundle (1992) and Ghosh (1992) both note a drop in the employment elasticities of output and the latter also refers to a negative employment elasticity in private formal sector manufacturing.[7] A more recent study by two of India's most distinguished economists endorses the view (see Bhaduri and Nayyar 1996; 100–101). Among other things, what a falling employ-

ment elasticity implies is a rising labor productivity. Here an argument could be made that the private entrepreneurs who are solely concerned with the profitability of their ventures would, of course, take measures to augment their economic position, rather than worry about providing employment. To some extent, these measures could entail the reorienting of the production structures of enterprises to incorporate a more capital intensive and/or a labor displacing technology.

The adjustment packages explicitly provide incentives for private sector growth. However, one cannot pin too much hope on the private sector to create employments especially in economies such as in South Asia where the state has, ever since independence, been the major employer in the organized sector and the private interests have only played a minor role in the overall employment picture. Under the circumstances, it is unreasonable to expect that the private sector could be transformed into the major provider of wage employments overnight.

Furthermore, there are obvious constraints to the growth of the private sector. For instance, it is noted that the private sector has been quite reluctant to enter into ventures where the returns to investment are seen as low in the long run, and particularly where the context suggests political and economic instability. The situation may hold less for India than for the other countries of the region. Even if the private sector is assisted by the State, there is the added problem (definitional) of underdeveloped capital markets, which either cannot raise the amounts that are needed or are reluctant to loan out funds, especially to those who cannot provide "adequate" collateral. This is fairly evident in the South Asian case.[8] Those who benefit in such a situation are the large firms — which is quite contrary to the espoused intention of fostering competition through deregulation — who then eliminate competition through ". . . acquisitions, mergers and takeovers."[9]

4) *Employment in the Informal Sector, Poverty and Migration*. The growing informalization of the economy has also been a characteristic of development in all South Asian countries in the '80s and '90s. However, it should be pointed out that though these activities may present certain avenues for employment, their income generation potential is variable and weak and their continued presence over long periods fairly precarious. As such the existence of most of these activities is dependent upon the velocity of monetary circulation (high level of transactions). So long as there are funds being spent on the services provided by the informal sector, the activities may prosper (relatively), but once the funds dry up, because of some monetary discipline being practiced and/or income sources diminishing because of increased levels of unemployment, their survival is put into question. The cutbacks in public expenditure and the consequent reduction in aggregate demand can only have serious nega-

tive impacts on employment in the sector. It should also be kept in mind, that there is a wide range of informal endeavors, ranging from fairly high skilled work to activities which may be described as fairly ubiquitous, e.g., hawking, vending, etc. All along the spectrum there are negative implications for employment, at least in the medium term of the implementation of adjustment reforms. However, it seems that the adverse impacts are more pronounced for those on the lower rungs of the social ladder undertaking the more "basic' activities.

Indeed, the discerned impact of adjustment in the developing world has suggested that the burden has been borne greatly by the disadvantaged groups and social classes in society. South Asia is no exception. By design, the adjustment policies have seriously hampered services which benefit the poorer element in society through cutbacks in public sector spending and also by switching expenditures to activities which are generally geared towards the employment of the relatively more skilled. With the worsening income distribution, the poor and vulnerable have sought to maintain their share in the "economic pie" in various ways. The increased labor force participation that is noted in the taking up of multiple employments and recourse to child labor — which is rampant in all the countries of South Asia — are but two cogent elements of what one author has described as, ". . . the outcomes of intense labor market survival strategies" (see Saith 1997).

There is a strong association between poverty and unemployment. Providing employment — in the formal or informal sectors — is the only way to ensure sustainable livelihoods and improve the quality of life. To quote Bhaduri and Nayyar (1996), ". . . ultimately, the process of economic growth must create employment and incomes for the poor. There is no alternative to this. No other sustainable means of eradicating poverty exists." The implications of this are straightforward. Employment creation should be the cornerstone of all policies designed to improve the general welfare of the people and alleviate poverty. But if employment cannot be provided, then among the poor, outmigration from their places of origin — whether internal and/or abroad — is an important element to consider in the design and implementing of survival strategies.

A Note on Government Policy in South Asia

Emigration pressure in a developing country has been defined as ". . . an excess labor supply in the presence of a negative per capita income differential" (Bruni and Venturini 1992: 4, quoted in Saith 1997). The excess labor supply is, of course, with respect to the domestic capacity of labor absorption and the latter with regard to the countries of destination. As can be gauged from the preceding presentation, the stock of labor supply in South Asia is hitting astronomical levels and, the excess labor supply, to varying degrees, is to be noted in all sectors of the economy. Thus definitionally, the supplementing factor of wide income differentials, coupled with other decisive "push" factors, should then be sufficient to motivate international movements from the South Asian countries.

Under the circumstances, most governments tend to look at international migration as an equilibrating mechanism. The general belief is that out-country movements of labor would not only alleviate the unemployment problem but there are further benefits to be derived through the inflows of remittances sent back which would not only augment the depleted foreign exchange coffers but would — or could — also be cycled into productive investments.[10] However, though a tacit encouragement is given — in that some countries have set up training institutes or vocational centres to train labor for employment opportunities abroad, and some agreements are reached by the governments with the prospective receiving states at the highest level of meetings — there is no cohesive and coordinated strategy with a long term outlook in any of the countries in the region; only selective and ad hoc measures exist.

It should also be mentioned that the main focus of policy concern in the South Asian countries are the blue collar workers whose excess supply dwarfs the surplus pool of white collar professionals and technical workers. The governments are well aware of the potential for social and civil disorder the unemployed represent and are more than eager to grant them permission to go abroad. However, this is largely done in absence of any vetting process for skill losses that might ensue, and as such it could be said that they follow a policy which gives scant attention to the management of human resources. Subsequently, it is inferred, that in their anxiousness in encouraging the out-country flows of labor, the governments have also implicitly endorsed, or at least tolerated, many undesirable labor market practices in the recruitment and supply of workers to overseas markets.

Future Prospects of South Asian Migration to Canada: Who Migrates?

However, though an inclination to effect an out-country movement may be ever present, it does not hold that all those wishing to move would emigrate. Emigration, to reiterate, is a "selective" process and the enabling of the movement needs to take into account both the supply side factors, as well as the demand side stipulations. If we now look at the emigration potential of South Asians from the Canadian perspective, it would seem that the various controls on migration would, by definition, exclude the majority of the movers whose profiles do not match up with the specificities of demand, particularly in the category of "independents." These would be the more unskilled and blue collar workers. Looking at the supply side, from the perspective of these relatively low skilled workers, it would seem that migration to Canada would also be accorded a very low priority, simply because effecting such a movement is well beyond their economic means. A cursory examination of the present situation suggests that within the nexus of their

calculations, the Middle Eastern oil producing region and the booming economies of Southeast Asia and even, to some extent, the Western European
countries offer a far more attractive option.

Nevertheless, some migration of the unskilled to Canada could be expected, particularly of those who come from the background of the earlier
Sikh settlers — and of similar rural based communities, who in the past may
have moved to Canada via a step migration from Britain — but the prospects of their moving to Canada would rest upon the strength of their kinship and social networks which would enable their migration. Perhaps, at
this juncture it would seem pertinent to detail some aspects of the working
of these networks.

A Note on Social Networks as Mediators in Migration

In the South Asian context, the role of social and kinship networks in
mediating migration cannot be underestimated. The networks are essentially
to be understood as integral parts of an "extended family" tying together the
fortunes of different households. The networks arise from social relationships which are either biologically referred, mainly through paternal descent,
and affinity described through marriage. They may also include a circle of
friends with similar caste affinities, and this is noted not just in its rigid
application among the Hindus, but also — presumably because of cultural
lineage — among many Muslim communities in Pakistan and Bangladesh.
The network ties are quite wide ranging and basically provide normative and
ideological support to households in need. They are also important as so-
cializing agents and as a source of guidance in the conduct of affairs, i.e., as
providers of welfare and as financial and advisory services.

The functioning of the networks is particularly strong in the rural areas
of South Asia, especially among the relatively poorer groups for whom they
constitute an indispensable mechanism of security. It becomes an obligation for members of one household to help another. Those who have migrated to Canada, have relatives and friends who need to be supported in
every which way and if this means enabling their migration then it is incumbent upon those already in the host country to find ways and means.[11] This
may mean bringing them over gradually either through the "family
reunification" category (enabling it through the betrothal of sons and daugh-
ters who are already citizens of Canada) and/or as "assisted relatives/se-
lected workers," where the guarantee of jobs can be made by local community businesses.

The influence of the networks weakens somewhat in the urban areas where
the families generally tend to be more nuclear. Here it is inferred that the
networks do not express a similar alignment and solidarity with other households as they do in the rural areas, but this is not to say that the ties are non-
existent; the family (or to be more exact the household, with parents and
siblings and their children) rather than the individual continues to be the

major unit of analysis within the social and cultural context of almost all South Asian ethnically distinct groups. This perhaps, may explain why "family reunification" constitutes the largest category of South Asian immigration to Canada.

Thus, apart from the movements for "family reunification" which are likely to continue, it would seem that emigration to Canada is more within the scope of those "independents" whose socio-economic profiles are better suited to meet the Canadian labor demand. These would tend to be the better-off elements in society — mostly professionals and business persons — displaying high skill qualifications and/or high asset worth. There are many factors which make Canada an attractive place for relocation and though it is difficult to say which reason generates what quantum of movement, a semblance of the decisions and their context may be provided.

From the supply side perspective, part of the reasons to move to Canada may be found in the recent developments in the world economy which have brought about a closer link-up of international markets. In the context of intense activity worldwide in the pursuance of "globalization," the more qualified just might feel that their interests are better served in the more developed markets where inter-job mobility is greater, and as a corollary, higher income earning opportunities, more abundant. Furthermore, the decision to move to Canada might be tinged by the fact that under the prevailing political and economic instability in many countries of the region, securing an employment, and/or a base for business operations, in a more stable economy like Canada would be more advantageous for them and their families in the long run. On the other hand, the decision to move could be swayed simply by the observed income differentials between the home country and Canada for similar employments, and the movement may be conceived of as a conduit to augmenting the standard of living. The various reasons could operate exclusively on their own in motivating migration and/or there might also be some aspects of each factored into one decision. But what is important here is the environment generated by the host country's immigration policies which provides the context for these decisions and their realization.

The future migration of South Asians to Canada will be essentially determined by demand-induced factors. The basic affirmation is that future migration streams will fundamentally be made up of those who will be migrating for "family reunification" given the already present stock of labor and the additional attributes of social networks. Apart from this, there is likely to be an acceleration in flows of "independents" from the South Asian region if the economic situation deteriorates — of which there are strong indications — and the states are not able, either to undertake investments — which is the sole provider of employments — or invite such from domestic and international sources. To what extent this is likely to happen is unclear, but it is clear that these migrants would not only be the highly qualified but also those with enough personal capital at their disposal to enable the movement. Another factor, which would enter into the calculation of the potential emigrants is, of course, the relative attractiveness of the Canadian labor market, with respect to other destinations. Some skilled and highly educated workers, particularly in the telecommunications and computer industry, might look eastward towards the Asian Pacific economies. However, as yet, the demand for such skills from the region is weak. The "selected workers" category may only be a minor concern, though some independents lacking the necessary means may utilize this and social networks to facilitate their movement.

A word needs to be said on the immigration of "refugees" and "asylum seekers." In the past two decades, Canada has been host to refugees mainly hailing from the Southeast Asian Pacific rim after the cessation of hostilities in the countries of the Indo-China region. Lately, it has also taken in refugees from the Middle East and Western Asia. So far as South Asian refugees to Canada are concerned, the only significant movements have been those of Tamil Sri Lankans fleeing the civil war. As the situation stands, the conflict shows no sign of abating and it is likely that a number of potential refugees escaping the war will move to Canada if their profiles satisfy the screening procedures. For here as well it is noted that Canadian authorities have only parsimoniously provided a right of entry to refugees, in the main accepting those who they feel will not be economically and socially handicapped in the Canadian environment or vice-versa. Those refugees who have been naturalized will, in all likelihood, use their positions to also enable the entry into Canada, of the other family members, relatives and friends. In any event, South Asia is a turbulent region of many ethnic groups. There is a high probability of many conflicts breaking out in the future.

Benefits and Costs for the Sending and Receiving Countries

Finally, a last word on the benefits derived by the sending and receiving countries through international migration. For the sending countries, the gains from emigration have to be weighed against the costs. For example, a country has more to gain in the emigration of the relatively less skilled labor — and who are unemployed — since their moving away would lower the unemployment levels and their remittances would be a welcome addition to the national economy. Similarly, it stands to loose a fair amount in the out-country movement of the relatively high skilled and educated on whose training certain costs were incurred unless these costs can be recovered through the inflow of capital.

The general analysis of migrant behavior has suggested that indeed, the sending developing countries have benefited significantly more from the migration of the relatively less skilled than from the movement of the relatively more skilled and highly educated population. Some studies, especially in the South Asian region, have found that the propensity to remit of the blue collar workers is higher, particularly those who come from disadvantaged groups and who have to regularly send money home to allow their families to meet a whole host of immediate needs (see Khan 1990). Furthermore, the temporariness of most employment opportunities for such skills also suggests that they tend to define their future livelihood at the home end, for which reason they send money back with greater frequency to avail of investment opportunities at home and/or bring back their savings when their temporary sojourn/work period is over.

Where the relatively high skilled and highly educated are concerned, the South Asian experience suggests that there is a certain permanence about their movement away from the home country, and particularly to developed countries. Generally — and definitionally — these people come from households which are economically well-off, at least, in the sense that units (families/households), don't have to rely on the remittances of the migrant members to sustain themselves. In such cases, the money earned by the migrants is saved to be utilized basically for improving their lifestyle at their place of destination and perhaps, also to bring over their families from the home country at some later point in time. Under these circumstances the sending countries, who have spent a great deal on the training of these migrants, get very little in return and therefore, it stands to reason that they tend to loose more than they gain from the emigration of such skills.

From the host country — particularly Canadian — perspective, the immediate costs of immigration would be high if substantial amounts have to be spent and expenditures undertaken for the welfare and upkeep of the immigrants until they become economically active. If the participation rates of the immigrants are high, which has generally been noted in quite a few cases, then it also implies that the immigrants would make fewer demands per person/immigrant on welfare, social security and unemployment compensation. In any event, it cannot be denied that the host country incurs certain costs in the short-run.

However, beyond a certain time frame, there are also significant benefits to be realized especially when the immigrants are gainfully employed. This happens because all employments generate a value-added which is well in excess of the wages received. The value-added is then paid out to other factors of production in various forms (i.e., wages, interest, rent, undistributed profit and dividends) and is also subject to taxation, and the additions to government revenues represent a potential increase in the per capita supply of public goods. Given the patterned movements of labor and people from South Asia to Canada, and the socio-economic profile of the immigrants, a balance sheet of migration accounts would suggest that Canada has actually benefited quite significantly, at the expense of the South Asian sending countries.

Endnotes

¹   Paper prepared for a conference on Asian Immigration and Racism in Canada: A Policy Conference, organized by the Institute of Asian Research, University of British Columbia, 24 to 27 June 1997, Vancouver, Canada.

²   To be eligible for immigration to Canada, one needs a minimum of 70 out of 100 points. The skill factor accounts for 15 points (see Stalker, 1994: 176).

³   This is not to suggest that the earlier South Asian immigrants did not belong to "white collar" occupations. Tinker, 1977, points out that ". . . where they were accepted and the process of adaptation (and socialization) went forward . . ." the latter generations acquired education and took up occupations which were, in the upper echelons of the social hierarchy of work. Nevertheless, the point is that the earlier pioneers came from a rural background and were most suited to semi-skilled activities which required hard labor under extreme conditions.

⁴   The program for refugees from Southeast Asia (particularly Vietnam, Laos and Cambodia) accounted for about a quarter of all immigration. In the late 1980s, immigration from Lebanon, Iran and, Sri Lanka may also be seen in this vein.

⁵   South Asia has been the most pronounced exporter of labor since 1834, when slavery was abolished in the British Empire. The export of workers from South Asia was tied to arrangements around the "indentured" work scheme which Tinker (1975) describes as being nothing more than another form of slavery. The excesses of the system led to the creation of other systemic forms of labor recruitment, the chief among which was the "Kangani" system. The "Kangani" was a foreman authorized to recruit labor on behalf of his employer. Often he procured labor from his own circle of family and friends and the society he came from. This "Kangani" system is the precursor to present day networks which are the most important mediators in international migrations from South Asia.

⁶   More recent analysis of the data reveals that the employment situation has taken a turn for the worse. In the Indian case, the data show that the rate of growth of employment in the organized sector dropped from 1.7 per cent per annum in the late 1980s to 1.2 per cent in 1991–92 and to 0.6 per cent in 1992–93.

⁷   Employment elasticities reflect a relationship between employment growth and output growth measured by a proportionate increase in employment and divided by a proportionate increase in output over a defined period.

⁸   In India it has been observed, that cuts in public sector investments cause a decline in private gross domestic investments. This may be because of the squeeze on public investments which, combined with monetary discipline, may have had a dampening effect on private investment. In a sense, a complementarity between the two is suggested, where the lack of investment by the private sector, in the absence of public sector investment particularly in infrastructure and associated services, may be construed as a lack of support for the private sector.

⁹   Bhaduri and Nayyar, 1996, cite four cases where the "big" firms have appropriated the benefits arising out of deregulation and captured ". . . a preponderant share of the market." These are: the acquisition of TOMCO by Hindustan Lever; the

takeover of Godrej and Boyce by Proctor and Gamble; the merger of Parle and Coca Cola; and the tie-up between Malhotras and Gillette. They further contend that: "In all these cases, the dominant market share so attained in a particular product range has tended to eliminate established competition or pre-empt potential competition" (p. 35).

[10] The data show that the remittances of migrant labor have played a major role in the foreign exchange earned by the South Asian countries (see Athukorala, 1993). For example, in Pakistan ever since the late 1970s they have been the largest single source of foreign exchange earnings. In 1982, they constituted almost 98 per cent of the total merchandise exports of the country. At present, a rough estimate suggests, on average, a remitted capital inflow of almost US$6 billion per year for the region. However, if the source of these remittances is taken into account then what becomes clear is that almost 80 per cent were from the Middle Eastern region, where almost 90 per cent of the South Asian labor stock could be identified with blue collar occupations. The inflows were the highest in the early and mid-80s when the stock of South Asian labor was also at its peak in the oil-producing countries. They tapered off somewhat in the later part of the '80s and early '90s, with the termination of employments and the repatriation of labor to the home countries. However, recently with the economic boom in the Southeast Asian region, the out-country movements have picked up again, and a certain accretion in the remittances inflow is also to be noted.

[11] There is a "tradition" of migration among many communities in South Asia, and particularly in Punjab. Such a "tradition" develops when a course of action becomes entrenched in the normal functions of the society. Connell et al. saw evidence of this in their general survey, and noted that: "(It is) not that some groups have specially migration-prone cultural values, but that their environments interlock with, and help to generate traditions of migration. Not just in groups, but base groups as a whole — villages or even areas — which have sent out migrants are likeliest to continue to do so. Early migrants establish the existence of income-earning opportunities outside the village, provide information and contacts for their successors, and — if young and temporary — can transform migration into an accepted part of the base groups' life cycle" (Connell et al. 1976). "This has an inherent logic of its own. Once a tradition of migration develops it facilitates future movements, through the creation of norms, beliefs and values which support migration as an ideal" (Hugo, 1981). Hugo also points out that in some places: ". . . the social function of migration has come to outweigh the economic aspects in that there may be alternative non-migratory solutions open to movers to improve their income, but they are not considered because migration has become habitual in that community" (*op. cit.*: 205).

8 Intra-regional Migration in Southeast Asia: Migration Patterns and Major Concerns in Malaysia

Azizah Kassim

INTRODUCTION

In the last three decades Southeast Asia saw an accelerated pace of labor mobility within and from the region. The political turmoil in the seventies in Vietnam and Cambodia led to an exodus of political refugees to the countries south of their borders. At the same time, movement of another kind was also taking place in other areas in the region. Many Southeast Asians left their homeland in search of a better life elsewhere. While the refugee problem has been dealt with, the latter form of migration persisted and became accentuated in the nineties. Such spatial mobility now involves a wide range of workers from the skilled "expatriates" to the unskilled manual labor and include also those who are not economically active. This chapter concerns itself largely with the economically active group, especially the non-expatriates whose number is relatively large and whose absence in the home country and presence in the hosts are often very problematical.

Today all countries in Southeast Asia are affected by cross border migration either as major labor importers, exporters or both. In this chapter the writer examines the movement of peoples across national boundaries in the region, viz. the nature, direction and volume of flow, patterns of foreign labor utilization and the way in which governments deal with labor mobility. The Malaysian experience is emphasized in this chapter to highlight some of the major concerns associated with such population mobility.

POPULATION MOVEMENT IN SOUTHEAST ASIA: AN OVERVIEW

In general Southeast Asian countries sanction labor mobility officially or tacitly and view it as a necessary panacea to overcome their problems of unemployment, underemployment, foreign exchange deficit or labor shortage. Such mobility is regarded as temporary and should be regulated. However, measures taken to regulate such mobility are often inadequate or have come too late when illegal inflow has increased in volume, have become widespread and entrenched. As a result there exists in the region today two equally dominant modes of labor mobility: legal and illegal which involve millions of people.

Differentials in levels of economic development appear to be the dominant factors in influencing the direction of voluntary migration flow. People move away from countries with high population and low GDP towards those with relatively lower population but higher GDP. While economic reasons are the main driving forces inducing people to move out, the direction of migration flow is influenced by many inter-related factors. Among these are close geographical proximity, historical and socio-cultural ties between the sending and receiving countries and their policy (or absence of a policy) on emigrants and alien labor employment, and the availability of an efficient transport and communication system. This explains why some countries are more attractive to a certain type of alien labor than others or why they are more prone to attract illegal labor.

Southeast Asian countries can be categorized according to their major role in relation to migration. Singapore and Brunei are main labor importers; the Philippines and Indonesia are major labor exporters and so are Cambodia, Myanmar and Laos. Malaysia and Thailand are both exporters and importers. The position of Vietnam is unknown in view of the lack of available literature on the subject.

Labor Importing Countries

Under its existing policy on overseas workers, Singapore can employ nationals from nine countries, viz. Malaysia, Hong Kong, Taiwan, Macau, South Korea, Thailand, India, Bangladesh and the Philippines[1]. In 1996, according to the Singapore Controller of Work Permits, the republic had about 350,000 foreign workers, an increase of about 50,000 on the previous year. Of these, about 80,000 are domestic maids. No breakdown of the workers based on their country of origin or job distribution is given. However, an indication of this can be gauged from the study by Pang in 1994. According to him, out of the 230,000 alien workers in Singapore then, the largest number comprised Malaysians (100,000) followed by those from the Philippines (Table 1). Pang also mentions a substantial number of Indonesians and nationals from mainland China working in the country. These workers are employed in domestic services, construction, manufacturing, services, hotels and shipyards. There appears to be specialization of labor based on gender and nationalities; female workers dominate domestic services and manufacturing, while male workers are found in the other sectors. Thais, Indians and Bangladeshis are generally engaged as general labor (Pang, E. F., 1995: 112). This pattern of job distribution among foreign workers is replicated throughout Southeast Asia. Singapore has a clear policy on migrant workers. Those who enter the country illegally and work without employment permits are subjected to a fine, a jail sentence and caning. Even with this tough policy the

Table 1: Labor Importing Countries in Southeast Asia

Country & Estimated Number of Alien Labor Utilization	Nationality	Sector of Labor
Singapore (1996) (350,000) 11.3 % of Total Population	Malaysian Filipinos Thais Indonesians Bangladeshis Indians Sri Lankans Chinese (Mainland)	Construction, Manufacturing, Services, Domestics, Shipyards
Brunei (1988) (37,000 inclusive of domestic helpers) 12.3 % of Total Population	Thais Filipinos Bangladeshis Indians Indonesians Singaporeans Malaysians	Construction, Domestics, Oil/Gas Industries

Source: Pang E.F., 1995 & personal correspondence with the Controller of Work Permits, Singapore, 1995 &1996; S. Gunasekaran 1994; and Mani (1996).

republic is not free of illegal alien workers. According to the Annual National Register of the Ministry of Labor, Singapore (1995: 50), over 2,148 illegal aliens were arrested throughout 1995. In addition there are ways in which the Singapore immigration and labor laws can be circumvented as shown by some small scale studies carried on Malaysian workers in Singapore. The latter show that some Malaysians work in Singapore while in the country on tourist passes. As the two countries are in close proximity and share a common border, these workers cross the causeway into Johore Bahru and renew their visit passes every three months to enable them to continue staying and working in Singapore (Ling, 1996/97).

Like Singapore Brunei imports labor from five of its neighbors as well as Bangladesh and India. In 1988, there were about 37,000 alien workers which included 3,000 domestic helpers. For the same year, 72 per cent of the country's private sector workforce is said to comprise alien workers (Gunasekaran 1994: 52–53, Mani 1996: 441–454). Recent data on the state of alien labor in the Sultanate are not available.

Labor Exporting Countries.

Major labor sending countries in the region are the Philippines and Indonesia. Filipinos began to move out in large numbers in the seventies and their number has been on the increase ever since. According to Go (1994), there were about 2.7 million Filipinos working abroad between 1975 and 1987. Of these, only about 417, 829 (16 per cent) were based in Asia and approximately 4 per cent worked in Southeast Asia. Between 1990 and 1995, the number rose to over 4.1 million of which 2.4 million are documented. Of the 2.9 million land based workers the largest number are in the Middle East especially in Saudi Arabia (40.2 per cent) followed by Asia and Oceanea (21.1 per cent). America and Europe are hosts to 1.8 per cent and 1.7 per cent respectively (Go, 1997). Filipino workers are relatively more widespread globally than other Southeast Asian migrant workers and cover a larger range of jobs which include the entertainment sector, clerical, sales, transport, forestry and fisheries, besides the "traditional" foreign labor domains (domestics, construction, manufacturing, etc.). This is made possible by their relatively higher educational attainment and their good command of English.

The writer has no access to recent figures on Indonesian emigrants. However, according to Hugo (1992a: 1–45), between 1969 and 1992, over 690,000 Indonesian overseas workers had been processed. Of the total, about 67 per cent worked in the Middle East and only 24 per cent were in Malaysia and Singapore. In view of the fact that in recent years the Indonesian government is actively encouraging more Indonesians to seek employment abroad to alleviate unemployment and underemployment at home and to acquire foreign exchange, it can be assumed that the number of documented Indonesians workers abroad must be considerably higher now. In addition to the documented workers, there is a high number of illegal Indonesian workers abroad especially in the neighboring ASEAN countries. In Malaysia for example, the Indonesian Embassy in Kuala Lumpur in mid May 1996, sought the Malaysian government's permission to carry out a registration drive of Indonesian voters in Malaysia in anticipation of the Indonesian general election in the middle of 1997. The result of the registration, as announced by the Embassy in May 1997, shows that there are about 1.4 million Indonesian workers in the country inclusive of clandestine ones. As the registrants are Indonesian nationals who are entitled to vote, they obviously represent only the adult Indonesian population, i.e., above twenty-one years of age, in Malaysia. Thus, the actual number of Indonesians in Malaysia must be a great deal higher. Unlike the Filipinos, the majority of Indonesian foreign workers are without or with little formal education and are confined largely to low status manual jobs. Aside from Indonesia and the Philippines, other labor exporting countries in Southeast Asia are Laos, Myanmar and Cambodia. Data on documented workers from these countries are not available.

Labor sending and receiving countries

Malaysia and Thailand export as well as import labor. In Thailand, the number of workers going abroad is on the increase astronomically in the last twenty years. In 1977, the number of Thai documented workers going abroad

Table 2: Labor Exporting Countries in Southeast Asia

Country of Origin		Country of Destination	%	Labor Utilization
Philippines (1990–1995)				
No. of Documented		Sea-based	20.0	Domestic maids;
Workers Abroad	4.1 million	Emigrants	9.0	production & related
Emigrants	377,260	Land based	71.0	workers; transport
Overseas Workers	3,817,829	Africa	0.4	equipment operators;
		Americas	1.8	laborers; clerical & related
		Asia	21.1	workers; agriculture,
		Europe	1.7	animal husbandry, forestry,
		Middle East	40.2	fishermen & hunters;
		Oceanea	0.2	administrative & manager-
		Not reported	4.6	ial and professional,
				technical & related workers
Indonesia (1969–92)		Middle East		
No. of Documented		Malaysia		Domestic maids,
Workers Abroad	690,000	Singapore		construction & services,
		Brunei		agriculture &
				manufacturing
Myanmar	n.a.	Thailand		Construction; agriculture;
Cambodia	n.a.	Thailand		fishing; production,
Laos	n.a.	Thailand		domestic maids

Source: Stella Go, 1997; Hugo G., 1992; & Chalamwong Y, 1997.

was only 3,831 and by 1995, it rose to 202,296. It is estimated that the number of documented Thai workers abroad was 428,178 of which 26 per cent were illegals. Their destinations, too, have broadened from two countries, viz. Saudi Arabia and Bahrain to at least fourteen major recipient countries. The last two decades also saw a shift in the direction of labor flow from Thailand. A large bulk of Thai labor was previously in Saudi Arabia. However, Saudi's position as the main importer in the Middle East has been superseded by Israel where over 50 per cent of Thai labor in the area were employed in 1995. The largest utilizer of Thai labor now is Taiwan which has about 120,360 Thai workers in 1995. ASEAN countries, in particular, Singapore, Malaysia and Brunei, have about one fourth. Apart from their somewhat prominent participation in the entertainment/sex related industry, Thai labor is utilized in the same sectors as other foreign labor in the region (Hiranpruk, 1993; Tingsabadh, C. 1995; and Chalamwong, 1997).

While Thais work abroad, an estimate of between 750,000 and one million nationals of Myanmar, Laos and Cambodia, are found working in Thailand. Most of them are undocumented workers having come to the country illegally. They are found in forty regions close to the border with the countries concerned. They work in construction, agriculture, and services, fishing, production, i.e., the very jobs done by Thais abroad.

Malaysia, on the other hand, is estimated to have between one million and 2.5 million alien workers in 1997. Of these, only about 813,000 are legal workers. In spite of its high employment rate, over 220,000 of its workers are working abroad.

LABOR MOBILITY IN MALAYSIA

By 1989, the Malaysian economy which was experiencing a recession in the mid-eighties began to recover and made substantial growth in the following years. Employment began to expand at a faster rate than labor supply resulting in a tight labor market. The situation became accentuated with the choosy attitude of Malaysians and a mismatch between available skills and employment, leaving numerous jobs unfilled. In 1993, for example, 77,031 job vacancies were registered at the manpower department against a total of 31,617 job seekers. Only one third of the registered job seekers found job placements, leaving over 52,000 jobs vacant. In 1995, a similar situation occured (Tables 4 & 5). This provided an opening for the importation of foreign labor.

In-migration: Mode of Entry

One major feature of alien employment in Malaysia is the high number of clandestine workers who, in official circles, are referred to as PATI (short for *Pendatang Asing Tanpa Izin* [2] (lit. people who come (in) without permission, i.e., illegal immigrants). PATI refers to three categories of workers: Firstly, those who entered the country illegally and subsequently worked without employment permit. Secondly, those who came on tourist or student visas, overstayed and sought employment. Thirdly, those who were directly and legally recruited but contravened the terms and conditions of their employment contract. Legal workers are those with valid employment permits. Such permits may have been obtained on being recruited directly by employment agencies or by their employers; or, in the case of the illegals, through regularization exercises which are carried out from time to time.

Because of the persistence of illegal entry and illegal employment and the poor and uncoordinated documentation of alien workers by the relevant authorities such as the departments of immigration, registration, manpower and the police, it is difficult to determine the actual number of alien workers at any one time. However, an estimate has been attempted based on some official data made available to the writer.

Estimating the Size of Foreign Work Force

According to the Malaysian Population Census 1991 there were in 1991, over 750,000 foreign nationals in the country accounting for about 4.4 per cent of the population of about 18.5 million (Table 6). A high percentage of

Table 3: Labor Importing & Exporting Countries

Labor Import		Labor Export	
MALAYSIA (January 1997)			
No. of Alien Workers		No. of Outmigrants (est.)	220,000
Documented	813,000		
Undocumented (estimates)	1.2 mil.		
Countries of Origin:		Countries of Destination:	
Indonesia, Philippines, Thailand, Myanmar, Bangladesh, Pakistan, India, Nepal & Others.		Singapore, Brunei, Japan Taiwan, Hong Kong, others.	
Sectors of Labor Utilization:		Sectors of Labor Utilization:	
Agriculture,domestic maids, construction, manufacturing & services		Domestic maids, transport, construction, manufacturing, shipyards, oil/gas, services.	
THAILAND (1995)			
No. of Alien Workers		No. of Outmigrants	
Documented Workers	11,446	Documented	316,541
Undocumented (estimates)	730,000 –1 mil.	Undocumented (estimates)	111,637
Countries of Origin:		Countries of Destination:	
Myanmar, Laos, Cambodia, Southern China.		East Asia: Japan, Taiwan, Hong Kong. Southeast Asia: Singapore, Malaysia, Brunei. Middle East: Saudi Arabia, Qatar, Bahrain, Kuwait, Utd. Arab Emirates, Libya, Israel, & Others.	
Sectors of Labor Utilization		Sectors of Labor Utilization:	
Agriculture, fishing, construction, domestic maids, production & services.		Construction, agriculture, domestic maids & services.	

Source: Chalamwong, Y. (1997); Pillai, 1994 and unpublished data from the Malaysian Department of Immigration Headquarters, Kuala Lumpur.

Table 4: Summary of Principal Statistics on Employment &
Unemployment, Malaysia (1980–1996)

Year	Labor Force	Employed	Unemploy- ment Rate	Labor Force Participation Rate
1980	5,122.2	4,835.2	5.6	37.2
1981	5,281.0	5,019.7	5.0	37.3
1982	5,410.0	5,142.5	5.1	37.5
1983	5,580.0	5,250.4	6.0	37.5
1984	5,743.0	5,382.0	6.3	37.6
1985	6,039.1	5,624.6	6.9	65.8
1986	6,222.2	5,706.5	8.3	65.8
1987	6,408.9	5,880.8	8.2	65.9
1988	6,622.2	6,087.5	8.1	66.1
1989	6,850.0	6,390.0	6.3	66.3
1990	7,042.2	6,686.0	5.1	66.5
1991	7,204.0	6,891.0	4.3	66.6
1992	7,370.0	7,096.0	3.7	66.7
1993	7,627.0	7,396.2	3.0	66.8
1994	7,834.0	7,603.1	2.9	66.8
1995	8,140.0	7,915.4	2.8	66.8
1996	8,398.2	8,180.8	2.6	66.9

Source: Social Statistics Bulletin Malaysia, 1984: 215; 1989: 229; 1993: 207; & 1996: 221.

foreign nationals are in the eastern state of Sabah where they form about 25 per cent of the population. However, these figures are conservative as they did not take into consideration illegal aliens. A more reliable estimate can be derived by examining the records of work permits issued to foreign nationals by the immigration department and records of the manpower department in Sabah. Between 1992 and 1997 a total of over 669,237 work permits have been issued in the Peninsula and in Sabah about 120,719 aliens were registered with the department of manpower in 1995. In Sarawak, there were about 24,000 alien workers in the state in 1994 and in view of the economic development in the state, their number must have risen by now. If we assume that all these workers are still working in the country, then the total number of registered alien workers in Malaysia is about 813,363. In addition, records at the Ministry of Home Affairs show that there are about 554,941 alien workers in the Peninsula who have been registered in the last regularization exercise between June and December 1996; and the Ministry estimates that between one million and 1.2 million illegal aliens are still at large[3]. Based on these, the number of registered workers is about 1.36 million and if one adds to this the number of illegals the total number of foreign workers in Malaysia can be estimated between 2.3 and 2.5 million, i.e., about 11 per cent of the population of about 20.3 million and 28 per cent of the labor

Table 5: Distribution of Job Vacancies and
Placement of Registrants, Malaysia, 1993 & 1995[1]

Industrial Group	1993		1995	
	Job Vacancies	Placement of registrants[2]	Job Vacancies	Placement of registrants[3]
Agriculture, Forestry, Livestock & Fishing	5,513	518	2,098	54
Mining & Quarrying	205	88	271	57
Manufacturing	50,939	16,646	36,237	10,573
Construction	3,629	684	2,953	498
Electricity, Gas & Water	19	10	71	11
Transport, Storage & Communication	3,506	679	1,660	402
Wholesale & Retail Trade, Restaurant & Hotels	5,203	2,136	6,047	1,266
Finance, Insurance, Business Services & Real Estate	1,457	1,749	3,779	1,009
Government Services	6,560	3,391	5,296	1,759
Total	**77,031**	**25,901**	**58,412**	**15,629**

Source: Social Statistics Bulletin, 1995: 221; 1993: 211.

Notes: [1] As registered with the Manpower Department
[2] Total number of registrants in 1993 was 31,617
[3] Total number of registrants in 1995 was 22,515

force of eight million. This figure is reasonable bearing in mind, as alluded to earlier, that there are about 1.4 million Indonesians of voting age who registered at the Indonesian Embassy in May 1997.

Geographical Distribution

In general employers of alien workers obtain work permits for their workers at the nearest immigration department to facilitate subsequent dealings with the authorities in matters such as permit extension, alien workers defaulting on their contracts, etc. Thus the register on the issuance of work permits in the Peninsula provides a rough guide to the spatial distribution of foreign workers (Table 7). As shown in the table, most of the permits, i.e., 58.6 per cent, were issued in the Kelang Valley, i.e., in Selangor, the most industrialized state in the country where the majority of the large physical development projects are located and in which is also located the Federal Territory of Kuala Lumpur which is the capital of Malaysia and the centre for administration, business and commerce. About 17 per cent of permits is-

Table 6: Foreign Population In Malaysia 1991 ('000)

Citizenship	Malaysia	Peninsula	Sabah & W.P. Labuan	Sarawak	% Growth of pop. over 12 yrs. (1980–91)
Malaysians:	16,812.3	13,833.0	1,353.7	1,625.6	2.9
	(95.7)	(97.9)	(75.7)	(99.0)	
Non-Malaysians:					
Singaporeans	18.8	16.9	1.3	0.6	
	(0.1)	(0.1)	(0.1)	-	(3.9)
Indonesians	405.0	162.0	230.6	11.6	
	(2.3)	(1.2)	(12.9)	(0.7)	(13.9)
Filipinos	203.5	5.6	196.8	1.1	-
	(1.2)	-	(11.0)	(0.1)	(13.0)
Thai	36.6	35.7	0.2	0.3	
	(0.2)	(0.3)			(12.0)
Bruneians	1.3	0.5	0.4	0.5	-
	-	-	-	-	-
Others	86.5	77.3	6.1	3.2	
	(0.5)	(0.5)	(0.3)	(0.2)	(4.5)*
Sub-Total	751.1	298.7	435.2	17.2	
	(4.3)	(2.1)	(24.3)	(1.0)	(11.3)
Total	**17,563.4**	**14,131.7**	**1,788.9**	**1,642.8**	**(3.0)**
	(100)	(100)	(100)	(100)	

Source: Adapted from Report on Population Census 1991, Vol. 1, pp. 37 & 39.
Note: *Includes Bruneians as well.

sued are in Johor, second most industrialized state, next door to Singapore. Perlis and Kelantan which share a common border with Thailand and which serve as gateways for illegal migrants especially from Myanmar and Bangladesh seem to be the least attractive to workers. These states are less developed. In Sabah the register of foreign workers at the Manpower Department does not provide the geographical locations of alien workers. However, an indication of where they are can be gauged from the census report 1991 (Table 8). As shown in the table, alien workers are found in varying numbers in all the 23 administrative districts in Sabah and in five districts the alien population forms over 25 per cent. In two districts, i.e., Kunak and Kinabatangan the number exceeds the locals. These districts are situated in the eastern part of the state close to the southern islands of the Philippines and where Sabah shares a common border with Indonesian Kalimantan.

Nationalities and Labor Utilization

Based on the register of work permits issued between June 1992 and January 1997, foreign workers came mainly from ten countries (Table 9). The

Table 7: Peninsular Malaysia: Issuance of Work Permits by State (June 1992–January 1997)

State	No. of WP Issued	%
Kuala Lumpur	352,971	52.5
Selangor	41,212	6.1
Negeri Sembilan	16,174	2.4
Melaka	17,502	2.6
Perak	15,614	2.3
Pulau Pinang	42,812	6.4
Kedah	15,940	2.4
Perlis	2,116	0.3
Johor	114,130	17.0
Pahang	32,272	4.8
Trengganu	17,563	2.6
Kelantan	4,347	0.6
Total for Peninsular Malaysia	**672,653**	**100.0**

Source: Unpublished data at the Immigration Department headquarters in Kuala Lumpur.
Note: WP = Work Permits.

largest contributor is Indonesia with 62.7 per cent, followed by Bangladesh with 24.4 per cent, while those from the Philippines and Thailand 6.4 per cent and 4.8 per cent respectively. Citizens of other countries such as India, Pakistan, Nepal and Myanmar form less than one per cent each. Registered alien labor are in the plantation sector (27.1 per cent), followed by construction (26.3 per cent), domestic services (22.1 per cent) and manufacturing (21.1 per cent). In each sector the range of jobs available varies. For example, in the manufacturing sector, foreign workers are mostly engaged as production operators. In the plantation sector which deals in rubber, oil palm, tea, flowers or vegetable growing, jobs are less varied. In the oil palm plantations, they work largely as harvesters, elsewhere as rubber tappers, tea pickers, or general agricultural workers. In addition some are also involved in animal husbandry, working on pig and fowl farms.

The construction sector, on the other hand, offers the migrant workers the widest choice of jobs such as general workers/laborers, masons, plasterers, tilers, bar-benders, carpenters, electricians and some are even able to move up to the post of supervisors (*kepala*). The service sector also covers quite a wide range of jobs. This includes working as petrol pump attendants, shop assistants, tailors, pressers at laundry shops, hair dressers, cooks and waiters. Jobs related to the hotel and recreation industry such as working as caddies in golf courses, receptionists and chambermaids at hotels are classified in the "others" category.

123

**Table 8: Geographical Distribution
of Foreign Population & In-migrants in Sabah
(1991)**

Administrative Districts	Population	% of migrants	% of in migrants (1986–91)
Papar	59,473	8.2	1.9
Kudat	56,047	4.2	0.9
Kota Marudi	42,747	4.2	0.9
Pitas	24,240	3.8	1.0
Beaufort	48,742	6.9	2.0
Kuala Penyu	14,271	3.1	0.4
Sipitang	24,349	15.4	5.5
Tenom	37,954	9.8	2.0
Nabawan	199,999	26.3	7.8
Keningau	88,456	21.6	6.2
Tambunan	19,726	3.3	1.1
Kunak	39,873	57.0	18.1
Tawau	244,728	37.6	10.9
Lahad Datu	118,096	46.0	16.5
Semporna	91,828	40.3	10.1
Sandakan	222,817	30.3	5.3
Kinabatangan	59,072	54.3	23.3
Beluran	54,539	31.6	9.9
Kota Kinabalu	209,175	17.7	4.2
Ranau	49,358	8.5	2.8
Kota Belud	58,259	1.6	0.6
Tuaran	63,995	5.1	1.2
Penampang	86,941	12.2	3.7
Total for Sabah	**1,914,685**	**24.4**	**7.0**

Source: Population & Household Census of Malaysia 1991. State Population Report, Sabah, March 1995: 6–7

**Table 9: Issuance of Work Permits between
July 1992–January 1997 by Country of Origin & Job Sector**

Country of Origin	Domestic	Planta-tion	Const-ruction	Services	Manu-facturing	Others	Total	%
Indonesia	79,167	108,778	94,561	3,062	30,568	1,347	317,483	62.7
Thailand	3,879	11,120	6,540	1,492	298	848	24,177	4.8
Philippines	28,537	49	1,160	828	1,401	668	32,643	6.4
Bangladesh	56	17,366	27,578	5,803	72,538	416	123,757	24.4
Pakistan	53	183	1,356	427	1,682	3	3,704	0.7
India	54	306	1,347	444	194	27	2,372	0.5
Sri Lanka	5	4	43	39	28	-	119	0.0
Myanmar	17	125	675	282	123	16	1,238	0.2
Nepal	-	25	17	97	262	-	401	0.1
Nigeria	-	-	-	-	-	5	5	
Others	7	-	137	11	54	526	735	0.2
Sub-total	111,775	137,956	133,414	12,485	107,148	3,856	506,634	100.0
Percentage	(22.1)	(27.2)	(26.3)	(2.5)	(21.1)	(0.8)	(100.0)	
Number without nationality & job sectors indicated							162,603	
Total							**669.237**	

Source: Adapted from unpublished data from the Bahagian Sistem Maklumat & Rekod, Immigration Department Headquarters, Kuala Lumpur.
Note: The total number of work permits shown here is lower than that in Table 7 as it does not include those issued in January 1997.

There appears to be a job concentration based on nationalities and gender. The two main nationalities, namely, Indonesians and Bangladeshis, dominate different sectors of the economy (Table 9). The Indonesians are largely in plantation and construction where they form 78.8 per cent and 70.8 per cent of the foreign workforce respectively. The Bangladeshis on the other hand form 67.7 per cent of the workforce in manufacturing. Women monopolize jobs as domestic maids and in the last few years have increased their number in manufacturing, services and also in construction. No gender breakdown of alien labor is available but it is reasonable to estimate that women account for about 40 per cent.

Illegal workers, as revealed by the register of regularized illegals in June 1992, originated from over thirty countries. Most came from the ASEAN region while others from Africa, China, the Middle East and Russia. Job distribution of the illegals is also more varied as they are not limited in their choice by government restrictions. They are often found in jobs which keep them away from the general public and therefore less susceptible to raids by the police. This includes working as domestic help, cooks, pressers in laundry shops, as laborers in the plantations and in the fishing industry in coastal areas. In the urban areas they are also engaged in informal economic activities working as or with petty traders, cobblers, tailors, hairdressers, etc. (see, among others, Junipah Wandi, 1991/92 & 1995; and Ayob Tamrin 1987/88; and Azizah Kassim, 1988).

In Sabah a clue to the nationalities of alien workers and their job distribution can be gauged from the register of foreign workers in the Sabah Labor Department (Table 10). Of the total 196,996 workers, 61.3 per cent were non-citizens. The largest number of legal workers are Indonesians who form over 47 per cent of the total workforce in the state. Filipinos, whose presence in the state is ubiquitous, form only 11.1 per cent; thus, by implication the majority of the Filipinos work illegally. Those in the "others" category, comprising Indians, Pakistanis, Bangladeshis and Chinese nationals account for only 2.8 per cent. Aliens are found in large numbers in all sectors of the economy. They form the majority in forestry and logging, agriculture (plantations, hunting and fishing) and constructions where they, respectively, form 74.9 per cent, 82.1 per cent and 61.1 per cent of the workforce. There is also a high number of foreign workers in mining and manufacturing. The heavy dependency on alien labor has been going on for more than a decade.

Outmigration

A significant number of Malaysians are employed abroad although there are ample job opportunities in the country. To date there is no attempt by the authorities to track this outflow and information on its magnitude and direction are based on records on labor force, overstayers and arrests made in the receiving countries such as Singapore, Brunei, Japan, Taiwan and Hong Kong, Australia, Canada and the United States of America.

Singapore is the major recipient of Malaysian labor by virtue of its close proximity, the high exchange value of its dollar in relation to the Malaysian ringgit as well as its strong historical link with Malaysia. Over 20,000 Malaysian workers commute to the republic every day. Latest estimates on the number of Malaysian workers are not available; however, a study by Pang (1994: 79–94) states that in the late eighties there were about 100,000 Malaysians in Singapore working largely in manufacturing, construction and shipyards. In spite of the strict enforcement of labor and immigration laws in Singapore, many Malaysians have found ways to circumvent these laws. Small scale studies carried out by academics reveal that many Malaysians work in the country illegally. They enter the country on tourist visas and work for short periods of time and shuttle back and forth between Singapore and Johor Baharu to renew their visas. Examples are university students on their long vacations or secondary school students waiting for their form six examination results (see Ling, 1996/97).

Brunei, which is next door to the Malaysian eastern state of Sabah, is another favorite destination for Malaysians. The sultanate which has a low number of population, around 300,000 in 1997, allows non-citizens to work in both the public and private sectors and provide relatively higher pay and

Table 10: Number of Registered Workers in Sabah by Nationality and Sector (December 1995)

Sectors	No. of Employers	Number of Workers → Bp	%	Ch	%	Foreign Workers → Ind'sia	%	Filipino	%	Oth	%	Total	%	Total
Forestry and Logging	506	4,964	25.0	1,601	8.1	10,365	52.2	2,531	12.7	392	2.0	13,288	66.9	19,853
Agriculture (Plantation, Hunting/Fishing)	2,582	15,079	16.4	1,299	1.4	63,019	68.5	10,786	11.7	1,776	1.9	75,581	82.1	91,959
Mining (including Quarry)	38	343	47.3	81	11.2	211	29.1	61	8.4	29	4.0	301	41.5	725
Manufacturing	687	18,239	49.9	2,502	6.8	11,258	30.8	2,965	8.1	1,639	4.5	15,862	43.4	36,603
Electricity/Gas/Water	56	208	45.4	108	23.6	93	20.3	31	6.8	18	3.9	142	31.0	458
Construction	622	2,238	26.1	1,099	12.8	2,745	32.1	1,899	22.2	582	6.8	5,226	61.1	8,563
Wholesale (Business Agents, Restaurant & Hotel)	5,051	11,214	46.0	6,726	27.6	3,061	12.5	2,593	10.6	818	3.4	6,472	26.5	24,412
Transport/Storage/Communication	324	1,492	46.9	543	17.1	714	22.4	355	11.1	80	2.5	1,149	36.0	3,184
Financial/Insurance/Commercial Services	231	583	54.4	309	28.9	97	9.1	79	7.4	3	0.3	179	16.7	1,071
Social/Community & Personal Services	2,744	4,255	47.8	2,656	29.8	1,835	20.6	444	5.0	164	1.8	2,443	27.4	8,904
Other Activities	159	526	41.8	207	16.4	383	30.4	135	10.7	8	0.6	526	41.9	1,259
Total	**13,000**	**59,141**	**30.0**	**17,131**	**8.7**	**93,981**	**47.4**	**21,879**	**11.1**	**5,509**	**2.8**	**121,109**	**61.3**	**196,991**

Source: Unpublished data, Jabatan Buruh Sabah

Note: Bp=Bumipatra; Ch=Chinese; Ind'sia=Indonesia; Oth=Others

generous benefits for them. This, along with the absence of many kinds of taxes, in particular income tax; and the high value of the Brunei dollar relative to the Malaysian ringgit, are the main attractions for Malaysians, as well as others, to migrate and work in the country. As the public sector engaged mainly professionals such as lecturers at its only national university, foreign labor are concentrated in the private sector where they form an average of 71.6 per cent of the workforce in 1988. Malaysians in Brunei, who form over 55.7 per cent of foreign born population in the country between 1981–86, account for about 50 per cent of the foreign work force of about 31,434 in 1988. Most of the Malaysians there are from the east Malaysian states of Sabah and Sarawak. Foreign workers in Brunei, in 1988, were largely in construction (92.4 per cent); mining, quarrying and manufacturing (78 per cent); coffee shop, restaurants and hotels (74.2 per cent); community, social and personal services (62.5 per cent); and wholesale and retail trading (61.8 per cent) (Gunasekaran, 1994: 45–56 & Mani, 1995: 441–455). It can be assumed that the job distribution of Malaysian workers conforms to this.

Outside the ASEAN region, popular venues for Malaysian workers are Japan, Taiwan and Hong Kong. The flow to these countries, which involves largely Malaysians of Chinese origin, began in the mid-eighties when the Malaysian economy was in a state of recession and Malaysia's unemployment rate was at its highest in the post-independence era, i.e., between 6 per cent and 8.3 per cent. With improved economic conditions in the nineties, the number of migrants to these countries declined.

In Japan, where there is no specific policy on the employment of foreign labor, alien workers, including Malaysians, work illegally. Writing on clandestine labor in Japan, Sazaki (1994: 151–164) shows that overstaying by Malaysians was first noted in 1984, but their number was too small to deserve special mention in immigration records. In 1987, 18 Malaysians were apprehended and the figure rose drastically to 1,691 in 1989. The number of Malaysian illegal residents (and workers) rose further subsequently. In 1992 there were 34,529 (see Iguchi, 1997). It declined gradually to 11,525 in November 1995 partly as a result of a crackdown by the Japanese authorities. Malaysian workers in Japan comprise both male and female workers with the latter forming about one third. Sazaki (1994: 565–577), reveals that Malaysian workers, like other foreign nationals in Japan, are confined to low-status jobs as construction, production, transport and other manual workers; cooks, dish washers, hosts and hostesses; waitresses or bartenders, prostitutes and other services.

In Hong Kong, Skeldon (1994: 543–554) notes that in the early nineties there were 11,700 Malaysians in the British territory and the number rose to 13,800 in 1994, accounting for over 3.7 per cent of the country's foreign population. Skeldon gave no indication as to what sort of jobs these Malaysians were engaged in.

In Taiwan, Malaysians entered the country in the mid-eighties as tourists, overstayed, and worked without employment permits. The only record on them was that on overstayers by the Taiwan Port Control Authority. Using these records, Tsay (1992: 637–655) believes that there were about 14,323 illegal Malaysian workers in Taiwan in August 1989, accounting for about 64 per cent of all Malaysians who went to Taiwan then. The number of overstayers rose to 17,177 in January 1990. In the early nineties, Taiwan launched an exercise to regularize illegal workers leading to a decline in the number of overstayers. Between 1992 and 1995, 5,148 Malaysian overstayers in Taiwan were repatriated. Statistics from the Council of Labor Affairs Taiwan, as provided by Tsay (1994: 613–619), indicate that there were 2,186 Malaysian workers in Taiwan, of whom 88.6 per cent were in manufacturing, 7.5 per cent in construction and the rest in social and personal services. Presumably these are legal workers. As in the case of Japan, almost all Malaysian workers in Taiwan are ethnic Chinese. No breakdown by gender is available but through reports in the Malaysian dailies, it may be surmised that quite a large number of women are employed in Taiwan. They are primarily in the entertainment/tourist industry.

A significant number of Malaysians are also found in other countries which include Australia, Canada, the United States of America and the United Kingdom, but those who went to these countries are usually in the managerial and professional groups. It seems ironic that Malaysian nationals are emigrating when the country is in a state of full employment and even more ironic that they are engaged in the very jobs filled by foreigners at home The lure to work abroad is the offer of comparatively higher wages in the receiving countries. As shown in my earlier work (Azizah Kassim, 1994) a factory worker in Japan earns about ten times more than those working in factories at home. For example, it is a known fact that a production operator, working for two years in a factory in Japan, would be able to save enough money to buy a low cost house (RM 25,000) or the smallest Malaysian made car, Kancil (RM 35,000). This is beyond the means of many production operators in Malaysia even after working at the factory all their life.

The Malaysian authorities make no attempt to arrest the labor outflow. The only deterrent imposed on such workers is to impound their passports once they return home if they have been arrested and deported abroad. This is because the outflow of labor is small compared to the size of in-migrants in the country. It has its adverse effects but these are confined to the negative publicity on Malaysia when its tourists abroad are refused landing for they are suspected of trying to enter a country with a view to work; or when they are arrested abroad for overstaying and working without employment permits. The problems posed by these migrants are extra-territorial, therefore not felt by the Malaysian public and as such the outflow is not seen as a problem or an issue. What is of grave concern in Malaysia is the inflow of alien labor.

MAJOR CONCERNS

While it is acknowledged that alien labor is essential in sustaining Malaysian economic growth, their presence and employment have created problems which, as discussed by the writer in an earlier paper (Kassim 1997b), compromise security directly or indirectly. This stems from a number of factors — the persistence of illegal entry by aliens; their large number and the tendency by some to contravene local laws and customs.

Persistence and Magnitude of Illegal Entry

In the post independence era, no provision was made in the immigration laws to accommodate the importation of foreign labor and as a result when there was a need for alien labor in the seventies they had to be brought in surreptitiously. This went on for about a decade and it was only in the early 1980s that the problem of illegal entry was first addressed with the formulation of an act to allow private companies to recruit foreign workers directly from their countries. This was followed by memoranda of understanding signed with Indonesia (1984), and subsequently with Philippines, Thailand and Bangladesh to facilitate such recruitments. But these measures were too late to be effective. By then there was already a large number of illegal aliens in the country; brought in by informal recruiting syndicates which have become entrenched and whose activities were difficult to curb. So the number of aliens continued to mount.

In an attempt to regulate and monitor the illegals and to encourage legal recruitment the government carried out a series of regularization exercises in the last decade. Between May 1987 and January 1991 an exercise was launched in the Peninsula to regularize Indonesian workers in the plantation industry. This was followed by another exercise to regularize illegals in the domestic and construction sectors between December 1991 and June 1992. The exercise was extended to 1994 to accommodate illegals in the service sector. This was accompanied by the establishment of on-going operations code named Ops Nyah I in January 1991 to patrol the western coastal areas and to stop further incursion; and the Ops Nyah II in July 1992 to carry out raids to root out the remaining illegals. In spite of these operations the number of aliens kept on rising. Thus another regularization exercise was launched between June and December 1996 to enable aliens from selected countries (Indonesia, Philippines, Thailand, Bangladesh and Thailand) to be legalized and others to surrender, pay a token fine and opt for voluntary deportation.

The results of these exercises show that between December 1991 and August 1994 a total of 483,784 illegals were registered, of which only a fraction were legalized.[4] Between June and December 1996, a total of 554,941 illegals registered. The Ops Nyah I arrested over 51,042 aliens trying to enter the country while Ops Nyah II rounded up and arrested 136,876 illegal aliens between July 1992 and December 1995. Thus over a period of about five years over 1.6 million illegals have been identified (Table 11). This means that on average about 325,000 illegals enter the country annually, most of whom come either by land from Thailand via Perlis, Kedah and Kelantan in the north or through the western coast in the states of Selangor, Johore, Perak,

Negeri Sembilan and Penang. The persistent and increasing illegal inflow indicates that Malaysia has a serious security problem which makes it vulnerable to foreign attack and subversion. This, as well as other reasons forced the government to classify alien labor as a security issue in October 1996.

In Sabah the issue of alien labor has been considered a security problem since the mid eighties. But due to difference in opinion on how the issue of illegal aliens and their employment were to be dealt with between the state and federal government, a crackdown on the illegals began only in 1990, after the formation of the Federal Special Task Force (FSTF). In an exercise carried out between April 1990 and August 1991, a total of 299,800 illegals were registered comprising 151,670 Indonesians and 148,130 Filipinos and the authorities believed then about 57,390 illegals were still at large (FSTF Report 1992). Another exercise, which began in March 1997 and is in progress, is scheduled to go on until the end of August 1997. In view of its small population size the problem of illegal entry is more serious in Sabah.

Apart from being a threat to security, the presence of illegal aliens has other attendant problems. Because they are illegal, they cannot get work permit and therefore have to work illegally and by doing so open themselves to exploitation by unscrupulous recruitment agents and employers. They also have no access to housing or public and social amenities; nor do they have recourse to justice and this quite often lead them to violate local custom and law and order.

Alien Involvement in Criminal Activities

Since the mid-eighties there has been a rise in the number of criminal activities involving aliens. Police records at its headquarters in Bukit Aman reveal that between 1985 and 1996, aliens accounted for between one and three per cent of all crimes committed in the country. What is of great concern to the authorities and Malaysians in general is the relatively high percentage of violent crimes committed by these migrants. In 1992, for example, the rate of aliens involvement in murder, armed gang robbery and armed robbery was 17 per cent, 27 per cent and 18 per cent respectively and in 1996, it was 27 per cent, 18 per cent and 16 per cent respectively. The last two years (1995 and 1996) also saw an increase in the rate of attempted murder by the alien workers (Table 12). Many of those involved in crimes are Indonesians and Filipinos and quite often crimes committed by them involve their own community. It has been suggested that the high rate of crime among alien workers is due to their lack of access to justice which forces them to take the law into their own hands when faced with problems involving other parties.

Associated with criminal activities is the expansion of syndicates with international links, which recruit, supply and harbor illegal aliens, manufacture and sell forged travel documents, identity cards, Malaysian work permits and other documents associated with immigration and employment. It

Table 11: Peninsular Malaysia: Illegals who were Legalized/Arrested by Country of Origin (1992–Dec. 1996)

Country	Registration Exercise (Jan. '92–Aug. '94) %	Registration Exercise (Jun. '96–Dec. '96) %	Ops Nyah I (Dec. '91–Dec. '95) %	Ops Nyah II (Jul. '92–Dec. '95) %
ASEAN				
Indonesia	83.20	59.4	99.8	70.0
Thailand	6.00	1.0	-	3.3
Philippines	0.10	1.2	-	0.1
Vietnam	-		-	0.4
Myanmar	2.50	3.2	0.2	9.5
East Asia				
Bangladesh	5.00	30.8	-	13.2
Nepal	0.05		-	0.6
Sri Lanka	0.30		-	0.2
Pakistan	0.50	1.5	-	1.2
India	2.30	2.9	-	1.3
Other Countries	0.05		-	0.2
Total	100.0	100.0	100.0	100.0
Total Number	483,784	554,941[1]	51,049[2]	136,876
Grand Total				1,686,093[3]

Source: Computed from unpublished data made available to the writer by the Malaysian Police Headquarters, Bukit Aman, Kuala Lumpur and the Ministry of Home Affairs.

Notes: [1] This percentage is based on the figure for the Kelang Valley which is 219,619. Percentage for the total number is not available.
[2] Total number of arrests was 53,571. Out of this total, 2,522 were later freed when their documents were authenticated by their respective embassies.
[3] This figure does not include those arrested for criminal offences and sent to prison.

has been found that they operated jointly with some government officials, some of whom have since been arrested or sent for restricted residence (*The Star* 19 October 1996 & *New Straits Times* 11 August 1995). The presence of these syndicates sustain illegal entry and employment and to some extent undermines the authority of the establishment.

Emerging Conflicts with the Local Population

Apart from the increasing crime rate, the last few years also saw many aliens contravening local law and customs which created a lot of resentment against them among the local population. These include:

1) Illegal occupation of state land for purposes of housing by aliens especially Indonesians, fraudulent transactions of Malay reserve land and the occupation of low cost accommodations meant for the local poor especially in the state of Selangor and Kuala Lumpur. These, as well as their involvement in non-designated economic activities especially in petty trading, put them in direct competition and conflict with the local population.

2) Cases of bigamy involving 120 Indonesian women in 1995 which is, to many, an affront to Muslim sensitivities. Not only do these marriages contravene Malaysian family law, they are also conducted by illegal marriage syndicates.

3) Marriages between illegal aliens and girls of the aboriginal groups, the *Orang Asli* allegedly as a way of escaping arrest and finding a foothold in Malaysia. In 1997, about 311 cases were reported and over 95 per cent involved Indonesians.[5] The number may be small but it is feared that it may create a precedence as well as encroach on special privileges accorded to the *Orang Asli*.

4) The involvement of some Bangladeshis with local Malay and Indian women, which created a lot of resentment and open conflict between them and local men. The Johore State Commissioner of Police said throughout 1996 that about 26 cases of assaults on Bangladeshis were reported. One such conflict involving groups of men from both sides which was widely publicized took place in Johore in September 1996. The anti-Bangladeshi attitude spread causing a backlash on the Bangladeshis in Selangor, Pahang and Penang.

5) Demonstrations held by some Bangladeshi workers at their work place to air their grievances over conditions of work and clashes between them and locals at the work place.

Vulnerability of the Economy to Foreign Subversion

With a large number of aliens among its workforce, the Malaysian economy is also subjected to the vicissitudes of Malaysia's diplomatic relations with and political stability in the sending countries. A severe rift between countries, like the Konfrontasi (confrontation) with Indonesia during the Sukarno regime in the mid sixties can seriously affect the Malaysian economy. The sending country can recall its citizens or stop further recruitment or worse still use its large reservoir of citizens in Malaysia for subversive purposes to destabilise the country. Even if only half of the foreign labor in Sabah's plantation and logging industry were withdrawn the effect could be devastating to the state's economy. In addition, in the event of political

Table 12: Criminal Activities Among Illegal Aliens
(1992–1996)

	1992		1993		1994		1995		1996	
	No.	%	No.	%	No.	%	No.	%	No.	%
Crimes vs Persons										
Murder	70	17.0	78	18.1	55	14.6	109	27.5	122	27.3
Attempted Murder	2	4.5	5	6.9	-	-	8	21.0	9	18.0
Armed[1] Gang Robbery	21	26.8	46	52.3	11	16.1	51	60.0	16	35.6
Gang Robbery	8	1.6	23	4.5	11	2.0	19.	3.5	38	4.6
Armed Robbery	64	18.2	105	11.6	27.	4.4	65	10.7	93	16.3
Robbery	128	2.7	114	2.2	68	1.4	181	3.8	161	2.9
Rape	57	7.9	83	9.6	48	5.0	64	6.2	63	5.6
Causing Injury (Sect. 324–326 PC[2])	163	5.7	118	3.8	92	3.2	131	4.2	193	5.1
Sub-total	513	5.1	564	5.1	312	3.0	628	5.9	639	5.6
Crimes Against Property										
Housebreaking (Day)	66	1.8	143	2.6	43	0.8	205	3.7	91	1.7
Housebreaking (Night)	221	1.5	337	2.0	59	0.4	361	2.2	311	1.9
Theft (Lorries/Vans)	23	2.5	37	3.4	9	0.9	12	1.0	20	1.5
Theft (Motorcars)	32	1.2	57	2.2	14	0.6	14	0.5	28	1.0
Theft (Motorcycles & Scooters)	31	0.3	62	8.5	5	0.1	23	0.1	29	0.1
Theft (Bicycles)	7	0.3	8	0.3	2	0.1	4	0.2	12	0.8
Other Forms of Theft	420	1.6	538	2.0	313	1.3	950	3.6	827	0.2
Sub-total	820	1.3	1,182	1.7	452	0.7	1,569	2.2	1,329	1.8
Total	**1.333**	**1.8**	**1,746**	**2.2**	**764**	**1.0**	**2,197**	**2.7**	**2,022**	**2.3**

Source: Adapted from unpublished data of crime index supplied by the Malaysian Police Headquarters, Bukit Aman
Notes: [1] Refers to the use of firearms
[2] PC=Penal Code

unrest in the sending country, Malaysia, with its "porous" border must also be prepared for an exodus of refugees.

Other Concerns

Other concerns relate to the drain to the economy through remittances sent to the home countries which amounted to at least 1.5 billion ringgit in 1995 and three billion ringgit in 1996. In addition, the government has to bear the mounting costs of arresting the illegals, maintaining them at the eight immigration depots and then deporting them. It costs the government on average 3 milion Malaysian ringgit a year previously, but in 1996 the figure rose to 14 million ringgit. There is also the extra cost of providing social amenities as hospitals; and schools for the rising number of alien children estimated at over 40,000 in 1996. Such strains on the country's economy cause many Malaysians to question the wisdom of depending heavily on foreign labor.

CONCLUSION

Intra-regional labor mobility in Southeast Asia which has accelerated in the last decade is characterised by two main features, i.e., a high volume of trafficking in illegal labor and an emerging relay outflow pattern beginning from the north in Cambodia, Laos and Myanmar and ending in Brunei and Singapore. While expanding cross-border migration intensifies economic interdependence between countries in the region, it also increases potential for conflicts. The continued flow of illegal labor and alleged maltreatment of alien labor abroad are some of the issues that can sow the seeds of future conflicts among the ASEAN nations. When people move in search of jobs, they very often take along their families with them or start a family in the receiving countries where they tend to stay permanently and not temporarily as sojourners as anticipated by the governments of the receiving and sending countries. The expansion of the alien population raises questions of their rights and that of the citizenship status of their offspring which in turn has implications on ethnic relations in the host countries, in particular Malaysia. Such issues, as well as others related directly to alien labor employment, need to be addressed and resolved bilaterally if such conflicts are to be avoided and if these countries are to benefit fully from international labor mobility.

Endnotes

[1] Personal correspondence with Public Relations Officer, Work Permit & Employment Department, Singapore (29 January 1996).

[2] In local parlance they are referred to as *pendatang haram*. The term is not used officially as the Indonesians, it seems, objected strongly to it. The term *haram* has negative religious connotations and is used, among other things to pigs which Muslims are prohibited to touch or eat. Hence the Indonesian objection.

[3] Personal correspondence with the Chief Secretary, Ministry of Home Affairs as per letter from the said Ministry to the writer (4 June 1997).

[4] The responsibility of legalizing the workers lies with the employers. After registration, the illegal workers are required to get travel papers from their respective embassies,and undergo a medical check-up. Only upon successful compliance with such requirements can they be legalized and be given a work permit. This process involves bureaucratic procedures, takes time and incurs expenses. As a result many employers do not bother to legalize their employees after registration. Aliens without employers and dependents of alien workers are not covered by this exercise.

[5] Personal correspondence with the Jabatan Hal Ehwal Orang Asli headquarters in Kuala Lumpur as per letter from the department to the writer (9 June 1997).

9 The Philippine Overseas Employment Program and its Effects on Immigration to Canada

Jose Brillantes

INTRODUCTION

Overseas employment is a global phenomenon. It is expected to continue as the modern world needs transnational movements to support the increasingly globalizing world economy. There will always be people who will perceive greater opportunities abroad and who will want to benefit from them. There will always be labor market gaps in some countries that are easier to fill with foreigners than with nationals.

The Philippines is certainly among the more active players in this international scenario. Most Filipinos desire to work abroad primarily because of better opportunities and higher pay than what the local jobs can offer. There are those who prefer to work overseas on a contract basis for the purpose of augmenting the family income. Others desire to settle in another country to try new experiences and broaden their horizon or to seek good fortune and stay permanently.

Among the country destinations that encourage immigration on a large scale and which has been a major player in the international movement of people in the world is Canada. It has a large and diverse migrant population creating a multicultural or multi-ethnic society. Recently Canada has intensified its campaign to attract immigrants worldwide. The absorption of human resources from different parts of the globe has definitely contributed to its flourishing and strong economy today.

This chapter seeks to examine the overseas employment and immigration policies of the Philippines and Canada, respectively and how they impact on the lives of their nationals both as a sending and receiving country. In particular, it hopes to determine whether there is congruence between such policies and to what extent they have influenced the immigration of Filipinos to Canada. It also hopes to put forward some issues and concerns which might be useful in the review of the immigration policies of Canada to make them more relevant to the needs of the Filipino immigrants and to its own economy.

THE PHILIPPINE OVERSEAS EMPLOYMENT PROGRAM

When the overseas employment program was launched in 1974, it was intended to be just a stop-gap measure to ease the high unemployment and foreign exchange problems. For some 20 years, contract labor migration effectively met this objective. On the average, around 650,000 people are deployed every year. Of this number, around 80 per cent are landbased workers, the rest are seabased. It is estimated that at any given time, there are at least 1.6 million documented Filipino workers abroad. By destination, the bulk of the Overseas Filipino Workers (OFWs) still go to the Middle East, although in recent years, deployment to East Asia and Southeast Asia has grown tremendously. Only a small percentage of OFWs go to the Americas and Europe.

A big factor in shoring up the country's balance of payments is OFW foreign remittances. Its percentage to total exports increased from 4.5 per cent in 1975 to around 19 per cent in 1995. As a proportion of GNP, remittances contributed about 2.5 per cent on the average. Remittances in 1995 totaled US$4.87 billion.

While the benefits from the overseas employment program are widely acknowledged, these are not without attendant costs. Among the pressing issues concerning the effective implementation of the program are:
- the need for protective mechanisms to keep the balance between the concerns of market development and workers' welfare;
- cases of illegal recruitment;
- job mismatch and deskilling;
- reintegration of returning workers;
- concentration of women migrants in vulnerable occupations; and
- consequences on social structures and value systems.

It is a fact that migration for employment will remain unabated because of the attraction of higher wages in labor-short economies. But in the context of pursuing international opportunities for Filipino manpower, it is the goal of the country to succeed in fully employing its labor force at home despite the attractions of the global market. The vision calls for a stable macro-economic environment that offers socially satisfying jobs at internationally competitive levels of income. A robust economy is therefore necessary, although not sufficient, to dampen the almost national preoccupation to get an overseas job. While the stage is being set for economic expansion and growth, it is recognized that the overseas employment program shall remain a viable and legitimate alternative for Filipino workers. Hence, the focus of government on the protection and welfare of migrant workers through the following program interventions:

1) **Implementation of Republic Act No. 8042**
   (Migrant Workers and Overseas Filipino Act of 1995). R.A. No. 8042 was passed by the Philippine Legislature to address the growing and persistent concern over the plight of Filipino overseas workers. The Act lays

down the minimum conditions under which the deployment of workers overseas may be allowed. It provides assurance that protective services will be given to both legal and undocumented overseas Filipino workers. Likewise, it recognizes and makes the "country team approach" a statutory policy for the operation of Philippine Missions in order to effectively protect workers' welfare. The policy makes clear two concurring conditions for allowing deployment of workers — skill and fitness of workers and hospitable country destinations.

2) **Worker empowerment through education.**
An effective way of helping workers to make right choices and become responsible for themselves is to empower them through education or information on matters about overseas employment. Pre-employment and predeparture orientation seminars, counseling and information services are made available for aspiring and hired contract workers with the help of people's organizations and other civic or religious groups. A mandatory orientation module has been developed on migration in the secondary level curriculum in cooperation with the Department of Education, Culture and Sports (DECS) and the Department of Foreign Affairs (DFA). The Commission on Filipinos Overseas (CFO) is also in place. The rationale behind this program is to equip entrants to the labor force with information to make intelligent decisions as to work and work site preferences.

3) **Development and adoption of standard employment contracts.**
Minimum standards on a country-specific and skill-specific basis, primarily for occupations most at risk, (domestic workers and entertainers) are prescribed. The same contracts undergo periodic review and revision to attune them to developments here and in the host country.

4) **"Professionalization" of domestics and entertainers.**
New systems of documentation and deployment for these two vulnerable skills are now in place. Additional requirements and procedures for the deployment of said workers by recruitment agencies, foreign principals and workers include setting of age requirements (25 years old for domestic workers in general, 30 years old if bound for Saudi Arabia and Bahrain and 21 years old for female entertainers) and setting of literacy requirements including the ability to speak, write and read English.

5) **Anti-illegal recruitment measures.**
With the view that the problem of illegal recruitment stems from the public's lack of information on the overseas labor markets and the rules and regulations governing overseas employment, an education and information dissemination program is in place. The anti-illegal recruit-

ment campaign is waged on all fronts utilizing multi-media and cooperative arrangements between local government units, police authorities and other private and government agencies.

6) **Stringent administrative measures in the selection of destination
countries and employers include the following:**

a) *Selective deployment of Filipino workers (Department Order No. 32 Series of
1996).* Destination countries are chosen on the basis of host country laws for foreign workers, mechanisms that allow protection to
these workers, bilateral and multilateral agreements; and other measures that ensure their protection. This policy also emphasizes non-
vulnerable occupations and the phasing out of occupations that
expose workers to abuse and exploitation.

b) *Full disclosure policy (Department Order No. 35 Series of 1996).* A mechanism whereby all parties to a contract declare the real terms and
conditions in all aspects of the worker's employment. It is on these
bases that workers in vulnerable occupations make well-informed
decisions on whether to pursue overseas work or not.

c) *Deployment ban/markets or skills restrictions.* Suspension of deployment,
restriction of markets/skills if the circumstances warrant the same, depending on the conditions, and peace and order situation at the post.

d) *Watchlisting/blacklisting of foreign principals and employers.* Employers,
principals and contracting partners including natural persons found
defaulting on their contractual obligations to workers, agencies
and/or violating rules and regulations on overseas employment or
committing grave misconduct and offenses involving moral turpi-
tude shall be prohibited from participating in the overseas employment program.

e) *Implementation of strict qualifications for agencies and employers of Filipino
Overseas Performing Artists* (Department Circular No. 01, Series of 1991:
Department Order No. 3, 3-A Series of 1994) which include set qualifications of legitimate performing artists; pre-qualification of prin-
cipals/promoters; pre-qualification of performance venues; post-
ing of escrow deposits by the foreign employers/promoters in the
amount of US$20,000 or its equivalent in Philippine currency to
answer for all claims for the artists against the employer/promoter;
and comprehensive training and certification of performing artists
prior to deployment to ensure that they are skills-ready and psy-
chologically/emotionally prepared for overseas employment.

f) *Establishment and management of* 21 *Filipino Workers Resource Centres* (FWRCs). The Centres offer overseas workers counseling as well as legal services, conciliation of disputes arising from employer-employee relations; translation and interpretation services during court hearings; procurement of medical and hospitalization services; information and orientation programs for overseas workers; human resource development including skills training and upgrading. Other services offered in the FWRCs include *Kabuhayan* services such as training and retraining referrals; livelihood loan referrals; and investment counseling.

g) *Reintegration services and programs.* These take off onsite through the Filipino Workers Resource Centres (FWRCs) which offer training courses and provide information on employment and livelihood options once workers decide to return to the Philippines permanently or temporarily. All the programs and services of the DOLE and its agencies are available for all overseas workers. These include skills training and upgrading courses, including its own placement services; employment placement and referral services; livelihood loan referrals and skills-for-employment scholarship baccalaureate course.

h) *Diplomatic negotiations with host governments on welfare and protection.* As a major sending country, the Philippines has sought and maximized various bilateral or multi-lateral arrangements to promote the welfare of Filipino workers. On the bilateral level, the government has secured social security agreements with Austria, Spain and the United Kingdom. Other social security agreements are being prepared and worked out with France, Italy, Indonesia, Canada and Quebec, the Republic of Palau and Micronesia. Such agreements are important since they provide extended social security coverage for Filipino workers even after they have returned to the Philippines.

i) *International cooperation and action.* On the multilateral level, the government has taken every opportunity to bring the plight of migrant workers to the attention of the international community. It assumed a very active role in the preparation of the final draft of the UN Convention on the Protection of All Migrant Workers and Members of their Families (November 1993).

j) *Ratification of* ILO *Convention No.* 19. Among others, the government has ratified ILO Convention No. 19. Equality of treatment for nationals and for migrant workers as regards workmen's compensations for accidents and ILO Convention No. 118 — Concerning equality of treatment of nationals and non-nationals in social security.

k) *Other Philippine initiatives.* Two resolutions were sponsored in the UN General Assembly and in the UN Commission on the Status of Women calling upon both sending and receiving states to conduct regular consultations for the purpose of adopting specific measures to prevent violence against migrant women and to set up mechanisms to implement those measures.

Moreover, the government is one with the international community in raising concern over the illegal trafficking in women and children and in finding solutions to violations against human rights and dignity.

The overseas employment program is principally being implemented by the Philippine Overseas Employment Administration (POEA) and the Commission on Filipinos Overseas (CFO). The former, created by Executive Order 797, is tasked to facilitate and monitor the overseas employment of Filipino workers, while the latter, created by *Batas Pambansa Blg.* 79, is responsible for promoting the general welfare of Filipino immigrants and overseas contract workers.

The Philippine Deployment Policy to Canada

The policy for the deployment of Canada-bound workers is to allow only for name-hiring. This means that only direct employers can apply for visas of Filipino workers who will be provided with jobs once they are qualified for the position. It is only then that the POEA facilitates the processing of documents and papers for the job seekers.

One of the current priority programs provides Canada with Filipino caregivers and skilled/professional workers. Following the standards set by the Canadian government for admission of caregivers, the POEA adopts a comprehensive foreign caregiver program where applicants are highly trained for eventual absorption in the Canadian economy.

Caregivers are in great demand in Canada due to the fact that women are also actively participating in the labor force with no one to take care of the children, elders and the household. It is a job where access to Canada is quite easy compared to other professional or skilled positions. Even if the applicants are overqualified for the job, they grab the opportunity not only for the good pay but also for the prospect of being able to change jobs after the required two-year contract. After working under the Canadian employers for two years, Filipino caregivers are given the opportunity to apply for permanent residency. This gives them the freedom to look for better jobs commensurate to their skills.

Meanwhile, job vacancies by other skill categories are reported by Canadian employers from time to time to POEA with requirements ranging from professional/technical/skilled workers to unskilled workers such as mine helpers and farm workers. In 1996, a total of 1,566 Filipino workers were deployed to Canada through the POEA (Table 1).

Table 1: Deployed Filipino Workers to Canada, 1988–1996

Year	Deployed Filipino Workers	Year	Deployed Filipino Workers
1988	1,722	1993	2,473
1989	2,562	1994	1,718
1990	2,836	1995	1,813
1991	3,954	1996	1,566
1992	2,959		

Source: Philippine Overseas Employment Administration

People who wish to settle in Canada but have no prospective employer may do so if their job specifications are among those indicated in the National Occupational Guide (NOG). They have to have a working visa in which they are classified as independent immigrants. This visa can be obtained from the Canadian Embassy after complying with prescribed standard requirements for entry to Canada. Another means of access is by way of the family reunification program where the immigrant should be a close member of the family of a naturalized Canadian citizen or permanent resident. These immigrants are classified as assisted relatives or family immigrants.

Before leaving for Canada, Filipino workers are required to attend the Predeparture Orientation Seminar conducted by the CFO. The seminar focuses on the living and social conditions of the host country, immigration policies, social security and employment concerns and the rights of immigrants, among others. With this seminar, immigrants are equipped with handy tips on job hunting, adaptation and survival in Canada. The CFO also conducts counseling, information assistance, inventory and follow-up services for Filipino migrants.

CANADA'S IMMIGRATION POLICY

With increasing skill gaps and mismatches in the labor market, Canada pursues an immigration policy that promotes its domestic and international interests. As embodied in Section 3 of the 1976 Immigration Act, Canada recognizes the need to facilitate the entry of visitors into the country for purposes of trade and commerce and to foster the development of a strong and viable economy and prosperity for all its regions. The skills required for the expansion of the vital sectors of the economy cannot be adequately addressed through domestic training and upgrading of workers. Hence, as a policy, Canada has opened its door to the world to be able to tap the vast pool of highly skilled migrants for its economic needs.

There are three categories of immigrants as indicated in the Immigration Act — independent, family class and refugees. Independent immigrants come to Canada primarily for economic reasons and are dominantly characterized by their skills or business abilities, possession of investment capital, advantageous profile and knowledge of one or both of the official languages. Family class immigrants, on the other hand, are often less qualified educationally and occupationally and less mobile than independents. Largely, they are consanguineous with those who sponsored them. Lastly, the refugees are involuntary movers who tend to have fewer human and material resources. Acceptance of these refugees to Canada is part of the country's international obligation and humanitarian tradition to assist displaced and persecuted foreigners.

The primary criterion for passage to Canada according to the current immigration system is occupational skills with strong emphasis on the educational, language skills and flexibility of the applicants to adapt to the dynamic labor market of Canada. The new immigration system focuses more on immediate economic benefits rather than humanitarian issues or family reunification. The ever changing labor market requires immigrants to be adaptable, flexible and willing to work in different occupations during their active working life. Classified as economic immigrants, these workers are expected to support the expansion of Canadian domestic and export-oriented industries. The new immigration policy is to increase the number of economic immigrants particularly those in the business category.

There are two types of immigrants currently admitted to Canada for permanent residency — Independent Category or Skilled Workers and Business Class. The first category covers those who possess a variety of attributes such as education and employment experience which are compatible with occupations listed under NOG (occupations which are open to prospective immigrants to Canada). There are a number of occupations within this category where an approved job offer from a prospective Canadian employer is not required. The second category, conversely, is further categorized into Entrepreneur, Investor, Self-employed and Family Business. This class has the entrepreneurial talents and capital resources which are the desirable qualifications for an immigrant.

Independent Category/Skilled Workers

Immigrants in this category are selected on the basis of their employment potential within a comprehensive listing of occupations. Their admittance to Canada must comply with the "point system" introduced in 1967. The points are based on the applicants' social and demographic profile which include 9 factors with corresponding numerical values; a) education, 16 points; b) vocational preparation, 18 points; c) experience, 8 points; d) occupation demand, 10 points; e) arranged employment, 10 points; f) demographic factor, 10 points; g) age, 10 points; h) language, 15 points; and i) personal suitability, 10 points with a total of 107 points. Successful applicants must receive a minimum of 70 units of assessment with at least one unit under the "Experience" factor.

Table 2: Announced and Actual Immigration Levels, 1979–1996

Year	Level	
	Announced	Actual
1979	100,000	112,096
1980	120,000	143,117
1981	130,000–140,000	128,618
1982	130,000–135,000	121,147
1983	134,000–144,000	89,157
1984	130,000–145,000	88,239
1985	100,000–110,000	84,302
1986	105,000–115,000	92,650
1987	115,000–125,000	152,751
1988	125,000–150,000	160,768
1989	150,000–175,000	189,199
1990	180,000–200,000	214,023
1991	175,000–200,000	229,730
1992	200,000–225,000	252,842
1993	245,000	254,321
1994	221,000	223,911
1995	215,000	212,154
1996*	212,000	88,165

Source: Government of Canada, 1993; Immigration Statistics, Employment and Immigration Canada, p.3, 1996; Employment and Immigration Canada, personal correspondence, Rick Carlton, Ottawa.
Note: *for first six months.

Business Class Category

Business Class immigrants are largely encouraged, given their expected significant contributions to the economy through the investments that could provide more jobs for Canadian citizens and prospective immigrants. Under this category are four sub-categories:

a)   *Entrepreneur.* Applicants under this sub-category must have a personal net worth of $300,000 and two to three years of business or upper managerial experience. The qualified applicant must have the ability to establish, purchase, or make a substantial investment in a business or commercial venture in Canada.

b)   *Investor.* Applicants under this sub-category may acquire permanent residence on the basis of a five-year irrevocable investment in a predetermined and approved Canadian company in the amount of $350,000 or

$250,000. They must also have a proven and successful business track record and have a personal net worth of $500,000 which they acquired from the management of a commercial enterprise.

c) *Self-Employed*. Falling under this sub-category are consultants, independent sub-contractors, artists, musicians, beauticians and the like who have demonstrated a track record of two to three years of experience in their line of expertise and must also possess a sufficient personal net worth for their kind of work. They are expected to create employment not only to himself/herself but also to others thereby contributing to the Canadian economy as well as to the culture and arts.

d) *Family Business*. This sub-category is one mode of family reunification where a Canadian resident businessman brings to Canada a family member immigrant. He must prove that by reason of trust, it is more sensible to employ a family member than to utilize the normal recruiting procedures to find an employee. The family member immigrant must have related work experience, aptitudes and sufficient abilities to perform the duties of the position intended to be filled.

Immigration Trends in Canada

Since the universalization of the Canadian immigration policy, the magnitude of immigrants going to Canada has greatly increased except during the recession period in the 1980s. Even if the government regulated their entry through the point system and controlled their concentration in preferred provinces, the actual count of entrants exceeded the annual targeted or announced allowable levels (Table 2). Because of the tremendous impact of immigrants on the demographic and cultural structure of Canada, a national consultation process was introduced in 1994 whereby the views and perspectives of the Canadian citizens toward the flow of immigrants were sought for purposes of reviewing the country's immigration policy. This led to the new immigration policy which encourages the admission of economic immigrants rather than refugees and family members under the family reunification program.

From 1969 to 1994 nearly four million immigrants were admitted into Canada. In 1996, 16 per cent of the total Canadian population comprised of immigrants. For over three decades, the demographic structure of immigrants has changed with respect to ethnic groupings. In 1965, 73 per cent of the total number of immigrants came from Europe. By 1992, immigrants from the Asia Pacific region already comprised 48 per cent of the total with only 18 per cent from Europe. Among the top ten countries of origin of immigrants to Canada in 1996, Hong Kong topped the list with 11,180 immigrants followed by India with 8,632 and the Philippines with 5,546 (Table 3).

Table 3: Immigration To Canada
All Classes Top Ten Countries, 1991–1996

Top Ten Countries	Jan.–Dec. 1991 Rank	No.	Jan.–Dec. 1994 Rank	No.	Jan.–Dec. 1995 Rank	No.	Jan.–Dec. 1996* Rank	No.
Hong Kong	1	22,340	1	44,174	1	31,740	1	11,180
India	4	12,848	3	17,228	2	1,6199	2	8,632
Philippines	5	12,335	2	19,098	3	15,137	4	5,546
Taiwan	-	(4,488)	5	7,412	6	7,691	5	4,950
China	3	13,915	4	12,487	4	13,276	3	7,001
Sri Lanka	10	6,826	6	6,671	5	8,914	6	3,158
Vietnam	7	8,963	9	6,230	9	3,929	9	1,158
U.S.A.	-	(6,597)	8	6,242	8	5,170	8	2,271
United Kingdom	8	7,543	7	6,325	7	6,376	7	2,458
Poland	2	15,731	10	3,425	10	2,297	10	856
Lebanon	6	11,987	-	2,674	-	1,908	-	721
El Salvador	9	6,997	-	1,167	-	715	-	328
Top 10 Total		**119,465**		**129,292**		**110,729**		**47,210**
		51.3%		57.7%		52.2%		53.5%
Other Countries		113,316		94,619		101,425		40,955
		48.7%		42.3%		47.8%		46.5%
Total		**232,781**		**223,911**		**212,154**		**88,165**

Sources: Personal Correspondence, Electronic Information Services, Citizenship and Immigration, 1996, Ottawa.   *Note*: *for first six months.

Demographic Profile of Filipino Immigrants to Canada

A total of 112,608 registered Filipinos emigrated to Canada from 1981 to 1996 with their presence most apparent in Ontario where 57,935 have already qualified as landed immigrants as of 1996 (Table 4). The number of entrants to Canada was highest in 1994 with a total of 14,303. Decreases were registered in 1995 and 1996 with 11,292 and 10,051 entrants, respectively. The decreases were, to some extent, attributed to the implementation of the policy to limit entry only to economic and business immigrants who can contribute fresh capital and investment to the Canadian economy.

Of the total 85,015 Filipinos who emigrated to Canada for the period 1988 to 1996, 51 per cent were male while 49 per cent were female (Table 5). By age group, 24 per cent of the immigrants were below 14 years of age and around 62 per cent belong to the 15–54 age group (Table 6). This indicates that many Filipinos below the age of 14 were able to gain access to Canada through the family reunification program. The 15–54 bracket, likely composed of independent migrants, made up the bulk.

Table 4: Registered Filipino Emigrants By Province and Year, 1981–1996

Province of Canada	1981	1982	1983	1984	1985	1986	1987	1988	1989	1990	1991	1992	1993	1994	1995	1996	Total No.	Total %
Alberta	722	666	505	352	252	370	587	610	696	884	771	829	1,263	1,619	1,227	770	12,123	10.5
British Columbia	958	921	789	454	399	652	881	1,089	1,237	1,304	1,101	1,280	2,069	2,883	2,414	2,515	20,946	18.6
Labrador			1		3				3	1	1	2	3	0		0	14	0
Manitoba	1,022	960	794	397	325	541	927	792	1,288	1,231	860	875	1,160	867	566	765	13,370	11.9
New Brunswick	7	4	5	3	2	5	4	6	15	4	4	9	14	17	6	12	117	0.1
Newfoundland	26	22	18	2	3	7	16	9	16	12	2	5	13	2	4	1	158	0.1
Nova Scotia	18	16	6	16	8	12	15	20	11	17	15	13	18	18	13	22	238	0.2
Northwest Territory			9	8	14	8	3	9	2	2	12	17	18	33	15	18	168	0.1
Ontario	2,042	1,970	1,502	1,037	923	1,304	2,978	3,651	4,322	4,393	3850	3,926	6,310	7,949	6,466	5,312	57,935	51.4
Orleans				4					3	5	1	0			1	0	14	0
Prince Edward Isl.							1	19		10	11	2	5	7	2	0	57	0.1
Québec	328	286	196	141	141	258	280	295	325	468	531	433	677	780	472	525	6,136	5.4
Saskatchewan	103	53	119	49	27	47	65	82	85	71	66	63	78	114	92	107	1,221	1.1
Yukon Territory		2				2		2	6	0	1		5	13	13	4	48	0
Did Not Specify								21	21	11	8				2	0	63	0.2
Total	5,226	4,898	3,946	2,463	2,097	3,206	5,757	6,608	8,032	8,409	7,233	7,454	11,633	14,303	11,292	10,051	112,608	100.0

Source: Commission on Filipinos Overseas (CFO)

**Table 5: Canada-Bound Registered
Filipino Emigrants By Sex, 1988–1996**

Year	Male	Female	Total
1988	3,185	3,423	6,608
1989	3,973	4,059	8,032
1990	4,158	4,251	8,409
1991	3,645	3,588	7,233
1992	3,711	3,743	7,454
1993	5,962	5,671	11,633
1994	7,443	6,860	14,303
1995	5,941	5,351	11,292
1996	5,237	4,814	10,051
Total	**43,255**	**41,760**	**85,015**

Source: Commission on Filipinos Overseas (CFO)

With regard to the type of work prior to departure of the immigrants for the same period, 37 per cent were previously employed while 63 per cent were unemployed. Those unemployed constitute the housewives (11 per cent), retirees (4 per cent), students (27 per cent), minors below 7 years old (9 per cent) and those with no occupation (12 per cent). Of those who were formerly employed, 13 per cent were professional or technical and related workers while 7 per cent were sales workers. Production and related workers, clerical, agricultural and managerial/administrative workers comprised the rest of the distribution (Table 7).

An evaluation of educational attainment of immigrants revealed that 29 per cent were college graduates, 1 per cent had post graduate studies, while 16 per cent and 14 per cent were in elementary and college levels, respectively (Table 8). This clearly shows that Filipinos are among the best educated among the immigrant groups and that compared to other Asians, the Filipinos are second only to Japanese immigrants in terms of educational qualification.

With respect to regional roots, 49 per cent of the immigrants came from the National Capital Region followed by 12 per cent and 16 per cent from Central and Southern Luzon, respectively (Table 9).

While there are no official statistics on the actual occupations engaged in by the immigrants, they are generally known to be in occupations related to the medical technology (med techs, caregivers and nurses), information technology (computer programmers and operators) and domestic services (nannies and domestic helpers).

Table 6: Canada-Bound Registered Filipino Emigrants By Age Groups
Prior To Migration, 1988–1996

Age Group	1988 No.	1989 No.	1990 No.	1991 No.	1992 No.	1993 No.	1994 No.	1995 No.	1996 No.	Total No.	%
14 - Below	1,861	2,374	1,659	1,360	1,267	2,693	3,198	3,065	2,730	20,207	23.77
15 - 24	1,095	1,124	1,190	1,131	1,249	2,071	2,730	2,179	1,884	14,653	17.23
25 - 34	1,373	2,031	2,445	1,951	2,109	2,677	2,898	2,261	2,331	20,076	23.62
35 - 44	1,122	1,558	1,550	1,172	1,118	1,937	2,132	1,776	1,633	13,998	16.46
45 - 54	329	314	412	334	400	671	851	671	527	4509	5.30
55 - 64	437	293	490	554	657	868	1,404	807	624	6,134	7.21
65 - Above	383	337	662	731	654	716	1,090	533	322	5,428	6.39
Not Reported	8	1	1							10	0.01
Total	**6,608**	**8,032**	**8,409**	**7,233**	**7,454**	**11,633**	**14,303**	**11,292**	**10,051**	**85,015**	**100.00**
Average Age	30	28	32	34	32	30	31	29	28	31	

Source: Commission on Filipinos Overseas (CFO)

150

Table 7: Canada-Bound Registered Filipino Emigrants
By Major Group Occupation Prior To Migration, 1988–1996

Age Group	1988 No.	1989 No.	1990 No.	1991 No.	1992 No.	1993 No.	1994 No.	1995 No.	1996 No.	Total No.	%
A. *Employed*											
Professional, Technical & Related Workers	955	1145	1227	1010	1002	1445	1536	1447	1661	11,428	13.44
Managerial, Executive & Admin. Workers	176	196	110	87	116	217	270	181	167	1,520	1.79
Clerical Workers	446	383	390	309	415	584	620	523	361	4,031	4.74
Sales Workers	398	550	695	472	610	814	906	673	538	5656	6.65
Service Workers	89	171	207	210	200	286	524	196	156	2,039	2.40
Agriculture, Animal Husbandry, Forestry Workers and Fishermen	99	97	199	181	146	203	296	235	180	1,636	1.92
Production Process, Transport Equipment Operators and Laborers	272	509	510	522	508	776	733	662	702	5,194	6.11
Members of the Armed Forces	33	76	47	49	16	20	22	11	15	289	0.34
Occupation Inadequately Defined		12		3						15	0.02
B. *Unemployed*											
Housewives	683	622	689	840	955	1316	1708	1170	989	8,972	10.55
Retirees	168	206	285	313	332	433	676	358	255	3,026	3.56
Students	1808	2015	1749	1514	1444	3229	4461	3883	3263	23,366	27.48
Minors (Below 7 years old)	799	1075	681	544	478	1004	948	960	976	7,465	8.78
No Occupation Reported	682	975	1620	1179	1232	1306	1603	993	788	10,378	12.21
Total	**6,608**	**8,032**	**8,409**	**7,233**	**7,454**	**11,633**	**14,303**	**11,292**	**10,051**	**85,015**	**100**

Source: Commission on Filipinos Overseas (CFO)

Table 8: Canada-Bound Registered Filipino Emigrants
By Educational Attainment, 1988–1996

Age Group	1988 No.	1989 No.	1990 No.	1991 No.	1992 No.	1993 No.	1994 No.	1995 No.	1996 No.	Total No.	%
Not of Schooling Age	—	—	—	512	466	986	970	943	957	4,834	5.69
No Formal Education	795	1101	802	115	85	88	179	63	42	3,270	3.85
Elementary Level	1193	1340	1213	1089	1027	1734	2411	1898	1561	13,466	15.84
Elementary Graduate	309	249	377	339	309	470	723	470	399	3645	4.29
High School Level	657	701	828	715	813	1301	1695	1487	1174	9,371	11.03
High School Graduate	444	560	720	697	668	1046	1357	986	856	7,334	8.63
Vocational Level	68	85	159	133	134	200	235	190	142	1346	1.58
Vocational Graduate	149	228	338	312	392	571	611	442	386	3429	4.03
College Level	829	1084	1211	1026	1057	1578	1977	1534	1329	11625	13.68
College Graduate	2014	2509	2588	2155	2390	3361	3762	2960	2873	24612	28.96
Post Graduate Level	89	104	105	82	63	181	231	200	191	1246	1.47
Post Graduate	61	71	68	58	50	117	152	100	141	818	0.96
Total	**6,608**	**8,032**	**8,409**	**7,233**	**7,454**	**11,633**	**14,303**	**11,292**	**10,051**	**85,015**	**100.00**

Source: Commission on Filipinos Overseas (CF0)

Table 9

Canada-Bound Registered Filipino Emigrants By Region Of Origin: 1988–1996

Region	1988 No.	1989 No.	1990 No.	1991 No.	1992 No.	1993 No.	1994 No.	1995 No.	1996 No.	Total No.	%
Ilocos Region	412	524	807	776	735	1,341	1,983	1,471	1,316	9,365	11
Cagayan Valley	86	113	99	119	133	211	407	398	332	1898	2
Central Luzon	658	875	972	850	859	1,403	1,780	1,411	1,270	10,078	12
Southern Luzon	909	1,103	1,321	1,090	1,247	1,938	2,376	1,814	1,687	13,485	16
Bicol Region	67	66	143	102	110	114	183	165	126	1,076	1
Western Visayas	118	172	252	219	204	346	395	364	304	2374	3
Central Visayas	221	233	308	209	195	309	383	301	295	2454	3
Eastern Visayas	22	32	45	56	48	78	94	72	89	536	1
Western Mindanao	4	19	28	24	32	41	69	22	31	270	0
Northern Mindanao	21	41	62	73	48	91	92	75	81	584	1
Southern Mindanao	56	53	47	45	53	93	141	106	107	701	1
Central Mindanao	7	12	7	12	13	28	27	30	38	174	0
National Capital Region	4,015	4,787	4,318	3,658	3,777	5,640	6,373	5,059	4,375	42,006	49
Total	**6,600**	**8,030**	**8,409**	**7,233**	**7,454**	**11,633**	**14,303**	**11,288**	**10,051**	**85,001**	**100**
No Response	8	2						4		14	

Source: Commission on Filipinos Overseas (CFO)

153

Issues and problems encountered. Despite prospective job vacancies in Canada for independent immigrants, Filipino professionals and skilled workers find it very difficult to obtain a working visa from the Canadian Embassy due to non-recognition of educational credentials and qualifications. The Philippines and Canada do not have a reciprocal accreditation of academic institutions. This hinders professional workers from qualifying for entrance to medical, nursing, teaching and other board examinations without going back to formal schooling in Canada for proper accreditation of units.

For those able to qualify for skills not requiring board examinations, the long waiting time for the approval of visa remains a perennial problem. Depending on the time of the year, the visa office and officer in charge, the processing of visa application takes between four to twenty months.

Obtaining a working visa and qualifying for the skills needed by the Canadian economy, however, are not assurances that jobs will be available for immigrants. While job opportunities abound in Canada, the difficulty in finding a job lies in the nonrecognition of the applicant's educational attainment and work experiences in the home country. Usually, employers require six months of Canadian work experience of any kind before they can be considered candidates for a vacancy. As a result, many Filipinos accept volunteer work outside of or below their skills and training just to comply with this job prequalification requisite.

In other cases, upon arrival in Canada, the immigrants have to undergo reassessment of their educational attainment. If found short of the Standards, they have to go back to school in Canada in order to qualifiy for the jobs sought.

Further, even while already employed, immigrants also need to undergo continuing education or re-training to keep pace with the dynamic Canadian labor market and respond to technology advancement and changing skills requirements. In fact, it is embedded in the Canadian culture that a person changes career during his/her working life, transferring from one type of job to another, which may be completely unrelated.

As in other countries with multi-ethnic inhabitants, racial discrimination is also found in Canada. Discrimination is commonly seen in work places where whites are preferred to non-whites. A Human Rights Commission has been put in each province to check reported acts of discrimination. Except for caregivers, most Filipinos have been able to cope with racism with their perseverance and adaptability.

From the perspective of a sending country, the emigration of its nationals, puts a drain on the Philippines' investments in human capital. Since people who emigrate are not really surplus workers but those who have gained years of work experience in their fields, the country is deprived of the manpower that could very well help in the attainment of its development and economic objectives.

The priority given by the Canadian immigration policy to skilled and well-educated workers has led to the brain and skills drain phenomenon and the deskilling of professional and skilled workers. Most of the immigrants are college degree holders or professionals who get jobs that are way below their qualifications just for the sake of getting a job.

At Canada's end, policies and laws need to be constantly reviewed and formulated to conform to the needs of the increasing multi-racial population. One of the tasks is to check and prevent racial disputes which may occur as a result of the interaction of peoples with diverse cultural backgrounds. The job requirements also need to be updated often to ensure that the skills required are adequately addressed.

On the one hand, the costs covering the selection and settlement of immigrants, including education, are shouldered by Canadian citizens and permanent residents throught their taxes. With the burgeoning population of immigrants, fiscal restraints resulting in the cutbacks of social, welfare and medical services to Canadians occur, causing deprivation to the locals who are also deprived of priority for jobs due to better qualified immigrants. These issues and concerns lead to the need to further review Canadian immigration policies to balance the costs and benefits as well as the advantages and disadvantages of the immigration process both to the sending and the receiving country.

CONCLUSIONS: IMPLICATIONS OF POLICY

The deployment policy of the Philippines is generally in congruence with the immigration policy of Canada. The Philippines has a policy of selective deployment sending only qualified Filipinos for positions that offer good pay. Canada, on the other hand, has a preference for economic or business immigrants who will be offered better pay once they qualify for the jobs. Both policies are geared toward enhancing the competency of human resources in the face of a borderless international economy.

What remains to be a source of inconsistency in the immigration policy of Canada lies in the non-recognition of educational qualifications and work experiences of Filipino professionals and skilled workers. For a better sharing of human resources, the mutual recognition of skills and qualifications between the two countries should be worked out and put in place.

Part Three

Comparative Aspects of Asian Immigration

1846

1997

10 Migration and Mobilization in Asia: An Overview

Graeme Hugo

INTRODUCTION

One of the most fundamental changes over the last quarter century has been that in every country in the Asian region personal mobility has increased greatly. As part of this, movement between nations inside and beyond the Asian region is now part of the calculus of choice of many millions of Asians as they respond to changes and consider their life chances. Many labor markets in Asia now overlap national boundaries not just for highly skilled workers but also unskilled workers. While the expansion of international migration has not matched the expansion of flows of capital, traded goods and information between nations it has nevertheless increased substantially. All countries in the region are now influenced to some degree by international migration although the nature and level of that impact varies greatly. International migration is a topic of unprecedented interest in the region among both governments and the population. With newspapers and other media reporting on it daily, the issue is constantly in the public consciousness.

This chapter firstly seeks to document recent major trends in the various types of international migration in the Asian region. It then argues that there are elements in the existing system, namely migrant social networks and the proliferation of an immigration industry in the region, which will lead to the perpetuation and enhancement of international migration in the region to some extent regardless of political and economic development and the interventions of government. Thirdly, the chapter discusses some of the major issues which are emerging in the region in relation to migration between nations. Any discussion of this kind is beset with a number of difficulties. Firstly, the vast size and cultural, ethnic, political, religious and economic complexity of the Asian region makes it difficult to generalize. Secondly, the data relating to international migration are incomplete or totally absent for most nations in the region[1] (Asia Pacific Migration Journal, 8, 4, 1995; Bilsborrow et al., 1997) and there is very limited empirical research base.

MAJOR TYPES OF INTERNATIONAL MIGRATION

An important characteristic of the burgeoning of international migration in Asia in the last decade or so has been the diversity of types of movement which have evolved. In this section some of the major elements in the contemporary Asia-Pacific migration system are briefly described and recent developments within them discussed. There are a number of reviews of international migration trends in the region available which provide more detail and descriptions of the emerging trends (e.g., Pongsapich, 1995; Bedford and Ligard, 1996; Martin, 1996; Rallu, 1996; Stahl and PECC-HRD Task Force, 1996; Martin, Mason and Tsay, 1995). These movements include very large flows to nations outside Asia (especially the Middle East, North America, Europe and Australasia), movements from other parts of the world into Asia and increasing migration *between* Asian countries. All of these flows are increasing significantly, but especially the latter. In this section all that will be attempted is a brief description of contemporary trends in each of the main types of international migration influencing the region.

South-North Migration.

For more than two centuries the United States, Canada, Australia and New Zealand have been receiving substantial numbers of immigrants and are among the very few countries in the world to have active immigration programs. Until the late 1960s, however, these programs discriminated in favor of Europeans and against Asians. Since the removal by the early 1970s, of discrimination on the basis of race, ethnicity or birthplace, and immigration selection now based mainly on skills and family reunion, Asian immigration has increased substantially. Moreover, Europe has also become a significant destination for Asian migrants, with movement partly being associated with previous colonial linkages. Asians now make up almost half of settlers in the traditional migration receiving countries. Figure 1 shows how in Australia, for example, Asia has replaced Europe as the main origin of settlers. The resulting growth of the Asian population in Australia is evident in Table 1 which shows that they more than doubled between 1985 and 1995. First and second generation Asian migrants now make up at least 7 per cent of the total Australian population.

However, the increased numbers of permanent settlers in more developed countries (MDCs) is only one dimension of Asian movements to North America, Europe and Australasia. There is a totally new paradigm of international population movement in the 1990s to that applying three decades ago due to the impact of globalization.

In countries such as Canada and Australia, where the dominant form of migration was permanent settlement, the contemporary pattern is much more complex. This can again be illustrated with respect to Australia. Table 2 shows that non-permanent movements have increased exponentially in recent years.

Hence, whereas permanent migration levels have changed little over the last decade, short term arrivals from Asia increased seven-fold and long term

**Figure 1: Australia: Settler Arrivals by Region/Country
of Last Residence, 1945–1995**

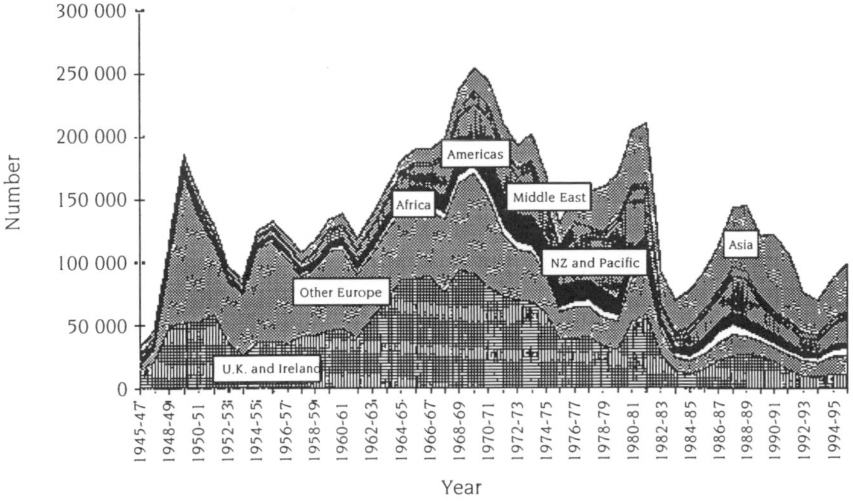

Source: *Australian Immigration Consolidated Statistics*, various issues; ABS unpublished
data
Note: * October 1945–June 1947.

Table 1: Australia: Asia-Born, 1985–1995

Country of Birth	1985 ('000)	1995 ('000)	Per cent Change
Vietnam	80.9	146.5	81
China	35.0	92.7	165
Philippines	29.1	91.8	215
Malaysia	46.4	91.5	97
Hong Kong	26.2	91.3	248
India	19.8	79.0	299
Sri Lanka	22.3	46.7	109
Indonesia	23.0	42.2	83
Singapore	15.8	36.4	130
Other	52.1	147.8	184
Total	**409.8**	**866.2**	**111**
%	2.6	4.8	
U.K./Eire	1180.8	1210.9	3
Italy	275.9	261.4	-5
Former Yugoslavia	158.5	179.8	13
Greece	148.8	144.7	-3

Source: ABS, 1996

Graeme Hugo

Table 2: Australia: Arrivals/Departures by Country of Residence/Main Origin/Destination, 1975, 1984–1985 and 1994–1995

	1975 Total		1975 To/From Asia		1984-1985 Total		1984-1985 To/From Asia		1994-1995 Total		1994-1995 To/From Asia	
	No.	%	No.	%	No.	%	No.	%	No.	%	No.	%
Short-term arrivals[1]	516 023	79.6	72 325	83.5	1 061 700	86.7	256 200	83.3	3 535 300	93.7	1 741 500	94.7
Long-term arrivals	78 210	12.1	5 756	6.6	85 750	7.0	21 380	7.0	151 095	4.0	62 119	3.4
Permanent settlers	54 117	8.3	8 566	9.9	77 510	6.3	29 780	9.7	87 428	2.3	30 911	1.7
Total	648 350	100.0	86 647	100.0	1 244 960	100.0	308 360	100.0	3 773 823	100.0	1 834 530	100.0
Short-term departures[2]	911 815	88.5	172 964	96.3	1 497 800	94.0	442 600	95.6	2 422 000	94.3	890 800	94.5
Long-term departures	89 815	8.7	6 088	3.4	74 870	4.7	19 300	4.2	118 533	4.6	47 687	5.1
Permanent departures	29 084	2.8	487	0.3	20 380	1.3	1 050	0.2	26 948	1.0	4 443	0.5
Total	**1 030 631**	**100.0**	**179 539**	**100.0**	**1 593 050**	**100.0**	**462 950**	**100.0**	**2 567 481**	**100.0**	**942 930**	**100.0**

Source: ABS *Overseas Arrivals and Departures Bulletins*; ABS, 1996

Notes: [1] These refer only to overseas visitors, not returning Australian citizens.
[2] These refer only to departures of Autralia-born persons, not departing overseas visitors.

**Table 3: Australia: Proportion of Arrivals and Departures
To or From Asia, 1975–1995**

		Per cent To/From Asia	
	1975	1984–85	1994–95
Short term arrivals[1]	14.0	24.1	49.3
Long term arrivals	7.4	24.9	41.1
Permanent settlers	10.8	38.4	35.4
Total	**13.4**	**25.1**	**48.6**
Short term departures[2]	19.0	29.6	36.8
Long term departures	6.8	25.8	40.2
Permanent departures	1.7	5.2	16.5
Total	**17.4**	**29.1**	**36.7**

Source: ABS *Overseas Arrivals and Departures Bulletins*; ABS, 1996,
Migration Australia 1994–95, Catalogue No. 3412.0
Notes: [1] These refer only to overseas visitors, not returning Australian citizens.
[2] These refer only to departures of Australia-born persons, not
departing overseas visitors

arrivals trebled. The huge increase in the volume of non-permanent movement between Asia and the MDCs is of considerable significance and its
linkages with more permanent migration little understood. Table 3 shows
that while Asians made up only a tenth of permanent arrivals in Australia in
1975, they accounted for more than a third two decades later.

However, the situation is more striking in the case of non-permanent
movements with Asians among long term arrivals increasing from 7.4 to 41.1
per cent and from 14 to 49.3 per cent of short term arrivals. Hence not only
has the paradigm of migration to Australia shifted toward a more complex
model in which non-permanent movement is more important, but the Asian
presence has increased more among non-permanent than among permanent migrations to Australia.

Refugees

Until recently Asia had more refugees than any other world region, reaching a peak in 1989 of seven million UNHCR recognized refugees. However,
the numbers have since declined to 4.48 million in 1996 — one third of the
world total. The reduction in UNHCR recognized refugees is largely due to
the success of the Comprehensive Plan of Action (signed in 1989 by Western
countries, countries of first asylum such as Indonesia, Malaysia etc. and Vietnam) in reducing the number of Indo-Chinese refugees in Asia to a handful. More than two million have been resettled in third countries, mainly in

North America, Europe and Australasia and most of the remainder repatriated to their home country (Stephan and Keenan, 1997).

More than half of the Asia Pacific region's refugees (2.35 million) are the longstanding groups from Afghanistan in Iran, Pakistan, the CIS and India. Afghanistan refugees have spent almost two decades in these neighboring countries and resettlement in third countries has been very limited. Repatriation is also still limited with 348,800 being sent back from Iran, Pakistan and India in 1995. In addition to the major refugee flows out of Afghanistan and Indo-China, there have been smaller but locally significant flows which have been important in recent years. Perhaps the most substantial of these has been the refugee outflow from Burma. There have been longstanding flows of Rohinga Muslims into Bangladesh due to persecution in predominantly Buddhist Myanmar (Burma). In 1992, some 300,000 entered Bangladesh (Rogge, 1993: 4). There has been movement across the Myanmar-Thailand border for many years but crackdowns by the military government in Myanmar saw in 1991 and 1992 large scale movements into Thailand, much of it of students and intellectuals and focusing upon Bangkok. Hence by 1991, the UNHCR recognized 70,000 Myanmar refugees in Thailand. Other Asian refugee flows include the movement of around 90,000 Tamils from Sri Lanka to India, a similar number of Muslim Filipinos in East Malaysia and some 10,000 Irianese from Indonesia to Papua New Guinea. One crucial point about the large numbers of Asian refugees who have settled in "Third nations" is that they have provided a basis for creating networks between the Asian region and North American, European and Australasian countries along which non-refugee migrants have subsequently flowed. These have included some 500,000 people who left Vietnam under the Orderly Departure Program. In more recent years there has also been an increase in the numbers of Asian asylum seekers arriving in Europe and North America.

Overseas Contract Workers (OCWs)

The largest international migrations influencing contemporary Asian countries are those involving largely non-permanent labor movements. These types of migrations have a long history in Asia (Hugo, 1997a) but entered a new era in scale and complexity with the 1973 increase in oil prices and the associated massive demand for workers in the Middle East with the development of infrastructure projects. While South Asian migrants had a long history of involvement in the Gulf area, after 1973 their numbers expanded and began to involve large numbers of East and Southeast Asians. In 1975 India and Pakistan contributed 97 per cent of Asian workers to West Asia but this is now less than a third with the Southeast Asian share growing from 2 per cent to more than half. This migration has continued through to the present with more Asian countries becoming involved as origins. Whereas workers in the early years were mainly involved in infrastructure development, those in more recent times have moved mainly into service occupations. Over time women have become more significant in the migration flows with many moving into domestic service. During the last decade the destinations of Asian migrant workers have become more diverse with Asian countries now accounting for more migrants than are directed to the Middle East. Much of the movement is undocumented and is not included in the available official statistics.

There are two systems of labor migration involving Asian OCWs. The first and the largest involves mainly unskilled and semi-skilled workers who are employed in low paid, low status, so-called 3D (dirty, dangerous and difficult) jobs that are eschewed by local workers in fast growing labor short nations of Asia and the Middle East. These are drawn predominantly from the South Asian nations, Indonesia, Thailand, Philippines, China, Burma and Vietnam. The second group are much smaller in number but still significant and involve highly skilled professionals drawn mainly from India, Bangladesh, Pakistan, Sri Lanka and the Philippines and are drawn not only to fast developing labor-short NICs and near-NICs but also to labor surplus nations like Indonesia where there is a mismatch between the products of the education and training system and the skilled labor demands of a rapidly restructuring and growing economy.

In the contemporary situation it is possible to classify the larger nations in the Asian region according to whether they have significant gains or losses of migrant workers to other Asian destinations. This classification is presented in Table 4 and shows the larger nations of Asia in which the transition to low fertility did not commence until the 1970s or later hence they remain labor surplus areas. On the other hand, in Japan and the Newly Industrializing Countries (NICs) fertility decline was much earlier and economic growth has been more rapid and sustained over a long period. Despite strict immigration regulations the shortage of labor in these countries has led to major inflows of workers both documented and undocumented. These countries were mainly regions of emigration in the first three decades of the post-war period but have been through a rapid transition to become substantial immigration nations. This transition has been much more rapid than the similar transition in Europe and is a distinctive feature of the Asian international migration situation (Martin, 1993, 1994; Fields, 1994; Skeldon, 1994; Vasuprasat, 1994).

Two countries, Malaysia and Thailand, currently are midway through this transition, which are both recording substantial emigration over a long period but also significant immigration of workers from nearby labor surplus nations (Indonesia, Bangladesh and Burma especially). In passing, however, it should be mentioned that in the contemporary situation all Asian nations are to some extent both emigration and immigration nations with highly skilled workers moving in to even labor surplus nations because of shortages of skills in fast growing economies and the spread of multinational corporations (MNCs). Brunei in many ways is more like the Middle East destinations of Asian migrants in that it has vast foreign exchange earnings which have meant that there are

Table 4: Intra-Asia: Classification of Asian Nations on the Basis of their International Migration Situation in the Late 1990s

Mainly Emigration

Philippines	India	Sri Lanka	Indonesia	Vietnam
China	Bangladesh	Pakistan	Burma	

Mainly Immigration

South Korea	Taiwan	Singapore
Japan	Hong Kong	Brunei

Both Significant Immigration and Emigration

Malaysia

Thailand

not enough local workers to meet the labor demands of the economy so that more than a third of the population are foreigners (Hiebert, 1995).

The Middle East remains an important destination of OCWs from Asia and is a major focus of migration from Pakistan, India, Sri Lanka, Indonesia and the Philippines. The estimated stocks of Asian origin migrant workers in the first half of the 1990s are shown in Table 5. It is likely that the figure of 4 million underestimates the numbers given that it takes no account of illegal migration and does not include all countries sending workers to the Middle East. Clearly, South Asians still dominate among Asians in the Gulf region but Filipinos and Indonesians are of increasing significance.

In several Asian countries, especially the Newly Industrializing Countries rapid economic growth and an associated growth in employment is outpacing the rate of growth of the workforce due to the substantial fertility declines of the 1960s and 1970s which resulted in cohorts of school leavers in the late 1980s and 1990s being smaller than the generations preceding them. Table 6 indicates that the stock of Asian migrant workers in Asian countries is larger than the numbers in the Middle East. It must be stressed, however, that these data vary greatly in quality (as do the Middle East data). Many destination countries are not anxious to reveal the extent to which their economies are reliant upon foreign workers,while in cases like Japan and Korea the countries' very strict immigration regulations have meant that the bulk of workers are clandestine.

Focusing attention on the sending countries, Table 7 shows that there would appear to be around 14 million Asian workers in other countries in the second half of the 1990s. Pre-eminent here is the Philippines where it is estimated (Bilsborrow, 1997) that over 6 million nationals are working overseas, only 1.2 million of them legally. In Indonesia, the second largest nation, only a tenth of those overseas went through official channels.

**Table 5: Estimated Stock of Asian Origin Workers
in Selected Countries, 1992**

Nationality	Number
Indians	1,426,438
Pakistanis	828,184
Bangladeshis	507,934
Sri Lankans	452,964
Filipinos	500,000
Indonesians	200,000
South Koreans	97,195
Thais	80,803
Total	**4,093,518**

Source: Birks and Sinclair, 1992; Stahl, 1995

In the case of many other sending nations (e.g., China) it is clear that the official data presented in Table 7 underestimate the actual flows because no estimates of undocumented migration are available. Similarly, the table does not include all labor exporting countries because of lack of information. For example, with respect to Vietnam, Hiebert (1990: 20) has written:

> Over 180,000 Vietnamese work in Eastern Europe, mostly in light industry and building construction, under bilateral labor co-operation agreements signed in 1980. Part of their salaries goes to repay Vietnam's debts to these countries, while the workers use the rest to feed themselves and buy local products to send home.

Estimates of the number of Vietnamese abroad vary between 100,000 and 600,000 with the official figure in mid-1990 being 195,000 and there has been some concern that many of these workers are moving into Western Europe following the changes in Eastern Europe in 1989–1990 (*Straits Times*, 10 May 1990). The rapid increase in recent years in the number of OCWs from China in Table 7 is of particular interest since the potential for that country, with 150 million underemployed workers to supply labor is enormous (Jayasankaran, 1997).

The increasing overlapping of labor markets in Asia is evident in Figure 2 which shows the results of a poll of executives in a number of Asian countries on the question "To what extent is the economy of your country dependent upon immigrant labor?" Clearly, several Asian nations are becoming heavily dependent upon foreign labor. This is not only a function of their rapid economic growth but also of their demography.

To focus specifically on Southeast Asia, Figure 3 shows that the age structures of the main labor importing nations of the region (especially Singa-

Table 6: Estimated Stocks of Foreign Labor
in Asian Countries in the Mid-1990s

Country	Year	Stock
Japan	1994	1,354,011
South Korea	1996	210,000
Taiwan	1995	296,745
Singapore	1994	300,000
Malaysia	1996	2,300,000
Thailand	1996	1,000,000
Brunei	1994	62,326
Hong Kong	1994	368,500
Total		**5,891,582**

Source: Abella, 1995; Stahl and PECC-HRD Task Force, 1996; Martin et al., 1995; Azizah, 1997; Asia Pulse, 21 May 1997; Stern, 1996

Table 7: Estimated Stocks of Migrant Workers Overseas
in the Mid-1990s

Origin	Year	Stock	Source
China	1996	380,000	Saywell, 1997, p.80
Nepal	1996	110,000	BBC, 14 February 1997
Philippines	1997	6,100,000	Saywell, 1997, p.80
Indonesia	1997	2,404,000	Depnaker, Indonesia
Thailand	1995	445,000	Stahl and PECC-HRD
Malaysia	1995	200,000	Azizah, 1997
Burma	1995	415,000	Stahl and PECC-HRD
South Korea	1995	190,000	Stahl and PECC-HRD
Japan	1995	18,000	Stahl and PECC-HRD
South Asia	1995	3,500,000	Stahl and PECC-HRD; Birks and Sinclair, 1992
Total		**13,762,000**	

pore and Thailand) are steep sided in the younger ages so that the numbers entering the workforce ages are not expanding. In the labor surplus nations on the other hand (e.g., Indonesia, Philippines), the age pyramids are much flatter indicating that the work-force is still growing quite rapidly, by each year more younger people ageing into the school leaving age groups than the year before. Hence Table 8 shows that there is a considerable range in the annual rate of growth of the population aged 15–59 over the next 5 years between countries of the region ranging from 0.8 per cent per annum in Singapore and 1.31 per cent in Thailand to 3.1 per cent in Cambodia and 2.9 per cent in Laos. These differences are maintained over the 2001–2010 period.

Moreover, it will be noted that in the labor surplus nations the workforce will grow at a faster rate than the total population over the next 15 years. Hence there appears to be a divergence in the demographic situation of labor surplus and labor shortage countries with respect to growth of their labor force age groups over the next decade or so. This obviously will expand the potential for labor migration between countries in the Asian region.

A crucial question relating to the burgeoning international labor migration impinging upon Asia is the extent to which the migration will remain temporary. At present the bulk of OCWs return to their homeland. However, the policy makers in destination nations are conscious of the experience with guestworkers in Europe in the 1950s and 1960s whereby temporary labor migration became transformed into permanent settlement (Castles, Booth and Wallace, 1984). There are signs that some Asian labor migrants are settling more or less permanently at their destinations (e.g., the Indonesians in Malaysia; Hugo, 1995). However, it is not clear as yet how widespread this pattern is.

Figure 2: Results of a Poll of Asian Executives' Responses to the Question "To What Extent is the Economy of Your Country Dependent Upon Immigrant Labor?"

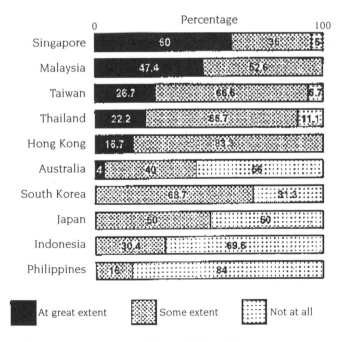

Source: Far Eastern Economic Review, 22 May 1997, p.37

167

Figure 3: Southeast Asian Nations: Age-Sex Structure, 1995

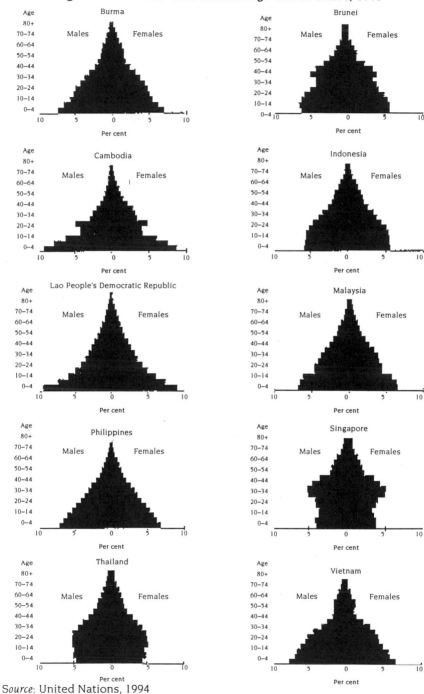

Source: United Nations, 1994

**Table 8: Southeast Asia: Projected Growth
of Labor Force Age Groups, 1995–2010**

	('000)				% p.a. Growth		Total Population % p.a. Growth	
	1995	2000	2005	2010	1995– 2000	1995– 2010	1995– 2000	1995– 2010
15–59 years								
Burma	26059	29097	32868	37033	2.23	2.37	2.07	1.89
Brunei	173	196	217	235	2.53	2.06	1.83	1.55
Cambodia	5212	6075	7179	8238	3.11	3.10	2.57	2.39
Indonesia	119086	131368	143325	154805	1.98	1.76	1.49	1.29
Lao People's Dem. Rep.	2460	2836	3312	3905	2.89	3.13	2.79	2.61
Malaysia	11303	12979	14819	16533	2.80	2.57	2.06	1.78
Philippines	38085	43196	48501	53852	2.55	2.34	1.99	1.79
Singapore	1915	1993	2080	2093	0.80	0.59	0.82	0.66
Thailand	37702	40235	42541	43887	1.31	1.02	1.04	0.89
Vietnam	41143	47267	53763	60788	2.81	2.64	2.09	1.87
Total	**283138**	**315242**	**348605**	**381369**	**2.17**	**2.01**	**1.71**	**1.52**

Source: United Nations, 1994

North-South Migration

In contemporary Asia the rapid growth and restructuring of national econo-mies has been accompanied by an increasing influx of skilled workers and business people from Europe, North America and Australasia on a mostly temporary, but long term, basis. This has been in addition to significant move-ment of professionals and other highly skilled workers *within* the Asian region largely from countries with education systems producing larger numbers of such workers than their own economies can currently absorb especially India, the Philippines, Pakistan, Sri Lanka and Bangladesh. The influx of profession-als, business people and technical workers from MDCs is associated with:

- The massive growth of investment by multinational operations in the region which has seen the MNCs transfer large numbers of MDC origin staff into Asia. For example, in 1994 there were 689,895 Japanese citi-zens officially regarded as living overseas (Okunishi, 1995: 141).
- The mismatches between the education and training systems and labor market skill needs in rapidly growing economies like Indonesia, notwith-standing high levels of underemployment and educated unemployment substantial numbers of expatriate engineers, technicians, accountants, fi-nance and management experts etc. have had to be imported (Hugo, 1997a).

The result has been a massive influx from MDCs of highly trained people into the rapidly growing economies of the Asian region. Hence in Hong Kong in 1994 there were: 23,700 British; 29,900 U.S.A.; 24,700 Canadians; 18,700

Australian people; as well as 115,000 from the Philippines; 23,800 from Thailand; 17,600 from Japan; 19,500 from India; 19,700 from Indonesia; and 13,800 from Malaysia.

In addition to documented overseas workers, there are also many expatriates who enter Asian nations under tourist visas but subsequently engage in some work (*Manila Chronicle*, 16 December 1994). The media in the region are increasingly carrying stories opposing the impact of foreign skilled workers for individual projects (e.g., *Economic and Business Review Indonesia*, 24 September 1994). However, in a survey of 3,000 *Far Eastern Economic Review* readers in April–June 1994 only in Malaysia was there a predominantly positive response to the statement "There are too many foreigners in my country."

An important element in the North-South flow of migrants is a reverse flow to the South-North migration. A common phrase used in contemporary Asian countries with fast growing economies in recent years is "reverse brain drain." It refers to the repatriation of nationals and former nationals who have lived and worked in an MDC for a considerable period. This movement has been gathering momentum throughout the late 1980s and 1990s and is partly associated with the burgeoning opportunities in the rapidly growing, restructuring and labor shortage economies of their home country. Moreover, the dynamism of the economies of their home countries has contrasted with the low growth and economic downturns experienced by some MDCs in the early 1990s. In addition, in several countries in the region there has been a deliberate policy to attract back former emigrants who have particular technical, professional and business skills. South Korea represents an important example of such government intervention (Hugo, 1996b).

The reverse brain drain is only one part of a complex pattern of return migration from MDCs, although the scale is difficult to establish since most MDCs do not keep comprehensive emigration statistics (Hugo, 1994). Australia is one of the few such nations which keeps accurate and comprehensive data sets on all persons leaving the country. In the case of more permanent emigrants from Asian countries, two patterns of return migration appear to be occurring:

- Return migration of the conventional type whereby migrants return to settle in their country of origin.
- "Astronauting" whereby migrants shuttle between their origin and destination countries, often keeping business interests in both countries.

The pattern of return migration of Asian migrants from Australia over the last decade is depicted in Table 9. This shows the origins of the 429,371 immigrants from Asia settling in Australia between 1984 and 1994 and the number of emigrants from Australia flowing in the opposite direction. The highest rate of return from Australia is among Japanese settlers, suggesting that many Japanese moving to Australia do so on transfer with a Japanese company and after a few years' service they return to Japan. This may also be the case with Singapore and Thailand. However, for the bulk of Asian birthplaces the backflow is very small indeed. Only some 5.7 per cent of migrants from Hong Kong to Australia have returned to their home country. However, it is clear that many Hong Kong migrants to not only Australia but also Canada and elsewhere, once they have obtained their foreign passports or obtained permanent residence status in another country have returned to Hong Kong to continue their business activities (Fong, 1993: 77). Some estimates put the proportion of Hong Kong residents who left in the 1980s who have returned, at 10–15 per cent (Ho, Liu and Lam, 1991: 40).

It is interesting that in 1993–1994 the number of return migrants to Hong Kong from Australia made up only slightly over a third of all permanent migrants moving from Australia to Hong Kong and that the numbers of Australia-born and other birthplace groups resident in Australia involved in the move was quite significant.

There has been some concern that a substantial number of business migrants from Hong Kong have established their citizenship of Canada or Australia as a form of insurance and then returned to Hong Kong. In the U.S., Arnold (1989: 890–891) has referred to similar developments:

> A large number of so-called immigrants to the United States have not really moved to the U.S. and therefore they are not immigrants in the traditional sense. There are many thousands of immigrants who have received their green cards, but still live in their country of origin. This is particularly true in several places in Asia such as Hong Kong, Korea and Taiwan. Many individuals from these areas keep one foot in each country and have not really established residency in the U.S.; although residency is a requirement of U.S. immigration law. Visits to the U.S. are only made often enough to keep the Immigration and Naturalization Service from revoking permanent residence status. These individuals prefer to live in their home countries at the present time, but want to keep open their future options for immigrating to the United States. Many merchants in Hong Kong, for example, want to continue to operate their businesses there, but have applied for green cards because of concerns about the future business climate in Hong Kong as the country reverts to China in 1997.

The phenomenon of "astronauting" among Hong Kong immigrants to Canada, U.S., Australia and elsewhere has become significant in recent years (Pe-Pua *et al.*, 1996). This involves Hong Kong people gaining residency or even citizenship in one of the immigration nations and establishing their family there but with some members of the family becoming bi-local in that they maintain substantial business interests in Hong Kong and spend quite a bit of time there. The significance of the "astronauting" phenomenon in Australia can be seen from results of the prototype Longitudinal Survey of Immigrants to Australia (LSIA). Of the 30 sampled, PAs (principal applicants for immigration visa) from Hong Kong who immigrated to Australia between July and September 1991 under the independent visa category; the follow-up

**Table 9: Australia: Immigration to, and
Emigration from, Asian Countries, 1984–1985 to 1993–1994**

Country of Origin/ Destination	Immigrants to Australia	Overseas-born Emigrants (Number)	As % of Immigrants	Australia- Born Emigrants	Ratio of Overseas to Australia- Born Emigrants
Southeast Asia					
Indonesia	11,719	1,103	9.4	977	1.13
Malaysia	40,697	1,276	3.1	1,027	1.24
Philippines	59,742	885	1.6	545	1.62
Singapore	11,867	1,476	12.4	1,809	0.82
Thailand	8,218	1,376	16.7	425	3.24
Vietnam	81,324	403	0.5	68	5.93
Other	14,551	295	2.0	339	0.87
Total	228,118	6,232	2.7	5,190	1.20
Northeast Asia					
China	31,591	449	1.4	170	2.64
Hong Kong	67,056	3,817	5.7	3,441	1.11
Japan	4,959	1,164	23.5	627	1.86
Korea	12,090	629	5.2	215	2.93
Taiwan	16,609	669	4.0	151	4.43
Other	1,563	45	2.9	19	2.37
Total	133,868	6,773	5.1	4,623	1.47
South Asia					
India	32,686	344	1.1	127	2.71
Pakistan	3,536	85	2.4	46	1.85
Sri Lanka	23,900	133	0.6	45	2.96
Other	7,263	41	0.6	49	0.84
Total	67,385	603	0.9	267	2.25
Total	**429,371**	**13,608**	**3.2**	**10,080**	**1.35**

Source: Calculated from Bureau of Immigration, Multicultural and Population Research sources

survey one year later was able to interview only one of these immigrants. Among reasons for non-contact the most frequent was "gone to former home country temporarily." An investigation of arrivals and departures data for the 28 uncontactable immigrants revealed that all returned to Hong Kong within several days or in some cases weeks. In fact, this phenomenon was found in the LSIA prototype to be not restricted to Hong Kong immigrants. Indeed 13.7 per cent of the 792 PAs interviewed a year after arrival had "returned home temporarily" while only 1.1 per cent had returned to their home country permanently (and 7.7 per cent could not be contacted at all).

Table 10 shows that the PAs were strongly concentrated in three Asian countries — Hong Kong, Malaysia and Taiwan accounted for 79 (72 per cent) of the people returning home on a temporary or permanent basis. Thus it is clear that this pattern of PAs returning temporarily to their home country soon after arrival in Australia is obviously highly specific to these destinations and thus tends to be mainly associated with settlers entering Australia under the Business, Employer Nomination Scheme and Independent policy categories.

Student Migration

The exponential increase in temporary international labor movements in the Asian region has been more than matched by expansion of other moves associated with tourism, business and education. Some indication of this can be gained by examining the flows into Australia from Asia shown in Table 2. One type of short term movement of particular significance is the increasing tempo of migration of Asian students (Shu and Hawthorne, 1996). Again the pattern in Australia is indicative. Figure 4 shows that over the 1983–1997 period the number of overseas students studying in Australia increased from 9,098 to 62,000. More than 95 per cent of these are from Asia. In the United States the number of foreign students enrolled in universities increased: from 82,709 in 1965 to 179,350 in 1975; 343,780 in 1985; 438,618 in in 1992; and 449,749 in 1993 while the equivalent figures for Canada were: 11,284; 22,700; 29,495; 37,478; and 35,451 (Kritz and Caces, 1989; UNESCO, 1995). It is estimated that in 1994 Malaysia paid out M$49.9 billion for education of its nationals, most of it flowing to MDCs (*Far Eastern Economic Review*, 27 April 1995: 44). Moreover, there is little evidence of a reduction in student migrations out of Asia. In the United States it is reported that the number of Americans earning advanced degrees has been declining in recent years, especially in science and technology and foreigners are making up an increasing proportion of graduate students. Since 1980 more than half of the doctorates in engineering in the U.S. were earned by foreigners and in 1990, 57 per cent of all mathematics doctorates were awarded to foreigners, and Asians are predominant among the overseas graduates (Tran, 1990). Similarly, there is an increasing flow of Asian students to Japan. For example, in 1990 it was reported that there were around 60,000 researchers from less developed countries (LDCs) based in Japan (Cross, 1990: 66).

There is undoubtedly a strong connection between student migration and eventual settlement of Asian origin groups in MDCs. It may occur through students:

- overstaying their education visas;
- gaining a change of status to a resident;
- returning to their home country on completion of their studies and subsequently immigrating officially to the country where they studied.

Unfortunately, there are little data available to establish the extent to which these three processes are occurring. In Australia the overstay rate among students is reported to have declined from 12.2 per cent in May 1989

**Table 10: Prototype LSIA: Proportion of Sample Respondents
Who Had Returned Home by Country of Birth**

	Per cent Returned Overseas	Sample Size
Hong Kong	48	102
Malaysia	37	59
Taiwan	36	22
South Africa	26	27
Total Other Countries	5	588
Total	**15**	**798**

Source: Hugo and Gartner, 1993, p. 50

to 0.5 per cent in December 1993 and at the latter date there were 13,687 student overstayers making up a fifth of all overstayers (DIEA, 1994). It is apparent from research in Australia that there is a connection between flows of students and flows of immigrants with the substantial recent migration from Malaysia and Singapore being associated with linkages established by previous student movements (Dawkins *et al.*, 1991: 21; Lewis 1994). The connection between student migration and eventual emigration from Singapore has been recognized in research by Singaporean academics (Low, Toh and Soon, 1991: 145):

> . . . studying abroad also exposes the young to external influences and may initiate ideas of migration to the extent that they can be practised. The brain drain problem is a real one in Singapore, and it is one which they can ill afford.

It is apparent also that availability of high quality educational opportunities for children is an important factor motivating Asian migrants who decide to settle in Australia under the economic categories of immigration. Sullivan and Gunasekeran (1993) found that among migrants from Singapore and Malaysia to Australia, a prime motivation was the superior educational and associated career opportunities which they perceived would be available to their children in Australia. Figure 5 shows that this was also a significant cause of emigration from Taiwan.

One major country in the Asian region which has major concerns about a student-led brain drain is China where it is estimated that of 220,000 Chinese students who have gone abroad since 1979 only 75,000 have returned (Plafker, 1995). This student loss was obviously exacerbated by the Tiananmen Square Uprising in 1989 (Goldstein, 1994) whereby many students overseas at the time of that event applied for residence in their country of study. In Australia alone there were 27,162 such applications. The State Education

Figure 4: Overseas Students in Australian Universities, 1983–1997

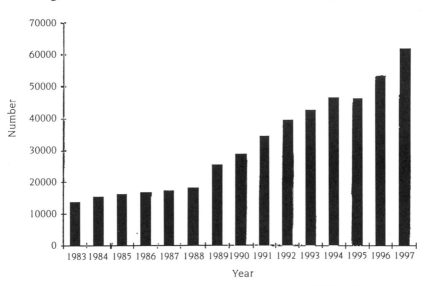

Source: DEETYA, 1996, p.103; *Campus Review*, 28 May–3 June 1997, p. 15

Commission in China has strict rules about return but only 40,000 of the 220,000 Chinese students going abroad were state funded (Plafker, 1995).

THE MOMENTUM FACTOR

It is important to appreciate that the acceleration of Asian international migration in recent years has developed a momentum which is in many ways self-perpetuating and which to some extent will continue to operate regardless of shifts in economic and political forces and in spite of government attempts at intervention. There are two common elements to all of the types of migration considered above which provide this self-perpetuating momentum and which are likely to continue to operate, probably at more intense levels in the future. The first element is the operation of migrant social networks and the second is the development of an immigration industry in the Asian region.

Firstly, regarding migrant social networks, it is not sufficiently acknowledged that the majority of international movers from Asia move along well trodden paths, which, if they have not travelled along them before themselves, have been traversed by family members and friends. Migrants tend to travel with friends or family and have a range of contacts at the destination. The networks that are established linking origin and destination become key elements in sustaining and enhancing population flows between them. These networks inject a self-perpetuating dynamism into flows of population, which allows movement to continue long after the original economic reasons for the flow have been superseded or rendered redundant. Whenever persons immigrate, every individual that they know acquires social capital in the form of a contact at the mover's destination which can be "cashed in" at any time to obtain help in getting a job or accommodation and social support while adjusting to the destination.

The networks established by earlier generations of movers from families and localities act as conduits to channel later generations of movers to those destinations in an atmosphere of certainty. Previous generations of movers have not only supplied valuable information and encouragement but often paid for, or arranged and eased, the passage. Moreover, when the immigrant arrives at the destination, the destination-end of the network lends valuable assistance in the adjustment process, especially through assisting in gaining access to housing and employment. The fundamental role of networks is to greatly reduce the risks associated with migration and, many movers from Asian origins thus operate in an environment of total certainty. This risk minimization factor is important. While other factors are necessary to initiate the beginning of a new limb of the network once the pioneer(s) is established at the destination, the increase in the subsequent flow can be rapid. The pioneer immigrants constitute anchors to which much larger numbers of subsequent immigrants are drawn. The pioneers can be people who gain access through some form of recruitment or refugee migration but then can facilitate substantial movement through legal family reunification movement. On the other hand, illegal migration is virtually impossible unless there is an informal network linking origin and destination to facilitate the clandestine movement. The pioneer immigration may have occurred for quite adventitious reasons but once established the flow may take on mass proportions.

Figure 5: Top Eight Reasons for Taiwanese Emigration

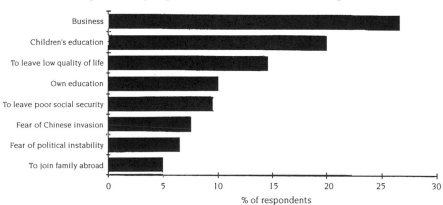

Source: Far Eastern Economic Review, 15 June 1995, p. 13

One of the most important features of the networks established by immigration is the role they have in sustaining population flows quite independently of objective economic conditions in origin and destination. Moreover, they can operate largely outside the arena of policy makers. Migration flows occurring along such networks are notoriously difficult to influence, let alone stop, by policy intervention. Almost all attempts to prevent such movements in the past have failed. The networks are enormously resilient and tenacious, even in the face of the most vigorous and draconian actions of governments. Once established, the networks become a very strong force for perpetuating particular streams of movement. As populations of previous Asian migrants build up in destination areas, the networks are expanded and lend a considerable element of momentum to ongoing migration patterns. However, our knowledge of the operation of migration networks remains limited. Such questions as what are the limits of assistance provided at the destination, how long after the initial migration do they operate, how different can the connection be to claim assistance remain largely unanswered.

Secondly, another of the most distinctive features in the explanation of much of the international migration occurring within Asia and out of Asia is the involvement of a complex varied group of recruiters, travel agents, lawyers, agents of various kinds, travel providers, immigration officials and an array of gatekeepers of various kinds. There can be no doubt that much of the migration in Asia is at least facilitated, and often initiated, by these crucial intermediaries and this is especially the case for international labor migration and especially for the segment of that movement which is clandestine. While recruitment activity has also been significant in the North American context (Massey *et al.*, 1994) it would appear to be more important in the contemporary Asian situation. Apart from genuine refugee movements it is difficult to think of a major contemporary Asian migration flow in which the immigration industry does not have a pivotal role. Yet this role is frequently overlooked or given only passing mention in studies of the causes of migration in Asia. This is partly a function of methodological approaches which involve study of the migrants and their families, communities of origin and destination etc. but fail to include interviewing or observation of the recruiters and other informal and formal institutional elements which initiate and facilitate migration. Moreover, these crucial intervening gatekeepers are very difficult (and even dangerous) to study because of commercial considerations and criminal involvement but especially because many operate outside the law. The high levels of profitability associated with people-smuggling and the "new slave trade" involving workers who are effectively indentured to their owners has led syndicates formerly involved in the drug trade to move into this arena.

The role of such groups goes back to the slave trade which prospered historically in Asia and also to the recruiters who were central to the "contract coolie" trade in the region in the latter part of the nineteenth and early twentieth centuries when most countries in the region were under colonial rule. For example, a variety of institutions were instrumental in the immigration of Chinese into Southeast Asia in the nineteenth and twentieth centuries. A complex group of shipping companies, shipping agents, shipping brokers, innkeepers and recruited carriers were key elements in the massive Chinese emigration extending over more than a century (Hicks, 1993, Chapter 2; Shozo, 1995). This has continued with many contemporary Chinese emigration flows being organized by human traffickers known as *shetou* or snakeheads (Pieke, forthcoming: 6; Thuno, 1996: 12) who are often associated with the triads.

The few studies which have examined the role of the immigration industry in Asia have shown how important the activities of recruiters can be in persuading potential migrants to move and thereafter greatly facilitating that process (Spaan, 1994; Hugo and Singhanetra-Renard, 1987; Goss and Lindquist, 1995). Private agencies are involved in most contract-labor immigration as well as in a great deal of the permanent migration out of Asia. The number of immigration agents and lawyers is growing rapidly in both origin and destination areas. However, the legal component is only part of the industry and, perhaps, the smaller part compared with the growing plethora of global "people smugglers." To use the Indonesian migration to Malaysia as an example, agents variously known as *calo*, *taikong*, *tauke* or *mandor* are highly organized and are crucial facilitators of the entire process. They operate both within and outside existing legal constraints. Habir (1984: 167) has described the range of important roles that the middlemen play in the migration process through recruitment of workers, arranging the moves, obtaining jobs at destination and settling in the workers. These agents have extensive networks on both sides of the border and Habir documents many cases where they have taken money from prospective migrants but not delivered all the services promised. One of the few detailed studies of the role of the *taikong* is that of Spaan (1994) which illustrates the complexity of the role of these mediators in the migration of East Javans to Malaysia. The illegal migrant is passed from one intermediary to another in a chain of contacts linking origin and destination. Each element in the chain receives a small payment in classic "involuntary" (Hugo, 1975) fashion. It is a safe and trusted network because it starts in the home village with a *calo* who has to bear the results of a failure in the system or of exploitation. Such illegal networks are often much more trusted and reliable than official systems, in which there is not the same degree of personalized local accountability, there are extended and costly delays in obtaining correct documentation and a great deal of waiting before the migration can actually take place. In the present context it is important to realize that there is a massive immigration industry in Asia involving many complex chains of people linking origin and destination countries. These are often operating outside official structures and are so ingrained that influencing them, let alone removing them through policy intervention, is extremely difficult. The industry is proliferating and gives a momentum to the current levels of migration which will be difficult to resist. Moreover, the industry often is penetrating particular migration networks so that those networks, formerly totally comprised of family and friends linkages are increasingly becoming institutionalized.

SOME EMERGING ISSUES IN ASIAN INTERNATIONAL MIGRATION

Remittances

There are many issues of significance associated with international migrations out of Asian countries but that of the flows of scarce foreign exchange into the sending countries is of particular importance. Remittances were once discounted as being of limited scale and impact but careful measurement of money sent back by migrants to their place of origin and of the first and second round impacts of that money has led to a significant revision of the conventional wisdom. Russell and Tietelbaum (1992) have shown that international remittances passing through official channels are second only to international trade in value globally. In several nations of the region (e.g., Pakistan, India, Sri Lanka, Bangladesh, Philippines), export of people has displaced export of commodities as the major foreign exchange earner. Table 11 shows the massive growth in remittances in three labor exporting nations in the 1980s and the ratio that they make up of merchandise export earnings. Moreover, official remittances are only the tip of the iceberg of all flows since the bulk of remittances are brought back by hand by migrant workers themselves or family members and friends. This is evident in Table 12 which shows the method of sending back remittances among a sample of 313 migrant workers from East Flores (Indonesia) to Sabah (Malaysia). It is apparent from Table 11 that remittances are only a small factor in the large Indonesian economy, although the official remittances severely underestimate the real flow. Nevertheless, it is shown elsewhere that remittances can and do have a significant effect on *regional* economies since migrants are selectively drawn from some of the poorest areas in Indonesia (Hugo, 1996a). For example, in a single *kabupaten* in East Java in 1995 remittances amounted to Rp 61.3 billion, several times larger than the entire government budget for the *kabupaten* Rp 2.3 billion (*Republika*, 19 February 1996).

Table 11 shows that remittances are a major factor in the Philippine national economy. In 1995, the 4.2 million Filipinos working overseas remitted US$4.93 billion through official channels, a substantial increase from the 3.01 billion sent in 1994 (*Xinhua News Agency*, 2 April 1996). The 65,000 female domestic workers in Singapore alone sent back US$106 million, an average of $1,630 each (*Straits Times*, 17 March 1996). Remittances increased by 32 per cent between 1993 and 1994 and 60 per cent between 1994 and 1995. The significance of international migration in the Philippine economy can be appreciated from the fact that in 1995 these remittances almost covered the nation's US$6 billion trade gap and was three times larger than net foreign investment inflows (Tiglao, 1996). It also needs to be appreciated that official remittances do not capture the probably larger amount of money and goods sent and brought home by Filipinos overseas through unofficial channels. The significance of unofficial channels can be seen from the fact that in 1990 when the Philippine National Bank extended its services to Italy, Amsterdam, Germany and Madrid, official per capita labor income from Europe more than doubled over 1989 levels (Russell, 1991: 20).

The macro-economic impact of remittances can also be seen in Pakistan where in the last half of 1995 official remittances totalled US$969 million (43 per cent up from the previous year) compared with the US$226 million direct foreign investment over the same period and a trade deficit over the first seven months of fiscal 1994–1995 of $1.1 billion (Rashid, 1996). In Malaysia outflows of remittances began to show up in the nation's current accounts in 1996 when remittances were estimated at M. Ringgit 3 billion (Jayasankaran, 1997).

Feminization of Migration

A distinctive feature of many of the international migration flows influencing contemporary Asia is the increasing involvement of women. This has included a number of elements. Women have been a major element in the Asian migration to MDCs — indeed they outnumber their male counterparts in such movement (Hugo, 1997b). However, this is only one component of a diverse range of movements involving varying distances, degrees of permanency of settlement at the destination, legality or illegality and a wide range of processes and motivations on the part of the women involved. A major type of movement involved has been the increasing involvement of women as OCWs. In Asia women dominate several of these labor flows. One of the most substantial and controversial of the OCW flows involving women are those who work in the destination nations as domestic servants.

Figure 6 shows the main origin nations are the Philippines, Indonesia, Sri Lanka, Thailand and Bangladesh. The major destinations of these women in the 1950s were Middle Eastern countries but increasingly other Asian destinations such as Hong Kong, Singapore and Malaysia have become very important. It is estimated that in the early 1990s there were up to 1.7 million Asian women working as maids outside of their own nation throughout Asia and the Middle East (*Straits Times*, 13 May 1995). Although women now dominate many of the major international migration flows in Asia, the gender dimension has been neglected in migration research in the region. The role and status of women in Asia is undergoing rapid and profound change especially with the spread of education, increasing participation in the workforce outside of the home and increased use of contraceptives. However, little is known about the impact of these changes on population mobility and whether migration is associated with an improvement in the status of women. Much research into international migration in the region remains gender-blind or relegates migration of women to being predominantly associational. However, it is clear that the independent migration of women is gathering pace but understanding of its implications for women and their families is limited. The fact that many Asian women move to other nations for marriage, to work as domestics or in the entertainment and sex industries means that they are often vulnerable to abuse and exploitation.

The sex trade has also become a significant element in female international migration in Asia. Women are recruited to work as entertainers or prostitutes in other Asian countries or in MDCs such as Japan and Australia. Thailand and the Philippines are important source countries of this movement. Brockett (1996) has shown how for Thai women there is a pattern of a circuit of movement to Japan, Taiwan and Australia and social networks link the sex industry across several nations. One insidious element in this is the increased scale of trafficking in women. Figure 7 shows some of the major flows of women involved in such trafficking in the Southeast Asian region.

Table 11: Main Southeast Asian Labor Exporting Countries: Workers' Remittances Relative to Exports and Imports in US$ Million, 1980–1995

Country	Year	Workers' Remittances (R)	Total Merchandise Exports (X)	Imports (M)	$\frac{R}{X}$	$\frac{R}{M}$
Indonesia	1980	33	21,908	10,834	0.1	0.3
	1995	356	40,054	31,985	0.9	1.1
Philippines	1980	421	5,744	8,295	7.3	5.0
	1995	4,930	13,304	22,546	37.1	21.9
Thailand	1979	191	5,240	7,158	3.6	2.7
	1995	1,900	45,262	54,459	4.2	3.5

Source: Hugo, 1996a, p. 8; Hugo, 1996c, p. 3; World Bank, 1996

Table 12: International Labor Migrants in East Flores: Method of Sending Remittances

Type of Migrant	Bank	Post	Sent With Family/Friend	N
Migrant Still Away	18.0	2.0	80.0	116
Single Migrant, Returned	21.3	8.5	70.2	125
Multiple Migrant, Returned	34.9	6.6	56.6	72

Source: 1996 East Flores OCW Survey

This trade is largely in the hands of organized crime, some of it involving diversification from the drug trade. There are an estimated 150,000 foreign sex workers in Japan alone, most of them Thais and Filipinos (Sherry, Lee and Vatikiotis, 1995: 24).

Although international movements out of Asian countries which are predominantly made up of women and place them in particularly vulnerable work situations are striking and of major policy significance, one of the most important trends has been in women becoming involved in the full gamut of international movements which have in the past not only been much smaller in scale but have been heavily dominated by males. Hence Asian women are now heavily represented in the massive numbers of students now spending several years in MDCs undertaking training of various kinds. This reflects the changing roles and status of women in LDCs. In Flores in Eastern Indonesia young men have been travelling for several decades to Sabah in East Malaysia to work on plantations and construction works. If women were involved at all it was to accompany or join their husbands. In the 1990s, however, young women from Flores are also migrating to Malaysia on an autonomous basis to work as domestic servants, mess cooks or housemaids etc. In the Flores study mentioned earlier, for example, 24.1 per cent of contemporary migrants were women.

Increasingly, governments are becoming involved in facilitating or controlling the international migration of women. The Philippines has long had training institutions to train nurses to a standard acceptable in the United States so that they can work overseas upon graduation. The Indonesian government has initiated a similar training program and has long provided a compulsory course that women going to work as domestic servants in the Middle East have had to take before being given an exit permit. Mail order bride schemes involving Filipino (and, to a lesser extent, Thai) women in Australia, Japan, Germany, the United States, Italy and elsewhere have come under increasing scrutiny of governments, both at the origin and destination (Cahill, 1990). There were 20,000 mail order brides from the Philippines to Japan in 1996.

The greatly increased scale of female international migration in Asia would appear on the surface to offer considerable opportunity for women to improve their economic and social situation. It frequently involves movement between contexts which, other things being equal, one would expect some empowerment to occur. Hence movement often involves a transition from a rural to an urban context, from a familial mode of production to an enterprise mode and from a "traditional" situation to a "modern" situation. It often involves women moving away from the immediate control of traditional forms of authority which are often patriarchal and in moving to a situation where they receive money for their work and where they have control over that money. For the first time they may be living in a situation which is not with their family. They are likely to be exposed to a range of experiences and influences different from the traditional way of life maintained in their village origins. They will probably meet people from a wider range of backgrounds and experience than would be the case in the home village. However, while such transitions can and do result in empowerment of the women involved, it is by no means an automatic result of migration. Indeed, migration can also operate so as to preserve, and even strengthen, the *status quo* with respect to gender position and relations (Hugo, 1997b). Indeed, many female international migrants from Asia move into vulnerable situations and there is a pressing need for appropriate policies and programs to protect their rights (Lim and Oishi, 1996).

Undocumented Migration

An important growing trend in recent years has been the increase of undocumented migration (especially of workers) within Asia. Table 13 presents recent estimates of the scale of this movement. It is especially strong in Japan and the Four NIC Tigers where strict immigration regulations have combined with substantial labor shortages in unskilled areas to encourage illegal movement from labor surplus areas.

One of the most substantial movements is from Indonesia to Malaysia (Azizah, 1997) involving over 1 million workers, making up more than 10 per cent of the Malaysian workforce and substantially more than 1 per

Figure 6: Major Female Migration Flows in the Mid-1990s

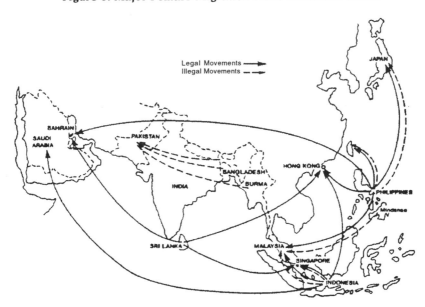

Source: Far Eastern Economic Review

cent of the Indonesian workforce. In recent years, China has become a significant source of illegal migrants with people smuggling estimated to number around 200,000 to the U.S., 150,000 to Russia, 100,000 to Thailand and smaller flows to several other nations (UNECE, 1994). Thailand also has become a major focus for illegal migration from Burma, Laos, Cambodia and Bangladesh. In 1994 it was estimated that Thailand had half a million illegal migrants — 300,000 from Burma, 100,000 from China, 50,000 from South Asia and 10,000 from Indo-China (*Straits Times*, 17 March 1994). In Japan it is possible to calculate the number of overstayers and Stahl and PECC-HRD Task Force (1996: 8) explain:

> Beginning in 1985 the number of illegal foreign workers was almost nil. However, by the end of 1994 there were 288,000 overstayers. If to this figure we add those who are working on currently valid non-work visas, then it is conceivable that the numbers working illegally would exceed 500,000, an estimate consistent with several Japanese sources.

Illegal migration in Asia is increasingly involving criminal syndicates. In some cases, especially in Thailand, criminals involved in the drug trade have turned to the migration and people trafficking industry. The illegal immigration industry is expanding and posing an increasing threat to security in the region.

Government Involvement

An important element in the initiation of international migration in the Asian region is the activity of governments in the region. It is one of the most distinctive features of all international migration that it is more strongly shaped by governments than is the case with internal migration but it is a distinctive feature of the Asian migration system that political factors have been highly influential in a direct way, not only in destination countries but also in origin nations.

Government policies can impinge upon international migration indirectly via its influence on employment opportunities, income levels, exchange rates etc. but increasingly in Asia, governments are directly intervening to initiate, facilitate and encourage international migration and this element must be considered in any comprehensive explanation of international migration in the Asian region. One of the most substantial differences between internal and international migration is the greater ability of governments to control the latter, although the growing volume of illegal migration in Asia (Hugo, 1996b) demonstrates that there are some limits to the ability of governments to control international migration. Nevertheless, government policy and practice is an important controlling factor in international migration in Asia. Examination of such policy is almost always focused upon destination countries' attempts to control the scale, composition and period of stay of flows of foreigners into their nation, and this must and does exert a significant influence on international migration in Asia. However, the most distinctive

Figure 7: Southeast Asia: Trafficking in Women and Children

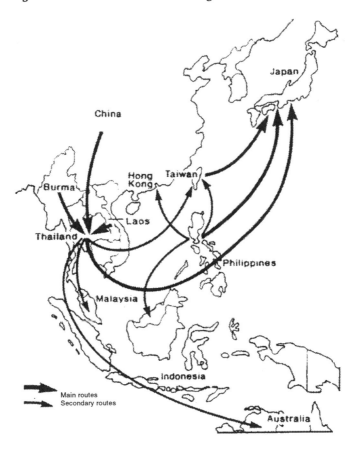

Source: Far Eastern Economic Review, 14 December 1995, p.26

element in Asia is the growing number of nations who are putting in place policies to encourage, facilitate and initiate international migration, usually non-permanent international labor migration. Labor export has become an important part of economic planning with the objectives of:

- reducing pressure upon national and regional labor markets,
- enhancing foreign exchange earnings,
- in some cases providing its workers with skills and training.

Indeed, as was pointed out earlier, labor export has become the largest single foreign exchange earning activity, outweighing commodity exports, in the national economy in a number of Asian labor surplus nations. To maximize the scale and benefits of labor export, national governments have put in place a number of policies and programs including the following:

- Establishing labor export agencies within the government bureaucracy. Almost all labor surplus nations within the region have such agencies although the functions they have vary between regulating the flow, controlling recruitment, training of potential migrants to exploring new markets for labor and active encouragement of nations to obtain work overseas.
- Initiation of special programs to maximize remittances — tax breaks, special banking facilities at destinations, forced remittance of a share of weekly earnings.
- Seeking out bilateral arrangements with destination countries to supply labor.
- Protection of migrant workers at the destination.
- Providing support services at destination.
- Assisting in readjustment back in to the home community after migration.
- Special programs to attract back former nationals, especially those with high level skills or wealth, to return to their home country.

Some countries have built in to their national and provincial economic planning target levels of international labor migration, the composition of the flows and levels of remittances (Hugo, 1995). In China each county has set up a labor export company to encourage and facilitate labor movement (Qian, 1996). Hence governments in some nations of Asia are not only facilitating and regulating international migration but also actively initiating and encouraging that movement.

Governments in destination areas are usually depicted as having policies to restrict and control immigration and this is certainly the case in the region. Many Asian nations have highly restrictionist immigration policies, with Japan being a striking example (Sassen, 1993). It is only in the traditional immigration countries that governments are also playing a role in initiating migration through economic and business migration, family reunion etc. Governments in labor shortage nations in Asia have generally initiated strong policies to prevent migrant workers settling permanently, although Singapore has allowed some Hong Kong Chinese and Western highly skilled people to settle there (Beng and Chew, 1995).

Brain Drain Issues
    In the early postwar decades there can be little doubt that several countries of Asia experienced a significant brain drain. International emigration from Asia was very limited in scale and had little demographic effect in origin countries, but most of the movement involved highly qualified personnel moving to MDCs, especially the United States (Hugo, 1996a). This movement often involved Asian nationals who had previously studied in the country

which they eventually settled in. The brain drain to the United States was greatly facilitated by the 1965 amendments to the Immigration Law (Pernia, 1976: 63; Fortney, 1972). In the 1980s and 1990s, however, when the scale of migration has greatly increased, the degree of educational selectivity of migration has decreased. The diversification of flows out of Asian nations has resulted in uneven brain drain effects. On the one hand it appears that refugee movements, family migration and contract labor (legal and illegal) have generally had limited impacts in depriving Asian nations of scarce talent crucial to their economic and social progress. On the other hand losses of skilled nationals through "economic" and business migration to MDCs and "leakage" of students remaining overseas after completing their courses undoubtedly represent a brain drain to some nations (Hugo, 1996a). Hence, in the Philippines there is concern that a substantial proportion of the best quality science graduates emigrate (*Manila Chronicle*, 24 March 1994).

In Hong Kong too there is considerable concern about the brain drain despite the influx of expatriate workers (Kwong, 1992; Do Rosario, 1995). In the early 1990s, as emigration peaked, there was considerable concern about skilled labor shortage and increasing concern about the competitiveness of the Hong Kong economy (Fong, 1993: 77). Moreover, in 1990 Hong Kong emigrants and investors are estimated to have transferred about US$4 billion to Australia and Canada (Ho, Liu and Lam, 1991: 38). Similarly, in Singapore the overall labor shortages have been exacerbated by a significant outflow of highly educated people. For example, the number of Singapore-born people resident in Australia has increased from 12,400 in 1981 to 32,700 in 1994. Beng (1990) shows that there was an increase in the number of emigrants leaving Singapore from 5,040 in 1986 to 11,770 in 1988 and shows why this is of concern to the government. In addition, around 30,000 Singapore citizens were living abroad in 1990 — mainly students, professionals and managers (Fong, 1993: 78).

Conventional views of the brain drain see it as both a cause and effect of underdevelopment (Adams [ed.], 1969). Many have argued with good cause

Table 13: Estimates of the Numbers of Asian Illegal Migrants in Selected Countries in the Early 1990s

Country	Numbers Involved	Source of Information
Australia	81,500 (1992)	Shu and Khoo, 1993: 4
Japan	300,000	*Japan Times*, 25 Feb. 1993
South Korea	68,000	*Asia Focus*, X, 8, 25 Feb. 1994
Philippines	100,000	*Manila Chronicle*, 10 Mar. 1994
Taiwan	200,000	Baum, 1993: 24
Malaysia	1,500,000	Azizah, 1997
Singapore	250,000	Prasai, 1993: 23
Thailand	500,000	*Straits Times*, 17 Mar. 1994

that the outflow of highly educated groups from Asia to MDCs constitutes a significant loss of resources which will reduce the country's productive capacity and "represents lost educational investment in that the sending country bears the cost of educating the highly skilled labor but does not directly benefit from it" (Carino, 1987: 316). On the other hand commentators (e.g., Adams, 1969; Carino, 1987; Pernia, 1976; Minocha, 1987) argue that the brain drain reflects the basic inability of the origin country's economy to absorb the going supply of certain high level skills (Pernia, 1976: 71). Hence, as Carino (1987: 317) points out:

> . . . the supply of professionals particularly engineers, scientists, physicians and surgeons — has obviously outpaced the economy's absorptive capacity. The extent of the drain would, therefore, seem to be far less than the actual volume of immigrant professionals. More significantly, this view has an important policy implication: the remedy for the brain drain seems to lie in a training and manpower policy that addresses itself to the sending country's actual development needs and objectives.

It has been argued elsewhere (Hugo, 1996a) that loss of highly trained personnel can, in some contexts in Asia, have beneficial impacts upon the sending countries because of:

- a mismatch between the origin country's supply of such labor and its economy's capacity to absorb them,
- the inflow of remittances from the migrants,
- the significant return migration of this group to their origin countries with enhanced skills and capacities,
- the other economic linkages which these migrants forge between their origin and destination countries,
- migrants can act as beachheads for origin country goods to be sold in the destination countries,
- migrants in influential positions in destination based MNCs can direct investment to their home country.

POLITICAL CONSEQUENCES OF INTERNATIONAL LABOR MIGRATION

It is apparent that international migration both influences, and is influenced by, bilateral political relationships between groups of countries. It is the essence of the conceptualization of international migration within a systems framework (Kritz and Zlotnik, 1992) that population movements are part of a wider series of flows and relationships linking nations with which they interact. Exactly how international migration impinges upon wider bilateral political relations and upon the networks of linkages among countries in the emerging political blocs in Asia like the ASEAN, APEC and other regional groupings, however, remains to be studied (Lim, 1994). Clearly, the type and context of the movement is important in this as are the numbers of migrants involved and their characteristics, and whether or not there are reciprocal flows. International migration can be the basis for building up a wider set of mutually beneficial flows between nations. However, they can also be the basis for souring relations between countries as where countries accept emigres fleeing from a neighboring nation and where those emigrants continue to actively oppose the regime in their home nation as is the case with some Burmese in Thailand for example. Similarly, the recent case of a female Filipino domestic worker in Singapore who was executed for the alleged murder of a fellow Filipino maid and her ward led to a significant cooling of relations between the two ASEAN partners (Arcellana, 1995). It would certainly seem that migration is going to figure more prominently in bilateral and multilateral relationships involving Asian countries.

One very important issue which has not been given enough prominence in the region relates to the rights of migrants, especially migrant workers. The issue is made all the more difficult in Asia by the high level of illegal migration. Clearly, migrants in a foreign country where they do not have the rights of citizens of that country are vulnerable to the risk of exploitation, discrimination and abuse. This vulnerability is increased if they are undocumented migrants. While there are well established regimes for dealing with some types of migrants such as refugees, there are not widely accepted and established regimes for dealing with other international migrants. This applies especially to international labor migration, although there is a UN international charter of Migrant Worker Rights which could serve as a blueprint for such a regime, it has not been identified by most nations in the region (only the Philippines and Sri Lanka). The difficult issue of protecting the rights of nationals in a foreign land is exacerbated when they work in contexts which are not even under the jurisdiction of local labor authorities such as is the case with domestic workers in Saudi Arabia or many workers in the so-called "entertainment" industry in Japan. The priority given to protection of the rights of migrant workers is clearly low in most countries in the region, and this especially applies to women (Goldberg, 1996). There may be greater scope for involvement of NGOs in these activities.

Backlash Against Migrants

One of the most discussed aspects of Asian migration to North America, Europe and Australasia has been the backlash which it has engendered from existing established communities. In all of the major destination areas there has been some backlash against the increased levels of Asian immigration. However, such responses have not been confined to these destinations. In Asia too influx of people, usually workers, from other Asian countries has produced a backlash from established communities. In Japan, South Korea, Singapore and, to a lesser extent, Taiwan very strict regulation of migrant workers, banning of them bringing families with them, prohibition of marrying locals and strict local control over their movement and activity in the destination is exercised for fear of a loss of social cohesion arising out of the dominance of Japanese, Korean or Chinese populations in those societies.

One of the most controversial issues associated with international migration in countries of destination is its impact upon social cohesion. Some established groups at destinations fear that an influx of migrants with different ethnic, cultural, language and religious backgrounds represents a threat to the existing social system. The extent to which change occurs among the migrants and among the community they join of course depends upon the scale and nature of the migration, the characteristics of the migrants, their degree of permanency and upon the socio-cultural systems of the migrants and the host community. In each of the countries of destination the main intention is for their international labor migrants' stay in their country to be a temporary one. However the experience in Europe has been that many guest-workers who originally in the 1950s and 1960s were recruited on a temporary basis have tended to settle in their host countries (Castles, Booth and Wallace, 1984). It is unclear as to whether this will happen to the same degree in Asia and indeed there are already some indications of labor migrants becoming more or less permanently settled in some destinations. This applies especially to Indonesians and Filipinos in Malaysia, although in both cases there are strong cultural and ethnic similarities between the migrant workers and the dominant Malay group. In Singapore too some concessions have been made to Hong Kong Chinese workers and some highly qualified workers. However in general the overwhelming attitude of governments is for labor migration to be temporary. To this end migrant workers tend to live separately from the local communities in destination countries and are not offered access to government provided services made available to citizens of the country. With a likely continuation of economic growth and lack of growth in the local workforce, however, it may well be that more labor migrants will establish themselves permanently in destination countries regardless of the wishes and policies of host governments and communities as has been the case in Europe.

As is the case worldwide, migrant workers in Asia often find themselves accused of misdeeds by the host populations. Hence Indonesian migrants in Malaysia are stereotyped as criminals although the relevant data do not show any above average involvement in crime. They have been accused of spreading the HIV AIDS virus and other infectious diseases, although again the evidence of this is at best inconclusive. The experience with international labor migration in the Asian region is that a backlash against migrant workers seems to occur when:

- there are some signs that the OCWs are settling permanently at the destination, establishing families, marrying locals etc.;
- the migrants begin to compete with local population by seeking work outside of the labor market segments originally set aside for migrant workers in low paid, low status dirty jobs;

- where the migrants begin to compete with the local population for services such as health, education etc.

THE IMPLICATIONS FOR CANADA

In conclusion we will attempt to draw some of the implications of trends in the evolving international migration system for the future of Asian migration to Canada. It is difficult to speculate about this, especially since much will depend upon developments in Canadian immigration policy. Nevertheless, there are some elements in the existing pattern of international movement in Asia which allow us to put forward a number of tentative statements regarding future Asian migration to Canada. The following would appear to be the most striking:

- Firstly, one has to stress the demographic underpinnings of Asian emigration. Elsewhere (Hugo, forthcoming) it has been shown that not only does Asia dominate the global demographic situation accounting for 57 per cent of the total population but that over the next decade or so its workforce age population will grow faster than the global average so that by 2011 nearly two thirds of the world's working age population will live in the region. Despite reductions in overall population growth in Asia the working groups will continue to grow rapidly for another two decades.
- Moreover, this generation of Asians will be the first to have experienced virtually universal primary education. It will contain an unprecedented number with advanced education, some of whom will become disgruntled because they cannot be absorbed into their countries' economies at a level which they consider appropriate to their training, skills and aspirations. Such groups not only have the motivation and assets to migrate and the information to select a destination, but also frequently they have the attributes (skills, business experience, education, etc.) which gives them a good chance of qualifying as settlers in Canada under one of the categories of economic and business migration available.
- It is also apparent that the doubling of the Asian origin population in Canada over the last decade has greatly increased the number of Asians with a relative established in Canada. The strength of social networks and their significance in Asian migration will mean that this not only will increase the flow of information about Canada back to Asian communities but also greatly expand the numbers eligible to emigrate to Canada under the family reunification element of the immigration program.
- The proliferation of the immigration industry in Asia will mean that the pressure placed on the legal immigration system by immigration agents and the like will increase. Equally, attempts of undocumented migrants to settle in Canada are also likely to increase as the Asian migration industry extends its arena of activity outside the Asia Pacific region.

- One intriguing area of speculation is the question of whether the exponential increase in intra-regional international movements in Asia leads to an increased emigration consciousness in the region which leads migrants to consider longer distance migration (e.g., to Canada) after being successful in a shorter distance migration *within* the Asian region. An example of this occurring is presented by Wong (1996: 103) who describes a Filipino maid in Singapore was weighing up her options about her future and one of these was migrating to Canada. Although the area needs more research it would seem that with increased international migration experience in Asia the numbers considering migration further afield to attractive destinations like Canada will increase.
- Canada has had a creditable record in accepting for settlement significant numbers of refugees from Asia. At the time of writing it would seem that the numbers of genuine refugees in Asia seeking resettlement in third countries has been substantially reduced. Of course, one cannot predict whether there will be another major political upheaval which will produce another outflow of refugees. Certainly it is hoped that in this post Cold War era the likelihood of this has been reduced, although the current situation in Burma may lead to some refugee outflows. On the other hand, the greatly increased knowledge of immigration regulations and processes in the region, together with the proliferation of migration lawyers and other intermediaries, may well lead to increased numbers of asylum seekers in Canada and other MDCs.

While each of these developments may or may not eventuate, it is crucially important to underline that future developments in Canadian immigration policy and variations in the immigration program should be undertaken with a full appreciation of the rapidly changing international migration situation with the Asian region in mind. This is imperative for the maintenance of good relationships with other Asian nations, to be fair and equitable to all potential immigrants and safeguard the well-being of all resident Canadians. All immigration policy formulation in Canada should be undertaken in full recognition of the fact that the world immigration situation of the 1990s is a totally new one. It is part of a set of powerful international processes which are creating strong new political, economic, financial, cultural and information linkages between countries. These forces of globalization are crucial to an understanding of changing Asian immigration trends. To view immigration as an autonomous process in isolation from other international flows and linkages could lead to the development of irrelevant and ineffective policies.

Endnotes

1 For a discussion of Asian international migration data, see the special issue of *Asia-Pacific Migration Journal* 8 (4) (1995) and Bilsborrow *et al.*, 1997.

11 Emigration Pressures in Selected Asian Countries: Some Preliminary Findings

Manolo I. Abella

At certain stages of economic development the propensity of people to emigrate has been observed not to decline, but to increase, with improvements in per capita incomes. This has led to some speculation that the economic dynamism of the Asian region would in the medium term give rise to more emigration pressures than what is being observed at present. Looming large in this concern is China because of its huge population, where a trickle might amount to a deluge to some of its neighbors. China has had over a decade and a half of rapid economic growth and per capita incomes have more than doubled during the period. Similarly significant is Indonesia, only next to China within the Asia-Pacific region in population, and also one where per capita incomes rose from very low levels in the 1970s to close to US$1000 today. The Philippines and Vietnam have both already experienced high rates of emigration in recent decades for different reasons but both still have large pools of surplus labor suggesting that despite recent economic gains their emigration potential remains large.

Emigration pressures have been observed to abate however with rapid economic growth and the question turns to whether one should foresee, if growth continues at current levels, a "migration transition" which refers to a country's transformation from being a supplier of labor to foreign countries to being an employer of foreign labor.[1] Some countries in the region have already experienced such a migration transition. It happened in Japan in the early sixties, in the Republic of Korea in the early 1980s, and it is now taking place in Malaysia and Thailand. In all these countries the transition occurred when their economies passed from a stage of surplus labor to one of full employment with real wages rising substantially all around.

ILO Studies on Emigration Pressures

Since 1990 the ILO has undertaken a number of studies to look into the question of migration pressure and in 1992 organized an international conference jointly with the UNHCR to draw the attention of the international community to the dimensions of the phenomenon and its implications for policy.[2] Actual migration flows generally reflect only the demand for foreign workers, a usually "constrained" one since there is always political resistance to letting the market decide how many people are to be allowed into one's borders. Since many more workers are seeking to obtain better employment outside their countries than the number that other countries are prepared to admit, pressures build up which often lead to illegal migration and the manifold problems for the migrants and the receiving societies.

In 1994 the ILO launched studies in four East Asian countries to look into the question of whether emigration pressures are rising and how domestic economic and social policies may be contributing to or modulating them. The countries chosen were China, Vietnam, Indonesia and the Philippines because of their importance in current labor migration flows in the sub-region.[3]

The studies aimed to provide some indication of the magnitude of emigration pressures in these countries and to identify structural and policy variables which may in one way or another be influencing them. Of particular interest was the impact, direct or indirect, of socio-economic policies such as measures to redistribute productive assets, to support agriculture with infrastructure and easier access to credit, to stimulate industrialization and to influence the geographic concentration of employment opportunities. This chapter summarizes the salient findings of these country studies and integrates them with the available evidence from other sources with a view to formulating more general conclusions about the dimensions and causes of emigration pressures.[4]

Defining Emigration Pressures

The notion of *emigration pressures* has been widely used in the literature but few have tried to give it a precise definition or to suggest quantitative measures.[5] Bohning defines it as a situation where more people want to leave a country than the countries that they wish to enter are willing to accept. His definition would mean that there is an excess supply of labor in an international labor market. Bruni and Venturini defined it as *excess supply* of labor in the presence of a negative per capita income differential. The qualification is meant to exclude wealthy countries where there may also be unemployment and underemployment (hence excess supply) but income differentials with other countries may be insignificant. The problem with this definition is that it would apply to most developing countries whereas in fact the actual incidence of migration is very minor or insignificant in some of them.

Schaeffer defined emigration pressures as the demand for opportunities by residents to leave for another country for a prolonged period of time.

Such a demand depends on the cost of migration, the characteristics of the destination country, and the migrants' expected economic, legal, and social status there relative to that at home, and other variables. Straubhaar, on the other hand, starts with the idea of restriction in defining pressure. Preferring the use of the term *migration* rather than only *emigration* pressure he defined it as the difference between migration potential and actual migration demand. Migration potential is a function of individual utility and macro factors. The individual migration utility is, in turn, a function of several factors some of which are non-economic that Straubhaar believed are more important. In theory his formulation can explain why some people would not migrate even if huge income differentials exist.

None of these attempts at defining emigration pressure have led to its actual measurement other than some notional representation of how it may have changed over time.[6] In the four country studies in Asia, the authors glossed over the question of how much emigration pressures existed. More attention was focused on how changing economic structures and the policies that gave rise to them are contributing to the successful absorption of workers in their national economies. In his study of the Philippines, Saith even questioned the notion that an excess supply of labor in the presence of negative income differential would constitute emigration pressure since it leads to the bizarre conclusion that the vast majority of the people in China or India are hankering to leave their countries in search of work.

Overview of Studies' Conclusions

Although the matter of measuring "emigration pressures" was not satisfactorily resolved, the notion itself was sufficiently intuitive to enable the authors to identify structural and policy variables that they felt determined it. A few important conclusions did emerge from the ILO country studies which merit attention.

One is that a large emigration potential remained in all the four countries. Because of their large populations and fast growing work forces it will still take some time for surplus labor to be productively absorbed in these economies. The four countries had a combined population of over 1.5 billion in 1993 and a labor force of over 840 million, of which China accounts for 78 and 79 per cent respectively. The utilization of the labor force is a difficult one to measure but estimates of the unemployed and the underemployed based on conventional definitions have reached some 170 million, or about one out of every five in the labor force. Table 1 shows that their combined labor force has been growing in recent years at 1.2 per cent or some 10.5 million more workers annually. By any reckoning these countries possess huge stocks of human resources and face daunting challenges on how to absorb them into productive employment.

A favorable global economic environment is critical to the success of these countries in coping with the challenge of labor absorption. Trade and

Table 1: Indicators of Migration Potential

	Population (millions)	ΔLF (millions)	GNP p.c.	Adult literacy %	rural-urban migration (millions)	Emig. flow (thousands)
China	1,178	12.1	$490		80 (cir. '95)	380
Indonesia	189	0.9	740	87	2.4('89–'94)	167
Vietnam	72	0.9	175			50
Philippines	69	0.7	981	93	2.5('80–'85)	720

Note: All data for 1994 except where indicated.

foreign direct investments have stimulated the rapid industrialization that is generating much of the jobs needed by their teeming populations. This was true even of the largest economy, China. For over a decade and a half from, 1979 to 1995, China's real GDP grew at an average of 9.2 per cent a year. While many factors contributed to this performance trade, which grew at 12.5 per cent a year, had certainly been a leading sector[7]. To sustain their growth, the other three countries are also dependent, if not more so, on the growth of the global market and continued flows of foreign capital.

Because economies of scale often require geographic concentration of production facilities and supporting infrastructure, the process of industrialization is, however, inherently de-stabilizing of the spatial distribution of the population. In China the massive population movement to the cities has emerged as a serious problem. Wakabayashi cited information that by 1990 some 60 to 80 million people nationwide were migrating to cities and towns every year.[8] In Vietnam Nguyen and Bandara found that economic reforms and structural changes over the past decade have increased labor mobility between industrial sectors and geographic areas. As a result the major cities like Hanoi and Ho Chi Minh City have witnessed "a burst of population growth." The studies have not demonstrated that urbanization raises emigration pressures but they all suggest that unless the trend is accompanied by rapid absorption into employment the trend towards greater internal mobility will have precisely that effect. In Saith's words "If an epicentre of high emigration pressure had to be located for that period in the Philippines, it would surely have been located in this vast pool of qualified, young aspirants but frustrated section of urban Philippines."

Another important conclusion is that the explanation for the large differences among the countries in terms of emigration pressures may lie in asset or wealth distribution and their consequences on income inequalities. In the Philippines, which had the highest rate of labor emigration, Saith noted an extremely high degree of landlessness among rural workers.[9] Together with anti-agricultural bias in macroeconomic policies, this structural problem has been the cause of heavy rural-urban migration flows and intensified labor market crowding. These would have worked together to create strong emigration pressures had it not been for the existence of opportunities for releasing them provided by the demand for foreign labor in the Middle East and later in the neighboring East Asian NICs. In Vietnam and China, the levels of absolute poverty were much more severe but inequalities did not arise on account of the maldistribution of land (agriculture was collectivized).[10] The disparities took the form of large differences in regional incomes, as in the large income differentials between China's coastal and interior provinces.

In their pursuit of more rapid growth and development the four States have employed a wide range of policies which are not neutral in their effects on emigration pressures. There are dangers in drawing quick conclusions from a cursory review of these policies, many of which have impacts that are, in the first instance, largely shaped by conditions specific to a country. There seems to be agreement, however, that some are more likely than others to worsen emigration pressures. These include spending policies which are urban-biased and neglect the rural economy, inward-looking industrialization policies especially those favoring early investments in capital-intensive heavy industries, and inflationary fiscal and monetary measures. The lack of policy may have the same effects such as neglect of the environment, tolerating inequities in asset and income distribution, and failure to restrain population growth.

Finally, all the four countries have active policies for sending workers abroad which could, in principle, make a difference to releasing emigration pressures. State intervention in emigration processes have tended, however, to have the effect of constraining rather than facilitating emigration. By raising the transaction costs of migrating for employment, states might be unwittingly making the supply of labor less elastic to wage stimulus from abroad. In this sense the impact of such interventions may be negative on emigration pressures.

Recent Migration Flows

Since the 1980s a small proportion of the workforce of these countries have gained entry into the labor markets of Japan and the Asian NIEs, as well as in the Middle East. Reported gross labor emigration flows from the four countries together reached 1.3 million in 1993 which is large compared with levels in the 1970s or early 1980s and is growing at a much faster rate than the growth of their respective labor forces. Starting from a negligible level in the 1970s, aggregate labor emigration is today already equivalent to more than 12 per cent of the total yearly addition to their combined labor force.

1)   *China*. Labor emigration flows from China were estimated by Huang at roughly 380,000 a year during the last two years, hardly a significant

number when viewed as a proportion of the country's total workforce but large when seen in terms of labor outflows during the 1960s to the 1980s. They comprise about 50,000 workers who settle permanently in another country through sponsorship by relatives; 250,000 who are sent to work abroad under the employ of Chinese corporations or recruited by them for foreign employers; about 75,000 who leave to work abroad without proper documents; and a few thousand who work abroad in connection with some Chinese investments. Highly organized migration through the overseas contracting activities of Chinese construction companies thus appears very important in the recent flows. At the beginning most of the workers brought out were in the employ of the Chinese companies, but lately the growth has been accounted for by the activities of many newly-licensed provincial corporations and local cooperatives who act as recruiters for foreign employers.

The region of origin of the emigrants, according to Huang, has perceptibly shifted to the coastal regions of China. This was revealed by the 1990 population census which, like the 1982 census, included a question on whether the household has members working abroad. Whereas regional differences were not notable in 1982, a bias in favor of the eastern provinces especially the major cities became apparent from the latter census. The total population of the eastern region reported to be overseas rose from 30,300 in 1982 to 194,900 in 1990. The regional bias of emigration reflects three factors which are evidently at play. One is the fact that the eastern provinces of China had a long history of emigration. Many of the Chinese in Southeast Asia originated from Guangdong, Fujian, Shandong, Zhejiang, and Hainan provinces. The second is the higher human capital stock of the region compared to the central and western regions. And thirdly, income levels are higher in the eastern region compared to the others.[11]

2) *Indonesia.* In Indonesia, as in China, labor emigration is a growing phenomenon but not a significant one for the absorption of its huge labor force. In 1990 recorded labor outflows amounted to 6 per cent of the increment in the workforce. There are no official estimates of the total stock of Indonesian workers abroad but it is most unlikely that their numbers would exceed 1.5 million, or barely 2 per cent of the country's labor force. What is significant however is the rate of growth of labor emigration which appears to have been quite high during the past decade and it is probably going to accelerate in the future because of economic development in the region.

Actual emigration from Indonesia is just as difficult to estimate as in China because a very large part of the outflows are clandestine movements. Studies by other scholars confirm what is well known that considerable labor emigration flows from Indonesia, especially to Sabah and West Malaysia, never get reported or recorded either in Indonesia or in Malaysia because they do not pass through official channels.[12] Recorded flows to Malaysia, for example, for the ten-year period between 1984 and 1993 totalled less than 180,000 but illegal Indonesian workers who came out and registered in 1992 in response to the amnesty offer by the Malaysian authorities reached close to half a million. If one were to disregard the outflows to Malaysia, the *recorded* labor emigration is probably a true reflection of the migration to other destinations. During the period *recorded* labor emigration from Indonesia to all destinations, except Malaysia, rose at a compound annual rate of about 15 per cent a year. If outflows to Malaysia are included the rate is probably much higher. In contrast the total labor force has been growing at about 2.7 per cent a year.

Nayyar did not attempt an estimate of the emigration potential from Indonesia, but the growth of reported emigration flows indicates very strongly that labor supply is very responsive to opportunities for emigration.

A very large proportion of both official and unreported flows appear to originate from the country's eastern provinces which have the highest incidence of poverty such as East and West Nusa Tenggara, Timur, South Sulawesi, and East Java. There has, for example, been a long history of emigration from Nusa Tenggara which, according to Hugo (1996), has the highest incidence of poverty among Indonesia's 27 provinces. Per capita GDP in East Flores was only around $220 in 1993.

Most of Indonesian labor emigrants are unskilled who are recruited to work as domestic workers mostly in the Middle East and neighboring Southeast Asian countries, as plantation workers in Malaysia, and as transportation and construction laborers in the Middle East and Southeast Asia. The proportions are difficult to ascertain because of the size of the clandestine flows but it is widely observed that domestic workers comprise over half of the total number of emigrants. The official records indicate anywhere from 65 to 70 per cent. Young women comprise a very large proportion of these flows since domestic helpers are almost all female.

3) **Vietnam.** Vietnam is one of the region's poorest countries with per capita income of only US$175. As much as 40 per cent of all Vietnamese households spend less than $400 a year and almost half of the entire population earn an annual per capita income of $75 or less. At this level of development the emigration potential would not normally be expected to be high, but an earlier history of large refugee migration has created anchors for chain migration in a large overseas population. There were about 425,000 Vietnamese admitted as refugees in the United States and are now settled there permanently, over a hundred thousand each in Canada and Australia, and another hundred thousand in Western Europe.

Table 2: Determinants of Emigration Pressures

	China	Indonesia (1990)	Vietnam (1992)	Philippines
Income (GNP p.c. 1980–92)	7.6	4.0		-1.0
Unemployment	2.8	3.2	17.3	8.6
Underemployment	20	22.5		19.9
Poverty (below poverty line)	65 mil	27 mil	37 mil	27 mil
Inequality (Gini coefficient)	0.296	0.32		0.45
Urbanization (1990) % of pop.	33.4	30.5	21.9	42.6
Income differential vis a vis Japan — ratio of p.c. GDPs (ppp)	6.6x	7.1x	15.5x	7.9x
Political instability	medium	medium	low	medium

According to official statistics the emigration of labor peaked in 1988 at 72,000 but the numbers quickly declined thereafter because of the political changes in the destination countries, namely the former U.S.S.R. and the then East Germany. This peak figure is undoubtedly a poor indicator of the emigration potential in the country for at least two reasons. The first is because it does not take into account migration to the neighboring states like Cambodia which became short of all types of skilled labor following the genocide under the Khmer Rouge in the mid to late 1970s. Emigration to other destinations was tightly controlled by the State. It was almost totally destined for Eastern Europe and the former U.S.S.R., and was fully organized by the Government of Vietnam in what amounted to a barter in exchange for the country's imports of capital equipment and consumer goods from these socialist states. At the turn of the 1990s, nearly two hundred thousand Vietnamese contract workers returned from Eastern Europe and the former U.S.S.R. after the labor agreements were abrogated in the aftermath of the political and economic changes in those countries.

4) **Philippines.** Of the countries under study the Philippines is probably the one where actual emigration comes closest to its emigration potential. From about 134,000 in 1984 recorded gross emigration of temporary contract labor, including seafarers, reached a peak of 301,000 in 1991 for the so-called "new-hires" while another 188,000 left for abroad as re-hires. Permanent immigration to the United States, Canada, and Australia reached 63,000 in 1991 of which 32 per cent were reported to have employment. Unrecorded flows perhaps represent another 30,000. Altogether they represented over half of the yearly addition to the labor

force.[13] The volume of outflows of circulating contract workers recorded by the authorities as "new hires" started receding in 1992 and was down to 207,000 in 1996.

The Filipino contract workers come disproportionately from a few regions, most of them on the richer end of the scale. These are the national capital region, the Southern Tagalog Region, Central Luzon, and the Ilocos. From the Family Income and Expenditures Survey of 1991 Saith noted that the representation of the lowest income classes is very low, but it rises sharply at the upper end of the income scale. Whereas one in six families among the richest class has a member working overseas, only one out of every 66 families among the poorest income class has one.

In terms of occupations the Philippines was different from the other three countries in the fact that professionals accounted for a fairly significant proportion of the contract migrants. One out of five went abroad to work as professionals, technical, and managerial workers in the mid 1980s. The distribution progressively became bi-modal in terms of skills as the demand shifted to service workers especially domestic helpers. Recent years have seen a growing feminization of the flows characterized by lower education-skill profile and the poorer regions as their origin. In his study Saith noted that the shift took place around 1988 when the incremental share of the richer regions became much lower than their average share. The much faster expansion in numbers from 1988 to 1991 "pushed the contours of recruitment into the poorer provinces."[14]

Supply-side Push Factors

The country studies identified a number of push-factors which are behind the emigration pressures in the countries studied. Table 2 shows some of the indicators of these push factors. Among these the most important are:

- large reserves of labor and unemployment;
- landlessness, poverty and income inequality;
- high rates of rural-urban migration; environmental degradation;
- reforms during economic transition;
- political instability.

1) *Labor Reserves and Unemployment.* China's labor force has been growing relatively slowly (below 1.5 per cent a year since 1990) but because of its absolute size (721 million in 1992) the numbers are still very large. For example, between 1983 and 1992 almost 138 million more workers joined the labor force. The period saw very rapid economic expansion and employment in China rose by 28 per cent against a labor force growth of 23 per cent. But the reorganization of agriculture with the dismantling of the peoples' communes and reforms in the state sector industries re-

vealed large stocks of surplus labor. Some 16 million workers of the state sector industries are estimated to have become redundant, while the surplus labor in agriculture is frequently placed at about 100 million. Huang estimated that unemployment and underemployment together still account for about 20 per cent of China's labor force.

Indonesia's labor force rose by some 17.4 million workers between 1985 and 1994 and at the end of that period stood at about 81.2 million. Thanks to rapid economic growth the economy was able to absorb this huge increase in numbers. Some 3.3 million more Indonesian workers were employed in manufacturing during the period which also saw wage employment growing at the rate of 6 per cent a year. Nayyar found however that economic development has so far not enabled Indonesia to make a transition from a labor surplus economy to full employment notwithstanding unemployment rates of 1.6 per cent. As evidence of this he points to the stagnation in real wages in the agricultural and manufacturing sectors during the 1980s. Much of the labor surplus is apparently hidden in the large percentage of workers (about 23 per cent who are working less than 25 hours a week) who are classified as underemployed.

Vietnam has one of the highest rates of population growth among the Asian countries and one of the highest population density rates in Southeast Asia. Although the official rate of unemployment was reported at 8.3 per cent the Ministry of Labor estimated that in 1992 about 17.2 per cent of the population of working age (or roughly about 7 million) were in one form of unemployment or another. A 1989 report by the General Statistics Office revealed that the problem was especially severe for young urban workers, among whom some 45.7 per cent of the age group 15 to 19 years and 19.8 per cent of the group 20 to 24 years were reported to be unemployed. As the proportion of the population of working age continued to rise, the rate of growth of the labor force increased from 2.1 per cent a year in the 1970s to 2.8 per cent in the 1980s and 3.3 per cent a year in the early 1990s. These compare with employment growth of only 2.1 per cent a year. Employment in the state sector declined from 3.86 million to 2.93 million employees between 1985 and 1994 as a consequence of economic re-structuring.

Three further developments have aggravated the problem. One is the demobilization of about half a million soldiers between 1989 and 1990, and a further 140,000 annually in the years that followed. Another is the return of about 200,000 migrant workers from Eastern Bloc countries and the Middle East in the aftermath of the Iraqi invasion of Kuwait.

In the Philippines the push factors were certainly very strong especially during the period 1980 to 1992. The period saw a severe economic crisis in the country during which per capita GDP fell by 1.0

per cent on the average every year. Reflecting survival strategies, the average Filipino "worked more in order to retain his or her claim to a shrinking pie." Employment figures actually showed a growth rate of 3.6 per cent a year, and unemployment and underemployment fell from 9.4 to 8.6 per cent, and from 25.5 to 19.8 per cent, respectively. The country's economic recovery since 1992 has greatly improved the employment picture, with more workers absorbed in the formal sectors of the economy even if aggregate employment only rose moderately.

Unemployment is foreseen to remain high in the Philippines for many years to come even with rapid growth. Projections made for the Medium Term Philippine Development Plan indicate that even if investments were to rise from 25.8 per cent of GDP in 1995 to 29.5 per cent in 1998 and these were to raise GDP growth from 6.2 per cent to 9.8 per cent, unemployment rates would still be at the level of 6.6 per cent (about 2.1 million workers). If a lower growth rate of GDP were assumed (8.1 per cent in 1998) unemployment rates would continue at the same level as in the early 1990s.

2) *Landlessness, poverty and income inequality.* At very low levels of income propensities to emigrate are probably very weak, so measures of poverty may not provide much help in assessing emigration pressures. However, significant improvements in income might, at certain stages, be meaningful indicators of growing capacities of people to invest in migration. Similarly, income inequalities within a country may not have any effect on propensities of people to emigrate. But where inequalities are along regional lines they do serve as the stimulus to internal migration which in some instances pave the way for emigration.

In China the last decade and a half have seen dramatic improvements in reducing the number of people considered poor. The State Council defined the poverty line for households as those receiving less than 200 yuan and staple food of 200 kg per annum. This definition perhaps understates the true number of poor people in China but it is nevertheless useful to compare the changes over time. At the end of 1985 the poor population was estimated at 102 million. In 1988, when the poverty line was adjusted to 260 yuan, the poor were estimated at 120 million. By 1995 the poor population had been brought down to 65 million.[15]

Rural-urban income differentials narrowed very substantially from 1978 to 1984, according to Huang, when agriculture led the economic reform. In that period the ratio of disposable income between urban residents and farmers dropped from 2.4 to 1.7. However, the income gap widened again thereafter and reached 2.6 in 1994. Generally, the income distribution was more equal in the urban than in the rural areas reflecting the impact of delayed reform and growth of the urban economy. The inequalities in income widened particularly dramatically between regions, notably between the coastal and the interior provinces.

In the case of Vietnam, data on trends in poverty and income distribution are unfortunately very scarce. A recent study (World Bank, 1995) found that 51 per cent of the population could be classified as poor if the poverty line was drawn at 1.09 million Vietnamese Dong (almost $100) per person per year. There are no similar studies done for earlier years with which these statistics can be compared. As far as regional inequalities are concerned, the World Bank study did reveal that large income differentials existed between the poorest regions and the rest of the country. In the North Central region the poverty incidence was as high as 71 per cent, and in the Northern Upland, as high as 59 per cent.

In Indonesia Nayyar reported that, contrary to trends observed elsewhere, rapid economic growth led to a sharp reduction in absolute poverty. The Household Expenditure Surveys revealed that the proportion of the rural population living below the poverty line declined from 40.4 per cent in 1976 to 14.3 per cent in 1990. For the urban population the decline was from 38.8 per cent to 16.8 per cent. In absolute numbers that meant that those classified as being poor went down from 54.2 million in 1976 to 27.2 million in 1990. The Gini coefficient estimated from the distribution of consumption expenditures went down from 0.35 in 1970 to 0.34 in 1980 and 0.32 in 1990. The share of the poorest 20 per cent of the population also increased from 6.9 per cent in 1970, to 7.7 per cent in 1980, and 8.9 per cent in 1990. Unfortunately, Nayyar did not say what has happened to regional income disparities. Some cursory information available from other studies such as Hugo (1995) suggest that large income differentials do exist between Java and the outlying islands.

3) **Rural Urban Migration.** The studies do not offer evidence that urbanization contributes to emigration pressures but do suggest, as Skeldon does, that international movements diffuse down through the urban hierarchy.[16] Cities draw people from the rural areas who then are drawn to the metropolitan centres, and from there to foreign countries. Skeldon observed that in the early stages of international contract labor migration from Asia, most of the migrants did come from the largest cities. How has urbanization proceeded in the countries under study?

As noted earlier, China has experienced a very rapid rate of urbanization since the turn of the 1980s. The reported proportion of the Chinese population in urban areas jumped from 20.8 per cent in mid-1982 to 36.9 per cent in mid-1987 (Zeng and Vaupel, 1989) reflecting rural to urban migration of a massive scale.[17] This has been attributed to the effects of China's economic reforms and the relaxation of the household registration system. In 1987 China was estimated to already have a "floating population" of some 62 million in 7 major cities.[18] Over the long-term the growing urbanization of Chinese population should contribute to further reducing fertility rates as more and more young people who migrate to urban areas adopt urban values and lifestyles. In 1986 the total fertility rate (TFR) in rural areas was 2.72 compared to 1.96 in the urban areas based on the 1987 One Per cent Population Survey.[19] From the same survey it was found that the TFR of women who reported their occupation as agricultural was 2.76 in contrast to 1.24 for those whose occupation was non-agricultural.

So far there have been no studies in China which can shed light on this possible linkage of domestic spatial mobility with external migration, but one can draw insights from studies of domestic migration. Drawing on the results of the 1986 National Migration Survey[20] Xiushi Yang analysed the dramatic rise of temporary migration in Zhejiang Province. He looked at whether the propensity to move temporarily was determined by certain individual and household characteristics, and whether the same factors determined the frequency of movement. He found that sex, educational attainment and prior migration experience have significant implications for multiple movements. Other things being equal, the probability of moving more than once is 14.4 percentage points higher among males than females; 5.0 percentage points higher with improvement in educational attainment by one level; and 7.4 percentage points higher among people with prior migration experience.

As in China, the economic reforms in Vietnam have "loosened the restrictions on such (rural to urban) mobility."[22] There are available estimates of the extent of internal migration but unfortunately what have been reported are the inter-provincial movements, not rural urban flows. It is well known however that populations of cities like Ho Chi Minh, Hai- phong and Hanoi have rapidly expanded in recent years. Movements have also been very notable from the uplands to the Red River Delta and the provinces of Lam Dong, Dac Lac, and Vung Tau-Con Dao.

In Indonesia Hugo observed the increasing tempo of urbanization in the last two decades compared to the previous five.[23] Indonesia's urban population swelled from 20 million in 1970 to 55.4 million in 1990. The growth rate rose from 3.6 per cent a year in the 1960s to 5.4 per cent in the 1970s and 1980s. Government efforts to counteract this tendency and spread the population away from densely populated Java to the frontier regions have evidently been unsuccessful.

In the Philippines there have also been very heavy internal migrations, both intra-rural as well as inter-sectoral. In the 1970s and early 1980s the major movements were to the frontier regions of the north and of Mindanao, but over the period 1980 to 1990 these movements, according to Saith, weakened while the shift to the National Capital Region (Metro Manila) increased. The main direction of the flows of migrants from the rural areas has been towards Manila, and to a much lesser extent, to the other developed regions. Saith noted a very significant "dualistic" pattern in labor migration where domestic migration involves shifts from poorer to the richer regions, but not abroad, and a separate one from the richer regions to overseas destinations.

The data from the National Income and Expenditures Surveys (which also obtained information on incomes received from abroad) disprove the assumption frequently made that migration to the metropolitan centre, namely Manila, is simply "transit" before moving on to overseas destinations. Saith observed that recipients of remittance incomes were largely from the richer regions. If the migrants were really just using Manila and its neighboring rich regions as stepping stones, then, argued Saith, one should expect families in the poorer regions to receive higher rates of income from abroad than they actually do.

4) *Economic Policies and Reforms.* The speed and nature of the development process and the strategies used to hasten it evidently have an impact on emigration pressures. It is clear that successful development has, as in the case of the Republic of Korea, eased the propensity of people to emigrate and led to an early "migration transition," transforming a country from being an exporter to an importer of labor. What is less clear is whether certain kinds of development policies are more likely than others to stimulate emigration even if they have the same impact on the rate of economic growth. For example, an agricultural surplus could be generated either by promoting plantation agriculture or alternatively by supporting owner-cultivated farms. The former may lead however to earlier mechanization or the substitution of capital for labor than the latter. Similarly, some industrialization strategies may contribute more to emigration pressures when they, for instance, create biases in locational choice (e.g. in subsidized special economic zones). Income distribution policies which take a variety of forms and modalities (from land reform to credit policies, taxation/subsidies, and public expenditures) directly affect motivations to migrate or emigrate, or to stay at home.

In Table 3 we attempt a summary of the impact of state policies on emigration pressures. Do policies contribute to (+) or help reduce (-) emigration pressures? Is the impact of the policy likely to be felt in the short-run (sr) or in the long-run (lr)? The list of policies identified is evidently not exhaustive, partly because we had no information on some and partly because some policies are expected to have only a very indirect or weak impact on emigration pressures. However, it is useful to have a more holistic view of the relevance of the state on emigration pressures than what one can get by looking at individual policies.

Systemic change impacts on emigration pressures because of the way they affect the social organization of production and the distribution of the product. In China and Vietnam these have meant the dismantling of the planning apparatus for centralized allocation of resources, decollectivization of agriculture, allowing private enterprise in some sectors, and greater autonomy to the management of state enterprises. In our view these policy shifts have contributed significantly to emigration pressures. The shift to the market economy has revealed huge pools of underemployed labor in the State sector and inevitably to massive job-shedding. In China it was estimated that 15 per cent of the work force of the State sector, about 16 million workers, was redundant. In Vietnam, close to a million workers were thrown out of jobs because of the restructuring in the State sector. Fortunately the impact on unemployment has not been as large as these figures suggest because of the growth of the private economy.

In both countries the shift to a market economy has also meant progressive abandonment of the "iron rice bowl" system which guaranteed life-long employment and all basic needs which have served in the past to lock in people to their economic units and thus kept in check all forms of labor migration.

Many policies affect population growth and its spatial distribution. In Table 3 are shown simply those policies that affect fertility such as family planning program, policies on rural urban migration, and schemes to redistribute the population such as Indonesia's *transmigrasi* program. It is extremely difficult to isolate the impact of population policies on other factors which influence fertility rates but it is undeniable that in China the one-child policy introduced in the early 1970s has brought down the rate of growth of the population. It is now having a palpable impact on the growth of the labor force which declined from high levels in the 1980s to under 1.5 per cent per annum by the early 1990s. Perhaps more importantly from the standpoint of migration pressure is the ageing of China's labor force. Over the two decades from 1990 to 2010 the proportion of young workers (15 to 39 years old) in China's labor force is projected to decline from 60.3 per cent to 44.6 per cent.

Although none of the other three countries took the drastic population control measures that China adopted, they all have population control programs which may be affecting the growth rate of their populations. The Philippines probably has the weakest program of all the four countries. Overall rates of population growth did go down to about 2 per cent a year in the Philippines and Vietnam and even lower in Indonesia. However, the growth rates of their labor forces remain high and can be expected to continue influencing emigration pressures positively in the medium term. Vietnam, for example, has a very young population with only 6.2 per cent of the male and 8.2 per cent of the female population over 60 years of age. About 52.5 per cent of the male and 55 per cent of the female population are in the working ages between 15 and 59 years, and 41.3 per cent and 36.8 per cent, respectively, below 14 years.

Table 3: State Policies Affecting Emigration pressures

Policy Area	China		Indonesia		Vietnam		Philippines	
Economic system								
Shift to a market-oriented economy	++	(lr)	n.a.		++	(lr)	n.a.	
Private enterprise/reform of state sector	+	(lr)	n.a.		+	(lr)	n.a.	
Population								
Population control measures	---	(lr)	---	(lr)	-	(lr)	-	(lr)
Policies on rural-urban migration	-	(lr)	-	(lr)	--	(lr)		
Subsidized migration to frontier provinces								
Agricultural and rural development								
Organization of agricultural/land distribution	-	(lr)	+	(lr)	---	(lr)	+++	(lr)
Rural industrialization	---	(lr)	-	(lr)	-	(lr)	-	(lr)
Pricing of agricultural products	+++	(sr)			--	(sr)	--	(sr)
Exchange rate policy affecting exports	+	(sr)	--	(sr)	--	(sr)	+	(sr)
Tariff protection	+	(sr)	--	(sr)			--	(sr)
Agricultural credit			-	(sr)			-	(sr)
Industrialization								
Tax incentives for export/labor intensive industries	---	(sr)	---	(sr)	---	(sr)	---	(sr)
Industry location/free trade zones	+++	(lr)	++	(lr)	++	(lr)	--	(lr)
Foreign direct investments	---	(lr)	---	(lr)	---	(lr)	---	(lr)
Restructuring of state enterprises	++	(sr)	n.a.		++	(sr)	n.a.	
Technology development	+++	(lr)						
Tariff protection	++	(sr)	++	(sr)	++	(sr)	++	(sr)
Labor market and human resource development								
Restricted labor mobility in domestic market	---	(lr)	n.a.		---	(lr)	n.a.	
Subsidies to tertiary education	++	(lr)	+	(lr)	+	(lr)	++	(lr)
Collective bargaining/trade unionism	--	(lr)	++	(lr)	-	(lr)	--	(lr)
Social safety nets/security	---	(lr)	-	(lr)	---	(lr)	-	(lr)
Foreign employment policy	+++	(lr)	+++	(lr)	+++	(lr)	+++	(lr)
Wealth and income distribution								
Land holding in agriculture	+(sr)--(lr)				---	(lr)	+++	(lr)
Wage policy	+++	(lr)	+++	(lr)	+++	(lr)	--	(lr)
Taxation of profits	--	(lr)	-	(lr)	--	(lr)	-	(lr)

Policies which raise labor absorption in agriculture should, *ceteris paribus*, also help reduce the push pressures behind migration. These include the policies on land tenure or land ownership policies, agrarian reform, (de)-collectivization of agriculture, exchange rate policies which affect returns to agricultural exports, pricing and credit policies, investments in irrigation and storage, the propagation of high-yielding crop varieties, agricultural extension, farm to market road networks, and rural industrialization schemes linking industries to farms, among others. The four studies did not systematically go into these issues but did touch on the impact of each country's policies on agricultural productivity. In China and Vietnam the reforms in agriculture have had an immediate impact on raising agricultural productivity. Vietnam, for instance, has developed large surpluses in rice production and emerged in recent years as the third largest exporter of rice in the world.

In China the productivity gains from the introduction of the Household Responsibility System may be short-lived however. Huang believes that land fragmentation is unfavorable for the adoption of modern techniques and commercialization of the agricultural sector. He also fears that the weakening of collective management may already have led to deterioration of agricultural infrastructure such as irrigation.

When there were still strict barriers to labor migration between rural and urban areas and across regions those who quit agricultural production set up industrial or service industries. In some areas the development of such township, village and private sector enterprises (TVPs) have been very successful, as in the coastal provinces. These enterprises are now reported to employ some 125 million rural workers, or about 28 per cent of all rural workers and have become one of the major sources of additional income for farmers. The output of these enterprises was reported to have grown at an annual rate of 27 per cent between 1984 and 1995. In 1995 the rural enterprises already accounted for nearly a third of China's GDP.

TVPs have mixed effects on emigration pressure in a rural economy but the overall impact is generally negative. It may have contributed negatively because it generated huge employment opportunities and provided higher or more stable incomes. Huang however suspects that it might also induce greater migration flows from the less successful to the more successful regions. Some provinces with successful experiences in the development of the TVP sector, such as Guangdong, Fujian, Jiangsu, Zhejiang and Shandong have in fact become major importers of labor coming from the central and western regions.

In the Philippines the failure of land reform has evident long-term consequences on the ability of agriculture to absorb the labor force. Table 3 shows positive impact on emigration pressures. Moreover, as Saith noted, several studies indicate that over the last two decades there has been a noticeable disinvestment in agriculture. This was the consequence of fiscal and monetary policies which supported an earlier regime of import substitution. High tariff protection for industrial goods plus, for a time, an overvalued exchange rate, caused a shift in the terms of trade against agriculture in favor of industry. Special tax levies on some exports like coconut products further compounded the bias against the sector.

The tariff protection policies for agriculture cause inefficiencies and in the long-run probably have adverse effects on emigration pressures, but in the short-run they do protect jobs in these countries. On the other hand, the agriculture sector does suffer from overvalued exchange rates and frequently from price-fixing policies of the state.

Some policies had a more direct impact on migration pressures because they deliberately aimed at fostering industrialization in a few regions ahead of the others. In China the policy of inviting foreign equity capital into certain special economic zones in the coastal provinces has led to unbalanced growth, creating large income disparities between the coastal and the interior provinces and thus inducing migration. The authorities had no choice but to relax earlier restrictions on people leaving their villages in search of jobs in the eastern coastal cities.

A worsening of income distribution would be expected to have on balance a positive effect on emigration pressures. Available evidence on the experience of the four countries seems to suggest that despite rapid growth (or probably because of it) income distribution has become less equal over the last decade. In the China study Huang cited other research which found rising Gini coefficient between 1981 and 1988 from 0.26 to 0.3.[23] Huang himself suspects that the income distribution became much less equal during the early 1990s especially in the urban areas.

Finally, the studies considered labor market policies especially the development of institutions for exporting labor. All the countries have adopted policies to send workers abroad to alleviate unemployment and to earn foreign exchange. The Philippines and Indonesia have from the very beginning left the organization of migration to the private sector because they were seen to be more effective in developing markets abroad. Their Governments however have taken measures to protect the migrant workers against recruitment abuses and exploitative employment. While China and Vietnam have not relinquished the function to the private sector, both are progressively liberalizing their policies to expand their respective labor exports. They now permit more state and township enterprises to engage in recruitment for employment abroad and actively seek out potential markets through their large contracting corporations.

Endnotes

[1] See Amjad, R., 1996, "Philippines and Indonesia: On the way to a migration transition?" *Asia Pacific Migration Journal* 5 (2–3). Also Abella, M., ed., 1994, "Turning Points in Labor Migration," Special issue of *Asian and Pacific Migration Journal* 3 (1).

[2] For a discussion of the key issues see Bohning,W. R. and M.L. Schloeter-Paredes (1994), *Aid in place of migration*, Geneva: ILO.

[3] The four studies on structural change and emigration pressures were by Yiping Huang on China, Deepak Nayyar on Indonesia, D. T. Nguyen and J. S. Bandara on Vietnam, and Ashwani Saith on the Philippines. This paper quotes extensively from their reports which are not yet published.

[4] In a still unpublished paper, Skeldon also draws on the four studies to review demographic and other developments in the region and their possible implications on emigration.

[5] See Bohning, Schaeffer, and Straubhaar, 1991; Bruni and Venturini, 1992.

[6] Straubhaar illustrated the dramatic increase of the Turkish migration potential since 1960 using some highly stylized facts.

[7] Foreign direct investment inflows to China grew by leaps and bounds from less than $400 million in 1981 to about $4.4 billion in 1991, raising the contribution of foreign savings flows to gross domestic capital formation from only 0.08 per cent in 1976–1980 to 2.3 per cent in the period 1986–1991.

[8] See Wakabayashi, K., 509.

[9] It was estimated that fifty per cent of rural workers are landless. Sharp inequality was also notable in the distribution of total cultivated farm land. See C. David, "Philippine agriculture: The difficult path to recovery," *Philippine Economic Journal* 31 (72): Nos. 1 & 2.

[10] The World Bank estimated that 51 per cent of Vietnam's population were poor — they earned less than US$100 a year.

[11] Higher income is favorable to international migration. Huang examined the statistical relationship between regional income levels and emigration. He found that for 1990, the correlation coefficient between provincial per capita income and total population overseas is 0.87 and that between per capita income and the share of population overseas is 0.89.

[12] In one province alone, East Nusa Tenggara, Hugo estimates that up to 100,000 workers may be employed overseas. See Hugo, 1996.

[13] The more relevant comparison should of course be with net labor emigration after all returns have been taken into account, but information on return flows is not available. But even if one assumes that returning emigrants number half of the gross figure, emigration would still represent a large proportion of the total annual increment to the labor force.

[14] The Special Survey of Overseas Contract Workers by the National Statistics Office (1991) provides systematic data, for the first time, on the regional origins of contract workers. Saith compared the findings with earlier studies notably by Jayme (See Jayme, R., 1979, "A study on the effects of temporary worker flows from the Philippines," MA thesis, Univ. of the Philippines).

[15] The poor population was reduced by 5 million in 1995 alone, according to the State Council. See Huang, Yiping, 1996.

[16] See Skeldon, Ronald, "The relationship between migration and development in the ESCAP Region," in *Migration and urbanization in Asia and the Pacific: Interrelationships with socio-economic development and evolving policy issues*, ESCAP Asian Population Studies series No. 111, Bangkok.

[17] Zeng and Vaupel did point out that due to administrative changes in the classification of areas as urban and rural a substantial part of the increase may be a statistical artifact. See p. 427.

[18] See Wakabayashi, K., 1990, "Migration from rural to urban areas in China," *The Developing Economies* 28 (4) (December).

[19] The One Per Cent Population Survey was conducted by the State Statistical Bureau in July 1987. Some 10,711,652 persons were surveyed, covering all provinces, autonomous regions, and municipalities.

[20] This was a major study of internal migration sponsored by the Population Research Institute at the Chinese Academy of Social Sciences with the support of the UN Population Fund.

[21] See Xiushi Yang, "Temporary migration and its frequency from urban households in China," *Asia-Pacific Population Journal* 7 (1): 44.

[22] See Nguyen and Bandara, 21.

[23] See Hugo, G., "Migration and rural-urban linkages in the ESCAP region," in *Migration and urbanization in Asia and the Pacific: Interrelationships with socio-economic development and evolving policy issues*, ESCAP Asian Population Studies series No. 111, Bangkok.

12 From Multiculturalism to Diaspora: Changing Identities in the Context of Asian Migration

Ronald Skeldon

Just as the real patterns of international migration have changed over recent years, so too have our interpretations of that migration. When emigration was dominated by movements out of Europe, and particularly from the United Kingdom and Ireland, towards North and South America and Australasia, the concerns were very different from those of the late twentieth century when international migration is much more complex, involving peoples from a much greater range of backgrounds, races and cultures. Although migration has not ceased from European sources, its character has changed, and Europe has emerged as an area of net immigration rather than of marked emigration. International movements in the global system towards the main destination societies in North America and Australasia have come to be dominated by movements from Asia and Latin America. In part, this transformation of the global migration system is associated with the demographic transition: the persistent low fertility in Europe has meant that there are fewer people in the cohorts most liable to migrate. On the other hand, those societies where fertility is highest, in sub-Saharan Africa, participate only tenuously in the global migration system and the changing origins of movement can be better understood in terms of the nature of the economic and political linkages between origins and destinations.

Immigration: Assimilation and Multiculturalism

When European peoples dominated the international flows, the concerns were more towards assimilation. The creation of a new national identity from the many old identities of the immigrant populations is captured in the motto of the seal of the United States which symbolizes the melting-pot of the American dream. Canada and Australia, as part of the then British Empire and later the Commonwealth, had much closer political, as well as social and cultural, ties with Britain. These self-governing parts of a wider polity never saw the same need to create a "new" and separate identity, although the ready assimilation of immigrants was the overt policy direction in the creation of essentially white societies (see Troper 1993 and Jupp 1995). Unlike the United States, with its long tradition of a separate identity, these Commonwealth nations reacted to the new migrations from Asian, Latin American and Caribbean origins by adopting policies of multiculturalism:

"Multiculturalism as an area of public policy can be defined as the official recognition by governments, expressed in legislation and/or in speeches and programmes, of the many different ethnic origins of their present population, combined with the stated intention to protect and assist those who are not members of the founding majority or charter groups. It emphasizes cultural freedom, social justice, and equality of opportunity for all within the existing political system" (Hawkins 1989: 214).

Multiculturalism has guided official immigration policy in Canada and Australia since the early to mid-1970s and, in New Zealand, from about a decade later. It was a logical continuation of the shifts in policy that had progressively dismantled the racist immigration controls from the end of the Second World War and the triumph of liberal democratic regimes. Exclusionary policies, or policies that might favor one ethnic or cultural group over another, were clearly incompatible with the ideals of liberal democracies. Multiculturalism also provided a moral high ground for states in international forums such as the United Nations. Its weakness, however, if it is indeed a weakness, is that a clear concept of a unique national identity remains obscure. The United States, on the other hand, while doing away with racist immigration policies, has persisted with the assimilationist ideal in the face of the increasingly diverse origins of its immigrants. The vigorous debate on recent American immigration avers that a "salad bowl" or a "mosaic," rather than a melting-pot, more accurately describes American society. These images presumably reflect a type of de facto multiculturalism. (See also Glazer1997, who argues, rhetorically, that "we are all multiculturalists now"). Recent research suggests, however, that much of the new migration might fit neither the assimilationist nor the multiculturalist ideals. The primary focus of this chapter is to examine some of this research in the context of one of the new regions of origin of international migration, Asia, and to consider the policy implications not only for the destination societies but also for the origin areas in Asia.

The Emergence of Diaspora as a Concern

Over the last decade, the word "diaspora" has come to such prominence in the field of international migration studies that it has virtually come to displace the word "migration" altogether: all international migrations now seem to be diasporas. Until about ten years ago, diaspora was rarely used outside the context of Jewish migration. Its meaning was clear. It indicated an expulsion on such a scale that the majority of a people, a nation, were outside their homeland. They were a people in exile, wandering alien lands with the dream of going home. The Jews were not alone, however. Other groups could be considered to have been forced out of their homelands, the Armenians and the Palestinians being among the most notable examples. Nevertheless, the word came to be associated with the Chinese, even though the majority of the Chinese living overseas had not been forced from their homes and only a tiny minority of Chinese lived outside their homeland. The rationale here was that the Chinese were sojourners, living in alien lands with the hope that one day they would go home. The vast majority of migrants from China in the second half of the nineteenth century were males who had either left their families in China or hoped to return to marry, thus giving some substance to the idea of a Chinese diaspora.

Many of the Chinese in Southeast Asia, like the Jews in Europe, became traders and entrepreneurs. It was a king of Thailand, Rama VI, who in 1914 wrote an extended essay on the Chinese as the "Jews of the East," outlining their said similarities in terms of attitudes to money, attitudes to outsiders and, in the vocabulary of the time, "racial loyalty" (see Landon 1941: 34–46). Interestingly, perhaps the first use of the term "diaspora" in English in a broader sense than the Jewish diaspora was its application to "trading diasporas," or transnational networks of traders, that were as common in the ancient world as they are today (Cohen 1971). Clearly, traders were not migrants in the sense of settlers but they moved into host societies on sufferance to deal in desired commodities. The Lebanese and Greeks, as well as the Jews and Chinese, fell into this category.

From trading diasporas, however, the term "diaspora" has been extended to include almost every conceivable type of migration. Robin Cohen, in his introductory book to a planned series of studies on global diasporas, identifies labor diasporas, imperial diasporas, cultural diasporas and diasporas in an age of globalization, as well as the more familiar trading and homeland diasporas (Cohen 1997). In a way, Cohen is following and systematizing the work of Kotkin (1992) who conceptualized global migrations in terms of transnational "tribes." One can legitimately ask whether we are simply dressing up in new clothes a perfectly good word, "migration," which exists in most languages, without changing the substance in any significant way. At the risk of appearing pedantic, I think that although almost everything that is proposed for inclusion under "diaspora" could be very properly examined under "migration," the use of the term "diaspora" does indeed draw our attention to several significant dimensions of the process of human mobility that until recently have received little attention from scholars of migration. Partly, this lack of attention has been due to very new features of the migration systems themselves and partly it has been due to the almost total preoccupation of migration scholars with but two of the components of the very complex migratory flows: settlers and labor migrants.

The Implication of Diaspora: of Victims and Achievers

The first implication of diaspora is that the migrant is a victim. Forced from his or her homeland into exile, the migrant is at the mercy of the whims of the host society. The increasing number of refugees and asylum-seekers consequent upon growing national sentiment towards the creation of homogeneous societies in the post-colonial era gave substance to this interpretation. The idea of diaspora can thus help to integrate forced migrations into the wider context of migration theory in general rather than seeing them as entirely separate from so-called "voluntary" population movements. Applying diaspora more widely draws attention to the prejudice and overt racism that migrants from the new diversity of backgrounds are facing in destination areas. However, and without denying the very real exploitation that many migrants indeed face, the image of the migrant as victim owes much to the current political correctness of postmodern thinking. The migrants appear helpless in the face of dominant and racist host groups, reactive rather than proactive, given their inferior position.

Nevertheless, not all migrants in the modern diaspora can be considered victims, as many of the proponents of the approach well recognize (Cohen 1996). The well-educated or entrepreneurial Asian, mainly ethnic Chinese or Indian, migrant can hardly be seen as simply reactive. Migrants from Hong Kong and Taiwan have dominated the business migration programs of Australia, Canada and New Zealand over the last decade. Fully two thirds of those who entered Canada during the 1980s as entrepreneurs were from Hong Kong and Taiwan and over 70 per cent of those entering New Zealand and some 44 per cent of those entering Australia in the late 1980s and early 1990s came from these two economies (Skeldon 1997a: 232). Immigrants with India as the place of birth made up the most highly educated and affluent immigrant group to the United States (Clarke, Peach and Vertovec 1990: 18). Nine of the top ten places of origin of foreign students to the United States in 1993/94, representing some 53 per cent of the total number of foreign students in that country, were Asian countries. These migrants are part of a global elite, those who shape local and regional economies, and can in no way be seen as victims. Yet, they can be seen as in diaspora, if from a very different point of view.

Of Astronauts and Parachute Kids

One of the characteristics of the elite migration out of East Asia towards North America and Australasia has been its tendency to split families. While whole families might migrate as complete units, shortly after arrival the husband, or both the husband and the wife, return to continue their employment in their place of origin, leaving the rest of the family at the destination. When only the husband returns, the phenomenon has led to the term "astronaut" being used to describe the family; where both parents return, the children left behind are known as "parachute kids." Observed primarily among

Hong Kong and Taiwan migrants to North America and Australasia, these phenomena are also seen amongst the Malaysian and Singaporean Chinese migrants to Britain, for example. The members of these split families virtually commute at regular intervals within transnational networks to create new extended, if spatially extended, families

It is difficult to assess just how significant this type of long-distance commuting might be. There is more anecdotal information than there are hard data, and it must surely be only the relatively wealthy who can afford to commute at regular intervals across the Pacific. It is a form of mobility that is only made possible through modern forms of mass air travel at relatively low real cost compared with the past. The numbers involved in such long-distance commuting may, however, be substantial. The sex ratios for the Hong Kong-born in Australia as a whole, and in Auckland and Vancouver, are significantly biased towards women in the adult age cohorts suggesting large numbers of female-headed "astronaut" households, and towards males in the older child cohorts suggesting the leaving or sending of male, in preference to female, children at destinations (Skeldon 1997a). For one of the few studies directly addressing this issue (see Pe-Pua et al.,1996).

Diasporas and National Security

The critical aspect of these bi-local families is one of national affiliation. Do they identify primarily with their country of origin or with their country of destination? With neither, or with both? Or with each at different times? Do these questions matter? Generalizing this pattern of transnational, individual and family migration to an aggregate level, we are immediately involved with issues of national security, the nation state and national identity. The application of the concept of diaspora to this pattern of migration shifts our focus away from a movement *from* an origin or *to* a destination towards movements *between* origin and destination. The emphasis is upon linkages and networks, and circulation within them, rather than on a migration between two points. The ideals of multiculturalism saw different cultures combining in unspecified ways but clearly within the fabric of the nation state. Diaspora draws attention to the weakness of the state as nations without coterminous territory come to take on the primary communities. Identities, rather than national, are transnational and bounded by circuits of transnational mobility, not the state (see Clifford 1994).

Diasporas, in the above sense, are seen to erode the identity of the nation state as the principal provider of communal identity in the modern world. They are diffusing identities and creating new ones, particularly where the concept of the nation state may be very recent or weakly developed within boundaries imposed by colonial powers rather than within political units that have centralized and evolved over long periods of time. Thus, diaspora would appear to be a further contributor to the "end of the nation state," although in ways very different from those envisaged by Ohmae (1995), who argued for their loss of sovereignty in the face of powerful multinational corporations which were creating regional rather than national economies. The two interpretations are certainly not exclusive as much international population migration is controlled through the networks of multinational corporations in the transfer of skilled personnel and the recruitment of labor. These circuits of mobility are creating, it can be argued, new "imagined communities" in which the limits of community, and hence of identity, are defined by the spatial networks of shared experience (see Anderson 1991). Diaspora thus redefines identity within transnational systems of circulation rather than within the boundaries of the nation state.

Thus, nation states can feel challenged by diasporas and issues of national security come to the fore (see Weiner 1993 and also Teitelbaum and Weiner 1995). Are immigrants following the interests of areas of origin and acting to undermine the host state? Are emigrants dissidents who manipulate the values of host states to undermine the state of origin? Migrants as "peoples in between" come to be viewed with suspicion by both host and origin states. Networks of international terrorism and crime take on sinister dimensions. Unquestionably, the power of international criminal syndicates has come to challenge, and even to surpass, that of states, particularly where the state is weak (Skeldon 1994a). International drug traffickers have created multinational corporations of fabulous wealth that have diversified into the trafficking of people and into legitimate activities in newly emerging stock and real estate markets. With increasing democratization and the decentralization of power, it is becoming increasingly easy for criminal groups to buy influence in government.

Certainly, global migrant networks such as those provided by a very few groups, the overseas Chinese or the Russians, for example, facilitate the dissemination of criminal activities that can be seen to be contrary to the best interests of the host societies. Herein lies the fundamental weakness of the diaspora approach. It assumes a communality of interest throughout the migrant or diaspora community. Just as criminal groups make up a tiny minority among migrants in any particular flow, so too are the flows composed of many disparate components. The concept of diaspora has highlighted some critical aspects of the process of migration that until now have received little attention, and for this the concept has proven useful. It has also reinforced, if any reinforcing was required, the continued importance of culture in global affairs. Nevertheless, it has not covered any single aspect that could not properly be included under the rubric of migration. It gives the impression that the linkages within the diaspora are strong enough to create unitary communities and that these linkages are stronger than any that link migrant groups to the wider polity, and particularly the state.

Diasporas: Persistent or Transitional?

Unquestionably, diaspora communities can prove resilient, and the example of the Jewish peoples is clearly a case in point. However, the establishment of the Jewish state and thus the removal of a pivotal unifying element in that diasporic community — the creation of a homeland — may well have a significant impact upon diaspora Jews. When the dream becomes a reality and there is freedom to move, subtle changes in authority occur. While Jewish Americans or Canadians remain American or Canadian Jews, they may decide not to associate themselves with the state of Israel. They choose to identify more fully with a multicultural America, or Canada, rather than thinking of themselves as an exile from a homeland. The state as a critical source of identity is certainly not dead. In a somewhat different situation, Wasserstein (1996) charts the decline of the Jewish communities in Europe since 1945, not simply in numbers, but also in terms of religious association, in what he calls the "vanishing diaspora."

The transnational circuits of circulation observed earlier either do not apply to all migrants in a certain group — some go with the idea of settling, for example — or they may be profoundly modified over time. What will happen to the second generation? Will it continue to move back and forth between two worlds even if these worlds themselves have been transformed at least partially through the process of migration (Skeldon 1997b)? On returning to their perceived roots, will they discover that they are American or Canadian or Australian rather than Indian or Chinese? The expatriate literary experience of Third World intellectuals reveals ambivalent attitudes towards their homelands. (For a clear examination of the difficulties involved in the analysis of the second generation, see the essays in Portes (1994).)

Return to homeland has been a characteristic of all immigrant groups to settler societies and is not just restricted to those from the "new" areas of origin. In one of the few detailed studies of emigration from a settler society, in this case Australia, Hugo (1994) shows the importance of return to origin among the emigrant flows. This return may be upon retirement or upon loss of employment during an economic downturn. Similar findings have been reported for Canada (Beaujot and Rappak 1989). Return movements are by no means a recent phenomenon. They were as characteristic among nineteenth-century migrants to North America as they appear to be today. Even if the technology of transportation available at the time did not allow frequent transnational commuting of the type observed above, regular seasonal movements took place across the Atlantic for agricultural labor in the early years of this century; the *golondrinas* (swallows) from Italy to Argentina, for example, took advantage of the inverse agricultural seasons in the two countries. There were high rates of return for supposedly settler migrants too. Baines (1991: 39) has estimated that the incidence of return for emigrants from Italy in the early twentieth century was 40-50 per cent and for the English in the late nineteenth and early twentieth centuries around 40 per cent (see also Nugent 1992). During the period when Chinese could move freely back and forth to America in the nineteenth century the incidence of return for the Chinese "sojourner" appears to have been little different from that of many European "settlers" (see Chan 1990).

219

The existence of these diaspora linkages of the time does not seem to have inhibited the emergence of powerful and influential nations. The current fears about lack of commitment to the Americas have their historical counterparts in northern European immigrant attitudes towards southern European immigrants. However, as Nugent (1992: 161) has perceptively observed, Americans never saw the transience of the immigrants in quite the same way that they saw the transient life style of the pioneers on *The Frontier* . While the former, according to American nativist opinion, was considered a threat to the nation and to the American identity, the latter created the American nation and identity. The concept of diaspora would seem to support nativist fears and nativist claims by imposing an unrelenting and unchanging homogeneity upon an extremely varied immigrant experience. Many migrants stay and contribute hugely to the success of the nation, integrating with and contributing to the national identity as they do so. Others return, some of them acting as profound agents for change in their societies of origin.

Assimilation Once More?

The incidence of intermarriage becomes a critical indicator of any emergence of new identities as the boundaries between many diaspora communities erode in host societies. The analysis of intercultural marriage is plagued by definitional problems and it may be too early to draw definite conclusions owing to the recency of so much of the migration from Asia in particular. The major changes in behavior may come only when the destination-born children of immigrants reach marriageable age. Cross-national marriages in France, for example, appear to have increased from less than 5 per cent in the late 1960s and early 1970s to around 10 per cent today (Barbara 1994: 572). Such marriages will depend not only upon the strength of feeling towards exogamous unions among the members of each migrant group but also upon the opportunity for people of marriageable age to meet. Although the proportion of the population of mixed ancestry has been shown to increase with continuing immigration and length of residence, the rate of crosscultural marriage can actually decline over time as social networks crystallize. There are indeed significant differences between first and second generation marriage patterns even if there are also significant differences from one part of a country to another depending upon opportunity for intermixing. (For a recent review of the difficulties in coming to an adequate assessment of changing patterns of intermarriage, see Roy and Hamilton 1997).

Although the old Chinatowns have been profoundly modified with more mixed Asian populations, areas of clear migrant concentration still exist in the principal cities of destination in North America and Australasia. In the United States, which still pursues an assimilationist ideal, the resultant impact of the recent international migration on internal movements may be leading to what one researcher terms the "balkanization" of the country (Frey

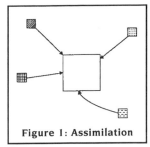

Figure 1: Assimilation

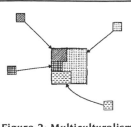

Figure 2: Multiculturalism

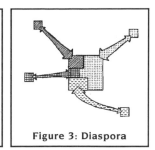

Figure 3: Diaspora

1995; 1996). This essentially implies a de facto spatial multiculturalism. Such analyses would certainly seem to support the spirit of the diaspora approach rather than any transition towards a more integrated state. Nevertheless, the historical perspective outlined earlier might guard against such ready fragmentationist interpretation. At the risk of oversimplifying an extremely complex situation, the essential differences between assimilation, multiculturalism and diaspora can perhaps be captured in diagrammatic form (see figures 1, 2 and 3).

A Diversion to Asia

The changing nature of the international migration system has seen not only the rise of Asia and Latin America as the major origins for movement to the settler societies, but also the emergence of significant destinations within Asia and Latin America themselves. Before attempting to draw some kind of order from the conflicting situation described above, it is worth briefly examining the situation within one part of one of these regions, Eastern Asia, to see whether there are relevant lessons for the analysis of diaspora and multiculturalism.

In East Asia, Japan, South Korea, Taiwan, Hong Kong, Singapore, Malaysia and Thailand have gone through a transition to low levels of fertility, as well as experiencing rapid and sustained economic growth over the last few decades. To a greater or lesser extent, these economies have also gone through a migration transition from being areas of net outmigration to being areas of net immigration (Fields 1994). Outmigration has not ceased from most of these economies, but its composition has changed from being primarily labor and settler migration to more highly skilled transfers associated with the export of capital and economic activities to areas of lower relative wage costs. While Thailand and Malaysia are still relatively minor players in these latter activities they too have emerged as labor-deficit economies with significant inmigration. There are probably over one million immigrants in each of these two economies: the majority from Indonesia in the case of Malaysia, and from Laos and Burma in the case of Thailand. All the economies import professional workers to meet skill shortages at the highest levels, often through the networks of transnational corporations.

Unlike the migration to the settler societies discussed earlier, the movement to these East Asian economies is seen as primarily circular, of labor, and much is clandestine and illegal. The only partial exceptions which allow for legal permanent settlement are the movement of skilled and semi-skilled ethnic Chinese to Singapore — provision was made for up to 25,000 workers from Hong Kong and their families to move to Singapore, for example, although it is likely that relatively few will take up this opportunity (Skeldon 1995) — and for ethnic Japanese from Latin America to settle with their families in Japan, becoming eligible to apply for Japanese citizenship. With the exception of these race-based admissions, the East Asian economies operate essentially closed-door immigration policies. Those who come in are expected to leave at some future date and, ideally, at the termination of their work permit, always assuming that they have one. East Asian policy makers are only too well aware of the European experience of guestworkers who turned into settlers.

It is perhaps too cynical to suggest that keeping large numbers of migrants as overstayers or illegals gives countries greater leverage than if these migrants resided legally, thereby being entitled to greater protection. Nevertheless, countries in the region certainly have ambiguous attitudes towards migrants. On the one hand, these countries wish to maintain their rapid rates of economic growth, based on low-cost labor in the case of Malaysia and Thailand, in the context of declining rates of growth of the indigenous labor force. On the other hand, they fear an influx of people of different ethnic groups who might erode the cultural identity of what have been predominantly homogeneous nations (Japan, South Korea, Taiwan and Thailand) or delicately balanced plural societies (Malaysia and Singapore). Already, in Thailand, there have been calls in the popular press to halt the family planning program as it has caused a shortage of labor which has led to the illegal importation of labor from Burma which will lead to the demise of Thai culture. Security concerns, because of migration, are looming large in parts of Asia, too. Thus, circular flows exist between origin and destination in East Asia in which the linkages within each migratory system are more important than linkages between migrants and host society. Can these movements therefore be considered diasporas?

No country in the region pursues an immigration policy that might lead to multiculturalism, but the concept of diaspora, too, has uneasy implications for many Southeast Asian countries. It is not just the European experience with labor migrants that is of concern to these countries: they are wary of one group which has indeed been considered to be in diaspora, the Chinese. For centuries, the Chinese established trading networks throughout the lands of Southeast Asia and beyond — trading diasporas? — and from the middle of the nineteenth century settled in large numbers throughout the region. When the migration out of China virtually ceased by the 1930s, there were probably just over 4 million ethnic Chinese in Southeast Asia

(Purcell 1965: 3). This number had increased to an estimated 8.5 million by 1947 (Purcell 1965: 3) and some 25.7 million by 1990 (Poston, Mao and Yu 1994). Even given problems of data comparability and of identifying ethnic Chinese as a separate category, these data indicate a very substantial increase in the overseas Chinese population over a period when there was almost no direct contact with China itself. Natural increase, intermarriage and incorporation into the group have accounted for the increase.

The numbers of ethnic Chinese are of secondary importance to their economic power. The Chinese still control between 40 and 50 per cent of the Malaysian economy even after more than 25 years, they control four of the five largest banks in Thailand, 163 of Indonesia's top 200 business groups, 16 of 28 private banks in the Philippines and over 80 per cent of that country's rice milling industry (Ch'ng 1993). The networks among overseas Chinese business groups within Southeast Asia which, through the new Chinese movements to North America and Australasia are now global activities, give substance to the idea of a trading diaspora (see Skeldon 1997a).

Sojourners thus became influential settlers throughout Southeast Asia and a critical question is whether the new sojourners from Burma, Laos, Indonesia, Bangladesh and elsewhere within Asia will similarly become long-term settlers as did the Chinese or, in a different context, the guestworkers of Europe. If so, then parts of Asia will become multicultural immigrant societies. There may be lessons, however, in how the Chinese have become incorporated into Southeast Asian economies and societies. Assimilation is not a one-way process in which the immigrant group becomes absorbed into the host society: both host and immigrant are modified and, at the interface of contact, identity and behavior will depend very much upon situation and context (Chan and Tong 1993). There is no contradiction between being a Chinese and a Thai or being a Chinese and a Singaporean or a Chinese and a Malaysian. Ethnic identity at the local level need not be associated with the same identity at the global, state level. Clearly, however, the attitude of the dominant political group(s) in a state will be critical to the acceptance or rejection of such a global-local mix of identities: identities that are not only constantly changing through contact and from situation to situation but also subject to deliberate change, which introduces the key issue of policy.

Towards a Policy-relevant Conclusion

The role of policy in the changing pattern of migration, both internal and international, is ambivalent. Unquestionably, policies can influence population movements, as evinced in exclusionary policies or those favoring reverse migration from cities in Maoist China, but migration can take on a momentum of its own which becomes increasingly difficult to control. Exclusionary policies in areas of origin can be seen as creating diasporas but exclusionary policies at destinations inhibit the development of diasporas in more ways than the obvious. As was clear in the Asian context, all countries implement exclusionary policies towards settlement but are struggling to design policies that will allow the importation of the required labor. Diaspora is not a term that is applied to migrations in Asia.

The discussions presented in this chapter lead to somewhat different perspectives on multiculturalism and diaspora. Diaspora is a logical outgrowth of multiculturalism to the extent that the acceptance of separate cultural groups encourages and sustains linkages back to the home area. Multiculturalism is a means to the creation of a transnational mosaic of mobile groups — travelling cultures? (Clifford 1992) — that interlocks in settler societies. The identity of the destination state becomes blurred. One can argue that such a trend is to be welcomed as it avoids the narrow and often racist prejudices of nationalism. Nevertheless, there are dangers. Multiculturalism, by officially endorsing cultural differences, may unintentionally reinforce the linkages back to areas of origin and weaken the development of ties at destination. Earlier migrant groups thus perceive a lack of commitment to the host nation on the part of more recent arrivals, which may promote and provoke racist attitudes. These prior migrant groups see their identities to be under threat as the new identities are given official sanction to remain different. Racist attitudes may thus be promoted by the very policies that were implemented to eliminate them. The process of internationalization, "globalization" as it is commonly known, creates new forms of racism and their persistence in multicultural society. See the essays in Vasta and Castles (1996).

However, diaspora, as well as multiculturalism, perhaps assumes too static a view of culture (see Castles 1992) and too homogeneous a view of immigrant populations. Some migrants indeed come to extend the business interests of their home area and home culture, but others come because the new country offers more than just a business opportunity: it offers the promise of something different and something that cannot easily be had in the origin areas. A clean environment with plentiful space, a less stressful education program, a perceived liberal and just society where individual freedoms are valued, and a lack of corruption in daily contacts are but some of the reasons given for moving to societies in North America or Australasia. For a discussion of the motivation of migrants to leave Singapore, see Yap (1991), and for studies of those leaving Hong Kong, see the essays in Skeldon (1994b). A danger with multiculturalism is that the origin society, through the continuous and intense contact between origin and destination, may be recreated in destination societies.

Without abandoning the clear strengths of multiculturalism in promoting migrant rights, governments of settler societies might like to shift the emphasis away from cultural relativism towards promoting the institutions for which the state and nation stand. This would not be a return to policies of assimilation (as we have seen, assimilation is a two-way process) but a clearer statement of national ideals and the way to implement them through the institutions of the state, particularly education and language policy, the legal system, civic participation and the system of government. The second generation of migrants is likely to be very different from the first and will need a broader reference than can be provided through multicultural policies. Thus, policies that create the idea of an integrated state may need to be emphasized at the expense of those that appear to favor a fragmented state.

That state institutions can come under pressure is clearly indicated in the United States, a country that has certainly never even promoted multicultural policies. Recent illegal donations of campaign funds from Asian sources, not only to the Democratic Party, but also to help the election of a Korean businessman and local councillor to the United States Congress (*Far Eastern Economic Review*, 15 May 1997), have brought political behavior that would be considered "normal" in Asia to the heart of American democracy. Given the financial power of many of the new groups and differences in values, it is essential that destination country institutions be as resilient as possible. These institutions come under pressure even where multiculturalism is not an ideal. The more flexible and liberal ethos of multiculturalism does not seem to provide a strong enough basis to provide necessary future guarantees against culturally accepted behavior in one culture being applied in the context of the culture of destination states, where it is interpreted in a quite different light

The focus on diaspora has highlighted some hitherto ignored aspects of the process of migration and placed circulation firmly in a transnational context. Its strengths lie in its emphasis on linkages back to the home areas and in the development of transnational communities. It draws attention to features of the new migration that policy makers may want to address, and particularly the implications of multiculturalism in a transnational context. It is perhaps currently in vogue as a concept because of its view of populations as victims and in the relativism so popular in postmodernist approaches. Its weakness is to see diaspora communities as unchanging and undifferentiated. Like multiculturalism (Glazer 1997), diaspora, as it is currently being understood, is but a temporary phase in the transition towards a more integrated nation. Despite the insights that the current usage has brought, the term diaspora is perhaps best restricted to a few forced and massive movements into exile in which the majority of a population is indeed dispersed. Other movements can still be more profitably examined, both theoretically and in terms of policy, under the rubric "migration."

Postscript

Since this chapter was written, the final report has appeared, after five years of work, of the U.S. Commission on Immigration Reform. Although a detailed assessment is not possible at this point, it seems that a key thrust of the recommendations is for a "new Americanization" of immigrants. This would appear to refer to a "renewed commitment to educating the newcomers in English and civics, improving the naturalization process and asserting the primacy of individual rights over the "collective" rights that are paramount in many parts of the world" (*International Herald Tribune*, 2 October 1997). Clearly, this new Americanization is precisely the policy direction identified in this chapter as evolving out of concerns about diaspora patterns of migration. However, whether this chapter has indeed captured the immigration mood of the times will depend very much upon whether Canada and Australia, with their much stronger multicultural traditions, attempt to follow suit. If Cornelius, Martin and Hollifield (1994) are correct in their identification of a general convergence among immigration policies, then this will be a significant trend indeed.

13 Asian Immigration, Public Attitudes and Immigration Policy: Patterns and Responses in New Zealand

Andrew Trlin, Anne Henderson and Regina Pernice

Since the mid-1980s, immigration policy changes implemented as part of a broad program of economic deregulation, restructuring and social reform, have produced a progressive and radical change in New Zealand's patterns of international migration. In August 1986 the removal of a traditional source countries preference (for skilled migrants from the United Kingdom, Europe and North America) was announced together with a new policy for business migrants. The latter policy, intended to encourage entrepreneurs with "demonstrated ability and investment capital" who could contribute to "the development of new competitive industries and markets" (Burke, 1986: 19), was not expected to have "a substantial or sudden impact in terms of [the] total numbers of business immigrants entering New Zealand" (Burke, 1986: 21). Within two years, however, the policy's success and the predominantly Asian composition of the inflow were abundantly clear (see Trlin and Kang, 1992). In 1991 further changes were implemented (see Trlin, 1997) and among these was the introduction of a new "General Category" (GC) distinguished by a points system that was heavily weighted toward educational qualifications, work experience and capital for both settlement and investment. Replacing an occupational program that had regulated the entry of skilled migrants in relation to labor force vacancies, the GC was the "key instrument" for attracting greater numbers of "quality migrants" who would make a positive contribution to economic and social development (Birch, 1991). It soon became the dominant avenue for residence, particularly for increasing numbers of Asians.

Statistics for 1995, albeit an exceptional year (Bedford, 1996), provide a graphic illustration of the volume and significance of Asian immigration. Including all types of arrivals and departures, a net migration gain of 36,200 was recorded (slightly more than 1 per cent of the total population) — the balance from a net loss of 23,300 New Zealand citizens and a net gain of 59,500 people of other nationalities. "White" nationals from New Zealand's traditional source areas, plus Australia and South Africa, accounted for 24,100

(40.5 per cent) of the latter group whereas Asian citizens accounted for 23,300 (39.2 per cent), the majority (17,300) coming from China, South Korea, Japan, Taiwan and Hong Kong. If only permanent and long-term migrants are considered, a net gain of 28,500 was achieved as a result of a net loss of 14,100 New Zealand citizens and a net gain of 42,600 other nationals. Significantly, the majority of the latter were Asian (23,700 or 55.6 per cent) rather than "White" nationals (13,600 or 32 per cent) — a far cry from the pattern that had prevailed for over 100 years.

This change has not escaped the attention of New Zealanders and has been central to a public debate on immigration. In this context, this chapter has three objectives. First, to trace patterns and trends in public attitudes to Asian immigration via a brief review of recent nationwide opinion polls. Second, to identify and discuss key factors underlying public concerns related to attitudes on Asian immigration. As the most important of these factors has been the nature and outcomes of immigration policy, particular attention will be given to a case study of two groups of Asian applicants approved for entry under the General Category. The final objective is to outline General Category changes implemented in October 1995, changes which can be identified as a response to both public and official government concerns.

PUBLIC ATTITUDES

Public opinion about Asian immigration was initially enthusiastic but in others more moderate or cautious. For example, a 1992 Insight nationwide survey found that while almost two-thirds thought Asian migrants made a positive contribution to New Zealand life, 44 per cent nevertheless believed that there were too many in the country (Yarwood, 1993: 39). Over the next four years, however, successive polls revealed a shift toward more cautious and negative views with regard to both the value and numbers of Asian immigrants.

The results of two National Research Bureau (NRB) surveys in 1994 and 1995, which included questions on the value of Asian immigration to New Zealand and the marketing of educational programs to attract Asian students, signalled the first changes in public attitudes. When asked for an opinion on the value of Asian immigration, 29 per cent of respondents said it was "Good" in early 1994 compared with 24 per cent in August 1995. Those with "Mixed feelings" increased from 33 to 38 per cent while the percentages expressing either a neutral or negative assessment remained stable (Table 1). The reasons for negative or mixed feelings were primarily expressed as concerns for: a) the nation's distinctive social and cultural characteristics (e.g., the perceived lack of integration by Asians, their failure to adapt to the New Zealand way of life, etc.); b) New Zealand's identity (e.g., being swamped and taken over by large numbers of arrivals who purchase land, businesses, and other resources); and c) for job losses or other forms of economic competition (especially in 1994). Such misgivings were most common among the less educated and older respondents (NRB, 1994: 54, 1995: 5).

**Table 1: Opinions of New Zealanders
on Aspects of Asian Immigration:**
National Research Bureau Polls
January/February 1994 and August 1995[1] (percentages)

	1994	1995
Opinions on Asian immigration		
Good for New Zealand	29	24
Neither good nor bad for New Zealand	25	25
Bad for New Zealand	13	13
Have mixed feelings about it	33	38
Reasons given for negative and mixed feelings toward Asian immigration (multiple responses recorded)		
Cultural/social threat	17	23
New Zealand identity threat	18	21
Economic threat	20	8
Opinions on attracting Asian fee-paying students		
Good for New Zealand	57	53
Neither good nor bad for New Zealand	11	12
Bad for New Zealand	11	10
Have mixed feelings about it	21	25
Reasons given for negative and mixed feelings toward attracting Asian fee-paying students (multiple responses recorded)		
Threat to New Zealand students	23	32
Long-term threat or problem	6	4

Source: National Research Bureau (1994; 1995).

Note: [1] Each poll involved 600 respondents obtained via a nationwide, stratified, random probability sampling procedure, with results weighted for individual age within sex sub-groups to reflect proportions in the 1991 Census.

A similar shift in opinion was found with regard to educational marketing programs designed to attract Asians as full fee-paying students (Table 1). Those approving of such programs dropped from 57 to 53 per cent, while those with mixed feelings increased from 21 to 25 per cent. The two other categories (neutral or negative) remained fairly stable. The main reason for negative or mixed feelings was the view that Asians would take the study places that New Zealanders should have. This reason and a number of others (e.g., that wealthy Asians might get preferential treatment, raise education costs, exacerbate the problems of already large and overcrowded classes, etc.) — that may reflect personal experience, observation or media attention — together comprised what the NRB defined as a "threat to New Zealand students" theme. The "long term threat" theme, though of minor importance, included concerns that educational programs were a means to secure residence and that the knowledge gained could be used by future competitors.

With regard to the numbers of Asian immigrants, a TV One-Colmar Brunton national poll provided clear evidence in March 1996 of an increase in opposition to Asian immigration when compared with the results of a 1990 survey. Only 4 per cent (12 per cent in 1990) favored an increase, while 42 per cent (50 per cent, 1990) wanted the numbers kept the same and 47 per cent (32 per cent, 1990) felt that the numbers arriving from Asia should be reduced. This negative shift in public opinion was confirmed by three National Business Review-Consultus polls conducted over the period October 1994 to September 1996. The percentage who felt there were too many immigrants from Asia increased from 42 to 46 per cent (with a peak of 51 per cent in October 1995), an interesting result highlighted by a parallel softening of opinion toward the number of Pacific Islanders and the high approval consistently expressed for the number of migrants from the United Kingdom (Table 2). Concern about the number of Asian immigrants was usually strongest among the young (18–24 years), the old (60 years and over), those on low incomes, residents of areas having limited contact with Asians, and supporters of the New Zealand First political party (Hunt, 1995a; 1996a).

FACTORS UNDERLYING PUBLIC CONCERNS

It would be easy to dismiss public attitudes toward Asian immigration as nothing more than evidence of racist xenophobia (see Hunt, 1995a). However, the influence of other concerns and underlying factors should also be acknowledged. Among these are issues which have attracted considerable media attention, namely: the reported presence and activities of Asian Triads; the exploitation of Asian women in Auckland's sex industry; the impact of wealthy Asians upon housing markets and residential patterns; the pressure placed on school resources by Asian students; and the apparent "abuse" of immigration policy by "astronaut" migrants who leave families to enjoy New Zealand's many advantages while they continue business interests in their country of origin. Nor can one ignore the impact of one political party's election campaign that challenged the desirability of immigration and overseas investment, thereby exacerbating fears of an economic "takeover" and the loss of New Zealand's socio-cultural identity.

There appear to be four key factors underlying public attitudes and concerns with respect to Asian immigration. They are: prejudice and a sense of national identity; socio-economic power and visibility; the politics of immigration; and the nature and outcomes of immigration policy. Of these, immigration policy is the most important; it has been the catalyst for change and the prime source of a broad array of public concerns. Therefore, while the first three factors are each briefly discussed below, more detailed attention is given to immigration policy via a case study of Taiwanese and Chinese applicants approved under the General Category points system.

Prejudice and National Identity

The marked contrast in attitudes toward the number of immigrants from Asia and the Pacific Islands as compared with the United Kingdom (Table 2), provides compelling evidence of ethnic and/or racial prejudice. This evidence is reinforced by the finding that respondents' opinions on British migrant numbers were closely matched by their views on the numbers of Australians and South Africans. In the September 1996 National Business Review-Consultus poll, for example, only 13 per cent of respondents felt there were too many Australians, whereas the numbers were judged to be about right by 50 per cent or not enough according to approximately 15 per cent. For South Africans, the responses were very similar: too many, 16 per cent; about right, 42 per cent; and not enough, 18 per cent.

**Table 2: Public Opinion on the Numbers of Immigrants
in New Zealand from Asia, the Pacific Islands
and the United Kingdom:**
National Business Review — Consultus Polls,
October 1994, October 1995 and September 1996[1] (percentages)

Question:	Are there too many, about the right number, or not enough immigrants from . . . ?			
		Asia	Pacific Islands	United Kingdom
Too many	1994	42	53	12
	1995	51	57	21
	1996	46	45	14
About right	1994	40	35	51
	1995	36	31	49
	1996	39	37	49
Not enough	1994	6	3	19
	1995	5	5	19
	1996	4	3	16
Unsure	1994	12	9	18
	1995	8	7	11
	1996	11	15	21

Source: Hunt (1995a; 1996a).
Note: [1] Conducted by UMR Insight, this poll employs a nationwide, random sample of 750 people aged 18 and over. The margin of error is ±3.5 %.

Commenting on these and previous poll results, Hunt (1996a) argued that traditional "white New Zealand attitudes toward immigration . . . still have currency in the 1990s." Support for Hunt's view can be found in New Zealand studies (conducted more than 20 years ago) of perceived social distance between the host and immigrant populations. Measuring degrees of tolerance or prejudice, these studies (McCreary et al., 1952; Vaughan, 1962; Trlin, 1971; Graves and Graves, 1974) revealed a hierarchy of preferences for interaction with different national, ethnic and racial groups; Northwest Europeans, North Americans and Australians were the most preferred while non-Europeans were the least preferred by New Zealanders. Implicit in this ranking is an expectation that immigrants should "fit in." The most acceptable, therefore, were those perceived to be the most similar in cultural characteristics or the least physically dissimilar; "race" was an important determinant of attitudes. As demonstrated in comparable research in the United States (Owen et al., 1981), and confirmed by the National Business Review-Consultus polls, a society's preference hierarchy remains remarkably stable over time. Accordingly, it may be argued that the outcomes of New Zealand's immigration policy since the mid-1980s have been out of line with the public's broad expectations and preferences for social interaction.

Could the attitudes of New Zealanders reflect a lack of contact with Asians and hence little appreciation of their attributes? Results from the two NRB polls appear to discount this possibility. Contact with a citizen of an Asian country in the past year or two was reported by 66 and 68 per cent of respondents in 1994 and 1995, respectively (NRB, 1995: 38). Furthermore, when asked to identify the characteristics they associated with Asian migrants, about 75 per cent identified favorable features (notably those consistent with a positive work ethic) but about 62 per cent also identified unfavorable characteristics (NRB, 1995: 39–40). Chief among the latter was a "cultural/social threat" theme that embraced the perceived tendency of Asians to "stick to themselves," their reluctance to adapt to a New Zealand lifestyle, language difficulties, criminal behavior, etc. Obviously many of these characteristics are closely related to the reasons given for negative and mixed feelings toward Asian immigration (Table 1). Coupled with negative features interpreted as an "economic threat," these characteristics could be perceived as a challenge to the fabric of New Zealand's socio-cultural and economic identity.

The sensitive issue of national identity had already been raised in 1993 in statements from Prime Minister Bolger. Broadly defining New Zealand as part of Asia, he identified himself as an "Asian leader." Bolger's statements were part of a strategy to enhance public awareness of Asia, rather than focusing exclusively on the West, and to position New Zealand as an integral part of the Asia-Pacific region. The strategy failed to win much support, especially after an over-enthusiastic colleague (Tony Ryall, MP East Cape) claimed that New Zealanders were now "a nation of white and brown Asians"

232

(*The New Zealand Herald*, 15 May 1993, p. 5). When respondents in an October 1995 National Business Review-Consultus poll were asked "Do you think New Zealand is part of Asia?" only 16 per cent said "Yes," 82 per cent answered "No" and 2 per cent were unsure (Hunt, 1995b). This response adds weight to Hunt's (1996a) comment on the poll results presented in Table 2; namely, that they reflected:

> ... the government's huge task to integrate New Zealand into Asia by, not least, encouraging Kiwis to become more Asia focused.

While accepting the need for New Zealanders to be more aware of Asia, Tarling — a staunch advocate of closer relations with Asia — believed the proper aim should be (Tarling, 1994: 21):

> ... to assert an identity as New Zealanders, anxious to be informed about Asian countries, to deal with them state-to-state and people-to-people and economy-to-economy.

The substance of his message was clear; avoid the hollow insincerity of over-anxious, misguided claims about New Zealand's Asian identity, and take pride in the nation's distinctive qualities. But what about the implications of this approach for Asian Immigration? From Tarling's viewpoint, Asian migrants have an educational role to perform, helping "New Zealanders to become more Asia literate" (Tarling, 1994: 22). This role, however, has figured little (if at all) in the thinking of policy makers.

Socio-economic Power and Visibility

From the viewpoint of successive Ministers of Immigration, immigration consultants, business leaders and interest groups (notably the Business Roundtable), a change in New Zealand's traditional patterns of immigration — particularly its ethnic composition — was long overdue. One reason frequently cited (Kerr, 1995; New Zealand Immigration Service, 1995a: 8-9; Yarwood, 1993: 38) is that a more diverse ethnic mix would be advantageous if it yielded substantial increases in capital investment and the expansion of international business, trade and tourism linkages.

There is some evidence of such gains being made in relation to Asia. Cremer and Ramasamy (1996) demonstrated this in terms of increased trade, foreign investment and with case studies of Asian-owned companies in New Zealand. Citing Overseas Investment Commission data, Ninness (1996) reported that:

> In 1992 the Commission approved $770 million worth of investments from Asia which was just 11.4% of total approvals by value ... and in 1994 ... Asian investment approvals had soared to $1.74 billion or 34% of the total ... Of all the land the commission has approved for sale to overseas interests ... between 1991 and 1994 ... 51% of the total has been to Asian buyers.

A more direct link with immigration is provided the New Zealand Immigration Service (NZIS) statistics. In 1995, Chinese, Hong Kong Chinese, Korean and Taiwanese applicants specified a total of NZ$611.5 million or 84.6 per cent of all investment funds for migrants approved under either the Business Investment Category or the General Category (NZIS, 1996).

The figures on Asian investment are certainly impressive but many New Zealanders were nevertheless concerned, as indicated by responses to the NRB surveys in 1994 and 1995 (Table 3). Despite a strong positive shift in opinion, almost half of the respondents in 1995 still reported mixed or negative feelings toward Asian investment. The reason most frequently given (25 per cent of cases in 1995), the one that provided the foundation for the "threat to New Zealand identity" theme, was that New Zealanders should retain ownership of their country. Other key reasons included the beliefs that investment profits would be taken out of the country, that there would be no benefit for New Zealand and that jobs could be taken away from its citizens — reasons which together comprised the theme of an "economic threat."

Overall, there was a striking similarity between the reasons given for mixed or negative attitudes to both Asian investment and immigration. This is not surprising. It marks a conflation of perceptions and thinking, a conflation that mistakenly links developments of the sort noted by Ninness (1996) to new immigrants rather than non-resident foreign investors. However, it is also understandable as a fusion fostered by casual personal observation, possible experience, the variable quality of nationwide media attention and political party exploitation of the issues (notably by the leader of New Zealand First).

The day-to-day basis for this conflation — the visible presence of Asian immigrants, their wealth, economic impact, and power to gain control of valued resources — is nowhere more evident than in Auckland. In a survey to which just 212 Asian immigrants responded, for example, it was revealed that they alone: (a) increased (via household consumption and growth of government services) annual economic output by $22 million for the Auckland regional economy and by $28 million for the wider New Zealand economy; and (b) provided a one-off increase in output (via initial asset purchases) of $133 million and $159 million for the Auckland regional and New Zealand economies, respectively. Each year their businesses had a turnover of $30 million, employing 402 Aucklanders who were paid $7.8 million in wages (Enterprise Auckland, 1996: 2–3). Some central city and suburban business areas have been transformed, in part by the concentration of new Asian enterprises but also by the visible response (street signs, advertising, staff appointments) of local companies, shops and services keen to cater for this new group of affluent clients.

Perhaps the most visible impacts, however, have been the consequences of a demand for high quality housing (a major initial asset purchase), with

Table 3: Opinions of New Zealanders on Asian Investment:
National Research Bureau Polls,
January/February 1994 and August 1995[1] (percentages)

	1994	1995
Opinions on Asian investment in New Zealand		
Good for New Zealand	25	34
Neither good nor bad for New Zealand	11	17
Bad for New Zealand	18	14
Have mixed feelings about it	46	35
Reasons given for negative and mixed feelings toward Asian investment (multiple responses recorded)		
New Zealand identity threat	44	32
Economic threat	23	16
Cultural/social threat	5	3

Source: National Research Bureau (1994; 1995).

Note: [1] Each poll involved 600 respondents obtained via a nationwide, stratified, random probability sampling procedure, with results weighted for individual age within sex sub-groups to reflect proportions in the 1991 Census.

selection often dictated by proximity to a good school (Boyer, 1995: 51–52). This demand, unlike previous experience with the residential patterns of ethnic minorities (see Trlin, 1984), has resulted in the concentration of new Asian arrivals in Auckland's upper status areas, especially the eastern and southeastern suburbs (see Boyer, 1995; Boswell, 1995). For some of these suburbs there is evidence that the Asian demand has significantly boosted real estate values (Wong, 1990; McLauchlan, 1991: 118) — a source of satisfaction for some Aucklanders and of dismay for others. Finally, although Asian students have often featured with distinction as high achievers, residential concentration has accentuated the pressure placed on local schools and teaching resources by those who initially lacked English language competency (McLauchlan, 1991: 121–122). It is a situation that has disadvantaged both migrant and New Zealand-born students. Citing Ministry of Education statistics for 1993, Phillips (1994) presented a stark picture in which over 12,000 students — about one-third of all those with a "non-English speaking background" (NESB) — required instruction in English. About 70 per cent of all NESB students were located in the Auckland region. The matter came to a much publicized head in early 1995 when the Epsom primary school board, facing the enrolment of still more Asian pupils, announced its intention to turn away students not fluent in English.

The Politics of Immigration

Winston Peters has been the key player in New Zealand's politics of immigration. A long-time member of the National Party, Peters was fired from the position of Minister of Maori Affairs by Prime Minister Bolger but in 1993 successfully held his seat as an independent candidate. During the long run-up to the country's first election with a mixed member proportional system of representation (October 1996), he founded his own party — New Zealand First. By late 1995, Peters had already established himself as a vigorous critic of National Government policy, winning attention for: his opposition to a surcharge on the retirement income of the elderly (which provided him with a "Grey Power" support base); his dramatic exposure of a Cook Islands-based corporate tax scam (the "Wine Box Affair"); and his attack on foreign ownership of New Zealand assets. The success of the latter campaign was evident as early as April/May 1995 when a public opinion poll found that 47 per cent thought that foreigners should not be allowed to own land in New Zealand and 51 per cent indicated they would support a law to ban such ownership. Predictably, these views were held by about 80 per cent of Peters' own party supporters, but about 50 per cent of both Alliance and Labor Party supporters were also of the same mind (Hunt, 1995c).

Although Peters had been attacking asset sales to foreigners for some time, his campaign on the immigration issue effectively started in February 1996. The immediate catalyst appears to have been the news that almost 55,000 applicants, of whom 60 per cent were Asian, had been granted per-

Figure 1

Source: The Dominion, Wellington, New Zealand, 3 April 1996: 6

manent residence in 1995. However, he could not have been unaware of the implications for voter support of either the publicity over previous years concerning immigration or the results of public opinion polls on the issue. Indeed, in the October 1995 National Business Review-Consultus poll, New Zealand First supporters were already in the vanguard of those who felt there were too many Asian immigrants (72 per cent), Pacific Islanders (69 per cent), South Africans (32 per cent) and others (Hunt, 1995a). Whatever the reason, Peters launched a series of speeches on the theme "Whose country is it anyway?" that: criticized the 1995 approvals given existing levels of unemployment (110,000 or 6.2 per cent of the labor force); questioned the mandate for a mass influx of foreigners; reiterated the well-known issues of Asian "astronauts," language difficulties and school resources, etc.; and contributed to the conflation of attitudes on immigration and investment with a continuing attack on foreign ownership or control of land and other assets. He concluded that immigration should be "cut to the bone" with only 10,000 (preferably skilled) migrants approved for permanent residence each year.

Political opponents, newspaper leader writers, media commentators, the Race Relations Conciliator and others quickly denounced this campaign. Peters was accused of appealing to the bigoted, the disaffected, and the elderly. He was personally attacked as a poll-driven, opportunistic demagogue and condemned by Prime Minister Bolger for playing "the race card." His policy of 10,000 per year was dismissed by critics as xenophobic or racist (charges strongly denied by Peters), and by the Minister of Foreign Affairs and Trade "as a closed door policy on immigration" (McKinnon, 1996: 12). Internationally, the response, exemplified by the *Wall Street Journal* (15 April 1996) description of New Zealand First as "the modern face of anti-immigrant discrimination," was also negative.

Nevertheless, increasing numbers of ordinary New Zealanders saw things differently. Between February and May of 1996, opinion poll support for New Zealand First soared. Ironically, this support grew at a time when public opposition to the number of immigrants was showing signs of waning. A poll at the end of March 1996 found that 46 per cent believed there were too many Asians compared with 51 per cent in October 1995, and a similar change of opinion (a drop of 5–7 per cent) was evident in terms of those who thought there were too many Pacific Islanders, Britons, Australians and South Africans (see Hunt, 1996b). In general this new pattern held steady until September (Table 2). It should be noted, moreover, that Peters' campaign was promulgated several months after the introduction of a more restrictive immigration policy (discussed below). By scratching a traditional anti-immigrant itch (not unique to New Zealand), therefore, what he accomplished was not an increase in antipathy toward immigrants but a shift in voter support, from one of the minor parties (Alliance) and from Labor. The outcome in the October election was that New Zealand First emerged as the third party, holding the balance of power and in a position to negotiate a coalition with Bolger and the National Party.

IMMIGRATION POLICY, 1991–1995: THE KEY FACTOR

The nature and outcomes of immigration policy, crucial to an understanding of the situation described above, are addressed here solely in relation to the General Category (GC) provision for permanent entry and residence. As noted earlier, the GC was: introduced as part of a new policy in 1991 (NZIS, 1991a); distinguished by a points system for selection; and described as the "key instrument" for attracting greater numbers of "quality migrants" (Birch, 1991). In 1995 the GC accounted for almost 72 per cent of all persons approved for residence — the bulk of the remainder being approved under the Family Reunion (16.2 per cent) or Business Investment (3.4 per cent) categories — and for 46 per cent of investment funds specified by successful applicants in both the GC and Business Investment Category. Salient details of the GC points system are presented below, together with a case study of the characteristics of approved applicants from Taiwan and the People's Republic of China to illustrate policy outcomes.

The General Category Points System

The main areas/attributes for the award of points are shown in Table 4 and may be summarized as follows:

1) *Employability*: the major element with an allocation of 25 out of 40 points; up to 15 for qualifications (biased toward degrees in any science or engineering area) and up to 10 for years of sound, continuous work experience gained after the qualification specified or experience in an approved occupation.
2) *Age*: up to 10 points, biased toward the young (notably those aged 25–29) and with an upper age limit of 55 years.
3) *Ability to settle*: based on the assessment of 13 points, but limited to a maximum allocation of 5, this area took account of: settlement funds for housing and establishment costs; sponsorship by either a close family relative or community group; funds that would be invested for at least two years; and an offer of skilled employment.

There were also the usual good health and character requirements, and the principal applicant had to meet a minimum level of English language ability (previously applied also to the applicant's spouse and children over 12 years of age).

In general, the GC points system followed closely but not precisely the proposals of a Working Party on Immigration. Compared with those proposals (Wilson et al., 1991: 10–13), the GC: a) gave a greater weighting to "employability," which had been narrowed down to qualifications and work experience without regard for special skills or an offer of skilled employment (the latter included in the settlement factors); and b) gave much less weight to settlement factors, with no points at all for English language skills. In other words, the GC points system implemented had a stronger human capital focus.

Table 4: Points System for Assessment of
General Category Principal Applicants,
November 1991–October 1995

Categories	Points
Qualifications (maximum of 15 points)	
Successful completion of 12 years schooling	2
Diploma/Certificate, at least 1 and under 2 yrs full-time study	4
Diploma/Certificate, 2–3 years full-time study	8
Bachelors degree (other than science, technical or engineering), trade certificate or advanced trade qualification	12
Postgraduate degree or Bachelors degree in science, technical or engineering area	15
Work experience (maximum of 10 points)	
1 point for every 2 years of relevant work experience up to 20 plus years of such experience	1–10
Age (maximum of 10 points)	
18–24 years	8
25–29 years	10
30–34 years	8
35–39 years	6
40–44 years	4
45–49 years	2
Settlement Factors (maximum of 5 points)	
NZ$100,000 settlement funds	2
NZ citizen/resident close family relative sponsor	2
Community sponsorship	3
Investment funds, 1 point each additional NZ$100,000 up to maximum of NZ$300,000	1–3
Offer of skilled employment	3
Maximum points, total all categories	40

Source: New Zealand Immigration Service (1991a; 1991b)

With applicants ranked on the basis of points scored, it was possible to: nominate a high automatic approval score or autopass; specify a minimum score below which applicants would be declined; and to define those between the two scores as a "pool" for additional approvals needed to reach an immigration target. Because applicants seeking entry under other categories (e.g., business investment, family reunion) were accepted if they met the relevant criteria, the GC acted as a residual category to make up the balance in the targeted number of approvals. By 1995 it was clear that the

GC was being used not only to attract a greater number of quality migrants but also to facilitate an increase in immigration. For example, the total number of migrants approved for entry jumped from 28,447 in 1993 to 54,811 in 1995, with the GC share rising from 68 to almost 72 per cent. The autopass level, it may be noted, increased with some fluctuations from 20 to 31 points between November 1991 and July 1995. In this respect the GC marked the impact of Poot et al. (1988) and Kasper (1990) who challenged previous thinking on the benefits of increased immigration.

General Category Case Study: Taiwanese and Chinese

Approximately 5,900 and 3,700 GC applications by Taiwanese and Chinese citizens, respectively, were approved over the period 1991–1995. Information for this case study was obtained from these approved applications, classified by date of receipt and held on file by the New Zealand Immigration Service. For each group a sample of 150–155 cases was drawn using a systematic sampling procedure (an interval of 1:38 for the Taiwanese and 1:24 for the Chinese) with a random starting point. This sampling procedure ensured that the cases drawn adequately represented chronological variations in both the number of applications approved and the characteristics of applicants.

1) *Similarities and Differences.* Tracing an increase in the "quality" of approvals since 1991, the NZIS (1995a: 42–43) reported that: 67 per cent of all GC applicants approved scored the full 15 points for qualifications; over 50 per cent were professionals, typically in the physical, mathematical and engineering sciences, life science and health fields; and that managers accounted for another 11 per cent, while only 5 per cent were trades workers. In these terms, overall both the Taiwanese and Chinese principal applicants (PAs) in the present case study were of an exceptionally high "quality."

   As shown in Table 5 the two groups had some features in common as well as marked differences between them. The PAs were usually: males, with a mean age in the 30s; married, and therefore normally accompanied by their family members; reasonably competent in English (self-declared ability), certainly more so than a spouse/partner; very well educated; and predominantly engaged in professional occupations. On the other hand, as compared with their Taiwanese counterparts, the Chinese PAs were: on average, almost 8 years younger; more likely to be single and to have both smaller nuclear and extended families (perhaps reflecting both age and home country constraints); more heavily concentrated in professional occupations and under-represented in the administrative/managerial category; and much more likely to have lodged their applications for residence when already in New Zealand (typically as postgraduate students — a feature that could confirm public suspicion of education programs as a means to gain residence).

Two further differences warrant closer attention. First, the apparent similarity of qualifications (implied by both the percentages with a Bachelors degree or better and the mean scores for qualifications) conceals what could be important differences for eventual settlement in New Zealand. A higher percentage of Chinese PAs scored the full 15 points for qualifications because they held either a postgraduate degree or a Bachelors degree in a science, technical or engineering area (91.4 vs 76.8 per cent of the Taiwanese), whereas a higher percentage of Taiwanese scored 12 points with a Bachelors degree in an area other than science or engineering, or a trade certificate or advanced trade qualification (20.6 vs 7.3 per cent of the Chinese). Second, with regard to the mean scores for settlement factors, the salient difference appeared to lie in the availability of capital. Here the Taiwanese PAs had a definite edge; 99.4 per cent (Chinese only 29.8 per cent) scored points for having NZ$100,000 settlement funds (e.g., for housing) and 54.2 per cent (Chinese only 1.3 per cent) scored points for funds that would be invested for at least two years. This difference, related to their national origins, is probably understated as many Taiwanese would not have sought points for additional funds if they already had enough points (for qualifications, etc.) to gain entry. Indeed, the files examined included numerous examples of applicants whose declared assets were well beyond the investment funds offered for GC points assessment.

Given the nature and weightings of the GC points system (Table 4), the features in common (age, qualifications, occupations) are to be expected. But so too are some of the differences which indicate the various combinations of assessment factors that enable applicants to attain equivalent points. Consider, for example, the contrast between the two groups in terms of mean scores for age and work experience (Table 5). These variables (each assigned 10 points) are to some degree inversely related. The younger Chinese, therefore, attained a higher mean score for age but a lower mean score for work experience compared with the older Taiwanese. The maximum 5 points for settlement factors could be accumulated via various combinations of points for funds, sponsorship or an offer of skilled employment and could be used to offset a points "deficit" for age and/or employability as illustrated by the Taiwanese (Table 5).

2) *Policy and Settlement Implications.* The PA characteristics outlined above confirm an official view (NZIS, 1995a) that the GC performed very satisfactorily as the "key instrument" for attracting quality migrants. It is necessary therefore to consider a number of points that serve to qualify this impression. Of these, the first concerns the PA's dependants and the family's potential for later chain migration. Both the PA and spouse/partner have parents and/or siblings in their extended families (Table 5) who represent a "pool" for later sponsorship. This growing "pool" could sub-

stantially increase applications under the Family Reunion provision with implications for immigration targeting and the residual role of a skills category. As for the PA's dependants, a partner (not necessarily as well qualified as the principal applicant) and accompanying children (an average of 1.6 and 0.5 for the Taiwanese and Chinese, respectively) will increase economic outputs via their initial and on-going demands for goods and services but may also exacerbate (as in Auckland) negative pressures for available housing, specialist educational resources and possibly employment.

The decision to require only the PA to meet a minimum level of English language ability, for which no points were awarded, proved to be a contentious flaw. For partners of both Taiwanese and Chinese PAs a mean score of 3 (i.e., "Conversational" on a self-declared ability scale ranging from 1 = "Mother tongue" to 5 = "None") signals that many would experience some difficulties in day-to-day communication and interaction, thereby possibly delaying their integration into the mainstream of New Zealand life. Among school-aged children the problem was more acute; for example, 64.6 and 31.3 per cent of the Taiwanese 5–9 and 10–14 year olds, respectively, were declared to have no English language ability and a further 29.2 and 51.8 per cent in these age groups were stated to have only limited ability. Such children would contribute to the resource problems of schools — especially as their New Zealand resident status exempted parents from the payment of additional fees. Even the PAs, with a mean score of 2.5 (i.e., midway between "Fluent" and "Conversational" ability), would be likely to encounter some problems. It must be stressed that the case study findings reported here relate only to PA declarations, and that in the files examined there was evidence of considerable variation in the procedures for verifying declared language ability. In her 1995 study of Taiwanese living in Auckland, Boyer (1996: 66) reports that:

> . . . [of those] who said they had, or were, experiencing difficulties in finding employment, 48 per cent cited language problems as their most significant hurdle.

Boyer's (1996: 66) finding that 43 per cent of her sample families were unemployed but would work if they could, pointed also to other serious weaknesses in the GC points system. The problem was that the GC selection criteria neither protected nor maximized the potential benefits of high quality migrants during settlement in New Zealand. To be more specific, the GC: a) produced a very narrow mix of occupations and skills, with an over-supply in some professions, because of the nature of the points weighting on academic qualifications; b) relegated the "insurance" of a skilled job offer to the position of an option in an undervalued set of settlement factors; c) gave no guidance concerning the recognition

**Table 5: Characteristics of Approved General Category
Principal Applicants (PAs) from Taiwan and the
People's Republic of China, 1991–1995**

Characteristics	Taiwan	P.R. China
Sex: % PAs male	78.7	70.8
Age: mean age (years) of PAs	39.0	31.1
Marital status: % PAs married	89.7	77.5
Unit of migration: % PA plus spouse, dependents	89.7	74.8
Children:		
mean family size	1.7	0.6
mean number coming to NZ	1.6	0.5
Extended family:		
PA mean number specified	4.8	3.7
PA's spouse mean number specified	4.4	2.9
English language ability[1]:		
PA's mean level	2.5	2.5
Spouse's mean level	3.1	3.0
Education:		
% PAs with Bachelors degree or better	92.9	97.3
Occupation:		
% PAs administrative, managerial	18.2	3.4
% PAs professional	66.9	88.6
Already in NZ: % PAs	2.0	19.8
Points assessment[2]: mean score qualifications	14.2	14.6
mean score work experience	5.9	3.7
mean score age	5.5	8.8
mean score settlement factors	3.1	1.3
overall mean score	28.7	28.4

Source: Applications for Entry to New Zealand, New Zealand Immigration Service, Wellington.

Notes: [1] English language ability, self-reported, ranges from 1 = Mother Tongue to 5 = None.

[2] Points assessment details are provided in Table 4 and should be carefully noted in the interpretation of mean scores presented here.

of occupational qualifications; and d) included no mandatory requirement to validate qualifications at the time of application by securing (where appropriate) statutory professional registration in New Zealand.

On the final point, the Working Party on Immigration (Wilson et al., 1991: 11) had specifically stated that the points system should:

> . . . not exclude persons who . . . because of the restrictions of trade associations and professional bodies, may not initially be able to practise their trade or profession.

The most widely reported outcome was the over-supply and unemployment of foreign medical practitioners who experienced persistent difficulties in securing recognition of qualifications and registration. Over 2,600 were approved for residence between 1991 and 1995. Among them were many Asians, including the 20 per cent of Taiwanese PAs in this case study who identified themselves as general practitioners, surgeons or other medical specialists. The issue of qualifications and registration applies, of course, to a wide range of professionals and has recently been the subject of a major survey in New Zealand (see Department of Internal Affairs, 1996).

Boyer (1996: 68) claimed that of the unemployed Taiwanese in her sample, 23 per cent were accounted for by an inability to have their qualifications recognized. Less obvious but no less important has been the occurrence of under-employment with downward occupational mobility and loss of status affecting those actually working in New Zealand (see Boyer, 1996: 71–72). The same problems have been reported for Hong Kong Chinese, Koreans and Taiwanese by Lidgard (1996). There is no reason to believe that the Taiwanese PAs in the present case study will have fared any better. Among the Chinese PAs, however, a more favorable situation could be expected given the high proportion who applied for residence while in New Zealand and who had local postgraduate experience.

Return migration, remigration (e.g., to Australia) and adverse social and psychological effects have all been noted as outcomes of unemployment (and possibly under-employment), as has the phenomenon of "astronaut" migrants. In the late 1980s and early 1990s the "astronaut," who left a wife and/or children comfortably settled in New Zealand while business interests were continued abroad, could be explained as a normal transition phase in the resettlement of business migrants. Time was needed to "wind up" previous activities, adjust to New Zealand conditions and so on. In the mid 1990s, however, as Lidgard (1996: 33) and especially Boyer (1996: 73–74) demonstrate, it is often a matter of survival. For households where the male breadwinner has been unable to obtain (any or suitable) employment because of problems with the recognition of qualifications and professional registration, a return to work in the country of origin may be the only way to minimize or avoid a loss of status and self-esteem. Clearly the GC points system was in need of an overhaul.

THE POLICY RESPONSE, 1995

Significant changes to provisions for the "economic" stream of immigration, embracing what were now called the General Skills (GSC) and Business Investor categories, were announced in July and came into effect in October 1995 (for a full discussion, see Trlin, 1997). There can be no doubt that the changes were primarily a response to difficulties, problems, tensions and issues in relation to Asian immigration during the previous 3–4 years. For GSC applicants the changes involved new prerequisites, an amended points system and a measure apparently directed against the "astronaut migrant" phenomenon.

Under the new prerequisites the GSC principal applicant is required to meet a minimum standard of English before arrival, namely level 5 of the General Module of the International English Language Testing System (IELTS). This standard is intended to ensure that applicants have at least "a partial command of the language," sufficient to cope in most situations. The same standard applies also to the PA's spouse or partner and children aged 16 years and over, though they can still qualify for residence upon payment of a NZ$20,000 fee per person failing to meet the standard. A fee refund can be obtained in full if the required standard is attained within 3 months of arrival, and in part ($14,000) if the standard is achieved 3–12 months after arrival (NZIS, 1995b: 10).

The rationale for these prerequisites was clear cut. A lack of language skills imposed costs on New Zealand, and the fee was an incentive for quick acquisition of basic skills (NZIS, 1995b: 10). However, while these changes appeared to address some problems — e.g., the language difficulty that impeded employment or daily interaction, the demands imposed upon secondary schools by senior NESB students — other issues either remained to be addressed or arose. Among these were the resource needs of schools catering for NESB students under 16 years of age and the implications for a national language policy (especially as the prerequisites did not apply to applicants in the Family, Humanitarian and Refugee categories).

Human capital factors remain dominant in the points system, accounting for 37 out of 44 points, but significant changes have been made to the previous GC assessment (NZIS, 1995b). First, there is a flatter points structure for qualifications (10–12 vs 2–15 points) with a 10 point minimum requirement that can be gained via any equivalent to a base degree, trade or recognized 3 year qualification. An advanced trade or professional qualification gains 11 points with 12 for a Masters degree equivalent or better. Second, where applicable, statutory registration is now required before an applicant can earn points for a professional qualification. Third, a validated skilled employment offer for at least 6 months gains 5 points (previously 3 points in a batch of optional settlement factors). And finally, several interesting adjustments have been made in the allocation of points for settlement factors (increased from a maximum of 5 out of 13 to 7 out of 9 points).

245

In particular: there are now 1–2 points for settlement funds (of NZ$100,000–$200,000); spousal human capital is recognized with 1–2 points for qualifications; New Zealand work experience gains 1–2 points (for 1–2 or more years); the sponsorship of a close family member gains 3 points; a previous provision for community sponsorship has been dropped; and no points (previously 3) are awarded for the transfer of investment funds.

Changes to the points system are obviously intended to tackle some of the previous shortcomings and problems identified. The flatter points structure redresses the bias towards academic qualifications and professional skills, presumably to encourage a broader skills mix in applications received and approved. Statutory registration tackles the problem of professionals (doctors, dentists, some engineers, etc.) and perhaps certain trades workers who gained residence but were unable to practice. The points value of a validated job offer indicates the perceived need to meet current labor market requirements and the importance of employment in resettlement and social integration. In the settlement factors, the community sponsorship provision has been dropped because of difficulties in "sifting genuine sponsors from ones contrived purely to gain points" (NZIS, 1995b: 14). The removal of points for investment funds was surprising. However, it reinforces the value of other factors (New Zealand work experience and the spouse's qualifications), perhaps in the belief that successful applicants will transfer funds either at times best suited to their resettlement or as a pragmatic act of commitment to New Zealand to secure a Returning Residents Visa.

A measure to encourage applicants genuinely committed to New Zealand, and to discourage others, was the final major component of the 1995 changes. Recent experience indicates that those to be discouraged included Asian "astronauts." These migrants, spending considerable periods abroad, were widely perceived to make a minimal contribution to the economy while family members enjoyed the benefits of New Zealand life. The force of circumstances described by Boyer (1996) and Lidgard (1996) were either unknown, not appreciated or believed to be countered by the new provision for professionals to secure statutory registration. Whatever the reason, principal applicants and their family members now approved for residence only qualify for a Returning Residents Visa if the principal applicant is "considered to have New Zealand residence status for tax purposes" (NZIS, 1995b: 15).

CONCLUSION

Changes in New Zealand's immigration policies since 1986, implemented as part of a broader program of social and economic development, have dramatically altered the nation's traditional patterns of immigration. In particular, the introduction of a General Category residence policy in 1991, which favored younger migrants with academic qualifications, work experience and capital for both settlement and investment, resulted in an immigrant in-flow that was predominantly Asian. A case study of approved Taiwanese and Chinese applicants (1991–1995) has confirmed both the success of this policy in attracting "quality migrants" to contribute to the attainment of development goals and policy flaws (reflected in migrant characteristics), the consequences of which have been noted and criticized by other researchers.

The changes, their implications and certain "negative" consequences, did not escape public attention. Public opinion polls revealed a hardening of attitudes toward Asian immigration and a conflation of these attitudes with those towards foreign investment. Four key factors underlying these public attitudes have been identified and discussed, namely: prejudice and an issue of national identity; Asian socio-economic power and its visibility; immigration politics, manifested in one political party's campaign in the run-up to the 1996 national election; and most importantly, the nature and outcomes of immigration policy — the source and catalyst for public concerns and attitudes. In response to both public pressure and official recognition of policy flaws, significant amendments to the General Category were implemented in 1995.

Have New Zealanders approved of the 1995 policy changes and what effect (if any) have the changes had upon Asian immigration? To gauge public opinion the National Research Bureau (1995: 34) included a question in its August 1995 poll and found that 63 per cent approved, 22 per cent disapproved and 15 per cent had no feelings either way. In the media most attention was given to the language ability prerequisite. Despite some initial concerns of possible discrimination and racism, it was generally agreed the provision would effectively test a basic knowledge of English among immigrants from non-English speaking backgrounds. In the business world, however, there were immediate concerns about the possible impact on the supply of highly skilled workers and the flow of investment capital.

These concerns proved to be justified. By the third quarter of 1996 the effects of the policy changes, perhaps accentuated by the anti-immigration campaign of Winston Peters, were undeniable. The numbers of applications received and approved, especially from Asia, had fallen dramatically compared with the previous year. The New Zealand Immigration Service was reported to be closing its office in Seoul and reviewing its staffing in other overseas posts (including Taiwan). Leading immigration consultants were doing likewise. Recent statistics show that the pattern of substantially lower immigration from Asia and elsewhere has continued into 1997.

Is this the end of a dramatic chapter in New Zealand's history of immigration? Or is it simply a pause during which potential Asian immigrants take stock of the new policy, public opinion and the political scene in New Zealand? At this time there is no unequivocal basis for a definitive answer to these questions. However, the continuing need for New Zealand to secure fragile political and economic ties with its prosperous Asian neighbors favors a pause rather than an end to reasonably high rates of Asian immigration.

Andrew Trlin, Anne Henderson and Regina Pernice

Acknowledgments

The research reported in this chapter is part of the "New Settlers Program" project supported by the New Zealand Foundation for Research, Science and Technology with a grant from the Public Good Science Fund. The authors also gratefully acknowledge the assistance of the New Zealand Immigration Service for permitting access to and facilitating examination of samples of applications for entry to New Zealand held on file at its Head Office, at other national branches or in secure storage.

14 "Australian Identity," Racism and Recent Responses to Asian Immigration to Australia[1]

Gavin W. Jones

The Evolution of National Identity

The history of Australia since European settlement in 1788 can be written from many perspectives, but one that would find considerable resonance among the Australian population at present would be a focus on the changing sense of national identity. The settlement of Australia, beginning at Botany Bay in present-day Sydney, involved the subjugation, displacement and to some extent organized extermination of an aboriginal population. In accord with the spirit of the times, the Australian aborigines were regarded by the early settlers as possessing a highly inferior culture (indeed many regarded them as sub-human). Unlike in New Zealand, no treaty was ever made with them recognizing their prior possession of the land; the attitude of white settlers until well into the 20th century was that they were destined to die out. White Australians suffered a collective amnesia with regard to Aboriginal Australians until a few decades ago. In my own school days they were almost invisible in our syllabus, and I gained no hint of the wrongs perpetrated on them by my ancestors until well after I had left school.

In the search for a national identity, the history of Aboriginal Australians has now come to play an important if controversial role. Recently Prime Minister John Howard took to task those promoting a "black armband" view of Australian history (i.e. giving excessive emphasis to the wrongs done the Aborigines, as well as to other shortcomings such as the environmental degradation caused by the farming systems adopted by the European settlers). He called for an emphasis on the positive accomplishments of nation building. Although Aboriginal Australians constitute only 2 per cent of the Australian population, their role in defining Australian identity is likely to loom much larger than this proportion might suggest.

Long-standing feelings of superiority, guilt, anger and confusion color the search for an appropriate and acceptable accommodation between Aboriginal and non-Aboriginal Australians. This background of relations between a white "master race" and a displaced non-white native people is not irrelevant to attitudes over the past century to neighboring Asian populations and the more recent issue of reactions to the growing proportion of Asians in the Australian population.

Throughout much of Australian history, the need to establish a large settler population has been an unquestioned goal. In the early days, there was fear of possible French invasion, as well as the need for a much larger population to occupy the land and open farming and pastoral leases. But over time, the "Britishness" of the settler population began to change, even when the population remained ethnically heavily Anglo-Celtic (a long-standing Australian term which reflects the important role of the Irish in the Australian population).

The Australian-born began to develop an identity separate from that of their old-world parents, and a sense of Australian nationalism began to develop quite early, notwithstanding what appears today as an extraordinary sense of loyalty to the "mother country" reflected in Australia's unquestioning rallying to the flag at the time of the Boer War and the First World War. The First World War — when Australian troops displayed heroism and suffered heavy casualties in Gallipoli, Europe and North Africa — strengthened the sense of Australian identity and left in its wake the Returned Sailors' and Soldiers' Imperial League of Australia (later the RSL) "to carry the banner of an aggressive and somewhat exclusive Australian nationalism" (Price, 1991: 4). This was the time of the independent "Australian Britons" — people of predominantly Anglo-Celtic origin who, though still proud of British connections, were determined to be independent of old world bonds and inequalities (Hancock, 1930, Chapter 3).

Australian nationalism has always had its racist elements.[2] *The Bulletin*, an important barometer of Australian aspirations, and one of Australia's most prestigious magazines, kept at its masthead the slogan "Australia for the White Man" over the entire period 1908 to 1961. It frequently argued that Australia should not receive non-European migrants at all. Prominent poets and novelists such as Joseph Furphy, Henry Handel Richardson and Henry Lawson presented racist themes and viewpoints that strike the modern reader as offensive but which were merely in tune with the tenor of their times. Until after the Second World War, all the countries to Australia's immediate north except Thailand were under colonial control, and a smug sense of superiority of Europeans to all non-white populations prevailed — a sense little affected by events such as Japan's victory over Russia in the Russo-Japanese War in 1905. The paradox is that, while writers such as C. J. Dennis and historian Charles Bean, a key figure in the creation of the Anzac legend, equated race consciousness and white supremacy with Australian fighting spirit, these sentiments co-existed with the emerging stress on egalitarianism, the fair go and taking individuals as they come. Of course, egalitarianism was being promoted in a very homogeneous society.

Postwar Immigration and the Demise of the White Australia Policy

During World War II Australia experienced near-invasion by the Japanese. Knowledge of atrocities perpetrated by the Japanese forces both before (in China and Manchuria) and during the conflict, many of the latter directly experienced by Australian prisoners of war, entrenched a longstanding attitude of fear of invasion from the north and was a potent element in the postwar immigration drive. Australia's population at the end of World War II was only seven and a half million, living on a land area almost as large as that of the United States (excluding Alaska). The need for a rapid increase in population appeared self-evident. Australia's postwar immigration policy was therefore simple: to bring in migrants from Britain, but from other European countries as well if numbers from Britain did not meet requirements.

The displaced persons, largely from Eastern Europe, came in large numbers in the years immediately following the end of the war. The search for immigrants was progressively widened to Southern Europe and even to Egypt, Lebanon and Turkey, which were accorded a kind of "honorary European" status, apparently by virtue of their proximity.to Europe. In the 1950s and 1960s, settlers from Italian or Greek peasant stock, with low levels of education and lacking English language, or later from Lebanon or Turkey, were clearly preferred to well educated, English-speaking, Christian potential settlers from "real" Asian countries such as Hong Kong, Sri Lanka or the Philippines.

The reason for this curious set of preferences was the abiding influence of the White Australia Policy[3], which was the centre point of Australian immigration policy from the 1880s[4] until the first real dent appeared in 1966. This policy was based on fashionable theories of racial superiority, and its objectives were to attain an ethnically homogeneous society. The Aboriginal population was expected to die out, with those of "mixed race" (the majority of the Aboriginal population) "assimilating into the majority population to the point of eventual invisibility" (Jupp, 1995: 208). The overall impact of exclusion of non-European migrants and a fairly modest immigration inflow during the 1930s was that by the time of the Second World War Australia was indeed a very homogeneous population, predominantly of Anglo-Celtic origin and with over 90 per cent local born.

In the postwar years, however, the White Australia Policy became dysfunctional in a number of respects: it thwarted the attainment of the national policy to achieve high migrant intake, by restricting that intake to European societies which eventually lost the incentive to migrate to Australia because of their growing prosperity; it was based on increasingly discredited theories and attitudes; "it restricted the thinking of Australians to a world view unduly focused on distant regions such as Britain" (Jupp, 1996: 209); it alienated newly independent Asian states (though this was hotly denied by successive Ministers for Immigration); and as neighboring Asian countries achieved rapid economic development and a more important place on the world stage, the policy became increasingly contrary to Australia's economic, social and political interests. Paradoxically, an important factor eroding support for White Australia was the success of postwar mass immigration programs composed of non-English-speaking Europeans, designed to sustain White Australia by supplementing British migration. Many of these migrants were culturally very different from the British, yet they appeared to fit into Australian society with little friction — and certainly improved its cuisine — thus strengthening the case for widening the source areas to include Asian countries. Some state governments moved towards multicultural approaches in their settlement policies, no longer requiring immigrants to become indistinct from Anglo-Australians. The widening of source areas of migrants to the Middle East and Turkey, already mentioned, made untenable the cultural arguments for White Australia and left exposed its officially-denied crude racist basis.

Under increasing pressure for modification, some minor changes were introduced in the White Australia Policy beginning in 1958, with a more important breakthrough in 1966.[5] The policy was finally fully dismantled in 1973, during the early days of the Whitlam labor government.

Immigration Patterns After Dismantling of the White Australia Policy

Before discussing the changing sources of migrants since the dismantling of the White Australia Policy, the overall volume of migration needs to be stressed. This has remained high throughout the postwar period, with net migration often exceeding 100,000 per year, adding close to one per cent to the rate of population growth (Fig. 1). The result is that migrants constitute a larger proportion of the Australian population than they do in Canada or the U.S.A. — indeed, larger than in any other industrialized nation except Israel.[6] However, over the period 1992–1995 Australia's per capita migrant intake has been only about half that of Canada.

Australia has had only a quarter century to adjust to a situation of substantial immigration from Asia. Since the late 1970s, at least one quarter and generally one third or more of annual settler arrivals have been from Asia. In 1971, only 167,000 Australians had an Asian birthplace — and a not insubstantial number of these were of European ethnicity. By 1981, the Asian birthplace population had increased to 370,000 and ten years later had reached 665,000. The Chinese and Vietnamese have become the sixth and seventh largest immigrant ethnic groups respectively, after the British, Germans, Italians, Greeks and members of the former Yugoslav republics.

Figure 1: The Natural Increase and Net Migration Component Population Growth Rates, Australia, 1948–1996

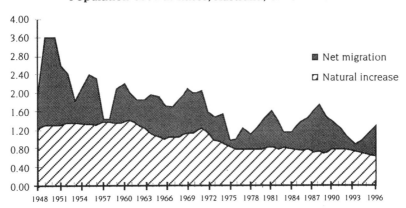

Figure 2 shows the 10 main countries of origin of immigrants in 1964, before the policy had changed, then in 1984, once the impact of the changed policy had had time to settle down, and finally in 1994. The most striking trends are the substantial fall in the absolute numbers, as well as the share, of British migrants, the rise of Asian source countries, and also the diverse sources of migrants in recent times. This, in fact, has been a marked characteristic of Australian immigration. Apart from the dominant British group, no one source of migrants has become very large, though total non-British are very numerous. The importance of different sources has risen and then fallen over the past half century — first the displaced persons, mainly of central and eastern European origin, then the Yugoslavs and Italians, then the Greeks, more recently the Vietnamese. Most recently of all, the Chinese and Filipinos have played an increasing role. The Chinese have come from a large number of countries other than China — Hong Kong, Vietnam, Malaysia, Singapore, even Papua New Guinea and East Timor. They joined a small population of ethnic Chinese of longer standing.[7] Although in terms of "ethnic strength,"[8] the Chinese in 1987 still lagged well behind the Germans, Italians, and Greeks, it seems certain that within another decade or so they will have passed all these groups and will be second only to the dominant Anglo-Celtic group in "ethnic strength" in Australia (for the projected situation in 2025, see Price, 1996, Table 4.1). Nevertheless, the point just made — the diversity of migrant sources — continues to hold. This has led to an extraordinarily diverse population at present, drawn from all the world's continents and most of the world's countries.[9]

In some ways, the scale of Asian migration following the change in policy has been surprising. In 1960, a group of liberal academics and public figures, the Immigration Reform Group, published a pamphlet entitled *Immigration: Control or Color Bar?* (Rivett (ed), 1962), in which it was proposed that, to "test the waters" of public tolerance, as it were, 1,500 non-European mi-

Gavin W. Jones

Figure 2: Top Ten Sources of Settler Arrivals
1964–65, 1984–85 and 1994–95

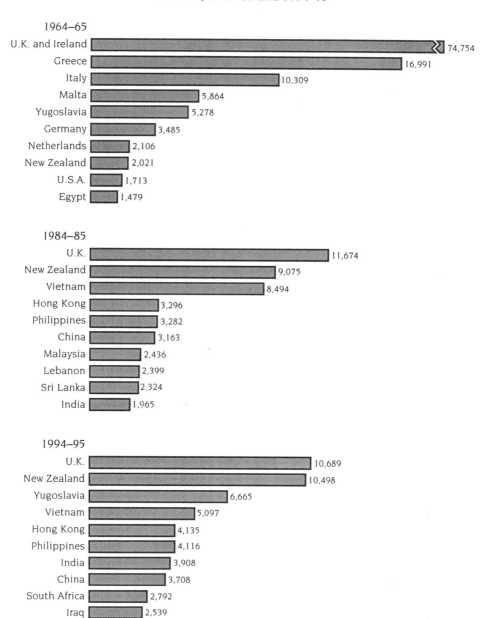

1964–65

U.K. and Ireland	74,754
Greece	16,991
Italy	10,309
Malta	5,864
Yugoslavia	5,278
Germany	3,485
Netherlands	2,106
New Zealand	2,021
U.S.A.	1,713
Egypt	1,479

1984–85

U.K.	11,674
New Zealand	9,075
Vietnam	8,494
Hong Kong	3,296
Philippines	3,282
China	3,163
Malaysia	2,436
Lebanon	2,399
Sri Lanka	2,324
India	1,965

1994–95

U.K.	10,689
New Zealand	10,498
Yugoslavia	6,665
Vietnam	5,097
Hong Kong	4,135
Philippines	4,116
India	3,908
China	3,708
South Africa	2,792
Iraq	2,539

Source: Australia's Population Trends and Prospects 1995, Bureau of Immigration, Multicultural and Population Research

grants should be let in annually for five years and the number be gradually increased thereafter. In the event, however, once the White Australia Policy was modified, this tentative number was very rapidly exceeded. In the late 1960s, about 9,000 non-Europeans and part-Europeans were admitted annually. The overturning of the policy in 1972 led to even greater changes: by 1979, over 20,000 Asian migrants were entering each year, and the number had exceeded 30,000 in a number of years in the late 1980s and early 1990s. Australia managed to adapt to these large inflows of Asian migrants with scarcely any overt signs of unrest.

An important aspect of the flow of Asian migrants to Australia is that these migrants have been, on average, more highly educated and have achieved higher income levels in Australia than the rest of the population. This is because a substantial proportion of them have been admitted under the business and skills categories of the Australian migration program, and because even in the case of family reunion, Asian migrants have been generally quite well educated. The only groups of Asians who are less educated than the Australian population have been the refugees from Vietnam, Cambodia and Laos[10], and some of the family reunion flow from the Philippines and China, because in the case of refugees in particular, the points-based criteria for assessing people seeking entry to Australia, which give considerable importance to education, are relaxed.

The relatively high socio-economic status of Asian groups in the Australian population has resulted from deliberate policy, based on fear of the consequences of the development of enclaves of economically disadvantaged Asian migrants for public perceptions about these migrant groups. Although there is certainly a (correct) perception that refugee groups are economically disadvantaged, this is not the case for Asian Australians as a whole. Indeed, there is perhaps a risk of jealousy stemming from the obvious signs of wealth and success in the case of much of the Asian population. An indicator of the remarkable educational success of Australia's Asian populations is that over the last five years, students with Asian ethnic backgrounds have captured approximately 40 per cent of the top 100 places in the NSW Higher School Certificate examination held at the end of secondary school (Jones, 1996a).[11] Since the 1981 Census, the Vietnamese have consistently been over-represented in University education, despite their economically disadvantaged situation.[12]

Assimilation, Integration, Multiculturalism: What next?

Official attitudes towards what is expected of migrants to Australia have undergone some striking modifications. In the early postwar years, refugees from Europe, be they professionals or of more modest background, were expected to serve on construction projects for two years after their arrival. The policy of the time was assimilation — i.e., adaptation to the culture of the host community. Involvement of migrant men in the workforce would require them to acquire English language and adapt to the work habits and other Australian customs. Compulsory enrolment in the education system would largely take care of the assimilation of the second generation. It was only a proportion of migrant women, left at home to raise families, who would be largely cut off from Australian society and have more trouble adapting than did their husbands or children.

From 1964 to 1973 integration was the accepted policy; it required less complete melding into the Australian population than did the earlier assimilation policy. Then in 1973, under the Whitlam Labor government, multiculturalism (drawing heavily on the Canadian model) became the official policy (Zubrzycki, 1991; Jupp, 1991, 1996). This policy was continued with enthusiasm during the Fraser liberal government, and was strongly supported during the Hawke and Keating Labor governments. In its early years, multiculturalism and the celebration of ethnic diversity began to be promoted as distinctively Australian symbols, indeed for some government members it was seen as the focus of a new kind of nationalism (Betts, 1988: 105). The contrast with the rather stultifying pro-British sentiments of the later Menzies era of the 1950s and early 1960s was marked; but it is likely that neither the Menzies emphasis nor the "showy" multiculturalism of Al Grassby, Whitlam's Minister for Immigration, reflected middle Australian attitudes.

Under the Keating government from late 1991 to 1996, there was a strong push for Australia to be accepted as a "part of Asia." Keating strongly believed that Australia's future lay in this rapidly developing region, and that the increasing share of Asians in the Australian population had very positive implications for enmeshing Australia economically in the region.[13] For those Australians who were closely involved with the dynamic countries of South-East and East Asia, Keating's vision seemed more like a commonsense statement (Jones, 1996). To be a part of Asia does not require Australians to deny their European heritage, but it does require the recognition that Australia's geography places us irrevocably as part of this region, and the growing economic and political clout of East Asia renders this an opportunity to be grasped rather than cause for regret and nostalgic backward glances.

Another important plank of Keating's policies was the push towards a republic. The monarchists — concentrated among the older Anglo-Celtic population — were offended by the joint republican push and the notion of Australia's Asian destiny. There were others with republican sentiments, who were in tune with the Keating goal of a republic by the centenary of Federation in 2001, who were nevertheless left offside by the Keating vision of Australia's Asian destiny. For them, the Republic was part and parcel of an aggressive nationalism that was not particularly tolerant of ethnic and cultural diversity.

Attitudes to Asian Immigration: the Polls

It would be useful to know whether Australian public attitudes towards immigration in general and towards Asian immigration in particular have been changing over time. It seems clear that the overall level of support for immigration fell between the 1960s and 1970s (Betts, 1988, Fig. 5.1), and opposition to immigration appears to have reached a new, higher plateau since the mid-1980s (Betts, 1996; Millbank, 1996:12–14). Nobody was quite sure about the level of public acceptance or rejection of Asian immigration at the time when the White Australia Policy was overturned in 1972, and despite the publication of the results of many public opinion polls since that time, it is not clear whether public support for Asian immigration increased or decreased during the period of increasing Asian immigration over the 1970s and 1980s. Support has probably decreased since the mid-1980s, along with decreased support for immigration as a whole.

Most of these polls on Asian immigration have been in the context of a broader question about whether the level of overall migration is too high, about right or too low. A similar question on Asian immigration is usually a follow-on question to this more general question. What is found is that the level of support for Asian immigration does not differ greatly from the level of support for immigration as a whole. This suggests that the answers regarding Asian immigration may frequently not be expressing any particular attitude about Asian immigration from a racial viewpoint, but rather from a broader set of views about whether substantial levels of immigration are a good or bad thing.

For what they are worth, the poll findings on Asian immigration show that, although there is considerable variability between polls, the proportion who answers "too many" is generally in the 40 to 60 per cent range, whereas the proportion replying "about right" or "too few" is generally in the 30 to 40 per cent range, though with some outliers above 50 per cent. After a thorough review of these poll results, Goot (1991) concludes that some of the differences might reflect changes over time, but others may reflect differences in the way the questions were worded.

> However the most remarkable if least obvious cause of the difference seems to be the contexts in which the questions were asked; more precisely, differences in the length and focus of the various questionnaires in which questions on immigration were embedded. Public opinion on the rate of immigration is not only "soft," it is created in the very attempt to measure it (Goot, 1991: 277).

Perhaps the more important finding is that people from non-English-speaking backgrounds and the tertiary educated were more likely to support immigration, including Asian immigration, than were less educated "middle Australians." Australians as a whole felt warmer towards British immigrants, who rated 63, or warmest, on a scale of feelings, followed by Italians (61) and Greeks (58). Feelings were cooler towards Chinese (50), Indians (48), Vietnamese (46) and Lebanese (45) (Evans, 1996).

A final point to be noted in this section is that although the majority of

Australians will say that immigration in general, and Asian immigration in particular, is too high when pressed to give an opinion in surveys, multiple issue opinion polling does not show migration to be an issue of major concern. For example, *The Bulletin* Morgan Poll of 28 November 1995, which surveyed the issues voters believed the Government should be addressing, immigration rated 15th, behind "interest rates" and above "child and youth issues" (Millbank, 1996: 14).

The Hanson Affair of 1996 and its Interpretation

A major controversy erupted in Australia in September 1996 following the maiden speech in Parliament by the independent member for Oxley in Queensland, Pauline Hanson. Ms. Hanson had been deselected by the Liberal Party before the election because of her racist views, and her maiden speech was a cocktail of grievances, concerning policy on Aborigines, Asian migration, foreign ownership and the need to do away with Australian foreign aid programs. Her speech (including the statement "I believe we are in danger of being swamped by Asians") flew in the face of accepted bipartisan support for an immigration program in which ethnic background was not a criterion. But it clearly resonated with a substantial body of opinion in Australia, and for months anti-Aboriginal and anti-Asian views, some of them of a crudely racist kind, filled talkback radio programs and letters to the editor. It was almost as if a dammed-up flow of opinion was breaking out. Some unpleasant verbal and physical abuse was experienced by some Asian students, tourists and Asian-Australians. Prime Minister Howard was slow to react, claiming that it would be inappropriate to dignify the Hanson speech by replying to it specifically. However, conscious of the harm that reporting of the speech and subsequent controversy was doing to Australia's reputation in Asia, a bipartisan motion on racism was finally passed by Parliament on 30 October 1996. It might be cited in full:

That this house
- Reaffirms its commitment to the right of all Australians to enjoy equal rights and be treated with equal respect regardless of race, color, creed or origin;
- Reaffirms its commitment to maintaining an immigration policy wholly non-discriminatory on grounds of race, color, creed or origin;
- Reaffirms its commitment to the process of reconciliation with Aboriginal and Torres Strait Islander people, in the context of redressing their profound social and economic disadvantage;
- Reaffirms its commitment to maintaining Australia as a culturally diverse, tolerant and open society, united by an over-riding commitment to our nation, and its democratic institutions and values; and
- Denounces racial intolerance in any form as incompatible with the kind of society we are and want to be.

258

The statement makes no mention of multiculturalism. This formerly bi-partisan policy had been dropped with alacrity by the incoming Howard conservative government.

A central element of the Hanson complaints was that the Asian proportion of the Australian population is likely to rise to unacceptable levels. How high will it rise? It is not easy even to establish the current proportion of the Australian population with an Asian ethnicity, let alone to project it forward in time. Birthplace figures certainly do not describe the ethnic mix, both because especially in earlier times, many migrants with Asian birthplaces were children of British or Australian colonial officials or business people and, more importantly, birthplace figures tell us nothing of the second and subsequent generations. Therefore the fact that, based on recent immigration patterns, by 2031, the Asian-born might be about 7.5 per cent of Australia's population (Khoo and Price, 1996: Table 7) is less relevant for most purposes than the proportion of the population that is ethnically Asian. According to careful estimates by Price (1996) this proportion was 3.2 per cent in 1987 (4.6 per cent if West Asians were included) and would be higher by at least 2 more percentage points today. Price projects the Asian ethnic proportion to 2025 on the assumption that both total immigration and its distribution by birthplace remain roughly at recent levels. These assumptions yield projections that by 2025, the proportion of the population with an Asian ethnicity will rise to 15 per cent, or 19 per cent including West Asians (Price, 1996, Table 4.1).

While Price's figure might appear alarmingly high to those who define Australian identity mainly in terms of a homogeneous ethnicity, it would not appear alarming at all to those who define it in terms of a common experience of Australian life, because well over half of the 19 per cent would have been Australian born and raised. Price also emphasizes that if the different ethnic groups in Australia continue to mix with each other, we will have a large and increasing number of persons of mixed ethnic origin who, in ethnic terms, can only describe themselves as "Australian."

What are we to make of the 1996–97 immigration controversy? (It can hardly be dignified by the term "debate"). It clearly revealed that racist sentiments are alive and well among a substantial section of the Australian population. But this was hardly a secret; indeed, as this paper has made clear, Australia's history has been built on racist foundations. It would appear that racism had long been a staple fare of certain popular talkback programs on commercial radio, but most of Australia's intelligentsia, who almost by definition would be listening to the ABC (Australian Broadcasting Commission) were oblivious to this (Jakubowicz, 1996).

Australia's popular culture, like that of any country we care to examine, contains subterranean racist elements. Although there have been no major public disorders based on racial tensions, many cases of small-scale violence, intimidation, abuse and discrimination have been documented, mainly directed against Aboriginal people but some against Asian migrants and students (Human Rights and Equal Opportunity Commission, 1991). The Hanson phenomenon has brought Australia's racism to the surface: even on the football field, racial vilification of Aboriginal players seems to have increased in the past year.

The more important issue is to decide whether the 1996-97 outpouring of racist sentiments has been to some extent cathartic, enabling the country to move forward on what is probably a more realistic basis of acknowledgment that ethnocentrism underlies our national ethos; or whether this airing of the dirty linen of the national psyche represents a dangerous lurch towards intolerance, opening the way for increased influence of right wing groups such as the League of Rights and Australians Against Further Immigration, or of more radical neo-fascist groups such as National Action, which are always looking to increase their national appeal.

In coming to terms with such issues, another question is whether attitudes to Asian immigration differ on the basis of age, ethnicity, education, class, rural-urban origin or any other characteristic. Some worrying fault lines have been opening in Australian society over the past two decades, with increasing income inequality (next worst to that in the United States among economically advanced countries, according to some accounts) and high youth unemployment (Karmel, 1997). If those who feel worse off economically also felt divorced from the rest of society in terms of their attitudes and basic beliefs, this would be a matter of great concern. There is some evidence that such a gulf in attitudes is indeed developing — for example, that anti-Asian sentiment was more prevalent in "middle Australia," among the Anglo-Australian working class, who feel "disenfranchised," as it were, by the emphases of multiculturalism, whereas among liberal intellectuals there is stronger support for multiculturalism and a more diverse society. Pauline Hanson certainly claimed to be representing the "forgotten people,"

> principally the Anglos — not the polished, cosmopolitan Anglos from politics and the Arts, transcendent cultural beings such as Paul Keating or Hilary McPhee, but the Anglos from the school of hard knocks -working class battlers or shopkeepers like herself, the unpolished white folk, what poet Les Murray has called "Vernacular Australia" with its vernacular heritage — billy tea, swags, Blue Hills and blue gums, the ute and the kelpie. *Australia All Over* territory (Cochrane, 1997).[14]

Pauline Hanson tended to be ridiculed by academics and by the establishment because of her ignorance. Ignorance she certainly displayed — the statement in her maiden speech that Malaysia's population is 100 million had to be edited out of the Hansard record, and in reply to a television interviewer's question, she clearly had no idea what the word "xenophobic" meant. But supercilious reactions to her ignorance are counterproductive; her ignorance is not a problem to her supporters, because she shares their basic reactions to what is happening in Australian society. "If she were educated she would belong to the enemy" (Cochrane, 1997).

Betts (1988, Chapters 5 and 7) argues persuasively that in the 1970s and 1980s, "liberal cosmopolitanism," drawing on a 1960s background of opposition to the White Australia Policy and to involvement in the Vietnam war, and support for women's liberation and other social movements, became an almost uncontestable value in intellectual circles. A dangerous gulf developed between middle Australians and the "liberal cosmopolitans" who took pains to denigrate aspects of Australian popular culture and to criticize it for its ethnocentrism, racism, and indifference to the needs of immigrant communities and (once the refugee intake built up after 1976) to the desperate needs of Indo-Chinese refugees.

After the policy of multiculturalism was introduced in 1973 under the Whitlam government, "racial and cultural tolerance and the celebration of ethnic diversity were now to be promoted as distinctively Australian symbols, and for at least some members of the Government a new kind of nationalism could be built around the idea of the 'family of Australia'" (Betts, 1988:105). This new nationalism, however, involved a tendency to denigrate parochial Australian values and living patterns, which were characterized as dull, conformist, materialist and essentially worthless. The fact is, of course, that these "worthless" values and patterns of living continue to be those of the majority of Australians, and will not be given up simply because some intellectuals rail against them. By the same token, the overturning of the White Australia Policy, involving the removal of discrimination on grounds of race in migrant selection, did not represent a victory in a closely argued debate. "White Australia supporters were not persuaded by reason and evidence. It was a political victory that left the racist parochial unconverted but outmanoevred" (Betts, 1988: 105).

At least ostensibly, it was a valid concern about whether Australian society was ready to deal with the strains resulting from a high level of Asian immigration in such a context that constituted the essence of the controversial speech by prominent historian Professor Geoffrey Blainey at Warrnambool in 1984. Blainey was "letting the side down" by raising such issues and he was attacked unmercifully by the intellectual establishment as a result (Betts, 1988: 160–168).[15] The issues deserved to be dealt with on their merits rather than on the assumption that Blainey was expressing racist views. The fact that subsequent events (or rather, lack of events) seem to have shown that Australia's limits of tolerance are higher than Blainey anticipated in no sense negates the validity of his raising the issue.

During the Hawke-Keating years (1983–1996), and especially under Keating, many people felt pressured into accepting, or at least not overtly opposing, "liberal" views on matters such as the Republic, the need for a new flag, and attitudes towards multiculturalism — all of which acquired an aura of "political correctness." Of all recent Australian Prime Ministers,

Keating was the most brilliant Parliamentary performer, putting down his opposition with cruel but effective riposte; there is little doubt that some of those who opposed the notion that Australia could really be accepted as part of the Asian region felt cowed into silence. Keating felt passionately that Australia's future lay in Asia, and he made the point strongly in speeches. He probably misjudged the proportion of people who felt threatened by the vision of the future which he promoted — or who at least needed more time to adjust to it. Political correctness was also the order of the day in the immigration debate. Many people who wanted to reduce the immigration intake because of genuine concerns about environmental sustainability or threats to social cohesion were unjustly accused of racism and felt constrained from speaking out. Those whose opposition to Asian immigration was crudely racist were similarly constrained. The Hanson controversy may represent, in one sense, a "breakout" as such people suddenly felt released to say all the things, nasty or otherwise, that they had been bottling up for so long.

The Future

The current prognosis for the future of racism in Australia is a mixed one. Australia's record over the past 50 years in absorbing migration flows from eastern and southern Europe, and more recently from Asia, has been remarkably good. These were, relative to the population, very large inflows indeed (larger than either the United States or Canada have experienced over the same period), and the cultural adaptations required in integrating Southern Italian and Greek migrants into Australian society were actually greater than those required in the case of most categories of recent Asian migrants.[16]

It has been argued that the relatively weak national identity of Australian society (lacking, as it does, national myths linked to major geopolitical crises, or a dominant national religion) may make it easier for immigrants to become integrated into Australian society, and for the host society to accept immigrants (Holton, 1994: 213). However, immigration policy cannot be settled on the assumption that Australia does not include racists or that they cannot poison race relations.

Does the 1996–97 race controversy represent a political aberration, or a harbinger of change for the worse that can only be avoided by a fundamental change in social and political direction? The answer is not clear. Early success in migrant absorption occurred in a rapidly expanding economy offering jobs to all, most children of migrants were rapidly integrated into the community through the public education system or parochial Catholic schools, and there was little resentment of the minority forced to rely on welfare. These fortunate conditions no longer prevail; for example, unemployment rates among refugee groups in Australia are very high indeed and they remain stubbornly high among young people in general. Added to this is the rise in political temperature resulting from the resentment of some in the white community with the High Court ruling on native land titles. As mentioned earlier in this paper, racism towards Aborigines and racism towards Asians cannot be totally separated.

Pauline Hanson has kept the heat on, founding her One Nation party, conducting speaking tours, mainly in country areas, and publishing an extraordinary ghost-written diatribe, *Pauline Hanson: The Truth*, which apart from revealing an extreme political paranoia on the part of its anonymous author, contains some vicious anti-Asian racism. A poll published on April 30, 1997 showed that 10 per cent of Australians said they would vote for Hanson's party (20 per cent in Queensland). This undoubtedly exaggerates the real support her party would get in an election. But the realities of the Australian parliamentary system are such that, although there is little danger of her party winning any seats in the lower house, they could well pick up a senate seat or two which could conceivably leave them holding the balance of power in this house of review. In any event, her party's existence means that extreme racist views will for the first time in decades be fed "legitimately" into the political debate. They may, however, be illegal. A Chinese-Australian group threatened to take Hanson to court under the Racial Discrimination Act.[17]

The year 1997 is therefore full of dangers with regard to race relations. Avoidance of divisiveness will demand more than status quo politics. It will require that the leaders of the major parties show statesmanship of a high order. The task should not be beyond them. Australia remains relatively free of terrorism, ethnic and religious hatreds and transplanted prejudices. It is arguably no more racist than any of its neighboring Asian countries, or other English-speaking countries with which it is most closely aligned.

The sectarianism of Anglo-Irish relations and the ethnic hatreds of the former Yugoslavia have tended to wither among these populations when transplanted to Australia. Australia remains basically a decent society, if a little self-righteous. Although Hanson has managed to raise the temperature on racism, for most Australians it is not a pressing issue. As respected commentator and ABC radio talk show host Philip Adams said in a recent speech, if we exclude the dyed-in-the-wool racists on one extreme and the committed multiculturalists on the other, public opinion is like a large blob of jelly, ready to wobble in whatever direction it is pushed. It is up to those who are committed to a harmonious society to push it in the direction of tolerance — or better still, of acceptance, even celebration, of difference.

Culturally, Australia is alive and evolving — already a multicultural society which must now forge a new Australian identity out of these diverse communities. Despite the Howard government's shrinking from the term "multiculturalism," and a great deal of uncertainty in the community about what the term really means (Goot, 1993), a poll published in the *Weekend Australian* on 3–4 May 1997 showed very strong public acceptance of whatever its respondents believed the concept to mean: 78 per cent agreed that multiculturalism had been good for Australia, and only 16 per cent felt that it had been bad. Certainly, there is an identity crisis of sorts: "a contradiction exists between the British historical tradition, the current Anglo-American cultural dominance and the Asia-Pacific geographic and economic location" (Jupp, 1995: 211). But not too many Australians worry about it when they go to bed at night. In time, more will appreciate Woolcott's (1997) point: "the tyranny of distance has been replaced by the opportunities of proximity."

Endnotes

[1]   The author thanks Terry Hull for useful comments on an earlier draft of this chapter.

[2]   Historian Humphrey McQueen argues provocatively that "racism is the most important single component of Australian nationalism" (McQueen, 1970: 42) and that "the Labor Party was racist before it was socialist" (McQueen, 1970: 53).

[3]   Although successive Australian governments strenuously denied that a "White Australia Policy" existed, in this case Australians' tendency to call a spade a spade prevailed in the persistence of the term in popular usage.

[4]   Obviously, before the time of Federation in 1901, when the Immigration Restriction Bill was adopted, the exclusionist policies (mainly directed at Chinese and Pacific Islander laborers) were separately instituted by the different Australian colonies (London, 1970: 3–23; Yarwood, 1964).

[5]   The most important change in 1966 was that non-Europeans already in Australia under temporary permits, but likely to be there indefinitely, could apply for resident status after five years instead of the previous fifteen year waiting period. Additionally, applications by "well qualified people" from non-European countries were to be "considered on the basis of their suitability as settlers, their ability to integrate readily and their possession of qualifications which are in fact positively useful to Australia" (London, 1970: 28). The Minister for Immigration expected only limited increases in non-European migration to result from the policy changes, and stated that "the basic aim of preserving a homogeneous population will be maintained."

[6]   The proportion of immigrants in the population of certain immigrant-receiving countries is as follows:

Australia	22.7%	U.S.A.	7.9%
Switzerland	18.1%	France	6.3%
Canada	15.5%	U.K.	3.5%
Germany	8.5%		

[7]   Australia experienced substantial inflows of Chinese immigrants onto the goldfields of Victoria and New South Wales during the 1850s and early 1860s. Most left when the gold rushes ended, and the Chinese population, which had reached 42,000 in Victoria alone in 1858–9 (one-sixth of the adult male population — Price, 1974: 71), had fallen to 17,000 in 1921. See Choi, 1975.

[8]   This is a term used by Price (1996) to define the ethnic origins of the Australian people. In the case of mixed ancestry, proportions are assigned according to the proportion of each ethnicity in the person's ancestry. See also Khoo and Price, 1996.

[9]   The diversity of the Australian population is well captured in a major book prepared for the Australian Bicentennial — Jupp, 1988.

[10]   Employed immigrants from Vietnam, Cambodia and Laos are also far less likely than other immigrant groups to be employed in professional occupations (Jupp, 1995, Table 3). See also Viviani, 1996.

[11] Although some students are sent to Australia from Asian countries for their high school education, it seems certain that ethnic Asian students would constitute fewer than 10 per cent of students sitting for the NSW Higher Certificate examination.

[12] Data for 1994 in the state of New South Wales show that Vietnam-born participation rates at University are double the general Australian rate (Parr and Mok, 1995), and this is likely to be even more pronounced as the Australian-born children of Vietnamese are now entering University. More than three times as high a proportion of the Vietnamese students in higher education were from a low socio-economic background than was the case with students of English speaking background (Dobson, Birrell and Rapson, 1996). In 1991, Vietnam-born students in medical faculties were 5.2 per cent of all medical students although the Vietnam-born were still less than 1 per cent of the Australian population in 1995 (Birrell, 1995: 30).

[13] Keating was by no means the first Labor Party figure to stress the need to enmesh Australia in the Asian region. In 1983, Bill Hayden, as Minister of Foreign Affairs, told *Asiaweek* that "we're an anomaly as a European country in this part of the world. There's already a large and growing Asian population in Australia and it is inevitable in my view that Australia will become a Eurasian country over the next century or two. I happen to think that's desirable. That means we are becoming part of the mainstream of this region" (Betts, 1988: 159).

[14] In this quote, Blue Hills refers to a long-running radio drama extremely popular with middle Australia; Australia All Over refers to a radio program equally popular with middle Australia, especially country people, in which ordinary Australians from all over the country talk about their lives and experiences. Swags were what the itinerant swagman (hoboe) carried. "Ute" = utility, a small pick-up truck used by farmers and tradesmen. The kelpie is an Australian sheepdog.

[15] For a subsequent elaboration of Blainey's arguments, see Blainey, 1984. For the academic counterattack on him and his views, see Markus and Ricklefs, eds., 1985.

[16] For example, many Greek families continue to use the Greek language at home even into the second and third generation; and Greek rates of outmarriage are very low (Clyne and Kipp, 1995; Price, 1994).

[17] This act was passed in 1975 and strengthened in 1995 by the addition of a section about the public expression of racial hatred (Zelinka, 1996: 19).

15 A Sensible Immigrant Policy in New York City

Angelica Oleg Tang

IMMIGRATION AND NEW YORK CITY

The City of New York has welcomed immigrants from every corner of the earth for close to 400 years. As of 1994, people born outside the United States make up a third of the total population of 7.3 million persons in New York City. In addition, between 50 per cent and 55 per cent of all persons in the city are either foreign-born or children of foreign born persons.[1] Fifteen per cent of all immigrants to the United States come to New York City.[2]

Immigration from Asia

The growth in immigration from Asia was consistent with overall increases in immigration. Asian immigrants constituted 22 per cent of immigrants to the city in the 1970s and 26 per cent in the 1980s and early 1990s.[3] Chinese immigrants from the Mainland, Taiwan and Hong Kong, were the largest group from Asia and averaged 12,000 annually in the early 1990s compared to 9,000 in the 1980s. This placed China as the third leading source of immigrants to the city, a position it has held since the 1970s. Although, only 26 per cent of all immigrants to New York City come from Asia, Asian immigrants comprise 42 per cent of all immigrants entering the U.S.

Population By Race And Ethnicity

Immigration continues to shape the character of New York City, as has been true throughout its history. Between 1980 and 1990, the large flow of immigrants helped stabilize the city's population. Within each race group, the pattern is similar: the native-born decline, either through death or migration, and are replaced by immigrants and their offspring.

The landmark *Immigration and Nationality Act of* 1965 abolished the national origins quotas of the 1920s, which had heavily favored northern and western Europeans. The Act also instituted a system of preferences that placed all countries on an equal footing. It emphasized family reunification, employment skills needed in the U.S., and the admittance of refugees and "asylees" (asylum seekers). As a result, immigration from non-European countries increased precipitously. Thus New York City's population has become more racially and ethnically diverse than perhaps, at any time in its history.

The population of the city was 63 per cent non-Hispanic white in 1970; by the year 2000, this is projected to decline to 35 per cent, making the City's population even more diverse. During this same period, the share of the Hispanic population is projected to grow from 16 to 29 per cent, non-Hispanic blacks are projected to increase from 19 to 26 per cent of the city's population, and the share of Asians is projected to quintuple from two to ten per cent.

Table 1: Population by Race and Ethnicity
New York City, 1970–2000

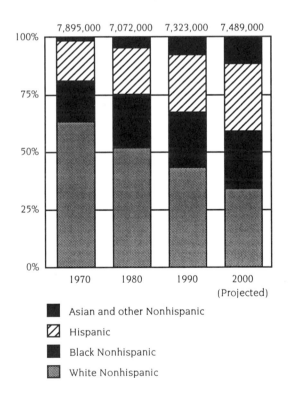

Sources:

1970 Census Fourth Count

1980 and 1990 Census STF1

2000 Projection: Dept. of City Planning, "Population Projection for the Year 2000." Technical Report 1

Population Division New York City Department of City Planning

E Pluribus Unum

New York continues to be America's largest city because it is a mecca for immigrants. No city in the United States matches the racial and ethnic diversity seen in New York. In comparison, many of the major cities were dominated by one racial group, according to the 1990 U.S. Census. Phoenix, for example, was over three-quarters white while in San Antonio, Hispanics comprised the majority. Even cities that are racially diverse cannot match New York's ethnic diversity. For example, Hispanics comprise about one-quarter of both Houston's and New York's populations. However, Hispanics in Houston are overwhelmingly Mexican, while New York's Hispanic population consists of several large subgroups, including Puerto Ricans, Dominicans, Colombians and Ecuadorians. Similarly, few major cities in the nation have the large numbers and diverse mix of Black West Indian groups that New York possesses.

**Table 2: The Ten Largest Cities
in the United States by Race and Ethnicity, 1990**

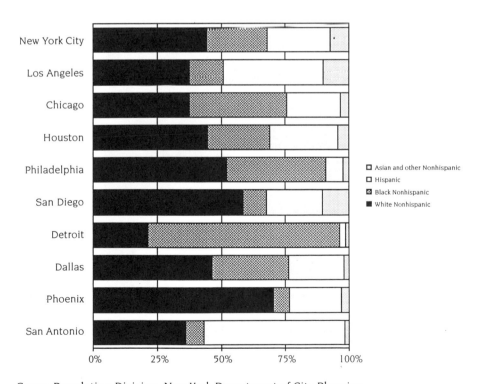

Source: Population Division, New York Department of City Planning

269

ASIANS IN NEW YORK

In the latest *Annual Report on Social Indicators*, published by the New York City Department of City Planning, the Asian race group is compared to other race groups, (white, black and Hispanic) in a study based on the 1990 census. Notable differences emerge in the demographic/social characteristics, measures of economic well-being, and household characteristics.[4] Moreover, statistical analysis bespeaks a wide range of differences that exists between several ethnic populations designated in the Asian race group. (Chinese, Korean, Indian, and Filipino)

Demographic/Social Characteristics

1) *Per cent Foreign-Born*. In 1990, over 28 per cent of the city's population was foreign-born. Asians, however were overwhelmingly foreign-born (80 per cent), compared to just 19 per cent of whites. Blacks and Hispanics, were 24 per cent and 35 per cent, respectively, born outside of the United States.

2) *Recency of Immigration*. A relatively high percentage of immigrants has been in the United States for a very short period of time. Among foreign-born Asians, 36 per cent came to the U.S. between 1985 and 1990, the highest of any race group, while 28 per cent of foreign-born Hispanics, 24 per cent of foreign-born blacks, and 18 per cent of foreign-born whites arrived during the same period. Among immigrant Asian groups, Koreans and Asian Indians were the most recent arrivals with around 40 per cent arriving between 1985 and 1990.

3) *Ability to Speak English*. Among the foreign-born, only 56 per cent reported strong English language proficiency. However, 88 per cent of foreign-born blacks were so categorized, compared to only 25 to 33 per cent of

Table 3: Race/Ethnic Groups by Nativity,
New York City, 1990

	Total	Foreign-born	Foreign-born as a Per cent of Total
Total	**7,322,564**	**2,082,931**	**28.4**
White nonhispanic	3,178,712	612,691	19.3
Black nonhispanic	1,874,892	444,335	23.7
Asian nonhispanic	496,287	399,022	80.4
Hispanic	1,737,927	615,272	35.4
Other Hispanic	34,746	11,811	34.0

Source: 1990 Census Public Use Microdata Sample and Summary Tape Files 3 and 4PB. Population Division, New York City Department of City Planning.

**Table 4: General Demographic and Social Characteristics
by Race, Nativity, and Ancestry, New York City, 1990**

	Total Persons	Foreign-born Persons		Per cent Strong English (5+ Years)	Per cent High School Graduates (25+ Years)
		Per cent	Per cent Arrived 1985–1990*		
Total	**7,322,564**	**28.4**	**25.5**	**80.0**	**68.3**
Native-born	5,239,633	n.a.	n.a.	91.1	73.2
White nonhispanic	2,566,221	n.a.	n.a.	97.4	83.1
Black nonhispanic	1,430,557	n.a.	n.a.	98.6	65.8
Asian nonhispanic	97,265	n.a.	n.a.	81.0	90.0
Hispanic	1,122,655	n.a.	n.a.	65.8	47.9
Foreign-born	2,082,931	100.0	25.5	55.6	59.8
White nonhispanic	612,491	100.0	18.0	61.2	60.6
Black nonhispanic	444,335	100.0	24.2	88.4	67.4
Asian nonhispanic	399,022	100.0	35.7	40.8	67.4
Hispanic	615,272	100.0	28.4	35.5	48.3
Selected Foreign Born Groups:					
Caribbean					
Jamaican	116,100	100.0	25.0	98.8	66.0
Guyanese	73,846	100.0	31.9	97.7	63.5
Haitian	70,987	100.0	21.7	45.5	65.9
Trinidadian	58,212	100.0	25.2	97.8	69.8
Asian					
Chinese	164,586	100.0	30.1	24.9	52.9
Korean	57,555	100.0	40.4	28.1	79.8
Asian Indian	42,674	100.0	39.2	64.4	80.6
Filipino	37,307	100.0	33.1	71.8	92.5
Hispanic					
Dominican	226,560	100.0	29.7	30.4	38.5
Colombian	68,787	100.0	28.2	31.6	58.4
Ecuadorian	60,119	100.0	26.4	33.3	51.8
Mexican	34,856	100.0	51.0	27.2	35.3
*Selected Ancestry Groups:***					
Italian	748,630	13.4	4.6	89.7	66.6
Irish	388,893	8.5	18.4	99.4	81.9
German	281,164	14.1	6.6	96.6	83.5
Russian	233,199	20.2	31.4	88.4	89.4
Polish	213,361	26.0	18.9	85.5	77.9
English	109,210	11.8	18.8	99.0	91.5
Greek	74,328	45.2	5.9	70.2	64.8
Hungarian	48,717	31.3	6.7	83.4	77.2
Austrian	47,053	17.3	5.4	95.4	86.2

Source: 1990 Census Public Use Microdata Sample and Summary Tape Files 3 and 4PB. Population Division, New York Department of City Planning.

* Refers to the share of all foreign-born persons arriving between 1985-90.

** Refers to first ancestry only, and includes both the native- and foreign-born.

Hispanic subgroups were proficient. Among immigrant Asians, the level of proficiency varied widely. Chinese and Koreans had very low levels of English proficiency (25 and 28 per cent respectively), while Asian Indians and Filipinos, many of whom were educated in English in their home countries, had much higher levels (64 and 72 per cent, respectively).

4) *Educational Attainment of Adults.* Native-born Asians had the highest educational attainment among all race groups, with 90 per cent graduating from high school. In comparison only 67 per cent of Asian immigrants were so categorized. Among immigrant Asians, Filipinos had the highest percentage graduating from high school (93 per cent). In contrast, just over one-half of Chinese immigrants received high school diploma.

Economic Well-Being

1) *Poverty Status and Median Household Income.* Nineteen per cent of residents were below the poverty line in 1989 in a city with a median household income of $29,800. Both foreign- and native-born Asians had household incomes above the city average, and while a nativity gap exists, it was not as substantial as that among whites. There were significant differences among Asian foreign-born subgroups. Chinese immigrants had a median income that was 93 per cent of the city median, and a poverty rate that was slightly less than the city average. On the other hand, Filipino immigrants had a median household income that was 168 per cent of the city median — the highest of any subgroup in the analysis — and a poverty rate of less than five per cent, lower than that of whites and virtually all European ancestry groups.

2) *Labor Force Participation.* The labor force participation rate is defined as the percentage of people working or looking for work. Foreign-born males had a higher labor force participation rate (83 per cent) than that of their native-born counterparts (76 per cent). Each foreign-born race group had a labor force participation rate of 82 per cent or higher. Eighty-three per cent of male Asian immigrants were participating in the labor force. Foreign-born females had an overall labor force participation rate of 64.4 per cent, slightly higher than that of native-born females at 64 per cent. Labor force participation among foreign-born race groups were at or above that of their native-born counterparts, with the exception of whites. Asian subgroups displayed varied female participation levels, ranging from 88 per cent for Filipinos, to 60 per cent for Korean women.

3) *Earnings.* Earnings consist of income derived from employment, either in the form of wages and salary or self-employment income. Other than native-born white males, native-born Asian males were the only other

Table 5: Selected Economic Characteristics
by Race, Nativity, and Ancestry,
New York City, 1990

| | Per cent Persons Below Poverty | Household Income | | Labor Force Participation Rate (16–64 Years) | | Earnings Persons Employed Full-time (25–54 Years) | | | |
| | | | | | | Males | | Females | |
		Median	Ratio: subgroup to total	Males	Females	Mean	Ratio: subgroup to total	Mean	Ratio subgroup to total
Total	19.3	$29,800	1.00	78.7	64.0	$35.500	1.00	$27,900	1.00
Native-born	19.4	30,000	1.01	76.4	63.8	40,200	1.13	31,000	1.11
White nonhispanic	8.0	38,000	1.28	83.2	70.4	48,000	1.35	36,700	1.32
Black nonhispanic	26.6	22,000	0.74	67.9	63.1	27,000	0.76	24,300	0.87
Asian nonhispanic	12.1	36,700	1.23	70.9	66.1	38,700	1.09	34,300	1.23
Hispanic	36.9	18,100	0.61	68.8	48.0	25,300	0.71	21,400	0.77
Foreign-born	17.8	27,00	0.91	82.9	64.4	27,700	0.78	21,900	0.78
White nonhispanic	14.3	27,900	0.94	83.4	58.6	38,500	1.08	28,600	1.03
Black nonhispanic	14.8	28,800	0.97	82.0	77.1	25,000	0.70	21,900	0.78
Asian nonhispanic	15.9	31,400	1.05	82.5	65.6	26,200	0.74	22.600	0.81
Hispanic	24.8	22,600	0.76	83.3	58.7	21,100	0.59	16,900	0.61
Selected Foreign Born Groups:									
Caribbean									
Jamaican	13.0	31,000	1.04	80.9	79.8	25,300	0.71	23,500	0.84
Guyanese	13.8	30,000	1.01	81.6	71.1	24,300	0.68	18,900	0.68
Haitian	17.5	29,000	0.97	82.3	76.8	24,000	0.68	19,500	0.70
Trinidadian	17.1	27,200	0.91	82.5	77.6	25,300	0.71	22,700	0.81
Asian									
Chinese	17.3	27,800	0.93	79.5	66.5	23,100	0.65	18,400	0.66
Korean	17.1	30,000	1.01	82.5	59.9	24,000	0.68	21,000	0.75
Asian Indian	11.0	38,600	1.30	84.8	60.5	33,200	0.94	25,100	0.90
Filipino	4.5	50,000	1.68	84.1	87.6	32,700	0.92	32,800	1.18
Hispanic									
Dominican	33.6	18,000	0.60	77.2	52.3	19,100	0.54	14,400	0.52
Colombian	16.5	27,000	0.91	87.6	66.7	21,200	0.60	16,700	0.60
Ecuadorian	17.9	25,700	0.86	89.5	61.9	19,900	0.56	16,000	0.57
Mexican	22.4	28,100	0.94	92.1	55.6	15,700	0.44	15,100	0.54
Selected Ancestry Groups: *									
Italian	7.6	34,000	1.14	83.3	63.4	41,000	1.15	29,900	1.07
Irish	6.5	39,000	1.31	84.6	71.7	43,600	1.23	35,200	1.26
German	6.8	38,800	1.30	86.5	74.9	49,400	1.39	37,400	1.34
Russian	9.9	39,800	1.34	83.9	75.6	56,900	1.60	41,900	1.50
Polish	7.4	35,500	1.19	85.5	69.5	46,600	1.31	33,300	1.19
English	6.4	42,900	1.44	88.8	77.3	56,300	1.59	44,300	1.59
Greek	8.2	35,000	1.17	82.3	58.3	35,800	1.01	33,300	1.19
Hungarian	10.8	34,000	1.14	82.3	69.9	51,900	1.46	36,400	1.30
Austrian	4.6	37,800	1.27	85.6	76.4	58,100	1.64	41,500	1.49

Source: 1990 Census Public Use Microdata Sample and Summary Tape Files 3 and 4PB. Population Division, New York Department of City Planning.
   * Refers to first ancestry only, and includes both the native- and foreign-born.

group whose earnings ($38,700) exceeded the city average. With the exception of whites, all foreign-born race groups had relatively low earnings, ranging from 59 per cent for Hispanics to 74 per cent for Asians, relative to the city average. As with so many characteristics, there was considerable variation in earnings levels among Asian subgroups: men born in China had average earnings ($23,000) about two-thirds that of all persons in the city, while the earnings for Filipinos and Asian Indians were over 90 per cent of the city average.

Among native-born females, whites and Asians had the highest earnings, 132 per cent and 123 per cent, respectively, of the city average of $27,900. On the other hand, foreign-born white women were just above the city average, and foreign-born Asian women were at 81 per cent. Again, there was much variation in the earnings of Asian female subgroups. Filipinas had the highest earnings, at 118 per cent of the city average; however Chinese women earned only 66 per cent of the city average.

Household Characteristics

1) *Average Household Size.* There was an average of 2.5 persons per household in the City of New York in 1990. In general, households headed by the foreign-born were larger than those headed by the native-born, irrespective of race. All foreign-born Asian subgroups had average household size above the city's average, from 3.0 persons in Filipino households to 3.5 persons in Chinese households.

2) *Household Tenure.* For the city overall, the average of the rates of ownership in 1990 was 29 per cent. After whites, Asians had the second largest home ownership levels, (30 per cent for native-born Asians and 31 per cent for the foreign-born). Among foreign-born Asian subgroups, only Koreans (21 per cent) were below the average for the City, while the Chinese (39 per cent), Filipinos (32 per cent), and Asian Indians (31 per cent) were all above the average.

3) *Overcrowding.* Overcrowding, as defined by federal standards, occurs when there is more than one person per room in a housing unit. Foreign-born persons are much more likely to live in overcrowded housing units; this holds for each race group. High levels of home ownership fail to dampen the effects of large household sizes on overcrowding. Among Asians, for example, despite similar levels of home ownership for foreign- and native-born household heads, the percentage of overcrowding among the foreign-born was almost four times that of the native-born (35 versus 9 per cent). Variation again existed among the foreign-born Asian subgroups, with Filipino overcrowding rate at 29 per cent and Koreans at 47 per cent.

Table 6: General Household Characteristics
by Race, Nativity, and Ancestry, New York City, 1990

	Total Households	Average . Household Size	Per cent Units Owner Occupied	Per cent Units Over- Crowded
Total	**2,816,274**	**2.5**	**28.6**	**12.3**
Native-born	1,933,988	2.3	29.4	7.3
White nonhispanic	1,147,365	2.0	38.2	2.4
Black nonhispanic	460,208	2.7	19.4	12.4
Asian nonhispanic	11,934	2.1	29.5	8.5
Hispanic	308,967	3.0	11.3	18.0
Foreign-born	882,286	3.0	27.2	21.3
White nonhispanic	323,031	2.3	37.0	6.7
Black nonhispanic	178,969	3.2	25.9	21.3
Asian nonhispanic	139,702	3.4	31.3	35.3
Hispanic	236,315	3.5	12.1	33.6
Selected Foreign Born Groups:				
Caribbean				
Jamaican	48,564	3.1	30.3	19.1
Guyanese	24,947	3.6	32.8	27.6
Haitian	27,604	3.7	23.7	34.3
Trinidadian	25,250	3.1	25.6	19.7
Asian				
Chinese	56,282	3.5	39.1	33.9
Korean	19,371	3.3	21.2	46.9
Asian Indian	15,990	3.4	31.4	30.9
Filipino	15,087	3.0	31.7	28.9
Hispanic				
Dominican	85,062	3.8	5.8	38.6
Colombian	26,075	3.3	16.3	35.4
Ecuadorian	21,441	3.6	13.7	34.4
Mexican	10,105	4.5	7.4	58.5
*Selected Ancestry Groups:**				
Italian	320,804	2.4	50.0	2.2
Irish	174,961	2.1	34.9	2.9
German	153,219	1.9	38.3	2.5
Russian	133,355	1.9	33.3	3.1
Polish	111,663	2.1	39.4	2.6
English	60,216	1.8	30.5	2.9
Greek	28,857	2.6	45.9	4.8
Hungarian	25,921	2.1	37.6	4.0
Austrian	30,306	1.7	37.8	1.0

Source: 1990 Census Public Use Microdata Sample and Summary Tape Files 3 and 4PB. Population Division, New York Department of City Planning.
  * Refers to first ancestry only, and includes both the native- and foreign-born.

Policy Issues

The demographic information in this chapter confirms the high percentage of immigrants residing in New York City and underscores the various positive contributions of immigrants. New York, in particular, benefits immensely from the economic, cultural, and social contributions of the immigrants. Immigrants fuel the City's economy by investing in businesses and homes in neighborhoods others have long abandoned. Moreover, immigrants stabilize the declining population of the City and buttress the housing stock in many neighborhoods[5] while infusing funds to maintain the extensive subway system by providing the needed level of ridership.[6]

The National Academy of Sciences published in June 1997 the most comprehensive study ever done on the impact of immigration on the U.S. economy and society. The Academy study found that immigrants contribute positively to the U.S. economy and that immigration benefits the U.S. economy overall and has little negative effect on the income and job opportunities of most native-born Americans. The study also concluded that immigration will positively alter the age structure of the U.S. population, making it younger and will increase the racial diversity of the nation.

Because immigration has been a vital component of the city, immigration policy, which is set at the federal level, affects not only the immigrant communities but also the City's ability to deliver its services effectively to its entire citizenry. This section explores the ramifications of federal policies on local governments like that of the City of New York. The City's aggressive response with several initiatives to mitigate impact of these federal policies is part of a cohesive immigrant policy to protect the interests and needs of immigrants in New York.

The Illegal Immigration Reform and Immigrant Responsibility Act of 1996 significantly reforms immigration laws of the United States. The new welfare law known formally as the Personal Responsibility and Work Opportunity Reconciliation Act of 1996, also eliminates many forms of assistance to legal immigrants. Taken together, these two laws impose extraordinary restrictions on legal immigrants and other non-citizens for many public benefit programs. Of additional concern, these laws would overturn New York City Executive Order No. 124, which protects the health and safety of all New Yorkers.

City Executive Order No.124

Since 1989 it has been the policy of the City of New York that its officers and employees would not report aliens to the federal immigration authorities except in those cases where an alien is suspected of engaging in criminal activity, or the reporting is required by law. The reasons for this policy, embodied in New York City Executive Order No. 124 are evident and compelling. It offers a safe haven in which undocumented aliens who are witnesses to or victims of crime can assist the Police Department; undocumented aliens who are infected with contagious diseases can obtain medical care; and undocumented parents can send their children to public schools, all without fear that by coming forward they risk deportation. The safety and public health and welfare of the entire City are dependent on all residents, regardless of their immigration status, cooperating with government and being able to access essential government services (Appendix 1).

The Welfare law and the Illegal Immigration Reform law each contains provisions that overturn significant portions of *Executive Order No. 124*, and preclude the City from directing its officers and employees not to report aliens to the federal Immigration and Naturalization Service. Without the important protection of *Executive Order No. 124*, aliens may be afraid to cooperate with the Police, seek medical care for contagious diseases, or seek an educational opportunity for their children. The new federal laws do not explicitly deny undocumented aliens access to these essential services. However, they effectively accomplish this result by outlawing state and local governments' reasonable and legitimate efforts to encourage aliens to seek necessary services.

Public Benefits to Legal Immigrants

The welfare reform law enacted in 1996 achieves a large portion of its projected savings by restricting benefits to legal immigrants. In fact, the U.S. Congressional Budget Office estimates that $23.7 billion in federal savings comes from barring non-citizens from two major federal cash assistance programs: food stamps, which are coupons that help feed the poor and Supplemental Security Income (SSI) which is the dependent income of many elderly, poor and disabled. The laws further limit non-citizens' access to means-tested benefit programs, and by imposing deeming restrictions which require a sponsor's income to be counted when determining benefit eligibility of an immigrant. In addition, the new immigration law sets the income level to sponsor family members as legal immigrants at 125 per cent of the poverty rate.

Denying benefits to legal immigrants is patently unfair to these taxpaying residents and will also result in considerable cost-shifting to local and state governments. The federal government has sole responsibility over immigration policy and should bear the ensuing responsibility of serving the legal immigrants it permits to enter states and localities. New York City believes that denying benefits to immigrants will not eliminate need and will, subsequently, force state and local governments to bear the financial consequences of these unwise policy decisions. According to the estimates made by the New York City Office of Management and Budget, New York immigrants' loss of federal benefits will cost the city $240 million in fiscal year 1998 and $2.7 billion cumulatively in the next five years.

Equal Educational Opportunity

The City remains concerned about proposals introduced in Congress last year aimed at denying undocumented immigrant children a public school education. This misguided idea ignores the dangers it would create for American cities, as it would engender an underclass of illiterate and unskilled individuals unable to be productive members of society. In addition, it would create distrust and suspicion in our public schools toward all school children who look foreign and would lead inevitably to discrimination.

New Restrictions on Legal Immigration

The sweeping reforms being proposed to the United States' immigration laws contradict America's overwhelmingly positive experience with legal immigrants. Instead of treating legal immigrants as assets and recognizing the invaluable contributions they make in communities across America, these proposals unfairly target and penalize them by seeking to reduce current immigration levels.

Restricting the number of visas issued annually will harm family reunification efforts, undercut the ability of many American companies to compete internationally, and adversely affect New York's revitalization efforts. Reform of this nature is simply a misguided response to the American public's growing frustration with the federal government's failure to adopt and implement comprehensive policies to reduce illegal immigration.

Aggressive Response To New Laws

The federal government's failure to control illegal immigration and its abdication of responsibility of caring for legal immigrants create a massive administrative and fiscal burden for states and localities. Lacking a practical and effective immigration policy, which is set only at the federal level, local governments still need to maintain a practical and humane immigrant policy.

In New York City, Mayor Rudolph Giuliani leads the country in opposing the unfair provisions of the new federal laws that adversely affect immigrants and cities with large immigrant populations. Largely as a result of an active plan of action with a combination of New York City efforts, some of the most harmful provisions were amended by the Balanced Budget Act of 1997 which President Clinton signed into law in August. The strategy consists of major efforts in five areas: public education, public information, legal challenges, legislative amendments, and naturalization assistance. These efforts are detailed in the section that follows.

Public Education

Mayor Giuliani has raised the issue of immigration and welfare reform to a national level of awareness by actively speaking out on the subject at cross-country and local public activities. The Mayor has helped balance the debate of the new reforms by exposing and publicizing the flaws in the federal policy. In so doing, the City galvanized substantial public support to convince legislators to amend provisions of the new laws.

Public Information

In an effort to provide the latest and most accurate information on the changes of the new laws and available alternative resources, several New York City agencies have produced a range of information literatures. In particular, the Mayor's Office of Immigrant Affairs and Language Services published an Immigration Fraud Alert brochure and a Directory of Services to Immigrants. The brochure on immigration fraud is available in seven languages and lists important guidelines for immigrants when shopping for immigration services. The directory of services is a compendium of about 300 community-based organizations that provide a gamut of services to immigrants. All of these materials are distributed extensively to immigrant communities through various direct channels. In addition, the Mayor's Office of Immigrant Affairs and Language Services has hosted numerous seminars, presentations and information sessions for immigration advocates, attorneys, services providers as well as immigrants themselves.

Legal Challenges

New York City has filed two lawsuits against the federal government seeking to enjoin the unfair provisions of the new federal laws on the grounds that they violate the principles embodied in the United States Constitution. The first lawsuit, filed in October 1996, charged that the federal government had violated the Tenth Amendment of the Constitution in overriding the City's Executive Order No. 124. The second lawsuit, filed in March of 1997, charged that provisions of the new laws barring legal permanent residents from public benefits are unconstitutional for denying equal protection of the laws to these immigrants, violating the due process clause of the Fifth Amendment. New York City's legal action has gained much support from the public and has successfully led similar lawsuits brought on by other local governments and civil organizations from across the country.

Legislative Amendments

Mayor Giuliani has urged a number of elected officials to introduce legislation in Congress on behalf of New York City. Two Congressional Representatives introduced a bill in support of retaining the City's Executive Order No. 124. A few other members of Congress introduced legislation to restore public benefits to legal permanent residents. New York City's Office in Washington actively advocates these concerns to the President and Congress.

Naturalization Assistance

In May of 1997, Mayor Giuliani launched the largest and most extensive naturalization assistance program in the country. *Citizenship* NYC is a $12-million initiative aimed at helping elderly and disabled immigrants who are at risk of losing critical public benefits. This is in addition to the annual $3 million that the City already funds in immigration-related services including literacy training. Under the new program, field offices have been set up in strategically located areas to assist immigrants access information on the new laws, citizenship, and available resources in the City. Staff at these offices help immigrants at risk of losing critical benefits and eligible to be naturalized with various procedures of the naturalization process from initial filling out of the application to the final oath ceremony.

In addition to the five-part action plan, Mayor Giuliani established in October 1996, a coalition of prominent individuals and organizations who oppose anti-immigrant initiatives. The coalition focuses its efforts on educating the public about the valuable contributions immigrants make to our society, and on opposing anti-immigrant legislation. The coalition also works with Congress and the President to overturn sections of the new welfare and immigration laws that discriminate against immigrants. The underpinning of the Mayor's immigration coalition is a unifying partnership between the city government and community based organizations.

Other Services to Immigrants

The municipal government of New York has been providing a range of services to its immigrant population long even before the enactment of the new federal welfare and immigration laws. The effective 5-part action plan works in tandem with existing city programs aimed to assist the immigrant populations of New York. A number of city agencies contract with community based organizations to target delivery of services to their immigrant constituencies.

The Department of Employment funds employment training programs for immigrants and refugees. The Mayor's Office of Adult Literacy coordinates the City's literacy and English as a Second Language (ESL) initiatives. The Department of Youth and Community Development administers the Citizenship NYC program and funds community organizations to provide immigration services. The Commission on Human Rights enforces the City's anti-discriminatory law which protects immigrants. The Department of Aging funds special ESL programs for seniors. The Department of Consumer Affairs monitors misleading advertisement of fraudulent immigration services providers. The Department of Cultural Affairs works closely with a registry of artists and organizations of diverse ethnic backgrounds. The Commission on the Status of Women assists immigrant women with accessing city services. The Police Department has a New Immigrant Unit which works with community police officers to highlight sensitivity to immigrant populations. The Department of City Planning conducts research on immigration trends of the city and demographics on the diverse communities of New York. The Departments of Health, Sanitation, and Business Services plus the Mayor's Office of Transportation and several other city agencies work with the Mayor's Office of Immigrant Affairs and Language Services to further outreach to the immigrant communities of New York. Together, these agencies work with community-based partners to make services more appropriate for and more accessible to newcomers and to increase immigrant participation in New York's political, economic, social and cultural arenas, creating a more productive, cooperative and prosperous community for all New Yorkers.

SUMMARY

The City of New York continues to be revitalized by immigration. As of 1994, 35 per cent of the City's population is foreign-born and 20 per cent are children of foreign-born persons. The first part of this chapter presents demographic information on Asian immigrants in New York City. An analysis of socioeconomic characteristics of several race groups provides a comparative perspective for Asians, a rapidly growing population in New York.

The second part of this chapter renders a policy discussion on provisions of the newly enacted federal welfare and immigration laws that unfairly discriminate against all immigrants including Asians. New York City Mayor Rudolph Giuliani's five-part action plan in response to the new laws comprises major efforts in public education, public information, legal challenges, legislative amendments and naturalization assistance. Mayor Guiliani's efforts successfully led the country in restoring most of the public benefits for illegal immigrants lost under the two new federal laws. The plan also reinforces the need for a practical and humane local immigrant policy because federal immigration policy has profound impact on cities and localities. This chapters's dicussion on policy is based on the distinction between immigration policy which governs the admission of immigrants, and immigrant policy, which directs the treatment of immigrants admitted to the country.

Appendix I

The City Of New York
Office Of The Mayor
New York, N.Y. 10007

Executive Order No. 124
August 7, 1989

City Policy Concerning Aliens
By virtue of the power vested in me as Mayor of New York, it is hereby ordered:

Section 1. Definitions.
As used herein,
a) "Alien" means any person who is not a citizen or national of the United States.
b) "Line worker" means a person employed by any City agency whose duties involve contact with the public.

Section 2. Confidentiality of Information Respecting Aliens.
a) No City officer or employee shall transmit information respecting any alien to federal immigration authorities unless
    1) such officer's or employee's agency is required by law to disclose information respecting such alien, or
    2) such agency has been authorized, in writing signed by such alien, to verify such alien's immigration status, or
    3) such alien is suspected by such agency of engaging in criminal activity, including an attempt to obtain public assistance benefits through the use of fraudulent documents.
b) Each agency shall designate one or more officers or employees who shall be responsible for receiving reports from such agency's line workers on aliens suspected of criminal activity and for determining, on a case by case basis, what action, if any, to take on such reports. No such determination shall be made by any line worker, nor shall any line worker transmit information respecting any alien directly to federal immigration authorities.
c) Enforcement agencies, including the Police Department and the Department of Correction, shall continue to cooperate with federal authorities in investigations and apprehending aliens suspected of criminal activity. However, such agencies shall not transmit to federal authorities information respecting any alien who is the victim of a crime.

Section 3. Availability of City Services to Aliens.
Any service provided by a City agency shall be made available to all aliens who are otherwise eligible for such service unless such agency is required by law to deny eligibility for such service to aliens. Every City agency shall encourage aliens to make use of those services provided by such agency for which aliens are not denied eligibility by law.

Section 4. Effective Date.
This order shall take effect 30 days after publication in the City Record.
Edward I. Koch
Mayor

Statement of Basis and Purpose of Executive Order

Section 3 of the New York City Charter provides that the Mayor "shall be the Chief executive officer of the city." The New York State Court of Appeals has stated that the Mayor's authority in that capacity "does, of course, include the power to enforce and implement legislative enactments." Under 21 v. City of New York, 65 N.Y. 2d 344, 356 (1985).

Many services provided by New York City, including education and police protection, are available to all City residents regardless of their citizenship or immigration status. However, many aliens who reside in the City fail to make use of such services, largely from fear that any contact with a government agency will bring them to the attention of federal immigration authorities. It is to the disadvantage of all City residents if some who live in the City are uneducated, inadequately protected from crime, or untreated for illness. Regardless of their immigration status, aliens should not be discouraged from utilizing those City services to which they are entitled. On the contrary, the public welfare requires that they be encouraged to do so. Yet many aliens will continue to avoid City agencies as long as they fear that they will be reported to federal immigration authorities.

Federal law places full responsibility for immigration control on the federal government. With limited exceptions the City therefore has no legal obligation to report any alien to federal authorities. The executive order, in recognition of this lack of obligation and the importance of providing the services covered herein, requires City agencies to preserve the confidentiality of all information respecting law-abiding aliens to the extent permitted by law. City agencies are also prohibited hereby from arbitrarily excluding aliens from eligibility for services which are available to all. In this way, it is hoped, aliens will be encouraged to make use of City services to which they are entitled by law.

Endnotes

[1] New York City Department of City Planning. 1996. *The Newest New Yorkers 1990–1994*, 157.

[2] *ibid.*, 8.

[3] *ibid.*, 12–13.

[4] New York City Department of City Planning. 1997. *1996 Annual Report on Social Indicators*, 1–9.

[5] *The Newest New Yorkers, op. cit.*, 155.

[6] *New York Times*. 1997. (February 11).

Part Four

Effects, Impact & Policy Implications

16 International Immigration as a Dynamic of Metropolitan Transformation: The Case of Vancouver

Thomas Hutton

Vancouver, and more generally the southwest region of British Columbia of which Vancouver is a part, has long-established and important associations with the societies and markets of the Asia Pacific realm, originating with the migration of aboriginal peoples over the Siberian-Alaska land-bridge some 10,000 years ago. In the modern historical period, initial references of association include the Nootka-Canton fur trade, and intriguing new evidence that the first Chinese settlers arrived over two centuries ago as part of a short-lived attempt by British fur-trader John Meares to colonize Nootka Sound in 1788 — several years in advance of Captain George Vancouver's arrival off (what is now) Point Grey in Vancouver in 1792.[1]

As is well known, Chinese immigrants played key roles in the development of Vancouver and British Columbia over the second half of the nineteenth century, during the gold rush of 1858 and then the construction of the British Columbia portion of the Canadian Pacific Railway, a project which linked Vancouver to other Canadian cities and which brought B.C. into confederation. The early years of the present century saw the arrival of Chinese, Japanese and East Indian immigrants, movements which found expression (although not without opposition from Caucasian elements of society) in the establishment of Vancouver's Chinatown and Japantown, and a Japanese fishing community at Steveston, in south Richmond.[2] The inter-war years also witnessed the expansion of trade and travel between Vancouver and the Asia Pacific, as exemplified by the Canadian Pacific steamship service to Japan, and other regularly-scheduled seaborne passenger and cargo services offered by other carriers.

These references acknowledge the historical associations between Vancouver and the Asia Pacific sphere, and reaffirm the reality that this association is not "new." What is new, however, is the breadth of rich and complex linkages that characterize the contemporary relationship between Vancouver and the Asia Pacific, and the transformative impacts of these associations upon contemporary Vancouver. The purpose of this chapter is to examine Vancouver's growing role within the broadly-defined Pacific Basin, to identify the most strategic aspects of linkage and interdependency between Vancouver and the Pacific realm, and to identify some of the defining outcomes for Vancouver's modern development.

Vancouver's association with the Asia Pacific has always included both an external dimension, expressed in terms of mercantile networks and the movement of peoples since the earliest period of contact; and an internal dimension represented by new settlement patterns and cultural expressions. The contemporary relationships are far more extensive, but can also be viewed within this kind of framework. First, the external dimension encompasses Vancouver's deepening engagement with Pacific Basin societies and markets and, more specifically, Asia Pacific trading systems, financial flows and "circuits," socio-cultural networks, and travel patterns. The sum of these linkage patterns within the Pacific Basin may even be conceptualized as an extensive urban network or system. Cities are playing increasingly important roles in economic development, financial mediation, and trade within the Pacific sphere; are characterized by intensive socio-cultural interaction, sustained by recent waves of large-scale migration and the formation of the "mobilized diasporas"; and thus collectively form internodal, trans-Pacific urban networks which feature aspects both of competition and complementarity.[3] Vancouver is widely seen as an exemplar of this network, whether as a "key player" or (alternatively) a remote outpost.

Secondly, the internal dimension of Vancouver's emergence as a Pacific Rim city encompasses intra-metropolitan attributes and outcomes of Vancouver's increasingly intimate association with Pacific markets, societies and city-regions. Here we can reference an important array of impacts, including the influence of Asia Pacific trade, investment and immigration on metropolitan Vancouver's economy, export base, industrial structure, settlement patterns, and built form.

Our focus will be necessarily selective, consisting initially of an outline of Vancouver's strategic roles within the Asia Pacific, with special emphasis on the "gateway" functions which define Vancouver's role as linchpin between Canada and the Pacific Basin. A following section will more specifically examine the services export component of Vancouver's linkages with Pacific markets, as this growing services trade underscores not only changes in market demand but, also, larger restructuring trends and, increasingly, the role of recent immigrants in specialized services production and exchange.

Next, an analysis of recent immigration trends will be offered, with particular attention to the specific character of Vancouver's new citizens, once again highlighting the interdependency between culture, community, and urban economic development. This discussion will include the role of recent immigrants in the formation of a new entrepreneurial class in Vancouver, a group which some see as representing a potentially dominant or hegemonic group. This narrative will in turn set the stage for an examination of representative impacts of immigration and cultural diversity upon Vancouver's built environment, within the larger context of Vancouver's spatial reconfiguration and physical redevelopment.

Vancouver's Strategic Asia Pacific Roles and Gateway Functions

Metropolitan Vancouver's contemporary transformation includes a profound and comprehensive process of economic and socio-cultural reorientation, within which Vancouver is assuming more important roles among the markets and urban societies of the Asia Pacific and the Pacific Basin as a whole. Vancouver's status within the hierarchy of Pacific cities hardly rivals that of Tokyo or Los Angeles, the dominant control centres of the western and eastern Pacific Rim respectively, or even "second order" metropolitan regions such as Sydney, Hong Kong, Singapore and Osaka. But Vancouver does perform roles within the Asia Pacific, of both a specialized and diverse character, that imply a more strategic niche than its size would suggest.[4]

These aspects of functional diversity and specialization are depicted schematically in Figure 1, which presents Vancouver's gateway functions, and Figure 2, which identifies the essentially complementary (but important on their own terms) educational, political and socio-cultural functions. Vancouver's growing significance as a Pacific Rim city is conventionally interpreted in terms of the specific trading and gateway functions, but the activities presented in Figure2 imply a considerable enrichment of the City's position within the broadly-defined Pacific realm. In fact, an articulation of both sets of functions, and the critical interdependencies between each, is essential to achieving a more balanced, comprehensive and nuanced profile of Vancouver's Pacific reorientation.

Vancouver's secondary and tertiary educational institutions increasingly reflect an Asia Pacific orientation, expressed in research, exchange programs, curriculum, and student representation. The University of British Columbia may be regarded as the lead institution with respect to research and teaching in this sphere, as articulated in UBC's Toward the Pacific Century mission statement (1988). UBC is also heavily engaged in training programs for cadres of (for example) educators, planners and property managers from many Asian societies. But other institutions also play key roles in support of Vancouver's expanding Pacific role: as an example, we can cite Capilano College's innovative "CanAsean" program, which involves exchanges of professionals, educators and business people between Vancouver and Southeast Asian countries. As another measure of Vancouver's developing educational role in the Pacific realm, the number of Asian stu-

Figure 1: Vancouver's Strategic Asia Pacific Roles: Gateway Functions

Strategic Functions and Roles	Facilitating Mechanisms and Underlying Dynamics	Key Institutions, Agencies and Programs	Major Markets Urban Connecting Points
I. Gateway Functions			
A. Trade 1. Resource commodities 2. Goods 3. Services	Globalization of commodity markets Growing demands among Pacific Basin markets Externalization of service demand, and Vancouver's competitive advantage in tradeable services	Port of Vancouver Rail and trucking facilities B.C. Trade Corporation Federal export marketing programs Vancouver Board of Trade/World Trade Centre	1. Japan, Hong Kong, China, Russia, South Korea, United States, Taiwan, ASEAN Nations, Australia 2. Yokohama, Hong Kong, Guangzhou, Vladivostok, Pusan, Los Angeles, Kaohsiung, Singapore, Sydney, Melbourne
B. Finance and Investment 1. Foreign direct investment (FDI) 2. Joint venture 3. Private banking	Liberalization of capital markets Role of multinationals Growth of 'surplus capital' accumulation within Pacific Stability of Canadian political and financial institutions	Hongkong Bank of Canada (HQ: Vancouver) Other "B" Banks and Canadian "big 6" International Finance Centre (IFC) Vancouver Vancouver Stock Exchange (VSE)	1. Japan, Hong Kong, China, U.S., Malaysia Australia, Taiwan, Singapore 2. Tokyo, Hong Kong, Shanghai, Los Angeles, Kuala Lumpur, Sydney, Taipei, Singapore
C. Immigration 1. "Business" category (entrepreneurial/investor) 2. Family reunification and "independents" 3. Refugees	Concern about political factors overseas Perception of Vancouver as prosperous multicultural society Canada's immigration policies and programs Canadian commitment to refugees	Federal Immigration and consular services Provincial overseas offices Vancouver-based consulates Community-based immigration services (e.g., SUCCESS, MOSAIC)	1. China, Hong Kong, India, Pakistan, Vietnam, Philippines 2. Guangzhou, Beijing, Hong Kong, New Delhi, Islamabad, Ho Chi Minh City, Manila
D. Travel and Tourism 1. Business travel 2. Conventions 3. Tourism (including cruise ships)	Income growth among APEC nations Bilateral air connections to key Asia-Pacific markets Vancouver as tourist destination and gateway to Whistler and wilderness resorts	Vancouver International Airport (YVR) Tourism B.C. Tourism Vancouver Port of Vancouver Cruise Ship terminal Vancouver Trade and Convention Centre/B.C. Place	1. U.S., Japan, Australia, New Zealand, Hong Kong, Singapore, Malaysia, Indonesia, Thailand, Mexico, China 2. Honolulu, Seattle, Los Angeles, Tokyo, Osaka-Kyoto, Sydney, Cairns, Auckland, Hong Kong, Singapore, Kuala Lumpur, Jakarta, Denpasar, Bangkok, Mexico City, Beijing, Shanghai
E. Communications 1. Business/personal	Emergence of "information economy" and knowledge economy	Telecommunications and trans-Pacific fibre-optic networks	Links to major Asia Pacific financial, business and trading centres

Figure 2: Vancouver's Strategic Asia Pacific Roles: Educational, Political and Socio-Cultural Functions

Strategic Functions and Roles	Facilitating Mechanisms and Underlying Dynamics	Key Institutions, Agencies and Programs	Examples of Important Groups and Constituents

I. Education
A. University
  1. Teaching
  2. Research
  3. Training
B. Colleges
C. Schools and Other Institutions
	Demand for education and knowledge among Pacific nations
	Role of R & D specialized information inputs to advanced production
	Human capital formation as priority among Asian societies
	"Openness" of Vancouver tertiary educational institutions to overseas students
		UBC's mission statement: "Toward the Pacific Century" (1988)
		UBC's strategic research programs and training
		UBC Asian Centre
		Capilano College's "CANASEAN" program
		Commonwealth Distance Learning Centre
			Overseas students
			Overseas faculty
			"Domestic" students
			Various businesses and industries

II. Political-Administrative A. Government of Canada B. Pacific-Rim Nation Representatives C. "Niche-Level" Institutions within Pacific	Vancouver's emergence as Canada's "Pacific City" Vancouver as "Gateway to Canada" Vancouver as specialized service centre within the Pacific Basin	Federal Foreign Affairs office in Vancouver Consulates of Asia Pacific nations International Centre for Commercial Arbitration; International Maritime Centre; Centre for the Reform of Criminal Law	Expatriate business interests Local/domestic businesses and industries Recent immigrants and prospective citizens Various client groups among commercial sectors
III. Social-Cultural A. Vancouver as Node of Pacific Basin Urban Network B. Vancouver as "Hosting Society" for Asian-Pacific Culture C. Vancouver as Canada's "Connecting Point" to Asian Culture and Society	High levels of immigration to Vancouver from the Asia Pacific region Growth of new ethnic communities and neighborhoods Development of networks among diasporas within Pacific Rim cities	Federal multicultural policies Asia Pacific Foundation of Canada (HQ: Vancouver) Ethno-cultural Association and bilateral business groups	Expatriate citizens New and expanding cultural groups General population in Vancouver Interested parties elsewhere in Canada

dents in British Columbia (a large majority of which are resident in Vancouver) tripled during the period 1985–1992, comprising by the latter year 17.3 per cent of the Canadian total (cf 11 per cent in 1985).[5]

Vancouver also plays increasingly important political-administrative roles in the Pacific domain. There are no fewer than sixty-four consulates in Vancouver, 18 of which have opened since 1990.[6] In the case of at least one important Asia Pacific jurisdiction, Singapore, the Vancouver consulate represents the only official government presence in Canada. These consulates can play facilitating roles in trade development between Vancouver, the Asia Pacific, and other external economies and markets. As another reflection of Vancouver's political role in the Pacific realm, the city hosted the 1997 conference of the Asia Pacific Economic Council.

Figure 1 sets out the basic structure of Vancouver's strategic Asia Pacific gateway functions, including trade, finance and investment, immigration, travel and tourism, and communications — each of which incorporates several more specific activities or facets — together with an identification of facilitating mechanisms, key institutions and programs and the major markets and urban "connecting points" relevant to each. These representative sets of cities serve to reinforce the significance of gateway centres within the burgeoning economies and trading systems of the Pacific Rim, and the membership of (somewhat different) sets of cities within each network: trade, finance and investment, immigration, and travel and tourism. In turn, contact, interaction and exchange between and among these gateway cities is facilitated by what Peter Rimmer has termed "multi-layered urban networks" of sea-borne trade, air connections, and telecommunications, the latter including fibre optics and satellite links.[7]

While each of these facets of Vancouver's gateway role is to some extent interdependent, we can also identify some distinctive factors relevant to each. With respect to Vancouver's crucial role as export centre for bulk commodities and resources, the dominant influences are clearly (on the supply side) British Columbia's massive reserves of staples, such as coal and other minerals, wood and forest products, and grains, and (on the demand side) the huge industrial and consumer markets of east and Southeast Asia and the United States. In the smaller (but growing) area of service exports and trade, the externalization of specialized services for intermediate markets (i.e., other businesses and industries rather than the general public) is prominent on the demand side, while Vancouver's competitive advantage in specialized services production is the most important feature of supply. "Macro-level" forces include the globalization of resource commodity markets, which has stimulated the export of resources from Vancouver, and the growth of capital accumulations among East Asian societies which are directed in part to Vancouver in the form of investment, and which facilitate the growth of tourism within the Asia Pacific, to the benefit of Vancouver and British Columbia as a whole.

Some Measures of Vancouver's Gateway Functions

The significance of Vancouver's strategic gateway functions and, more specifically, the increasing orientation toward Asia Pacific markets, can be illustrated by reference to recent trade and travel statistics. The natural starting point is the Port of Vancouver, by far Canada's largest and one of the major deep-sea ports of the Pacific Rim. It exports 60 to 70 million tons of commodities annually, the largest portion of which is shipped to Asia Pacific ports and markets. In fact, the growth of commodity exports to Japan and other Pacific markets ". . . was a decisive factor in the growth of the Port of Vancouver to the status of the largest in Canada, as well as the largest on the Pacific coast of North America by tonnage."[8] Typically, the top three destinations for Port of Vancouver shipments include Japan, South Korea and China (Table 1).

The Port of Vancouver also handles a substantial volume of imports, much smaller in tonnage, but high in value, as these imports are typically high value-added consumer items such as automobiles, electronics, and apparel (as well as foodstuffs). Vancouver is thus tightly bonded to a Pacific network of major gateway ports such as Tokyo-Yokohama, Hong Kong, Pusan, Vladivostok, and Singapore.

Over the longer-term, the Port of Vancouver faces an increasingly competitive situation vis-à-vis the other principal west coast ports of Seattle-Tacoma, San Francisco-Oakland, and Los Angeles-Long Beach. As in other transportation and distribution sectors, the major carriers are consolidating their routings and destinations, and it is possible that one or two of the leading west coast ports could experience a substantial decrease in volume over the next decade or so. At the same time, the Port of Vancouver has an

**Table 1: Principal Export Destinations for the Port of Vancouver
In Metric Tons**

	1994	Rank	1993	Rank	1992	Rank	1991	Rank	1990	Rank
Japan	20,978,874	1	20,586,032	1	20,641,772	1	23,710,766	1	23,573,700	1
S. Korea	8,553,949	2	8,603,667	2	6,586,235	2	9,234,483	2	6,601,460	2
China	4,535,949	3	2,976,889	3	4,274,381	3	4,572,139	3	3,839,328	3
Brazil	2,589,710	4	1,923,078	4	1,884,897	4	1,499,081	7	1,535,944	7
Taiwan	1,956,986	5	1,741,707	5	1,706,100	6	1,997,857	4	1,925,452	4
U.S.A.	1,602,481	6	1,332,195	6	1,762,392	5	1,699,606	6	1,395,532	8
Mexico	1,582,352	7	1,047,500	8	-	-	-	-	-	-
U.K.	1,381,544	8	-	-	1,284,258	7	1,386,301	8	1,576,802	6
Indonesia	1,129,390	9	1,153,034	7	1,239,236	9	-	-	-	-
Australia	975,963	10	916,298	10	-	-	-	-	1,213,068	9

Source: Port of Vancouver, 1990–1994 Statistics, Vancouver Port Corporation, Corporate Communication

Table 2: Growth of Asia Pacific Passenger Traffic for Vancouver International Airport, 1990–1995*

	1990	1991	1992	1993	1994	1995
Total passengers (Asia-Pacific Region) (000s)	790	950	1,095	1,233	1,407	1,590
Percentage increase		20%	15%	13%	14%	13%

Source: Vancouver International Airport Authority Marketing Department
   * 1995 figures preliminary estimate

aggressive long-range capital investment and marketing program designed to enhance its competitive advantage, and has also achieved a measure of diversification. As evidence of Vancouver's competitive position, two major container lines recently commenced service to the Port of Vancouver, Maersk Line of Denmark (which dropped Portland from its rotation) and South Korea's Hanjin Line.[9] We can also cite the example of the Alaska cruise business, which has experienced throughput increases in each of the past ten years and now stands at 240 sailings and over one-half million revenue passengers per annum.[10]

As important as the Port is to Vancouver's economy, to its gateway role and to its position within Pacific Rim trading networks, air travel represents the most dynamic component of metropolitan Vancouver's gateway functions. In this regard it is important to acknowledge that the quality and frequency of direct flights to major business centres is seen as a crucial measure of a city's "connectivity" within international markets, and is also deployed as an important measure of an urban area's "global" or "international" city status.[11]

Over the past decade Vancouver International Airport has emerged as one of the leading aviation gateways in Canada and on the west coast of North America, ranking second overall to Toronto in Canada, and second to Los Angeles in terms of international traffic among west coast airports. Vancouver International Airport handles about twice as many international air travellers as does SeaTac Airport in Seattle, a considerably larger facility.[12] More specifically, Vancouver International Airport's business within the Asia Pacific has doubled over the 1990s, again reinforcing Vancouver's Pacific gateway role, as reflected in Table 2.

There are a number of demand-related factors associated with the rapid expansion of Vancouver International Airport's Asia Pacific air travel, including the growth of business travel, increases in tourism among prosperous citizens of Asian societies, the high levels of immigration to Vancouver from Asian nations, and the sustained patterns of personal and family travel associated with new migrants to Vancouver.

**Table 3: Vancouver's Network of Air Connections
with Principal Asia Pacific Gateway Cities**

City	Airline	Flights/Week	Aircraft Type
Bangkok	Canadian	6[2]	B747
Beijing	Air China	1[1]	B747
	Canadian	1	DC10
	Canadian	2[1]	DC10
Hong Kong	Cathay Pacific	8	B747
	Canadian	12	B747/DC10
	Air Canada	3	B747
Kuala Lumpur	Malaysia	2[3]	B747
Nagoya	Canadian	2	B747/DC10
Osaka	Air Canada	7	A340
Seoul	Korean Airlines	3	B747
	Air Canada	3	B747
	Singapore Airlines	2	B747
Shanghai	Air China	1	B747
	Canadian	2	DC10
Singapore	Singapore	2[4]	B747
Taipei	Canadian	4	B747
	Mandarin Airlines	4	B747
Tokyo	Japan Airlines	12	B747
	Canadian	9	B747/DC10
11 Cities	**9 Airlines**	**72 Direct Flights/Week**	

Source: *Vancouver's Network of Air Connections with Principal Asia Pacific Gateway Cities.*
Notes: [1] Via Shanghai
[2] Via Hong Kong
[3] Via Taipei
[4] Via Seoul

On the supply side, we can reference improvements to Vancouver's airport (including a $1 billion dollar capital plan which includes a second parallel runway, and a new international terminal) as well as the expansion of Vancouver's tourism and convention infrastructure (hotels and convention facilities), and nearby international tourist destinations such as the Whistler-Blackcomb resort, now rated as the top ski resort in North America,[13] and for which Vancouver International Airport serves as the principal gateway or connecting point.

The expansion of capacity on trans-Pacific flights represents an essential supply-side factor contributing to the expansion of air passenger traffic between Vancouver and other Pacific Rim gateway cities. Table 3 shows the frequency of weekly flights between Vancouver and eleven major Asia Pacific metropolitan cities. The nine air carriers combine for a total of 72 direct flights a week to the 11 listed cities, representing a particularly crucial connecting system between Vancouver and the Asia Pacific sphere. To these we can add the numerous daily flights to Los Angeles and San Francisco, and daily Canadian/Qantas flights to Sydney and Melbourne, to obtain a full profile of Vancouver's Pacific Rim air network.

Aside from the direct and indirect economic benefits of this increasing volume of trans-Pacific air traffic, which include substantial income derived from fees, salaries, concessions and the like, the pattern of connections presented in Table 3 emphasizes the quality of Vancouver's contact with the Asia Pacific's principal business centres, notably Tokyo, Hong Kong, Seoul, and Singapore, and with "emergent" Asia Pacific business centres such as Kuala Lumpur and Shanghai.

In addition to the trans-Pacific patterns noted above, Vancouver also has non-stop and direct air connections with major European financial and business cities such as London, Paris and Milan. These inter-continental air connections, coupled with location within a time zone that enables overlapping contact with the world's global financial centres of London, New York, and Tokyo, represents an element of comparative advantage with respect to banking and finance. Vancouver has been relatively underdeveloped as a financial centre, reflecting the primacy of Montréal and Toronto, and still lacks the concentration of indigenous financial institutions of a major regional financial centre. However, Vancouver has made significant gains as a financial intermediary centre. Vancouver's institutional complex in the realm of finance, banking and investment includes the Vancouver Stock Exchange, one of North America's principal exchanges for venture capital in the resource sector; major regional offices of Canada's "big six" chartered banks; about 20 foreign banking (or "Class B") banks; and VanCity Savings, one of Canada's largest financial co-ops.

Other Vancouver-based institutions are engaged in Asia Pacific merchant banking and/or trade financing. Here, the Japanese connection is quite substantial: of the twelve major Japanese trading companies or *sogo shosha* which established in Canada following the war, no fewer than seven selected Vancouver as their local headquarters (with the others being domiciled in Montréal or Toronto). This in turn reflects the powerful Japanese trade orientation of British Columbia's economy; Japan represented less than five per cent of Canada's exports in 1994, but accounted for fully 24.8 per cent of B.C.'s exports in that year. The concentration of these key Japanese trading corporations in Vancouver provides another confirmation of Vancouver's strategic Asia Pacific gateway role.[14]

Perhaps the most influential single financial institution underpinning Vancouver's recent transformation as a Pacific Rim city and gateway centre is the Hongkong Bank of Canada (HKBC). In less than two decades, HKBC has become Canada's seventh largest bank. Technically a foreign banking subsidiary (of the London-based Hong Kong and Shanghai Banking Corporation), HKBC stands out from other "Class B" or foreign banks domiciled in Canada by virtue of its size, asset base, links to the Asian market, retail network, and association with B.C. business people, especially, but by no means exclusively, those of Chinese ethnicity. Headquartered in Vancouver, HKBC gives Vancouver a measure of strength within the Canadian financial system, as well as links to Asia Pacific markets. With assets of $17.6 billion and over 100 branches across Canada, HKBC is the only foreign bank rated by the Dominion Bond Rating Service without reference to its parent company.[15]

The growth of HKBC's operations in Vancouver outside the CBD demonstrates both the strength of the Bank in retail markets as well as the recent dispersion of the Chinese community and its commercial operations. The Chinatown branch of the HKBC serves over 20,000 clients, of which more than 1,000 were reported to have millionaire status.[16] As another measure of the Bank's significance in Canada, the manager of the Chinatown branch suggested that 70 per cent of the City's developers are Chinese, and the HKBC "is financing 70 per cent of them."[17] Even discounting for a measure of exaggeration, these estimates underscore both the status of HKBC in Vancouver's burgeoning financial sector, and its role as capital provider for local development, as well as its status as key institutional connecting point between Vancouver and the Asia-Pacific.

Vancouver's Asia Pacific gateway role also incorporates a number of small, "niche-level" institutions which may nonetheless perform strategic service functions (Figure 2). These initiatives tend to feature co-operative ventures between business interests and the public sector. Vancouver's International Financial Centre (IFC Vancouver) is a well-known case in point. IFC Vancouver was created simultaneously with a similar agency in Montréal, involving both federal and provincial legislative initiatives to allow international transactions to be undertaken, without entering the domestic Canadian taxation regime.[18] A second example is the British Columbia International Maritime Centre, established in 1991 with a view to encouraging and assisting foreign shipping lines and owners to transfer head operations to Vancouver. At least six Hong Kong shipping line owners have applied to move their respective head offices to Vancouver to achieve a domicile within a politically stable jurisdiction, as well as being exempt from paying Canadian taxes on profits earned from international operations.[19]

Vancouver's Service Exports and Pacific Rim Markets

Consistent with the development of an advanced, highly-tertiarized urban economy is an increasing role for services within the metropolitan economic (or export) base. In many cities, the loss of manufacturing export capacity associated with the decline of traditional industrial production has been partially offset by the growth of service exports. These service exports can take the form of 1) the direct sale of specialized services to clients outside the producing region,[20] 2) services embodied in goods and commodities (for example, the "knowledge" or informational component of computer software), 3) capital (in the form of fees, investments, commissions and banking and financial services), and 4) services consumed within the producing region by non-residents (as in the case of tourism and convention services; or foreign students enrolled in colleges and universities).

Service exports are of particular importance among the "global gateways" like London and New York, which have experienced massive contractions of their traditional manufacturing and port functions, and which contain the largest concentrations of head office, banking and financial activities,[21] but they are also of increasing significance to dynamic, medium-size metropolitan regions. In the case of the Seattle-Central Puget Sound region, for example, Beyers has discovered that more workers are dependent on the export of services than on manufacturing exports, despite the presence of industrial megafirms such as Boeing and Weyerhaeuser.[22]

In the Vancouver case, the growth of service exports generally reflects an advanced stage of metropolitan tertiarization, and the pervasive tendency of firms to contract out (or "externalize") for specialized service inputs like accountancy and legal services. More specifically, the growth of Vancouver's service exports, and the market destinations of these services, underscores 1) Vancouver's comparative advantage in specialized services production, 2) producer services as a complement to Vancouver's gateway functions, 3) Vancouver's accelerating orientation toward Asia Pacific markets, and 4) the key role of immigrants in the growth of service exports and trade.

Service firms active in export markets may include establishments which originally catered to local markets. A substantial number of producer service firms — consulting engineers, management consultants, and geological firms — provided services for corporations associated with the expansion of British Columbia's resource sector. Accounting firms and legal establishments located in the downtown core in order to provide specialized service inputs to the head offices of the province's major resource corporations. At the same time, property development firms in the ICI (industrial, commercial and investment) sector catered to the needs of firms wishing to locate in Vancouver, either in purpose-built or "spec-built" premises.

The increasing export orientation of these specialized service firms and, more particularly, the accelerating penetration of markets within the Asia Pacific region, can be illustrated with reference to several empirical studies undertaken since the early 1970s. The results of these five survey-based studies point to several distinct stages of export activity by Vancouver service firms.

First, a major input-output (I-O) study by Davis in 1971, which included firms with fully one-quarter of metropolitan Vancouver's total employment, disclosed that the vast bulk of services were destined almost equally to the local and provincial markets, on the order of 44 per cent each.[23] These findings support the status of Vancouver as regional service point and as control centre for a vast provincial resource economy, but with relatively little presence in international markets (or even domestic markets outside B.C.).

A second survey, conducted by Hutton and Ley in the mid-1980s, disclosed considerable growth of inter-provincial and even international service exports from Vancouver. More specifically, 11 per cent of the firms surveyed reported sales to the Asia Pacific,[24] a trend also identified in a separate survey in the mid-1980s by Barnes and Hayter.[25] Interviews with firms in both samples disclosed a "push-pull" dynamic motivating service exports, the "push" factors including concerns about the future of the B.C. economy (and more particularly the prospect of a contracting resource sector) following the severe downturn of the early 1980s, while the "pull" factors included the dynamism of new markets within the Asia Pacific.

Another survey of 251 producer service firms (supplemented by some 30 structured interviews) by Davis and Hutton in 1990 confirmed the powerful attraction of Asia Pacific markets for Vancouver companies. Of 251 firms surveyed, no fewer than 64 reported sales in the Asia Pacific, including, notably, engineering, management consulting and computer service firms.[26] A final, separate survey of 133 environmental industry firms in B.C. ". . . overwhelmingly indicated that the markets that provide the greatest export opportunity are in the Asia Pacific region."[27] This latter finding reinforces the crucial interdependency between environment and economic development in the Vancouver case. Indeed, these Vancouver-based environmental services companies are active in providing environmental impact analysis for projects in places like China and Indonesia, and constitute an important element of Vancouver's competitive advantage in specialized service production and trade at international as well as regional levels.

To illustrate the nature of this activity in the Asia Pacific, Kilborn Engineering (Pacific Division), headquartered in Vancouver, is heavily engaged in several Asia Pacific jurisdictions. This activity includes participation in about $1 billion worth of projects, each in the $100 million — $500 million range in Russia, China, Indonesia, Vietnam and Thailand. This export success followed major activity in domestic markets, a process observed earlier, including the $1 billion Quintette Mine in northern B.C.[28]

It is important to acknowledge the intersection of private sector marketing with public sector trade promotion policies in interpreting the growing presence of Vancouver service companies in the Asia Pacific region. About one-third of the firms in the Davis-Hutton sample in1990 confirmed that government trade promotion efforts were significant in the initiation of export marketing within the Pacific realm.[29] More recently, the B.C. Trade Development Corporation has collaborated with the Consulting Engineers of B.C. to form the Asia Marketing Group. This approach draws on the European example of small- and medium-size service firms which form "flexible networks" of complementary service establishments to more effectively market internationally.[30] By " pooling their expertise and resources and maximizing their financial investment, companies can get benefits that may have been previously denied to them by virtue of their size or other limitations."[31] The successful export marketing of services depends, therefore, on realizing "economies of scope" as well as economies of scale.

The Role of Immigrants in the Export of Services

The growth of Vancouver's service exports reflects the pervasive trend toward externalizing demand (contracting out) but, more specifically, the export potential of specialized expertise within firms, Vancouver's comparative advantage in export-oriented service industries and institutions, and public sector trade support programs.[32] At the same time, high levels of immigration from Asia over the past fifteen to twenty years may also stimulate the export of services from Vancouver, and export trade more generally.

We can identify several ways in which immigrants to Vancouver contribute to the growth of Vancouver's service exports and trade, as follows: 1) in establishing new businesses engaged wholly or in part in export trade, 2) in enhancing the expertise and exportable specializations of existing firms, 3) in more generally increasing the entrepreneurial quality of metropolitan Vancouver's "human capital" base, and 4) in enriching the commercial networks between Vancouver, the "host" society, and overseas societies of origin.

With respect to (1), many immigrants to Vancouver have established new businesses with trade potential. Relative to other Canadian cities, Vancouver's immigrants includes both larger proportions of "investor" or "entrepreneur" individuals, as well as large contingents (for example, Cantonese and Punjabis) with strong entrepreneurial skills and traditions of trading.

Secondly, many immigrants have significantly augmented the expertise of existing firms and have stimulated their export efforts. These include immigrants employed within export-active professions and trading companies. Many of Vancouver's accounting, legal and management consulting firms, for example, have designated "Asian practice" units, frequently staffed with immigrant professionals.[33] To illustrate this point, a recent study of the contribution of Asian immigrants to the export of services from Australia estimated that firms active in Asia Pacific markets have on average 3.5 times as many employees of Asian ethnicity as those not currently active in the Asia Pacific.[34]

Thirdly, a somewhat less direct (but perhaps still important) contribution of immigrants to the export of services relates to the overall enhancement of entrepreneurship within metropolitan Vancouver's human capital base. The suggestion here is that with more multicultural urban societies comes an increase in "productive diversity."[35] The export skills and trading propensities of new immigrant groups can in essence "spill over" to the general business population, facilitated by partnerships, informal meetings, the media, bilateral and other business associations, and "social learning" over time.

Given the nature of new and emerging Asian enclaves and groups within metropolitan Vancouver, this transmission of entrepreneurship and trading stimulus is powerfully enhanced by the operations of complex networks (family, cultural, commercial) between immigrants and their societies of origin. These networks can certainly take the form of active systems of production, exchange and distribution, but can also include the conscious or incidental flow of market intelligence of many kinds.

The Role of Asia Pacific Immigration in Vancouver's Transformation

Migration has been a central force in the formation of society in Canada, from the establishment of New France, to the arrival of Acadians, to the massive inflows following this century's two world wars, and to the current wave of new immigrants.

Over the past five centuries, international migration has been instrumental within the most consequential processes of history, including colonialism, industrialization, the rise of nation-states, and the emergence of global capitalism.[36] At present, however, we are witnessing especially massive flows of population across national boundaries, motivated by complex mixtures of economic, political, socio-cultural and environmental factors, and so the last decade of the present century (and at least the first decade of the new millennium) can be termed "The Age of International Migration."[37] With respect to Canada, we can identify three attributes which differentiate the current phase of immigration from others over the past century.

1) *Urban focus and degree of concentration.* A significant proportion of immigrants to Canada in the earlier part of this century settled in agricultural regions and small communities, reflecting the more agrarian character of the nation. In the late twentieth century, immigrants settled mainly in urban areas. As a further measure of concentration, Toronto and Vancouver, with about 20 per cent of the national population, have accommodated 50 per cent or more of Canada's total immigrants in recent years.

2) *Origin of recent immigrants.* The highly Eurocentric character of immigrants in earlier migration periods has given way to a much more diverse pattern, with a particular increase in visible minority groups. It is estimated that the share of visible minorities in the Toronto and Vancouver CMAs will at least double between 1986 and 2001, attaining levels of 45 per cent and 39 per cent respectively.

3) *Socio-economic status.* The bulk of earlier waves of immigrants to Canada were drawn from the less well-off, even impoverished elements of originating societies, and were clearly motivated by the goal of an improved standard of living. Recent immigrants include, to be sure, poor people,

as well as refugees, but also incorporate significantly wealthier contingents, some coming under various "business categories" (investor and entrepreneurial immigrants).[38]

It seems clear, then, that although Canada has experienced large-scale influxes of immigrants before, the current phase differs from these previous periods in important qualitative terms.

The Pattern of Asian Immigration to Vancouver

An important feature of current immigration to Canada is the different structure of ethnicity among groups destined for various regions of the country, and consequent impacts on the ethnic profile of specific cities and city-regions. With respect to the leading metropolitan "receptor" areas, for example, Toronto's immigrants include large numbers of Caribbean and Latin American citizens, as well as Asians, while the ethnic profile of Vancouver's recent immigrants is preponderantly Asia Pacific.

The impact of these contrasting immigrant profiles is clearly reflected in Table 4, which depicts Asian ethnicity (both in absolute numbers and as a proportion of total population) for five major Canadian CMAs: Vancouver, Toronto, Montréal, Edmonton and Calgary, for 1991. The proportion of metropolitan residents of Asian ethnicity ranges from a low of 3.65 per cent in Montréal, to Vancouver at over a fifth of its total population — just under 21 per cent. The 1991 census data show that the proportion of Vancouver residents of Asian ethnicity (including single and multiple ethnicity responses) exceeds that for Toronto by 5 per cent, confirming Vancouver's status as a leading "host society" for Asian immigrants in the larger Canadian context. While a more precise empirical measure of current levels of Asian ethnicity must await the publication of 1996 mid-census results, some estimates place the Asian proportion of metropolitan Vancouver's total population as high as one-quarter.[39]

Table 5 shows the top ten source countries of immigrants to British Columbia for 1994.[40] In 1980, Vietnam was the country of origin for the largest single group of immigrants to British Columbia, with India ranking second, and England, the dominant source for much of Vancouver's early history, at third place. (The Netherlands was the tenth leading source country for B.C. immigrants in 1980, but neither it nor any other European country has approached top ten status since, with the single exception of Yugoslavia in 1993.[41])

In the recent period Hong Kong has been the most important originating jurisdiction for foreign immigrants to British Columbia, with double or even triple the number of immigrants from the second leading source country (China in 1991, Taiwan in 1992, and India in 1993 and 1994). In 1994, Hong Kong immigrants totalled 16,159, about one-third of British Columbia's total of 48,529. The latter figure is almost double British Columbia's

Table 4: Asian Ethnicity in Selected Canada Census
Metropolitan Areas, 1991

Ethnic Origin (Asian)	Single and Multiple Ethnicity Responses				
	Calgary	Edmonton	Montréal	Toronto	Vancouver
Punjabi	1,175	1,520	960	7,560	7,600
East Indian	17,045	17,555	20,050	166,715	72,490
Pakistani	2,525	2,315	4,665	20,745	3,210
Sri Lankan	510	520	4,090	22,500	835
Chinese	36,145	36,270	38,365	252,440	178,820
Filipino	8,670	7,935	10,950	72,425	28,385
Cambodian	945	1,100	7,225	1,925	1,100
Laotian	350	385	3,550	3,025	715
Vietnamese	7,255	6,780	19,265	24,550	10,095
Japanese	2,855	1,820	2,365	17,065	19,845
Korean	1,395	2,257	2,580	22,160	8,825
Total Population of Asian Ethnic Origin	**78,870**	**78,457**	**114,065**	**611,110**	**331,920**
Total CMA Population	**754,033**	**839,924**	**3,127,242**	**3,893,046**	**1,602,502**
% of City's Population of Asian Ethnicity	10.46%	9.34%	3.65%	15.70%	20.71%

Source: Asia Pacific Foundation of Canada, 1991 Census of Canada

foreign immigration total of 24,474 in 1980 underscoring the dramatic growth of migrants to the province and the importance of immigration to overall population growth over the past decade-and-a-half.

The large contingent of Hong Kong citizens to British Columbia is linked powerfully to concerns regarding its reversion to Chinese control in 1997, and related fears about economic stability and social order. Since the signing of the Sino-British accord in 1984, which confirmed and set the terms for China's reassertion of control over Hong Kong, almost one-half million of Hong Kong's 6 million inhabitants have applied for passports from off-shore jurisdictions, principally Canada, the United States, Australia, New Zealand and Britain. Of the 430,000 Hong Kong residents who have obtained passports and visas from other countries since 1987, about 67,700 (or almost one-sixth) have arrived in British Columbia, with the vast majority of those settling in Vancouver.[42] Seen in this light, Vancouver clearly has a special place in the hearts and minds of Hong Kong citizens, with far-reaching and multi-faceted implications.

Table 5 also shows a large increase in Taiwanese immigration over the past 15 years. In 1980, a comparative handful of only 230 Taiwanese settled in Vancouver, while by 1993 the annual total had reached almost six thousand — an increase of more than twenty-fold. This growing influx of Taiwanese citizens (along with ethnic Chinese from the Philippines, Malaysia and elsewhere) serves to enlarge the overall growth of residents of Chinese ethnicity in Vancouver, although of course there are significant socio-cultural differences between the largely Cantonese Hong Kong immigrants and others. Some estimates place the Taiwanese expatriate population in Vancouver at about forty thousand.[43] This figure is certainly large enough to provide a certain "critical mass" or threshold level for a strong, vibrant and distinctive Taiwanese culture, expressed in (for example) business and social organizations and other reflections of collective identity.

As important as the ethnic Chinese are to the formation of Vancouver's new social profile, other Asian groups are certainly significant, and must be acknowledged in even the most cursory of narratives. The South Asian population of Vancouver, including Indians, Pakistanis, Bangladeshis and Sri Lankans, number over 75,000 and have made a distinctive impact on metropolitan Vancouver's social morphology, economic base, and cultural landscape. South Asians are less well-represented in Vancouver's metropolitan core than the Chinese, but are prominent elements of communities in south and southeast Vancouver, in Richmond and Surrey, and in the central Fraser Valley, just outside the GVRD proper. Many South Asians are engaged in professional, commercial and industrial endeavors, while a substantial number of Punjabis are agricultural workers, representing occupational continuity with their original homeland in northern India, and per-

Table 5: The Ten Principal Source Countries of Immigrants to Vancouver for 1994: Comparative trends, 1980–1993

Country	1994	1993	1992	1991	1990	1980
Hong Kong	16,159	11,288	10,051	6,301	7,714	1,677
India	5,530	6,036	3,198	3,542	2,862	3,124
Taiwan	4,755	5,932	4,131	2,617	1,699	230
Philippines	3,787	3,726	2,460	1,950	1,992	973
China	2,998	2,175	2,231	3,544	1,424	2,163
England	1,366	-	-	-	-	2,569
U.S.A.	1,352	1,715	1,538	1,346	1,260	2,103
South Africa	1,267	8	-	-	-	-
Korea, South	880	820	-	-	-	-
Vietnam	826	93	912	1,058	977	4,013

Sources: Immigration Statistics Division, Dept. of Citizenship & Immigration Government of Canada,
B.C. Stats, Ministry of Government Services, Government of British Columbia,
Immigration Highlights, April 1995.

haps explaining as well the growth of the agricultural labor force in Vancouver CMA, against the broader Canadian metropolitan trend of decline in this sector.

Impacts of Asian Immigration on Vancouver's Transformation

The dramatic expansion of immigration from the Asia Pacific region especially over the past fifteen or twenty years represents a major growth impulse for metropolitan Vancouver. The influx of such large immigrant contingents cannot fail to generate large-scale impacts on Vancouver's growth in terms of population, employment, income, demand for housing and public services, and production and exports.

But as crucial as these growth impacts clearly are to Vancouver's development, foreign immigration is also a potent agent of transformational change. At a broader level, Sassen has emphasized a strong link between immigration, economic restructuring and the emergence of the post-industrial city. To illustrate, immigrants may enter professional and managerial occupations, characteristic of the upper echelons of the urban service labor force in advanced service economies, but many others perform the menial or "small scale, low profit" entrepreneurial functions which are also concomitant features of post-industrial societies. Because of that responsiveness to opportunity and demand, these immigrants ". . . are almost akin to a rapid deployment force" within the restructured, post-industrial urban economy.[44]

As a way of identifying the complex and multiple relationships between immigration and Vancouver's contemporary transformation, we can deploy a framework of metropolitan change. Figure 3 presents a selective representation of the impacts of immigration (and foreign investment) for Vancouver, and underscores the crucial interdependencies between immigration and each of the five principal dimensions of structural change relevant to the Vancouver case.

Great care must be taken to maintain some analytical distance between the effects of immigration and investment, as by no means are all immigrants wealthy,[45] and a considerable portion of the capital flows which are transforming Vancouver are in the form of foreign direct investment (FDI) from offshore corporations. At the same time, there are significant connections between foreign immigration and investment. With respect to economic restructuring, for example, DeVoretz found that each investor-class immigrant to British Columbia brought in an average of $2.1 million.[46] Over the recent period, this combination of immigration and capital inflow contributed over four billion dollars in new income to B.C. (preponderantly to Vancouver), "an investment pool that helped British Columbia escape the recession . . . (of the early 1990s)."[47]

These large capital inflows from the Asia Pacific, in the form of FDI from corporations, from investor-class immigrants, and from financial assets brought in by numerous independent-class immigrants, also imply another important facet of economic restructuring. These large capital flows create demand for the mediation and management of financial assets on a very large scale, with the effect of stimulating growth in financial and producer services in Vancouver. In a recent review of the "invisible empire of the overseas Chinese," Seagrave predicted that the building of Vancouver's capital base derived from FDI and immigrants and the associated institutional impacts ". . . will soon transform Vancouver into a leading world financial centre, as the Overseas Chinese have done for Hong Kong and Singapore."[48] This prediction may be overstated, but serves to reinforce the correlation between foreign investment from the Asia Pacific and the expansion of Vancouver's (hitherto underdeveloped) status as a banking and financial centre.

While the financial impacts of Asia Pacific investment and immigration certainly carry the highest profile, we can cite other significant implications for Vancouver's economic restructuring. Over the past decade or so, investments associated both with immigrants and with FDI have experienced some measure of diversification, to include industrial development as well as the more established realm of property and construction. The role of Asian immigrants in the revival and growth of Vancouver's garment district, concentrated in the City's inner city and east end, is well known, but there is also substantial involvement on the part of new immigrants in more advanced production industries. More specifically, immigrants from Hong Kong and Taiwan (and to a somewhat lesser extent Singapore and Malaysia) are engaged in modern manufacturing industries, especially in the inner suburban municipality of Richmond. Examples include a television assembly plant built on Annacis Island by Hong Kong's Great Wall Electronics, that will employ 250 workers; MTC Electronic Technologies in Richmond, which manufactures fax machines; and Qualidux Industrial, a plastics plant in the inner suburban municipality of North Vancouver, controlled by the Ting family of Hong Kong.[49] These and other investments contribute, in the aggregate, to Vancouver's industrial diversification and economic restructuring.

As significant as these economic impacts clearly are, arguably the most consequential implications of immigration for Vancouver's transformation lie in the realm of social and cultural change. The scale and pace of immigration from Asia Pacific nations especially has effectively restructured metropolitan Vancouver's social morphology, with respect to the region's ethnic diversity. But beyond this basic empirical reality of Vancouver's social recomposition, we can identify a complex spectrum of transformational implications.

Socio-cultural impacts of foreign immigration on Vancouver may include, for example, contrasts between immigrants and the "host society" in terms of behavior, values, tastes and preferences, social organization (at the level of communities, extended families, and households), occupational choices, religion and belief, and so on. It is exceedingly difficult to generalize about the impacts of immigration on Vancouver in light of such factors as:

Figure 3: Asia Pacific Investment and Immigration and the Transformation of Metropolitan Vancouver

Representative Impacts

	Immigration	Investment
Economic Restructuring (*urban economy, export base, labor force*)	1. Growth of human capital 2. Enhancement of entrepreneurship in production, trade and small business 3. Increase in market intelligence – economic responsiveness and "resilience"	1. New capital formation – production and infrastructure 2. Stimulus to growth in banking and finance 3. Stimulus to growth in producer and other intermediate services
Social Recomposition (*social morphology, class, community*)	1. Greater ethnic diversity and cultural enrichment 2. Introduction of new values, preferences 3. Emergence of new cultural groups, social institutions, business networks	1. New contingent of capital owners 2. Displacement effects among more vulnerable classes and communities 3. Rise of new social-economic hegemony?
Spatial Reconfiguration (*metropolitan structure*)	1. New ethnic enclaves and neighborhoods 2. Impetus to suburban growth (selective) 3. New "consumption landscapes" in metro core and suburbs	1. Internationalization of the CBD 2. Megaprojects and transformation of the inner city 3. New production spaces (e.g. inner city garment district)
Physical Reconstruction (*urban form and the built environment*)	1. Reconsideration of residential landscapes 2. New cultural landmarks and institutions 3. Metropolitan "densification" or intensification	1. Transformation impact of large capital investments 2. "Ethnic" retail centres and markets (e.g. Cantonese, Punjabi, Filipino) 3. Introduction of new architectural motifs
External Reorientation (*linkages and "connectivity"*)	1. Growth of "mobilized diasporas" 2. Expansion of linkages between Vancouver and originating societies, cultures, communities 3. Vancouver as a key node in international network of diasporas	1. Vancouver's development as "Gateway" center 2. Acceleration of Vancouver's integration within Pacific Rim capital markets and investment flows 3. Vancouver as "transmission point" in Asia Pacific urban system and information networks

1) important cultural contrasts among different ethnic groups; 2) significant contrasts within groups, e.g., in terms of class, occupation, and other distinctions; 3) the "blurring" of inter-cultural distinctions because of assimilation and integration; and 4) the effect of individual actions. With respect to the latter, the range of behaviors among members of any specific ethnocultural group are likely to be greater than those between the various groups.

While it is clearly beyond the scope of this study to specify detailed impacts of immigration on Vancouver's socio-cultural milieu, we can at least identify some of the principal implications for Vancouver's social composition, as follows:

1) *Diversity*. The nature and scale of immigration to Vancouver has profoundly enhanced the ethnic diversity of the City and metropolitan region as a whole. Vancouver is not merely implicated within trading systems and urban networks of the Pacific Basin, it is swiftly and visibly becoming an Asia Pacific city.

2) *Class*. While the impacts of immigration upon Vancouver's structure of social classes is highly complex, an important feature is certainly the contribution of Asian immigrants especially to the formation of a new entrepreneurial cohort. This new entrepreneurial class represents a marked departure from the pre-existing business elite of resource corporation executives (Figure 4) and owners of capital, and may even represent a potentially dominant sector over time.

3) *Culture*. The impact of Asian immigration on Vancouver's culture has been profound, manifested not only by the important institutional symbols such as the Suzhou classical Chinese garden downtown, the Sikh temple on Marine Drive in Southeast Vancouver, and the Nitobe (Japanese) Garden at UBC; but also in popular culture, for example, the "Cantopop" vocalists favored by Vancouver's Chinese population, featuring star performers from Hong Kong and the Pearl River Delta Region.[50]

4) *Organization*. The large-scale Asian immigration of the past two decades has stimulated new institutional and organizational responses among the individual ethno-cultural groups. These include, generically, a) agencies designed to facilitate the accommodation of new immigrants to the "host society," such as SUCCESS and MOSAIC; b) social clubs, which provide a forum for maintaining cultural contact and for networking; c) religious institutions, which are crucial to the maintenance of ethno-cultural identity, as well as to the expression of faith, and observance of collective ritual; and d) business organizations, including bilateral business and professional associations that represent important networking institutions.

5) *Connectivity*. While the impacts cited in 1 to 4 above represent a sampling of the more important in situ social impacts, immigration also carries with it the construction and enrichment of socio-cultural networks between the "host city" and the immigrants' society of origin. Thus, immigration can powerfully reinforce the external "reorientation" of an urban society, as well as transforming the city's internal social composition.

As a final point, the growth of new immigrant enclaves and communities within suburban municipalities represents another important facet of Vancouver's "reconfiguration." More specifically, the growth of immigrants of Chinese ethnicity is a defining feature of Richmond's social morphology, culture, and economy, while south Asians are central to the development of the suburban municipality of Surrey. In short, the enrichment of business and social networks linking Vancouver's Asian communities with other ethnic enclaves represents another crucial element of connectivity between Vancouver and the Asia Pacific, as well as contributing powerfully to Vancouver's spatial reconfiguration, economic restructuring, and social recomposition. This new suburban phase of immigrant settlement is also evident in a limited number of other North American cities, perhaps most notably Toronto and Los Angeles. With respect to the latter, Chinese immigrants have formed a new "transnational business enclave" in the San Gabriel Valley, an important node in the international Chinese economy ". . . linking Vancouver, Sydney, Singapore, Kuala Lumpur, Bangkok and Manila."[51] Vancouver is clearly an important node of this complex, interactive network.

The Progression of Public Policy Responses

The growth of Vancouver's Pacific Rim gateway roles, its deepening engagement with Pacific markets, cultures and urban networks, and its manifest transformation as an Asia Pacific society serve to raise the question of what roles the public sector has played in this process. At the federal level, we can cite open foreign immigration policies, expenditures in external market development and export trade support programs, and investments in infrastructure (for example the City's trade and convention centre) as influential policies and actions. Bilateral air travel agreements between the federal Government and Asia Pacific nations have also helped Vancouver.

The government of British Columbia has actively supported Vancouver's roles as a Pacific gateway city, and node of the Pacific urban system during the 1960s and 1970s when it favored large capital programs within interior regions (including highways, rail connections, hydroelectric projects and other large-scale investments) in an effort to "open up" a vast, resource-rich hinterland, but the 1980s saw a significant shift in priorities toward Vancouver and the metropolitan south-west of the province. Here, important provincial government initiatives included funding for the "Expo 86" world's fair, the development of an initial, 22-kilometre fixed-rail rapid transit system, a 60-thousand seat stadium and exhibition centre, and a series of promotional policies undertaken (in conjunction with the federal government and local authorities) within the rubric of the "Asia Pacific Initiative."

While the senior levels of government exercise the big "policy levers" in support of Vancouver's Asia Pacific roles and activities, various local governments have also been active. The Greater Vancouver Regional District (GVRD) has focused on growth management issues, strategic land use prob-

Figure 4: Contrasting Attributes of Vancouver's
Two Dominant Business Elites

Traditional Corporate Elite		Entrepreneurial Asian Business Culture
resource extraction, processing, and export	Industry focus	property, retail, light manufacturing, trade
corporate	Business organization	family, partnerships
hierarchical	Management structure	patriarchal or collegial
class "A" office in CBD	Operating environments	diverse range of commercial and industrial buildings
price-taking (mercantile/engineering tradition)	Business approach	deal-making (entrepreneurial tradition)
management consultants	Market intelligence	informal networks
head/branch/ representative offices	Communication networks	"transnational business enclaves"
chambers of commerce, industry associations, private business clubs	Business associations	business bilaterals, service clubs, fraternal organizations
legalistic/contractual	Agreements	based on personal relationships and trust

lems, transportation, environmental enhancement programs and the shaping of regional structure.but has played a modest role in informational services, and inter-municipal liaison in Pacific Rim marketing.

A number of municipal agencies, notably the inner suburban municipalities of Richmond and Burnaby, have also been active in promoting both Pacific Rim trade and Asia Pacific cultural events, but the City of Vancouver itself offers the most instructive story. The City's policy approach toward the realization of its Pacific roles and opportunities over the past decade and a half can be generally structured in terms of three more or less distinct periods.

Prior to 1980, the City was generally content to have the senior levels of government act on its behalf to undertake the necessary investments and initiatives in the realm of the Pacific, apart from a "sister city" relationship with Yokohama, characterized largely by routine ceremonial events and exchanges. The City established an Economic Development Office (EDO) in 1978, but its initial mandate was to stem a (perceived, rather than actual) flight of industry to the suburbs, rather than to pursue opportunities in foreign markets, much less to promote Vancouver City's Pacific Rim destiny.

With the election of Michael Harcourt as Mayor in 1980, Vancouver embarked upon a more active exploration of opportunities within the Pacific realm. A municipal economic strategy was approved by Council in 1983, and emphasized benefits to be derived from supporting Vancouver's Pacific gateway functions, the export of services as well as resource commodities, and new relationships with other urban centres of the Pacific Basin. The latter objective was realized in part with the establishment of formal sister city relationships with Los Angeles and Guangzhou, and the designation of other Pacific "strategic cities" such as Hong Kong, Singapore and Kuala Lumpur.

Reflecting Harcourt's personal view of Vancouver's potential destiny within the Pacific realm, the City also engaged in what Patrick Smith has termed a kind of "para-diplomacy."[52] Mayor Harcourt and senior City officials, in partnership with the Montréal Urban Community, (successfully) lobbied the senior levels of government to enact legislation creating an international banking centre, against the strenuous objections of Toronto. As another example of this para-diplomacy, the City actively encouraged the negotiation of bilateral air agreements between Canada and Asia Pacific nations, with a view to expanding the roster of Pacific cities with which Vancouver enjoys direct air connections. Harcourt met with senior officials of Singapore Airlines and the Canadian High Commissioner in Singapore in 1986, to press for a direct link between Vancouver and Singapore.

Following Harcourt's departure for provincial politics after the municipal elections of 1986, the City under Mayor Gordon Campbell began to articulate a new policy approach toward the City's Asia Pacific role, initiating a third phase in Vancouver's overall posture toward the Pacific. Under the Campbell administration, the City continued to support trade, investment and cultural relationships with Asia, but with sharply-reduced budgets, and with discernibly less conviction. The City was generally content to leave the more strategic elements of Vancouver-Asia Pacific responsibilities to senior government and to business interests, and began to shift its attention to the accommodation of the new immigrant populations from Asia and elsewhere.

This new policy direction, influenced to be sure by a belief that external trade development was properly within the purview of senior governments and, also, by a sense of civic complacency about the City's economic prospects after years of sustained growth, implied a reallocation of resources to social planning and to more regulatory, rather than developmental, policy approaches.

The City (as well as suburban municipalities, notably Richmond) was increasingly concerned about the integration of the large-scale inflows of foreign and domestic immigrants and began to explore models of social interaction within the context of an increasingly multi-cultural and, more specifically, Asia Pacific, society. There was also a growing sense of confidence among City Council and the community at large that, following a decade of large-scale increments in Asia Pacific trade, investment and immigration, Vancouver had achieved a "critical mass" of connectivity and status within the dynamic Pacific realm. The growth of infrastructural, financial and human capital accruing from the immigration and investment flows of the 1980s and early 1990s provided Vancouver with a powerful "induced" measure of competitive advantage which would enable it to assume at least a more strategic niche within the Pacific urban hierarchy. Thus, Vancouver is now an "active participant" among Pacific markets and societies, rather than merely a "facilitator."[53]

The City's policy attention was thus increasingly directed toward the management of growth and change within the municipality, rather than developing Vancouver's position within external networks and systems. These aspects of internal change included consideration of widely-experienced urban growth pressures, and changes in urban form and structure, but also comprised new issues associated with the *in situ* impacts of Asia Pacific trade, immigration and investment.

(This paper was prepared for the forthcoming book *The Transformation of Canada's Pacific Metropolis: A Study of Vancouver* to be published by the Institute for Research on Public Policy, Montréal, Québec.)

* *With respect to terminology in this chapter, The "Pacific Rim" (or "Pacific Basin") is a geographical term (with somewhat weaker application as an economic or trading entity concept), encompassing the nations of the western and eastern Pacific sphere, i.e., North and Central America, the Pacific coast South American nations, northeast Asia (Russian Far East, Japan, North Korea and South Korea), the People's Republic of China, Taiwan, Hong Kong, Southeast Asia, and Australasia. The "Asia Pacific" realm includes the nations of northeast and Southeast Asia, as well as South Asia (principally, India, Pakistan, Bangladesh, Sri Lanka, and the smaller Himalayan states).*

Endnotes

1   Bolan, K. 1995. "Chinese first settled in B.C. 200 years ago, exhibit shows." *The Vancouver Sun* (September 27): B6.

2   See MacLeod, S., D.W. Edgington, and T.G. McGee, 1993,"Vancouver on the edge: Vancouver and the outside world," in *Vancouver and Yokohama, emerging cities in the Pacific Rim,* ed. T.G. McGee, Vancouver: Univ. of British Columbia (UBC) Yokohama: Yokohama City Univ..

3   Douglass, M. 1989. "The future of cities on the Pacific Rim." In *Pacific Rim cities in the world economy: Comparative urban and community research* 2:9-67, ed. Smith., M. P. New Brunswick, NJ: Transaction Publishers.

4   Puri, T. R..1993. "Urban development: New towns around the Pacific Rim." Paper presented at Fifth Annual Conference of the Pacific Rim Council on Urban Development, San Francisco (October).

5   Edgington, D. W., and M. A. Goldberg. Forthcoming. "Vancouver: Canada's gateway to the Rim." Ch. 5 in *New cities of the Pacific Rim,* ed. E. J. Blakely and R. J. Stimson. Routledge.

6   Will, G. 1995. "Consular corps finds province a busy place." *The Vancouver Sun* (June 6).

7   Rimmer, P. J 1991. "Megacities, multilayered networks and development corridors in the Pacific Economic Zone." *Proceedings of the Third Annual Conference of the Pacific Rim Council on Urban Development.* Vancouver: CHS.

8   Edgington and Goldberg, *op. cit.*

9   Daniels, A. 1996. "Port acquires new Asia link." *The Vancouver Sun* (January 3): A-i.

10 Vancouver Port Corporation. 1994. 2010 *Port land use management plan.* Vancouver: VPC. (January).

11 Sassen, S. 1991. *The global city.* Princeton, NJ: Princeton Univ. Press.

12 Edgington and Goldberg, *op. cit.*

13 This includes rankings from the leading American magazine *Skiworld,* as well as from Japanese tour operators.

14 Edgington and Goldberg, *op. cit.*

15 *The Globe and Mail.* 1995. "DBRS rates Hong Kong Bank of Canada." Report on Business. (November 14).

16 *Pacific Business.* 1995. "Hong Kong Bank eyes Taiwanese cash in B.C. with new branches." (October/November): 14.

17 *ibid.*

[18] Goldberg, M.A., R. Helsley, and M. Levi. 1988. "Factors influencing the development of financial centres." Mimeograph. Vancouver: Faculty of Commerce and Business Administration, UBC. (The City of Toronto vigorously opposed the Federal Government's IFC legislation on the grounds that it discriminated against Toronto, Canada's principal banking and financial center. Part of the Government rationale for the legislation was the notion that Vancouver would offer a special window for Canada on the Asia Pacific, while Montréal could perform an analogous role within the French-speaking nations of la Francophonie)

[19] Daniels, A. 1993. "Tide turns in favor of shipowners: Hong Kong firms closer to moving staff, jobs here." *The Vancouver Sun* (March 12): D1.

[20] These flows comprise transactions between firms or agencies, but there is, of course, also a substantial volume of specialized informational inputs transmitted between units of the same firm, located in different centres.

[21] See, for example, Daniels, P. W., 1987, "Foreign banks and metropolitan development: A comparison of London and New York," *Tijdschrift voor economische en sociale geografy* 78: 269–287; and Drennan, M. P., 1992, "Gateway cities: The metropolitan source of U.S. producer service exports," *Urban Studies* 29: 217–235.

[22] Beyers, W. B. 1985. *The service economy: Export of services in the Central Puget Sound Region*. Seattle: Central Puget Sound Economic Development Department.

[23] Davis, H. C. 1976. *An inter-industry study of the Metropolitan Vancouver economy*. Vancouver: Urban Land Economics Report No. 6., Faculty of Commerce and Business Administration, UBC.

[24] Ley, D. F., and T. A. Hutton. 1987. "Vancouver's corporate complex and producer services sector: Linkages and divergence within a provincial staple economy." *Regional Studies* 21: 413–424.

[25] Hayter, R., and T. Barnes. 1990. "Innis' staple theory, exports, and recession: British Columbia,1981–86." *Economic Geography* 66 :156–173.

[26] Davis, H. C., and T. A. Hutton. 1991. "An empirical analysis of producer service exports from the Vancouver Metropolitan Region." *Canadian Journal of Regional Science* 14: 375–394.

[27] Price Waterhouse. 1988. *Export market capabilities of the British Columbia environmental industry*. Vancouver: Asia Pacific Initiative.

[28] Chow, W. 1995. "Engineering firm finding Asia market its goldmine." *The Vancouver Sun* (June 21): D1 and D4.

[29] Davis, H. C., and T. A. Hutton. 1994. "Marketing Vancouver's services to the Asia Pacific." *The Canadian Geographer* 38: 18–28.

[30] The fostering of a "culture of cooperation" within societies can lead to gains in regional economic competitiveness by (for example) providing a supporting context for inter-firm collaboration in export marketing. For a discussion of the role of inter-firm networks in the development of advanced service industries, see Maye're, A., and F. Vinot, 1993, "Firm structures and production networks in intel-

lectual services," in *The geography of services*, ed. Daniels, P. W., S. Illeris, J. Bonamy, and J. Philippe, London: Frank Cass.

[31] Exell, O. 1995. "B.C. businesses flex muscle in Asia." *Pacific Business* (October/November).

[32] For a more detailed discussion, see Davis, H. C., and M. A. Goldberg, 1988, "An empirical estimation of Vancouver's comparative economic advantages," School of Community and Regional Planning Paper No. 16, Vancouver, University of British Columbia.

[33] As an example, the Vancouver office of Price Waterhouse features a "Chinese Practice Group," with five professionals of Chinese ethnicity, a unit which networks ". . . with local offices in Hong Kong, Taiwan and other countries in Asia" (Price Waterhouse Chinese Practice Group brochure, n.d.).

[34] Dawkins, P., S. Kemp, and H. Cabalu. 1995. *Trade and Investment with East Asia in selected service industries: The role of immigrants*. Canberra: Bureau of Immigration, Multicultural and Population Research.

[35] Aislabee, C. J., Lee, and J. Stanton. 1994. *Australian cultural diversity and export growth*. Canberra: Office of Multicultural Affairs.

[36] Castles, S., and M. J. Miller. 1994. "The age of international migration." *The Urban Age* 3.

[37] *ibid*.

[38] Discussion summarized in part from Hiebert, D., D. F. Ley, and D. DeVoretz, 1995, "The Metropolis Project-immigration and integration in Vancouver," (Annex D, Introduction: Immigration and the Metropolis) Vancouver: UBC and Simon Fraser University.

[39] Cernetig, M., and R. Williamson. 1996. "Vancouver feels impact of rising Asian influence." *The Globe and Mail* (January 9): Al + A4.

[40] Although we cannot be precise about the specific geography of immigrant destinations within British Columbia, the vast majority certainly settle in metropolitan Vancouver, with secondary but significant numbers locating in the central and eastern Fraser Valley, Victoria, and major interior urban centres such as Prince George, Kamloops, and Kelowna.

[41] This anomaly would appear to be clearly associated with the war in Bosnia, reinforcing the notion that immigration has many motivations, for different groups.

[42] Yaffe, B. 1995. "As '97 approaches, we must let China know we're watching." *The Vancouver Sun* (July 22): B3.

[43] Bramham, D. 1996. "Taiwan cash pouring into Vancouver." *The Vancouver Sun* (March 14): Dl + D4.

[44] Sassen, S. 1994. "International migration and the post-industrial city." *The Urban Age* 3.

⁴⁵ To illustrate, foreign-born residents of the Vancouver CMA had incomes only 82 per cent of those of Canadian-born Vancouver citizens in 1991. (Heibert, Ley, DeVoretz, *et al.*, The Metropolis Project - Immigration and Integration in Vancouver.")

⁴⁶ DeVoretz, D. Forthcoming. *Diminishing returns: Immigration policy in the 1990s.* Ottawa: C.D. Howe Institute.

⁴⁷ Lee, R. Mason. 1995. "One bad apple in Toronto costs the West millions in investment." *The Globe and Mail* (October 27): D4.

⁴⁸ Seagrave, S. 1995. *Lords of the Rim: The invisible empire of the overseas Chinese.* New York: G. P. Putnam's Sons.

⁴⁹ Lamphier, G. 1992. "Vancouver's new power elite." *Financial Times of Canada* (June 1).

⁵⁰ Cernetig and Williamson, "Vancouver feels impact of rising Asian influence." A recent "Cantopop" concert in Vancouver raised over $1 million for charities.

⁵¹ Tseng, Y. F. n.d. "Chinese ethnic economy: San Gabriel Valley, Los Angeles County." *Journal of Urban Affairs* 16(2): 169–189. Tseng observes that Monterey Park, emerged as "the nation's first suburban Chinatown" (172), with 37 per cent of its population of Chinese ethnicity. Spillover population from Monterey Park contributed to the growth of a new Chinese enclave in the proximate San Gabriel Valley.

⁵² Smith, P. J. 1992. "The making of a global city: Fifty years of constituent diplomacy — the case of Vancouver." *Canadian Journal of Urban Research* 1 (1).

⁵³ Barnes, T., D. W. Edgington, and K. G. Denike. 1992. "Vancouver, the province, and the Pacific Rim." Ch. 6 in *Vancouver and its region*, Oke, T., and G. Wynn. Vancouver: UBC Press.

17 The New Entrepreneurs and Investors from Hong Kong: An Assessment of the Business Program

Edward Woo

Canada's business immigration program aims at attracting investors and entrepreneurs who would bring direct economic contribution to its economy. Of the 220,000 immigrants expected to reach Canada in 1997, about 10 per cent will be principal applicants and family members of the business class.[1] Immigrants in this category differ from other immigrants by having a price tag attached to their permanent residence status. This relates to the amount of wealth they possess and the subsequent investment of part of that wealth into the Canadian economy.

Such wealth has been gathered by the immigrants from their successful professional or entrepreneurial practices in their place of origin. Of the 4,042 business immigrants who landed in Canada in 1996, more than 80 per cent came from Asia, particularly East Asia, which is considered to have the most promising growth into the next century. That the expertise and wealth of these immigrants would invigorate the Canadian economy is the goal of the business immigration program.

How much this program has accomplished has been debated from time to time.[2] Those who think positively of the program base their argument on the amount of investment brought into Canada, and the desire of the immigrants to make Canada their home. Those who think otherwise see the lack of commitment of these immigrants to Canada, especially those from Asia, and challenge their "arrogance:" building "monster" houses in traditional neighborhoods, driving expensive imported cars and chatting loudly in public in their native language.[3] Similarly, there are business immigrants who complain about the fraudulent handling of their investment, and the unfavorable Canadian business environment.

From a study of a group of Hong Kong business immigrants who have come to Canada in the past five years, it was found that a quarter of them make frequent trips back to Hong Kong to attend to their business there while their families reside permanently in Greater Vancouver.[4] Another one-quarter has thought about returning to Hong Kong. What then is the implication of this on the business immigration program? Is the federal government over-estimating the contribution of these immigrants or under-recognizing their potentials? What have these immigrants really brought to Canada and what do they think about the program?

The Business Immigration Program: An Overview

Canada has always been a country of immigrants. Immigration policies in the past encouraged people to make their home in this land of abundance but seldom demanded that they bring their wealth or entrepreneurial skills along. In the 1970s, Canada began to attract entrepreneur immigrants by offering immediate settlement for investment. The business immigration program launched in 1978 introduced the entrepreneurs and the self-employed categories. In 1986, the federal government added a separate investors category.

The self-employed are those who can contribute their professional talents to Canada's economy. The entrepreneur immigrants come with their management skill and capital to set up a business in Canada. While playing an active role in managing the business themselves, they also maintain existing jobs or create new opportunities for one or more Canadian residents. The investor immigrants are expected to augment the pool of capital, to create jobs for Canadians by establishing or expanding businesses and industries, and to bring needed skills and demand for goods and services.[5] But they differ from the entrepreneurs by having a price-tag of at least $500,000 in personal wealth and of at least $150,000 of business investment (later changed to $250,000 and rose to $350,000 after 1 July 1997) for a duration of three years. Although business experience is required, a management role in the invested business is not. Investment from these immigrants is targeted at small and medium sized businesses which find difficulty in raising adequate capital.[6]

Table 1: Number of Principal Business Immigrants

Categories	1992	1993	1994	1995	1996
Entrepreneurs	3528	3245	3696	2997	2699
Investors	3397	1103	1542	1344	1373
Self-employed	1072	1062	1432	951	1211
Total	**7997**	**5410**	**6670**	**5292**	**5253**

Source: Citizenship and Immigration Canada
Notes: 1) Dependents not included.
2) The significant drop in the number of investors in 1993 is due to the eradication of the $150,000 category of investment.

Table 1 shows the number of immigrants under these categories in the past five years. Table 2 shows the countries attracted to the program with Hong Kong topping the list and accounting for more than one-third.

The business immigration program has injected substantial investment in Canada. The investor program alone has induced over $3.7 billion since 1986 and created over 33,000 jobs. Around half of the funds and of the jobs went to the two provinces of Quebec and Saskatchewan. However, when the

Table 2: Top Business Immigrant Sources

Sources	1992	1993	1994	1995	1996
Hong Kong	46.50%	42.20%	44.40%	33.70%	37.00%
Taiwan	19.70%	21.10%	16.40%	17.30%	20.10%
South Korea	7.60%	7.00%	5.60%	10.00%	6.80%
China	n.a.	n.a.	n.a.	3.60%	6.80%

Source: Citizenship and Immigration Canada

Notes: 1) The inclusion of China in 1995 was primarily due to the opening of business immigrant application to the country in that year.

Table 3: Accomplishments of the Investor Program, 1986–96

Province	Subscriptions ($)	Investors	Jobs Created
Newfoundland	44,550,000	11	397
P.E.I.	207,700,000	44	838
Nova Scotia	291,100,000	283	2,237
New Brunswick	130,300,000	115	663
Québec	1,470,000,000	2,188	9,825
Ontario	130,550,000	3,030	991
Manitoba	224,700,000	115	2,448
Saskatchewan	570,400,000	185	7,045
Alberta	318,450,000	633	3,546
B.C.	360,200,000	7,431	5,767
Yukon-N.W.T.	3,150,000	n.a.	11
Total	**3,751,100,000**	**13,915**	**33,768**

Source: Citizenship and Immigration Canada

Notes: 1) Number of investors refers to destination intended by principal applicants.

2) Jobs created refers to figure reported by fund managers. The entrepreneur immigration program is more effective in job creation or retention. In 1995 alone, the entrepreneurs invested over $435 million in businesses which employed 12,850 workers.

Table 4: Investment and Jobs Created or Maintained by Entrepreneurial Immigrants

Year	1992	1993	1994	1995
Investment ($)	200,358,315	148,672,292	266,872,167	435,643,527
Jobs	8,193	3,919	8,476	12, 850

Source: Citizenship and Immigration Canada

number of investors is considered, B.C. province has captured more than 50 per cent and Ontario a little over 20 per cent. Tables 3 and 4 summarize the accomplishment of the programs.

Indeed, few immigrant investors chose the destination of investment as their home, which, though not prohibited by the program, is not encouraged either. The choice of location to invest is mainly based on the ease in getting the immigration approval while the choice of location for settlement is mainly influenced by the favorable living environment. In the case of British Columbia, the mild weather, the concentration of Chinese residents and, above all, the shorter distance from Hong Kong to where the immigrants make frequent trips, were the main attractions.

Hong Kong Business Immigrants: Who are They?

1) *Personal Background.* The new business immigrants are ethnic Chinese who owned or still own small and medium sized operations in Hong Kong, and who might also have ventures in China. Most of their businesses are related to services (retailing, medical clinic, shipping, printing, insurance, import/export trading and government) or manufacturing. Manufacturing concentrates on light industries (garment, plastics and electrical goods) which are the leading domestic exports from Hong Kong. All these immigrants have been in business for over ten years. Ranging in age from mid-thirties to fifties, they have had ample time to acquire their wealth and entrepreneurship skills.

They have had a reasonable amount of schooling to at least junior high but their entrepreneurial skills are acquired from the complex business world at home. Some have attained university education and are more proficient in the English language. But businessmen in Hong Kong do not need much English in their daily work. The lawyers, accountants and other professionals often take care of the language issue.

None of the business immigrants have come to Canada alone. Unlike the pioneering Chinese who came in the prime of their life and returned home with some savings to raise a family, the contemporary Hong Kong business immigrants come with their family. In fact, providing their children with a good education is one of the major reasons for coming to Canada. The business immigrants are particularly attracted to the Canadian liberal educational system which imposes little pressure of frequent examinations and competition that often caused stress at home. Some immigrants consider it cheaper to invest in a resident status and enrol their children in local schools and universities than to pay for the education of their children in Canada under a foreigner status.

Freedom, whether in education or otherwise, is often the concern of most of these business immigrants. With the turnover of Hong Kong to China on 1 July 1997, many of them wanted to find a secure place to raise their family and to pursue their business.[7] Those who have experienced the hardship under the Communist regime in China before fleeing to Hong Kong have even more to worry about, though interestingly, many of these entrepreneurs have established business relations with China since the 1980s. Their distrust of what is promised for Hong Kong after the transition is built on that intimate understanding of the Chinese system.

Few of the immigrant entrepreneurs would admit that bright prospects in the Canadian economy were what attracted them to this country. In fact, before emigrating, many have heard about the difficulties in making money in Canada. They were driven here mainly by their enterprising spirit — the spirit of risk-bearing in particular, while hoping to see that what they heard was wrong. Some of the business immigrants would consider Canada as a stepping stone to the U.S. market and the abundant opportunities for quality education for their children there. But most would prefer the safer and more pleasant living environment of Canada to the U.S.

2) *Life-style.* Most of the business immigrants live in houses built within the last 5 years before they moved in. The houses are of good size, with a floor area averaging between 2,500 sq. ft. to 3,500 sq. ft. That land is much cheaper in Canada than in Hong Kong has prompted the immigrants to be more generous with living space but that does not necessarily mean extravagance. In fact, with the price of a 600 sq. ft. apartment in Hong Kong, these immigrants can well buy a luxurious and comfortable detached home in British Columbia. There is yet another practical consideration for a spacious house. Often, these immigrants would entertain friends and relatives at home and for those coming from abroad, they would provide lodging, too. It is not uncommon for the immigrants' home to become a guest house in the summer when Hong Kong relatives like to visit Canada.

Besides allowing room for visitors, a bigger house with four- to-five-bedrooms and a similar number of bathrooms would provide enough space and ensure privacy for immigrants' children and parents or in-laws who have come with them. In Hong Kong, limited living space often inhibits having the extended family together under one roof.

The preference for new houses is also understandable. In Hong Kong, houses over 20 years old are regarded as "old-timer" and often are poorly maintained. Newer homes would mean less maintenance and repair which the immigrants from Hong Kong are not familiar with, and do not enjoy undertaking themselves. Newer homes have more modern facilities which make life more enjoyable; intercommunication and burglar alarm systems are just two examples.

There is a questionable supposition that the business immigrants would prefer to live in expensive districts. The truth is that there is quite a diffused location of their homes. Budget is an important consideration for location. Many choose to live in Burnaby or Coquitlam because of the lower property prices and living expenses. Those who are better off would consider Vancouver West or West Vancouver. Proximity to relatives and friends is another factor. That the immigrants need immediate support in starting up their new home and new life is obvious. Often upon their arrival, they would stay for a short time with relatives or friends who would then show them around and help them look for a home in their neighborhood. Thus clustering effect occurs.

Other locational factors include nearness to "good" schools, public transport and shopping facilities. The importance of "good" schools has been outlined above. Reliance on public transport arises as the immigrants need time to obtain a B.C. driver's licence This becomes more necessary as there are senior family members living with them who do not drive. Being able to travel around by public transport or to go shopping in the neighborhood makes life easier for these family members. Nonetheless, the recommendation from the real estate agent is also a decisive factor in the location of the new home for the immigrant.

Hong Kong people have a passion for high quality cars, particularly those from Japan and Germany. On the roads in Hong Kong, almost 90 per cent of the cars are imports from these two countries. Though more expensive than American ones, they are regarded as more reliable, more trouble-free and having more friendly service. No doubt the immigrants will trust their experience. To these immigrants, Japanese and German cars are also more affordable here than in Hong Kong where the price would be double. For those who did not own cars before, the influence of friends and relatives who own Japanese and German cars will motivate them into buying the same. The young adults in the family also feel that it's more fashionable to drive a BMW or Mercedes than a Chevrolet or Ford. This affects the choice of cars in the household. It is not uncommon for immigrant families to own more than one car. The second car would probably be an American-made minivan.This is a practical vehicle for bigger families. Many find the van also more handy when driving with visitors. Entrepreneurs, on the other hand, find it useful in handling cargo.

Most of the business immigrants lost their well-earned social contacts after leaving Hong Kong. Therefore, they tend to pick up whatever contacts they can have in Canada. Relatives and friends are important resources for them to start up their new life and thus the social engagements of the business immigrants are frequently related to social gatherings with these contacts. Going out for a dim-sum lunch or a Chinese dinner, or visiting each other becomes a common pastime.

Another source of social activity is the church. The business immigrants with Christian faith in particular would find many opportunities to meet new friends at the numerous Chinese Christian churches here. Many will also volunteer in church activities and have luncheon gatherings with other church-goers after Sunday service. Few, however, would attend English church services because of the language barrier. Although most of the business immigrants know some English, they are shy to converse with others in that language. They find greeting their neighbors or brief shopping dialogues manageable but when it comes to other functions, they prefer using Chinese if possible. This is also why activities conducted in Chinese by the immigrant and settlement agencies are so popular among the business immigrants.

However, it is this language barrier which has driven many of them to attend English as a second language (ESL) classes. The wives are usually more active in such classes because the husbands may either be more fluent in English or are too shy to catch up. These classes also offer opportunities for gatherings such as having tea or playing mahjong after class as popular social events. Some would even attempt to repeat the class just to find more opportunities to make new friends.

Other occasions where these immigrants would mix with others is at their children's school functions. Many of them would volunteer there where they get acquainted with other parents while watching their children in the skating rink, the swimming pool or the baseball field. Of course, on some occasions, the parents they meet are also Chinese, especially in Chinese language classes, piano or ballet lessons. Seldom do these business immigrants take part in Community Centre activities or volunteer there. In fact, volunteering is not a common practice among the business people in Hong Kong.

Some of these immigrants have become members of Chinese business associations to extend their business network. However, they realize that these associations cannot do much for them when it comes to assistance in business.[8] Even fewer are members of the "mainstream" business associations like the Vancouver Board of Trade.

Business Immigrants as a Resource

It is not hard for entrepreneurs and professionals in Hong Kong to acquire adequate assets to qualify for business immigration to Canada. The spectacular growth of the Hong Kong economy has no doubt created exceptional opportunities to make money. As the latest figures in Hong Kong show, for example, anyone owning a 600 sq. ft. new apartment unit in a new town district would already possess a personal asset of almost one million Canadian dollars![9] The low tax rate plus a fluid trade-led economy with a substantial export-oriented manufacturing sector are the major reasons for the economic boom in Hong Kong. China, which has received the relocation of most of Hong Kong's manufacturing plants since the 1980s by offering cheap land and labor, has also created a great deal of opportunities for Hong Kong business people. Their entrepreneurial skills and capital from their wealth are what the Canadian business immigration program is looking for.

1) *Capital.* Calculating the amount of investment funds is one way of assessing the contribution of the business immigrants. For the investor immigrants, their approved investment ranges from $150,000 to $500,000 each, paid up before the visa is granted. There must also be evidence of a personal net worth of at least $500,000. This means each immigrant would have at least $350,000 to bring into Canada upon arrival. The entrepreneurs, on the other hand, have to establish their own business or buy a substantial share of a business' equity also for at least $150,000, but would still have at least $350,000 of other disposable assets.[10]

A rough calculation would confirm that amount. Besides investment in business, the immigrants will need money for two other expenses. One is on the house and car, and the other is on household expenses . On the house, business immigrants would spend not less than $300,000 and many in fact spend more than $500,000. On cars, seldom would they spend less than $30,000. It is not uncommon for each family to have two imported cars at an investment of $70,000–$100,000.[11]

On household expenses, the amount depends on the number of people in the household and the habit of consumption. A family of four would easily spend around $36,000–48,000 per year, or a total of $108,000–144,000 within three years when the investment is locked. These expenses, combined with those on the house and car, would amount to at least $350,000 per immigrant family just in three years. This investment can set off a series of linkage effects in the economy. The boom in the property market in the past ten years in Vancouver is one testimony to the influence of the business immigrants. The property market itself is linked to the construction industry and a whole range of services including banking, real estate and other professions. Demands created by household consumption also lead to growth in retail businesses.

2) *Entrepreneurial Experiences and Skills.* Besides capital, entrepreneurial skill is also a pre-requisite for business immigration application. However, it is impossible to quantify and difficult to see its effect. The type of activities the business immigrants previously engaged in varies but their experience and skill are certain. The vibrant Asian market has provided both good investment opportunities and fierce competition. Surviving these challenges require exceptional diligence, perseverence and adaptiveness from them. Few entrepreneurs were born with great wealth. Their success is chiefly due to their entrepreneurial qualities.

However, the majority of investment projects fail to match up with the experience of the business immigrants. The top two projects, for example, are in the accommodation industry including food and beverage services and in construction which are not popular business areas for the Hong Kong immigrants (Table 5). Not only that investment projects are not matching their experience, regulations in the investor program further strip the immigrants of the chance to manage the business altogether. This may look good for investor immigrants who need more time to take care of more profitable ventures they still run in Hong Kong, or those looking for retirement. But for those who have decided to settle down in Canada or are younger in age, this would be quite disappointing. While accepting the regulation, they find little encouragement to demonstrate their entrepreneurial skills in their new homeland.

Entrepreneur immigrants are required to set up business before being granted permanent residence. It is not a secret that some of them do so merely to fulfil this requirement. Many of these businesses are set up in haste and are not profitable. Nearly all of them anticipate that they would lose money in the short-run and they feel that purchasing a business from an existing owner would run more risk of loss. They prefer to set up their own business if they can. Once the immigration condition is removed, these entrepreneurs would either move into some other business or return to Hong Kong.

Table 5: Top Investment Projects by Amount of Funds Contributed (1986–1991)

Type	Amount Invested ($)
Accommodation, Food and Beverage Services Industries	267,814,905
Construction Industry	191,776,031
Manufacturing Industries	86,548,343
Mining, Quarrying and Oil Well Industries	39,151,595
Retail Trade Industries	18,794,479

Source: Citizenship and Immigration Canada

3) *Language and Culture.* Another asset the immigrants bring to Canada is their language and culture. All the business immigrants from Hong Kong speak Cantonese and some also speak Mandarin. Except those who have received post-secondary education, the business immigrants find their English level inadequate. Some tackle the language problem by taking ESL classes. Some, however, are less aggressive and prefer to restrict their social and business contacts in the Chinese community instead. In social life, the attachment of these immigrants to the Chinese language has not caused them too much inconvenience. In fact, it has been claimed that some Chinese immigrants in Richmond can pass the day, and indeed the year, doing whatever they have to do, without having to utter a single word of English.

Most of the immigrants read Chinese language newspapers published in Vancouver. *Singtao* and *Mingpao* are more popular among the dailies. Occasionally they may read the *World Journal* which appeals more to the Taiwanese. Both *Singtao* and *Mingpao* carry rather detailed news of Hong Kong and China. The immigrants also listen to the Chinese radio broadcast from three local stations and watch the two Chinese TV channels. A few of them also enjoy singing Chinese karaoke or listening to Chinese popular songs. Their most preferred meals outside of home are in Chinese restaurants and the dishes they cook at home are almost exclusively Chinese cuisine.

There are two major reasons why these immigrants have strong ties to the Chinese language and culture especially those prevalent in Hong Kong. The first is out of familiarity; the second is out of need. Many of these immigrants still want to maintain close ties with Hong Kong and feel that they would be lagging behind their Hong Kong friends or relatives should they lose touch with their roots. That would be seen as an embarrassment.

The preservation of the Chinese language among their children is also valued. Though not required by the School Board, most Chinese business immigrants send their school-age children to after-school Chinese classes. There is every practicality to do so. They speak Chinese at home and would like their children to do so. Moreover, the Chinese language will be useful to their children if they choose to work in Hong Kong in the future. Chinese (also known as Mandarin) has now become a recognized language subject in the provincial examination. Students can fulfil the language requirement when entering university using their credit in Chinese. Many mainstream corporations also recruit employees with Chinese language ability.

Though not explicitly admitted by all the business immigrants, one major cultural element they have brought to Canada is "Hong Kong consumerism." Generally speaking, this would mean the preference for shopping, especially for fashionable products and novelties. The increase in the number of "Asian malls" basically reflects such preference. Dining out is also a popular pastime of the Hong Kong Chinese and the remarkable boom of Chinese restaurants in Greater Vancouver, especially in Richmond, illustrates this fact.

Issues Facing the Business Immigrants

Getting a Canadian business immigrant visa may take only a few months. But it may take much longer to adjust to life as a Canadian business immigrant. The first few years are particularly taxing. Their business initiatives in their adopted homeland could be affected by a number of issues, and these initiatives would in turn affect their investment and settlement in the long run.

1) **Loss through scams.** To the investors, the worst problem to face is the loss of their principal through scams and mismanagement of investment projects. There are particularly serious problems in Manitoba where loss is substantial.[12] In most of these cases, the "high risk" ventures were poorly managed or budgeted. The investors were also not properly informed of the risk involved. The project overspent or were under-budgeted, or did not work as planned. Eventually the project would stop unless the investors poured in new funds. One immigration consultant estimates that more than 25 per cent of the funds incurred losses.

    While understanding the risk in investment and being prepared to accept a loss as "fee" for entry into Canada, most of the investors blame the government for failing to supervise investments. The off-handedness of the government is interpreted as irresponsibility or foolishness. They agree that it is better for the Canadian government to charge them an admission fee into Canada than to take part in the un-regulated projects. Some investors would advise the government to make use of the immigrants' capital in funding government or community projects. The building and maintenance of roads, schools and running education and training programs are regarded as more worthwhile areas of investment than those "high risk" businesses.

2) **Taxation.** Canada has a higher tax rate than many Asian countries. Hong Kong, in particular, has enjoyed one of the lowest tax rates in the world. More than a quarter of the business immigrants interviewed expressed the view that Canadian taxes are too heavy leaving them with little profit while in Hong Kong they could earn more than 20 per cent. The high tax rate affects pricing and makes business less competitive. The high income tax rate also poses a problem as the workers lose their incentives to earn more by working harder. This would impede productivity and affect production or service plans. Some immigrants, however, argue that the tax rate is all right as long as they do not compare

it with Hong Kong's. In fact, they say that all Hong Kong investors and entrepreneurs who applied under the business program knew about the high taxes before arriving in Canada and choosing to come anyway means they have to accept the existing tax system.

3) *Labor.* Another factor which affects business initiative is labor cost. Again, about one quarter of the immigrants interviewed complained of high wages, even though wage rates in Hong Kong have risen a great deal in the past years. In manufacturing and other labor-intensive services, many Hong Kong business immigrants feel that the lack of cheap labor, which they enjoyed in Hong Kong and China and is partly responsible for the business boom there, would seriously dampen their initiatives. And moreover, the highly unionized labor force in Canada does not provide the same production flexibility as in Hong Kong or China and that, they think, is the major reason why Canada is losing its competitiveness in the world market.

4) *Declaration of Overseas Assets.* Though not directly related to their business, the regulation for Canadian residents to declare overseas assets worth over $100,000 has adversely affected not only the Hong Kong business immigrants' interest in investing more in Canada but also their will to stay. Most of them regard the regulation as "unreasonable" or a "big problem." Many business immigrants still maintain strong ties with Hong Kong: some have parents or relatives there, others, businesses. Maintaining assets in Hong Kong particularly in the form of real estate is considered natural by the business immigrants. The Chinese familial system necessitates these people to have a registered share of a house, an office or factory in a domestic partnership. Some have not given up their business operations in Hong Kong or China and would wait to find out what opportunities they could have here. These business immigrants would face heavy taxes as their assets are in excess of the allowance. If taxed, depending on the rate, many would not hesitate to leave Canada altogether, although few would like to see that happen. However, those who have brought all their assets to Canada would not be affected.

Commitment to Canada

Almost a quarter of the business immigrants interviewed are "astronauts," flying to and fro to care for their business and their family located on the two shores of the Pacific Ocean. While there is more money for the principal immigrants to earn on the other side of the Ocean, their families prefer to live in Canada.

There are several factors which would determine the commitment of the business immigrants to Canada. First and foremost is whether or not they still have business or work back home. Although Hong Kong has returned to Chinese sovereignty, business booms as usual and the property market is also booming. In China, inflation is curbed and investment opportunities abound. Those immigrants who still have business in Hong Kong are the least decided to settle in Canada, though risking separation from their families. Their general notion is that making money takes priority. It can be expected that they would continue to do so until either they have saved enough to retire or the situation back home has become so unfavorable that they really have to leave.

The second factor is related to the first, that is, whether or not they could set up and develop a profitable business in Canada. For the investors who do not have the obligation to set up their business though, the question would be whether or not they could make a living, either by starting off another business or by gaining employment. Many are just too young to retire. If there is nothing they could do here, they would try to return to Hong Kong. Connections and experience back home would still give them some business or job opportunities.

In any case, most business immigrants would like to continue the ideal arrangement of maintaining both their business and family in Canada. Three reasons for this are: First, their family, especially their children, like to stay in Canada. The education system, though some complaints apply, is more suited to individual development. Second, the pleasant and safe living environment which money cannot buy. Added to this is the comfort of living in a large house with a beautiful yard and garden which one can only dream of in Hong Kong. Third, the freedom of movement is another plus. The traffic jam here seems trivial compared to that in Hong Kong.

So, those who have brought everything here with them, whether they be investors or entrepreneurs, would be most content to live in Canada and would be the least likely to return to Hong Kong. Those who have good business in Hong Kong or China are the most vulnerable and could consider leaving and applying for non-resident status once they have their citizenship conferred. Their family, however, would most likely remain in Canada. A lot still depends on how Hong Kong fares after its return to China.

Conclusion

Few people would disagree that the business immigration program has brought in the targeted people and resources to Canada. But besides mere numbers, what do the immigrants really mean to Canada and what does immigration mean to the investor or entrepreneur?

To the business immigrants, the most serious concern is that their investment would not be used effectively. Some of the investment programs are not making any gain for the Canadian economy nor for the investors but causing frustration to both. Even with the risk factor, the hard-earned savings deserve some guarantee that it is put to proper use. It is suggested that the funds supplement investment in public projects. This would give the investors a sense of commitment to their new homeland.

Then, there is the question of the proper use of their entrepreneurial experience and skills. The segregation between investment and management in the investors' program deprives the business immigrants the opportunity to exercise those skills. There is also no encouragement for them to use their entrepreneurship in other endeavors. Most investors have other financial resources over the $150,000 they spent on investment funds but they do not find many profitable businesses attractive to them here. Some, therefore, may decide to return to Hong Kong where the business environment is much more encouraging (despite the political uncertainty). Some may simply enjoy an early retirement. Others, weary of leisure, may try to find jobs with little use of their entrepreneurial expertise. All this means a loss to Canada and the entrepreneurs.

There is also the issue of the immigrants' culture as not being understood and often treated as alien rather than as a business opportunity or social asset. The business immigrants' roots in Hong Kong and China and their experience in the Asian region could be tremendous assets to the business community in Canada which is boosting its Asia Pacific relationship. The strength of these business immigrants lies not only on their individual capital and skills but also on their extensive social and business network in the fastest growing region of the world.[13]

Allowing the investor immigrants a place on the board of the investment project or in the management of the project itself would give them a chance to demonstrate their skill, at least for those who want to do so. This will also attract the immigrant to settle in the target area of investment. Facilities which could help these investors to make further investment in the Canadian economy are also lacking. Many investors feel there is no interest in the business community in their assets.

The entrepreneur immigrant may have different concerns. Most of them hope to set up a business here but that is not often possible. Eager to establish themselves, they would rush into buying a business unfamiliar to them. They know the risks but would consider subsequent loss to be the price of removal of their immigration condition. Afterwards, they will sell their business and either return to Hong Kong or find other opportunities here. This would be a waste of their time or their entrepreneurial effort. Why, then, could they not be guided into setting up some business which could be more permanent and rewarding?

Those entrepreneurs who have burned their bridges would look more seriously into the possibility of starting a new business which they could rely on for profit in the years to come. Some will even consider pooling together resources from friends and acquaintances and roll off their joint-venture. Nevertheless, often the entrepreneurs find the two years will pass by very quickly and that business which they buy or start up to fulfil the condition is by no means their preference. They would need more time to adjust to the business environment here.

To the Hong Kong immigrants, the business immigration program is not a bad idea but it lacks proper guidance and facilities to put capital and entrepreneurship into more profitable endeavors in Canada. Are the public and private sectors here prepared to do a little bit more on this?

Endnotes

[1] Citizenship and Immigration Canada. 1996. *Staying the course, 1997 annual immigration plan*. Online. Available at http://cicnet.ingenia.com/english/pub/anrep97e.html#plan1.

[2] *Financial Post* (24 November 1995); *The Globe and Mail* (2 August 1992); and *The The Vancouver Sun* (7 August 1992, 11 June 1994, 22 May 199).

[3] Lam, Lawrence. 1994. "Searching for a safe haven: The migration and settlement of Hong Kong Chinese immigrants in Toronto." In *Reluctant exiles? Migration from Hong Kong and the new overseas Chinese*, ed. Skeldon, Ronald, 163–179. New York: Armonk.

[4] The study is based on personal interviews in April-May 1997 with twenty business immigrants from Hong Kong, half of whom belong to the investor category and the rest entrepreneur category. Though not representing a significant sample, information from these immigrants provides a better understanding of the nature of Hong Kong business immigrants and highlights the need to further research on their roles and potentials.

[5] Employment and Immigration Canada. 1995. Report to Parliament on the review of future directions for immigration levels. Ottawa: Employment and Immigration Canada.

[6] Employment and Immigration Canada. 1989. *A guide to Canada's business immigration program*. Ottawa: Employment and Immigration Canada

[7] Lam, Lawence, *op. cit.*

[8] Kunin, Roslyn, and Diana Lary. 1997. *Succeeding: Profiles of Chinese Canadian entrepreneurs*. Vancouver: Asia Pacific Foundation of Canada.

[9] *Singtao Daily* (British Columbia edition) (14 June 1997).

[10] Business Immigration Branch, Government of British Columbia. January 1996.

[11] The immigrant may put up a mortgage on the house but often pays up the car in full.

[12] *The Vancouver Sun* (7 August 1992); *Financial Post* (2 November 1994, 24 November 1995). See also Deloitte and Touche, 1993, *Immigrant investor program review*, Winnipeg.

[13] Government of British Columbia. 1995. *Immigrant investment in British Columbia: New partnerships for our economic future*. Victoria: Province of British Columbia.

18 The Rhetoric of Racism and the Politics of Explanation in the Vancouver Housing Market

David Ley

These remarks on the rhetoric of racism are offered with some apprehension. I do not want to minimize the actual incidence of racist attitudes and practices which continue, as they always have, to poison intergroup relations and pose unacceptable obstacles to individual life chances at all four corners of the Pacific Basin and beyond. The exposure of these deviations remains a significant moral and intellectual responsibility. Moreover, I am well aware that in the emotional and political crucible of identity politics, few issues are as highly charged as those around race and ethnicity. Yet It remains important, if necessary against the grain, to challenge influential streams of popular and intellectual culture around their representations of racism. What motivates this intervention is a perception of flawed scholarship that has consequences in practice. My argument will be to suggest that in its discussion of race and racism scholarly culture too often is in agreement with an uncritical popular culture that errs, for sometimes strategic reasons, toward simple reductions of complex relations and ends up by offering premature closure in an all-too-coherent narrative. This intellectual error is compounded as it develops into an ethical judgment that readily slips into implicit or explicit political declarations. The irony in this slippage is that, however unwittingly, it reproduces the cruel fashioning of racist categories: from simplification and reduction to typification and the ascription of a singular, usually prejudicial, characteristic to a broad community. In its eagerness to expose racism, this genre courts the danger of reproducing the mind of the racist.

This at least will be my argument. Rather than remain at the safe level of abstraction, I wish to develop this thesis in a concrete setting: the immigration over the past decade of members of the Chinese diaspora into upper middle-class districts of Vancouver and certain of its middle-class suburbs, particularly the municipality of Richmond, and the simultaneous conflict over landscape transformation in these districts as large modern houses have replaced an older landscape expressing longer-established Anglo-Canadian sentiments. In its polemical form, this debate has been represented in the media for some time in the idiom of the "monster house." My discussion concerns the flawed representation and interpretation of that debate in the media, in strategic interventions, and in scholarship.

Context

An important context of these circumstances is the changing social geography of immigration to Canada over the past generation. A first factor is the remarkable place specificity of immigrant destinations, with Toronto and Vancouver dominating destinations to a degree not equalled before. Over the past three years, in particular, British Columbia has received new entrants at a level well in excess of its share of the national population. With some 13 per cent of the Canadian population, B.C. has been the destination for between 21 and 23 per cent of new arrivals between 1994 and 1996, while Greater Vancouver, with half the provincial population, has become home to 85 per cent of these new Canadians.[1] In other words, Greater Vancouver, with something over 6 per cent of the national population is receiving 18–20 per cent of all newcomers.[2] Recent immigrants are highly concentrated and thereby highly visible both in appearance and in their impacts. A second geographic factor has been the transformation of immigrant origins. In 1966, and continuing a pattern that had existed since before Confederation, between 80 and 90 per cent of new arrivals to Canada originated in Europe and the United States, led by Great Britain. These well-established channels were redirected, however, by immigration reform during the 1960s that redefined the terms of entry, and by 1986 these traditional sources were contributing only 30 per cent of immigrants; by 1996 the figure had fallen to 20 per cent. As is well known, the new legislation has favored entry from other continents, and particularly Asia. Immigrants from Asia have risen from less than 10 per cent of the national total in 1966 to over 40 per cent in 1986 and close to 65 per cent in 1996. In British Columbia, on the Pacific rim, these trends are understandably accentuated, and in recent years 80 per cent of new arrivals to the province have originated in Asia, led by Hong Kong and India, with Taiwan close behind. The British contribution is now under four per cent.

A second context is the growing size of the immigrant pool in absolute terms, accentuating the incidence as well as the perception of change. National immigration totals in the 1990s are at their highest level in the post-1945 period, while in B.C., 1996 represented the first year since 1912 that immigrant landings exceeded 50,000 persons. The result has been that the ethno-cultural transformation of urban space is both quickened and deepened. One projection by a demographer at Carleton University suggested that the share of visible minorities in the population of Metro Toronto would increase from 21 per cent in 1986 to 45 per cent in 2001, while the Vancouver share would also more than double, from 17 to 39 per cent.[3] Most authorities today would regard this estimate as exaggerated, but nonetheless indicative of the degree of transformation that is underway. Changes of this magnitude are measureable at the scale of everyday life, as some schools, for example, have moved from 95 per cent Caucasian to less than 30 per cent over a fifteen year period or less. Students enrolled in English as a second language (ESL) classes in Greater Vancouver have increased in number from around 10,000 in 1987 to over 60,000 in 1995. In the City of Vancouver ESL enrolment now accounts for just over half the student body, and in Richmond, where ESL numbers quintupled between 1990 and 1995, for over 40 per cent.[4] Studies of several subdivisions in Richmond, the suburb closest to the international airport, have observed Chinese-origin residents increasing from one in twenty households to almost one in four in the brief span between 1988 and 1992.[5] For a province historically settled from Europe these are very substantial changes over a short period in the urban milieu.

There is a third context that has introduced a new complexion to immigration in the Vancouver region. The composition of entry categories among immigrants shows marked regional variation in Canada. Since 1990, British Columbia has received between only six and eight per cent of refugees landing in Canada, the most disadvantaged of the immigrant categories. In contrast the province has been the destination of choice for a steadily rising share of economic immigrants, over 27 per cent of those landing nation-wide in 1996. The wealthiest groups of new Canadians are included among the economic classes of entrepreneurs and investors, and here B.C. is dominant, the destination in 1996 of 35 per cent of the entrepreneur class and 54 per cent of the investor class. The declared wealth of these new Canadians, three-quarters of whom have moved to B.C. from Hong Kong or Taiwan, is impressive, amounting to almost $3 billion in 1996 and between $20 and $25 billion since 1990.[6] The scale of this personal wealth brings an entirely new dimension to post-1945 immigration. When we recall its geographic concentration in the largest Canadian cities, and in particular, in Vancouver, then the opportunity exists for a significant impact upon patterns of consumption, including the consumption of land and housing.[7] As we shall see, this is an opportunity that has been fully realized.

The Transformation of Upper Middle-class Districts

For a number of years immigration has been the largest single component of population growth in Greater Vancouver area, and has grown steadily in absolute values to a peak of 42,500 in 1996.[8] Consequently it has become the leading shaper of the regional housing market (Figure 1). Moreover, the distinctive submarket of wealthy business class immigrants, numbering from 50,000 to 55,000 persons between 1990 and 1996, have set up residence in Greater Vancouver with declared funds of the order of $18–20 billion.[9] While this cohort of business immigrants accounts for only 20 per cent of the entire immigrant cohort, its economic power has made it of special significance.

Figure 1: Immigration and Population Growth in Greater Vancouver

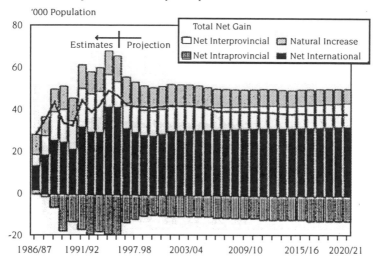

GVRD Population Gain by Component

Projection: PEOPLE Projection 21 — BC STATS
Estimates: Statistics Canada
Source: BC STATS (1996)

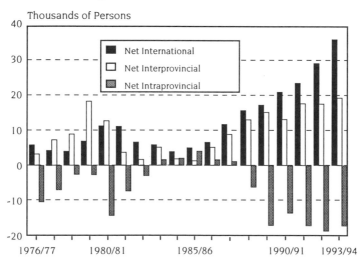

GVRD Net Migration

Source. Statistics Canada; City of Vancouver (1995)

As a group business immigrants have shown particular interest in Vancouver's blue-chip residential districts, notably the old Anglo-Canadian upper-class area of Shaughnessy and its middle-class neighbors Kerrisdale and Oakridge, all conveniently close to downtown and the airport. As prices rose rapidly in these westside districts, attention turned at the end of the 1980s to the middle-class airport suburb of Richmond immediately to the south. Immigrants in these districts favor a new large house on a cleared lot, usually in excess of 4,000 square feet. House layout and design are shaped in part by the traditional metaphysic of feng shui, but as part of the modern urban world, these buyers share modernity's fascination with the new. The home is an important opportunity to demonstrate one's purchase upon progress, to advertise a successful, forward-looking modern identity.

Small building firms have accommodated this new market by purchasing and demolishing existing detached homes, clearing the lot and constructing a new residence to the maximum area permitted by city by-laws, a mass often significantly larger than the previous property on the site. These dimensions have been accommodated by large houses, initially with minimal facade articulation and lightly sloping roofs. Symbols of success include Greek columns, a spiral staircase and spacious cathedral entry hall, multiple bedrooms and bathrooms, and in larger properties an entertainment room and a second Chinese kitchen. With minimal vegetation screening the cleared lot, the opulence of these homes is clearly visible.

This house form first began to appear in the mid-1980s in the westside district of Oakridge, an area that included a middle-class Jewish population, and a preponderance of low-profile ranch style homes built in the 1950s on good-sized lots. The aging of the community was creating vacancies that were already being occupied by Canadian-born Chinese business and professional families by the early 1980s. A second attractive feature of Oakridge to new business immigrants was the existence of Vancouver's only International Baccalaureate program at the neighborhood secondary school, an enriched curriculum that permits successful graduates entry to study at international as well as Canadian universities, and is eminently suited for transnational families interested in global networking. The population turnover is far advanced in Oakridge and has attracted no public expression of concern.

As the immigrant population has grown, it has moved westwards into Kerrisdale and Shaughnessy, neighborhoods that also contain an aging Caucasian population and thus the potential for considerable turnover. Unlike Oakridge, these elite westside districts have a well-defined Anglo-Canadian heritage; in 1971, 76 per cent of the Kerrisdale population defined themseves ethnically in this category, with 69 per cent in Shaughnessy, well above the average for the entire city. The landscape reflects this heritage, with an emphasis upon European design precedents, especially 1910s and 1920s neo-Tudor mansions and smaller arts and crafts-influenced homes. Mature landscaping and manicured gardens express what Turner called an elegant pastoralism, a picturesque green veil of English deciduous trees and shrubs, integrated by an historicist inclination, a "valuation of places according to their connections with a presumed or inferred history."[10] There is a tight bonding of landscape and identity in these districts, marked by the vigilance of the Shaughnessy Heights Property Owners' Association since the 1930s, whose aim has been consistently to perpetuate the landscape symbols of an elite anglophilia. From the 1970s, well before the arrival of trans-Pacific business immigrants, the Association lobbied City Council for protective legislation controlling redevelopment and was rewarded in 1982 with the passage of the First Shaughnessy Plan covering the northernmost and oldest section of the district, a plan whose design guidelines forbade new structures that did not follow the model of "the English picturesque landscape tradition."[11]

Consequences

Immigration to these privileged westside districts has led to the internationalization of this local colony of a national elite. Exposure to a system of global flows has introduced marked inflationary pressures to real estate. Analysis of the residential land market in British Columbia has shown that over the past twenty years there has been a strong positive relationship between net migration and real housing prices (Figure 2).[12] Because immigration has been the major contributor to growth in every year since 1986 in Greater Vancouver it has also been the leading factor affecting house prices. Core areas — downtown districts and the westside in particular — have been the major target of immigrant and off-shore investor interest. According to Alan Liu, Hong Kong-based sales executive of Colliers Jardine, "the areas in Vancouver most popular with Hong Kong buyers are the westside, downtown, False Creek, Yaletown, and Oakridge."[13] Downtown condominium projects, especially those developed by Hong-Kong based companies, are regularly marketed there; photographed in his Hong Kong office behind a model of twin residential towers in downtown Vancouver, Liu noted that his company had just sold 70 per cent of the units of a separate Yaletown condominum to Hong Kong buyers. This international exposure of the city's residential real estate is accomplished through an intricate network of relations between builders, investors and realty companies with strong trans-Pacific connections.[14] Similar networks function in the westside detached housing market, led by Manyee Lui's Kerrisdale-based company, Hallmark Properties. In the summer of 1996, Ms. Lui noted that for the immigrant market she specialized in, "Vancouver's westside is still most popular."[15] In 1995 Ms. Lui sold 16 homes valued at over $1 million, 90 per cent of them to Asian immigrants, a pace she was substantially improving upon in 1996.

The internationalization of westside real estate has led to substantial price increases, but also sharp (if smaller) price losses during downturns

**Figure 2: Relations between Net Migration and
House Prices in British Columbia**

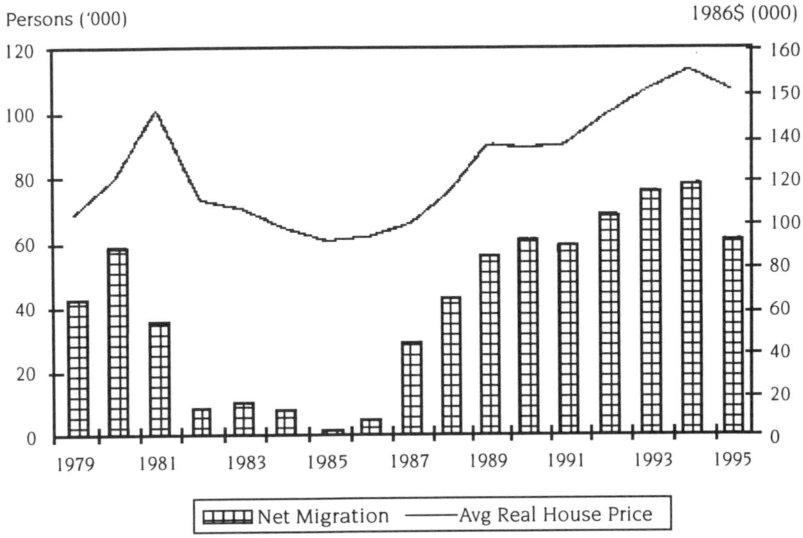

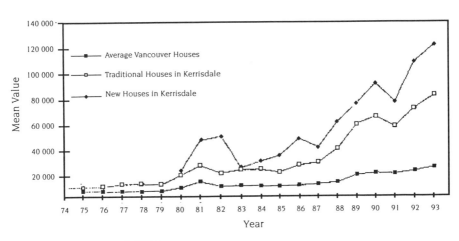

Persons ('000)   1986$ (000)

Net Migration ——— Avg Real House Price

Source: BC STATS (1996)

**Figure 3: Average Value of New and Traditional Houses
in Kerrisdale Compared with Vancouver Mean**

(Translated from Brosseau et al., 1996)

Average Vancouver Houses
Traditional Houses in Kerrisdale
New Houses in Kerrisdale

Year

Source: Brosseau et al. 1996

(Figure 3). In each instance, Shaughnessy and Kerrisdale appear to be leading the Vancouver regional market, the site of marked upturns ahead of other
districts through much of the past decade, but also the locale of exaggerated
downturns in 1991, and again in 1997 when the combination of an unfavorable
tax decision in Canada concerning the disclosure of overseas assets together
with rising optimism about the future of Hong Kong, led to a decline of over
ten per cent in westside median house prices "in areas of high Asian
activity."[16] Interestingly this oscillating pattern has also been observed in
price movements in elite districts in comparable world cities including Sydney, Melbourne and Toronto.[17]

In economic terms, the impact of immigration in the housing market
has been a mixed blessing. Households have been burdened by increased
municipal taxes as their land values have risen; a number have rued that
price increases have disenfranchised their children from homeownership in
the district of their upbringing. But there have been substantial economic
gains as well. Elderly households have found that their home has become a
nest egg of scarcely imagined value; some younger households have decided
to cash in their real estate assets, "to move to Langley and become rich."[18]
Moreover, construction and real estate companies have operated at high
capacity, firming up a critical area of the regional labor market.

But the issue of neighborhood change has not typically been engaged in
economic terms. The message of the Shaughnessy Property Owners' Association, and similar groups in Kerrisdale, together with a legion of unattached
individuals, has had everything to do with the symbolic economy. These interventions over neighborhood redevelopment have a common refrain: the
need for public regulation to protect a heritage landscape; the requirement
that new buildings be "neighborly" in their design; an insistence that mature
trees and landscaping be protected. There is not space here to detail the
letters to the media, to city council, the delegations to the city, the lobbying
of planners, and briefs to public hearings that have occurred since the mid
1980s. Two examples will have to suffice, letters selected from among the
hundreds sent to the City over the issue of the transformation of the
Shaughnessy and Kerrisdale landscapes.[19] The theme of protecting symbolic
value against exchange value is persistent in these interventions:

> We've raised our family here, sent our children to the neighborhood schools,
> participated in all kinds of community events over the years. Now many of
> the people who own homes in the area don't live here. The homes are empty.
> These homes are investments, perhaps one of many. You feel differently
> about a place when you live there, form friends there, become part of the
> neighborhood and the community . . .

> We don't mind change but we want to see it fit into the neighborhood. We
> don't like to see good homes with years of livability in them destroyed if
> something not appropriate is put up in their place. We want the area to

remain a livable and lovely neighborhood for the families that live here now and will live here in the future. We want to stress that this is a place to live not just a place to make money out of.[20]

The elision of family and neighborhood and the desire for compatibility with a community norm is apparent. Community guardians establish a defence against what they see as the raw deployment of economic power. A second letter to Council is quoted because it was one of a minority that placed landscape change into a broader narrative of economic power and citizenship rights and also was unusually direct in its imputation of blame:

The wail of the chain saw yesterday prompted me to write to you. I spent several sleepless hours thinking about our home, our neighborhood and our city . . .

I have come to accept the fact that these huge and generally unattractive houses are a reality. However, I will not sit back and watch every tree being cut down in order to accommodate these monsters . . .

The face of Vancouver is changing far too quickly. We — fairly reasonable people — fear the power that the Hong Kong money brings. We resent the fact that because they come here with pots of money they are able to mutilate the areas they choose to settle in. Our trees are part of our heritage. These people come — with no concern for our past — they have not been part of the growth and development of our beautiful city — they have not been paying taxes for years. They have no right to devastate the residential areas.[21]

An extended interpretation could accompany this letter alone. It is not without its ironic moments, for it shows a blindness to the far greater exercise of erasure practised by Europeans little over a century earlier as they removed the people of the First Nations from their seasonal camps and traditional hunting areas in precisely this location. Nor does it acknowledge the free market principles that these conservative homeowners pursue at work while seeking the protection of state regulation at home. But these have not been the principal objections directed at the positions of the Shaughnessy and Kerrisdale homeowners.

Representations: The Rhetoric of Race
Media representations of neighborhood transition have rarely been subtle. The English-language media have typically traded in slogans around the "monster house," a term offensive to the immigrant Chinese community. On occasion the racialization of land use and social change has become extreme. The sensational headline "White flight, Chinese distress," part of what was meant to be an in-depth interpretation of population change in Richmond, revealed in its simplification, stereotyping and polarization (fuelled by the entirely inappropriate evocation of racial change — "white

flight" — in the United States) many of the ingredients of the racist mind, a capacity to see social and land use processes only in ethno-cultural terms.[22]

But perhaps racialized accounts flow readily in a city that in its early years showed serious manifestations of racist sentiment, and where racial exclusion was institutionalized against Asian-origin people, for example in the right to vote, until the late 1940s.[23] The salience of race is perpetuated by media sensationalism and a public culture where the legitimacy of anti-racism makes trading in accusations of racism a particularly powerful tool. As a consequence charges of racism need to be deconstructed, though of course in asserting their social construction I am not accepting the full constructionist position that racist accusations have no neccessary empirical reference. What I am saying is that their material reality needs to be empirically demonstrated, not uncritically assumed. For as we shall see, the deployment of charges of racism can be a strategic intervention to silence critics where other matters may be at stake. In taking this position I am in agreement with Wimmer's recent statement that the interpretation of racism needs to consider not only ideas but also undergirding economic, political and social interests.[24]

So we see charges of racism being authored by groups who are economic beneficiaries of recent immigration. Accusations have been laid against their neighbors by some Anglo-Canadians concerned about land values and property rights. The most publicized charge, however, has come from the West Side Builders' Association, representing small contractors who have secured profits from the development boom in westside neighborhoods. A letter to Council, later repeated in a widely-cited brief, declared that proposed rezoning bylaws for the areas of Shaughnessy and Kerrisdale were "discriminatory, racist and unfair."[25] This allegation was picked up in Hong Kong's *South China Morning Post* under a characteristically inflammatory headline "Vancouver planning law fuels racist fire."[26] This was not the first time for a strategic intervention, for earlier a brief to Council from a separate builders' group had been titled "Racism and the dilemma of changing neighborhoods."[27]

This argument has been writ large in the pro-business media. The local business magazine *Equity* published a theme issue under the provocative title, "Racism: will it kill investment billions?"[28] Left-wing municipal politicians who maintained their traditional support for community interests over international capital were branded as racists by pro-business figures.[29] As Katharyne Mitchell has observed ". . . control over race construction and the meanings of race and racism has thus become an extremely desirable and highly contested prize. Capitalists and politicians seeking to attract Hong Kong Chinese investment target "localists" as racist and endeavor to present themselves as non-racist . . . In examining race and nation in Vancouver in the past decade, the social relations of power involved in the struggles over meaning become immediately apparent."

Aware of the political fallout from the "creative destruction" of rapid development, some corporate interests have been particularly vigilant in denying the role of trans-Pacific investment in Vancouver's neighborhood changes and rapidly inflating housing market.[30] In 1989 the business-funded Laurier Institute was formed, in its own words, as "a national non-profit, non-advocacy research and education organization dedicated to the advancement and dissemination of information concerning economic and social implications of cultural diversity. It has no political or business affiliations."[31] The Institute's sponsors were major corporate players in trans-Pacific finance, real estate, trade and transportation. It immediately commissioned a six-part research project from neo-liberal land economists to ascertain "factors affecting real estate prices in the Greater Vancouver area," and to interrogate "controversial suggestions that a particular cultural group — the Chinese — were the cause of increased real estate prices."[32]

The methodology of this research was flawed, as were inferences drawn from it. The mandate to examine price inflation immediately drew attention to current events, for prices had only begun to recover in 1986 from a four-year decline during the economic recession that followed the 1981 boom. The implication, then, was that research would examine current conditions — a rapidly inflating land market and a growth in trans-Pacific immigrants to Greater Vancouver[33] — and such indeed were the inferences drawn from the report. But in fact the migration data used in the analysis were a time series that ended in 1986, prior to the immigration and real estate upturn of the post-1986 period. The analysis absolved international capital as a principal factor in residential land price movements, and this finding was ideologically transferred to the present. Immediately following the Institute's press release, the region's *Real Estate Weekly*, a free publication delivered to homeowners, used the analysis to refute "complaints that high immigration to Vancouver was the root cause of soaring home prices," a thesis that the research had been unable to investigate.[34] The implication was quite clear: anyone who held other views of the changing housing market was negating scientific research, and thereby guilty of prejudice, or worse.[35] Some of the media fell into the trap; a television station acknowledged that "we revised our coverage in short order" concerning the impact of off-shore property investment following publication of the Laurier reports.[36]

This labelling was evident to residents of Shaughnessy and Kerrisdale who resisted neighborhood change. Responding to the charge of racism from the West Side Builders' Association, the leader of the Kerrisdale-Granville Homeowners' Association affirmed that the land use dispute was "not an issue of 'race' but of 'greed,'" thereby deflecting the protest from race to class concerns.[37] A neighbor opened up a new front: "I am not racist. I tell myself this over and over again to loosen the creeping fingers of intimidation that Mr. Hersh and his developer friends are attempting to tighten around my voice box."[38] On the defensive, residents sought to activate the option of voice usually claimed by marginalized groups. "Discrimination is a widely and loosely used word these days. I would like to use it for myself for a change. In my family's situation I feel we are being discriminated against as well as harassed and would like to receive the same consideration (so abundantly given by us Canadians to others)."[39]

Another view, then, would agree with the position expressed by an Indo-Canadian speaker at the 1992 public hearing over the rezoning of Shaughnessy, a move intended to preserve existing streetscapes through design guidelines while permitting demolition and redevelopment to continue: "While it's true pockets of racism can rear their ugly heads during times of tension, for anyone in a position of clout to imply that racism is at the base of this issue or that such pockets are the sole monopoly of one specific group, is in itself racist and an affront to us all."[40] This conclusion seemed to be shared by David Lam, the former Lieutenant-Governor of the province of British Columbia, who declared in an influential statement "When a Canadian is concerned about his own way of living, this concern is not racism."[41]

How plausible is this position? One response is to consider recent land use conflict in Shaughnessy and Kerrisdale as part of a longer established and more widely-based anti-growth movement of which race is neither a necessary nor a sufficient cause .[42] Greater Vancouver has experienced periods of particularly rapid growth over the past 30 years that have seen recurrent flashpoints of resistance to (re)development. The regional population surged by 16 per cent between 1966 and 1971 and prompted persistent anti-growth sentiments. Around 1970 the extent and character of downtown redevelopment and urban renewal gave rise to sustained opposition to demolition, including struggles in heritage districts that included Gastown and Chinatown and landmark sites like Christ Church Cathedral and the Orpheum Theatre. Shortly after, redevelopment pressures moved into old inner city districts where sustained opposition was raised over gentrification in Kitsilano in particular. A pro-neighborhood and slow growth movement was mobilized and came to power at City Hall during the early mid-1970s.

It was this reform movement that initiated a program of local area planning that reached Shaughnessy and was institutionalized in the preservation-oriented First Shaughnessy Plan in 1982. A proposal to construct a light rapid transit line through the westside neighborhoods along an established right of way was roundly rejected by residents of Shaughnessy and Kerrisdale in public hearings that attracted hundreds of residents, despite the advantages of fast access to downtown and the airport and the promise of significant capital gains to property owners living near stations. The line would have run via the airport to Richmond, where the municipality was gripped by an acrimonious anti-growth dispute over the development of the Terra Nova farm lands, a dispute that went all the way to the Supreme Court of Canada.

From 1971 to 1986, five-year growth figures fell to 8–9 per cent, but following the recession of the early to mid-1980s, a renewed round of rapid growth took place. From 1986–91 the regional population surged by 16 per cent, and added another 14 per cent in the next five years. Once again conflict emerged where pressures for change were marked: in the poverty district of the Downtown Eastside where gentrification was first triggered by the destabilizing forces of Expo '86, once again in Kitsilano, in the Kerrisdale apartment district where hundreds of tenants were evicted, and in several of the fastest growing suburbs, including Richmond, Delta and Surrey. In the 1990 municipal elections slow- or anti-growth advocates were elected in a number of the suburbs. Matching the reform movement of the 1970s a neighborhood movement led by a community activist, Jim Green, challenged the existing pro-business majority at Vancouver's City Hall with the arresting localist slogan "the Neighborhood Green." It was in this context that the land use tensions I have described in the detached housing districts of Shaughnessy and Kerrisdale occurred. Responses there showed continuity with earlier resistance to growth. The preservation objectives of the Shaughnessy Property Owners' Association (and similar groups in Kerrisdale) and their methods in the late 1980s and early 1990s mirrored exactly their successful strategy in First Shaughnessy a decade earlier. One thing of course had changed. Between the first round of resistance and the second, race had become part of the composition of neighborhood change, and now monopolized the rhetoric of explanation.

Conclusion

What I am suggesting is that charges of racism need to be interrogated, first for their own ideological motivation, and second, in light of a broader empirical examination that opens up the issue to more nuanced interpretation. The intent is not to deny the existence of racism but rather to make charges of racism themselves accountable to ideological analysis and empirical verification. Such an exercise indicates that a far more complex story needs to be told.

Unfortunately, the simplifications expressed by the media and some business groups occur also in several social science accounts. I have already noted how reports by neo-liberal land economists have avoided the self-evident conclusion that the internationalization of the land market has had inflationary effects in Vancouver as it has in other global cities. Migration has a strong correlation with house prices, but as the dominant contribution over the past dozen years to migration has been immigration, so it is immigration that is the principal factor influencing price movements, both up and down. The ideological use of these real estate reports has been to question the motives of anyone who reaches this conclusion. But several anti-racist critics have been even more direct in their imputation of an un-complicated racism. In Richmond, one group of authors identify "a reinvented articulation of old racist concepts;" they continue, "We believe that the constructed images and popular discourse surrounding change in Richmond bear only a weak relationship to the actual nature of change and the Chinese population. In many ways this popular discourse has relatively little to do with physical change per se, and instead is reflective of a long history of ideas about immigrants, race and place in the suburbs,"[43] a declaration without supporting evidence. It is the belief of these authors that received cultural images around race and place rather than material land use changes provide the fundamental motive for protest. Just like the neo-liberal economists the issues of growth and land use change are marginalized in order to racialize the interpretation.

A second manuscript is in agreement, joining also with the neo-liberal economists in raising doubts that recent immigration has contributed significantly to price inflation in the westside neighborhoods.[44] As with the land economists and the Richmond study, the objective of devaluing the role of material land use change is to inflate the explanatory power of non-material cultural change, to orchestrate the interpretation of protest around the arbitrary nexus of race and racism. The result is an argument that is itself highly racialized, as the author speaks of white flight, white response, white neighborhoods, adopting through the processes of simplification, homogenization, and polarization what Bonnett has recently criticized as "the myth of whiteness" found in some anti-racist literature: "anti-racists have often placed a myth of whiteness at the centre of their discourse. The myth views 'being white' as an immutable condition with clear and distinct moral attributes. These attributes often include: being racist; not experiencing racism; being an oppressor; not experiencing oppression; silencing; not being silenced."[45]

In this chapter I have argued against such reduction of anti-development protest to a single dimension. A longer time horizon reveals that anti-growth politics in Shaughnessy and Richmond predated the arrival of trans-Pacific migration. Moreover, enhanced tree protection and compromise housing design bylaws in Shaughnessy and Kerrisdale have removed most of the steam from neighborhood protest since 1993, even as ethno-cultural change has continued. A thicker interpretation of the present indicates a variety of motives for resistance. My case, however, is not to deny the role of racist motivations as having some part in the protests of the past decade. Just as the 1992 public hearings over neighborhood change in Shaughnessy introduced a more democratic public sphere to land use decision-making where all voices had access, the intent of this paper has also been to open up discussion in a research arena where a single perspective has been unduly privileged in imputing racialized response to those changes — a state of affairs where forms of rhetoric serve a particular politics of explanation.

Endnotes

[1] Data in the following paragraphs are taken from Province of British Columbia, 1997, B.C. *stats: Immigration highlights 96–4*, Victoria: Ministry of Finance and Corporate Relations; and Province of British Columbia, 1995, *Profile 1995: An analysis of immigration to British Columbia*, Victoria: Ministry Responsible for Multiculturalism and Immigration.

[2] Immigrant numbers are in fact greater than this because of secondary migration from other Canadian centres to Vancouver after landing. In addition, immigrants are not uniformly distributed throughout the metropolitan area but are heavily concentrated in Vancouver and a few inner suburbs — introducing a further scale of locational specificity.

[3] Picton, J. 1992. "Visible minority population soaring, study finds." *The Toronto Star* (May 30): A2; Lowrie, W. 1992. "Immigrants putting new face on nation." *The Vancouver Sun* (May 30): A1.

[4] Rinehart, D. 1996. "ESL." *The Vancouver Sun* (November 2): D4–5. Only 44 per cent of school children in Vancouver public schools spoke English as their normal home language in 1996; 32 per cent spoke one of the Chinese languages: Ouston, R. 1996. "English now a minority language in Vancouver." *The Vancouver Sun* (November 2): A1.

[5] Ray, B., G. Halseth, and B. Johnson. 1997. "The changing face of the suburbs: Issues of ethnicity and residential change in suburban Vancouver." *International Journal of Urban and Regional Research* 21: 75–99.

[6] These raw figures do, however, need qualification. They underestimate the true net worth of immigrants for they do not necessarily include the full portfolio of world-wide assets; on the other hand there is no guarantee that even the declared basket of assets will be brought into Canada. Moreover, B.C. does not receive close to its proportionate share of mandated investments — less than six per cent of investor-class funds in 1996 — due to politically-inspired advantages in other provinces, particularly Québec. While the 54 per cent of investor-class immigrants specifying B.C. as a destination make private consumption expenditures in the province, they also consume public services. Muddying the waters further there is a marked secondary migration of investors out of Québec and into Ontario and B.C., so that the true level of investor-class residence in the province exceeds even the high specified level. See, among others, Wong, L., 1993, "Immigration as capital accumulation: The impact of business immigration to Canada," *International Immigration* 31: 171–90; Ley, D., 1995, "Between Europe and Asia: The case of the missing sequoias," *Ecumene* 2: 185–210; Nash, A., 1996, "The economic impact of Canada's business immigration program: A critical reappraisal of theory and practice," Paper presented at Symposium on Immigration and Integration, Winnipeg (October); Province of British Columbia, 1997, "Proposed new immigrant investor program," B.C. *stats: Immigration highlights 96–4*, Victoria: Ministry of Finance and Corporate Relations.

[7] The first consumer profile of new Chinese immigrants in Vancouver for 1995 showed that "Chinese immigrants to Canada are younger, better educated and financially better off than the average Canadian," DJC Research, 1995, Chinese Media Index.

[8] For the composition of population growth in Greater Vancouver since 1977, see City of Vancouver, 1995, *Vancouver Trends*, Vancouver: City Planning Department.

[9] Probably an underestimate for this figure does not include the funds of the more than 4000 persons who landed under the self-employed business category (and who are incorporated into the population of 50,000–55,000).

[10] Lowenthal, D., and H. Prince. 1965. "English landscape taste." *Geographical Review* 55: 186–222.

[11] Quoted from the city bylaw, in Duncan, J., and N. Duncan, 1984, "A cultural analysis of urban residential landscapes in North America: The case of the Anglophile elite," In *The city in cultural context* ed. J. Agnew, J. Mercer, and D. Sopher, 255–76, Boston: Allen and Unwin.

[12] Province of British Columbia. 1996. "Migration and housing demand." B.C. *stats*. Victoria: Ministry of Finance and Corporate Relations.

[13] Chow, W. 1996. "Hong Kong still sees Vancouver as red-hot market for real estate." *The Vancouver Sun* (November 14): A1.

[14] The best known Vancouver example is the marketing relationship between Anson Realty, owned by Grace and Stephen Kwok, and condominium developer Andre Molnar. Anson's trans-Pacific network has internationalized the market for Molnar's Vancouver projects. Kris Olds has discussed the Pacific Rim linkages binding investment, development and immigration for downtown residential megaprojects: Olds, K., 1996, "Developing the Trans-Pacific property market: Tales from Vancouver via Hong Kong," Working papers No. 96–02, Vancouver: Centre of Excellence for Immigration Studies. At one point new downtown condominium projects could be placed on the market in Hong Kong before they could be bought in Vancouver, a controversial usurpation of local discretion: for the cause célèbre, see Mitchell, K., 1993, "Multiculturalism, or the united colors of capitalism?," *Antipode* 25: 263–94.

[15] Chow, W. 1996. "Lower mainland real estate rides new influx of immigrants." *The Vancouver Sun* (August 23): D6.

[16] Brosseau, M., P. Garvie, L. Chen, and A. Langlois. 1996. "Les mega-maisons de Kerrisdale, Vancouver: Chronique d'un quartier en transformation." *Le Geographe Canadien* 40: 164–72; Chow, W. 1997. "Westside prices continue month-on-month slide." *The Vancouver Sun* (February 5): D1.

[17] For Sydney and Melbourne, see Maher, C., 1994, "Housing prices and geographical scale: Australian cities in the 1980s," *Urban Studies* 31: 5–27; for Vancouver and Toronto, see Ley, D., 1996, *The new middle class and the remaking of the central city*, Oxford: Oxford University Press. An intriguing issue, that unfortunately there is not space to develop further here, is the relation between the internationalization of the land market in central city elite districts and earlier rounds of gentrification by a Canadian-born middle class in adjacent inner city areas. For further discussion, see Ley, 1996, ch. 9, and Badcock, B., 1995, "Building upon the foundations of gentrification: Inner-city housing development in Australia in the 1990s," *Urban Geography* 16: 70–90.

[18] The comment of one of my neighbors in Kerrisdale; Langley is a distant suburb.

[19] I have examined almost 400 letters sent to City Hall between 1987 and autumn 1992. Over half of these were received in the few months between summer and late autumn 1992, when concerns peaked and a public hearing on downzoning

Shaughnessy was held by Council. Interestingly, though in the earlier period 90 per cent of letters were critical of redevelopment, in the latter half of 1992, this figure fell to just over half and Chinese names rose to 30 per cent of correspondents. The public hearing showed the full political articulation of the voice of new immigrants. For a discussion, see Ley, 1995.

[20] Letter to City Council from husband and wife in South Shaughnessy (October 1992).

[21] Letter to City Council from a South Shaughnessy resident (August 1988).

[22] Cernetig, M. 1995. "White flight, Chinese distress." *The Globe and Mail* (September 30): D1. Such a racialized view of Vancouver (in this case from Toronto) seems particularly prevalent among media from other regions of Canada.

[23] Amongst a range of studies of Vancouver's unhappy racist history, an impressive contribution is Anderson, K., 1991, *Vancouver's Chinatown: Racial discourse in Canada, 1875–1980*, Montréal: McGill-Queen's University Press.

[24] Wimmer, A. 1997. "Explaining xenophobia and racism: A critical review of current research approaches." *Ethnic and Racial Studies* 20: 17–41.

[25] Letter to Council from B. D. Hersh, Westside Builders Association of B.C., (September 1992).

[26] *South China Morning Post.* 1992. "Vancouver planning law fuels racist fire." (October 4).

[27] Hennessey, M. 1986. "Racism and the dilemma of neighborhood change." Brief to City Council by Allied Builders.

[28] Equity. 1989. "Racism: Will it kill investment billions?" *Equity* 7: 20–35.

[29] See Mitchell, 1993 for a fuller discussion.

[30] *There was considerable anxiety in the business community that left-liberal neighborhood interests would win the 1990 Vancouver civic election, and institute slow growth or even anti-growth bylaws. For an interpretation of sustained attempts to maintain a pro-business hegemony through a media campaign, see Mitchell, K., 1996, "Visions of Vancouver: Ideology, democracy, and the future of urban development,"* Urban Geography 17: 478–501.

[31] The Laurier Institute. 1989. "Fact sheet" (November).

[32] The Laurier Institute. 1989. "Press release: Laurier Institute releases findings of UBC study into Vancouver real estate prices." (November 15).

[33] Average annual immigration from Hong Kong alone rose from 1,500 persons during 1981–1986 to 5,500 in 1988–1990, before reaching a peak of 15,500 in 1994.

[34] "Blame 'boomers' for boom." 1989. *Real Estate Weekly* (November 24): 1.

[35] In fact there was criticism of these findings within the real estate industry. A presentation of the findings of one report drew laughter from an audience of realtors; the results of a second were dismissed as "naive" by a prominent realtor: Pettit, B., 1992, "Zoning, the market and the single family landscape: Neighborhood change in

Vancouver, Canada," Ph.D. dissertation in Planning, University of British Columbia (UBC), and personal communication.

[36] Statement by Russ Froese for UTV at the Symposium on Citizenship and Immigration, Vancouver (June 1997).

[37] Letter to Council (October 1992). Interestingly a similar judgment has been reached in a critical essay by Wong and Netting: "most of the apparent racism is in fact class antagonism wrapped in a race envelope;" See, Wong, L., and N. Netting, 1992, "Business immigration to Canada: Social impact and racism," in *Deconstructing a nation: Immigration, multiculturalism and racism in '90s Canada*, ed. Satzewich, V., 93–121, Halifax: Fernwood Publishing.

[38] *Vancouver Courier.* 1992. "Good taste not racist." Letter to the Editor. (October 11): 7.

[39] Letter to Council from Kerrisdale resident (11 October 1988).

[40] Brief presented to Council (October 1992) (emphasis in original).

[41] "Lam advises Hong Kong on Canada," 1989, *The Vancouver Sun* (December 13), quoted in Pettit, 1992: 107. Unfortunately there is not space here to discuss the diverse responses by long-established immigrants like Mr. Lam or Canadian-born ethnic Chinese. Their relationship with recent immigrants is complex, converging on matters of ethnic solidarity, but diverging on matters of sensitivity to established Canadian values.

[42] See Ley, D., D. Hiebert, and G. Pratt, 1992, "Time to grow up? From urban village to world city, 1966–91," in *Vancouver and its region*, ed. G. Wynn and T. Oke, 234–66, Vancouver: UBC Press.

[43] Ray *et al.*, 1997.

[44] However, data introduced in the text show that in Shaughnessy, until recently heavily Anglo-Canadian, a third of homeowners with the most expensive houses had Chinese family names: Li, P., 1994, "Unneighborly houses or unwelcome Chinese: The social construction of race in the battle over 'monster homes' in Vancouver, Canada," *International Journal of Comparative Race and Ethnic Studies* 1: 14–33. The view that recent immigrants were not key buyers in the market was no longer tenable in real estate circles by the mid-1990s: "Recent immigrants major players in market," *Real Estate Weekly* (6 January 1995): 1.

[45] Bonnett, A. 1996. "Anti-racism: The critique of 'white' identities." *New Community* 22 (1): 97–110.

19 The Role of Education in Combating Racism in Canada

Kogila Moodley

For an agnostic like myself, there is a prayer that nonetheless is appealing: "God help me to find the truth, but protect me from those who have already found it." I wish I had the certainty of definite answers. Not being a single factor explanation freak, one can only hope that by careful analysis of the workings of racism, more successful strategies for the elusive goal of a racism-free society can be discerned.

Teachers and administrators throughout Canada experience various forms of racism among the multi-ethnic populations they teach. Sometimes this is blatant, explicit,overt, while at other times tensions are covert and less visible. Individual pupils engage in name calling or violence, sometimes entire groups battle each other. These animosities may emanate from a range of sources: more powerful groups take advantage of less empowered ones, majority group students line up against newer minorities, recent immigrants attempt to assert a threatened identity. Throughout, First Nations students continue as victims in one form or another. The question is how to deal with these issues in a school system that is already "stretched" with numerous demands such as for different kinds of instruction and recognition of difference. Nor are these problems only present in inner city, lower income schools. They now invade the peaceful surroundings of suburbia as well. All this takes place within a culture of "politeness" and "tolerance" which chooses to overlook such unpleasantries in the hope that "things will work themselves out" and the widespread belief that if adults keep out of it, students will work things out by themselves. To locate this we need to understand what racism is all about, how it fits within the context of a multicultural society, how schools and educators respond.

Racism Defined

What is racism? It can be defined as the ideology of ascribing inferior characteristics to physically different people. In the 19th century version of racism people of color or different origin (Jews) were said to behave in distinct ways because of their inherent "nature." European colonialism and slavery justified its conquest with the superior racial qualities of the colonizers. The alleged superior products of genetic evolutionary selection were destined to rule over intellectually backward humans. Nowadays a new racism is said to use cultural difference instead of biology for discrimination. Lately, any attitudes that rely on universally valid norms originating in the European tradition are considered racist or ethnocentric because of the European history of exclusion and subjugation with its in-built arrogance for people of color. Yet racism or ethnocentricism are not confined to Europeans alone. Indians or Japanese are known to be racist toward outsiders as are Tutsis toward Hutus or Arabs toward Africans. What is common to all these intergroup relations is that some groups have greater power and cultural currency to affect the lives of others; their greater power translates into higher status and denigration of inferior, low status outgroups.

Oppression and racism are heavy accusations. They should not be bandied around lightly and without evidence, notwithstanding the fact that victims know when they are being discriminated against and it is not always easy to demonstrate the barriers and hostilities experienced. As Morton Weinfeld reminds us "if everything is harassment, racism and genocide, then nothing is harassment, racism or genocide."[1] Analytical insights cannot be free of passion but must not be distorted by inflationary language and dubious categories. A rhetoric of indignation should not substitute for an analysis of why people denigrate others. Preaching hardly ever penetrates an authoritarianism predisposed to hate. Those individuals harbor deep seated resentments. They are often persons with low self esteem who try to make themselves superior by debasing others. As Bettleheim has argued, racists almost need more empathy than contempt. Nor can reprehensible attitudes be legislated. Only their behavioral expressions need to be criminalized.

"Zero tolerance," as advocated in Britain, allows anti-racism advocates to claim victory in public, "whilst the informal cultures of racism which actually sustain these practices are relegated to an untouchable realm of 'private attitudes.'"[2] When racism awareness training attempted to intervene at this level with the same procedures as were applied in the public realm, this enforced privatization "in many cases resulted in more secretly coded forms of expression, which actually strengthened popular resistence to antiracism."[3] "Political correctness" pressure drives unpopular expressions underground. Contested issues such as immigrant quotas become a taboo instead of being subject to an informed public debate and input.

Particularly for the learning experience in the classroom it would seem important that students are allowed to work through their own stereotypes without being embarrassed or silenced from the outset. All too often anti-racism advocates display a self-righteous superior morality that by definition exempt the speaker from the sins of racism. Anti-racist pedagogues patronizingly lecture others in proper behavior, spread enlightenment about neglected voices and hope that their own indignation or alleged victimhood would either persuade or cow racists into submission. This assumption is not only naive but may well be counterproductive.

Racism in Canada

How prevalent is racism in Canadian society? Are we more or less prone to xenophobia and stereotyping of others than the U.S., Britain, France or Germany? Is our ethnocentrism different from the distrust of "uncivilized foreigners" in China or the disdain and social distance of a Brahmin towards lower caste members in the Hindu caste system?

The evidence from representative opinion surveys among Canadians is contradictory. All opinion surveys reveal substantial approval of multiculturalism and at the same time some anxiety about the pace of ethnic transformation. In a 1996 Angus Reid Poll, 80 per cent agreed with the statement: "Canada's multicultural make-up is one of the best things about this country." However 41 per cent also approved that "Canada is changing too quickly because of all the minorities we have now."

A 1993 poll shows that a significant minority of the general public feels that new Canadians should be restricted in terms of how much influence they are permitted to exercise over the future of this country. Over one third say they are angered when they see new immigrants on television demanding the same rights as other Canadians. Contrary to the goals of official multiculturalism 57 per cent of Canadians urge minorities to become more like most other Canadians rather than preserve their cultural or linguistic traditions. Canadians are particularly angered when they perceive immigrants importing their political troubles from "back home." However only 15–20 per cent can be described as hard core anti-immigrant in the sense that they wish to preserve a white Canada, deny the material benefits from immigration and advocate a (hypothetical) return of immigrants. This figure is not higher than comparable right wing support for LePen in France, the National Front in Britain or neo-Fascist parties in Germany. All Western democracies have to cope with antidemocratic populist fringe groups, who are generally not a threat by themselves but by their subtle pressure in pushing establishment parties to the right.

The best indicator for the levels of racism in Canada is provided in a survey among potential victims. While a majority of Canadians as a whole label racism as a significant problem in this country and 60 per cent "sense racism has been growing" (Reid Report, 6, 9, October 1991) only 39 per cent of urban Chinese-Canadians in Toronto and Vancouver report that they have experienced discrimination (Reid Report, 9, 4, April 1994). This low figure of a representative sample of 800 Chinese is truly surprising and could lead to the suspicion that many victims engage in denial or blame themselves in order to live with an unpleasant reality. The low 39 per cent of reported personal discrimination remains constant with length of stay in the city and is slightly lower in Toronto (where Blacks seem a more obvious target) than in Vancouver, without a significant Black population, but with Indo-Canadians and First Nations people as equally ready targets. However, the explanation of self-denial of outsider status cannot be upheld in light of the fact that in the same sample 81 per cent of Chinese Canadians report that they "do not feel accepted" in Canada. Obviously Canadian racism nowadays expresses itself less in direct personal discrimination but much more in a cultivated social distance to the constructed other. Our every day language reflects this distance between us and them, the ingroup and the outgroup: the term ethnic is used only for third world immigrants as if Scottish or French people had no ethnicity.

Stereotypes about Visible Minorities

Euphemisms about the unfamiliar arrivals abound. Since racist discourse became a taboo, a government Green Paper on immigration in the 1980 s focused all its attention on "people with novel and distinct features," as if those phenotypical characteristics were the cause of all problems. Derrick Thomas, a former senior immigration official also stresses the obvious when he points to color as the potential barrier for integration: "Third World immigrants diverge more radically from the host population, making them visibly and permanently different from the existing majority in at least this respect."[4] The difference however lies always in the eye of the beholder who socially constructs otherness. It is not the color difference that matters but the stereotypes we attribute to and associate with different appearance.

Visible minority members are confronted with the majority attitude that they "own" the country. The "visibly different" are expected to be forever grateful to be let in. They are seen to never truly belong, because the sense of belonging includes the imagined prior ownership in which the visibly different immigrants do not partake by the very history of initial European settlement. This makes the "visibles" eternal trespassers, both in the view of the dominant group but also sometimes in the eyes of the "intruders" who internalize majority attitudes towards them.

A dialectic of multiculturalism results in similar unintended consequences. Multiculturalism is intended to ensure equity through representation by highlighting origins elsewhere. At the same time origins of dominant white groups wane into irrelevance as they exercise dominance and a "natural" claim to ownership. However, the more the culture of the others is celebrated, the less their claim to the local is emphasized.

Racism in the Educational System

How is everyday racism produced and reproduced within the educational system? The school simultaneously holds out the promise of mobility and opportunity, yet at the same time teaches and reinforces hierarchy and stratification in its day to day operations. What are the social processes in everyday practices through which ideologies of superiority and inferiority are reproduced? Three areas stand out: firstly the content of education, secondly, hierarchies of language and thirdly the hidden curriculum.

Most curricula privilege whiteness as the norm, and in that sense is a racial text. Like women, ethnic minorities are seldom portrayed as active agents in history, geography or literature for instance. They seldom transcend stereotyped roles. As Toni Morrison puts it "Certain absences are so stressed, are so ornate, so planned, they call attention to themselves: arrest us with intentionality and purpose like neighborhoods that are defined by the population held away from them."[5] In literature, writing by ethnic minorities is referred to as postcolonial or Commonwealth writing, seldom entering the hallowed confines of "literature." For the most part colonialism is not presented as economic exploitation, conquest and slavery but almost a form of paternalistic benevolence through which primitive savages became civilized, westernized Christians. Yet the very term "privileging" is inaccurate, if one considers as Pinar points out that it is not only the marginalized who suffer, but the privileged as well in so far as they live in ignorance that their knowledge is racial knowledge.[6]

The culture of *de facto* monolingualism, albeit in a bilingual, multicultural country, implicitly teaches a ranking of other languages. Other languages are benignly labelled "heritage" languages, as though English or French are not "heritage" languages as well.

However, beyond this is the informal culture of a carefully learned "embarrassment" which non-English or French speaking students, experience when their languages are used in the public domain of school. What is it that is communicated in the hidden curriculum that transmits this lack of value to difference? How does this laundering of difference take place? What happens to those who can launder their accents but not their skin color?

Internalized domination and self racism are indelibly etched in students' conceptions of themselves and "received as truth because they are transmitted in the context of authority, that is the classroom."[7] Furthermore, these views are also shaped by the family and wider society. In B.C. Lower Mainland schools, students in group discussions speak openly about their experiences with racism. They speak of routine racist slurs in school corridors, classrooms and on the sports grounds. This is frequently reported to be accompanied by acts of violence.

Graffiti in gyms, on playground walls and toilet doors even include swastikas. What some students find abhorrent is that no provisions are made to remove them immediately. Others complain that school "supervisors" within whose hearing range racist slurs are made, do nothing about this. As one Indo-Canadian student put it "You see these supervisors wearing antiracism badges, but what's the worth in that if you're going to stand around and not do anything." All too often schools see racial incidents as a conflict of personalities, and as nothing more than that. Teachers should be given workshops to know what racism is all about, so that they can detect their own biases. A student of Filipino descent who claims to have been roughed up and demeaned by name-calling, speaks of how it shattered his confidence and left him with "no courage to go to school." The hardest thing for him was like many other minority children he kept the hurt to himself, since he did not wish to burden his immigrant parents with the problem. "They don't have the language to face the school system, so it's better if they're left out of it . . . they believe in schools as fair places . . . why should I shatter that belief! The most difficult thing for me though is when my mother makes a racist comment, and I have to say, don't do that, it's racist." Other outcomes of a racially charged climate are when minority students engage in outbursts of self hate, putting down their own group members and joining more powerful peer groups in denigrating people like themselves. ESL students are often the victims of scapegoating by other group members who have become acculturated and learnt the new currency of intra group dominance. The following comment by a Canadian-born man of Chinese origin, who lives in Vancouver, makes the point well in his description of newer Chinese immigrants as irritants:

> These "foreign" kids from Hong Kong and Taiwan mostly have no care at all; they drive their expensive cars with recklessness and feel they can flaunt their wealth in front of us and do anything they want and get away with it . . . What's even more frustrating for me is that I can't believe how unfair it is that my sons who do really well, get first-class marks in school and have problems getting into their program of study because these foreign students are taking away their seats . . . I pay my taxes, I've always supported and encouraged immigration, yet this is so frustrating for me, as a parent to have what should rightfully be ours — be given away to them since they have the money and power to do that . . . I even took (name of son) out of public school and into a private school since they had to slow down the curriculum since there were too many ESL students in that class."[8]

Anti-Racism and Multicultural Education

In a recent study by Solomon and Levine-Rasky[9] the views of over 1000 teachers, school administrators, multicultural and anti-racism advisors in 57 elementary and secondary schools from five school boards across Canada were sought on the subject of multicultural and anti-racist education. Educators varied widely in their philosophies, concepts and practices on anti-racism and multicultural education. In many instances these ideas were seen as unwelcome challenges to their teaching practices. For the most part, anti-racist education was viewed as merely reactive to potentially explosive racial conflicts. Multicultural education was perceived as additive in nature, not a core issue for all sensitive teachers.

Solomon and Levine-Rasky reiterate the findings of several previous studies, such as the Echols and Fisher(1992) study of the Vancouver School Board, that while there was a good deal of support in principle for anti-racism and multicultural education, when considered from the view of practice, responses ranged from accommodation to resistance. Accommodation they point out "takes the shape of passive acceptance of multicultural education and anti-racist education, to active advocacy and risk taking." Accommodating educators were engaged in revising their pedagogic orientations, classroom and school-wide practices, and challenging conservative political views represented by various school staff members. Educator resistance, which predominated in the study, involves anything from a seemingly harmless denial of the need for multicultural education or anti-racist education, claims of curricular overload or inaccessibility of resource materials to a more provocative unwillingness to "question beliefs and philosophy." Those who resisted expressed a desire to adhere to a traditional interpretation of provincial curriculum guidelines. They viewed suggestions about curriculum innovation or intervention as a violation of their professional autonomy, and saw monitoring of anti-racism programs as superfluous and disruptive of their collegial relations. They feared "affirmative action" as a way of addressing inequity, and were critical of paid race relations consultants to advise school boards about reform.

Lack of rewards for effective implementation of equity policies as well as vague imprecise policies caused discontent. Compared to their preference for ethnocultural equity, the language of anti-racism education was experienced as negative. The articulation of race, racialization and racism in the schools was considered "discomforting material for an educational arena."[10] The use of terms like racial anger and accusations of racism were considered offensive. Anti-racism education, in their view, would be necessary if we had problems, but we dont, so "if it isn't broke, don't fix it!" Multicultural and anti-racism education were seen as antithetical to teaching literacy and numeracy within an assimilative context. Contrary to its espoused goal of critical thinking, anti-racism education was considered to be reverse indoctrination which was potentially inflammatory in creating social conflict and likely to be counterproductive. Another source of dissension was the inadequate provision of empirical evidence to convince teachers of the need for innovation. This was an affront to their professionalism. What they were expected to do in these anti-racism programs, it was argued, was simply good teaching practice, so why have a separate program? Indifference, lack of time and need to focus on exam preparation were cited as reasons for non-compliance. Finally, the prevailing assimilative tone underlying practice is best summed up in the statement of one educator, "Peoplehood can only be based on an absolute and ironic erasure of difference."[11]

It is not surprising therefore, that attempts to bring about change in education through professional development programs meets with considerable resistence. Such transformative initiatives in pluralistic societies touch at the personal locus of teachers in terms of class, political ideologies, value orientations, and membership within the dominant-subordinate group spectrum. The Solomon study reaffirms this situation for Canadian schools as well.

On the subject of racialization and children and its implications for schools, Hatcher and Troyna make five useful points: firstly they recognize the significance of racism for minority children, secondly, that "race" is a significant element in the lives of the majority group children both in their social relationships as well as in their understanding of society, thirdly "race" does not work in isolation but is "interfused with other ideologies and social processes in children's lives," fourthly, among white children there is a spectrum both of beliefs about "race" and of ways in which "race" operates in social interaction. The relationship between the two is not one of simple correspondence: interactional processes have their own dynamics. Finally processes of racialization of children's attitudes and social behavior are often fluid, fragmented and inconsistent.[12]

They therefore argue "that schools need to establish effective procedures to implement a clear and firm policy to deal with racist incidents, as part of a wider policy addressing issues of conflict between children." Yet while this may reduce the occurrence of racist incidents , it may not get at the roots of racism. "Schools therefore need to find ways in the curriculum to help children to engage with how race works in their lives. To reflect cultural diversity positively and to teach about racism in society are both vital, but it is equally important to connect these interventions with children's own lives by bringing children's relationships and the conflicts within them including racialized forms, into the curriculum itself."[13]

Does official multiculturalism facilitate or obfuscate the school's struggle against racism? As a state policy designed by Trudeau's Liberals in 1971, it was meant to cope with the residual hostility towards immigrants, to garner the immigrant vote for the ruling party and to address the interests of the third force of non-English, non-French Canadians by elevating their claims to equal status with the charter groups. It is therefore no wonder that Quebec separatists as well as First Nations nationalists reject multiculturalism because it equalizes their charter entitlement as well as undermines aboriginal rights. However, Canadian multiculturalism has undergone many changes from the song and dance days of its beginnings. An essentialist museums culture has given way to official equity and anti-racism efforts that are supposed not only to celebrate life styles but guarantee equal life chances as well.[14]

Multiculturalism's right wing critics deplore an imagined divisiveness resulting from the official state policy that is said to undermine national unity. Left wing critics point to the symbolic manipulation that pretends power and class differentials in a common consumer society can be overcome by the celebration of diversity and mutual tolerance.

Both perspectives ignore valuable benefits of official multiculturalism. Psychologically, multiculturalism levels the traditional hierarchy. Official multiculturalism includes the newcomers in the cultural construction of Canadianness. Multiculturalism makes immigrants officially welcome at little cost to the state. The symbolic acceptance prevents the official status of permanent strangers, both in the definition of "the other" by the dominant majority but even more importantly in the eyes of the newly arrived themselves.

At the same time the official tolerance patronizes. The tolerant majority and its state wallows in a self-congratulatory confirmation of its open-mindedness. The graciously accepted others are expected to be thankful for the multicultural generosity. As Vijay Agnew has pointed out: "Multiculturalism offers compensation to the powerless by 'accepting' them but not by giving them power or privilege. Rather than challenging Canadian political and social structures, it reinforces them."[15] Such a challenge can hardly be expected from official state policy, unless its targets exploit its contradictions.

You may well ask what recommendations can we take home tonight about the most successful strategy for combating racism? Apart from the obvious sensitivity and leadership expected from opinion makers like educators in racist incidents, there is only one recommendation I can wholeheartedly endorse: The best way to eliminate prejudice is the sociological understanding of racism, its functions and ever changing forms. Racism is neither eradicated by preaching tolerance nor reduced by providing information that contradicts the stereotypes of the other. Unless the predisposing conditions for denigration are addressed, the racist mind finds rationalizations for inferiorizing ever changing targets. The behavior or appearance of the minority hardly influences the authoritarian character who is conditioned to hate. Just as psychoanalytic therapy aims at making conscious the unconscious — transforming the id into ego, in Freud's terms — so the most lasting cure is to make the prejudiced individual understand why she or he cherishes such deep resentments. As we are all prejudiced to varying degrees, this political education in the most genuine sense should be geared to everyone, not just individuals singled out for special consciousness raising. Political literacy immunizes against racist temptations.

Policies, procedures, consequences and accountability for racist incidents obviously need to be in place in all schools. So too should compulsory education in the skills to deal with a multi-ethnic clientele for teachers, police personel, social workers or hospital staff. Sadly, with few exceptions, this is not the case, despite all the lip service to cross cultural communication. Deterrence and communication skills, as necessary as they are, however, do not substitute for political literacy.

It is this wider context of understanding racist behavior that is missing in all the noble attempts to fight an obvious evil. Instead of self-righteously demonizing racism, the need for such a mentality has to be understood. The need grows out of unfulfilled individuals who have no other options to establish a secure identity, but to debase others. Social conditions increasingly deprive people of the security and self-confidence that would have no need to stigmatize others. With the decline of such self-realization in a political economy where more and more people are declared superfluous, scapegoating and other artificial forms of self realization increase.

Such insights link individual psychology with the social structure at large in which character development is always embedded. Successful anti-racism in this sense is predicated upon societal transformation. However, an apolitical consumerism that glorifies the private realm at the exclusion of the "tainted" public sphere does not grasp the political significance of racism, let alone envisage the alternative that would eliminate the need for racial stigmatization. In short, the best job we as educators can do to combat racism is to ensure a cosmopolitan political literacy.

Endnotes

[1] Weinfeld, Morton. 1996. "Social identity in the 1990's." *Clash of identities*, ed. James Littleton, 122. Prentice Hall/CBC.

[2] Cohen, Philip. 1996. "Hidden narratives in theories of racism." *'Race,' culture and difference*, ed. Donald, James, and Ali Rattansi, 62–103, 96. London: Sage.

[3] *ibid*: 97.

[4] *Immigration Dilemma*, 118.

[5] Morrison, Toni. 1989. "Unspeakeable things unspoken: The African-American presence in American Literature." *Michigan Quarterly* 28 (1): 1–34, 11.

[6] Pinar, William F. 1993. "Notes on understanding curriculum as a racial text." In *Race identity and representation in education*, ed. McCarthy, Cameron, and Warren Crichlow, 60–70, 68. New York: Routledge.

[7] Brittan, Arthur, and Mary Maynard. 1985. *Sexism, racism and oppression*, 158. Oxford: Blackwell.

[8] Yee, Lili Anne. 1996. "The social construction of identity: Theorizing intra-group identification." Term paper. (November).

[9] Solomon, R. Patrick, and Cynthia Levine-Rasky. 1994. "Accomodation and resistance: Educators' response to multicultural and anti-racist education." Report, 89. (August).

[10] *ibid*, 9.

[11] *ibid*, 36.

[12] Hatcher, Richard, and Barry Troyna. 1993. "Racialization and children." In *Race, identity and representation in education*, ed. McCarthy, Cameron, and Warren Crichlow.

[13] *ibid*, 124.

[14] Moodley, Kogila. 1983. "Multiculturalism as ideology." *Ethnic and Racial Studies*.

[15] Agnew, Vijay. 1996. *Resisting women from Asia, Africa, and the Caribbean and the women's movement in Canada*, 35. Toronto. N.p.

20 Globalization and International Migration in the Asia Pacific Region: Policy Implications

Terry McGee

Whether migration is controlled by those who send, by those who go, or by those who receive, it mirrors the world as it is at that time. (Davis 1974: 96).

Just over twenty years ago I took part in a symposium sponsored by the American Academy of Arts and Sciences entitled "Human Migration: Patterns Implications and Policies" (see McNeil and Adams, 1978). In his introduction to the conference, William McNeil, a distinguished historian from the University of Chicago and a Canadian émigré sketched a wide historical panorama of human migration from the earliest days of human evolution. He reminded us that, "humankind could not have become the earth-girdling, dominant species we are without roving and without the migrations that followed successful discovery of new possibilities made manifest by such roving. Human occupation of the Americas and of previously islanded lands of Oceania is only the most recent — and geographically most extensive — example of processes that are as old as humankind" (McNeil, 1978: 3).

Twenty years later, it is understandable that this focus upon the history of migration should shift to the ongoing acceleration of international migration at a global scale. Many commentators argue that this current phase of international migration is a consequence of a new era of globalization which is characterized by technological innovations in transportation and the transfer of information which have led to a collapse of space and time. More practically these developments have reduced the cost of movement thus spurring increased mobility. Another facet of this globalization is a growing integration of global economic, social and cultural activities which provides channels of convergence and contact for migrants. Writers such as Ohmae (1995), Elkens (1995) and Kennedy (1993) see these processes of globalization as increasingly challenging the power of the nation state. The territory these states control is becoming increasingly "contestable" and their border more permeable.

Thus globalization creates an environment which is very facilitative of mobility and the types of migration become more diverse. The short-term visitors to Japan turn into long-term illegal workers. Refugees invade borders by land, air and sea. Transnational migrants are in a constant state of circulation between global nodes of commerce. International migrants who have moved for economic reason use "telematics" to reinforce their networks with their homeland and strengthen their cultures and opportunities within their emigrant society. In this situation the environment of migration is different from the nineteenth and early twentieth centuries and poses new challenges to nation-states to develop effective policies to cope with this situation.

Turning to the Asia-Pacific region which is the focus of the essays in the volume, one can argue forcibly that these processes of globalization are shaking loose an increasing volume of population and movements of migrants in the region which are generally similar to other regions of the world. While the dominant search for economic opportunity which characterizes the movement of migrants from the poorer countries (or perhaps more accurately the poorer parts of countries) such as the Mexican migration to the United States, and Indian migration to Canada remains intact. These flows are increasingly augmented by middle and upper income migrants who search for educational and amenity advantages for their families and children. Much of the recent Taiwan migration to Canada falls into this category.

In an excellent overview of migration in the Asia Pacific region Hugo (Chapter 5) identifies five main types of migration. First, South-North migration which represents the largest of the flows; secondly, overseas contract workers who until recently were employed mainly in the Middle East but now are becoming more important in the developed economies of East Asia; a third type are refugee migrants where until recently Asia has supplied a major proportion of global refugees; fourthly, there is the student migration to the countries of the North; and finally, there are the growing numbers of transnational migrants moving from the developed to developing countries. This complex typology of migration suggests that governments need to "fine grain" their immigration policies to cope with this diversity.

However, there are several distinctive characteristics of the Asia Pacific region which must be taken into account in a discussion on international migration. The first is the overwhelming demographic importance of Asia in the actual and potential movements of international migration. Today almost 60 per cent of the global population are located in the Asian subcontinent; a majority concentrated in the population giants of India and China which when combined make up more than a quarter of the world's population (See McGee 1978, 1993). A second, and no less important, fact is that the generation of income is highly unequally distributed in this region. Thus, 86 per cent of the Gross Domestic Product of the Asia Pacific region in 1992 was generated in Japan, the U.S.A., Canada, Australia and

New Zealand. While this situation is beginning to change with the growth of economies such as Singapore, Taiwan, Hong Kong and the Republic of Korea, there is a massive challenge of economic growth in the region if this Asian sub-continent is to increase its share of the production of wealth even to the proportion of its population.

In the past, this dramatic differential between population and share of wealth has fueled concerns in the wealthy states of the region which is reflected in the strident warnings of anti-immigration factions. This was one factor fueling the so-called "yellow peril" of the nineteen-thirties. This attitude slides over into the thinly veiled racism of Pauline Hanson and her supporters in contemporary Australia which is discussed by several writers in this volume. It is reasonable that in a conference convened in Canada focusing on international migration as it affects Canada that much attention should be focused upon the migration issues that are emerging in Canadian society. But it is also important to see this migration as part of a broader process occurring at a regional level. The movement of migrants to Canada is often an insignificant proportion of the total out migration of Asians. The movement of Indians and Pakistanis to the United Kingdom; the movement of Filipinos to the United States; the movement of Indonesians to Malaysia and the flows of short-term labor to the Middle East are far more significant in the terms of the flows of wealth transfer to the sending societies than any migration to Canada. Globalization presents the opportunities for states to encourage migration as well as to structure the type and characteristics of the migration. For example, Canada has been remarkably humane and generous in its policy to refugee claimants. But equally, globalization presents greater opportunity for migrants to switch their allegiances and follow opportunities. For example, the government of India has established policies that encourage Indians living outside India to invest capital in India with tax incentives, etc. In a similar manner, the Taiwan computer industry has been built-up by hiring expatriate Taiwanese from Silicon Valley in the U.S.A. This poses major policy questions with respect to the reception, absorption and encouragement of migrants into host societies.

A third aspect of Asia Pacific migration relates to the issue of the feminization of international migration in the region. Increased female labor force participation rates in the developed countries in the region are leading to a considerable increase of women in transnational and student migration in both North-South directions. At the same time the ongoing "niche migration" of domestic labor particularly from the Philippines is predominantly female. The movement of women within the region who are engaged in the sex trade is also an important social issue. In Australia the so-called Filipino bride issue has become an important social issue. There are also substantial numbers of women who are moving from South to North as part of family reunification schemes. In the case of some Asian émigré communities they present problems of social adjustment because, for example, of limited language skills. Thus the growing "feminization" of migrant streams needs more awareness and research.

The papers presented in this volume present ample evidence of the complexity of international migration in the Asia Pacific region and it is not my task to summarize these aspects in great detail. Rather I want to identify four research issues that surfaced in the discussions of the Conference and which need greater elaboration which will ultimately involve much more subtle policy responses than those already in place in the region.

Four main policy research issues were identified. The first issue was concerned with the definition of international migrants; the second issue concerned the role of migrant networks both within reception countries and internationally. Thirdly there was the important issue of the economic role of migration. And finally, the emergence of transnationality as a feature of international migration.

The first issue concerns the "constant blurring" of the term international migrant. Conventional definitions of international migration are based on the idea of the taking-up of residence in the country and eventually, depending upon the regulatory environment, becoming a citizen of the host society. But the increased possibility of mobility that improved communication provides means that short-term visitors such as tourists, visitors, business and student arrivals often use these short-term visits as bridging opportunities to more permanent migration. The increasing permeability of national boundaries causes increasing illegal migration blurring the difference between immigrant and refugee status. In this situation, the whole category of "international migrant" becomes difficult to apply only to those "formal" migrants who have permission to take-up residence in their host society. Increasingly in a country such as Canada the institutional legal environment becomes more and more "cluttered" as the processing of non-legal migrants clog up the courts.

The second issue concerns the "role of networks" in international migration. While research into the role of networks (ethnic, linguistic, religious or regional) has been an ongoing part of migratory research, the Conference recognized that the "telematics revolution" which allows the instantaneous transfer of information through these informal networks is increasing the efficiency of these networks (See Krotkin, 1992 and Castells, 1960). Some commentators see the use of networks at both national and international level as a form of parallel information system which gives international migrant communities many advantages. But equally these networks may be regarded as flexible mechanisms for social and economic adjustment in the host societies. They also offer opportunities in host countries to engage competitively in Asia Pacific business opportunities.

The economic role of international migration still remains a major research thrust. Clearly, international migrants perform three types of economic role. First, they contribute to the economy of their host societies, through their involvement in the labor market, investment and business activity. However, there is still much debate over the issue of net economic gains of international migration for the social costs that are incurred in the absorption of migrants can be considerable. A second contribution is the flow of remittances that move between host societies and sending societies. Much of the research on remittances has focused on the important role that short-term labor migration remittances plays in contributing to the poorer economies in the Asia-Pacific region such as the Philippines, India and Pakistan. But there is now a growing flow of transfer in the transnational flows. For example, the more than 100,000 Canadian nationals now resident in the Special Autonomous Zone of Hong Kong transmit substantial funds to Canada. The third way in which international migrants contribute to the economy is the so-called "hidden dimension" of knowledge of global and regional markets that previous experience, cultural understanding and linguistic knowledge contribute to a country such as Canada. Again some commentators see this knowledge as forming part of a kind of "parallel economy" which does not always flow easily into the mainstream activities of business at a national level. As yet there seems to be insufficient evidence to support or disprove this assertion.

The last issue which emerges in several of the papers is much more difficult to pin down. Skeldon grapples with this idea when he discusses the growing popularity of the term "diaspora" as a description of international migration. As he comments, "one of the characteristics of the elite migration out of east Asia towards North America and Australia has been the tendency to split families" which leads to a form of long distance commuting. Even transnational and individual migration begins to assume some of these features which are creating migrants as "peoples in between." While these migrant groups may not be as large as the settler migrants groups, they wield much influence because of their wealth and education. Skeldon's essay suggests that they pose challenges to the host societies in that they find it difficult to cope with the concept of circulation and movement which is central to these transnational circuits and networks.

In what way do these issues in migration research inform policy formation by governments in the Asia Pacific region? If one were to accept Meyer Burnsteins's (p. 68) distinction between what he labels the instrumental view of immigration practiced by Canada, the U.S., Australia and New Zealand and those defined in terms of ethnic affiliation (most of Europe and most of the Asian states) then the view of priorities in research concerning international migration is very different in these two types of policy environments. However, in economies such as Japan, the Republic of South Korea, Malaysia, Singapore, Taiwan and Hong Kong that are experiencing labor shortages, there is a move toward a range of instrumental views of immigration ranging from short-term tightly controlled labor contracts to the avoidance of enforcement of restrictive measures on illegal migration (See Azizah Kassim's description of the Malaysian experience in this volume, Chapter 8).

It would be an overstatement to argue that the impact of the forces of "globalization" will automatically force all governments in the region towards an instrumental package of policies as they become more developed and need to attract more migrants that will provide required skills and make their countries more competitive at a global scale. But if this policy change does occur, then governments in the region will have to become more competitive and attractive to potential migrants. Arguments that international migrants will only move because the country of immigration has higher wages or a more secure environment will not be enough. Increasingly, international migrants will want the opportunity to keep their "translocality" stretching from "places of origin" to "places of international migration."

How governments balance their concerns about nation-building and labor market needs will be an important consideration in this process of policy formation.

Turning to Canada, the focus of the volume, the present Canadian government has made a firm commitment to globalization in endorsing NAFTA and engaging in the active support of free trade regimes such as APEC and the WTO. The Canadian government is firmly committed to the concept of making its economy globally competitive. A necessary corollary of this process is the creation of a facilitative environment for international labor movement which is necessary to make Canada more competitive. Of course political realities do not permit the Canadian government to embrace the concept of relatively free movement of international labor. High and persistent rates of unemployment, incipient racism (particularly well analyzed in this volume) and the priority given to fiscal strengthening all erode the Canadian government's flexibility in immigration policy.

But these political realities should not prevent a constant evaluation of present policies so as not to make them more responsive to changing conditions of international labor mobility which globalization provokes.

For example, there may have to be flexible policies with respect to labor conditions, family reunification, accreditation, taxation of off-shore earnings, requirements for entry to educational institutions and many other such issues. These are discussed in great detail in this book. It is significant that, for example, Australia and New Zealand have much more flexible policies than Canada in this respect. It is also clear that targeted programs such as the Business Entrepreneur Program while clearly formulated to take advantage of the mobility of capital have been open to abuse (Woo, Chapter 17).

There is another aspect of the impact of international migration which is discussed in great detail in this volume. This is the issue of what kind of society will emerge as a consequence of international migration. In Canada, Australia, New Zealand and the U.S.A., there has been a dramatic shift in the source of migrants from Europe to Asia. Today migrants from Asia form significant minorities in cities such as Vancouver, Los Angeles, New York, Sydney and Auckland. In every case the influx of Asian migrants has proven to be of benefit economically, to have enriched the societies culturally and in some cases, such as Vancouver, (See Hutton, Chapter 16) been of critical importance to the economic growth of the city and its region.

In Australia and New Zealand this influx of Asians has reinforced a commitment to be part of Asia. This is, at least in part, because of the dominance of Asia in these two countries' global trade. In the U.S.A. and Canada on the other hand, while trade with Asia is important, this process of Asian immigration is seen much more as part of wide commitment to the concept of globalization and human rights. It is unlikely that the question raised by an Australian academic in his recent book "Is Australia Asian?" would be asked in the U.S.A. and Canada.

Nevertheless despite these differences one can argue that all four societies are variously committed to policies of "multiculturalism" which are directed to enhancing the cultures and heritage of immigrant societies. Tepper (Chapter 3) suggests that Canada's application of these policies is strengthened by the recognition of the cultural duality of Canada with its significant French language component and "distinct" culture within Quebec and to a lesser extent in other parts of Canada such as the Maritimes. The discussions in this volume, at least with respect to Canada, in my view make a strong case that the support of multiculturalism can be of considerable value as migrants become more "transnational." These policies provide a supportive social environment of adaptation for migrants but they act equally as an entry point for non-migrant Canadians into an understanding of the diversity and cultural richness of both Canadian and Asian societies.

Another aspect of this policy of "multiculturalism" which is of value is the opportunity for immigrant communities to become more responsible for developing their own adaptation strategies. This often involves substantial devolution of programs designed for immigrant communities. Many examples of these developments are cited in this volume. This "empowerment" of immigrant communities further enhances their capacities to interact with various strategic coalitions that are being formed to develop a strategic union, for example, of cities in which they reside. This also finds expression in increased participation in politics at various levels of government. Thus, for example, in Vancouver, the immigrant communities are playing a greater role in the vision of the city (See Ley and Hutton in this volume).

One consequence of the earlier dominance of European migration has been school and university programs which have emphasized the hegemony of the knowledge of Anglo-European traditions. In Canada, this is a situation which is only slowly changing. Australia and New Zealand have been much more responsive to their need to teach more about Asia in their curriculum.

But while "multiculturalism" provides an important policy framework for migrant adaptation, it must be stressed that adaptation is intergenerational

and at the same time as the "cultural roots" of former homelands are re-
tained, there is also a process of cultural fusion occurring in virtually every
cultural area: architecture, literature, film, theater, art, dance and last but
not least, food. There is an exciting innovative feel about the fusion of Asian
culture with host societies which is far different from the emphasis upon the
continuities that cultural heritage assumes. Why should this development
be surprising? The creation of fused cultures seems a far more probable consequence of globalization than a persistence of "parallel cultures." This is
because globalization encourages a public culture which is global.

A careful reading of the essays presented in this book leads to the conclusion that governments of the Asia Pacific region are having great difficulties in devising the flexible immigration policies that accelerate globalization demands. In part, at least, writers of the volume recognize that this
difficulty stems from a limited range of information that can be used for
policy making.

The concluding session of this Conference clearly indicated some general principles on which research should be conducted and the issues that
should be prioritized. The most important principle is that research on the
international migration has to be internationalized. There is a requirement
to establish research networks of country researchers who carry out joint research on international migration issues. A second principle is the capacity
to recognize the changing conditions of international migration that enforce
an evaluation of concepts such as migrant, citizenship, residence, and economic contribution in a host society. A third principle to incorporate is the
evaluation of international migration as an inevitable and positive aspect of
the emergence of "fused societies" in which "parallel cultures" play an important transition role in immigrant absorption.

It follows from these principles that research priorities may be listed
as follows:

- research on the concept and definition of migration which includes more
  critical analysis of conventional statistical analysis of international
  migration trends
- research on the particular role of Asian societies in international migration
  necessitated by these demographic importance at a global level
- research on the manner in which migrant networks operate both within
  host societies and internationally to facilitate the economic and social
  empowerment of international migrants
- research on the economic role of international migration, particularly as
  it relates to the flow of capital and information internationally in addition
  to more conventional research on the economic constitution of migrants
  to host societies
- research on the concepts of "transnationalism" and "translocality" as they
  impinge upon international migration

As is often the case, such research may not always lead to immediate policy consequences. This research agenda, while broad, is forward looking and is in fact an agenda for the 21st century. It is the decision of the authors of this volume that we should keep and enlarge this original network of researchers as a basis for developing an ongoing research agenda. However, it is a research agenda that must be enlarged by the participation of the many non-governmental organization and immigrant associations that are actively participating in this process of international migration. In the process of international migration "the views from within" are far more important than "the views from without" and the Asia Pacific network of researchers will actively seek to add international migrant NGOs to the network.

It may be too much to claim but if ongoing research can inform policies on international migration that will reduce racism, social injustice and inequality, this will be a significant accomplishment. A first step will be to recognize the "internationalization" of international migration. This is the path forward.

The Yuen Family

Photos: Donna Chin

Chapter References

1. **Asian Immigration and Racism in Canada — A Search for Policy Options**
   Aprodicio A. Laquian and Eleanor R. Laquian

Angus Reid Group. 1989. *Immigration to Canada: Aspects of public opinion.* Winnipeg: Angus Reid Group Inc. Also, results of public opinion polls in 1991, 1993, 1994 and 1997.

Backhouse, Constance. 1994. "White female help and Chinese-Canadian employers: Race, class, gender and law in the case of Yee . . ." *Canadian Ethnic Studies* 26 (34).

Bergman, Brian. 1993. "A nation of polite bigots?" *Maclean's* 106 (52) (December 27): 42.

Bolaria, B. Singh, and Peter S. Li, eds. 1988. *Racial oppression in Canada.* 2d ed. Toronto: Garamond Press.

Brandt, G. 1986. *The realization of anti-racist education.* London: Palmer Press.

Brillantes, Jose. 1997. "The Philippine overseas employment program and its effects on immigration to Canada." Ch. 9.

Canadian Council of Christians and Jews. 1993. *Survey of Canadian attitudes towards ethnic and race relations in Canada.* Toronto: Decima Research.

Citizenship and Immigration Canada. 1997. *Citizenship and immigration statistics, 1994.* Catalogue No. MP22–1/1997. Ottawa: Minister of Public Works and Government Services Canada.

——.1994. *Immigration consultations report.* Ottawa: Ministry of Supply and Services Canada.

Economic Council of Canada. 1991. *Report of the Economic Council of Canada.*

Elliot, Jean Leonard, and Augie Fleras. 1992. *Unequal relations: An introduction to race and ethnic dynamics in Canada.* Scarborough: Prentice-Hall Canada, Inc.

Employment and Immigration Canada. 1988. *Demographic considerations in determining future levels of immigration to Canada.* Report prepared for the Experts' Group Meeting on Demography and Migration, OECD, Paris (October 3–4).

Environics. 1988. *Focus Canada Survey.*

Foot, David K. 1986. *Population aging and immigration policy in Canada: Implications and prescriptions.* Ottawa: Employment and Immigration Canada, Policy and Program Development, Immigration.

Goldberg, D. S. 1990. *The anatomy of racism.* Minneapolis: Univ. of Minnesota Press.

Hall, S. 1978. "Racism and reaction." In *Five views of multi-racial Britain.* London: Macmillan.

Hawkins, Freda. 1972. *Canada and immigration: Public policy and public concern.* Montréal: McGill-Queen's Univ. Press.

Henry, Frances, and Carol Tator. 1994. "The ideology of racism — democratic racism." *Canadian Ethnic Studies* 26.

Henry, Frances, Carol Tator, Winston Mattis, and Tim Rees. 1995. *The color of democracy: Racism in Canadian society*. Toronto: Harcourt Brace and Company.

Jones, Gavin. 1997. "'Australian identity,' racism and recent responses to Asian immigration to Australia." Ch. 14.

Laquian, Eleanor. 1973. *A study of Filipino immigration to Canada, 1962–1972*. Ottawa: United Council of Filipino Associations in Canada.

Li, Peter. 1994. "A world apart: The multicultural world of visible minorities and the art world of Canada." *The Canadian Review of Sociology and Anthropology* 31 (4): 365–391.

Li, Zong. 1994. "Structural and cultural dimensions of racism: Towards an alternative perspective." *Canadian Ethnic Studies* 26.

Moodley, Kogila. 1997. "The role of education in combating racism in Canada." Ch. 19.

New Democratic Party. 1995. "Multiculturalism, anti-racism, human rights." Vancouver: B.C. New Democrats Home Page.

Palmer, Douglas L. 1994. *Anatomy of an attitude: Origins of the attitude toward the level of immigration to Canada*. Ottawa: Citizenship and Immigration Canada, Strategic Research, Analysis and Information, Policy Sector.

Roy, Reginald H. 1996. *David Lam: A biography*. Vancouver: Douglas and McIntyre.

Simmons, Alan B. 1997. "Globalization and backlash racism in the 1990s: The case of Asian immigration to Canada." Ch. 2.

Sunahara, Ann Gomer. 1981. *The politics of racism: The uprooting of Japanese Canadians during the Second World War*. Toronto: James Lorimer.

Tang, Angelica O. 1997. "A sensible immigrant policy in New York City." Ch. 15.

Taylor, K. W. 1991. "Racism in Canadian immigration policy." *Canadian Ethnic Studies* 23 (1): 1.

Trlin, Andrew, A. Henderson, and R. Pernice. 1997. "Asian immigration, public attitudes and immigration policy: Patterns and responses in New Zealand." Ch. 13.

The Vancouver Sun

Campbell, Charles. 1996. "Immigration policies show a rate of diminishing returns." (November 25).

Chow, Wyng. 1995. (April 23).

Gardner, Dan. 1997. "Immigration ignored in election despite its impact on the future." (June 1).

Smith, Dave. 1996. "UI used less by immigrants." (September 10).

1997a. "Vancouver is Canada's most racially tolerant city, report says." (October 6).

1997b. "Immigrants tolerated for their wealth, Fry says." (7 October).

1997c. "B.C. leads in opposition to immigration, poll finds." (9 October).

2. Globalization and Backlash Racism in the 1990s: The Case of Asian Immigration to Canada *Alan B. Simmons*

Angus Reid Group. 1989. *Immigration to Canada: Aspects of public opinion*. Winnipeg: Angus Reid Group Inc.

Beaujot, Roderic, K. G. Basavarajappa, and Ravi Verma. 1988. *Income of immigrants in Canada: A census data analysis*. Ottawa: Statistics Canada.

Bolaria, B. Singh, and Peter S. Li. 1988. "Capitalist expansion and immigrant labor: Chinese in Canada." Ch. 5 in *Racial oppression in Canada*, ed. Bolaria and Li. 2d ed. Toronto: Garamond Press.

——. 1988. "Colonialism and labor: East Indians in Canada." Ch. 7 in *Racial oppression in Canada*, ed. Bolaria and Li. 2d ed. Toronto: Garamond Press.

Citizenship and Immigration Canada. 1995. A *broader vision: Immigration plan* (1996 annual report to Parliament). Ottawa: Minister of Supply and Services.

——. 1994. A *broader vision: Plan 1995–2000*. Ottawa: Supply and Services Canada.

Economic Council of Canada. 1991. *Economic and social impacts of immigration*. Ottawa: Supply and Services Canada.

Employment and Immigration Canada. 1992. *Managing immigration: A framework for the 1990s*. Ottawa: Employment and Immigration Canada.

Frobel, F., with J. Heinrichs, and O. Kreye. 1980. *The new international division of labor*. New York and Cambridge: Cambridge Univ. Press.

Hawkins, Freda. 1988. *Canada and immigration: Public policy and public concern*. 2d ed. Kingston and Montréal: McGill-Queen's Univ. Press.

Jackubowski, Lisa. 1994. *Immigration and the legalization of racism*. Ph.D. diss., Sociology. Toronto: York Univ.

Kalbach, Madeline, and Warren Kalbach. 1995. "Ethnic diversity and persistence as factors in socio-economic inequality: A challenge for the twenty-first century." In Proceedings of the 1995 Federation of Canadian Demographers symposium, *Towards the XXIst Century: Emerging socio-demographic trends and policy issues in Canada*. Ottawa: St. Paul Univ.

Li, Peter. 1988. *The Chinese in Canada*. Toronto: Oxford Univ. Press.

Marr, William L., and Pierre L. Siklos. 1994. "Immigration and unemployment." In *Diminishing returns: The economics of Canada's recent immigration policy*, ed. Don DeVoretz, 293–330. Ottawa: Renouf, for C.D. Howe Institute.

Oziewicz, Estanislao. 1991. "Ottawa urged to slow immigration: Racism, unemployment will grow otherwise, study says." *The Globe and Mail* (February 21): A1.

Richmond, Anthony. 1988. *Immigration and ethnic conflict*. New York and Toronto: Macmillan.

——. 1994. *Global apartheid: Refugees, racism, and the new world order*. Oxford: Oxford Univ. Press.

Samuel, T. John. 1990. "Third World immigration and multiculturalism." Ch. 20 in *Ethnic Demography*, ed. Shiva Halli, Frank Travato, and Leo Dreiger, 383–98. Ottawa: Carleton Univ. Press.

Sarick, Lila. 1995a. "Canada strives to woo upscale immigrants." *The Globe and Mail* (June 7): A1.

——. 1995b. "Increase in fees for immigrants called new 'Chinese head tax.'" *The Globe and Mail* (March 1): A6.

Sassen-Koob, Saskia. 1983. "Labor migrations and the new international division of labor." In *Women, men and the international division of labor*, ed. June Nash and Maria Patricia Fernandez-Kelly. Albany: State Univ. of New York.

Satzewich, Vic. 1991. *Racism and the incorporation of foreign labor: Farm labor migration to*

Canada since 1945. London: Routledge.

Simmons, Alan. In press. "Racism and immigration policy." In The racist imagination: The sociology of racism in Canada, ed. Vic Satzewich.

——. 1994. "Canadian immigration policy in the early 1990s: A commentary on Veuglers and Klassen's analysis of the breakdown in the unemployment-immigration linkage." Canadian Journal of Sociology 19 (4): 525–34.

Simmons, Alan, and Dwaine Plaza. 1995. "Breaking through the glass ceiling: The pursuit of university training among Afro-Caribbean migrants and their children in Toronto." Montréal: Canadian Learned Societies Meetings.

Verma, Ravi, and Chan Kwok Bun. 1996. "The economic adaptation of Asian immigration to Canada." Paper presented at Symposium on Immigration and Integration. Department of Sociology, Univ. of Manitoba.

Windsor, Hugh. 1990. "Forty-six per cent want immigration levels reduced, poll finds." The Globe and Mail (October 29): A7.

Wong, Jan. 1997. "Immigration: Death of a paper carrier." The Globe and Mail (April 19): D1.

3. Multiculturalism and Racism: An Evaluation   Elliot L. Tepper

Abu-Laban, Yasmeen, and Daiva Stasiulis. 1992. "Ethnic pluralism under siege: Popular and partisan opposition to multiculturalism." Canadian Public Policy 18 (4) (January): 381.

Berry, J. W., and Rudolf Kaplin. 1993. "Multicultural and ethnic attitudes in Canada: An overview of the 1991 National Survey." Paper presented at Canadian Psychological Association Annual Meetings, Montréal (May).

Breton, Raymond. 1989. "Collective dimensions of the cultural transformation of ethnic communities and the larger society." Paper presented at UNESCO Conference, Calgary.

——. 1985. "Multiculturalism and Canadian nation-building." In The Politics of gender, ethnicity and language in Canada, ed. Alan Cairns and Cynthia Williams, 27–66. Toronto: The Univ. of Toronto Press.

——. 1984. "The production and allocation of symbolic resources: An analysis of the linguistic and ethnocultural fields in Canada." Canadian Review of Sociology and Anthropology 21 (2): 123–144.

Corriere Canadese. 1993. "Multiculturalism, I will clarify everything: There will be a true minister while immigration will not be attached to public security." (October 22).

Elliott, Jean Leonard, and Augie Fleras. 1992. Unequal relations: An introduction to race and ethnic dynamics in Canada. Scarborough: Prentice-Hall Canada Inc.

Fleras, Augie, and Jean Leonard Elliott. 1992. The challenge of diversity: Multiculturalism in Canada. Scarborough: Nelson Canada.

Kalin, Rudolf, and John W. Berry. 1991. "Ethnic and multicultural attitudes in Canada, outside Quebec." Draft prepared for State of the art review of research on Canada's multicultural society. (September).

Tepper, Elliot. 1994. "Immigration policy and multiculturalism." In Multiculturalism in Canada: The research landscape, ed. John Berry and Jean Laponce. Toronto: Univ. of

Toronto Press.

——. 1991. "Facing the future." *Infoshare* I (February).

——. 1990a. "The future of Canadian cities." *Currents* 6 (October): 2.

——. 1990b. *Symbolism and pluralism in Canada*. Multiculturalism Department of the Secretary of State.

——. 1990c. "Ethnicity in Canada: Accessibility of research." Multiculturalism Canada, Secretary of State.

——. 1990d. "Race relations and the cities: Vancouver." Multiculturalism Canada, Secretary of State.

——. 1990e. "Race relations and the cities: Montréal." Multiculturalism Canada, Secretary of State.

——, co-ed., & contributor. 1989a. *Canada 2000: Race relations and public policy.* Univ. of Guelph.

——, co-authored. 1989b. *Training as a tool for change in a polyethnic and multiracial society.* Study for the Ministry of Citizenship. Government of Ontario.

——. 1989c. "Demographic change and ethnicity." In *Multiculturalism and policing in British Columbia.* Proceedings of a conference held in Richmond, B.C. (January 1988). Government of British Columbia.

——. 1988a. "Changing Canada: The institutional response to polyethnicity." *The Review of Demography and its Implications for Economic and Social Policy* (December). Health and Welfare Canada.

——. 1988b. *Self employment in Canada among immigrants of different ethno-cultural backgrounds.* Canada Employment and Immigration Commission.

——. 1988c. "Predicting future international migration." Report of the Chairman, Academic Review Panel, Employment and Immigration Canada.

——. 1987. "Demographic change and pluralism." *Canadian Studies in Population* 14 (2).

——. 1986a. "Japanese redress: Philosophical issues." Paper prepared for the Secretary of State and Minister Responsible for Multiculturalism (August).

——. 1986b. "Race relations in Canada: A national strategy." Policy proposals, Race Relations Unit, Secretary of State, Multiculturalism Canada.

——. 1983. "Racism and racial discrimination in Canada: A selective and interpretive bibliographic survey." Race Relations Unit, Secretary of State, Multiculturalism Canada (May).

——. 1982. *Asia's refugees and the Western tradition: The political and constitutional legacy of Indo-China.* Citizenship Branch, Secretary of State.

——. 1981. "Is Ottawa different? Perceptions of discrimination and race relations in the National Capital." Paper prepared for the Multiculturalism Directorate, Secretary of State (Winter).

——. 1980a. "Southeast Asian exodus: From tradition to resettlement." *Canadian Asian Studies Association.* Univ. of Chicago Press.

——. 1980b. D'*un continent à un autre: Les réfugiés du Sud-Est asiatique.* L'Association Canadienne des Etudes Asiatiques.

Wilson, V. Seymour. n.d. "Canada's evolving multicultural policy: A stalled omnibus in the 1990s?" Unpublished paper.

——. 1993. "The tapestry of Canadian multiculturalism." Presidential address, Canadian

Political Science Association. (June).

The Globe and Mail.

Barber, John . 1993. "Manning welcome to be first to leave." (October 15).

1993a. "Canadians want mosaic to melt, survey finds." (December 14): A1–2.

1993b. "Liberals turf out three Tory ad managers." (November 24): A3.

1993c. "Reform Candidate says new immigrants are a burden." (October 15).

1993d. "Tories hunting flawed Reformers." (October 15).

1993e. "Women's minority groups called 'parasites' by Reform official." (October 29).

The Toronto Star

Cardozo, Andrew. 1993. "PM delivered more talk than action on minorities." (May 3).

——. 1993a. "The tory way: See no diversity hear no diversity." (September 9).

——. 1993b. "Reform quietly setting agenda on immigration." (October 5).

——. 1993c. "Minorities in a majority government." (November 2).

The Liberal Party of Canada. 1993. "Creating opportunity: The liberal plan for Canada." Ottawa. (September).

The Reform Party of Canada. 1990. *Principles and Policies.*

——. 1989. *Platform and Statement of Principles.* (June).

Documents

Angus Reid Group. 1991. *Multiculturalism and Canadians: National attitudes study* 1991.

Canadian Ethnocultural Council (CEC). 1993a. "Prime Minister sending mixed message on multiculturalism." News release (November 8). Ottawa.

——. 1993b. "CEC urges new Prime Minister to affirm his government's support for multiculturalism." News release (October 28). Ottawa.

——. 1993c. "Ethnic leaders pleased with Liberal majority, but worried that multiculturalism will be sidelined in Parliament." News release (October 26). Ottawa.

Citizenship and Immigration Canada. 1997. News release (September 16).

Office of the Prime Minister of Canada. 1993a. *Release* (November 4).

——. 1993b. *Release* (June 25).

Multiculturalism and Citizenship, Corporate Policy and Research. 1993a. *Selected charts — 1986 and 1991 census data.* (February 8).

——. 1993b. *Projection of Canada's 1991 people in 2006.* (October).

Multiculturalism and Citizenship Canada. 1993–94. *Estimates: Expenditure plan part III.*

——. 1991–92 *Estimates: Expenditure plan part III.*

——. 1990. *Public opinion research on multiculturalism and immigration: An overview.* Marjorie E. Lambert. (January).

——. 1988. *Analysis of Thompson Lightstone Survey of public attitudes towards multiculturalism.* (April).

Statistics Canada. 1993a. "Age and sex aboriginal data, 1991 Census of Canada." *The Daily* (Tuesday, June 1).

——. 1993b. "Mobility and migration, 1991 Census of Canada." *The Daily* (Tuesday, May 11).

——. 1993c. "Immigration and citizenship (the national series), 1991 Census of

Canada." *The Daily* (Tuesday, March 30).

——. 1993d. "Home language and mother tongue knowledge of languages (the nation), 1991 Census of Canada." *The Daily* (Tuesday, January 12).

5. Conditions in China Influencing Outmigration *Zeng Yi and Zhang Qinwu*

Chen Chexian. 1963. "Popular outmigration of contract labor workers during the 19th century." *History Research* No. 1.

Chen Da. 1939. *Overseas Chinese in South-East Asia and society of Guangdong and Fujian provinces.* Shanghai: Business Affairs Publisher.

Liang, Zai, and Abigail Mandel. 1997. "Market transition and emigration from China in the 1990s." Paper presented at 1997 Annual Meeting of Population Association of America, Washington, D.C. (March 27–29).

Liang, Zai, and Wenzhen Ye. 1997. "From Fujian to New York: Understanding the new Chinese immigration." Paper presented at conference on Transnational Communities and the Political Economy of New York in the 1990s at New School of Social Research, New York City (February 21–22).

Ma Xia. 1993. "On brain drain problems." *Population Research* No. 3.

Sha Jichai. 1995. "International migration and mobility." In *Studies on population problems during the process of economic reform and opening the door to the outside world,* ed. Sha Jichai and Chao Jinchun. Beijing: Peking Univ. Press.

Sha Jichai, and Chao Jinchun, eds. 1995. *Studies on population problems during the process of economic reform and opening the door to the outside world.* Beijing: Peking Univ. Press.

Skeldon, Ronald. 1996. "Migration from China." *Journal of International Affairs* 49 (2): 434–455.

Zhu Guohong. 1989. "Historical review of international migration of Chinese population." *Historical Research* 6: 159–177.

6. From Brain Drain to Guest Workers and Refugees: The Policies and Politics of Outmigration from Sri Lanka *Sisira Pinnawala*

Ariyawansa, D.M. 1989. *Report of the survey on changes in economic and social habits of expatriate labor for unskilled occupations.* Colombo: Friedrich-Ebert Foundation.

Central Bank. 1970. *Annual report of the Central Bank of Sri Lanka.* Colombo: Central Bank.

De Fontgalland, S. G. 1986. *Sri Lankans in exile: Tamils displaced.* Madras: Cerro Publications.

Dias, M. 1986. "The community of outmigration." In *Middle East interlude: Asian workers abroad — a comparative study of four communities,* ed. M. I. Abella and Y. Attal, 202–246. Bangkok: UNESCO Regional Office.

Diggs, B. J. 1974. *The state, justice and the common good.* Glenview: Scott Foresman and Co.

Eelens, F., and J. D. Speckmann. 1990. "Recruitment of labor migration for the Middle East: The Sri Lankan case." *International Migration Review* 24: 297–322.

Government Press. 1974. *Report of the cabinet sub-committee inquiring into the problems of technologically, professionally and academically qualified personnel leaving Sri Lanka.* Sessional Paper 10. Colombo: The Government Press.

Greenberg, R. 1986. *No island is an island any more: International ramifications of the ethnic conflict in Sri Lanka (mémoire)*. Genève: Institut Universitaire De Hautes Etudes Internationales.

ILO Report. 1971. *Matching employment opportunities and expectations — A program of action for Ceylon*. Report of an inter-agency team organized by ILO. Geneva: International Labor Organization.

Jacobsen, K. 1996. "Factors influencing the policy responses of the host governments to mass refugee influxes." *International MigrationReview* 30 (3): 655–678.

Karunathilake, H. N. S. 1987. *Sri Lanka, migration of talent: Causes and consequences of brain drain: Three studies from Asia*, 189–240. Bangkok: UNESCO Principal Regional Office for Asia and Pacific.

Korale, R. B. M. 1984. *Middle East migration: The Sri Lankan experience*. Colombo: Employment and Manpower Division, Ministry of Plan Implementation.

Labour Migration. 1996. "Migrant labor exploitation: Does any one have the housemaid's welfare at heart?" *Economic Review* 1 (10): 14–20.

Lakshman, W. D. 1993. "The Gulf Crisis of 1990–91: Economic impact and policy responses in Sri Lanka." In *The Gulf Crisis and South Asia: Studies in the economic impact*, ed. P. Wickreinasekere, 144–172. Bangkok: UNDP, ARTEP.

Ministry of Plan Implementation. 1985. *Foreign employment: Sri Lankan experience*. Colombo: Ministry of Plan Implementation.

Newland, K. 1993. "Ethnic conflict and refugees." *Survival* 35 (1): 81–101

Ruhunage, L. K. 1996. "Sri Lankan labor migration: Trends and threats." *Economic Review* 21 (10): 3–7.

Sivarajah, A. n.d. "Internationalization of Sri Lankan ethnic conflict." *Ceylon Studies Seminar*. Univ. of Peradeniya.

United Nations. 1951. *Convention relating to the status of refugees*, Article 1. A. (2). *United Nations Treaty Series* 189:ʾ150 .

7. **In the Maelstrom of Hope and Despair; The Prospects for South Asian Migration to Canada** *Azfar Khan*

Athukorala, P. 1993. *Enhancing developmental impact of migrant remittances: A review of Asian experiences*. New Delhi:ILO/ARTEP.

Bhaduri, A., and, D. Nayyar. 1996. *The intelligent person's guide to liberalization*. New Delhi: Penguin Books India.

Cohen, R., ed. 1996. *The Cambridge survey of world migration*. Cambridge, U.K: Cambridge Univ. Press.

Connell, J., B. Dasgupta, R. Laishley, and M. Lipton. 1976. "Migration from rural areas: The evidence from village studies." Draft manuscript. Institute of Development Studies, Univ. of Sussex.

Ghosh, A. 1992. "Economic restructuring, employment and safety nets: A note." In *Social dimensions of structural adjustment in India*. New Delhi: ILO/ARTEP.

Hugo, G. 1981. "Village community ties, village norms and ethnic and social networks: A review of evidence from the Third World." In *Migration decision making*, ed. G. De Jong and R. Gardner. New York: Pergamon Press.

Immigration Canada. 1990. *Immigration to Canada: A statistical overview*. Ottawa-Hull: Employment and Immigration Canada.

Jalan, B., ed. 1992. *The Indian economy: Problems and prospects*. New Delhi: Penguin Books.

Khan, A. 1991. "International migration and the 'moral economy' of the 'Barani' peasantry." *Pakistan Development Review* 30 (4).

Mundle, S. 1992. "The employment effects of stabilization and related policy changes in India, 1991–92 to 1993–94." In *Social dimensions of structural adjustment in India*. New Delhi: ILO/ARTEP.

Saith, A. 1997. "Structural change and migration pressures: Case study of the Philippines." *International Migration Papers*. Geneva: ILO Employment and Training Department.

Samuel, J. 1995. "Temporary and permanent labor migration into Canada: Selected aspects." In "The jobs and effects of migrant workers in North America," J. Samuel, P. L. Martin, and J. E. Taylor. *International Migration Papers* 10. ILO, Geneva: Employment Department, ILO.

Samuel, J., and M. Jansson. 1988. "Canada's immigration levels and the economic and demographic environment, 1967–1987." In *European Journal of International Migration and Ethnic Relations* 2 (87).

Stalker, P. 1994. *The work of strangers: A survey of international labor migration*. Geneva: ILO.

Tatla, D. S. 1996. "Sikh free and military migration during the colonial period." In R. Cohen, ed.

Tinker, H. 1977. *The Banyan tree*. London: Oxford Univ. Press.

——. 1975. *A new system of slavery*. London: Oxford Univ. Press.

8. Intra-regional Migration in Southeast Asia: Migration Pattern and Major Concerns in Malaysia Azizah Kassim

Ayob Tamrin. 1988. *Pendatang Indonesia di kampung Baharu: Satu tinjauan latar belakang sosio–ekonomi*. Graduation exercise, Department of Anthropology and Sociology, Univ. of Malaya.

Azizah Kassim. 1997a. "Illegal alien labor in Malaysia: Its influx, utilization and ramifications." *Indonesia and the Malay world*, no. 71 (March): 50–82. London: Oxford Univ. Press.

——. 1997b. "International migration and its impact on Malaysia." Paper presented at ISIS 11th Asia-Pacific Roundtable, Hotel Istana, Kuala Lumpur, Malaysia (June 5–8).

——. 1997c. "International migration and alien labor employment in Southeast Asia: An insight from the Malaysian experience." Paper presented at conference on India, Southeast Asia and the United States: New Opportunities for Understanding and Co–operation, Singapore (January 31–February 1).

——. 1996. "Alien workers in Malaysia: Critical issues, problems and constraints." In *Movement of people within and from Southeast Asian Countries; Trends, causes and consequences*, ed. M. F. Carunia, 3–38. Jakarta: Toyota Foundation and Southeast Asian Studies Program, Indonesian Institute of Sciences.

——. 1995a. "From neglect to legalization: The changing state response to the inflow of illegal labor into Malaysia." Paper presented at conference on Globalization: Local Challenges and Responses organized by the Malaysian Social Science

Association, Penang (January).

——. 1995b. "Recruitment and employment of foreign workers in Malaysia." In *Dimensions of traditions and development in Malaysia*, ed. Rokiah Talib and C. B. Tan, 163–202. Kuala Lumpur: Pelanduk Publications.

——. 1994. "Malaysian illegal workers in Japan." In *Indonesia Circle* no. 63 (June): 156–173. London: Oxford Univ. Press.

——. 1988. "Immigrant workers and the informal sector in West Malaysia: A case study of the Indonesian workers in Kuala Lumpur." In *Current issues in labor migration in Malaysia*, 232–254. Kuala Lumpur: NUPW and PSU, Faculty of Economics and Administration, Univ. of Malaya.

Dorall, R. F. 1989. "Issues and implications of recent illegal economic migration from the Malay world." In *Trade in domestic helpers: Causes, mechanisms and consequences* (Selected papers from the Planning Meeting on International Migration and Women). Kuala Lumpur: Asia Pacific Development Centre.

Gooneratne et al., eds. 1994. "Regional development impacts of labor migration in Asia." UNCRD *Research Report Series No. 2*. Nagoya, Japan.

Gunasekaran, S. 1994. "Cross-national labor flows within ASEAN: Patterns and problems." In Gooneratne et al. eds., 45–56.

Hugo, G. 1993. "Indonesian labor migration to Malaysia: Trends and policy implications." *Southeast Asian Journal of Social Science* 21 (1): 37–70.

Iguchi, Y. 1997. "Labor market development and international migration in Japan." Paper presented at Workshop on International Migration and Labor market in Asia, Tokyo (January 30–31).

Junipah Wandi. 1995. "Pendatang Indonesia di Selangor: Proses penghijrahan dan Penyesuaian." MA thesis, Department of Anthropology and Sociology, Univ. of Malaya.

——. 1992. "Kegiatan sosio-ekonomi penghijrah Indonesia di kampung Kerinci." Graduation exercise, Department of Anthropology and Sociology, Univ. of Malaya.

Lim, V. K. E. and S. Balachandran. 1997. "The impact of migrant workers on patterns of infectious diseases in Malaysia." Paper presented at National Conference on Infection and Infection Control, Ipoh, Malaysia (March 14).

Ling, P. L. 1997. "Penghijrahan tenaga buruh Cina ke Singapura. Satu kajian kes di kampung Balai, Jerantut, Pahang." Graduation exercise, Department of Anthropology and Sociology, Univ. of Malaya.

Loke, S. Y. 1991. "Pekerja wanita Malaysia di sebuah kilang elektronik Singapura." Graduation exercise, Department of Anthropology and Sociology, Univ. of Malaya.

Mani, A. 1996. "Filipino migrant workers in Brunei Darussalam." *Philippine Sociological Review* 44 (1–4): 194–209.

——. 1995. "Migration in Brunei Darussalam." In *Crossing borders: Transmigration in Asia Pacific*, ed. J. H. Ong and S. B. Chew, 441–455. Singapore: Prentice Hall.

Pang, E.F. 1994. *Foreign workers in Singapore*. In Gooneratne et al., eds, 79–94.

Pillai, P. 1992. *People on the Move*. ISIS Malaysia.

Razali Ismail. 1996. "Pekerja Bangladesh dalam industri: Satu kajian kes di Tongkang Pechah, Batu Pahat, Johore Darul Ta'zim." Graduation exercise, Department of

Anthropology and Sociology, Univ. of Malaya.

Ryan, C. 1997. "Wanita Indonesia dalam sektor perkhidmatan: Satu kajian kes di Lembah Kelang." Graduation exercise, Dept. of Anthropology and Sociology, Univ. of Malaya.

Sazaki, S. 1994. "Clandestine labor in Japan: Sources, magnitude and implications." In *Regional development impact of labor migration in Asia*, ed. Gooneratne et al., 151–162. Nagoya, Japan: United Nations Centre for Regional Development.

———. 1995. "Data on international migration in Japan." *Asian and Pacific Migration Journal* 4 (4): 565–577.

Skeldon, R. 1995. "Recent changes in migratory movements and policies in Hong Kong." *Asian and Pacific Migration Journal* 4 (4): 543–554.

Tsay, C. L. 1995. "Data on international migration to Taiwan." *Asian and Pacific Migration Journal* 4 (4): 613–619.

———. 1992. "Clandestine labor migration to Taiwan." *Asian and Pacific Migration Journal* 1 (4): 637–655.

Zulkifly Hassan. 1995. "Kegiatan ekonomi pendatang Filipina di Sabah: Satu kajian kes di Pulau Gaya." Graduation exercise, Department of Anthropology and Sociology, Univ.of Malaya.

Official Reports/Publications and Other Documents

Government Printers. 1996. *Seventh Malaysia plan, 1996–2000*. Kuala Lumpur: Government Printers.

———. 1996. *Social Statistics Bulletin, Malaysia*. Kuala Lumpur: Government Printers.

———. 1993. *Social Statistics Bulletin, Malaysia*. Kuala Lumpur: Government Printers.

———. 1991. *General Report of the Population Census 1*. Kuala Lumpur: Government Printers.

———. 1989 *Social Statistics Bulletin, Malaysia*. Kuala Lumpur: Government Printers.

———. 1984. *Social Statistics Bulletin, Malaysia*. Kuala Lumpur: Government Printers.

Malaysian Employers Federation. 1996. *Report on the survey of labor shortage and manpower requirements in MEF member companies*. Kuala Lumpur: Malaysian Employers Federation. (June).

Pendatang Luar Negeri Di Sabah dan W.P. Labuan-Langkah-Langkah dan Penyelesaian. 1992. Pasukan Petugas Khas Persekutuan, Majlis Keselamatan Negara, Jabatan Perdana Menteri, Kota Kinabalu.

Population and Household Census of Malaysia. 1995. *State population report, Sabah, 1991*. Kuala Lumpur: Government Printers.

Newspapers

Berita Harian

1996. "Gaduh: Warga Bangladesh mati di tikam." (October 5).

Business Times

1995. "Council to discuss Bangladeshi issue." (October 5).

Harian Metro

1996. "Pindah Milik Tanah di disiasat." (March 23).

1995. "120 Indo bersuami dua." (December 7).

New Straits Times

1995. "Immigration chiefs under probe." (August 11).

1997a. "Employers warned about replacing local workers." (February 1).

1997b. "Local staff who quit replaced with foreigners." (February 2).

1997c. "Foreign workers not encouraged to join unions." (February 19).

1997d. "Civil servants behind immigrant-smuggling syndicates held." (February 19).

1997e. "Proposal for cheaper way to repatriate illegals." (March 6).

1997f. "Immigration deploys 15 officers to clear backlog." (March 25).

1997g. "Alien workers sent home RM3b in '96." (April 25).

The Star (Malaysia)

1997a. "One million illegals miss the boat under amnesty offer." (February 1).

1997b. "Sabah illegals may get a reprieve." (February 5).

1997c. "New policy on illegals in Sabah." (February 22).

1997d. "RM14 million spent on detained illegals." (February 25).

1997e. "Blitz on illegal professionals." (March 9).

1997f. "Scam to retrench local workers." (March 11).

1997g. "329 illegals married Orang Asli." (April 22).

1997h. "Prostitution among oil palm trees." (May 25).

1997i. "1.4 million Indons in Malaysia to vote." (May 29).

1996a. "Indon given the go-ahead on registration." (May 28).

1996b. "Illegal settlements in most districts." (June 5).

1996c. "Review over intake of Bangladeshis." (September 22).

1996d. "Police looking for trio over killing of Bangladeshi." (December 21).

1996e. "Ong: 33 gov't. servants held over issuance of fake ICs." (October 17).

The Sun (Malaysia). 1996. "Bangladeshi: We were assaulted while sleeping." (October 3).

10. Migration and Mobilization in Asia: An Overview   *Graeme Hugo*

Abella, M. I. 1995. "Asian labor migration: Past, present and future. ASEAN *Economic Bulletin* 122: 25–138.

Adams, W. 1969. *The brain drain.* New York: Macmillan.

Arcellana, E. Y. 1995. "The Maga-Contemplacion case: Beyond forgetting." *The Manila Chronicle* (June 4).

Arnold, F. 1989. "Unanswered questions about the immigration multiplier." *International Migration Review* 23: 89–92.

Australian Bureau of Statistics (ABS). 1996. *Migration Australia, 1994–1995.* Catalogue No. 3412.0. Canberra: ABS.

———. n.d. *Overseas arrivals and departures.* Catalogue No. 3402.0 (various issues). Canberra: ABS.

Azizah Kassim. 1997. "International migration and its impact on Malaysia." Paper presented at ISIS 11th Asia-Pacific Roundtable, Hotel Istana, Kuala Lumpur (June 5–8).

Baum, J. 1993. "Human wave." *Far Eastern Economic Review* (August 5), 24.

Bedford, R., and J. Ligard. 1996. *International migration in the Asia-Pacific Region in the 1980s and 1990s: Two New Zealand perspectives.* Population Studies Centre Discussion Paper No. 19. Hamilton, New Zealand: Univ. of Waikato.

Beng, C. S. 1990. "Brain drain in Singapore: Issues and prospects." *Singapore Economic*

Review 35 (2): 55–77.

Beng, C. S., and R. Chew. 1995. "Immigration and foreign labor in Singapore." ASEAN *Economic Bulletin* 12 (2): 191–200.

Bilsborrow, R. E., G. Hugo, A. S. Oberai, and H. Zlotnik. 1997. *International migration statistics: Guidelines for improving data collection systems.* Geneva: International Labor Office.

Birks, Sinclair, and Associates. 1992. GCC *market report 1992.* Durham, U.K.: Mountjoy Research Center .

Brockett, L. 1996. "Thai sex workers in Sydney." MA thesis, Department of Geography, Univ. of Sydney.

Cahill, D. 1990. *Intermarriages in international contexts: A Study of Filipino women married to Australian, Japanese or Swiss men.* Quezon City, Philippines: Scalabrini Migration Centre.

Cariño, B. V. 1987. "The Philippines and Southeast Asia: Historical roots and contemporary linkages." In *Pacific bridges: The new immigration from Asia and the Pacific islands,* ed. J. T. Fawcett and B. V. Cariño, 305–326. Staten Island, New York: Center for Migration Studies.

Castles, S., H. Booth, and P. Wallace. 1984. *Here for good: West Europe's ethnic minorities.* London: Pluto Press.

Cross, M. 1990. "A magnet in Asia." *Far Eastern Economic Review* 66 (December 6).

Dawkins, P., P. Lewis, K. Noris, M. Baker, F. Robertson, N. Groenewold, and A. Hagger. 1991. *Flows of immigrants to South Australia, Tasmania and Western Australia.* Canberra: Australian Government Publishing Service (AGPS).

Department of Employment, Education, Training and Youth Affairs. 1996. *Selected higher education student statistics 1996.* Canberra: AGPS.

Department of Immigration and Ethnic Affairs (DIEA). 1994. *Overseas students in Australia,* Fact Sheet 18. Canberra: DIEA.

Department of Immigration and Multicultural Affairs. n.d. *Australian immigration consolidated statistics* (various issues). Canberra: AGPS.

Do Rosario, L. 1995. "Futures and options." *Far Eastern Economic Review* (June 15): 21.

Fields, G.S. 1994. "The migration transition in Asia." *Asian and Pacific Migration Journal* 3 (1): 7–30.

Fong, P.E. 1993. *Regionalization and labor flows in Pacific Asia.* Paris: OECD.

Fortney, J. 1972. "Immigrant professionals: A brief historical survey." *International Migration Review* 6 (1): 50–62.

Goldberg, P. 1996. "International projections for migrant women as a human rights issue." In *Asian women in migration,* ed. G. Battistella and A. Paganoni, 165–182. Quezon City, Philippines: Scalabrini Migration Center.

Goldstein, C. 1994. "Innocents abroad." *Far Eastern Economic Review* (September 15): 22–27.

Goss, J., and B. Lindquist. 1995. "Conceptualizing international labor migration: A structuration perspective. *International Migration Review* 29 (2): 317–351.

Habir M. 1984. "A migration equation." *Far Eastern Economic Review* (April 26): 116–172.

Hicks, G. L., ed. 1993. *Overseas Chinese remittances from Southeast Asia, 1910–1940.* Singapore: Select Books .

Hiebert, M. 1995. "Do not disturb." *Far Eastern Economic Review* 50 (August 24).

——. 1990. "Comrades go home." *Far Eastern Economic Review* 20 (May 17).

Ho, L., P. Liu, and K. Lam. 1991. "International labor migration: The case of Hong Kong." Paper presented at Second Japan-Asean Forum on International Labor Migration in East Asia, Tokyo, Japan (September 26–27).

Hugo, G. J. 1997a. "International migration in the Asia-Pacific Region: Emerging trends and issues." Paper prepared for the Conference on International Migration at Century's End: Trends and Issues, organized by the International Union for the Scientific Study of Population, Barcelona, Spain (May 7–10).

——. 1997b. "Migration and female empowerment." First draft of a paper prepared for International Union for the Scientific Study of Population's Committee on Gender and Population's Seminar on Female Empowerment and Demographic Processes: Moving beyond Cairo, Lund, Sweden (April 21–24).

——. Forthcoming. "The demographic underpinnings of current and future international migration in Asia." *Asian and Pacific Migration Journal.*

——. 1996a. "Brain drain and student movements." In *International trade and migration in the APEC region,* ed. P. J. Lloyd and L. S. Williams, 210–228. Melbourne: Oxford Univ. Press.

——. 1996b. "Economic impacts of international labor emigration on regional and local development: Some evidence from Indonesia." Paper presented at Annual Meeting of the PAA, New Orleans (May).

——. 1996c. Remittances in Southeast Asia. Mimeo.

——. 1995. "Labor export from Indonesia: An overview." *ASEAN Economic Bulletin* 12 (2): 275–298.

——. 1994. *The economic implications of emigration from Australia.* Canberra: Bureau of Immigration and Population Research, Australia Government Publishing Service.

——. 1975. Population mobility in West Java, Indonesia. Ph.D. thesis, Department of Demography, Australian National University, Canberra.

Hugo, G. J., and M. Gartner. 1993. *Evaluation of the prototype survey first wave and some recommendations for the full survey.* Bureau of Immigration Research prototype survey for a Longitudinal Survey of Immigrants to Australia (LSIA) Working Paper Series, Working paper no.7 (April).

Hugo, G. J., and A. Singhanetra-Renard. 1987. *International migration of contract labor in Asia — Major issues and implications.* Ottawa: IDRC.

Jayasankaran, S. 1997. "Blunt talk." *Far Eastern Economic Review* (April 10): 60.

Kritz, M. M., and C. Caces. 1989. *Science and technology transfers and migration flows.* Population and Development Program 1989 Working Paper Series 1.02. Ithaca: Cornell Univ.

Kritz, M. M., and H. Zlotnik. 1992. "Global interactions: Migration systems, processes and policies." In *International migration systems: A global approach,* ed. M. M. Kritz, L. L. Lim, and H. Zlotnik, 1–18. Oxford: Clarendon Press.

Kwong, K. 1992. "Study shows brain drain on rise again." *Sunday Morning Post* (June).

Lewis, P. E. T. 1994. "Singaporean entrepreneurs — The Australian connection." *Journal of Enterprising Culture* 2 (2): 709–733.

Lim, L. L. 1994. *Growing economic interdependence and its implications for international migration in population distribution and migration.* Proceedings of the UN Expert Meeting on Population Distribution and Migration, Bolivia (January): 334–354.

Lim, L. L., and N. Oishi. 1996. "International migration of Asian women: Distinctive characteristics and policy concerns." In *Asian women in migration*, ed. G. Battistella and A. Paganoni, 23–54. Quezon City, Philippines: Scalabrini Migration Center.

Low, L., M. H. Toh, and T. W. Soon. 1991. *Economics of education and manpower developments, issues and policies in Singapore*. Singapore: McGraw-Hill.

Martin, P. L. 1996. *Migrants on the move*, Asia-Pacific Issues No. 29. Honolulu: East-West Center.

——. 1994. Migration and trade: Challenges for the 1990s. *Work and family life of international migrant workers* 4 (3): 1–21.

——. 1993. *Trade and migration: NAFTA and agriculture*. Washington, D.C.: Institute for International Economics.

Martin, P. L., A. Mason, and C. L. Tsay. 1995. "Overview." ASEAN *Economic Bulletin* 12 (2): 117–124.

Massey, D., J. Arango, G. Hugo, A. Kouaouci, A. Pellegrino and J. E. Taylor. 1994. "The evaluation of international migration theory: The North American case." *Population and Development Review* 20 (4): 699–752.

Minocha, U. 1987. "South Asian immigrants: Trends and impacts on the sending and receiving societies." In *Pacific bridges: The new immigration from Asia and the Pacific Islands*, ed. J. T. Fawcett and B. V. Cariño, 347–374. Staten Island, New York: Center for Migration Studies,

Okunishi, Y. 1995. "Japan." ASEAN *Economic Bulletin* 12 (2): 139–162.

Pe Pua, R., C. Mitchell, R. Iredale, and S. Castles. 1996. *Astronaut families and parachute children: The cycle of migration between Hong Kong and Australia*. Canberra: AGPS.

Pernia, E. M. 1976. "The question of the brain drain from the Philippines." *International Migration Review* 10 (1): 63–72.

Pieke, F. N. Forthcoming. Introduction. In *The Chinese in Europe*, ed. G. Beaton and F. N. Pieke. Basingstroke: Macmillan.

Plafker, T. 1995. "China fights brain drain." *International Herald Tribune* (April 24).

Pongsapich, A. 1995. *Recent trends in international migration in Asia*. Asian Population Studies Series No. 137. New York: United Nations.

Prasai, S. B. 1993. "Asia's labor pains." *Far Eastern Economic Review* (April 29): 23.

Qian, W. 1996. "The features of international migration in China." Paper presented at Conference on European Chinese and Chinese Domestic Migrants, Oxford (July 3–7).

Rallu, J. L. 1996. "Recent trends in international migration and economic development in the South Pacific." *Asia-Pacific Population Journal* 11 (2): 23–46.

Rashid, A. 1995. "Slippery slope." *Far Eastern Economic Review* (March 23): 53.

Research and Documentation Centre for Manpower and Development (RDCM-YTKI). 1986. *The prospects of labor market in Saudi Arabia for Indonesian workers*. Jakarta: RDCM-YTKI in cooperation with National Development Planning Agency (BAPPENAS).

Rogge, J. R. 1993. "Refugee migration: Changing characteristics and prospects." Paper presented at Expert Group Meeting on Population Distribution and Migration, Santa Cruz, Bolivia (January 18–22).

Russell, S. S. 1991. "Population and development in the Philippines: An update." Washington, D.C.: Population and Human Resources Division, The World Bank Asia Country Department II.

Russell, S. S., and M. S. Teitelbaum. 1992. *International migration and international trade.* World Bank Discussion Paper 160. Washington, D.C.: The World Bank.

Sassen, S. 1993. "Economic internationalization: The new migration in Japan and the United States." *International Migration Review* 31 (1): 73–102.

Saywell, T. 1997. "Workers' offensive." *Far Eastern Economic Review* (May 29): 50–52.

Sherry, A., M. Lee, and M. Vatikiotis. 1995. "For lust or money." *Far Eastern Economic Review* (December 14): 22–23.

Shozo, F. 1995. *With sweat and abacus: Economic roles of Southeast Asian Chinese on the eve of World War II.* Singapore: Select Books.

Shu, J., and L. Hawthorne. 1996. "Asian student migration to Australia." *International Migration* 24 (1): 65–96.

Shu, J., and S. E. Khoo. 1993. *Australia's population trends and prospects 1992.* Canberra: AGPS.

Skeldon, R. 1994. "Turning points in labor migration: The case of Hong Kong." *Asian and Pacific Migration Journal* 3 (1): 93–118.

Spaan, E. 1994. "*Taikongs* and *Calos*: The role of middlemen and brokers in Javanese international migration." *International Migration Review* 28 (1): 93–113.

Stahl, C. W. 1995. "Trends of international labor migration: An overview." *Asian and Pacific Migration Journal* 4 (2–3): 211–232.

Stahl, C. W., and PECC-HRD Task Force. 1996. "International labor migration and the East Asian APEC/PECC Economies: Trends, issues and policies." Paper presented at PECC Human Resource Development Task Force Meeting, Brunei (June 7–8).

Stephan, K., and F. Keenan. 1997. "Handover leftover." *Far Eastern Economic Review* (June 19): 17–20 .

Stern, A. 1996. "Thailand's illegal labor migrants." *Asian Migrant* 9 (4): 100–103.

Sullivan, G., and S. Gunaskeran. 1993. "The role of ethnic relations and education systems in migration from Southeast Asia to Australia." *Sojourn* 8 (2): 219–249.

Thuno, M. 1996. "Origins and causes of emigration from Qingtian and Wenzhou to Europe." Paper presented at Conference on European Chinese and Chinese Domestic Migrants, Oxford (July 3–7).

Tiglao, R. 1996. "Newborn tiger." *Far Eastern Economic Review* (October 24): 66.

Tran, M., 1990. "Brains behind the U.S. — brought from abroad." *Guardian Weekly* (December 30).

United Nations. 1994. *The sex and age distribution of the world populations.* New York: United Nations.

United Nations Educational Scientific and Cultural Organization. 1995. *Statistical yearbook 1995.* Paris: UNESCO.

United Nations Economic Commission for Europe. 1994. *International Migration Bulletin* 4. Geneva: United Nations.

Vasuprasat, P. 1994. "Turning points in international labor migration: A case study of

Thailand." *Asian and Pacific Migration Journal* 3 (1): 93–118.

Wong, D. 1996. "Foreign domestic workers in Singapore." In *Asian women in migration,* ed. G. Battistella and A. Paganoni, 87–108. Quezon City, Philippines: Scalabrini Migration Center.

World Bank. 1996. *World development report.* New York: Oxford Univ. Press.

11. Emigration Pressures in Selected Asian Countries: Some Preliminary Findings
Manolo Abella

Amjad, R. 1996. "Philippines and Indonesia: On the way to a migration transition?" Paper presented at Conference on the Dynamics of Labor Migration in Asia, Nihon University (March); *Asian and Pacific Migration Journal* 5 (2–3).

Bohning,W. R., and M. L. Schloeter-Paredes. 1994. *Aid in place of migration.* Geneva: ILO.

Bohning, W. R., P. V. Schaeffer, and Th. Straubhaar. 1991. "Migration pressure: What is it? What can one do about it?" WEP *Working Paper* (October). Geneva: ILO.

Bruni, M., and Venturini. 1992. "Pressure to migrate and propensity to migrate: The case of the Mediterranean Basin." WEP *Working Paper* (January). Geneva: ILO.

Chen, Zhongsheng. 1994. *Income distribution in economic development under public ownership.* Shanghai: Shanghai People's Press.

David, C. 1992. "Philippine agriculture: The difficult path to recovery." *Philippine Economic Journal* 31 (72) Nos. 1&2.

Huang, Yiping. 1996. "Economic reform and emigration pressures in China." Draft report (April). Bangkok: ILO.

Hugo, G. 1996. "Economic impacts of international labor emigration on local development: Some evidence from Indonesia." Paper presented at Annual Meeting of the Population Association of America, New Orleans (May).

——. 1992. "Migration and rural-urban linkages in the ESCAP region." *Migration and urbanization in Asia and the Pacific: Interrelationships with socio-economic development and evolving policy issues.* ESCAP Asian Population Studies series No. 111. Bangkok.

Jayme, R. 1979. "A study on the effects of temporary worker flows from the Philippines." MA thesis, Univ. of the Philippines.

Nayyar, Deepak. 1996. "Emigration pressures and structural change in Indonesia." Draft report (April). Manila: ILO.

Nguyen, D. T., and J. S. Bandara. 1996. "Emigration pressures and structural change in Vietnam." Draft report (September). Bangkok: ILO.

Saith, Ashwani. 1996. "Emigration pressures and structural change in the Philippines." Draft report (April). Manila: ILO.

Schiller, G. 1992. "Reducing emigration pressure in Turkey: Analysis and suggestions for external aid." WEP *Working Paper* (March). Geneva: ILO.

Skeldon, Ronald. 1992. "The relationship between migration and development in the ESCAP Region." In *Migration and urbanization in Asia and the Pacific: Interrelationships with socio-economic development and evolving policy issues.* ESCAP Asian Population Studies Series No. 111. Bangkok.

Wakabayashi, K. 1990. "Migration from rural to urban areas in China." *The Developing*

Economies 28 (4) (December).

Xiushi Yang. 1992. "Temporary migration and its frequency from urban households in China." *Asia-Pacific Population Journal* 7 (1): 44.

Zeng Yi, and J. Vaupel. 1989. "The impact of urbanization and delayed childbearing on population growth and aging in China." *Population and Development Review* 15 (3) (Sept.).

12. From Multiculturalism to Diaspora: Changing Identities in the Context of Asian Migration   Ronald Skeldon

Anderson, B. 1991. *Imagined communities: Reflections on the origin and spread of nationalism.* 2d ed. London: Verso.

Baines, D. 1991. *Emigration from Europe 1815–1930.* London: Macmillan.

Barbara, A. 1994. "Mixed marriages: Some key questions." *International Migration* 32 (4): 571–84.

Beaujot, R., and J. P. Rappak. 1989. "The link between immigration and emigration in Canada, 1945–1986." *Canadian Studies in Population* 16 (2): 201–16.

Castles, S. 1992. "The challenge of multiculturalism: Global changes and Australian experiences." *Working Papers on Multiculturalism* 19.

Chan, K. B., and C. K. Tong. 1993. "Rethinking assimilation and ethnicity: The Chinese in Thailand." *International Migration Review* 27 (1): 140–68.

Chan, S. 1990. "European and Asian immigration into the United States in comparative perspective, 1820s to 1920s." In *Immigration reconsidered: History, sociology and politics,* ed. V. Yans-McLaughlin, 37–75. New York: Oxford Univ. Press.

Ch'ng, D. C. L. 1993. *The Overseas Chinese entrepreneurs in East Asia: Background, business practices and international networks.* Melbourne: Committee for Economic Development Australia.

Clarke, C., C. Peach, and S. Vertovec. 1990. "Introduction: Themes in the study of the South Asian diaspora." In *South Asians: Overseas migration and ethnicity,* ed. Clarke C., C. Peach, and S. Vertovec, 1–29. Cambridge: Cambridge Univ. Press.

Clifford, J. 1992. "Traveling cultures." *Cultural Studies,* ed. L. Grossberg, C. Nelson, P. A. Treichler, with L. Bangham, and J. Macgregor, 96–116. New York: Routledge

——. 1994. "Diasporas." *Current Anthropology* 9 (3): 302–38.

Cohen, A. 1971. "Cultural strategies in the organization of trading diasporas." In *The development of indigenous trade and markets in West Africa,* ed. C. Meillassoux, 266–81. International African Institute, Oxford Univ. Press.

Cohen, R. 1996. "Diasporas and the nation state." *International Affairs* 72 (3): 507–20.

——. 1997. *Global diasporas: An introduction.* London: UCL Press.

Cornelius, W., P. L. Martin, and J. F. Hollifield, eds. 1994. *Controlling immigration: A global perspective.* Stanford: Stanford Univ. Press.

Fields, G. S. 1994. "The migration transition in Asia." *Asian and Pacific Migration Journal* 28 (1):7–30.

Frey, W. H. 1995. "Immigration and internal migration 'flight' from U.S. metropolitan areas: Toward a new demographic balkanization." *Urban Studies* 32 (4/5): 733–57.

——. 1996. "Immigration, domestic migration, and demographic balkanization in America: New evidence for the 1990s." *Population and Development Review* 22 (4):

741–63.

Glazer, N. 1997. *We are all multiculturalists now*. Cambridge: Harvard Univ. Press.

Hawkins, F. 1989. *Critical years in immigration: Canada and Australia compared*. Kingston and Montréal: McGill-Queen's Univ.Press.

Hugo, G. 1994. *The economic implications of emigration from Australia*. Canberra: Bureau of Immigration and Population Research, Australian Government Publishing Service.

Jupp, J. 1995. "From 'white Australia' to 'part of Asia': Recent shifts in Australian immigration policy towards the region." *International Migration Review* 29 (1): 207–28.

Kotkin, J. 1992. *Tribes: How race, religion and identity determine success in the new global economy*. New York: Random House.

Landon, K. P. 1941. *The Chinese in Thailand*. London: Oxford Univ. Press.

Nugent, W. 1992. *Crossings: The great transatlantic migrations, 1870–1914*. Bloomington: Indiana Univ. Press.

Ohmae, K. 1995. *The end of the nation state: The rise of regional economies*. New York: The Free Press.

Pe-Pua, R., C. Mitchell, R. Iredale, and S. Castles. 1996. *Astronaut families and parachute children: The cycle of migration between Hong Kong and Australia*. Canberra: Bureau of Immigration Multicultural and Population Research, Australian Government Publication Service.

Portes, A., ed. 1994. "The new second generation." *International Migration Review* 28 (4) (Special issue).

Poston, D. L., X. Mao, and M-Y. Yu.1994. "The global distribution of the overseas Chinese around 1990." *Population and Development Review* 20 (3): 631–45.

Purcell, V. 1965. *The Chinese in Southeast Asia*. 2d ed. Oxford: Oxford Univ. Press.

Roy, P., and I. Hamilton. 1997. "Interethnic marriage: Identifying the second generation in Australia." *International Migration Review* 31 (1): 128–42.

Skeldon, Ronald. 1997a. "Migrants on a global stage: The Chinese." In *Integration and globalization in the Asia-Pacific economy*, ed. P. Rimmer, 222–39. St Leonard's, NSW: Allen and Unwin.

——. 1997b. *Migration and development: A global perspective*. London: Longman.

——. 1995. "Singapore as a potential destination for Hong Kong emigrants before 1997." In *Crossing borders: Transmigration in Asia*, ed. O.J. Hui, C. K. Chan, and C. S. Beng, 223–38. Singapore: Prentice Hall.

——. 1994a. "East Asian migration and the changing world order." In *Population migration and the changing world order*, ed. W. T. S. Gould and A. M. Findlay, 173–93. London: Wiley.

——, ed. 1994b. *Reluctant exiles? Migration from Hong Kong and the new overseas Chinese*. New York: M. E. Sharpe; Hong Kong: Hong Kong Univ. Press.

Teitelbaum, M. S., and M. Weiner, eds. 1995. *Threatened peoples, threatened borders: World migration and U.S. policy*. New York: Norton.

Troper, H. 1993. "Canada's immigration policy since 1945." *International Journal* 48 (2): 255–81.

Vasta, E., and S. Castles, eds. 1996. *The teeth are smiling: The persistence of racism in multicultural Australia*. St Leonard's NSW: Allen and Unwin.

Wasserstein, B. 1996. *Vanishing diaspora: The Jews in Europe since 1945*. London: Penguin

Books.

Weiner, M., ed. 1993. *International migration and security*. Boulder: Westview.

Yap, Y. M. 1991. "Singaporeans overseas: A study of emigrants in Australia and Canada." IPS *report series, report No.* 3. Singapore: The Institute of Policy Studies.

13. Asian Immigration, Public Attitudes and Immigration Policy: Patterns and Responses in New Zealand Andrew Trlin, Anne Henderson and Regina Pernice

Bedford, R. 1996. "International migration, 1995: Some reflections on an exceptional year." *New Zealand Journal of Geography* 101: 21–33.

Birch, B. 1991. "General category 'the key instrument.'"Media release (November 5). Wellington: Office of the Minister of Immigration.

Boswell, S. J. 1995. "An ethnogeography of Japanese immigrants in Auckland." In *An Ethno-Geography of Taiwanese, Japanese and Filipino immigrants in Auckland* (Occasional paper 28: 89–147), ed. H-k. Yoon. Auckland: Department of Geography, Univ. of Auckland.

Boyer, T. M. 1996. "Problems in paradise: Taiwanese immigrants to Auckland, New Zealand." *Asia Pacific Viewpoint* 37 (1): 59–79.

——. 1995. "Home sweet home? An analysis of Taiwanese immigration since 1986, and the present status of the Taiwanese community in Auckland." In *An Ethno-Geography of Taiwanese, Japanese and Filipino immigrants in Auckland* (Occasional paper 28:19–88), ed. H-k. Yoon . Auckland: Department of Geography, Univ. of Auckland.

Burke, K. 1986. *Review of immigration policy, August 1986*. Appendix to the Journals of the House of Representatives, G.42. Wellington: Government Printer.

Cremer, R. D., and B. Ramasamy. 1996. *Tigers in New Zealand? The role of Asian investment in the economy*. Wellington: Institute of Policy Studies, Victoria University of Wellington

Department of Internal Affairs. 1996. *High hopes: A survey of qualifications, training and employment issues for recent immigrants in New Zealand*. Ethnic Affairs Information Series No. 2. Wellington: Department of Internal Affairs.

Enterprise Auckland. 1996. *Asian immigrants: Economic and social survey*. Auckland: Enterprise Auckland, Auckland City Marketing.

Graves, T. D., and N. B. Graves. 1974. *New Zealanders' images of themselves and of immigrant groups*. Research Report No. 4. Auckland: South Pacific Research Institute Inc.

Hunt, G. 1995a. "Xenophobia alive and well in New Zealand." *The National Business Review* (October 27): 12.

——. 1995b. "Most New Zealanders say we're not part of Asia." *The National Business Review* (November 3): 10.

——. 1995c. "Kiwis want foreign ownership of land banned." *The National Business Review* (May 26): 10.

——. 1996a. "Public says no to Asians, Islanders." *The National Business Review* (Sept. 13): 16.

——. 1996b. "Xenophobia fades despite NZ First campaign." *The National Business Review* (April 19): 14.

Kasper, W. 1990. *Populate or languish? Rethinking New Zealand's immigration policy*. Wellington: New Zealand Business Roundtable.

Kerr, R. 1995. "Long-term immigration benefits." *The Dominion* (August 3): 10.

Lidgard, J. M. 1996. *East Asian migration to Aotearoa/New Zealand: Perspectives of some new arrivals.* Population Studies Centre Discussion Papers No. 12. Hamilton: Univ. of Waikato.

McCreary, J. R., et al. 1952. *The modification of international attitudes: A New Zealand study.* Psychology Publications No. 2. Wellington: Victoria Univ. of Wellington.

McKinnon, D. 1996. "Human rights, sovereignty and migration." *New Zealand Foreign Affairs and Trade Record* 5 (1): 9–12.

McLauchlan, M. 1991. "Far eastern suburbs." *Metro* 125 (November): 114–124.

National Research Bureau (NRB). 1994. *International orientation survey.* Auckland: NRB Ltd.

——. 1995. *International orientation survey.* 1995. Auckland: NRB Ltd.

New Zealand Immigration Service (NZIS). 1996. *Immigration fact pack* 4 (February). Wellington: NZIS.

——. 1995a. *Background paper: A review of New Zealand's residence policies: The 'targeted' immigration streams.* Wellington: NZIS.

——. 1995b. *New Zealand's 'targeted' immigration policies: Summary of October 1995 policy changes* (July). Wellington: NZIS.

——. 1991a. *New Zealand's immigration policy.* Wellington: NZIS.

——. 1991b. *A guide to applying for residence in New Zealand under the general category.* Wellington: NZIS.

Ninness, G. 1996. "Asians set to become NZ's top investors." *Sunday Star Times* (March 24): D1.

Owen, C. A., et al. 1981. "A half-century of social distance research: National replication of the Bogardus studies." *Sociology and Social Research* 66 (1): 80–98.

Phillips, K. 1994. "Can't even say 'hello.'" *Vista* 3: 18–19.

Poot, J., et al. 1988. *International migration and the New Zealand economy: A long-run perspective.* Wellington: Victoria Univ. Press for the Institute of Policy Studies.

Tarling, N. 1994. "New Zealand, Asia 2000 and beyond." *New Zealand International Review* 19 (3): 20–22.

Trlin, A. D. 1997. "For the promotion of economic growth and prosperity: New Zealand's immigration policy, 1991–1995." In *New Zealand and international migration: A digest and bibliography* No. 3, ed. A. D. Trlin and P. Spoonley, 1–27. Palmerston North: Department of Sociology, Massey Univ.

——. 1984. "Changing ethnic residential distribution and segregation in Auckland." In *Tauiwi: Racism and ethnicity in New Zealand,* ed. Spoonley, P., et al., 172–198. Palmerston North: Dunmore Press.

——. 1971. "Social distance and assimilation orientation: A survey of attitudes towards immigrants in New Zealand." *Pacific Viewpoint* 12 (2): 141–162.

Trlin, A. D., and J. Kang. 1992. "The business immigration policy and the characteristics of approved Hong Kong and Taiwanese applicants, 1986–1988." In *New Zealand and international migration: A digest and bibliography,* No. 2, ed. A. D. Trlin and P. Spoonley, 48–64. Palmerston North: Department of Sociology, Massey Univ.

Vaughan, G. M. 1962. "The social distance attitudes of New Zealand students towards Maoris and fifteen other national groups." *Journal of Social Psychology* 57: 85–92.

Wilson, W. M., et al. 1991. *Report of the working party on immigration*. Wellington: GP Print Ltd.

Wong, K. K. 1990. "Chinese business migrants — their effect on the property market." *New Zealand Real Estate* 41 (4): 21–26.

Yarwood, V. 1993. "Why Asians expand our economic horizons." *Management* 40 (4): 34–41.

14. "Australian Identity," Racism and Recent Responses to Asian Immigration to Australia *Gavin W. Jones*

Betts, Katharine. 1988. *Ideology and immigration: Australia 1976 to 1987*. Melbourne: Melbourne Univ. Press.

——. 1996. "Immigration and public opinion in Australia." *People and Place* 4 (3): 9–20.

Birrell, Bob. 1995. "Immigration and the surplus of doctors in Australia." *People and Place* 3 (3).

Blainey, G. 1984. *All for Australia*. Sydney: Methuen Haynes.

Choi, C. Y. 1975. *Chinese migration and settlement in Australia*. Sydney: Sydney Univ. Press.

Clyne, Michael, and Sandra Kipp. 1995. "The extent of community language maintenance in Australia." *People and Place* 3 (4): 4–8.

Cochrane, Peter. 1997. "Race memory." *The Australian's review of books*. N.p.

Dobson, Ian, Bob Birrell, and Virginia Rapson. 1996. "The participation of non-English-speaking-background persons in higher education." *People and Place* 4 (1): 46–54.

Evans, M. D. R. 1996. "Attitudes towards immigrants in Australia: Evidence from the ISSS/A." Paper presented at Immigration and Australia's Population in the 21st Century Workshop, Research School of Social Sciences, Australian National University (May 20–21).

Goot, Murray. 1993. "Multiculturalists, monoculturalists, and the many in between: Attitudes to cultural diversity and their correlates." *Australian and New Zealand Journal of Sociology* 29 (2): 226–253.

——. 1991. "Public opinion as paradox: Australian attitudes to the rate of immigration and the rate of Asian immigration, 1984–1990." *International Journal of Public Opinion Research* 3 (3): 277–294.

Hancock, W. K. 1930. *Australia*. London. N.p.

Holton, Robert. "Social aspects of immigration." In *Australian immigration: A survey of the issues*, ed. Mark Wooden et al. Canberra: Australian Government Publishing Service.

Human Rights and Equal Opportunity Commission. 1991. *Racist violence: Report of the National Enquiry into Racist Violence in Australia*. Canberra: Australian Government Publishing Service.

Jakubowicz, Andrew. 1996–97. "Fear and loathing in Ipswich: Exploring mainstream and a branch in the race debate." *Australian Rationalist* 42 (Summer).

Jones, Gavin W., ed. 1996. *Australia in its Asian context*. Occasional Paper Series 1. Canberra: Academy of the Social Sciences in Australia.

Jupp, James. 1996. *Understanding Australian multiculturalism*. Canberra: Australian Government Publishing Service.

——. 1995. "From 'white Australia' to 'part of Asia': Recent shifts in Australian immigration policy towards the region." *International Migration Review* 29 (Spring): 207–228.

———. 1991. "Multicultural public policy." In Price, ed.

———. 1988. *The Australian people*. Sydney: Angus and Robertson.

Karmel, Peter. 1997. "Opinion: Australia and the economic paradigm: 30 years of change." *Newsletter*, Academy of the Social Sciences in Australia 16 (1).

Khoo, Siew-Ean, and Charles A. Price. 1996. *Understanding Australia's ethnic composition*. Canberra: Department of Immigration and Multicultural Affairs.

London, H. I. 1970. *Non-white immigration and the "White Australia" policy*. New York: New York Univ. Press.

Markus, A. and M. C. Ricklefs, eds. 1985. *Surrender Australia? Essays in the study and uses of history: Geoffrey Blainey and Asian immigration*. Sydney: Allen and Unwin.

McQueen, Humphrey. 1970. *A New Britannia*. Hammondsworth: Penguin.

Millbank, Adrienne. 1996. "Asian Immigration." *Current Issues Brief* 16. Canberra: Parliamentary Research Service.

Parr, Nick, and Magdalena Mok. 1995. "Differences in the educational achievements, aspirations and values of birthplace groups in New South Wales." *People and Place* 3 (2).

Price, Charles A. 1996. *Immigration and ethnicity*. Canberra: Commonwealth Department of Immigration and Multicultural Affairs.

———. 1994. "Ethnic intermixture in Australia." *People and Place* 2 (4): 8–10.

———, ed. 1991. *Australian national identity*. Canberra: Academy of the Social Sciences in Australia.

———. 1974. *The great white walls are built: Restrictive immigration to North America and Australasia 1836–1888*. Canberra: Australian National Univ. Press.

Rivett, Kenneth, ed. 1962. *Immigration: Control or color bar?* Melbourne: Melbourne Univ. Press.

Shu, Jing et al. 1996. *Australia's population trends and prospects 1995*. Canberra: Australian Government Publishing Service.

Woolcott, Richard. 1997. "Advance Australia where?" *The Australian* (January 25–26).

Yarwood, A. T. 1964. *Asian migration to Australia: The background to exclusion 1896–1923*. N.p.

Zelinka, Sue. 1996. *Understanding racism in Australia*. Canberra: Australian Government Publishing Service.

Zubrzycki, Jerzy. 1991. "The evolution of multiculturalism." In Price, ed.

20. Globalization and International Migration in the Asia Pacific Region: Policy Implications *Terry McGee*

Castells, Manuel. 1996. *The rise of network society — the information age: Economy, society and culture* Vol. 1. Cambridge Massachusets: Blackwell.

Davis, Kingsley. 1974. "The migration of human populations." *Scientific American* 231 (3): 93–97.

Elkens, David. 1995. *Beyond sovereignty, territory and political economy in the Twenty-First Century*. Toronto: Univ. of Toronto Press.

Fitzgerald, Stephen. 1996. *Is Australia Asian?* N.p.

Kennedy, Paul. 1993. *Preparing for the Twenty-First Century*. Toronto: Harper-Collins

Publishers Ltd.

Kotkin, Joel. 1992. *Tribes: How race, religion and identity determine succession in the global economy.* New York: Random House.

McGee, T. G. 1978. "Rural-urban mobility in South and Southeast Asia: Different formulations, different answers." In *Human migration: Patterns and policies,* ed. William H. McNeill and Ruth S. Adam, 199–224. Bloomington and London: Indiana Univ. Press.

McGee, T. G., and Mathur Om Prakash. 1993. "Urbanization trends, patterns and impacts." Ch. 2 in *State of urbanization in Asia and the Pacific,* 2–66. New York: United Nations Economic and Social Commission for Asia and the Pacific 1993.

McNeill, William H. 1978. "Human migration: A historical overview." In *Human migration: Patterns and policies,* ed. William H. McNeill and Ruth S. Adam, 3–19. Bloomington and London: Indiana Univ. Press.

McNeill, William H. and Ruth S. Adams, eds. 1978. *Human migration: Patterns and policies.* Bloomington and London: Indiana Univ. Press.

Ohmae, Kenichi. 1995. *The end of the nation state, the rise of regional economies.* New York: The Free Press.

Bibliography

Abella, M. I. 1995. "Asian labor migration: Past, present and future." ASEAN *Economic Bulletin* 122: 25–138.

Abu-Laban, Yasmeen, and Daiva Stasiulis. 1992. "Ethnic pluralism under siege: Popular and partisan opposition to multiculturalism." In *Canadian Public Policy* 18 (4) (January): 381.

Adams, W. 1969. *The brain drain*. New York: Macmillan.

Agnew, Vijay. 1996. *Resisting women from Asia, Africa, and the Caribbean and the women's movement in Canada*, 35. Toronto. N.p.

Aislabee, C. J. Lee, and J. Stanton. 1994. *Australian cultural diversity and export growth*. Canberra: Office of Multicultural Affairs.

Amjad, R. 1996. "Philippines and Indonesia: On the way to a migration transition?" Paper presented at Conference on the Dynamics of Labor Migration in Asia, Nihon Univ. (March); *Asian and Pacific Migration Journal* 5 (2–3).

Anderson, B. 1991. *Imagined communities: Reflections on the origin and spread of nationalism*. 2d ed. London: Verso.

Anderson, K. 1991. *Vancouver's Chinatown: Racial discourse in Canada, 1875–1980*. Montréal: McGill-Queen's Univ. Press.

Angus Reid Group. 1991. *Multiculturalism and Canadians: National attitudes study 1991*. Angus Reid Group Inc.

——. 1989. *Immigration to Canada: Aspects of public opinion*. Winnipeg: Angus Reid Group Inc.

Arcellana, E.Y. 1995. "The Maga-Contemplacion case: Beyond forgetting." *The Manila Chronicle* (June 4).

Ariyawansa, D. M. 1989. *Report of the survey on changes in economic and social habits of expatriate labor for unskilled occupations*. Colombo: Friedrich-Ebert Foundation.

Arnold, F. 1989. "Unanswered questions about the immigration multiplier." *International Migration Review* 23: 889–92.

Athukorala, P. 1993. *Enhancing developmental impact of migrant remittances: A review of Asian experiences*. New Delhi: ILO/ARTEP.

Australian Bureau of Statistics (ABS). 1996. *Migration Australia, 1994–1995*. Catalogue No. 3412.0. Canberra: ABS.

——. n.d. *Overseas arrivals and departures*. Catalogue No. 3412.0. (various issues). Canberra: ABS.

Ayob Tamrin. 1988. *Pendatang Indonesia di kampung Baharu: Satu tinjauan latar belakang sosio-ekonomi*. Graduation exercise, Department of Anthropology and Sociology, Univ. of Malaya.

Azizah Kassim. 1997a. "Illegal alien labor in Malaysia: Its influx, utilization and ramifications." *Indonesia and the Malay world*, no. 71 (March): 50–82. London: Oxford Univ. Press.

——. 1997b. "International migration and its impact on Malaysia." Paper presented at ISIS 11th Asia-Pacific Roundtable, Hotel Istana, Kuala Lumpur (June 5–8).

——. 1997c. "International migration and alien labor employment in Southeast Asia: An insight from the Malaysian experience." Paper presented at conference on

India, Southeast Asia and the United States: New Opportunities for Understanding and Co-operation, Singapore (January 31–February 1).

———. 1996. "Alien workers in Malaysia: Critical issues, problems and constraints." In *Movement of people within and from Southeast Asian Countries; Trends, causes and consequences*, ed. M. F. Carunia, 3–6. Jakarta: Toyota Foundation and Southeast Asian Studies Program, Indonesian Institute of Sciences.

———. 1995a. "From neglect to legalization: The changing state response to the inflow of illegal labor into Malaysia." Paper presented at conference on Globalization: Local Challenges and Responses organized by the Malaysian Social Science Association, Penang (January).

———. 1995b. "Recruitment and employment of foreign workers in Malaysia." In *Dimensions of traditions and development in Malaysia*, ed. Rokiah Talib and C. B. Tan, 163–202. Kuala Lumpur: Pelanduk Publications.

———. 1994. "Malaysian illegal workers in Japan." In *Indonesia Circle*, no. 63 (June): 156–173. London: Oxford Univ. Press.

———. 1988. "Immigrant workers and the informal sector in West Malaysia: A case study of the Indonesian workers in Kuala Lumpur." In *Current issues in labor migration in Malaysia*, 232–254. Kuala Lumpur: NUPW and PSU, Faculty of Economics and Administration, Univ. of Malaya.

Backhouse, Constance. 1994. "White female help and Chinese-Canadian employers: Race, class, gender and law in the case of Yee . . ." *Canadian Ethnic Studies* 26 (34).

Badcock, B. 1995. "Building upon the foundations of gentrification: Inner-city housing development in Australia in the 1990s." *Urban Geography* 16: 70–90.

Baines, D. 1991. *Emigration from Europe 1815–1930*. London: Macmillan.

Barbara, A. 1994. "Mixed marriages: Some key questions." *International Migration* 32 (4): 571–84.

Barber, John. 1993. "Manning welcome to be first to leave." *The Globe and Mail*. (October 15).

Barnes, T., D. W. Edgington, and K. G. Denike. 1992. "Vancouver, the province, and the Pacific Rim." Ch. 6 in *Vancouver and its region*, ed. T. Oke and G. Wynn. Vancouver: UBC (Univ. of British Columbia) Press.

Baum, J. 1993. "Human wave." *Far Eastern Economic Review* (August 5).

Beaujot, Roderic, and J. P. Rappak. 1989. "The link between immigration and emigration in Canada, 1945–1986." *Canadian Studies in Population* 16 (2): 201–16.

Beaujot, Roderic, K. G. Basavarajappa, and Ravi Verma. 1988. *Income of immigrants in Canada: A census data analysis*. Ottawa: Statistics Canada.

Bedford, R. 1996. "International migration, 1995: Some reflections on an exceptional year." *New Zealand Journal of Geography* 101: 21–33.

Bedford, R., and J. Ligard. 1996. *International migration in the Asia-Pacific Region in the 1980s and 1990s: Two New Zealand perspectives*. Population Studies Centre Discussion Paper No. 19. Hamilton, New Zealand: Univ. of Waikato.

Beng, C. S. 1990. "Brain drain in Singapore: Issues and prospects." *Singapore Economic Review* 35 (2): 55–77.

Beng, C. S., and R. Chew. 1995. "Immigration and foreign labor in Singapore." ASEAN *Economic Bulletin* 12 (2): 191–200.

Bergman, Brian. 1993. "A nation of polite bigots?" *Maclean's* 106 (52): 42 (December 27).

Berita Harian. 1996. "Gaduh: Warga Bangladesh mati di tikam." (October 5).

Berry, J. W., and Rudolf Kaplin. 1993. "Multicultural and ethnic attitudes in Canada: An overview of the 1991 National Survey." Paper presented at Canadian Psychological Association Annual Meetings, Montréal (May).

Betts, Katharine. 1988. *Ideology and immigration: Australia 1976 to 1987*. Melbourne: Melbourne Univ. Press.

——. 1996. "Immigration and public opinion in Australia." *People and Place* 4 (3): 9–20.

Beyers, W. B. 1985. *The service economy: Export of services in the Central Puget Sound Region*. Seattle: Central Puget Sound Economic Development Department.

Bhadur A., and D. Nayyar. 1996. *The intelligent person's guide to liberalization*. New Delhi: Penguin Books India.

Bilsborrow, R. E., G. Hugo, A. S. Oberai, and H. Zlotnik. 1997. *International migration statistics: Guidelines for improving data collection systems*. Geneva: International Labor Office.

Birch, B. 1991. "General category 'the key instrument.'" Media release (November 5). Wellington: Office of the Minister of Immigration.

Birks, Sinclair, and Associates. 1992. GCC *market report* 1992. Durham, U.K.: Mountjoy Research Centre.

Birrell, Bob. 1995. "Immigration and the surplus of doctors in Australia." *People and Place* 3 (3).

Blainey, G. 1984. *All for Australia*. Sydney: Methuen Haynes.

Bohning, W. R., and M. L. Schloeter-Paredes. 1994. *Aid in place of migration*. Geneva: ILO.

Bohning, W. R., P. V. Schaeffer, and Th. Straubhaar. 1991. "Migration pressure: What is it? What can one do about it?" WEP *Working Paper* (October). Geneva: ILO.

Bolan, K. "Chinese first settled in B.C. 200 years ago, exhibit shows." *The Vancouver Sun* (September 27): B6.

Bolaria, B. Singh, and Peter S. Li. 1988a. "Capitalist expansion and immigrant labor: Chinese in Canada." Ch. 5 in *Racial oppression in Canada*, ed. Bolaria and Li. 2d ed. Toronto: Garamond Press.

——. 1988b. "Colonialism and labor: East Indians in Canada." Ch. 7 in *Racial Oppression in Canada*, ed. Bolaria and Li. 2d ed. Toronto: Garamond Press.

Bonnett, A. 1996. "Anti-racism: The critique of 'white' identities." *New Community* 22 (1): 97–110.

Boswell, S. J. 1995. "An ethno-geography of Japanese immigrants in Auckland." In *An ethno-geography of Taiwanese, Japanese and Filipino immigrants in Auckland* (Occasional paper 28: 89–147), ed. H-k. Yoon. Auckland: Department of Geography, Univ. of Auckland.

Boyer, T. M. 1996. "Problems in paradise: Taiwanese immigrants to Auckland, New Zealand." *Asia Pacific Viewpoint* 37 (1): 59–79.

——. 1995. "Home sweet home? An analysis of Taiwanese immigration since 1986, and the present status of the Taiwanese community in Auckland." In *An ethno-geography of Taiwanese, Japanese and Filipino immigrants in Auckland* (Occasional paper 28:19–88), ed. H-k. Yoon. Auckland: Department of Geography, Univ. of Auckland.

Bramham, D. 1996. "Taiwan cash pouring into Vancouver." *The Vancouver Sun* (March 14): D1 + D4.

Brandt, G. 1986. *The realization of anti-racist education*. London: Palmer Press.

Brillantes, Jose. 1997. "The Philippine overseas employment program and its effects on immigration to Canada." Ch. 9.

Breton, Raymond. 1989. "Collective dimensions of the cultural transformation of ethnic communities and the larger society." Paper presented at UNESCO Conference, Calgary.

———. 1985. "Multiculturalism and Canadian nation-building." In The Politics of gender, ethnicity and language in Canada, ed. Alan Cairns and Cynthia Williams, 27–66. Toronto: The Univ. of Toronto Press.

———. 1984. "The production and allocation of symbolic resources: An analysis of the linguistic and ethnocultural fields in Canada." Canadian Review of Sociology and Anthropology 21 (2): 123–144.

Brittan, Arthur, and Mary Maynard. 1985. Sexism, racism and oppression, 158. Oxford: Blackwell.

Brockett, L. 1996. "Thai sex workers in Sydney." MA thesis, Department of Geography, Univ. of Sydney.

Brosseau, M., P. Garvie, L. Chen, and A. Langlois. 1996. "Les mega-maisons de Kerrisdale, Vancouver: Chronique d'un quartier en transformation." Le Géographe Canadien 40: 164–72

Bruni, M., and Venturini. 1992. "Pressure to migrate and propensity to migrate: The case of the Mediterranean Basin." WEP Working Paper (January). Geneva: ILO.

Burke, K. 1986. Review of immigration policy, August 1986. Appendix to the Journals of the House of Representatives, G. 42. Wellington: Government Printer.

Business Times. 1995. "Council to discuss Bangladeshi issue." (October 5).

Cahill, D. 1990. Intermarriages in international contexts: A Study of Filipino women married to Australian, Japanese or Swiss men. Quezon City, Philippines: Scalabrini Migration Center.

Campbell, Charles. 1996. "Immigration policies show a rate of diminishing returns." The Vancouver Sun (November 25).

Canadian Council of Christians and Jews. 1993. Survey of Canadian attitudes towards ethnic and race relations in Canada. Toronto: Decima Research.

Canadian Ethnocultural Council. 1993a. "Prime Minister sending mixed message on multiculturalism." News release (November 8). Ottawa.

———. 1993b. "CEC urges new Prime Minister to affirm his government's support for multiculturalism." News release (October 28). Ottawa.

———. 1993c. "Ethnic leaders pleased with Liberal majority, but worried that multiculturalism will be sidelined in Parliament." News Release (October 26). Ottawa.

Cardozo, Andrew. 1993a. "PM delivered more talk than action on minorities." The Toronto Star (May 3).

———. 1993b. "The tory way: See no diversity hear no diversity." The Toronto Star (September 9).

———. 1993c. "Reform quietly setting agenda on immigration." The Toronto Star (October 5).

———. 1993d. "Minorities in a majority government." The Toronto Star (November 2).

———. n.d. "Chain reactionaries: How Reform Party policies on immigration and multiculturalism have influenced the Tory and other parties." Discussion paper, Draft 2. Council of Canadians and the Asian Canadian Caucus.

Cariño, B. V., 1987. "The Philippines and Southeast Asia: Historical roots and contemporary linkages." In *Pacific bridges: The new immigration from Asia and the Pacific islands*, ed. J. T. Fawcett and B. V. Cariño, 305–326. Staten Island, New York: Center for Migration Studies.

Castells, Manuel. 1996. *The rise of network society — the information age: Economy, society and culture* Vol. 1. Cambridge Massachusetts: Blackwell.

Castles, S. 1992. "The challenge of multiculturalism: Global changes and Australian experiences." *Working papers on multiculturalism* 19.

Castles, S., H. Booth, and P. Wallace. 1984. *Here for good: West Europe's ethnic minorities.* London: Pluto Press.

Castles, S., and M. J. Miller. 1994. "The age of international migration." *The Urban Age* 3.

Central Bank. 1970. *Annual report of the Central Bank of Sri Lanka.* Colombo: Central Bank.

Cernetig, M. 1995. "White flight, Chinese distress." *The Globe and Mail* (September 30).

Cernetig, M., and R. Williamson. 1996. "Vancouver feels impact of rising Asian influence." *The Globe and Mail* (January 9): A1 + A4.

Chan, K. B., and C. K. Tong. 1993. "Rethinking assimilation and ethnicity: The Chinese in Thailand." *International Migration Review* 27 (1): 140–68.

Chan, S. 1990. "European and Asian immigration into the United States in comparative perspective, 1820s to 1920s." In *Immigration reconsidered: History, sociology and politics*, ed. V. Yans-McLaughlin, 37–75. New York: Oxford Univ. Press.

Chen Chexian. 1963. "Popular outmigration of contract labor workers during the 19th century." *History Research* No. 1.

Chen Da. 1939. *Overseas Chinese in South-East Asia and society of Guangdong and Fujian provinces.* Shanghai: Business Affairs Publisher.

Chen, Zhongsheng. 1994. *Income distribution in economic development under public ownership.* Shanghai: Shanghai People's Press.

Chinese Media Index. n.d. DJC Research 1995. Chinese Media Index. N.p.

Ch'ng, D. C. L. 1993. *The Overseas Chinese entrepreneurs in East Asia: Background, business practices and international networks.* Melbourne: Committee for Economic Development Australia.

Choi, C. Y. 1975. *Chinese migration and settlement in Australia.* Sydney: Sydney Univ. Press.

Chow, Wyng. 1997. "Westside prices continue month-on-month slide." *The Vancouver Sun* (February 5): D1.

——.1996a. "Hong Kong still sees Vancouver as red-hot market for real estate." *The Vancouver Sun* (November 14): A1.

——.1996b. "Lower mainland real estate rides new influx of immigrants." *The Vancouver Sun* (August 23): D6.

——.1995a. *The Vancouver Sun* (April 23).

——. 1995b. "Engineering firm finding Asia market its goldmine." *The Vancouver Sun* (June 21): D1 and D4.

Citizenship and Immigration Canada. 1997a. *Citizenship and immigration statistics, 1994.* Catalogue No. MP22–1/1997. Ottawa: Minister of Public Works and Government Services Canada.

——. 1997b. News release (September 16).

——. 1996. *Staying the course, 1997 annual immigration plan*. Online. Available at http://cicnet.ingenia.com/english/pub/anrep97e.html#plan1

——. 1995. A *broader vision: Immigration plan* (1996 annual report to Parliament). Ottawa: Minister of Supply and Services.

——. 1994a. *Immigration consultations report*. Ottawa: Ministry of Supply and Services Canada.

——. 1994b. A *broader vision: Plan 1995–2000*. Ottawa: Supply and Services Canada.

City of Vancouver. 1995. *Vancouver Trends*. Vancouver: City Planning Department.

Clarke, C., C. Peach, and S. Vertovec. 1990. "Introduction: Themes in the study of the South Asian diaspora." In *South Asians: Overseas migration and ethnicity*, ed. Clarke, C., C. Peach, and S. Vertovec, 1–29. Cambridge: Cambridge Univ. Press.

Clifford, J. 1992. "Traveling cultures." In *Cultural studies*, ed. L. Grossberg, C. Nelson, P. A. Treichler, with L. Bangham, and J. Macgregor, 96–116. New York: Routledge

——. 1994. "Diasporas." *Current Anthropology* 9 (3): 302–38.

Clyne, Michael, and Sandra Kipp. 1995. "The extent of community language maintenance in Australia." *People and Place* 3 (4): 4–8.

Cochrane, Peter. 1997. "Race memory." *The Australian's review of books*. N.p.

Cohen, A. 1971. "Cultural strategies in the organization of trading diasporas." In *The development of indigenous trade and markets in West Africa*, ed. C. Meillassoux, 266–81. International African Institute, Oxford Univ. Press.

Cohen, Philip. 1996. "Hidden narratives in theories of racism." *'Race', culture and difference*, ed. James Donald and Ali Rattansi, 62–103,96. London: Sage.

Cohen, R. 1997. *Global diasporas: An introduction*. London: UCL Press.

——, ed. 1996a. *The Cambridge survey of world migration*. Cambridge, U.K.: Cambridge Univ. Press.

——. 1996b. "Diasporas and the nation state." *International Affairs* 72 (3): 507–20.

Connell, J., B. Dasgupta, R. Laishley, and M. Lipton. 1976. "Migration from rural areas: The evidence from village studies." Draft manuscript. Institute of Development Studies, Univ. of Sussex.

Cornelius, W., P. L. Martin, and J. F. Hollifield, eds. 1994. *Controlling immigration: A global perspective*. Stanford: Stanford Univ. Press.

Corriere Canadese. "Multiculturalism, I will clarify everything: There will be a true minister while immigration will not be attached to public security." (October 22).

Cremer, R. D., and B. Ramasamy. 1996. *Tigers in New Zealand? The role of Asian investment in the economy*. Wellington: Institute of Policy Studies, Victoria Univ. of Wellington.

Cross, M. 1990. "A magnet in Asia." *Far Eastern Economic Review* 66 (December 6).

Daniels, A. 1996. "Port acquires new Asia link." *The Vancouver Sun* (January 3): A-i.

——. 1993. "Tide turns in favor of shipowners: Hong Kong firms closer to moving staff, jobs here." *The Vancouver Sun* (March 12): D1.

Daniels, P. W. 1987. "Foreign banks and metropolitan development: A comparison of London and New York." *Tijdschrift voor economische en sociale geografy* 78: 269–287

David, C. 1992. "Philippine agriculture: The difficult path to recovery." *Philippine Economic Journal* 31 (72): Nos. 1 & 2.

Davis, H. C. 1976. *An inter-industry study of the metropolitan Vancouver economy*. Vancouver: Urban Land Economics Report No. 6, Faculty of Commerce and Business Administration, Univ. of British Columbia.

Davis, H. C., and M. A. Goldberg. 1988. "An empirical estimation of Vancouver's comparative economic advantages." School of Community and Regional Planning Paper No. 16. Vancouver: Univ. of British Columbia.

Davis, H. C., and T. A. Hutton. 1994. "Marketing Vancouver's services to the Asia Pacific." *The Canadian Geographer* 38: 18–28.

——. 1991. "An empirical analysis of producer service exports from the Vancouver Metropolitan Region." *Canadian Journal of Regional Science* 14: 375–394.

Davis, Kingsley. 1974. "The migration of human populations." *Scientific American* 231 (3): 93–97.

Dawkins, P., P. Lewis, K. Noris, M. Baker, F. Robertson, N. Groenewold, and A. Hagger. 1991. *Flows of immigrants to South Australia, Tasmania and Western Australia*. Canberra: Australian Government Publishing Service (AGPS).

Dawkins, P., S. Kemp, and H. Cabalu. 1995. *Trade and investment with East Asia in selected service industries: The role of immigrants*. Canberra: Bureau of Immigration, Multicultural and Population Research.

De Fontgalland, S.G. 1986. *Sri Lankans in exile: Tamils displaced*. Madras: Cerro Publications.

Department of Employment, Education, Training and Youth Affairs. 1996. *Selected higher education student statistics 1996*. Canberra: AGPS.

Department of Immigration and Ethnic Affairs (DIEA). 1994. *Overseas students in Australia, Fact Sheet 18*. Canberra: DIEA.

Department of Immigration and Multicultural Affairs. n.d. *Australian immigration consolidated statistics (various issues)*. Canberra: AGPS.

Department of Internal Affairs. 1996. *High hopes: A survey of qualifications, training and employment issues for recent immigrants in New Zealand*. Ethnic Affairs Information Series No. 2. Wellington: Department of Internal Affairs.

DeVoretz, D. Forthcoming. *Diminishing returns: Immigration policy in the 1990s*. Ottawa: C. D. Howe Institute.

Dias, M. 1986. "The community of out migration." In *Middle East interlude: Asian workers abroad — a comparative study of four communities*, ed. M. I. Abella and Y. Attal, 202–246. Bangkok: UNESCO Regional Office.

Diggs, B. J. 1974. *The state, justice and the common good*. Glenview: Scott Foresman and Company.

Dobson, Ian, Bob Birrell, and Virginia Rapson. 1996. "The participation of non-English-speaking-background persons in higher education." *People and Place* 4 (1): 46–54.

Dorall, R. F. 1989. "Issues and implications of recent illegal economic migration from the Malay world." In *Trade in domestic helpers: Causes, mechanisms and consequences* (Selected papers from the Planning Meeting on International Migration and Women). Kuala Lumpur: Asia Pacific Development Centre.

Do Rosario, L. 1995. "Futures and options." *Far Eastern Economic Review* (June 15).

Douglass, M. 1989. "The future of cities on the Pacific Rim." In *Pacific Rim cities in the world economy: Comparative urban and community research* 2: 9–67, ed. M. Smith. New Brunswick, NJ: Transaction Publishers.

Drennan, M. P. 1992. "Gateway cities: The metropolitan source of U.S. producer service exports." *Urban Studies* 29: 217–235.

Duncan, J., and N. Duncan. 1984. "A cultural analysis of urban residential landscapes in North America: The case of the Anglophile elite." In *The city in cultural context* eds. J. Agnew, J. Mercer, and D. Sopher, 255–76. Boston: Allen and Unwin.

Economic Council of Canada. 1991. *Economic and social impacts of immigration*. Ottawa: Supply and Services Canada.

———. 1991. *Report of the Economic Council of Canada*. Ottawa: Supply and Services Canada.

Edgington, D. W., and M. A. Goldberg. Forthcoming. "Vancouver: Canada's gateway to the Rim." Ch. 5 in *New cities of the Pacific Rim*, ed. E. J. Blakely and R. J. Stimson. Routledge.

Eelens, F., and J. D. Speckmann. 1990. "Recruitment of labor migration for the Middle East: The Sri Lankan case." *International Migration Review* 24: 297–322.

Elkens, David. 1995. *Beyond sovereignty, territory and political economy in the Twenty-First Century*. Toronto: Univ. of Toronto Press.

Elliot, Jean Leonard and Augie Fleras. 1992. *Unequal relations: An introduction to race and ethnic dynamics in Canada*. Scarborough: Prentice-Hall Canada, Inc.

Employment and Immigration Canada. 1995. Report to Parliament on the review of future directions for immigration levels.

———. 1992. *Managing immigration: A framework for the 1990s*. Ottawa: Employment and Immigration Canada.

———. 1989. *A guide to Canada's business immigration program*. Ottawa: Employment and Immigration Canada.

———. 1988. *Demographic considerations in determining future levels of immigration to Canada*. Report prepared for the Experts' Group Meeting on Demography and Migration, OECD, Paris (October 3–4).

Enterprise Auckland. 1996. *Asian immigrants: Economic and social survey*. Auckland: Enterprise Auckland, Auckland City Marketing.

Environics. 1988. *Focus Canada Survey*. N.p.

Equity. 1989. "Racism: Will it kill investment billions?" *Equity* 7: 20–35.

Evans, M. D. R. 1996. "Attitudes towards immigrants in Australia: Evidence from the ISSS/A." Paper presented at Immigration and Australia's Population in the 21st Century Workshop, Research School of Social Sciences, Australian National Univ. (May 20–21).

Exell, O. 1995. "B.C. businesses flex muscle in Asia." *Pacific Business* (October/November).

Fields, G. S. 1994. "The migration transition in Asia." *Asian and Pacific Migration Journal* 3 (1): 7–30.

Fitzgerald, Stephen. 1996. *Is Australia Asian?* N.p.

Fleras, Augie, and Jean Leonard Elliott. 1992. *The challenge of diversity: Multiculturalism in Canada*. Scarborough: Nelson Canada.

Fong, P. E. 1993. *Regionalization and labor flows in Pacific Asia*. Paris: OECD.

Bibliography

Foot, David K. 1986. *Population aging and immigration policy in Canada: Implications and prescriptions*. Ottawa: Policy and Program Development, Employment and Immigration Canada.

Fortney, J. 1972. "Immigrant professionals: A brief historical survey." *International Migration Review* 6 (1): 50–62.

Frey, W. H. 1995. "Immigration and internal migration 'flight' from U.S. metropolitan areas: Toward a new demographic balkanization." *Urban Studies* 32 (4/5): 733–57.

——. 1996. "Immigration, domestic migration, and demographic balkanization in America: New evidence for the 1990s." *Population and Development Review* 22 (4): 741–63.

Frobel, F., with J. Heinrichs and O. Kreye. 1980. *The new international division of labor*. New York and Cambridge: Cambridge Univ. Press.

Froese, Russ. 1997. Statement for UTV at the Symposium on Citizenship and Immigration, Vancouver (June).

Gardner, Dan. 1997. "Immigration ignored in election despite its impact on the future." *The Vancouver Sun* (June 1).

Ghosh, A. 1992. "Economic restructuring, employment and safety nets: A note." In *Social dimensions of structural adjustment in India*. New Delhi: ILO/ARTEP.

Glazer, N. 1997. *We are all multiculturalists now*. Cambridge: Harvard Univ. Press.

Globe and Mail.

1995. "DBRS rates Hong Kong Bank of Canada." Report on Business (November 14).

1993a. "Canadians want mosaic to melt, survey finds." (December 14): A1–2.

1993b. "Liberals turf out three Tory ad managers." (November 24): A3.

1993c. "Reform candidate says new immigrants are a burden." (October 15).

1993d. "Tories hunting flawed Reformers." (October 15).

1993e. "Women's minority groups called 'parasites' by Reform official." (October 29).

Goldberg, D. S. 1990. *The anatomy of racism*. Minneapolis: Univ. of Minnesota Press.

Goldberg, M. A., R. Helsley, and M. Levi. 1988. "Factors influencing the development of financial centres." Mimeograph. Vancouver: Faculty of Commerce and Business Administration, Univ. of British Columbia.

Goldberg, P. 1996. "International projections for migrant women as a human rights issue." In *Asian women in migration*, ed. G. Battistella and A. Paganoni, 165–182. Quezon City, Philippines: Scalabrini Migration Center.

Goldstein, C. 1994. "Innocents abroad." *Far Eastern Economic Review* (September 15): 22–27.

Gooneratne et al., eds. 1994. "Regional development impacts of labor migration in Asia." *UNCRD Research Report Series* No. 2. Nagoya, Japan.

Goot, Murray. 1991. "Public opinion as paradox: Australian attitudes to the rate of immigration and the rate of Asian immigration, 1984–1990." *International Journal of Public Opinion Research* 3 (3): 277–294.

——. 1993. "Multiculturalists, monoculturalists, and the many in between: Attitudes to cultural diversity and their correlates." *Australian and New Zealand Journal of Sociology* 29 (2): 226–253.

Goss, J., and B. Lindquist. 1995. "Conceptualizing international labor migration: A structuration perspective." *International Migration Review* 29 (2): 317–351.

Government of British Columbia. 1995. "Immigrant investment in British Columbia:

New partnerships for our economic future." N.p.

Government Press. 1974. *Report of the cabinet sub-committee inquiring into the problems of technologically, professionally and academically qualified personnel leaving Sri Lanka.* Sessional Paper 10. Colombo: The Government Press.

Government Printers. 1996. *Seventh Malaysia plan, 1996–2000.* Kuala Lumpur: Government Printers.

——. 1996. *Social Statistics Bulletin, Malaysia.* Kuala Lumpur: Government Printers.

——. 1993. *Social Statistics Bulletin, Malaysia.* Kuala Lumpur: Government Printers.

——. 1991. *General Report of the Population Census 1.* Kuala Lumpur: Government Printers.

——. 1989. *Social Statistics Bulletin, Malaysia.* Kuala Lumpur: Government Printers.

——. 1984. *Social Statistics Bulletin, Malaysia.* Kuala Lumpur: Government Printers.

Graves, T. D., and N.B. Graves. 1974. *New Zealanders' images of themselves and of immigrant groups.* Research Report No. 4. Auckland: South Pacific Research Institute Inc.

Greenberg, R. 1986. *No island is an island any more: International ramifications of the ethnic conflict in Sri Lanka,* (*mémoire*). Genève: Institut Universitaire De Hautes Etudes Internationales.

Gunasekaran, S. 1994. "Cross-national labor flows within ASEAN: Patterns and problems." In Gooneratne et al. eds., 45–56.

Habir M. 1984. "A migration equation." *Far Eastern Economic Review* (April 26): 116–172.

Hall, S. 1978. "Racism and reaction." In *Five Views of multi-racial Britain.* London: Macmillan.

Hancock, W. K. 1930. *Australia.* London. N.p.

Harian Metro. 1996. "Pindah Milik Tanah di disiasat." (March 23).

——. 1995. "120 Indo bersuami dua." (December 7).

Hatcher, Richard, and Barry Troyna. 1993. "Racialization and children." In *Race, identity and representation in education,* ed. Cameron McCarthy and Warren Crichlow. N.p.

Hawkins, Freda. 1989. *Critical years in immigration: Canada and Australia compared.* Kingston and Montréal: McGill-Queen's Univ. Press.

——. 1988. *Canada and immigration: Public policy and public concern.* 2d ed. Kingston and Montréal: McGill-Queen's Univ. Press.

——. 1972. *Canada and immigration: Public policy and public concern.* Montréal: McGill-Queen's Univ. Press.

Hayter, R., and T. Barnes. 1990. "Innis' staple theory, exports, and recession: British Columbia,1981–86." *Economic Geography* 66: 156–173.

Hennessey, M. 1986. "Racism and the dilemma of neighborhood change." Brief to City Council by Allied Builders.

Henry, Frances, and Carol Tator. 1994. "The ideology of racism — democratic racism." *Canadian Ethnic Studies* 26.

Henry, Frances, Carol Tator, Winston Mattis, and Tim Rees. 1995. *The color of democracy: Racism in Canadian society.* Toronto: Harcourt Brace and Company.

Hersh, B. D. (Westside Builders Association of B.C.). 1992. Letter to Council, Vancouver, B. C. (September).

Hicks, G. L., ed. 1993. *Overseas Chinese remittances from Southeast Asia, 1910–1940.* Singapore: Select Books.

Hiebert, D., D. F. Ley, and D. DeVoretz. 1995. "The Metropolis Project — immigration and integration in Vancouver." (Annex D, Introduction: Immigration and the Metropolis). Vancouver: Univ. of British Columbia and Simon Fraser Univ.

Hiebert, M. 1990. "Comrades go home." *Far Eastern Economic Review* 20 (May 17).

———. 1995. "Do not disturb." *Far Eastern Economic Review* 50 (August 24).

Ho, L., P. Liu, and K. Lam. 1991. "International labor migration: The case of Hong Kong." Paper presented at Second Japan-Asean Forum on International Labor Migration in East Asia, Tokyo, Japan (September 26–27).

Holton, Robert. "Social aspects of immigration." In *Australian immigration: A survey of the issues*, Mark Wooden et al. Canberra: AGPS.

Huang, Yiping. 1996. "Economic reform and emigration pressures in China." Draft report (April). Bangkok: ILO.

Hugo, G. Forthcoming. "The demographic underpinnings of current and future international migration in Asia." *Asian and Pacific Migration Journal*.

———. 1997a. "International migration in the Asia-Pacific Region: Emerging trends and issues." Paper prepared for the Conference on International Migration at Century's End: Trends and Issues, organized by the International Union for the Scientific Study of Population, Barcelona, Spain (May 7–10).

———. 1997b. "Migration and female empowerment." First draft of a paper prepared for International Union for the Scientific Study of Population's Committee on Gender and Population's Seminar on Female Empowerment and Demographic Processes: Moving beyond Cairo, Lund, Sweden (April 21–24).

———. 1996a. "Brain drain and student movements." In *International trade and migration in the APEC region*, ed. P. J. Lloyd and L. S. Williams, 210–228. Melbourne: Oxford Univ. Press.

———. 1996b. "Economic impacts of international labor emigration on regional and local development: Some evidence from Indonesia." Paper presented at Annual Meeting of the PAA, New Orleans (May).

———. 1996c. Remittances in Southeast Asia. Mimeo.

———. 1995. "Labor export from Indonesia: An overview." ASEAN *Economic Bulletin* 12 (2): 275–298.

———. 1994. *The economic implications of emigration from Australia*. Canberra: Bureau of Immigration and Population Research, AGPS.

———. 1993. "Indonesian labor migration to Malaysia: Trends and policy implications." *Southeast Asian Journal of Social Science* 21 (1): 37–70.

———. 1992. "Migration and rural-urban linkages in the ESCAP region." *Migration and urbanization in Asia and the Pacific: Interrelationships with socio-economic development and evolving policy issues*. ESCAP Asian Population Studies Series No. 111. Bangkok.

———. 1981. "Village community ties, village norms and ethnic and social networks: A review of evidence from the Third World." In *Migration decision making*, ed. G. De Jong and R. Gardner. New York: Pergamon Press.

———. 1975. "Population mobility in West Java, Indonesia." Ph.D. thesis, Department of Demography, Australian National Univ., Canberra.

Hugo, G. J., and M. Gartner. 1993. *Evaluation of the prototype survey first wave and some recommendations for the full survey*. Bureau of Immigration Research prototype survey for a Longitudinal Survey of Immigrants to Australia (LSIA) working paper series,

Working paper No. 7 (April).

Hugo, G. J., and A. Singhanetra-Renard. 1987. *International migration of contract labour in Asia — Major issues and implications.* Ottawa: IDRC.

Human Rights and Equal Opportunity Commission. 1991. *Racist violence: Report of the National Enquiry into Racist Violence in Australia.* Canberra: AGPS.

Hunt, G. 1996a. "Public says no to Asians, Islanders." *The National Business Review* (September 13): 16.

——. 1996b. "Xenophobia fades despite NZ First campaign." *The National Business Review* (April 19): 14.

——. 1995a. "Xenophobia alive and well in New Zealand." *The National Business Review* (October 27): 12.

——. 1995b. "Most New Zealanders say we're not part of Asia." *The National Business Review* (November 3): 10.

——. 1995c. "Kiwis want foreign ownership of land banned." *The National Business Review* (May 26): 10.

Iguchi, Y. 1997. "Labor market development and international migration in Japan." Paper presented at Workshop on International Migration and Labor market in Asia, Tokyo (January 30–31).

ILO Report. 1971. *Matching employment opportunities and expectations — A program of action for Ceylon.* Report of an inter-agency team organized by ILO. Geneva: ILO.

Immigration Canada. 1990. *Immigration to Canada: A statistical overview.* Ottawa-Hull: Employment and Immigration Canada.

Jackubowski, Lisa. 1994. *Immigration and the legalization of racism.* Ph.D. diss., Sociology. Toronto: York Univ.

Jacobsen, K. 1996. "Factors influencing the policy responses of the host governments to mass refugee influxes." *International Migration Review* 30 (3): 655–678

Jakubowicz, Andrew. 1996–97. "Fear and loathing in Ipswich: Exploring mainstream and a branch in the race debate." *Australian Rationalist* 42 (summer).

Jalan, B., ed. 1992. *The Indian economy: Problems and prospects.* New Delhi: Penguin Books.

Jayasankaran, S. 1997. "Blunt talk." *Far Eastern Economic Review* (April 10).

Jayme, R. 1979. "A study on the effects of temporary worker flows from the Philippines." MA thesis Univ. of the Philippines.

Jones, Gavin. 1997. "'Australian identity,' racism and recent responses to Asian immigration to Australia." Ch. 14.

——, ed. 1996. *Australia in its Asian context.* Occasional Paper Series 1/1996. Canberra: Academy of the Social Sciences in Australia.

Junipah Wandi. 1992. "Kegiatan sosio-ekonomi penghijrah Indonesia di kampung Kerinci." Graduation exercise, Department of Anthropology and Sociology, Univ. of Malaya.

——. 1995. "Pendatang Indonesia di Selangor: Proses penghijrahan dan Penyesuaian." MA thesis, Department of Anthropology and Sociology, Univ. of Malaya.

Jupp, James. 1996. *Understanding Australian multiculturalism.* Canberra: AGPS

——. 1995. "From 'white Australia' to 'part of Asia': Recent shifts in Australian immigration policy towards the region." *International Migration Review* 29 (1): 207–28.

——. 1991. "Multicultural public policy." In Price, ed.

——. 1988. *The Australian people*. Sydney: Angus and Robertson.

Kalbach, Madeline, and Warren Kalbach. 1995. "Ethnic diversity and persistence as factors in socio-economic inequality: A challenge for the twenty-first century." In *Proceedings of the 1995 Federation of Canadian Demographers symposium, Towards the XXIst Century: Emerging socio-demographic trends and policy issues in Canada*. Ottawa: St Paul Univ.

Kalin, Rudolf, and John W. Berry. 1991. "Ethnic and multicultural attitudes in Canada, outside Québec." Draft prepared for *State of the art review of research on Canada's multicultural society*. (September).

Karmel, Peter. 1997. "Opinion: Australia and the Economic Paradigm: 30 years of change." *Newsletter*, Academy of the Social Sciences in Australia 16 (1).

Karunathilake, H. N. S. 1987. *Sri Lanka, migration of talent: Causes and consequences of brain drain: Three studies from Asia*, 189–240. Bangkok: UNESCO Principal Regional Office for Asia and Pacific.

Kasper, W. 1990. *Populate or languish? Rethinking New Zealand's immigration policy*. Wellington: New Zealand Business Roundtable.

Kennedy, Paul. 1993. *Preparing for the Twenty-First Century*. Toronto: Harper-Collins Publishers Ltd.

Kerr, R. 1995. "Long-term immigration benefits." *The Dominion* (August 3): 10.

Khan, A. 1991. "International migration and the 'moral economy' of the 'Barani' peasantry." *Pakistan Development Review* 30 (4).

Khoo, Siew-Ean, and Charles A. Price. 1996. *Understanding Australia's ethnic composition*. Canberra: Department of Immigration and Multicultural Affairs.

Korale, R. B. M. 1984. *Middle East migration: The Sri Lankan experience*. Colombo: Employment and Manpower Division, Ministry of Plan Implementation.

Kotkin, Joel. 1992. *Tribes: How race, religion and identity determine success in the new global economy*. New York: Random House.

Kritz, M. M., and C. Caces.1989. *Science and technology transfers and migration flows*. Population and Development Program 1989 Working Paper Series 1.02. Ithaca: Cornell Univ.

Kritz, M. M., and H. Zlotnik. 1992. "Global interactions: Migration systems, processes and policies." In *International migration systems: A global approach*, ed. M.M. Kritz, L.L. Lim and H. Zlotnik , 1–18. Oxford: Clarendon Press.

Kunin, Roslyn, and Diana Lary. 1997. *Succeeding: Profiles of Chinese Canadian entrepreneurs*. Vancouver: Asia Pacific Foundation of Canada.

Kwong, K.1992. "Study shows brain drain on rise again." *Sunday Morning Post* (June).

Labour Migration. 1996. "Migrant labor exploitation: Does any one have the housemaid's welfare at heart?" *Economic Review* 1 (10): 14–20.

Lam, Lawrence. 1994. "Searching for a safe haven: The migration and settlement of Hong Kong Chinese immigrants in Toronto." In *Reluctant exiles? Migration from Hong Kong and the new overseas Chinese*, ed. Ronald Skeldon, 163–179. New York: Armonk.

Lamphier, G. 1992. "Vancouver's new power elite." *Financial Times of Canada* (June 1).

Landon, K. P. 1941. *The Chinese in Thailand*. London: Oxford Univ. Press.

Laquian, Eleanor. 1973. *A study of Filipino immigration to Canada, 1962–1972*. Ottawa: United Council of Filipino Associations in Canada.

Laurier Institute. 1989. "Fact sheet" (November).

——. 1989. "Press release: Laurier Institute releases findings of UBC study into Vancouver real estate prices." (November 15).

Lee, R. Mason. 1995. "One bad apple in Toronto costs the West millions in investment." *The Globe and Mail* (October 27): D4.

Lewis, P. E. T. 1994. "Singaporean entrepreneurs — The Australian connection." *Journal of Enterprising Culture* 2 (2): 709–733.

Ley, D. 1996. *The new middle class and the remaking of the central city.* Oxford: Oxford Univ. Press.

——. 1995. "Between Europe and Asia: The case of the missing sequoias." *Ecumene* 2: 185–210.

Ley, D., D. Hiebert, and G. Pratt. 1992. "Time to grow up? From urban village to world city, 1966–91." In *Vancouver and its region*, ed. G. Wynn and T. Oke, 234–66, Vancouver: UBC Press.

Ley, D. F., and T. A. Hutton. 1987. "Vancouver's corporate complex and producer services sector: Linkages and divergence within a provincial staple economy." *Regional Studies* 21: 413–424.

Li, Peter. 1994a. "A world apart: The multicultural world of visible minorities and the art world of Canada." *The Canadian Review of Sociology and Anthropology* 31 (4): 365–391.

——. 1994b. "Unneighborly houses or unwelcome Chinese: The social construction of race in the battle over 'monster homes' in Vancouver, Canada." *International Journal of Comparative Race and Ethnic Studies* 1: 14–33.

——. 1988. *The Chinese in Canada.* Toronto: Oxford Univ. Press.

Li, Zong. 1994. "Structural and cultural dimensions of racism: Towards an alternative perspective." *Canadian Ethnic Studies* 26.

Liang, Zai, and Abigail Mandel. 1997. "Market transition and emigration from China in the 1990s." Paper presented at 1997 Annual Meeting of Population Association of America, Washington, D.C. (March 27–29).

Liang, Zai, and Wenzhen Ye. 1997. "From Fujian to New York: Understanding the new Chinese immigration." Paper presented at conference on Transnational Communities and the Political Economy of New York in the 1990s, New School of Social Research, New York City (February 21–22).

Liberal Party of Canada. 1993. "Creating opportunity: The liberal plan for Canada." Ottawa (September).

Lidgard, J. M. 1996. *East Asian migration to Aotearoa/New Zealand: Perspectives of some new arrivals.* Population Studies Centre Discussion Papers No. 12. Hamilton: Univ. of Waikato.

Lim, L. L., 1994. *Growing economic interdependence and its implications for international migration in population distribution and migration.* Proceedings of the UN Expert Meeting on Population Distribution and Migration, Bolivia (January): 334–354.

Lim, L. L., and N. Oishi. 1996. "International migration of Asian women: Distinctive characteristics and policy concerns." In *Asian women in migration*, ed. G. Battistella and A. Paganoni, 23–54. Quezon City, Philippines: Scalabrini Migration Centre.

Lim, V. K. E., and S. Balachandran. 1997. "The impact of migrant workers on patterns of infectious diseases in Malaysia." Paper read at National Conference on Infection and Infection Control, Ipoh, Malaysia (March 14).

Ling, P. L. 1997. "Penghijrahan tenaga buruh Cina ke Singapura. Satu kajian kes di kampung Balai, Jerantut, Pahang." Graduation exercise, Department of Anthropology and Sociology, Univ. of Malaya.

Loke, S. Y. 1991. "Pekerja wanita Malaysia di sebuah kilang elektronik Singapura." Graduation exercise, Department of Anthropology and Sociology, Univ. of Malaya.

London, H. I. 1970. *Non-white immigration and the "White Australia" policy.* New York: New York Univ. Press.

Low, L., M. H. Toh, and T. W. Soon. 1991. Economics of education and manpower developments, issues and policies in Singapore. Singapore: McGraw-Hill.

Lowenthal, D., and H. Prince. 1965. "English landscape taste." *Geographical Review* 55: 186–222.

Lowrie, W. 1992. "Immigrants putting new face on nation." *The Vancouver Sun* (May 30): A1.

MacLeod, S., D. W. Edgington, and T. G. McGee. 1993. "Vancouver on the edge: Vancouver and the outside world." In *Vancouver and Yokohama, emerging cities in the Pacific Rim,* ed. T. G. McGee. Vancouver: Univ. of British Columbia; Yokohama: Yokohama City Univ.

Maher, C. 1994. "Housing prices and geographical scale: Australian cities in the 1980s." *Urban Studies* 31: 5–27.

Malaysian Employers Federation. 1996. *Report on the survey of labor shortage and manpower requirements in MEF member companies.* Kuala Lumpur: Malaysian Employers Federation. (June).

Mani, A. 1996. "Filipino migrant workers in Brunei Darussalam." *Philippine Sociological Review* 44 (1–4): 194–209.

———. 1995. "Migration in Brunei Darussalam." In *Crossing borders: Transmigration in Asia Pacific,* ed. J. H. Ong and S. B. Chew, 441–455. Singapore: Prentice Hall.

Markus, A., and M. C. Ricklefs, eds. 1985. *Surrender Australia? Essays in the study and uses of history: Geoffrey Blainey and Asian immigration.* Sydney: Allen and Unwin.

Marr, William L., and Pierre L. Siklos. 1994. "Immigration and unemployment." In *Diminishing returns: The economics of Canada's recent immigration policy,* ed. Don DeVoretz, 293–330. Ottawa: Renouf, for C.D. Howe Institute.

Massey, D., et al. "The evaluation of international migration theory: The North American case." *Population and Development Review* 20 (4): 699–752.

Martin, P. L. 1996. *Migrants on the move* (Asia-Pacific Issues No. 29). Honolulu: East-West Center.

———. 1994. Migration and trade: Challenges for the 1990s. *Work and family life of international migrant workers* 4 (3): 1–21.

———. 1993. *Trade and migration: NAFTA and agriculture.* Washington, D.C., Institute for International Economics.

Martin, P. L., A. Mason, and C. L. Tsay. 1995. "Overview." *ASEAN Economic Bulletin* 12 (2): 117–124.

Ma Xia. 1993. "On brain drain problems." *Population Research* No. 3.

Maye're, A., and F. Vinot. 1993. "Firm structures and production networks in intellectual services." In *The geography of services,* ed. P.W. Daniels et al. London: Frank Cass.

407

Bibliography

McCreary, J. R., et al. 1952. *The modification of international attitudes: A New Zealand study.* Psychology Publications No. 2. Wellington: Victoria Univ. of Wellington.

McGee, T. G. 1978. "Rural-urban mobility in South and Southeast Asia: Different formulations, different answers." In *Human migration: Patterns and policies,* ed. William H. McNeill and Ruth S. Adam, 199–224. Bloomington and London: Indiana Univ. Press.

McGee, T. G., and Mathur Om Prakash. 1993. "Urbanization trends, patterns and impacts." Ch. 2 in *State of urbanization in Asia and the Pacific,* 2–66. New York: United Nations Economic and Social Commission for Asia and the Pacific 1993.

McKinnon, D. 1996. "Human rights, sovereignty and migration." *New Zealand Foreign Affairs and Trade Record* 5(1): 9–12.

McLauchlan, M. 1991. "Far eastern suburbs." *Metro* 125 (November): 114–124.

McNeill, William H. 1978. "Human migration: A historical overview." In *Human migration: Patterns and policies,* ed. William H. McNeill and Ruth S. Adam, 3–19. Bloomington and London: Indiana Univ. Press.

McNeill, William H. and Ruth S. Adams, eds. 1978. *Human migration: Patterns and policies.* Bloomington and London: Indiana Univ. Press.

McQueen, Humphrey. 1970. *A New Britannia.* Hammondsworth: Penguin.

Millbank, Adrienne. 1996. "Asian Immigration." *Current Issues Brief* 16. Canberra: Parliamentary Research Service.

Ministry of Plan Implementation. 1985. *Foreign employment: Sri Lankan experience.* Colombo: Ministry of Plan Implementation.

Minocha, U. 1987. "South Asian immigrants: Trends and impacts on the sending and receiving societies." In *Pacific bridges: The new immigration from Asia and the Pacific Islands,* ed. J. T. Fawcett and B.V . Cariño, 347–374. Staten Island, New York: Center for Migration Studies.

Mitchell, K. 1996 "Visions of Vancouver: Ideology, democracy, and the future of urban development." *Urban Geography* 17: 478–501.

———. 1993. "Multiculturalism, or the united colors of capitalism?." *Antipode* 25: 263–94.

Moodley, Kogila. 1997. "The role of education in combating racism in Canada." Ch. 19.

———. 1983. "Multiculturalism as ideology." *Ethnic and Racial Studies.*

Morrison, Toni. 1989. "Unspeakeable things unspoken: The African-American presence in American Literature." *Michigan Quarterly* 28 (1): 1–34, 11.

Multiculturalism and Citizenship, Corporate Policy and Research. 1993a. *Selected charts* — 1986 *and* 1991 *census data.* (February 8).

———. 1993b. *Projection of Canada's* 1991 *people in* 2006. (October).

Multiculturalism and Citizenship Canada. 1993–94 *Estimates: Expenditure plan part* III.

———. 1991–92 *Estimates: Expenditure plan part* III.

———. 1990. *Public opinion research on multiculturalism and immigration: An overview.* Marjorie E. Lambert (January).

———. 1988. *Analysis of Thompson Lightstone Survey of public attitudes towards multiculturalism.* (April).

Mundle, S. 1992. "The employment effects of stabilisation and related policy changes in India, 1991–92 to 1993–94." In *Social dimensions of structural adjustment in India.* New Delhi: ILO/ARTEP.

Nash, A. 1996. "The economic impact of Canada's business immigration program: A critical reappraisal of theory and practice." Paper presented at Symposium on Immigration and Integration, Winnipeg (October).

National Research Bureau (NRB). 1994. *International orientation survey*. Auckland: NRB Ltd.

———. 1995. *International orientation survey*. Auckland: NRB Ltd.

Nayyar, Deepak. 1996. "Emigration pressures and structural change in Indonesia." Draft report (April). Manila: ILO.

New Democratic Party. 1995. "Multiculturalism, anti-racism, human rights." Vancouver: B.C. New Democrats Home Page.

Newland, K. 1993. "Ethnic conflict and refugees." *Survival* 35 (1): 81–101

New Straits Times

1997a. "Employers warned about replacing local workers." (February 1).

1997b. "Local staff who quit replaced with foreigners." (February 2).

1997c. "Foreign workers not encouraged to join unions." (February 19).

1997d. "Civil servants behind immigrant-smuggling syndicates held." (February 19).

1997e. "Proposal for cheaper way to repatriate illegals." (March 6).

1997f. "Immigration deploys 15 officers to clear backlog." (March 25).

1997g. "Alien workers sent home RM3b in '96." (April 25).

1995. "Immigration Chiefs under probe." (August 11).

New Zealand Immigration Service (NZIS). 1996. *Immigration fact pack* 4 (February). Wellington: NZIS.

———. 1995a. *Background paper: A review of New Zealand's residence policies: The 'targeted' immigration streams*. Wellington: NZIS.

———. 1995b. *New Zealand's 'targeted' immigration policies: Summary of October 1995 policy changes* (July). Wellington: NZIS.

———. 1991a. *New Zealand's immigration policy*. Wellington: NZIS.

———. 1991b. *A guide to applying for residence in New Zealand under the general category*. Wellington: NZIS.

Nguyen, D. T., and J. S. Bandara. 1996. "Emigration pressures and structural change in Vietnam." Draft report (September). Bangkok: ILO.

Ninness, G. 1996. "Asians set to become NZ's top investors" *Sunday Star Times* (March 24): D1.

Nugent, W. 1992. *Crossings: The great transatlantic migrations, 1870–1914*. Bloomington: Indiana Univ. Press.

Office of the Prime Minister of Canada. 1993a. *Release* (November 4).

———. 1993b. *Release* (June 25).

Ohmae, Kenichi. 1995. *The end of the nation state: The rise of regional economies*. New York: The Free Press.

Okunishi, Y., 1995. "Japan." *ASEAN Economic Bulletin* 12 (2): 139–162.

Olds, Kris. 1996. "Developing the Trans-Pacific property market: Tales from Vancouver via Hong Kong." *Working papers* No. 96–02. Vancouver: Centre of Excellence for Immigration Studies.

Ouston, R. 1996. "English now a minority language in Vancouver." *The Vancouver Sun* (November 2): A1.

Owen, C. A., et al. 1981. "A half-century of social distance research: National replication of the Bogardus studies." *Sociology and Social Research* 66 (1): 80–98.

Oziewicz, Estanislao. 1991. "Ottawa urged to slow immigration: Racism, unemployment will grow otherwise, study says." *The Globe and Mail* (February 21): A1.

Pacific Business. 1995. "Hong Kong Bank eyes Taiwanese cash in B.C. with new branches." (October/November): 14.

Palmer, Douglas L. 1994. *Anatomy of an attitude: Origins of the attitude toward the level of immigration to Canada.* Ottawa: Strategic Research, Analysis and Information, Policy Sector, Citizenship and Immigration Canada.

Pang, E. F. 1994. *Foreign workers in Singapore.* In Gooneratne et al. eds. 79–94.

Parr, Nick, and Magdalena Mok. 1995. "Differences in the educational achievements, aspirations and values of birthplace groups in New South Wales." *People and Place* 3 (2).

Pendatang Luar Negeri Di Sabah dan W.P. Labuan — Langkah–Langkah dan Penyelesaian. 1992. Pasukan Petugas Khas Persekutuan, Majlis Keselamatan Negara, Jabatan Perdana Menteri, Kota Kinabalu.

Pe-Pua, R., et al. 1996. *Astronaut families and parachute children: The cycle of migration between Hong Kong and Australia.* Canberra: AGPS.

Pernia, E. M. 1976. "The question of the brain drain from the Philippines." *International Migration Review* 10 (1): 63–72.

Pettit, B. 1992. "Zoning, the market and the single family landscape: Neighborhood change in Vancouver, Canada." Ph.D. diss., Univ. of British Columbia.

Phillips, K. 1994. "Can't even say 'Hello'." *Vista* 3: 18–19.

Picton, J. 1992. "Visible minority population soaring, study finds." *The Toronto Star* (May 30): A2.

Pieke, F. N. Forthcoming. Introduction. In *The Chinese in Europe*, ed. G. Beaton and F. N. Pieke. Basingstroke: Macmillan.

Pillai, P. 1992. *People on the Move.* ISIS Malaysia.

Pinar, William F. 1993. "Notes on understanding curriculum as a racial text." In *Race identity and representation in education*, ed. Cameron McCarthy and Warren Crichlow, 60–70, 68. New York: Routledge.

Plafker, T. 1995. "China fights brain drain." *International Herald Tribune* (April 24).

Pongsapich, A. 1995. *Recent trends in international migration in Asia.* Asian Population Studies Series No. 137. New York: United Nations.

Poot, J., et al. 1988. *International migration and the New Zealand economy: A long-run perspective.* Wellington: Victoria Univ. Press for the Institute of Policy Studies.

Population and Household Census of Malaysia. 1995. *State population report, Sabah,* 1991. Kuala Lumpur: Government Printers

Portes, A., ed. 1994. "The new second generation." *International Migration Review* 28 (4) (Special issue).

Poston, D. L., X. Mao, and M-Y. Yu.1994. "The global distribution of the overseas Chinese around 1990." *Population and Development Review* 20 (3): 631–45

Prasai, S.B., 1993. "Asia's labor pains." *Far Eastern Economic Review* (April 29).

Price, Charles A. 1996. *Immigration and ethnicity.* Canberra: Commonwealth Department of Immigration and Multicultural Affairs.

———. 1994. "Ethnic intermixture in Australia." *People and Place* 2 (4): 8–10.

———. ed. 1991. *Australian national identity.* Canberra: Academy of the Social Sciences in Australia.

———. 1974. *The great white walls are built: Restrictive immigration to North America and Australasia* 1836–1888. Canberra: Australian National Univ. Press.

Price Waterhouse. 1988. *Export market capabilities of the British Columbia environmental industry.* Vancouver: Asia Pacific Initiative.

Province of British Columbia. 1997a. B.C. *stats: Immigration highlights 96–4.* Victoria: Ministry of Finance and Corporate Relations.

———. 1997b. "Proposed new immigrant investor program." B.C. *stats: Immigration highlights 96–4.* Victoria: Ministry of Finance and Corporate Relations.

———. 1996. "Migration and housing demand." B.C. *stats.* Victoria: Ministry of Finance and Corporate Relations.

———. 1995. *Profile 1995: An analysis of immigration to British Columbia.* Victoria: Ministry Responsible for Multiculturalism and Immigration.

Purcell, V. 1965. *The Chinese in Southeast Asia.* 2d ed. Oxford: Oxford Univ. Press.

Puri, T. R. 1993. "Urban development: New towns around the Pacific Rim." Paper presented at Fifth Annual Conference of the Pacific Rim Council on Urban Development, San Francisco (October).

Qlan, W. 1996. "The features of international migration in China." Paper presented at conference on European Chinese and Chinese Domestic Migrants, Oxford (July 3–7).

Rallu, J. L. 1996. "Recent trends in international migration and economic development in the South Pacific." *Asia-Pacific Population Journal* 11 (2): 23–46.

Rashid, A. 1996. "Slippery slope." *Far Eastern Economic Review* (March 23): 23.

Ray, B., G. Halseth, and B. Johnson. 1997. "The changing face of the suburbs: Issues of ethnicity and residential change in suburban Vancouver." *International Journal of Urban and Regional Research* 21: 75–99.

Razali Ismail. 1996. "Pekerja Bangladesh dalam industri: Satu kajian kes di Tongkang Pechah, Batu Pahat, Johore Darul Ta'zim." Graduation exercise, Department of Anthropology and Sociology, Univ. of Malaya.

Real Estate Weekly. 1995. "Recent immigrants major players in market." (6 January): 1.

———. 1989. "Blame 'boomers' for boom." (November 24): 1.

Reform Party of Canada. 1989. *Platform and Statement of Principles.* June.

———. 1990. *Principles and Policies.*

Research and Documentation Centre for Manpower and Development (RDCM-YTKI). 1986. *The prospects of labor market in Saudi Arabia for Indonesian workers.* Jakarta: (RDCMD-YTKI) in cooperation with National Development Planning Agency (BAPPENAS).

Richmond, Anthony. 1988. *Immigration and ethnic conflict.* New York and Toronto: Macmillan.

———. 1994. *Global apartheid: Refugees, racism, and the New World Order.* Oxford: Oxford Univ. Press.

Rimmer, P. J. 1991. "Megacities, multilayered networks and development corridors in the Pacific Economic Zone." *Proceedings of the Third Annual Conference of the Pacific Rim Council on Urban Development.* Vancouver: CHS.

Bibliography

Rinehart, D. 1996. "ESL." *The Vancouver Sun* (November 2): D4–5.

Rivett, Kenneth, ed. 1962. *Immigration: Control or color bar?* Melbourne: Melbourne Univ. Press.

Rogge, J. R. 1993. "Refugee migration: Changing characteristics and prospects." Paper presented at Expert Group Meeting on Population Distribution and Migration, Santa Cruz, Bolivia (January 18–22).

Roy, P., and I. Hamilton. 1997. "Interethnic marriage: Identifying the second generation in Australia." *International Migration Review* 31 (1): 128–42.

Roy, Reginald H. 1996. *David Lam: A biography*. Vancouver: Douglas and McIntyre.

Ruhunage, L. K. 1996. "Sri Lankan labor migration: Trends and threats." *Economic Review* 21 (10): 3–7.

Russell, S. S. 1991. *Population and development in the Philippines: An update*. Washington, D.C.: The World Bank Asia Country Department II.

Russell, S. S., and M. S. Teitelbaum. 1992. *International migration and international trade*, World Bank Discussion Paper 160. Washington, D.C.: The World Bank.

Ryan, C. 1997. "Wanita Indonesia dalam sektor perkhidmatan: Satu kajian kes di Lembah Kelang." Graduation exercise, Department of Anthropology and Sociology, Univ. of Malaya.

Saith, Ashwani. 1997. "Structural change and migration pressures: Case study of the Philippines." *International Migration Papers*. Geneva: ILO

——. 1996. "Emigration pressures and structural change in the Philippines." Draft report (April). Manila: ILO.

Samuel, J. 1995. "Temporary and permanent labor migration into Canada: Selected aspects." In "The jobs and effects of migrant workers in North America," J. Samuel, P. L. Martin and J. E. Taylor. *International Migration Papers* 10. Geneva: ILO

Samuel, J., and M. Jansson. 1988. "Canada's immigration levels and the economic and demographic environment, 1967–1987." In *European Journal of International Migration and Ethnic Relations* 2 (87).

Samuel, T. John. 1990. "Third World immigration and multiculturalism." Ch. 20 in *Ethnic Demography*, ed. Shiva Halli, Frank Travato, and Leo Dreiger, 383–98. Ottawa: Carleton Univ. Press.

Sarick, Lila. 1995a. "Canada strives to woo upscale immigrants." *The Globe and Mail* (June 7): A1.

——. 1995b. "Increase in fees for immigrants called new 'Chinese head tax'." *The Globe and Mail* (March 1): A6.

Sassen-Koob, Saskia. 1983. "Labor migrations and the new international division of labor." In *Women, men and the international division of labor*, ed. June Nash and Maria Patricia Fernandez-Kelly. Albany: State Univ. of New York.

Sassen, S. 1994. "International migration and the post-industrial city." *The Urban Age* 3.

——. 1993. "Economic internationalization: The new migration in Japan and the United States." *International Migration Review* 31 (1): 73–102.

——. 1991. *The global city*. Princeton, NJ: Princeton Univ. Press.

Satzewich, Vic. 1991. *Racism and the incorporation of foreign labor: farm labor migration to Canada since 1945*. London: Routledge.

Saywell, T. 1997. "Workers' offensive." *Far Eastern Economic Review* (May 29): 50–52.

Sazaki, S. 1994. "Clandestine labor in Japan: Sources, magnitude and implications." In *Regional development impact of labor migration in Asia*, ed. Gooneratne et al., 151–162. Nagoya, Japan: United Nations Centre for Regional Development.

———. 1995. "Data on international migration in Japan." *Asian and Pacific Migration Journal* 4 (4): 565–577.

Schiller, G. 1992. "Reducing emigration pressure in Turkey: Analysis and suggestions for external aid." WEP *Working Paper* (March). Geneva: ILO.

Seagrave, S. 1995. *Lords of the Rim: The invisible empire of the overseas Chinese.* New York: G. P. Putnam's Sons.

Sha Jichai. 1995. "International migration and mobility." In *Studies on population problems during the process of economic reform and opening the door to the outside world*, ed. Sha Jichai and Chao Jinchun. Beijing: Peking Univ. Press.

Sha Jichai and Chao Jinchun, eds. 1995. *Studies on population problems during the process of economic reform and opening the door to the outside world.* Beijing: Peking Univ. Press.

Sherry, A., M. Lee, and M. Vatikiotis. 1995. "For lust or money." *Far Eastern Economic Review* (December 14): 22–23.

Shozo, F. 1995. *With sweat and abacus: Economic roles of Southeast Asian Chinese on the eve of World War II.* Singapore: Select Books.

Shu, J., and L. Hawthorne. 1996. "Asian student migration to Australia." *International Migration* 24 (1): 65–96.

Shu, J., and S. E. Khoo. 1993. *Australia's population trends and prospects 1992.* Canberra: AGPS.

Shu, Jing et al. 1996. *Australia's population trends and prospects 1995.* Canberra: AGPS.

Simmons, Alan. In press. "Racism and immigration policy." In *The racist imagination: The sociology of racism in canada*, ed. Vic Satzewich.

———. 1997. "Gobalization and backlash racism in the 1990s: The case of Asian immigration to Canada." Ch. 2.

———. 1994. "Canadian immigration policy in the early 1990s: A commentary on Veuglers and Klassen's analysis of the breakdown in the unemployment-immigration linkage." *Canadian Journal of Sociology* 19 (4): 525–34.

Simmons, Alan, and Dwaine Plaza. 1995. "Breaking through the glass ceiling: The pursuit of university training among Afro-Caribbean migrants and their children in Toronto." Learned Societies Meetings.

Sivarajah, A. n.d. "Internationalization of Sri Lankan ethnic conflict." *Ceylon studies seminar.* Univ. of Peradeniya.

Skeldon, Ronald. 1997a. "Migrants on a global stage: The Chinese." In *Integration and globalization in the Asia-Pacific economy*, ed. P. Rimmer, 222–39. St Leonard's, NSW: Allen and Unwin.

———. 1997b. *Migration and development: A global perspective.* London: Addison Wesley Longman.

———. 1996. "Migration from China." *Journal of International Affairs* 49 (2): 434–455.

———. 1995a. "Recent changes in migratory movements and policies in Hong Kong." *Asian and Pacific Migration Journal* 4 (4): 543–554.

——. 1995b. "Singapore as a potential destination for Hong Kong emigrants before 1997." In *Crossing borders: Transmigration in Asia*, ed. O. J. Hui, C. K. Chan, and C. S. Beng, 223–38. Singapore: Prentice Hall.

——. 1994a. East Asian migration and the changing world order. In *Population migration and the changing world order*, ed. W. T. S. Gould and A. M. Findlay, 173–93. London: Wiley.

——, ed. 1994b. *Reluctant exiles? Migration from Hong Kong and the new overseas Chinese.* New York: M. E. Sharpe; Hong Kong: Hong Kong Univ. Press.

——. 1994c. "Turning points in labor migration: The case of Hong Kong." *Asian and Pacific Migration Journal* 3 (1): 93–118.

——. 1992. "The relationship between migration and development in the ESCAP Region." In *Migration and urbanization in Asia and the Pacific: Interrelationships with socio-economic development and evolving policy issues.* ESCAP Asian Population Studies Series No. 111. Bangkok.

Smith, Dave. 1996. "UI used less by immigrants." *The Vancouver Sun* (September 10).

Smith, P.J. 1992. "The making of a global city: Fifty years of constituent diplomacy — the case of Vancouver." *Canadian Journal of Urban Research* 1 (1).

Solomon, R. Patrick, and Cynthia Levine-Rasky. 1994. "Accomodation and resistance: Educators' response to multicultural and anti-racist education." Report. (August).

South China Morning Post. 1992. "Vancouver planning law fuels racist fire." (October 4).

Spaan, E. 1994. "*Taikongs* and *Calos*: The role of middlemen and brokers in Javanese international migration." *International Migration Review* 28 (1): 93–113.

Stahl, C. W. 1995. "Trends of international labor migration: An overview." *Asian and Pacific Migration Journal* 4 (2–3): 211–232.

Stahl., C. W., and PECC-HRD Task Force. 1996. "International labor migration and the East Asian APEC/PECC Economies: Trends, issues and policies." Paper presented at PECC Human Resource Development Task Force Meeting, Brunei (June 7–8).

Stalker, P. 1994. *The work of strangers: A survey of international labor migration.* Geneva: ILO.

Star (Malaysia)

1997a. "One million illegals miss the boat under amnesty offer." (February 1).

1997b. "Sabah illegals may get a reprieve." (February 5).

1997c. "New policy on illegals in Sabah." (February 22).

1997d. "RM14 million spent on detained illegals." (February 25).

1997e. "Blitz on illegal professionals." (March 9).

1997f. "Scam to retrench local workers." (March 11).

1997g. "329 illegals married Orang Asli." (April 22).

1997h. "Prostitution among oil palm trees." (May 25).

1997i. "1.4 million Indons in Malaysia to vote." (May 29).

1996a. "Indon given the go-ahead on registration." (May 28).

1996b. "Illegal settlements in most districts." (June 5).

1996c. "Review over intake of Bangladeshis." (September 22).

1996d. "Police looking for trio over killing of Bangladeshi." (December 21).

1996e. "Ong: 33 gov't. servants held over issuance of fake ICs." (October 17).

Statistics Canada. 1993a. "Age and sex aboriginal data, 1991 Census of Canada." *The Daily* (Tuesday, June 1).

——. 1993b. "Mobility and migration, 1991 Census of Canada." *The Daily* (Tuesday, May 11).

——. 1993c. "Immigration and citizenship (the national series), 1991 Census of Canada." *The Daily* (Tuesday, March 30).

——. 1993d. "Home language and mother tongue knowledge of languages (the nation), 1991 Census of Canada." *The Daily* (Tuesday, January 12).

Stephan, K., and F. Keenan. 1997. "Handover leftover." *Far Eastern Economic Review* (June 19): 17–20.

Stern, A. 1996. "Thailand's illegal labor migrants." *Asian Migrant* 9 (4): 100–103.

Sullivan, G., and S. Gunaskeran. 1993. "The role of ethnic relations and education systems in migration from Southeast Asia to Australia." *Sojourn* 8 (2): 219–249.

Sun Malaysia. 1996. "Bangladeshi: We were assaulted while sleeping." (October 3).

Sunahara, Ann Gomer. 1981. *The politics of racism: The uprooting of Japanese Canadians during the Second World War.* Toronto: James Lorimer.

Tang, Angelica O. 1997. "A sensible immigrant policy in New York City." Ch. 15.

Tarling, N. 1994. "New Zealand, Asia 2000 and beyond." *New Zealand International Review* 19 (3): 20–22.

Tatla, D. S. 1996. "Sikh free and military migration during the colonial period." In *The Cambridge survey of world migration*, ed R. Cohen. Cambridge, U.K.: Cambridge Univ. Press.

Taylor, K. W. 1991. "Racism in Canadian immigration policy." *Canadian Ethnic Studies* 23 (1): 1.

Teitelbaum, M. S. and M. Weiner, eds. 1995. *Threatened peoples, threatened borders: World migration and U.S. policy.* New York: Norton.

Tepper, Elliot. 1994. "Immigration policy and multiculturalism." In *Multiculturalism in Canada: The research landscape*, ed. John Berry and Jean Laponce. Toronto: Univ. of Toronto Press.

——. 1991. "Facing the future." *Infoshare* I (February).

——. 1990a. "The future of Canadian cities." *Currents* 6 (October): 2.

——. 1990b. *Symbolism and pluralism in Canada.* Multiculturalism Department of the Secretary of State.

——. 1990c. "Ethnicity in Canada: Accessibility of research." Multiculturalism Canada, Secretary of State.

——. 1990d. "Race relations and the cities: Vancouver." Multiculturalism Canada, Secretary of State.

——. 1990e. "Race relations and the cities: Montréal." Multiculturalism Canada, Secretary of State.

——, co-ed., and contributor. 1989a. *Canada 2000: Race relations and public policy.* Univ. of Guelph.

——, co-authored. 1989b. *Training as a tool for change in a polyethnic and multiracial society.* Study for the Ministry of Citizenship. Government of Ontario.

——. 1989c. "Demographic change and ethnicity." In *Multiculturalism and policing in British Columbia.* Proceedings of a conference held in Richmond, B.C. (January 1988). Government of British Columbia.

——. 1988a. "Changing Canada: The institutional response to polyethnicity." *The Review of Demography and its Implications for Economic and Social Policy* (Dec.). Health & Welfare Canada.

——. 1988b. *Self employment in Canada among immigrants of different ethno–cultural backgrounds.* Canada Employment and Immigration Commission.

——. 1988c. "Predicting future international migration." Report of the Chairman, Academic Review Panel, Employment and Immigration Canada.

——. 1987. "Demographic change and pluralism." *Canadian Studies in Population* 14 (2).

——. 1986a. "Japanese redress: Philosophical issues." Paper prepared for the Secretary of State and Minister Responsible for Multiculturalism (August).

——. 1986b. "Race relations in Canada: A national strategy." Policy proposals, Race Relations Unit, Multiculturalism Canada, Secretary of State.

——. 1983. "Racism and racial discrimination in Canada: A selective and interpretive bibliographic survey." Race Relations Unit, Multiculturalism Canada, Secretary of State (May).

——. 1982. *Asia's refugees and the Western tradition: The political and constitutional legacy of Indo–China.* Citizenship Branch, Secretary of State.

——. 1981. "Is Ottawa different? Perceptions of discrimination and race relations in the National Capital." Paper prepared for the Multiculturalism Directorate, Secretary of State (Winter).

——. 1980a. "Southeast Asian exodus: From tradition to resettlement." *Canadian Asian Studies Association.* Univ. of Chicago Press.

——. 1980b. *D'un continent à un autre: Les réfugiés du Sud–Est asiatique.* L'Association Canadienne des Etudes Asiatiques.

Thuno, M. 1996. "Origins and causes of emigration from Qingtian and Wenzhou to Europe." Paper presented at Conference on European Chinese and Chinese Domestic Migrants, Oxford (July 3–7).

Tiglao, R. 1996. "Newborn tiger." *Far Eastern Economic Review* (October 24): 66.

Tinker, H. 1977. *The Banyan tree.* London: Oxford Univ. Press.

——. 1975. *A new system of slavery.* London: Oxford Univ. Press.

Toronto Star. 1996. "Tories want to discourage diversity, but not in Quebec." (July 31): A5.

Tran, M., 1990. "Brains behind the U.S. — brought from abroad." *Guardian Weekly* (Dec. 30).

Trlin, Andrew. D. In press. "For the promotion of economic growth and prosperity: New Zealand's immigration policy, 1991–1995." In *New Zealand and international migration: A digest and bibliography* No. 3, ed. A. D. Trlin and P. Spoonley. Palmerston North: Department of Sociology, Massey Univ.

——. 1984. "Changing ethnic residential distribution and segregation in Auckland." In *Tauiwi: Racism and ethnicity in New Zealand,* eds. Spoonley, P., et al., 172–198. Palmerston North: Dunmore Press.

——. 1971. "Social distance and assimilation orientation: A survey of attitudes towards immigrants in New Zealand." *Pacific Viewpoint* 12 (2): 141–162.

Trlin, Andrew D., A. Henderson and R. Pernice. 1997. "Asian immigration, public attitudes and immigration policy: Patterns and responses in New Zealand." Ch. 13.

Trlin, Andrew D., and J. Kang. 1992. "The business immigration policy and the characteristics of approved Hong Kong and Taiwanese applicants, 1986–1988." In

New Zealand and international migration: A *digest and bibliography*, No. 2, ed. A. D. Trlin and P. Spoonley, 48–64. Palmerston North: Department of Sociology, Massey Univ.

Troper, H. 1993. "Canada's immigration policy since 1945." *International Journal* 48 (2): 255–81.

Tsay, C.L. 1995. "Data on international migration to Taiwan." *Asian and Pacific Migration Journal* 4 (4): 613–619.

——. 1992. "Clandestine labor migration to Taiwan." *Asian and Pacific Migration Journal* 1 (4): 637–655.

Tseng, Y. F. n.d. "Chinese ethnic economy: San Gabriel Valley, Los Angeles County." *Journal of Urban Affairs* 16 (2): 169–189.

United Nations. 1994. *The sex and age distribution of the world populations*. New York: United Nations.

——. 1951. *Convention relating to the status of refugees*, Article 1. A. (2). *United Nations Treaty Series* 189: 150.

United Nations Economic Commission for Europe (UNECE). 1994. *International Migration Bulletin* 4. Geneva: United Nations.

United Nations Educational Scientific and Cultural Organization (UNESCO). 1995. *Statistical yearbook 1995*. Paris: UNESCO.

Vancouver Courier. 1992. "Good taste not racist." 1992. Letter to the Editor. (October 11): 7.

Vancouver Port Corporation..1994. 2010 *Port land use management plan*. Vancouver: VPC. (Jan.).

Vancouver Sun

1997a. "Vancouver is Canada's most racially tolerant city, report says." (October 6).

1997b. "Immigrants tolerated for their wealth, Fry says." (7 October).

1997c. "B.C. leads in opposition to immigration, poll finds." (9 October).

1989. "Lam advises Hong Kong on Canada." (December 13).

Vasta, E., and S. Castles. eds. 1996. *The teeth are smiling: The persistence of racism in multicultural Australia*. St Leonard's NSW: Allen and Unwin.

Vasuprasat, P. 1994. "Turning points in international labor migration: A case study of Thailand." *Asian and Pacific Migration Journal* 3 (1): 93–118.

Vaughan, G. M. 1962. "The social distance attitudes of New Zealand students towards Maoris and fifteen other national groups." *Journal of Social Psychology* 57: 85–92.

Verma, Ravi, and Chan Kwok Bun. 1996. "The economic adaptation of Asian immigration to Canada." Paper presented at Symposium on Immigration and Integration. Department of Sociology, Univ. of Manitoba.

Wakabayashi, K. 1990. "Migration from rural to urban areas in China." *The Developing Economies* 28 (4) December.

Wasserstein, B. 1996. *Vanishing Diaspora: The Jews in Europe since 1945*. London: Penguin Books.

Weiner, M., ed. 1993. *International migration and security*. Boulder: Westview.

Weinfeld, Morton. 1996. "Social identity in the 1990's." *Clash of identities*, ed. James Littleton, 122. Prentice Hall/CBC.

Will, G. 1995. "Consular corps find province a busy place." *The Vancouver Sun*. (June 6).

Wilson, V. Seymour. 1993. "The tapestry of Canadian multiculturalism." Presidential address, Canadian Political Science Association. (June).

——. n.d. "Canada's evolving multicultural policy: A stalled omnibus in the 1990's?" Unpublished paper.

Wilson, W. M., et al. 1991. *Report of the working party on immigration*. Wellington: GP Print Ltd.

Wimmer, A. 1997. "Explaining xenophobia and racism: A critical review of current research approaches." *Ethnic and Racial Studies* 20: 17–41.

Windsor, Hugh. 1990. "Forty-six per cent want immigration levels reduced, poll finds." *Globe and Mail* (October 29): A7.

Wong, D. 1996. "Foreign domestic workers in Singapore." In *Asian women in migration*, eds. G. Battistella and A. Paganoni, 87–108. Quezon City, Philippines: Scalabrini Migration Center.

Wong, Jan. 1997. "Immigration: Death of a paper carrier." *The Globe and Mail* (April 19): D1.

Wong, K. K. 1990. "Chinese business migrants — their effect on the property market." *New Zealand Real Estate* 41 (4): 21–26.

Wong, L. 1993. "Immigration as capital accumulation: The impact of business immigration to Canada." *International Immigration* 31: 171–90.

Wong, L., and N. Netting.1992. "Business immigration to Canada: Social impact and racism." In *Deconstructing a nation: Immigration, multiculturalism and racism in 90s Canada*, ed. V. Satzewich: 93–121, Halifax: Fernwood Publishing.

Woolcott, Richard. 1997. "Advance Australia where?" *The Australian* (January 25–26).

World Bank. 1996. *World development report*. New York: Oxford Univ. Press.

Xiushi Yang. 1992. "Temporary migration and its frequency from urban households in China." *Asia-Pacific Population Journal* 7 (1): 44.

Yaffe, B. 1995. "As '97 approaches, we must let China know we're watching." *The Vancouver Sun* (July 22): B3.

Yap, Y. M. 1991. "Singaporeans overseas: A study of emigrants in Australia and Canada." IPS *report series, report* No. 3. Singapore: The Institute of Policy Studies.

Yarwood, A. T. 1964. *Asian migration to Australia: The background to exclusion 1896–1923*. N.p.

Yarwood, V. 1993. "Why Asians expand our economic horizons." *Management* 40 (4): 34–41.

Yee, Lili Anne. 1996. "The social construction of identity: Theorizing intra-group identification." Term paper. (November).

Zelinka, Sue. 1996. *Understanding racism in Australia*. Canberra: AGPS

Zeng Yi and J. Vaupel. 1989. "The impact of urbanization and delayed childbearing on population growth and aging in China." *Population and Development Review* 15 (3) September.

Zhu Guohong. 1989. "Historical review of international migration of Chinese population." *Historical Research* 6: 159–177.

Zubrzycki, Jerzy. 1991. "The evolution of multiculturalism." In *Australian national identity*, ed C. Price. Canberra: Academy of the Social Sciences in Australia.

Zulkifly Hassan. 1995. "Kegiatan ekonomi pendatang Filipina di Sabah: Satu kajian kes di Pulau Gaya." Graduation exercise, Department of Anthropology and Sociology, Univ. of Malaya.

Authors

Manolo Abella is a senior migration specialist at the International Labor Organization, Geneva. He has written extensively on Asian labor migration to the Gulf States and more recently on the growing flows of labor within East Asia. His latest book, *Sending Workers Abroad* serves as an ILO policy guide for low and medium income countries wishing to formulate a policy on foreign employment. For many years he was the coordinator of ILO's Asian Regional Program on International Labor Migration based in Bangkok which provided technical assistance to 13 countries in the Asia Pacific region. Lately he has been devoting his time to assessing the objectives and outcomes of state policies on migration.

Azizah Kassim holds a Ph.D. in Social Anthropology as well as a Certificate in Development Planning from the University of London. She is presently professor at the University of Malaya and specializes in urban studies, women studies and international migration. She has been researching and writing on foreign labor migrants in Malaysia since 1985 and has 15 papers on the subject to her credit. She has served as a consultant to ILO, UNCRD, ESCAP and the Japanese Ministry of Justice. Recent papers she has published include: "Illegal Alien Labor in Malaysia: Its Influx, Utilization and Ramifications," *Indonesia and The Malay World* Number 71, March 1997, Oxford University Press; and "Foreign Labor in Malaysia," *Regional Development Impacts of Labor Migration in Asia*, UNCRD Research Report Series No. 2, Nagoya, Japan, 1994.

Jose Brillantes is the current Philippine Ambassador to Malaysia where a large number of Filipinos are working as overseas contract workers. He was Undersecretary of Labor during the Cory Aquino administration in the '80s and Secretary of Labor and Employment during the current Ramos administration before being posted to Malaysia. His interest in Philippine immigration to Canada goes back to when he was Labor Attache at the Philippine Embassy in Ottawa in the 1970s. He received his law degree from the Ateneo de Manila University.

Meyer Burstein is the Executive Head of the Metropolis Project of Citizenship and Immigration Canada in Ottawa. Metropolis is a cooperative, international research project that seeks to stimulate interdisciplinary research on the effects of international migration on urban centres.

Graeme Hugo, Professor and Head of Geography Department at the University of Adelaide, received his Ph.D. in demography from the Australian National University. His main research interests are: population geography and demography, social geography, demographic trends (especially population mobility) and development in Southeast Asia, population trends and their implications in Australia and the changing patterns of immigration, their causes and implications for social and economic change. He is the author of some 100 books, articles in journals and chapters in books, as well as a large number of conference papers and reports. Among his recent publications on migration are: "Environmental Concerns and International Migration," *International Migration Review*, 30, 1, (1996) and "Asia on the Move: Research Challenges for Population Geography," *International Journal of Population Geography*, June, (1996).

Thomas Hutton is Associate Professor in the School of Community & Regional Planning at the University of British Columbia. He holds a D.Phil. in Geography and Planning from Oxford University. His research is focused on urban and regional change, with special reference to the role of service industries in economic restructuring, new division of labor, the emergence of new urban production spaces, and new patterns of exports and trade. Recent works include a book, *The Transformation of Canada's Pacific Metropolis: A Study of Vancouver*, and an article on models of metropolitan restructuring and strategic policy approaches for *Policy Options*. Current projects are on the impact of immigration on Vancouver and the role of services industries and economic restructuring in the reconfiguration of Asia Pacific city-regions.

Gavin Jones received his Ph.D. from the Australian National University and is currently Professor and Coordinator, Demography Program at the same university. He has authored 15 books and monographs and over 100 articles in professional journals, or chapters of books. He is a Fellow of the Academy of Social Sciences in Australia; member of Population Association of America; International Union for the Scientific Study of Population; Asian Studies Association of Australia and past president of the Australian Population Association. He has served as a consultant to the following organizations: Ford Foundation, World Bank, Population Council, Australian Development Assistance Bureau, United Nations Population Fund, International Labor Organization, United Nations Centre for

Human Settlements, Asian Development Institute and Malaysian Centre for Development Studies. He has lived and worked in Thailand, Sri Lanka, Malaysia and Indonesia for over 10 years.

Azfar Khan received his B.A. (Honors in Economics) and M.A. (Economics) from McGill University, Montreal, Canada, and D.Phil. from the Institute of Development Studies (IDS) at the University of Sussex, U.K. Since 1995, he has been working as a Technical Support Services Specialist on Migration, Urbanization and Population Distribution in the Development Policies Department of the International Labor Organization (ILO) in Geneva, Switzerland. Prior to that, he was a Senior Lecturer at the Institute of Social Studies (ISS) in the Hague, the Netherlands (1989–1994), where he was also the Convenor of the United Nations Population Fund's (UNFPA) Global Program of Training in Population and Development from 1991 to 1994. He also served with Global Studies Branch of the Division for Industrial Studies at the United Nations Industrial Development Organization (UNIDO), 1980–82.

Aprodicio Laquian, Director of the UBC Centre for Human Settlements from 1991 to 1997 and Professor at the School of Community and Regional Planning, has a Ph.D. in Political Science from Massachusetts Institute of Technology. He worked with the United Nations for 11 years with postings in New York, China and the South Pacific. Prior to that he worked for 10 years in Ottawa and Nairobi, Kenya, in the field of urban studies for IDRC. He has been a visiting professor at De La Salle University, University of the Philippines, University of Nairobi and University of Hawaii and is an Honorary Professor at Peking University. He has published 10 books, 50 articles and book chapters on population, migration, urban politics and governance. He is currently writing a book on the planning and governance of Beijing, Shanghai and Guangzhou.

Eleanor Laquian is Coordinator of the Asian Immigration Project at the Institute of Asian Research at UBC. She planned and managed the conference on Asian Immigration and Racism in June 1997. Her interest in immigration started when she immigrated to Canada in 1969. She conducted the first nationwide survey of Filipino immigrants in Canada for her master's thesis. She received her M.A. in Public Administration in 1973 from the University of the Philippines with the thesis "Administrative and Policy Aspects of Philippine Immigration to Canada." The United Council of Filipinos in Canada, Ottawa, published it as A *Study of Filipino Immigrants in Canada,* 1962–1972. She also wrote "Filipinos in Canada" in *The Canadian Encyclopedia* (Hurtig Publishers, Alberta) in 1985 and continues to update the article in the succeeding editions with the 1997 edition now available in CD-ROM.

David Ley is Professor of Geography at UBC and co-Director of the Vancouver Centre of Excellence for Immigration Studies, a federally funded research centre jointly administered by UBC and Simon Fraser University. His current research includes studies of immigration and deprivation in Vancouver and Toronto, the role of churches in immigrant settlement and integration, and the experience of business-class immigrants in Vancouver's upper middle-class neighborhoods. He is the author of *The New Middle Class and the Remaking of the Central City* (Oxford University Press, 1996), and co-author of *Neighborhood Organizations and the Welfare State* (University of Toronto Press, 1994).

Terry McGee holds a Ph.D. in Geography from Victoria University in Wellington and is currently Professor of Geography and Director of the Institute of Asian Research at UBC. He was former President of the Canadian Geographical Association and the Canadian Council of Southeast Asian Studies. For the past 30 years, he has concentrated his research on urbanization in Southeast Asia and development studies in the Asia Pacific. He is author/editor of more than 10 books and 150 articles dealing with these subjects. His latest publications include: *The Extended Metropolis: Settlement Transition in Asia* (University of Hawaii Press, 1991); *The Mega-Urban Regions of Southeast Asia, Policy Changes and Response* (UBC Press, 1995); and *New Geographies of the Asia Pacific Region* (London Hurst, in press).

Kogila Moodley, holder of the UBC's David Lam Chair of Multicultural Studies since 1995, is a widely published scholar on race and ethnic relations. Her publications include: *Race Relations and Multicultural Education* (UBC, 1984), *Beyond Multicultural Education: International Perspectives* (Detselig, 1992), *The Opening of the Apartheid Mind: Options for the New South Africa*, with Heribert Adam, (University of California Press, 1993) and "Multicultural Education in Canada: Historical Development and Current Status," a chapter in James A. Banks and Cherry A. McGee Banks (Eds.) *Handbook of Research on Multicultural Education*, N.Y. McMillan, 1995: pp. 801–820.

Sisira Pinnawala is a Senior Lecturer and Head of the Sociology Department, University of Peradeniya, Sri Lanka. He earned his Ph.D. from the Australian National University for which he did a study of Sri Lankan immigrants in Australia. His academic and research interests are development studies as well as ethnic and immigration studies. He was a Fulbright Senior Fellow in the Peace Studies Program at Cornell University.

Alan Simmons is Associate Professor of Sociology and a Fellow at the Centre for Research on Latin America and the Caribbean at York University,

Toronto. His current research is on globalization and international migration, Canadian immigrant policies and settlement. He has a Ph.D. from Cornell University. He served as Director of the Graduate Program in Sociology (1994–95), and Director of the Centre for Research on Latin America and the Caribbean (1985–1989), both at York, President of the Canadian Population Society (1984–1986) and Associate Director of the Social Sciences Division, International Development Research Centre (1974–1984). His latest work is an edited volume: *International Migration, Refugee Flows and Human Rights in North America: The Impact of Trade and Restructuring* (New York: Center for Migration Studies, 1996).

Ronald Skeldon is a Visiting Professor at the Institute for Population and Social Research, Mahidol University, Thailand. He was previously a Professor in the Department of Geography and Geology at the University of Hong Kong. He began his study of population migration in 1969 with work in Peru for his doctoral dissertation at the University of Toronto. This led to a series of research on migration-related issues in Peru and Papua New Guinea. Since 1979, he has been working on Asian migration. His latest book *Migration and Development: A Global Perspective* was published by Longman in September 1997.

Angelica Oleg Tang received her Bachelor of Arts degree from Princeton University. She is the Executive Director of the Mayor's Office of Immigrant Affairs and Language Services in New York City and a member of the Mayor's cabinet and an advisor to the Mayor on all immigrant and immigration-related issues. She develops special initiatives for the city and its immigrant communities. She also leads a comprehensive public information and education campaign on immigration issues. She was elected term member of the U.S. Council on Foreign Relations for her expertise on the Asia Pacific region.

Elliot Tepper, a Professor in the Department of Political Science, Carleton University, Ottawa, has a lengthy involvement in studies on immigration, multiculturalism, race relations and human rights in Canada. His latest publications include "Multiculturalism in an Evolving Society" in A. Cardoza & L. Musto, eds, *The Battle over Multiculturalism* (Pearson-Shoyama Institute, 1997) and "Immigration Policy and Multiculturalism" in J. Berry and J. Laponce, eds, *Multiculturalism in Canada: The Research Landscape* (University of Toronto Press, 1994).

Andrew Trlin is an Associate Professor in the Department of Social Policy and Social Work at Massey University, New Zealand. His research interests are social demography, social change and social policy in contemporary New Zealand but he is best known for his work on immigration policy and immigrant settlement as co-editor of *Immigrants in New Zealand* (Massey University Press, 1970), author of *Now Respected Once Despised: Yugoslavs in New Zealand* (Dunmore Press, 1979) and as co-editor of the series *New Zealand and International Migration: A Digest and Bibliography* (Dept. of Sociology, Massey University, 1986, 1992, 1997). He is currently leading "The New Settlers Program," a longitudinal study of the resettlement experiences of new arrivals from the People's Republic of China, India and South Africa. His co-authors in this book chapter are members of the research team for this project. **Anne Henderson,** project research officer, is working on a doctoral thesis on aspects of the sociocultural adaptation of skilled Chinese immigrants in New Zealand. From 1991–1996, Anne taught at the Shanghai International Studies University. **Dr. Regina Pernice** is a senior lecturer, Dept. of Rehabilitation Studies, Massey University. Her research interests are immigration adaptation, long-term unemployment and cross-cultural issues of rehabilitaiton. She is involved in an ILO-supported study on job retention and return to work of people with disabilities.

Edward Woo is the Executive Director of the Chinese Entrepreneurs Society of Canada, a national organization of Chinese-Canadian business people. He is also the General Manager in Administration of the 1997 World Chinese Entrepreneurs Convention held in Vancouver. He graduated from the University of Hong Kong with a M.S. degree in Comparative Asian Studies and a M.Ed. in Educational Management. He received his Ph.D. from the University of Leeds in England focusing on the development of non-state enterprises in China. He has taught human geography courses in the University of Hong Kong and the University of British Columbia.

Zeng Yi is Professor of Demography and Director, Institute of Population Research at Peking University in China, and Distinguished Research Scholar and Head of Research on Family Demography and Population Aging at Max Planck Institute for Demographic Research in Germany. He is also an adjunct professor at Humphrey Institute, University of Minnesota, U.S. He has a Ph.D. (*summa cum laude*) from Brussels Free University. He was awarded the Frank Notestein Fellowship by the Population Council and conducted his Post-Doctoral study at Princeton University. He has published nine books, including one text book, and 75 professional papers. Among his recent publications are: *Family Dynamics in China: A Life Table Analysis* (University of Wisconsin Press) and *China's Population Trends and Strategies* (Peking University Press).

Index

Index

Index

Index

Early Asian Immigrants in B.C.

A *Chinese "Joss House" or temple in Revelstoke*, B.C., 1895. — Vancouver Public Library

Imperial Cannery, Steveston, B.C., c. 1900-1910. — Vancouver Public Library

Chinese men laying Canadian Pacific Railway track near Glenogle, B.C., 1924.
— Vancouver Public Library

Japanese Canadian children in an internment camp somewhere in the interior of B.C.
— UBC Special Collections (Japanese Canadian Collection)